SOFTWARE PROCESS DYNAMICS

SOFTWARE PROCESS DYNAMICS

Raymond J. Madachy

IEEE PRESS

WILEY-INTERSCIENCE
A JOHN WILEY & SONS, INC., PUBLICATION

Library of Congress Cataloging-in-Publication Data is available.

ISBN 978-0-471-27455-1

10 9 8 7 6 5 4 3 2 1

CONTENTS

PART 2   APPLICATIONS AND FUTURE DIRECTIONS

FOREWORD

The pace of change in software-intensive systems continues to accelerate at a dizzying rate. This presents a huge challenge for people trying to develop useful software. In the early days of software development, developers could freeze the requirements for the software, develop the software to the requirements, and deliver the resulting software two years later with confidence that the requirements would still be relevant and the software would be useful. Most of our software engineering processes, methods, and tools were developed and used under the assumption of relatively stable requirements. Examples are formal specification languages, performance-optimized point-solution designs, fixed-requirements software-cost estimation, earned-value management systems, requirements traceability matrices, fixed-price/fixed-requirements contracts, and a general attitude that "requirements creep" was bad in that it destabilized software development.

However, as these practices became increasingly institutionalized, the accelerating rate of software change made them increasingly risky to use. Projects would use them for two years and become extremely frustrated when the users were not interested in the obsolete capabilities that resulted. Projects would fall behind schedule and use static models (time to complete = work remaining divided by work rate) to try to make up time by adding people, and run afoul of Brooks's law (adding people to a late software project will make it later). Or they would sprint for the finish line using a point-solution design that satisfied the initial requirements but was extremely difficult to modify when trying to satisfy users' changing requirements.

Ironically, even with all of these difficulties, organizations would increasingly turn to software and its ability to be electronically upgraded as their best way to adapt their products, services, and systems to the increasing pace of change in their business or operational environment.

In order to keep up with this increased demand for software and the rapid pace of change, software organizations and projects need better ways to reason about the effects of change on their software products, projects, and processes. This is often very difficult to do, as software changes often have complex second-order and higher-order interaction effects that are hard to visualize and reason about. Thus, for example, a project with high rates of change in its requirements, being developed by a team with high rates of change in its personnel, will need to understand and control the interactions of decreased productivity due to change processing, decreased productivity due to new staff members' unfamiliarity with the project and product, and loss of productivity when key staff members are diverted from project work to train and mentor new people in order to develop increased downstream productivity.

One of the best techniques for reasoning about the effects of such complex interacting changes is the System Dynamics modeling framework that Ray Madachy presents in this book. As I have found in numerous applications of the method, it enables project personnel to model such effects and run the models to better understand the implications of candidate project strategies and decisions.

From the pioneering application of Jay Forrester's System Dynamics approach to software project modeling by Tarek Abdel-Hamid and Stuart Madnick in their 1991 book *Software Project Dynamics,* system dynamics modeling has been applied to many aspects of software development and management. These include the analysis of the effects on software system cost, schedule, and quality of alternative approaches to software process sequencing, software requirements determination, software architecture and design, software project organization and staffing, software development and integration, software quality assurance, and software change management. These applications have constituted the major source of solution approaches in the software process simulation community and its annual series of ProSim conferences (recently combined with the Software Process Workshop into the International Conference on Software Process, held concurrently with the International Conference on Software Engineering).

Ray Madachy has been a major contributor to this body of work. His experience in applying system dynamics modeling as a technical leader in such diverse organizations as the aerospace corporation Litton Systems, the e-commerce system development company C-Bridge Institute, and the software tools company Cost Xpert Group have given him a broad and deep perspective on the critical success factors of developing and applying system dynamics models to various classes of software decision situations. His experience in teaching and researching these techniques at USC has enabled him to develop an integrating framework and set of techniques that make system dynamics modeling much easier and cost-effective to learn and apply to a software decision situation.

His resulting book begins with an overview of the systems dynamics modeling framework, and an example application showing how to develop a system dynamics model that helps explain the conditions under which you can add people to a software project with or without having Brooks's Law apply. Next is an extensive chapter on the modeling process that introduces concepts and techniques used to develop system dynamics models, with illustrations of how they are developed and applied. The next chapter provides and explains a full range of model structures from modeling molecules to large infrastructures and flow chains that can be used in new models. Once this framework is established, there are three chapters that apply it to the most significant classes of system dynamics applications.

The first of these chapters covers useful applications to software personnel decisions: workforce levels and team composition, learning, burnout, skills, motivation, retention, and rotation effects. The second chapter covers software process and product decision situations: peer reviews, software reuse, COTS-based system development, software architecting, and software process improvement effects. The third chapter covers project and organization applications, such as business case analysis, defect reduction strategies, and staffing management strategies. The final chapter projects likely future uses and research challenges in software process modeling and simulation, including how system dynamics models can add value via integration with other classes of models.

The appendices also provide important and one-of-a-kind material. The first appendix covers statistics of simulation, which is not covered in traditional references on system dynamics. Next is a thorough annotated bibliography of work using system dynamics for software processes, and is the definitive compendium for the field. Finally, the last appendix lists executable models provided with the book. These are used in examples and can be used for further exercises or for incorporation into your own models. These are valuable, reusable, and fun assets to go along with the book.

Overall, the book brings together a tremendous amount of useful process modeling material and experience in using it in practical software decision situations. It organizes this material into a unifying framework that makes it easier to apply and explain, and illustrates it with a wide variety of useful examples. I believe that the book will serve as a standard reference for the software process dynamics field and a great help to practitioners and researchers for a good long time.

BARRY BOEHM
University of Southern California

Los Angeles, California
June 2006

PREFACE

This book is designed for professionals and students in software engineering or information technology who are interested in understanding the dynamics of software development, or in assessing and optimizing process strategies. Its purpose is to improve decision making about projects and organizational policies by making its readers better informed about the dynamic consequences of decisions. Decisions may involve setting project budgets and schedules; return-on-investment analysis; trade-offs between cost, schedule, and quality or other factors; personnel hiring; risk management decisions; make, buy, or reuse; process improvement strategies; and so on.

The importance of process dynamics is hard to refute given the well-known (but too often ignored) combined effects of schedule pressure, communication overhead, changing business conditions, requirements volatility and user requests, experience, work methods such as reviews and quality assurance activities, task underestimation, bureaucratic delays, organizational shifts, demotivating events, other sociotechnical phenomena, and the feedback therein. These complex and interacting process effects are elegantly modeled with system dynamics using continuous quantities interconnected in loops of information feedback and circular causality. Knowledge of the interrelated technical and social factors coupled with simulation tools can provide a means for organizations to improve their processes.

The objectives of this book are to:

- Provide methods, tools, models, and examples to improve management decision making at all levels. Simulation can support corporate strategy and investment analysis, business case development, project and portfolio management, and training, for example.

- Illustrate *systems thinking* in action to develop increasingly deep understandings of software process structures and behaviors.

- Describe the modeling process, including calibration of models to software metrics data.

- Show basic building blocks and model infrastructures for software development processes.

- Review the field of software process modeling with system dynamics. Show how others have used the principles of system dynamics to analyze and improve processes in organizations.

- Provide practical lessons learned about the dynamics of software processes.

- Provide sufficient introductory material, including exercises and executable models on the Internet. Software practitioners who are brand new to simulation can immediately get their hands dirty and start modeling. Students can learn at their own pace, delving into the models as deeply as time and interest dictate.

- For those experienced in software process simulation, provide more detail of critical implementation issues and future research motivations.

The book is mostly new material, except for some example applications, and synthesizes previous work in the area. There has been much growth in the field; it has evolved to a state of maturity, and this book addresses the need to communicate findings. It draws from over 100 publications from practitioners and researchers experienced in system dynamics modeling of processes in organizations (all of them summarized in Appendix B). It is written to be a self-contained learning experience, and a comprehensive reference for modeling practitioners. The sections are structured so that readers can approach the subject from different perspectives and gain valuable knowledge for further study and practice depending on their needs.

A constructive understanding of process dynamics is provided by the illustrated models. Where appropriate, guidelines are presented for process improvement and general software management strategies (common threads include risk management and concentrating on people). The perspective in the book addresses the *dynamics* of software development, and best practices are described from that view. Some of these practices are illuminated through simulation experiments herein, and some will become foci of further study.

Readers may be involved in software process improvement, project planning and management, software development, testing, quality assurance, strategic corporate planning, organizational learning, education, or simply desire to understand the interrelated factors of software development. There is no need for sophisticated math skills, but a passing knowledge of numerical integration concepts will make the introductory material easier. Readers will increase their understanding of the complexities of software development and be able to use system dynamics for modeling and improving processes in their particular organizations. They will gain insight into the real-world mechanics behind the modeling equations.

For academic uses, this book may serve as an upper-level or graduate textbook for Software Process Modeling or other simulation courses. It can be used to support curriculums in Software Engineering, Software Project Management, Software Quality Assurance, Systems Engineering or related subjects.

Part 1 of the book presents modeling fundamentals for software processes. These chapters may constitute an entire course for those new to system dynamics modeling. Advanced students should cover applications and future directions in Part 2. These topics can be studied in whole or as selected subjects. Other disciplines or focused studies may choose relevant application topics. For example, researchers in organizations or sociology might want to cover people applications, engineering process groups might investigate selected process applications, while senior managers could focus on project or organizational applications.

The sequence and depth of subjects should be tailored accordingly for any of these uses. The variety of exercises in the book may serve as homework assignments, exam questions, or even major research projects. Except for the introductory chapters, detailed equations are generally omitted from the text and left for the reader to study from the models.

Though a primary objective is to instruct in computer-aided analysis, several identified exercises early in the book should be done without a computer. This is to help develop intuition of process dynamics, and to strike a balance by not becoming overly reliant on blindly using the computer during model development and evaluation of simulation results. The structure of the book is explained in more detail below.

BOOK ORGANIZATION AND HIGHLIGHTS

This section provides a sequential outline of topics with selected highlights. Each chapter includes numerous graphics, charts, and tables to help illustrate the material. The book is also supplemented on the Internet containing the sample models and simulation tools, exercises, extra references, and updates to the material. The book is divided into two major parts per the outline below:

Part 1—Fundamentals
    Chapter 1—Introduction and Background
    Chapter 2—The Modeling Process with System Dynamics
    Chapter 3—Model Structures and Behaviors for Software Processes
Part 2—Applications and Future Directions
    Introduction to Applications Chapters
    Chapter 4—People Applications
    Chapter 5—Process and Product Applications
    Chapter 6—Project and Organization Applications
    Chapter 7—Current and Future Directions
Appendices and References
    Appendix A—Introduction to Statistics of Simulation
    Appendix B—Annotated Bibliography
    Appendix C—Provided Models
    References

Chapter 1 establishes the context and foundation of the book, with a goal of helping people use models to quantitatively evaluate processes in order to make better decisions. The chapter presents an introduction and background including motivational issues and a capsule history of the field. Definitions of terms are provided for reference throughout the book. The concepts of systems thinking are introduced, so one can see how simulation can be used to leverage learning efforts and improve organizational performance. Control systems principles are introduced, and then a simple motivational example of modeling Brooks's Law is shown. A review of software process technology covers process modeling, lifecycle models, and process improvement.

A description of the iterative modeling process with the system dynamics simulation methodology is provided in Chapter 2. Basic modeling elements and classical system behaviors are shown. The underlying mathematical formulation of system dynamics is covered with its ramifications for software process models.

The activities of problem definition, model formulation (including calibration), simulation, assessment, communication to others, and challenging the model for the next iteration are elaborated on. Since simulation is both art and science, guidelines and modeling heuristics are discussed. It is seen that there is much in common with software engineering principles in general such as iteration, abstraction, aggregation, and so on, yet there are also aspects of simulation that require somewhat different skills.

This chapter also details the multiperspective validation of system dynamics models, which is of paramount importance before drawing policy conclusions from simulation experiments. Different modeling tools and environments are overviewed to help modelers in choosing appropriate tools for their different needs. Also see Appendix A on the use of statistics in the modeling process.

Chapter 3 presents patterns of model structures and behaviors for software processes. Included is a detailed description of levels, flows, auxiliaries, infrastructures, and feedback loops instantiated for software processes. State variables of interest include software work artifacts, defect levels, personnel levels, effort expenditure, schedule date, and others. Corresponding rates over time include software productivity, defect introduction and elimination rates, financial flows for costs and revenue, and so on. Project reference behaviors for different structures and management policies are introduced.

An important contribution of this chapter is the explication of basic flow processes for software development. Common structures for software processes ferreted out of the major models (upcoming in Chapters 4 through 6) are shown. Together with prototypical feedback loops such as learning and project controlling, these infrastructures can be (re)used to develop models relevant to any software process. This section also illustrates a major advantage in system dynamics models over other modeling techniques: inherent cost, schedule, and quality trade-offs by modeling their interactions.

Part 2 covers modeling applications in the field and future directions. Chapter 4 focuses on people applications, Chapter 5 covers process and product applications, and Chapter 6 is about projects and organizations. Each chapter contains applications of varying complexity. An overview of applications and research to date is provided, including history, a list of different implementations, and critiques of the various work.

Modeling examples from the field are shown with sample insights. The examples are further instances of the generic structures from Chapter 3.

The application examples show threads of simulation modeling with actual model implementations and worked out examples. These original examples should be of particular value to system dynamics novices, and more experienced modelers can study them for additional ideas. Many also amplify some lessons learned regarding the software process. Some of the example models are also contained on the accompanying website. Additional exercises are provided for students to work out and practitioners to implement. Note that the applications chapters will also be updated online to keep up with new work.

Chapter 7 presents current and future directions in software process modeling and simulation. These include advances in simulation environments and tools, model structures and component-based model development, new and emerging trends for application models, model integration (not just system dynamics models), empirical research, theory building, and putting it all together in process mission control centers and training facilities.

Appendix A introduces statistics for simulation as an addendum to the modeling fundamentals about which simulation analysts, researchers, and graduate students studying broader aspects of simulation must be knowledgeable. Statistical methods are used to handle the stochastic inputs and outputs of simulation models. The appendix covers the principles of probability distributions, sample size, confidence intervals, and experimental design applied to continuous system simulation. Monte Carlo simulation is described and recommended probability distributions for software process modeling are also provided.

Appendix B is an annotated bibliography of using system dynamics for software processes and is the most complete set of references for the field. It demonstrates well the breadth of applications to date and is a convenient place to start researching particular topics. These same citations are identified in the References in boldface.

Appendix C lists the provided models referenced in the chapters or exercises. These go along with the examples, and can be executed and modified by readers for their own purposes. These models will be updated and replaced on the Internet as improvements are made. Models provided by other readers will also be posted.

INTERNET SITES

The referenced models, tools, updates, discussion, and color book information are available on the world wide web at http://csse.usc.edu/softwareprocessdynamics and at a mirror site http://softwareprocessdynamics.org.

ACKNOWLEDGMENTS

I would like to extend sincere appreciation to all the other people who contributed to this work. I initially learned system dynamics for physiological modeling in a graduate biomedical engineering course at UCSD in 1982 under the excellent direction of Drs. Alan Schneider and James Bush. This book would not be complete without the accomplishments of other researchers and support of colleagues including Dr. Tarek Abel-Hamid, Richard Adams, Dr. Vic Basili, Dr. James Collofello, Scott Duncan, Dr. Susan Ferreira, Dr. David Ford, Tobias Haberlein, Jim Hart, Dr. Dan Houston, Dr. Marc Kellner, Peter Lakey, Dr. Manny Lehman, Dr. Robert Martin, Dr. Margaret Johnson, Emily oh Navarro, Dr. Nathaniel Osgood, Dr. Dietmar Pfahl, Oliver Pospisil, Dr. David Raffo, Dr. Juan Ramil, Dr. Stan Rifkin, Dr. Howard Rubin, Dr. Ioana Rus, Dr. Walt Scacchi, Dr. Neil Smith, Dr. Greg Twaites, Dr. Wayne Wakeland, Dr. Gerry Weinberg, Dr. Paul Wernick, and Ed Yourdon; Litton personnel including Dr. Denton Tarbet, Wayne Sebera, Larry Bean, Frank Harvey, and Roy Nakahara; Charles Leinbach from C-bridge Institute; Benny Barbe from Cost Xpert Group; and Dr. Julian Richardson and Dr. Michael Lowry for their support at NASA. USC graduate students who contributed to this work are Ashwin Bhatnagar, Cyrus Fakharzadeh, Jo Ann Lane, Dr. Nikunj Mehta, Kam Wing Lo, Jason Ho, Leila Kaghazian, Dr. Jongmoon Baik (also including post-graduate contributions), and Wook Kim. Profound thanks goes to Dr. Barry Boehm, who has served as a mentor and been my biggest influence since the middle of my Ph.D. studies. This book owes much to his continual support, penetrating insights, and inspiration to contribute. Many thanks to the anonymous IEEE reviewers for their long hours and detailed constructive reviews, and IEEE staff including Jeanne Audino, Cathy Faduska, Chrissy Kuhnen, Cheryl Baltes, and Matt Loeb. I also am most grateful to my wife Nancy for her long-term support and lots of patience, and my young daughters Zoey and Deziree for extra motivation and lessons on adaptation to change.

BOOK UPDATES AND MAKING CONTRIBUTIONS

The field of software process modeling itself is quite dynamic, with much happening in conjunction with other software process work. It has been a challenge keeping up with the times as this book has progressed, and the rate of change in the industry has increased over these years. It is inevitable that some things will continue to change, so the reader is urged to access the Internet site for updates at any time, including new and improved models.

Updates to the chapters will be put on the book's Internet site until the next published edition. The application Chapters 4–6 will have substantial updates and entire sections replaced. The goal is to keep the applications current and presented in a uniform format. Chapter 7 on current and future directions is a wild card in terms of predicted changes, and the annotated bibliography will be updated continuously.

It is an exciting time with much opportunity and more work to be done. Hopefully, some of the ideas and exercises in this book will be used as a basis for further practice and research. People will provide new and better exercises and those will be posted too. Your comments on this book and experiences with modeling actual processes are of great interest to this author, and your feedback will help in developing the next edition. You are encouraged to send any ideas, improvement suggestions, new and enhanced models, or worked out exercises from this book. They will be included in future editions as appropriate.

RAYMOND J. MADACHY

Los Angeles, California
November 2007

Part 1

FUNDAMENTALS

1

INTRODUCTION AND BACKGROUND

Everything is connected to everything.
—Anonymous

Software and information technology professionals, managers, executives, and business analysts have to cope with an increasingly dynamic world. Gone are the days when one's software technology, hardware platforms, organizational environment, and competitive marketplace would stay relatively stable for a few years while developing a system. Thus, the ability to understand and reason about dynamic and complex software development and evolution processes becomes increasingly valuable for decision making.

Particularly valuable are automated aids built upon knowledge of the interacting factors throughout the software life cycle that impact the cost, schedule, and quality. Unfortunately, these effects are rarely accounted for on software projects. Knowledge gleaned from a global perspective that considers these interactions is used in executable simulation models that serve as a common understanding of an organization's processes. Systems thinking, as a way to find and bring to light the structure of the organizational system that influences its dynamic behavior, together with system dynamics as a simulation methodology, provide critical skills to manage complex software development.

System dynamics provides a rich and integrative framework for capturing myriad process phenomena and their relationships. It was developed over 40 years ago by Jay

Forrester at MIT to improve organizational structures and processes [Forrester 1961]. It was not applied in software engineering until Tarek Abdel-Hamid developed his dissertation model, which is featured in the book *Software Project Dynamics* [Abdel-Hamid, Madnick 1991].

Simulation usage is increasing in many disparate fields due to constantly improving computer capabilities, and because other methods do not work for complex systems. Simulations are computationally intensive, so they are much more cost-effective than in the past. Simulation is general-purpose and can be used when analytic solutions are extremely difficult if not impossible to apply to complex, nonlinear situations. Simulation is even more powerful with improved data collection for the models. Example areas where increased processing power combined with improved models and data include meteorology to better predict hurricane paths, environmental studies, physical cosmology, chemistry to experiment with new molecular structures, or archaeology to understand past and future migrations. These are practical applications but simulation can also be used for experimentation and theory building.

The simulation process in an organization involves designing a system model and carrying out experiments with it. The purpose of these "what if" experiments is to determine how the real or proposed system performs and to predict the effect of changes to the system as time progresses. The modeling results support decision making to improve the system under study, and normally there are unintended side effects of decisions to consider. The improvement cycle continues as organizational processes are continually refined.

Simulation is an efficient communication tool to show how a process works while stimulating creative thinking about how it can be improved. The modeling process itself is beneficial; it is generally acknowledged that much of the reward of modeling is gained in the early stages to gather data, pose questions, brainstorm, understand processes, and so on.

There are many practical benefits of performing simulation in organizations. Besides individual project planning, simulation can help evaluate long-run investment and technology strategies. Companies can use simulation for continuous process improvement, regardless of their current process maturity. It can support organizational learning by making models explicit in a group setting, where all participants can contribute and buy into the model. Such collaboration can go a long way to effect team-building.

Simulation can also be used in individual training, since participants can interact with executing models in real time to see the effects of their decisions. Simulations are used extensively for training in aerospace, military, and other fields. Student awareness is heightened when virtual "games" with simulations are used, particularly when they participate interactively. Visual dynamic graphs or virtual rendering provide faster and more easily remembered learning compared to the traditional lecture format. Exploration is encouraged through the ability to modify and replay the models.

Another significant motivation is that simulation can help reduce the risk of software development. Particularly when used and cross-checked with other complementary analyses that embody different assumptions, process modeling can minimize the uncertainties of development. Previously unforeseen "gotchas" will be brought to the forefront and mitigated through careful planning.

System dynamics modeling can provide insights by investigating virtually any aspect of the software process at a macro or micro level. It can be used to evaluate and compare different life-cycle processes, defect detection techniques, business cases, interactions between interdisciplinary process activities (e.g. software and nonsoftware tasks), deciding "how much is enough" in terms of rigor or testing, and so on. Organizations can focus on specific aspects of development cost, schedule, product quality, or the myriad trade-offs, depending on their concerns.

The issues of software processes are very wide-ranging, so the scope and boundaries of this book will be defined. The focus is not on technical fundamentals of software programming or specific methodologies, but on the *dynamics* of software processes. The second definition from Webster's dictionary describes the prime focus of this book, particularly the relations between forces:

Dynamics—1. The branch of mechanics dealing with the motions of material bodies under the action of given forces **2. a) the various forces, physical, moral, economic, etc. operating in any field b) the way such forces shift or change in relation to one another c) the study of such forces.**

Essentially, this book is about understanding the dynamics of software processes with the help of simulation modeling. *Software process dynamics* is a more general term than *software project dynamics,* which is limiting in the sense that dynamics occur outside of project boundaries such as continuous product line development, organizational reuse processes contributing to many projects, or other strategic processes. A project is also considered an execution of a process, roughly analogous to how a programming object is an instance or execution of a class.

When simulation is used for personnel training, the term *process flight simulation* is sometimes used to invoke the analogy of pilots honing their skills in simulators to reduce risk, with the implicit lesson that software managers and other personnel should do the same. Use of the system dynamics method may on occasion be referred to as *dynamic process simulation, dynamic simulation,* or *continuous systems simulation.*

Alternative titles for this book could be *The Learning Software Organization* or *Software Process Systems Thinking,* depending on the camp de jour. System dynamics and, particularly, organizational learning gained wider public exposure due to Peter Senge's bestselling book *The Fifth Discipline* [Senge 1990]. Organizational learning in the context of a software process involves translating the common "mental model" of the process into a working simulation model that serves as a springboard for increased learning and improvement. This learning can be brought about by applying system dynamics to software process and project phenomena.

There are other excellent references on system dynamics modeling that one could use to learn from, but why should a busy software engineer studying the software process spend so much time with examples outside of his/her field? This book uses examples solely from the software process domain to minimize modeling skill transfer time. Organizational learning and systems thinking are also well documented elsewhere (see the popular books by Peter Senge and collaborators [Senge 1990], [Senge et al. 1994]).

1.1 SYSTEMS, PROCESSES, MODELS, AND SIMULATION

Important terminology for the field is defined in this section. A systems orientation is crucial to understanding the concepts herein, so system will first be defined generally as a subset of reality that is a focus of analysis. Technically, systems contain multiple components that interact with each other and perform some function together that cannot be done by individual components. In simulation literature, a system is typically defined as "a collection of entities, e.g., people or machines, that act and interact together toward the accomplishment of some logical end" [Law, Kelton 1991]. Forrester's system definition is very close: "a grouping of parts that operate together for a common purpose" [Forrester 1968].

Systems exist on many levels; one person's system is another person's subsystem. Since systems are influenced by other systems, no system is isolated from external factors. How to define system boundaries for meaningful analysis is discussed later in this book.

Systems are classified as "open" if the outputs have no influence on the inputs; open systems are not aware of their past performance. A "closed" system is also called a feedback system; it is influenced by its own behavior through a loop that uses past actions to control future action. The distinction between open and closed systems is particularly important in the context of system dynamics.

A system can be characterized by (1) parameters that are independent measures that configure system inputs and structure, and (2) variables that depend on parameters and other variables. Parameters in human systems are directly controllable. The collection of variables necessary to describe a system at any point in time is called the *state* of the system. Examples of state variables for a software process are the number of personnel executing the process; the amount of software designed, coded, and tested; the current number of defects; and so on.

Real-world systems can be classified as static or dynamic depending on whether the state variables change over time. The state of a static system does not change over time, whereas the state of a dynamic system does. Dynamic systems can be further classified as continuous, discrete, or combined, based on how their variables change over time.

Variables change continuously (without breaks or irregularities) over time in a continuous system, whereas they change instantaneously at separated time points in a discrete system. A lake is an example of a continuous system since its depth changes continuously as a function of inflows and outflows, whereas a computer store queue would be considered discrete since the number of customers changes in discrete quantities. A software process arguably has continuous quantities (personnel experience, motivation, etc.) and discrete ones (lines of code, defects, etc.)

Whether a system is seen as continuous, discrete, or combined depends on one's perspective. Furthermore, the choice of a continuous or discrete representation depends on the modeling purpose, and some discrete systems can be assumed to be continuous for easy representation. For example, some would consider a software process to be a system with discrete entities since it can be described by the number of people working, number of units/lines/objects produced, defects originated, and so on, but much difficulty will be avoided if each entity does not need to be traced individually. Hence, the approach in this book and system dynamics in general is to treat the "flow" of the software process as continuous.

A software process is a set of activities, methods, practices, and transformations used by people to develop software. This is a general definition from the commonly accepted Software Engineering Institute's Capability Maturity Model (SEI CMM) [Paulk et al. 1994]. In the context of this book, the software process is the system under study.

A system must be represented in some form in order to analyze it and communicate about it. A *model* in the broadest sense is a representation of reality, ranging from physical mockups to graphical descriptions to abstract symbolic models. Software programs are themselves executable models of human knowledge. A model in the context of this book is a logical, quantitative description of how a process (system) behaves. The models are abstractions of real or conceptual systems used as surrogates for low cost experimentation and study. Models allow us to understand a process by dividing it into parts and looking at how they are related.

Dynamic process models can be discrete, continuous, or a combination of the two. The essential difference is how the simulation time is advanced. Continuous systems modeling methods such as system dynamics always advance time with a constant delta. Since variables may change within any time interval in a continuous system, the delta increment is very small and time-dependent variables are recomputed at the end of each time increment. The variables change continuously with respect to time. Discrete modeling normally is event based. State changes occur in discrete systems at aperiodic times depending on the event nature, at the beginning and end of event activities. The simulation time is advanced from one event to the next in a discrete manner.

All classes of systems may be represented by any of the model types. A discrete model is not always used to represent a discrete system and vice versa. The choice of model depends on the specific objectives of a study. Models of the software processes are either static,[1] in which time plays no role, or dynamic, in which a system evolves over time. The dynamic process models described this book are classified as symbolic, or mathematical ones.

Models may be deterministic, with no probabilistic components, or stochastic, with randomness in the components. Few, if any, software processes are wholly deterministic. Stochastic models produce output that is random and must be handled as such with independent runs. Each output constitutes an estimate of the system characteristics.

---

[1] A cost model such as COCOMO II [Boehm et al. 2000] is traditionally a static model since the cost factors are treated as constant for the project duration. However, there is a continuum between static and dynamic versions of COCOMO. There are variations that make it possible to introduce time into the calculations.

Simulation is the numerical evaluation of a mathematical model describing a system of interest. Many systems are too complex for closed-form analytical solutions, hence, simulation is used to exercise models with given inputs to see how the system performs. Simulation can be used to explain system behavior, improve existing systems, or to design new systems too complex to be analyzed by spreadsheets or flowcharts.

Finally, *system dynamics* is a simulation methodology for modeling continuous systems. Quantities are expressed as levels, rates, and information links representing feedback loops. Levels represent real-world accumulations and serve as the state variables describing a system at any point in time (e.g., the amount of software developed, number of defects, number of personnel on the team, etc.) Rates are the flows over time that affect the levels. See Table 1.3-1 for a preview description of model elements. System dynamics is described in much more detail in Chapter 2.

A complete and rigorous reference for terms related to modeling and simulation can be found at [DMSO 2006].

1.2 SYSTEMS THINKING

Systems thinking is a way to ferret out system structure and make inferences about the system, and is often described as an overall paradigm that uses system dynamics principles to realize system structure. Systems thinking is well suited to address software process improvement in the midst of complexity. Many organizations and their models gloss over process interactions and feedback effects, but these must be recognized to effect greater improvements.

Systems thinking involves several interrelated concepts:

- A mindset of thinking in circles and considering interdependencies. One realizes that cause and effect can run both ways. Straight-line thinking is replaced by closed-loop causality.
- Seeing the system as a cause rather than effect (internal vs. external orientation). Behavior originates within a system rather than being driven externally, so the system itself bears responsibility. It is the structure of a system that determines its dynamic behavior.
- Thinking dynamically in terms of ongoing relationships rather than statically.
- Having an operational vs. a correlational orientation; looking at how effects happen. Statistical correlation can often be misleading. A high correlation coefficient between two factors does not prove that one variable has an impact on the other.

Systems thinking is, therefore, a conceptual framework with a body of knowledge and tools to identify wide-perspective interactions, feedback, and recurring structures. Instead of focusing on open-loop, event-level explanations and assuming cause and effect are closely related in space and time, it recognizes the world really consists of multiple closed-loop feedbacks, delays, and nonlinear effects.

1.2.1 The Fifth Discipline and Common Models

Senge discusses five disciplines essential for organizational learning in [Senge 1990]: personal mastery, mental models, shared vision, team learning, and systems thinking. Systems thinking is the "fifth" discipline that integrates all the other disciplines and makes organizational learning work. Improvement through organizational learning takes place via shared mental models.

Mental models are used in everyday life for translating personal or organizational goals into issues, questions, and measures. They provide context for interpreting and acting on data, but seldom are stated explicitly. Mental models become more concrete and evolve as they are made progressively explicit. The power of models increases dramatically as they become more explicit and commonly understood by people; hence, process modeling is ideally suited for organizational improvement.

For organizational processes, mental models must be made explicit to frame concerns and share knowledge among other people on a team. Everyone then has the same picture of the process and its issues. Senge and Roberts provide examples of team techniques to elicit and formulate explicit representations of mental models in [Senge et al. 1994]. Collective knowledge is put into the models as the team learns. Elaborated representations in the form of simulation models become the bases for process improvement.

1.2.2 Systems Thinking Compared to System Dynamics

Systems thinking has been an overloaded term in the last 15 years with many definitions. Virtually any comparison with system dynamics is bound to be controversial due to semantic and philosophical issues. Barry Richmond addressed the differences between systems thinking and system dynamics mindsets in detail in [Richmond 1994a]. His major critique about "the historical emphasis of system dynamics" is that the focus has been on product rather than transferring the process (of model building). Only a privileged few developed models and presented them to the world as "the way" as opposed to educating others to model and letting them go at it.[2] His prescription is a systems thinking philosophy of providing skills rather than models per se. Relevant aphorisms include "Give a fish, eat for a day; teach to fish, eat for a lifetime," or "power to the people."

His definition of systems thinking is "the art and science of making reliable inferences about behavior by developing an increasingly deep understanding of underlying structure." It is both a paradigm and a learning method. The paradigm is a vantage point supplemented with thinking skills and the learning method is a process, language, and technology. The paradigm and learning method form a synergistic whole. System dynamics inherently fits in as the way to understand system structure. Thus, system dynamics is a methodology to implement systems thinking and leverage learning efforts.

We prefer not to make any hard distinctions between camps because it is a semantic issue. However, this book is architected in the spirit of systems thinking from the perspective of transferring the process. The goal is to teach people how to model and give

---

[2]It should be noted encouragingly that the system dynamics pioneer Jay Forrester and others at MIT are involved in teaching how to model with system dynamics in K–12 grades.

them tools to use for themselves, rather than say "here is the model for you to use." This is a major difference between *Software Project Dynamics* and this book. Abdel-Hamid and Madnick present a specific model with no guidance on how to develop a system dynamics model, though very few organizations are content to use the model as-is. Their work is still a seminal contribution and it helped make this book possible.

1.2.3 Weinberg's Systems Thinking

Gerry Weinberg writes about systems thinking applied to software engineering in *Quality Software Management, Volume 1: Systems Thinking* [Weinberg 1992]. It is an insightful book dealing with feedback control and has a close kinship with this book, even though it is almost exclusively qualitative and heuristic. Some academic courses may choose his book as a companion to this one. It provides valuable management insights and important feedback situations to be modeled in more detail.

Weinberg's main ideas focus around management thinking correctly about developing complex software systems—having the right "system model" for the project and its personnel. In a restatement of Brooks's dictum that lack of schedule time has doomed more projects than anything else, Weinberg writes in [Weinberg 1992], "Most software projects have gone awry from management's taking action based on *incorrect system models* than for all other causes combined."

One reason management action contributes to a runaway condition is the tendency to respond too late to deviations, which then forces management to take big actions, which themselves have nonlinear consequences. In order to stay in control of the software process, Weinberg advises to "act early, act small." Managers need to continually plan, observe the results, and then act to bring the actuals closer to planned. This is the prototypical feedback loop for management.

Weinberg was working on his book at the same time that Abdel-Hamid and Madnick were working on theirs, unknown to each other. The day after Weinberg submitted his work to the publisher, he met Abdel-Hamid and realized they were working on parallel and complementary paths for years. Weinberg describes the relationship between the two perspectives as follows. He starts from the low end, so projects get stable enough so that the more precise, high-end modeling exemplified by system dynamics can be even more useful.

Much of Weinberg's book discusses quality, on-the-job pressures, culture, feedback effects, dynamics of size and fault resolution, and more. He proceeds to describe the low-level interactions of software engineering, which are the underlying mechanics for many of the dynamic effects addressed by various process models described in this book. His work is referenced later and provides fodder for some exercises.

1.3 BASIC FEEDBACK SYSTEMS CONCEPTS APPLIED TO THE SOFTWARE PROCESS

Continuous systems modeling has a strong cybernetic thread. The word cybernetic derives from "to control or steer," and cybernetics is the field of science concerned with processes of communication and control (especially the comparison of these processes in biological and artificial systems) [Weiner 1961]. Cybernetic principles are relevant to many types of systems including moving vehicles (ground, air, water, or space), biological systems, individuals, groups of individuals, and species.

We are all familiar with internal real-time control processes, such as when driving down a road. We constantly monitor our car's position with respect to the lane and make small adjustments as the road curves or obstacles arise. The process of monitoring actual position against desired position and making steering adjustments is similar to tracking and controlling a software project. The same mathematics apply, so system dynamics can be used to model the control aspects of either human driving or project management.

Control systems theory provides a rigorous framework for analyzing complex feedback systems. This section will introduce some basic system notations and concepts, and apply to them to our system of study—the software process. The purpose is to realize a high-level analogy of control principles to our domain, and we will forego mathematical formulae and more sophisticated feedback notations.[3] System dynamics is our chosen method for modeling feedback systems in a continuous-time fashion, as used in the rest of this book.

Figure 1.1 shows the most basic representation of an open system, whereby a black-box system transforms input to output per its internal processing functions. Input and output signals are treated as fluxes over time. It is open because the outputs have no system influence (frequently, it is also called an *open-loop* system despite the absence of any explicit loops). Figure 1.2 shows the closed-loop version with a controller implementing feedback. A decomposition of the controller shows two major elements: a sensor and a control device, shown in Figure 1.3.

The borrowing of these standard depictions from control systems theory can lead to misinterpretation about the "system" of interest for software processes. In both Figures 1.2 and 1.3, the controller is also of major concern; it should not be thought of as being "outside" the system. One reason for problems in software process improvement is that management is often considered outside the system to be improved. Therefore, the boundary for a software process system including management should encompass all the elements shown, including the controller.

Applying these elements to the software process, inputs traditionally represent requirement specifications (or capabilities or change requests), the system is the software development (and evolution) process with the management controller function, and the outputs are the software product artifacts (including defects). The sensor could be any means of measuring the output (e.g., analyzing software metrics), and the control device is the management action used to align actual process results with intended. This notation can represent either a one-time project or a continual software evolution process.

If we consider all types of inputs to the software process, the vector includes resources and process standards as well as requirements. Resources include people and

---

[3]We are not covering signal polarities, integrators, summers, transfer functions, Laplace transforms, cascaded systems, state space representation, and so on.

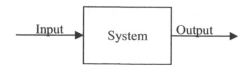

Figure 1.1. Open system.

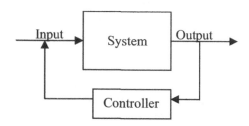

Figure 1.2. Closed system with controller.

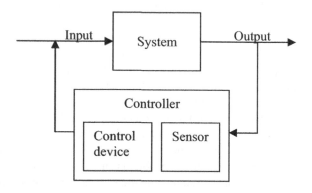

Figure 1.3. Closed system with controller elements.

machines used to develop and evolve the software. Process standards include methods, policies, procedures, and so on. Even the process life-cycle model used for the project can be included (see Section 1.3.2). Requirements include functional requirements, project constraints like budget and schedule, support environment requirements, evolution requirements, and more. Process control actions that management takes based on measurements may affect any of these inputs.

Substituting software process elements into the generic system description produces Figures 1.4, keeping the controller aggregated at the top level representing internal process management.

However, the management controller only represents endogenous process mechanisms local to the development team. These are self-initiated control mechanisms. In reality, there are external, or exogenous feedback forces from the operational environ-

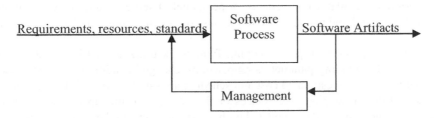

Figure 1.4. Software process control system with management controller.

ment of the software—global feedback. The feedback can be user change requests from the field, other stakeholder change mandates, market forces, or virtually any external source of requirements evolution or volatility. The exogenous feedback is a very important effect to understand and try to control. An enhanced picture showing the two sources of feedback is in Figure 1.5.

The outer, global feedback loop is an entire area of study in itself. Of particular note is the work of Manny Lehman and colleagues on software evolution, which is highlighted in Chapter 5 and referenced in several other places (also see their entries in Appendix B).

These feedback mechanisms shown with control systems notation are implemented in various ways in the system dynamics models shown later. Feedback is represented as information connections to flow rates (representing policies) or other parameters that effect changes in the systems through connected flow rates.

1.3.1   Using Simulation Models for Project Feedback

Projects can proactively use simulation models to adapt to change, thereby taking advantage of feedback to improve through models. This is one way to implement operational control through simulation. A simulation model can be used for metrics-based feedback during project execution since its input parameters represent project objec-

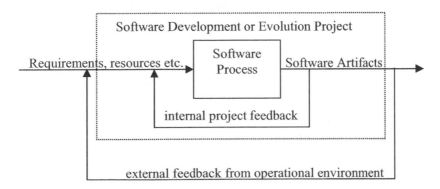

Figure 1.5. Software process control system with internal and external feedback.

tives, priorities, available components, or personnel. It serves as a framework for project rescoping and line management to reassess risks continuously and support replanning.

Figure 1.6 shows a project rescoping framework utilizing metrics feedback and simulation. By inputting parameters representing changed conditions, one can assess whether the currently estimated cost and schedule are satisfactory and if action should be taken. Either rescoping takes places or the project executes to another feedback milestone, where the model is updated with actuals to date and the cycle repeats.

1.3.2 System Dynamics Introductory Example

Table 1.1 is a heads-up preview of system dynamics model elements used throughout this book. The capsule summary may help to interpret the following two examples before more details are provided in Chapter 2 (this table is a shortened version of one in Chapter 2). We are jumping ahead a bit in order to introduce a simple Brooks's Law model. Novices may also want to consult the system dynamics introduction in Chapter 2 to better understand the model elements.

Throughout this text and in other references, levels are synonymous with "stocks" and rates are also called "flows." Thus, a stock and flow representation means an elaborated model consisting of levels and rates.

A simple demonstration example of modeling process feedback is shown in the Figure 1.7 system diagram. In this model, the software production rate depends on the number of personnel, and the number of people working on the project is controlled via a feedback loop. The linear *software production rate* is expressed as

$$\text{software production rate} = \text{individual productivity} \cdot \text{personnel}$$

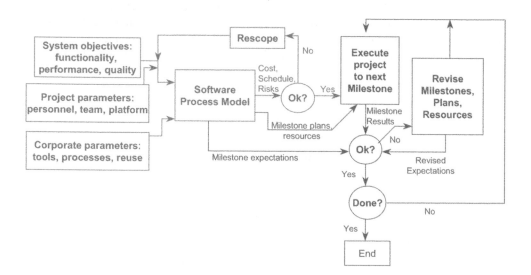

Figure 1.6. Project rescoping framework.

Table 1.1. System dynamics model elements (capsule summary)

Element	Notation	Description
Level		A level is an accumulation over time, also called a stock or state variable. They are functions of past accumulation of flow rates. Examples include software tasks of different forms, defect levels, or personnel levels.
Source/Sink		Sources and sinks indicate that flows come from or go to somewhere external to the process. They represent infinite supplies or repositories that are not specified in the model. Examples include sources of requirements, delivered software, or employee hiring sources and attrition sinks.
Rate		Rates are also called flows. They are the "actions" in a system. They effect the changes in levels and may represent decisions or policy statements. Examples include software productivity rate, defect generation rate, or personnel hiring and deallocation rates.
Auxiliary		Auxiliaries are converters of input to output, and help elaborate the detail of stock and flow structures. Auxiliaries often represent "score-keeping" variables and may include percent of job completion, quantitative goals or planned values, defect density, or constants like average delay times.
Information Link		Information linkages are used to represent information flow (as opposed to material flow). Links can represent closed-path feedback loops between elements. They link process parameters to rates and other variables. Examples include progress and status information for decision making, or knowledge of defect levels to allocate rework resources.

The management decision that utilizes feedback from the actual work accomplished is the following equation for personnel allocation:

personnel allocation rate = if (completed software < planned completion) then 1 else 0

This highly oversimplified feedback decision says to add a person whenever actual progress is less than planned. If actual progress meets or exceeds the planned progress, than no changes are made to the staff (zero people are added). Presumably, this management policy would keep a project on track, assuming a productivity increase when

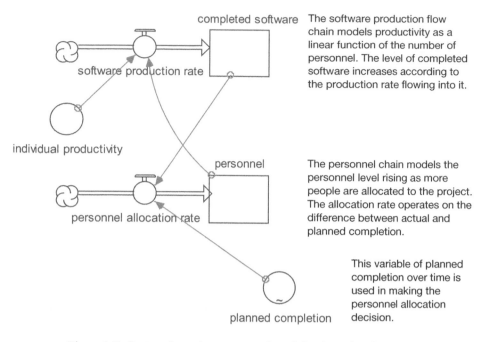

completed software   The software production flow
chain models productivity as a
linear function of the number of
personnel. The level of completed
software increases according to
the production rate flowing into it.

software production rate

individual productivity

personnel   The personnel chain models the
personnel level rising as more
people are allocated to the project.
The allocation rate operates on the
difference between actual and
planned completion.

personnel allocation rate

This variable of planned
completion over time is
used in making the
personnel allocation
decision.

planned completion

Figure 1.7. System dynamics representation of simple project feedback.

someone is added. It does not consider other ripple effects or nonlinearities of adding
extra people, which is addressed in the next example.

1.4 BROOKS'S LAW EXAMPLE

A small motivational example of modeling Brooks's Law is described here. In the early software engineering classic *The Mythical Man-Month* (it was also updated in 1995), Fred Brooks stated, "Adding manpower to a late software project makes it later" [Brooks 1975]. His explanation for the law was the additional linear overhead needed for training new people and the nonlinear communication overhead (a function of the square of the number of people). These effects have been widely accepted and observed by others. The simple model in Figure 1.8 describes the situation, and will be used to test the law. Model equations and commentary are in Figure 1.9.[4] This model is

---

[4]Mathematically inclined readers may appreciate differential equations to represent the levels. This representation is *not* necessary to understand the model. The following integrals accumulate the inflow and outflow rates over time to calculate a level at any time *t* using the standard notation:

$$\text{level} = \text{level}_{t=0} + \int_0^t (\text{inflow - outflow}) \, dt$$

$$\text{requirements} = \text{requirements}_{t=0} - \int_0^t (\text{software development rate}) \, dt$$

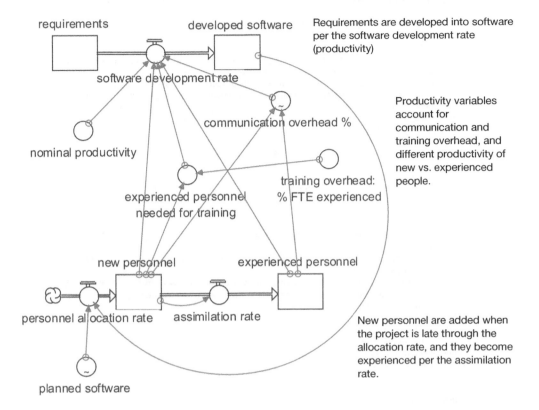

requirements   developed software   Requirements are developed into software
                                                      per the software development rate
                                                      (productivity)

software development rate

communication overhead %   Productivity variables
                                    account for
                                    communication and
nominal productivity   training overhead, and
                                    different productivity of
                                    new vs. experienced
training overhead: people.
% FTE experienced

experienced personnel
needed for training

new personnel   experienced personnel

personnel allocation rate   assimilation rate

New personnel are added when
the project is late through the
allocation rate, and they become
experienced per the assimilation
rate.

planned software

Figure 1.8. Brooks's Law model.

described below assuming no background in systems dynamics. More detail on model notations and equations are discussed in Chapter 2.

The model is conceived around the following basic assumptions:

- New personnel require training by experienced personnel to come up to speed.
- More people on a project entail more communication overhead.
- Experienced personnel are more productive than new personnel, on average.

It is built on two connected flow chains representing software development and personnel. The software development chain assumes a level of *requirements* that needs to

---

$$\text{developed software} = \text{developed software}_{t=0} + \int_0^t (\text{software development rate}) \, dt$$

$$\text{new personnel} = \text{new personnel}_{t=0} - \int_0^t (\text{assimilation rate}) \, dt$$

$$\text{experienced personnel} = \text{experienced personnel}_{t=0} + \int_0^t (\text{assimilation rate}) \, dt$$

☐ developed_software(t) = developed_software(t - dt) + (software_development_rate) * dt
    INIT developed_software = 0

    DOCUMENT: This level represents software function points that have been implemented.
    INFLOWS:
        ⇨ software_development_rate =
            nominal_productivity*(1-communication_overhead_%/100.)*(.8*new_personnel+1.2*(experi
            enced_personnel-experienced_personnel_needed_for_training))
            DOCUMENT: The development rate represents productivity adjusted for communication
            overhead, weighting factors for the varying mix of personnel, and the effective number of
            experienced personnel.
☐ experienced_personnel(t) = experienced_personnel(t - dt) + (assimilation_rate) * dt
    INIT experienced_personnel = 20

    DOCUMENT: The number of experienced personnel.
    INFLOWS:
        ⇨ assimilation_rate = new_personnel/20
            DOCUMENT: The average assimilation time for new personnel is 20 days.
☐ new_personnel(t) = new_personnel(t - dt) + (personnel_allocation_rate - assimilation_rate) * dt
    INIT new_personnel = 0

    DOCUMENT: The number of new project personnel.
    INFLOWS:
        ⇨ personnel_allocation_rate = if ((developed_software - planned_software) < - 75 and time
            <112) then 10 else 0
            DOCUMENT: If the gap between developed software and planned software becomes 15% of
            the plan (75 function points), then add people. The time condition constrains the correction
            to one time, for demonstration.
    OUTFLOWS:
        ⇨ assimilation_rate = new_personnel/20
            DOCUMENT: The average assimilation time for new personnel is 20 days.
☐ requirements(t) = requirements(t - dt) + (- software_development_rate) * dt
    INIT requirements = 500

    DOCUMENT: The project size is 500 function points. This level represents the number left to be
    implemented.
    OUTFLOWS:
        ⇨ software_development_rate =
            nominal_productivity*(1-communication_overhead_%/100.)*(.8*new_personnel+1.2*(experi
            enced_personnel-experienced_personnel_needed_for_training))
            DOCUMENT: The development rate represents productivity adjusted for communication
            overhead, weighting factors for the varying mix of personnel, and the effective number of
            experienced personnel.
○ experienced_personnel_needed_for_training =
    new_personnel*training_overhead:_%_FTE_experienced/100
    DOCUMENT: Training overhead is the effort expended by experienced personnel to bring new
    people up to speed. It is the number of new personnel * the percent of an experienced person's
    time dedicated to training.
○ nominal_productivity = .1
    DOCUMENT: The nominal (unadjusted) productivity is .1 function points/person-day.
○ total_personnel = experienced_personnel+new_personnel
○ training_overhead:_%_FTE_experienced = 25
    DOCUMENT: Percent of full-time equivalent experienced person's time dedicated to training new
    hires.
⊘ communication_overhead_% = GRAPH((experienced_personnel+new_personnel))
    (0.00, 0.00), (5.00, 1.50), (10.0, 6.00), (15.0, 13.5), (20.0, 24.0), (25.0, 37.5), (30.0, 54.0)
    DOCUMENT: Percent of time spent communicating with other team members as a function of team
    size. This graph represents the n^2 law in this size region, and was used in the Abdel-Hamid
    model.
⊘ planned_software = GRAPH(time)
    (0.00, 0.00), (20.0, 50.0), (40.0, 100), (60.0, 150), (80.0, 200), (100, 250), (120, 300), (140, 350), (160,
    400), (180, 450), (200, 500)
    DOCUMENT: Plan assumes a constant productivity of 2.5 function points per day.

Figure 1.9. Brooks's Law model equations.

be implemented (shown as the upper left box in Figure 1.8). The *requirements* are transformed into *developed software* at the *software development rate* (rates are shown as the circular pipe-valve symbols). Sometimes, this rate is called "project velocity" (especially by practitioners of agile methods). The level of *developed software* represents progress made on implementing the requirements. Project completion is when *developed software* equals the initial *requirements*. Software size is measured in function points, and the development rate is in function points/day. A function point is a measure of software size that accounts for external inputs and outputs, user interactions, external interfaces, and files used by the system [IFPUG 2004].

The *software development rate* is determined by the levels of personnel in the system: *new project personnel* who come onto the project at the *personnel allocation rate*, and *experienced personnel* who have been assimilated (trained) into the project at the assimilation rate. Further variables in the system are shown as circles in the diagram. Documentation for each model element is shown underneath its equation in Figure 1.9. When constructing the model, the time-based level equations are automatically generated by visually laying out the levels and rates with a simulation tool.

1.4.1 Brooks's Law Model Behavior

The model is a high-level depiction of a level-of-effort project. It allows tracking the *software development rate* over time and assessing the final completion time to develop the requirements under different hiring conditions. When the gap between *developed software* and the *planned software* becomes too great, people are added at the *personnel allocation rate*. All parameters are set to reasonable approximations as described below and in the equation commentary. The overall model represents a nominal case, and would require calibration to specific project environments.

As time progresses, the number of *requirements* decreases since this represents requirements still left to implement. These requirements are processed over time at the *software development rate* and become *developed software,* so *requirements* decline as *developed software* rises. The *software development rate* is constrained by several factors: the *nominal productivity* of a person, the *communication overhead %,* and the effective number of personnel.

The effective number of personnel equals the *new project personnel* plus the *experienced personnel* minus the amount of *experienced personnel needed for training* the new people. The *communication overhead %* is expressed as a nonlinear function of the total number of personnel that need to communicate ($0.06 \cdot n^2$, where n is the number of people). This overhead formulation is described in [Abdel-Hamid, Madnick 1991]. The *experienced personnel needed for training* is the training overhead percentage as a fraction of a full-time equivalent (FTE) experienced personnel. The default of 0.25 indicates that one-quarter of an experienced person's time is needed to train a new person until he/she is fully assimilated.

The bottom structure of the personnel chain models the assimilation of *new project personnel* at an average rate of 20 days. In essence, a new person is trained by one-fourth of an experienced person for an average of 20 days until they become experienced in the project.

The *nominal productivity* is set to 0.1 function points/person-day, with the productivities of new and experienced personnel set to 0.8 · *nominal productivity* and 1.2 · *nominal productivity,* respectively, as a first-order approximation (the fractions roughly mimic the COCOMO II cost model experience factors [Boehm et al. 2000]).

Static conditions are present in the model when no additional people are added. These conditions are necessary to validate a model before adding perturbations (this validation is shown as an example in Chapter 2). The default behavior of the model shows a final completion time of 274 days to develop 500 function points with a constant staff of 20 experienced personnel.

The first experiment will inject an instantaneous pulse of 5 new people when a schedule variance of 15% is reached at about day 110. On the next run, 10 people will be added instead. Figure 1.10 is a sensitivity plot of the corresponding software development rates for the default condition and the two perturbation runs.

Figure 1.10 now shows some interesting effects. With an extra staff of five people (curve #2), the development rate nosedives, then recovers after a few weeks to slightly overtake the default rate and actually finishes sooner at 271 days. However, when 10 people are added the overall project suffers (curve #3). The initial productivity loss takes longer to stabilize, the final productivity is lower with the larger staff, and the schedule time elongates to 296 days. The smooth recovery seen on both are due to the training effect. The extra staff productivity gains in the first case are greater than the communication losses, but going from 20 to 30 people in the second case entails a larger communication overhead compared to the potential productivity gain from having more people.

This model of Brooks's Law demonstrates that the law holds only under certain conditions (Brooks did not mean to imply that the law held in all situations). There is a

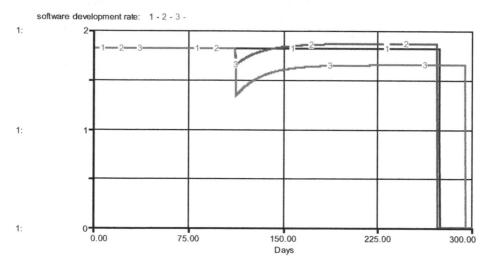

Figure 1.10 Sensitivity of software development rate to varying personnel allocation pulses (1: no extra hiring, 2: add 5 people on 110th day, 3: add 10 people on 110th day).

threshold of new people that can be added until the schedule suffers, showing the trade-off between adding staff and the time in the life cycle. Note that only schedule time was analyzed here, and that effort increased in both cases of adding people. The effort may also be taken into account for a true project decision (though schedule may often be the primary performance index regardless of the cost).

There is a trade-off between the number of added people and the time in the life cycle. The model can be used to experiment with different scenarios to quantify the operating region envelope of Brooks's Law. A specific addition of people may be tolerable if injected early enough, but not later. The project time determines how many can be effectively added.

The model uses simplified assumptions and boundaries, and can be refined in several ways. The parameters for communication overhead, training overhead, assimilation rate, and other formulations of personnel allocation are also important to vary for a thorough sensitivity analysis. A myriad of different combinations can and should still be tested. This model is analyzed in more detail in Chapter 2 to illustrate the principles of sensitivity analysis, and Chapter 6 has an advanced exercise to extend it.

This exercise has demonstrated that a small-scale and simple model can help shed light on process phenomena. Even though the model contains simple formulations, the dynamic time trends would be very time-consuming for a person to manually calculate and all but impossible to mentally figure.

Based on the insight provided, we may now clarify Brooks's Law. *Adding manpower to a late software project makes it later if too much is added too late.* That is when the additional overhead is greater than productivity gains due to the extra staff, as subject to local conditions.

This model is a microcosm of the system dynamics experience. Simplifying assumptions are made that coincide with the simple purpose of this model. Many aspects of the model can be challenged further, such as the following:

- Determining the adequacy of the model before experimenting with it
- Boundary issues: where do requirements come from, and why is there no attrition of people
- Accounting for new requirements coming in after the project has begun
- Varying the starting levels of new and experienced personnel
- Alternate representations to model learning by new hires
- Effects of different hiring scenarios (e.g., step or ramp inputs rather than a single pulse)
- Different relative productivities for experienced and new personnel
- Different communication overhead relationship
- Team partitioning when more people are added
- The policy of determining schedule variance and associated actions

All of these issues will be addressed in subsequent chapters that discuss this Brooks's Law model and others.

1.5 SOFTWARE PROCESS TECHNOLOGY OVERVIEW

Software process technology encompasses three general and overlapping areas: process modeling, process life-cycle models, and process improvement. These areas address highly critical issues in software engineering. A typical example of overlap is modeling of life-cycle processes to achieve process improvement. This book involves all three areas, but the major focus is process modeling with the given technique of system dynamics. Lessons learned from the modeling will give insight into choosing life-cycle models and improving processes. Background on each of these related areas follows in the next subsections.

The term *process model* is overloaded and has meaning in all three contexts. A simulation process model is an executable mathematical model like a system dynamics model, which is the default meaning for process model in this book. However, life-cycle approaches that define the steps performed for software development are sometimes called process models, so the term life-cycle process is used here. Finally, frameworks for process improvement such as Capability Maturity Models, Six Sigma, or ISO 9000 described in Section 1.3.3 are sometimes called process models.

1.5.1 Software Process Modeling

A high-level overview of the software process modeling field is contained in this section, and the remainder of the book expounds on process modeling with system dynamics. Process modeling is representing a process architecture, design, or definition in the abstract. Concrete process modeling has been practiced since the early days of software development [Benington 1956]. Abstract software process modeling started in earnest after Leon Osterweil's landmark paper titled "Software Processes are Software Too" [Osterweil 1987]. The title of Osterweil's statement neatly captures some important principles. As software products are so complex and difficult to grasp, processes to build them should be described as rigorously as possible (with the same precision and rigor used for the software itself). "Process programming" refers to systematic techniques and formalisms used to describe software processes. These techniques to produce process objects are very much the same as those used for software artifacts. The resulting process objects are instantiated and executed on projects. Hence, process descriptions should be considered software and process programming should be an essential focus in software engineering.

Since Osterweil's argument that we should be as good at modeling the software process as modeling applications, software process modeling has gained very high interest in the community among both academic researchers and practitioners as an approach and technique for analyzing complex business and policy questions.

Process modeling can support process definition, process improvement, process management, and automated process-driven environments. Common purposes of simulation models are to provide a basis for experimentation, to predict behavior, answer "what if" questions, or teach about the system being modeled [Kellner et al. 1999]. Such models are usually quantitative. As a means of reasoning about software processes, process models provide a mechanism for recording and understanding processes, and evaluating, communicating, and promoting process improvements. Thus, process models are a vehicle for improving software engineering practice.

A software process model focuses on a particular aspect of a process as currently implemented (as-is), or as planned for the future (to-be). A model, as an abstraction, represents only some of the many aspects of a software process that potentially could be modeled, in particular those aspects relevant to the process issues and questions at hand.

Models can be used to quantitatively evaluate the software process, implement process reengineering and benchmark process improvement since calibrated models encapsulate organizational metrics. Organizations can experiment with changed processes before committing project resources. A compelling reason for utilizing simulation models is when the costs, risks, or logistics of manipulating the real system of interest are prohibitive (otherwise one would just manipulate the real system).

Process models can also be used for interactive training of software managers; this is sometimes called "process flight simulation." A pilot training analogy is a handy one to understand the role of simulation. Before pilots are allowed to fly jet planes or space vehicles, they are first required to spend thousands of hours in flight simulation, perfecting their skills and confronting different scenarios. This effective form of risk minimization is needed due to the extremely high risks of injury, death, and damaged vehicles. Unfortunately, software managers are too often required to confront project situations without really training for them (despite the very high risks). Why not use simulation to prepare them better?

A model result variable is a primary output of a process simulation. Typical result variables for software process simulation include effort, cycle time, defect levels, staffing requirements over time, return on investment (ROI), throughput, productivity, and queue lengths. Many of these variables may be reported for the entire simulation or any portion thereof. Some result variables are best looked at as continuous functions (e.g., staffing requirements), whereas others only make sense at the end of the process being simulated (e.g., ROI). A more detailed overview of the what, why, and how of software process modeling can be found in [Kellner et al. 1999].

1.5.1.1 *Modeling Approaches*

To support the aforementioned objectives, process models must go beyond static representation to support process analysis. Unfortunately, there is no standard approach for process modeling. A variety of process definition and simulation methods exist that answer unique subsets of process questions.

Five general approaches to representing process information, as described and reviewed in [Curtis et al. 1992], are programming models (process programming), functional models, plan-based models, Petri-net models (role interaction nets), and system dynamics. The suitability of a modeling approach depends on the goals and objectives for the resulting model. No current software process modeling approach fully satisfies the diverse goals and objectives previously mentioned. Most of these approaches are still used. Over the years, experience has shown that Petri-net models do not scale very well for software processes [Osterweil 2005].

An earlier technique for process modeling is the Articulator approach [Scacchi-Mi 1993]. They created a knowledge-based computing environment that uses artificial intelligence scheduling techniques from production systems for modeling, analyzing, and simulating organizational processes. Classes of organizational resources are modeled using an object-oriented knowledge-representation scheme. Simulation takes place through the symbolic performance of process tasks by assigned agents using tools and other resources.

Other simulation modeling variants that have been applied to software processes include state-based process models, general discrete event simulation, rule-based languages, scheduling approaches, queueing models, and project management (CPM and PERT).

Process modeling languages and representations usually present one or more perspectives related to the process. Some of the most commonly represented perspectives are functional, behavioral, organizational, and informational. They are analogous to different viewpoints on an observable process. Although separate, these representations are interrelated and a major difficulty is tying them together [Curtis et al. 1992], [Kellner 1991]. Ideally, a single approach combines process representation, guidance, simulation, and execution capabilities.

A discrete process modeling approach that combines several language paradigms was developed by Kellner, Raffo, and colleagues at the Software Engineering Institute (SEI) [Kellner 1991], [Raffo 1995]. They used tools that provide state transitions with events and triggers, systems analysis, and design diagrams and data modeling to support representation, analysis, and simulation of processes. This approach enables a quantitative simulation that combines the functional, behavioral, and organizational perspectives.

The two main techniques to gain favor over the last decade are system dynamics and discrete-event simulation. A comparison of the relative strengths and weaknesses between the two are provided in [Kellner et al. 1999], and subsequent chapters in this book discusses their trade-offs for some applications. Recently, agent-based approaches have also been used, and they are expected to increase in popularity [Smith et al. 2006].

Various hybrid approaches have also been used. System dynamics and discrete-event models were combined in a hybrid approach in [Martin-Raffo 2001], [Martin 2002]. Another hybrid two-level modeling approach in [Donzelli, Iazeolla 2001] combines analytical, continuous and discrete-event methods. At the higher abstraction level, the process is modeled by a discrete-event queuing network, which models the component activities (i.e. service stations), their interactions, and the exchanged artifacts. The implementation details of the introduced activities are given at the lower abstraction level, where the analytical and continuous methods are used.

Little-JIL is a graphical method for process programming inspired by Osterweil. It defines processes that coordinate the activities of autonomous agents and their use of resources during the performance of a task [Wise et al. 2000], [Wise et al. 2006]. It uses pre-conditions, post-conditions, exception handlers and a top-down decomposition tree. Programs made with Little-JIL are executable so agents can be guided through a process and ensure that their actions adhere to the process. It is a flexible and adaptive language initially used to coordinate agents in software engineering [Wise et al. 2000], though recently the process formalism has been applied to other domains besides software demonstrating "ubiquitous process engineering" [Osterweil 2006].

1.5.1.1.1   STATIC VERSUS DYNAMIC MODELING. Traditional analysis approaches are static and cannot capture the dynamic feedback loops that cause real-world complexity. Static modeling techniques assume that time plays no role. Factors are invariant over the duration of a project or other applicable time horizon. However, the dynamic behavior of a system is one of the complexities encountered in real systems. Dynamic models are used when the behavior of the system changes over time and is of particular interest or significance.

For example, static cost and schedule estimation models such as COCOMO II derivatives [Boehm et al. 2000], SEER [Galorath 2005], True-S (formerly PRICE-S) [PRICE 2005], or others provide valuable insight for understanding software project trade-off relationships, but their static form makes it difficult to help reason about complex dynamic project situations. These may include hybrid processes with a mix of life cycles, agile and open-source development methods, or schedule optimization focusing on critical-path tasks. These situations may require understanding of complex feedback processes involving such interacting phenomena as schedule pressure, communication overhead, or numerous others.

1.5.1.1.2   SYSTEM DYNAMICS. The discipline of modeling software processes with system dynamics started with Tarek Abdel-Hamid developing his seminal model of software development for his Ph.D. at MIT. His dissertation was completed in 1984, and he wrote some intervening articles before publishing the book *Software Project Dynamics*[5] with Stuart Madnick in 1991 [Abdel-Hamid, Madnick 1991]. Since then, over 100 publications have directly dealt with software process modeling with system dynamics (see Appendix B for an annotated bibliography of these).

System dynamics is one of the few modeling techniques that involves quantitative representation. Feedback and control system techniques are used to model social and industrial phenomena. Dynamic behavior, as modeled through a set of interacting equations, is difficult to reproduce through modeling techniques that do not provide dynamic feedback loops. The value of system dynamics models is tied to the extent that constructs and parameters represent actual observed project states.

System dynamics addresses process improvement and management particularly well. It also helps facilitate human understanding and communication of the process, but does not explicitly consider automated process guidance or automated execution support. Some system dynamicists stress that *understanding* of system behavior and structure is the primary value of system dynamics as opposed to strict prediction.

As will be detailed in subsequent sections, software process modeling with system dynamics has been used in a large number of companies, governmental agencies

---

[5]Abdel-Hamid's model and book describe project dynamics for a single fixed process. The title of this book, *Software Process Dynamics,* conveys a more general view of processes and provides assets to analyze a variety of processes, including those outside of project boundaries.

around the world, university research and teaching, and other nonprofit institutions, and has been deployed in marketable software engineering toolsets. It has been used in numerous areas for software processes. The reader is encouraged to read Appendix B to understand the breadth of applications and work in this area.

1.5.1.1.2.1 Why Not Spreadsheets? Many people have tried to use spreadsheets to build dynamic models and failed. Spreadsheets are designed to capture discrete changes rather than a continuous view. It is extremely difficult to use them to model time-based relationships between factors and simulate a system continuously over time. Additionally, they are not made to easily generate different scenarios, which are necessary to analyze risks.

Using spreadsheets for dynamic modeling is a very tedious process that requires each time step to be modeled (e.g., four rows or columns are needed to simulate a week using a standard time step of 0.25). Additionally, this method is actually modeling a difference equation, not a continuous-time model. There is much peril in this approach and it is very easy for errors to creep in with all the related time equations. Some of the basic laws of system dynamics can innocently be violated such as requiring a stock or level in each feedback loop.

But spreadsheets can be important tools for modeling and used in conjunction with simulation tools. They can be used for a variety of purposes, most notably for analyzing outputs of many simulation runs, optimizing parameters, and for generating inputs for the models (such as a stream of random variables). Some system dynamics tools include these capabilities and some do not (a list of available tools is in Chapter 2).

1.5.1.2 Process Model Characterization

Software process modeling can be used in a wide variety of situations per the structure of Table 1.2. The applications shown are representative examples of major models and, thus, are only a sliver of all possible applications. The matrix structure was originated by Marc Kellner as a framework for characterizing modeling problems and relevant modeling work in terms of scope (what is covered) and purpose (why) for the annual Software Process Simulation (ProSim) workshops. System dynamics can be used to address virtually every category, so the table is incompletely populated (it would grow too big if all applications in Appendix B were represented). The matrix can also be used to place the result variables of a simulation study in the proper categorization cell.

The primary purposes of simulation models are summarized below:

- *Strategic management* questions address the long-term impact of current or prospective policies and initiatives. These issues address large portfolios of projects, product-line approaches, long-term practices related to key organizational strengths for competitive advantage, and so on.

- *Planning* involves the prediction of project effort, cost, schedule, quality, and so on. These can be applied to both initial planning and subsequent replanning. These predictions help make decisions to select, customize, and tailor the best process for a specific project context.

Table 1.2. Process modeling characterization matrix and representative major models

	Scope				
Purpose	Portion of Life Cycle	Development Project	Multiple, Concurrent Projects	Long-Term Product Evolution	Long-Term Organization
Strategic Management				Global Feedback [Wernick, Lehman 1999]	Acquisition [Greer et al. 2005]
				Progressive and Anti-Regressive Work [Ramil et al. 2005]	
				Value-Based Product [Madachy 2005]	
Planning	Architecting [Fakharzadeh, Mehta 1999]	Integrated Project Dynamics [Abdel-Hamid, Madnick 1991] Reliability [Rus 1998]	Hybrid Processes [Madachy et al. 2007]		IT Planning [Williford, Chang 1999]
		Requirements Volatility [Pfahl, Lebsanft 2000] [Ferreira 2002]			
		Hybrid Project Modeling [Martin 2002]			
		Operational Release Plans [Pfahl et al. 2006]			
Control and Operational Management		Risk Management [Houston 2000]	Time-Constrained Development [Powell 2001]		

(continued)

Table 1.2. *Continued*

			Scope		
Purpose	Portion of Life Cycle	Development Project	Multiple, Concurrent Projects	Long-Term Product Evolution	Long-Term Organization
Process Improvement and Technology Adoption	Sociological Factors in Requirements Development [Christie, Staley 2000]	Inspections [Madachy 1994b] [Tvedt 1996]			Organizational Improvement [Rubin et al. 1994] [Burke 1996] [Stallinger 2000] [Pfahl et al. 2004] [Ruiz et al. 2004]
Training and Learning		Project Management [Collofello 2000] [Pfahl et al. 2001] [Barros et al. 2006]			

- *Control and operational management* involves project tracking and oversight once a project has already started. Project actuals can be monitored and compared against planned values computed by simulation, to help determine when corrective action may be needed. Monte Carlo simulation and other statistical techniques are useful in this context. Simulation is also used to support key operational decisions such as whether to commence major activities.
- *Process improvement and technology adoption* is supported by simulation both *a priori* or *ex post*. Process alternatives can be compared by modeling the impact of potential process changes or new technology adoption before putting them into actual practice. The purpose is process improvement, in contrast to planning. Simulation can also be used ex post to evaluate the results of process changes or selections already implemented.
- *Training and learning* simulation applications are expressly created for instructional settings. Simulations provide a way for personnel to practice or learn project management, similar to pilots practicing on flight simulators.

The original taxonomy also had a purpose category for "understanding" [Kellner et al. 1999]. That designation is not used here because all models fit in that category. All simulation models promote understanding in some way or another (training and learning are also particularly close semantically). Though some applications may be more dedicated to "theory building" than actual process or project applications (notably the work of Manny Lehman and colleagues on software evolution theory), those efforts are mapped to their potential application areas. More details on the specific categorizations can be found in [Kellner et al. 1999].

The questions and issues being addressed by a study largely determine the choice of result variables, much like choosing a modeling approach. For example, technology adoption questions often suggest an economic measure such as ROI; operational management issues often focus on the traditional project management concerns of effort, cycle time, and defect levels. It is common to produce multiple result variables from a single simulation model.

1.5.2 Process Life-Cycle Models

Broadly speaking, a process life-cycle model determines the steps taken and order of the stages involved in software development or evolution, and establishes the transition criteria between stages. Note that a life-cycle model can address portfolios of projects such as in product-line development, not just single projects. An often perplexing problem is choosing an appropriate process for individual situations. Should a waterfall or iterative process be used? Is an agile process a good fit for the project constraints and goals? What about incremental development, spiral risk-driven processes, the personal software process, specific peer review methods, and so on? Should the software be developed new or should one buy COTS or use open-source components? Dynamic simulation models can enable strategic planners and managers to assess the cost, schedule, or quality consequences of alternative life-cycle process strategies.

The most commonly used life-cycle models are described in the following subsections. Knowing about the alternative processes is important background to better understand process behavior and trade-offs in the field. From a pragmatic modeling perspective, it also helps to understand the different life cycles in order to have a good modeling process for given situations. Chapter 2 describes the modeling process as being iterative in general, but aspects from other life cycles may also be important to consider. The spiral process in particular is a good fit for modeling projects (also see Chapter 2).

The proliferation of process models provides flexibility for organizations to deal with the wide variety of software project situations, cultures, and environments, but it weakens their defenses against some common sources of project failure, and leaves them with no common anchor points around which to plan and control. In the iterative development section, milestones are identified that can serve as common anchor points in many different process models.

1.5.2.1 Waterfall Process

The conventional waterfall process is a single-pass, sequential approach that progresses through requirements analysis, design, coding, testing, and integration. Theoretically, each phase must be completed before the next one starts. Variations of the waterfall model normally contain the essential activities of specification, design, code, test, and, frequently, operations/maintenance. Figure 1.11 shows the commonly accepted waterfall process model.

The first publication of a software process life-cycle model was by Winston Royce [Royce 1970]. In this original version of the waterfall, he offered two primary enhancements to existing practices at the time: (1) feedback loops between stages and (2) a "build-it-twice" step parallel with requirements analysis, akin to prototyping (see next section). The irony is that the life-cycle model was largely practiced and interpreted without the feedback and "build-it-twice" concept. Since organizations historically implement the waterfall sequentially, the standard waterfall definition does not include Royce's improvements.[6]

The waterfall was further popularized in a version that contained verification, validation, or test activity at the end of each phase to ensure that the objectives of the phase were satisfied [Boehm 1976]. The phases are sequential, none can be skipped, and baselines are produced throughout the phases. No changes to baselines are made unless all interested parties agree. The economic rationale for the model is that to achieve a successful product, all of the subgoals within each phase must be met and that a different ordering of the phases will produce a less successful product.

However, the waterfall model implies a sequential, document-driven approach to product development, which is often impractical due to shifting requirements. Some other critiques of the waterfall model include: a lack of user involvement, ineffectiveness in the requirements phase, inflexibility to accommodate prototypes, unrealistic separation of specification from design, gold plating, inflexible point solutions, inability to accommodate reuse, and various maintenance-related problems.

Some of the difficulties of the waterfall life-cycle model have been addressed by extending it for incremental development, parallel development, evolutionary change, automatic code generation, and other refinements. Many of these respond to the inadequacies of the waterfall by delivering executable objects early to the user and increasing the role of automation. The following sections describe selected enhancements and alternatives to the waterfall model. Note that process models can be synthesized into hybrid approaches when appropriate.

1.5.2.2 Incremental Development

The incremental approach is an offshoot of the waterfall model that develops a system in separate increments versus a single-cycle approach. All requirements are determined up front and subsets of requirements are allocated to individual increments or releases. The increments are developed in sequential cycles, with each incremental release adding functionality. The incremental approach reduces overall effort and provides an initial system earlier to the customer. The effort phase distributions are different and the overall schedule may lengthen somewhat. Typically, there is more effort in requirements analysis and design, and less for coding and integration.

---

[6]His son, Walker Royce, has modernized life-cycle concepts in [Royce 1998], but also defends the original waterfall model and describes how practitioners implemented it in wrong ways that led to failures.

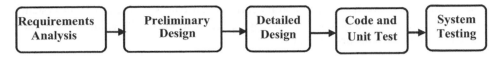

Figure 1.11. Conventional waterfall process.

The incremental process is sometimes called staged delivery, since software is provided in successively refined stages. Requirements analysis and preliminary architectural design is done once up front for all increments. Once the design is complete, the system can be implemented and delivered in stages. Some advantages of staged delivery include: (1) it allows useful functionality to be put into the hands of the customer much earlier than if the entire product were delivered at the end, (2) with careful planning it may be possible to deliver the most important functionality earliest, and (3) it provides tangible signs of progress early in the project. Almost all large projects use some form of incremental development.

1.5.2.3 Evolutionary Development

Evolutionary life-cycle models were developed to address deficiencies in the waterfall model, often related to the unrealistic expectation of having fully elaborated specifications. The stages in an evolutionary model are expanding increments of an operational product, with evolution being determined by operational experience. Evolutionary approaches develop software in increments, except that requirements are only defined for the next release. Such a model helps deliver an initial operational capability and provides a real-world operational basis for evolution; however, the lack of long-range planning often leads to trouble with the operational system not being flexible enough to handle unplanned paths of evolution.

With evolutionary prototyping, development is begun on the most visible aspects of the system. That part of the system is demonstrated, and then development continues on the prototype based on the feedback received. This process is useful when requirements are changing rapidly, when the customer is reluctant to commit to a set of requirements, or when neither the developer nor the customer understands the application. Developers find the model useful when they are unsure of the optimal architecture or algorithm to use. The model has the advantage of producing steady visible signs of progress, which can be especially useful when there is a strong demand for development speed.

The main disadvantage of the model is that it is not known at the beginning of the project how long it will take to create an acceptable product. The developer will not know how many iterations will be necessary. Another disadvantage is that the approach lends itself to becoming a code-and-fix development.

In evolutionary delivery, a version of the product is developed; it is shown to the customer, and the product is refined based on customer feedback. This model draws from the control obtained with staged delivery and the flexibility afforded by evolutionary prototyping. With evolutionary delivery, the developer's initial emphasis is on the visible aspects of the system and its core, which consists of lower-level system functions that are unlikely to be changed by customer feedback. Plugging holes in the system's foundation occurs later on.

1.5.2.4 Iterative Development

An iterative process uses multiple development cycles to produce software in small, usable pieces that build upon each other. It is often thought that iterative development is a modern concept; however, it was first documented in 1975 [Basili, Turner 1975]. Development proceeds as a series of short evolutionary iterations instead of a longer single-pass, sequential waterfall process for fixed requirements. The difference with incremental development is that iterative approaches do not lay out all the requirements in advance for each cycle. Each iteration may resemble a very short waterfall, and prototyping is an essential aspect for the vast majority of applications containing a user interface. The first iteration usually implements a core capability with an emphasis on addressing high-risk areas, stabilizing an architecture, and refining the requirements. The capabilities and architecture are built upon in successive iterations.

Iterative development helps to ensure that applications meet user needs. It uses a demonstration-based approach in order to refine the user interface and address risky areas [Royce 1998]. Programming starts early and feedback from real end users is integral to the evolution of a successful application. For example, working slices of the software architecture will be assessed early for areas of high risk (e.g. security, throughput, response time).

When defining the user interface for a new application, the project team will gather requirements and translate them quickly into an initial prototype. Next, the team will step through the prototype to validate the results and make changes. By rapidly iterating and refining "live" code, the final application is ensured to meet the needs and expectations of the users. This approach is how we successfully developed user-intensive e-commerce systems at C-Bridge Internet Solutions [Madachy 2001].

Some implementation examples of an iterative process include the Rational Unified Process (RUP) [Kruchten 1998], the USC Model-Based Architecting and Software Engineering (MBASE) framework (see Section 1.5.2.5.2), and most forms of agile methods. A typical profile of activities in iterative development is shown in Figure 1.12, adapted from RUP documentation. The milestone acronyms at the top stand for Life-Cycle Objectives (LCO), Life-Cycle Architecture (LCA), and Initial Operating Capability (IOC). The milestones and their criteria are described in [Boehm 1996] and [Royce 1998].

This life-cycle process reduces the entropy and large breakage associated with the waterfall. An overall functionality is delivered in multiple iterative pieces with the highest payback features first, and the overall scope is delivered in a shorter time frame compared to using the waterfall. Incremental application releases allow early return on investment and ease the burden of change management in the user's environment. The project loops through multiple development cycles until the overall scope of the application is achieved.

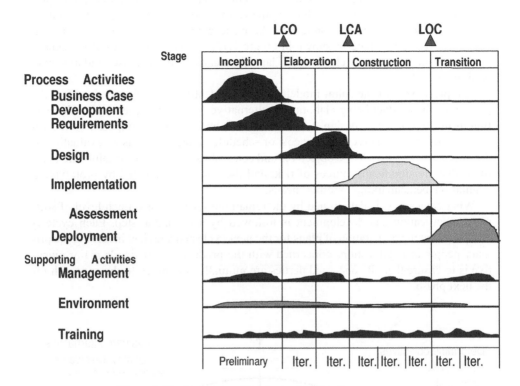

Figure 1.12. Activity profiles for typical iterative processes.

Business trends continue to place more emphasis on being first to market. Iterative software development processes are well suited for schedule-driven projects, and provide users with working systems earlier than waterfall processes.

1.5.2.5   Spiral Model

The spiral model is a risk-driven variation of evolutionary development that can function as a superset process model. It can accommodate other models as special cases and provides guidance to determine which combination of models best fits a given situation [Boehm 1988]. It is called risk-driven because it identifies areas of uncertainties that are sources of project risk and structures activities based on the risks. The development proceeds in repeating cycles of determining objectives, evaluating alternatives, prototyping and developing, and then planning the next cycle. Each cycle involves a progression that addresses the same sequence of steps for each portion of the product and for each level of elaboration. Development builds on top of the results of previous spirals.

A major distinction of the spiral model is having risk-based transition criteria between stages in contrast to the single-shot waterfall model in which documents are

the criteria for advancing to subsequent development stages. The spiral model prescribes an evolutionary process, but explicitly incorporates long-range architectural
and usage considerations in contrast to the basic evolutionary model. The original
version of the spiral model is shown in Figure 1.13. The process begins at the center,
and repeatedly progresses clockwise. Elapsed calendar time increases radially with
additional cycles.

A typical cycle of the spiral model starts with identification of objectives (for the
portion of the product being elaborated), alternative means of implementing the portion of the product (e.g., design A, design B, buy) and constraints imposed on the application of the alternatives such as cost or schedule budgets. Next is an evaluation of
the alternatives relative to the objectives and constraints. Areas of uncertainty are identified that are significant sources of risk, and the risks are evaluated by prototyping,
simulation, benchmarking, or other means.

What comes next is determined by the remaining relative risks. Each level of software specification and development is followed by a validation step. Each cycle is
completed by the preparation of plans for the next cycle and a review involving the primary people or organizations concerned with the product. The review's major objective is to ensure that all concerned parties are mutually committed to the approach for
the next phase.

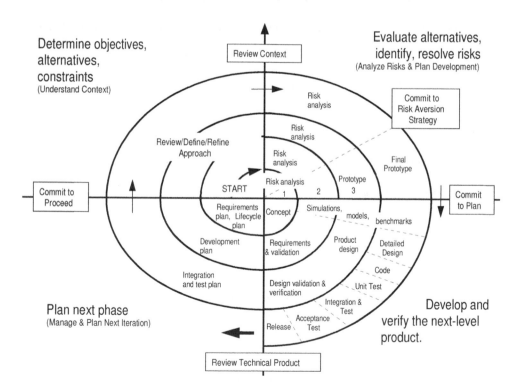

Figure 1.13: Original spiral model.

1.5.2.5.1 WINWIN SPIRAL MODEL. The original spiral model of software development begins each cycle by performing the next level of elaboration of the prospective system's objectives, constraints, and alternatives. A primary difficulty in applying the spiral model has been the lack of explicit process guidance in determining these objectives, constraints, and alternatives. The more recently developed WinWin spiral model [Boehm et al. 1998] uses the Theory W (win–win) approach [Boehm, Ross 1989] to converge on a system's next-level objectives, constraints, and alternatives. This Theory W approach involves identifying the system's stakeholders and their win conditions, and using negotiation processes to determine a mutually satisfactory set of objectives, constraints, and alternatives for the stakeholders.

Figure 1.14 illustrates the WinWin spiral model. The original spiral had four sectors, beginning with "Establish next-level objectives, constraints, alternatives." The two additional sectors in each spiral cycle, "Identify Next-Level Stakeholders" and "Identify Stakeholders' Win Conditions," and the "Reconcile Win Conditions" portion of the third sector, provide the collaborative foundation for the model. They also fill a missing portion of the original spiral model, the means to answer, "Where do the next-level objectives and constraints come from, and how do you know they're the right ones?" The refined spiral model also explicitly addresses the need for concurrent analysis, risk resolution, definition, and elaboration of both the software product and the software process.

An elaborated cycle of the WinWin spiral includes the following:

- Identify the system or subsystem's key stakeholders.
- Identify the stakeholders' win conditions for the system or subsystem.

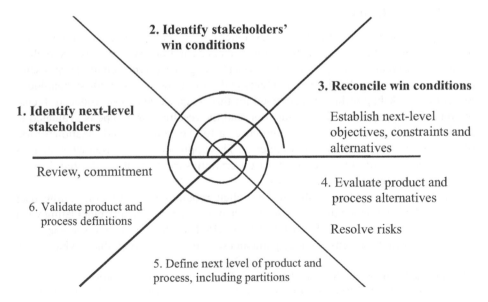

Figure 1.14. WinWin Spiral (additions to spiral model shown in bold).

- Negotiate win–win reconciliations of the stakeholders' win conditions.
- Elaborate the system or subsystem's product and process objectives, constraints, and alternatives.
- Evaluate the alternatives with respect to the objectives and constraints. Identify and resolve major sources of product and process risk.
- Elaborate the definition of the product and process.
- Plan the next cycle and update the life-cycle plan, including partition of the system into subsystems to be addressed in parallel cycles. This can include a plan to terminate the project if it is too risky or infeasible. Secure the management's commitment to proceed as planned.

1.5.2.5.2 MBASE Framework. At the USC Center for Systems and Software Engineering we have been developing the Model-Based[7] Architecting and Software Engineering (MBASE) framework. MBASE addresses debilitating dynamics of software development that often lead to project downfalls by embodying a risk-driven iterative approach, heavily involving project stakeholders per the WinWin spiral model, and evolving a system architecture compatible with changes and future evolution. Its milestones can be used in many different process life-cycle models. For an iterative process, the milestones are used to achieve stakeholder concurrence on the current project state.

MBASE has many features in common with the RUP, and is fully compatible with the iterative life cycle described in Walker Royce's book *Software Project Management—A Unified Approach* [Royce 1998]. Chapter 5 of this book has an application model for the MBASE architecting process.

1.5.2.6 Prototyping

Prototyping is a process whereby the developer creates a quick initial working model of the software to be built to support requirements definition. The objective is to clarify the characteristics and operation of a system using visual representations and sample working sessions. Partial requirements gathering is done first with stakeholders. Structured workshop techniques are good for this. A quick design is produced, focusing on software aspects visible to the user, and the resulting prototype is evaluated to refine the requirements. Prototyping produces a full-scale model and functional form of a new system, but only the part of interest. This approach may be used when there is only a general set of objectives, or other uncertainties exist about the desired form of an interface or algorithmic efficiencies.

Prototyping is highly valuable to help elicit requirements by incorporating user feedback. A phenomenon that often occurs when users have difficulty elucidating what they want is "I'll Know It When I See It" (IKIWISI). Not until they see some exploratory or sample screens can they point and say "that looks good, that's what I want

---

[7]The term "Model" in the name is a general descriptor referring to a large variety of models used in software (e.g., success models, development standards, and many others), and is not at all limited to simulation models or life-cycle models.

now." Prototyping is used heavily in modern user-interactive systems, and is an essential component of Rapid Application Development (RAD) and iterative development.

There are drawbacks to prototyping. Often, canned scenarios are used to demonstrate a particular functionality, and compromises are inevitably made to accommodate the quick development. A customer may think that the prototype is more robust than it is in reality, and may not understand why it cannot be used in the actual system. Prototyping has similar aspects to simulation. Neither produces the software product per se, but they are complementary ways to address project risk. Prototyping helps with product risks and process simulation helps with process risk.

1.5.2.7 Agile Methods

Agile methods are a set of iterative processes that have gained much favor in recent years. They have been advocated as an appropriate "lightweight" programming paradigm for high-speed and volatile software development [Cockburn 2001]. Some examples of agile methods include Extreme Programming (XP), SCRUM, DSDM, Adaptive Software Development, Crystal, Feature-Driven Development, and Pragmatic Programming.

As opposed to more plan-driven approaches espoused by the Capability Maturity Models (see Section 1.5.3.1), agile development is less document-oriented and more focused on programming. The so-called "agile manifesto" [Agile 2003] identifies an agile method as one that adopts the four value propositions and twelve principles in the agile manifesto. All of the concepts in the value propositions below are important and valid but, in general, agilists value the ones on the left over the right:

1. Individuals and interactions over processes and tools
2. Working software over comprehensive documentation
3. Customer collaboration over contract negotiation
4. Responding to change over following a plan

The twelve principles behind the agile manifesto are:

1. Our highest priority is to satisfy the customer through early and continuous delivery of valuable software.
2. Welcome changing requirements, even late in development. Agile processes harness change for the customer's competitive advantage.
3. Deliver working software frequently, from a couple of weeks to a couple of months, with a preference for the shorter timescale.
4. Business people and developers must work together daily throughout the project.
5. Build projects around motivated individuals. Give them the environment and support they need, and trust them to get the job done.
6. The most efficient and effective method of conveying information to and within a development team is face-to-face conversation.

7. Working software is the primary measure of progress.

8. Agile processes promote sustainable development. The sponsors, developers, and users should be able to maintain a constant pace indefinitely.

9. Continuous attention to technical excellence and good design enhances agility.

10. Simplicity—the art of maximizing the amount of work not done—is essential.

11. The best architectures, requirements, and designs emerge from self-organizing teams.

12. At regular intervals, the team reflects on how to become more effective, then tunes and adjusts its behavior accordingly.

The title of a relevant article characterizes agile methods as "Agile Software Development: It's about Feedback and Change" [Williams, Cockburn 2003]. In this sense, agile methods go hand in hand with using system dynamics to model feedback and adapt to change. Agile methods are a manifestation of fine-tuned process feedback control. Agile methods have drawbacks and trade-offs like other methods, and the interested reader can consult [Boehm, Turner 2004] for a balanced treatment.

1.5.2.8   Using Commercial-off-the-Shelf (COTS) Software or Open-Source Software

Software development with third-party components has become more prevalent as applications mature. The components help provide rapid functionality and may decrease overall costs. These components may be purchased as COTS or obtained from open-source repositories. COTS is sold by vendors and is generally opaque, whereas open source is from the public domain with full access to its source code. Both process strategies pose new risks and different life-cycle activities.

COTS-based or COTS-intensive systems utilize commercial packages in software products to varying degrees. Using COTS has unique challenges. Developers do not have access to the source code and still have to integrate it into their systems. Development with COTS requires assessment of the COTS offerings, COTS tailoring, and, quite possibly, glue-code development to interface with the rest of the software.

Frequently, the capability of the COTS or open-source software determines systems requirements, instead of the converse. Another challenge is timing the product "refresh" as new releases are put out. A system with multiple COTS will have different release schedules from different vendors. See [Abts 2003] for a comprehensive (static) COTS cost model. Chapter 5 describes some dynamic COTS application models. Chapter 7 discusses current and future directions of developing COTS-based systems and open-source software development, and makes important distinctions between their life-cycle impacts.

1.5.2.9   Reuse and Reengineering

Reuse-based development uses previously built software assets. Such assets may include requirements, architectures, code, test plans, QA reviews, documents, and so on. Like COTS, reuse has the potential to reduce software effort and schedule. Though extra costs are incurred to make software reusable, experience has shown that the investment is typically recouped by about the third round of reuse. Reuse is frequently incorporated in other life-cycle models, and a number of process models dedicated to reuse and reengineering have been published. Some are risk-driven and based on the spiral model, while others are enhanced waterfall process models. A process for reusing software assets can also improve reliability, quality, and user programmability.

Reengineering differs from reuse in that entire product architectures are used as starting points for new systems, as opposed to bottom-up reuse of individual components. A software process model for reuse and reengineering must provide for a variety of activities and support the reuse of assets across the entire life cycle. It must support tasks specific to reuse and reengineering, such as domain analysis and domain engineering.

1.5.2.10 Fourth-Generation Languages and the Transform Model

Fourth-generation languages (4 GLs) and transformational approaches specify software at a high level and employ automatic code generation. They automatically convert a formal software specification into a program [Balzer et al. 1983]. Such a life-cycle model minimizes the problems of code that has been modified many times and is difficult to maintain. The basic steps involved in the transform process model are: (1) formally specify the product, (2) automatically transform the specification into code (this assumes the capability to do so), (3) iterate if necessary to improve the performance, (4) exercise the product, and (5) iterate again by adjusting the specification based on the operational experience. This model and its variants are often called operational specification or fourth-generation language (4GL) techniques. Chapter 5 has an example application model for 4GLs.

1.5.2.11 Iterative Versus Waterfall Life-Cycle Comparison

A modern iterative life-cycle process, when practiced right, is advantageous to a conventional waterfall life cycle for a majority of applications. It is particularly recommended for user-interactive systems, where the IKIWISI principle applies. The difference between a modern iterative process versus a conventional waterfall process in terms of project progress is idealized in Figure 1.15, which is adapted from [Royce 1998]. Progress is measured in terms of the percent of software demonstrable in target form.

Figure 1.15 also calls out the significant contrasting dynamics experienced between the two life-cycle processes. Notable are the larger breakages and elongated schedule of the waterfall life cycle. No software is produced during requirements analysis, so nothing is demonstrable until design or coding. During design, there is apparent progress on paper and during reviews, but the system architecture is not really assessed in an implementation environment. Not until integration starts can the system be tested to verify the overall structure and the interfaces. Typically there is a lot of breakage once integration starts, because that is the first time that unpredictable issues crop up and interfaces are finally fleshed out. The late-surfacing problems stretch out the integration and testing phase and resolving them consumes many resources. Last-minute

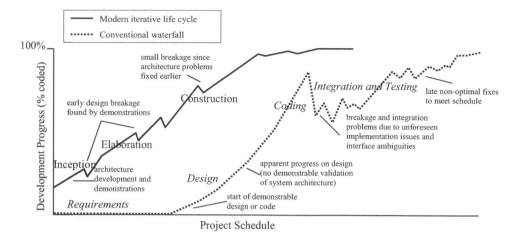

Figure 1.15. Progress dynamics for iterative life cycle versus waterfall life cycle (adapted from Walker Royce).

fixes are necessary to meet an already slipped schedule, so they are usually quick and dirty, with no time to do things optimally.

The iterative life cycle focuses on developing an architecture first, with frequent demonstrations that validate the system. The demonstrations may be in the form of prototypes or working slices that validate the proposed architecture. The working demonstrations help to mitigate risk by identifying problems earlier when there are still options to change the architecture. Some breakage is inevitable, but the overall life-cycle impact is small when the problems are addressed at this stage. The system architecture is continually being integrated via the executable demonstration of important scenarios. There is minimal risk exposure during construction since there are many fewer unknowns, so the final integration and transition proceed smoothly.

1.5.3   Process Improvement

In order to address software development problems, the development task must be treated as a process that can be controlled, measured, and improved [Humphrey 1989]. This requires an organization to understand the current status of their processes, identify desired process change, make a process improvement plan, and execute the plan. All of these process improvement activities can be supported with simulation.

Industrial initiatives to reengineer and improve software processes through metrics is helping to motivate modeling efforts. Initially, the Software Engineering Institute Capability Maturity Model (SEI CMM) process maturity framework was an important driver of these efforts [Paulk et al. 1994], but it has been superseded by the CMM-Integrated (CMM-I) [SEI 2003], which brings systems engineering into the process improvement fold among other improvements. Frameworks for process enhancements are described next.

1.5.3.1 *Capability Maturity Models*

The Software Capability Maturity Model (CMM or SW-CMM) was developed by the Software Engineering Institute (SEI) to improve software engineering practices [Paulk et al. 1994]. The more recent CMMI ("I" stands for integration) is a broader framework based on experience with the SW-CMM that includes systems engineering practices [SEI 2003]. They are both models of how organizations can mature their processes and continually improve to better meet their cost, schedule, and quality goals. They are frameworks of management, engineering, and support best practices organized into process areas. Capabilities in the process areas can be improved through generic practices outlined in the frameworks.

The SEI was initially tasked by the U.S. government to develop the CMM, and it has become a de-facto standard adopted by commercial and defense companies worldwide. CMMI has been a collaborative effort among members of industry, government, and the SEI. CMMI is also consistent and compatible with ISO/IEC 15504, an emerging standard on software process assessment.

The CMM framework identifies five levels of organizational maturity, where each level lays a foundation for making process improvements at the next level. The framework utilizes a set of key practices and common features. The CMM staged representation offers a road map for improvement one predetermined step at a time. Process areas are grouped at maturity levels that provide organizations with a sound approach for process improvement. The staged representation prescribes the order of implementation for each process area according to maturity levels.

CMMI also allows for either the traditional staged improvement or a continuous improvement path within a specific process area. The continuous representation offers a more flexible approach to process improvement. It is designed for organizations that would like to choose a particular process area or set of process areas. As a process area is implemented, the specific practices and generic practices are grouped into capability levels.

A primary intent of CMMI is to provide an integrated approach to improving an organization's systems engineering and software functions. CMMI covers the same material as the SW-CMM, although some topics like risk management and measurement and analysis are given more extensive treatment that reflects the engineering community's learning over the past 10 years. In CMMI, systems engineering is defined as "The interdisciplinary approach governing the total technical and managerial effort required to transform a set of customer needs, expectations, and constraints into a product solution and support that solution throughout the product's life."

Related maturity models include the Software Acquisition CMM (SA-CMM), the People Capability Maturity Model, the FAA-iCMM, and others. Though the CMMI is intended to supercede the SW-CMM, the SW-CMM will still be in use for a while. The subsequent sections are predicated on the software CMM but apply just as well to CMMI.

At level one in the maturity models, an organization is described as ad-hoc, whereby processes are not in place and a chaotic development environment exists. The second level is called the repeatable level. At this level, project planning and tracking is established and processes are repeatable. The third level is termed the defined level because processes are formally defined. Level 4 is called the managed level, whereby the defined process is instrumented and metrics are used to set targets. Statistical quality control can then be applied to process elements. At level 5, the optimized level, detailed measurements and analysis techniques are used to guide programs of continuous process improvement, technology innovation, and defect prevention. The CMMI key process areas and their general categories are shown in Table 1.3.

To make the process predictable, repeatable, and manageable, an organization must first assess the maturity of the processes in place. By knowing the maturity level, organizations can identify problem areas to concentrate on and effect process improvement in key practice areas. The SEI has developed assessment procedures based on the maturity models and standardized the assessments using ISO/IEC 15504.

Software process modeling is essential to support improvements at levels 4 and 5 through process definition and analysis. Process models can represent the variation among processes, encapsulate potential solutions, and can be used as a baseline for benchmarking process improvement metrics.

Table 1.3. CMMI key process areas

| Level | Process area category | | | |
	Engineering	Project Management	Process Management	Support
5—Optimizing			• Organizational Innovation & Deployment	• Causal Analysis and Resolution
4—Managed		• Quantitative Project Management	• Organizational Process Performance	
3—Defined	• Requirements Development • Technical Solution • Product Integration • Verification • Validation	• Integrated Project Management • Risk Management • Integrated Supplier Management	• Organizational Process Focus • Organizational Process Definition • Organizational Training	• Decision Analysis and Resolution • Organizational Environment for Integration
2—Repeatable	• Requirements Management	• Project Planning • Project Monitoring and Control • Supplier Agreement Management		• Configuration Management • Process & Product Quality Assurance • Measurement and Analysis
1—Ad hoc	No process areas defined for this level			

Table 1.4 identifies some general uses of simulation at the different levels and the type of data available to drive the models. Though dynamic process simulation is not absolutely necessary at the lower levels, some process modeling capability is needed to advance in levels 4 and 5. As maturity increases, so does the predictive power of the organizational models. Highly mature organizations can test their improved processes via simulation rather than through costly trial and error in the field.

The distinction between open and closed feedback systems described in Section 1.3 typifies the difference between an ad-hoc CMM Level 1 organization and higher maturity organizations in which past process performance data is used to control the current process. The essence of CMM levels 4 and 5 can be summarized as using process feedback. This implies that a mature organization would desire some model of that feedback. See Chapter 5 for an example of process maturity modeling.

Table 1.4. Simulation uses at the CMM levels

CMM Level	Simulation Uses	Calibration Data Available
5—Optimizing	• Testing new processes offline before project implementation and performing process trade-off studies • Modeling impacts of new technology adoption • Comparing defect prevention techniques • Interdepartmental collaboration and widespread usage of simulation • Organizational modeling • Product line analysis • Model change management	• Continuous stream of detailed data tailored for organizational goals • Results of previous simulations and decisions against actuals
4—Managed	• Time-based process predictions to determine planned values • Determination of process control limits through variance analysis • More widespread usage of simulation among software and managerial staff	• Finer detail and more consistent data • Specific process and product measures targeted to environment • Previous model estimates
3—Defined	• Defect modeling • Peer review optimization • Training • Increased validity and confidence in process models allow supplanting some expert judgment	• Phase and activity cost and schedule data • Size, requirements, and defect data • Peer review data
2—Repeatable	• Cost and schedule modeling • Earned value setting • Evaluating requirements	• Project-level cost and schedule • Expert judgment
1—Ad hoc	• Improve awareness of process dynamic behavior • Role playing games	

1.5.3.2 Other Process Improvement and Assessment Frameworks

ISO 9000 and ISO/IEC 15504 are other process assessment frameworks. These consist of standards and guidelines as well as supporting documents that define terminology and required elements, such as auditing and assessment mechanisms. Neither CMM, ISO 9000, nor ISO/IEC 15504 are product standards. They focus on processes under the assumption that if the production and management system is right, the product or service that it produces will also be correct. Six Sigma is a defined process for improving products and processes.

1.5.3.2.1 ISO 9000. The International Organization for Standards (ISO) published ISO 9000 in 1987 for quality management certification [ISO 2005]. ISO 9000 is primarily concerned with the establishment of a quality management system. The definition of quality is captured in twenty "must address" clauses and enforced by a formal, internationally recognized, third-party audit and registration system. ISO 9000 requires the organization to "walk the talk": say what it does, do what it says, and be able to demonstrate it. It requires the organization to write specific procedures defining how each activity in their development process is conducted.

Processes and procedures must address control, adaptability, verification/validation, and process improvement. Organizations must always be able to show objective evidence of what has been done, how it was done, and the current status of the project and product, and it must be able to demonstrate the effectiveness of its quality system.

An accreditation schema for software, motivated by ISO 9000's apparent lack of applicability to the software industry, led to the TickIT method, which is limited to the United Kingdom and Sweden. A more powerful assessment-based certification standard for software was developed under the informal name of SPICE. It was eventually formalized as the ISO 15504 standard described next.

1.5.3.2.2 ISO/IEC 15504. The aim of the ISO/IEC 15504 standard is to perform process assessment, process improvement, and capability determinations [SEI 2005]. ISO/IEC 15504 combines the CMM and ISO 9000 approaches into a single mechanism for developing a quality system for software. It embodies the reference framework of the ISO 9000 approach with the capability assessment and process maturity features of CMM. In addition, it establishes a migration path for existing assessment models and methods that wish to come into the 15504 domain. It intentionally does not specify a particular assessment methodology. Its architecture is designed to permit and encourage the development of methods and models that serve specific domains or markets. See [Stallinger 2000] for a system dynamics modeling application for ISO/IEC 15504.

1.5.3.2.3 SIX SIGMA. Six Sigma is a methodology initially used to manage process variations that cause defects, defined as unacceptable deviation from the mean or target, and to systematically work toward managing variation to eliminate those defects. Six Sigma has now grown beyond defect control. The objective of Six Sigma is to deliver high performance, reliability, and value to the end customer. See

[Motorola 2006] for details, but there are also many other online sources, books, and guides.

The methodology was pioneered at Motorola in 1986 and was originally defined as a metric for measuring defects and improving quality, and a methodology to reduce defect levels below 3.4 defects per million opportunities. Hence, "Six Sigma" refers to the ends of a probability distribution that correspond to these odds. The principles and techniques of using probability distributions (see Appendix A) are important to understand when implementing Six Sigma.

When deploying Six Sigma for improvement in an organization, there are clearly defined roles for executive and project sponsors, black belts, green belts, yellow belts, and so on (the belts correspond to levels of Six Sigma training and skill). On a project, a common road map for developing new processes or products is Define, Measure, Analyze, Design/Build, Verify (DMADV). The road map for improving products or processes that already exist is known as Define, Measure, Analyze, Improve, Control (DMAIC).

Six Sigma is a natural application for software process modeling to quantify and forecast effects of variation on new processes and designs. Key factors that drive uncertainty can be illuminated with simulation to better explain the effects of variation without expensive trials.

1.6   CHALLENGES FOR THE SOFTWARE INDUSTRY

We have just scratched the surface of the potential of dynamic modeling to help improve the software process. Accounting for all the dynamic factors on a software project far outstrips the capability of the human mind. For example, Capers Jones has identified about 250 different factors that can affect schedule, cost, quality, and user satisfaction [Jones 2000]. Clearly, one cannot mentally calculate all the influences from so many factors; thus, we resort to computer simulation technology.

Correspondingly, there are formidable challenges for the industry and pitfalls to avoid. The ability to handle more phenomena and have high confidence in models will help system dynamics make powerful impacts. Simulation models need their own verification, validation, and accreditation just like other software products. There are confidence limits associated with the calibration of models, and it is harder to verify and validate highly detailed models. Methods for model certification and ways to converge on acceptable models must be considered. As will be described later, some possibilities include the rigorous use of the Goal–Question–Metric (GQM) process, getting user buy-in and consensus on key model drivers, model assessment techniques per Chapter 2 and Appendix A, incremental validation, and cross-validation with other types of models. Many of these topics are explored in more detail in Chapter 2 and case studies in subsequent chapters. Chapter 7 discusses some automated model analysis techniques.

The field is continuously getting more complex for decision makers. Software development is becoming even more dynamic with agile methods, increasing use of COTS, complex systems of systems, open-source development via the Internet, distributed 24/7 global development, new computing devices, model-driven development, Rapid Application Development (RAD) processes, and increasingly shorter increments of development. New management techniques are needed to keep up with the changing environment, as well as available professionals trained in new techniques. Most of these topics are treated later in the book and Chapter 7 discusses their current and future directions. Some present-day decision scenarios are described next to illustrate the wide array of decision contexts and help set the stage.

Planners and managers need to assess the consequences of alternative strategies such as reuse and COTS, fourth-generation languages (4GLs), application generators, architectural refactoring, rapid prototyping, incremental or iterative development, or other process options before actual implementation. And what are the effects of interactions between requirements elicitation, software implementation, testing, process improvement initiatives, hiring practices, and training within any of these strategies?

In projects with multiple COTS packages, one problem is synchronizing releases from several products with different update schedules. How frequently the components should be "refreshed" and the overall software rebuilt is a complex decision. Will different COTS packages integrate well with each other, or do we need to develop special interface glue code? COTS glue code development is modeled in Chapter 5. Will the vendors be able to support future versions and upgrades?

There are countless individual strategies to improve the software process (e.g., formal inspections, object-oriented development, cleanroom engineering, automated testing, iterative development, etc.). But what are the conditional effects of combined strategies? Can they be separated out for analysis? For example, there are overlaps between methods for finding defects. What are the types of defects found by different means and what are the reduced efficiencies of single methods when used in conjunction with others? See Chapter 5 for examples on defects.

Trying to find the right balance between process flexibility and discipline is a large challenge. How much of a project should be performed with an agile approach and how much should be plan-driven? See Chapter 4 for an example application. It would also be valuable to understand the limits of scaling up agile methods to decide when best to use them.

Companies that are looking for ways to accelerate their processes can assess various RAD techniques through simulation. Methods are also needed, for example, to evaluate how many people are required to maintain a software product at a specified level of change, whether a modification to the inspection process will result in higher defect yields, or if a process can be implemented with fewer reviews and still maintain quality.

In today's interconnected world, large, complex systems of systems have their own unique dynamics. Trying to manage a globally distributed project involving many teams and interfaces is a unique challenge. What are the best ways to accomplish this process management in order to get successful systems out the door?

It would be useful to model the complex adaptation behavior of projects and the ripple effects of decisions made. In order to salvage runaway projects, teams sometimes incorporate more reused software and COTS software. Often, managers have to perform midstream corrections to "design to cost" or "design to schedule." This could mean a reduction in scope by dropping features, or finding ingenious shortcuts to lessen the effective size, such as incorporating middleware from another source (a ripple effect may be the extra time incurred to do so). These shortcuts can often be attributed to the ideas of "top people." Such individuals are invaluable to organizations, but they are in short supply and may cost a lot. The effects of having such people need to be better understood to capitalize on their talents.

People are the most valuable resources in software; as such, a lot of attention should be paid to their training and retention. Having a national or global supply of skilled workers requires cooperation between many organizations and educational institutions. Modeling can help assess different ways to achieve skill development, and to keep people motivated to address these industry challenges (see Chapters 4 and 7 on people resource issues).

These are just a few examples of complex decision scenarios that the software industry is currently grappling with. Things will get even more complex and dynamic as software technology and business conditions keep changing. The rest of the book will address how to achieve better understandings of the process interrelationships and feedback, in order to cope with a fast-changing software world.

1.7   MAJOR REFERENCES

[Abdel-Hamid, Madnick 1991]   Abdel-Hamid, T., and Madnick, S., *Software Project Dynamics,* Englewood Cliffs, NJ: Prentice-Hall, 1991.

[Boehm et al. 1998]   Boehm, B., Egyed, A., Kwan, J., Port, D., Shah, A., and Madachy, R., Using the WinWin Spiral Model: A Case Study, *IEEE Computer,* July 1998.

[Brooks 1975]   Brooks, F., *The Mythical Man-Month,* Reading, MA: Addison-Wesley 1975 (also reprinted and updated in 1995).

[Forrester 1961]   Forrester, J. W., *Industrial Dynamics,* Cambridge, MA: MIT Press, 1961.

[Kellner et al. 1999]   Kellner, M., Madachy, R., and Raffo, D., *Software Process Simulation Modeling: Why? What? How? Journal of Systems and Software,* Spring 1999.

[Kruchten 1998]   Kruchten, P., *The Rational Unified Process,* Reading, MA: Addison-Wesley, 1998.

[Osterweil 1987]   Osterweil, L., Software Processes are Software Too, *Proceedings ICSE 9,* IEEE Catalog No. 87CH2432-3, pp. 2–13, March 1987.

[Paulk et al. 1994]   Paulk, M., Weber, C., Curtis, B., and Chrissis, M., *The Capability Maturity Model: Guidelines for Improving the Software Process,* Reading, MA: Addison-Wesley, 1994.

[Royce 1998]   Royce, W., *Software Project Management—A Unified Approach,* Reading, MA: Addison-Wesley, 1998.

[Senge 1990]   Senge, P., *The Fifth Discipline,* New York: Doubleday, 1990.

[Weinberg 1992]   Weinberg, G., *Quality Software Management, Volume 1, Systems Thinking,* New York: Dorset House Publishing, 1992.

CHAPTER 1 SUMMARY

Simulation is a practical and flexible technique to support many areas of software processes to improve decision making. It can be used to model different aspects of processes in order to assess them, so that the dynamic (and unintended) consequences of decisions can be understood. Through simulation, one can test proposed processes before implementation. It is effective when the real system is not practical to use or is too expensive. Often, simulation is the only way to assess complex systems. Systems are becoming more complex and computer capabilities continue to improve, so it is expected that the use of simulation will continue to increase over the years in software engineering and other fields.

Systems come in a variety of types (discrete/continuous/mixed, static/dynamic), and there are different techniques for modeling them. This book will focus on the system dynamics technique for modeling dynamic continuous systems.

Systems thinking is an allied discipline that leverages system dynamics. Though it may have several different meanings depending on the perspective, for this context we consider it to be a thinking process that promotes individual and organizational learning.

The software process is a real-time process with feedback control elements. Treating it as such allows us to explicitly consider its inputs, outputs, and feedback loops in order to better understand and control it. System dynamics is well suited for modeling these aspects of the software process control system.

An example of modeling Brooks's Law was introduced. The model illustrates an important management heuristic for late projects that is frequently misunderstood, and sheds light on some reasons why adding people to a late project can make it later. These dynamic effects are increased communication overhead, training losses, and lower productivity for new personnel. This modeling example will be broken down more in Chapter 2.

Software process technology involves process modeling, life-cycle models, and process improvement. A variety of simulation approaches and languages are available. Continuous systems modeling (such as with system dynamics) is generally more appropriate for strategic, macro-level studies. Discrete event modeling is usually better suited for studying detailed processes. Simulation tools have been improving over the years and often are used in a visual manner.

Software process simulation is increasingly being used for a wide variety of purposes. These include strategic management, planning and control, process improvement, and training. Process models can focus on narrow portions of the life cycle, entire projects, multiple projects, product lines, and wide organizational issues. Simulation in software development has been used for decades to support conceptual studies, requirements analysis, assess architectures, support testing, and verification and validation activities.

Process life-cycle models define process activities, their order and dependencies. There are many different life-cycle models available to be used. A risk-driven approach to deciding on an appropriate process will help ensure that the process best matches the project needs. Simulation can be used to assess candidate processes. It is also important to understand the different life-cycle characteristics to make better modeling process decisions (see Chapter 2 on the modeling process). In particular, the WinWin spiral life cycle is a good fit for many modeling situations.

Process frameworks like the CMMI and ISO are important vehicles for process improvement that are fully compatible with simulation. They identify best practices and provide paths for organizations to improve. Modeling and simulation support continuous process improvement every step of the way.

It is an exciting time in the software industry, with many opportunities, but techniques are needed to deal with the ever-increasing dynamic aspects and complexities of software processes. Project time lines are shortening, there are an increasing number of new processes and techniques, new technology keeps coming along, and projects keep increasing in complexity. We also need to keep focused on people and sustain a large enough pool of skilled workers to develop software in an efficient fashion that meets user needs. Simulation can help us see the forest through the trees, find the right balance of methods or people for particular project environments, and, ultimately, help software projects make better decisions.

1.19 EXERCISES

Some of the exercises in this chapter and others ask for analysis with respect to "your environment," which may take on different interpretations. If you are a practitioner, it may refer to the software process environment on your project or in your company, a government acquisition agency, an open-source project, or any software development you wish to study.

If you are a pure student, your assignment may be a specific project, company, or a segment of the software industry for case study. An assignment may also be to do the problems for more than one environment, then compare and analyze the differences.

1.1. List some benefits of using software process simulation in your environment.

1.2. Explain any impediments to using simulation for software processes in your environment. How might these impediments be mitigated?

1.3. What are the advantages and disadvantages of using simulation as an approach to a dynamics problem versus an analytical solution?

1.4. What is the difference between open and closed systems? Can you identify both kinds in your environment? You may use pictures to help illustrate your answer.

1.5. Identify organizational systems that may influence the software process in your enviroment, and especially focus on those that are not normally considered to have anything to do with software development or engineering.

1.6.   Define the boundary of your process environment and create a comprehensive list of external factors that may influence the software process.

1.7.   If you have experience in an environment in which software process modeling has been used, what have been the results? What went right and what went wrong? Provide lessons learned and suggest how things could have been improved.

1.8.   What are the process state variables that are tracked in your environment?

1.9.   Can you name any aspects of the software process that are completely static?

1.10. Can you name any aspects of the software process that are completely deterministic?

1.11. Identify some critical issues or problems in your environment that might be addressed by simulation and place them in the process modeling characterization matrix.

1.12. What other types of models and simulations are used in software development?

1.13. Draw a software process control system and expand/instantiate the inputs and outputs for your environment. For example, what is the specific source(s) of requirements, what types of resources are used, what standards are used, and what artifacts are produced?

1.14. Draw a software process control system for your environment, paying attention to the controllers. Does the depiction help show what maturity level you are at?

1.15. Review the table of system dynamics model elements and add more examples from the software process domain.

1.16. Trace the feedback loops in the simple project feedback model and in the Brooks's Law model. For each loop, outline the entire path of feedback, including the information connections, rates, levels, and auxiliaries in the path. Describe how the feedback loops impact the system behaviors.

1.17. In the Brooks's Law model, what are some other ways to add people besides an instantaneous pulse?

1.18. Write your own summary of the differences between the major life-cycle models, and outline them in a table format.

1.19. What are some drawbacks to the life-cycle process(es) currently being used in your environment or elsewhere?

1.20. Explain whether your environment could settle on a single life-cycle model or whether it needs more than one.

1.21. Critically analyze the life-cycle comparison figure for the iterative versus waterfall process. Does it seem reasonable and match your experience? Why or why not?

1.22. Describe the pros and cons of using COTS software. What happens if COTS is no longer supported by the vendor? What must be anticipated before designing COTS into a system?

Advanced Exercises

1.23. Make a comprehensive list of software process measures and assess whether they are continuous or discrete. For those that are deemed discrete, discuss whether they can be modeled as continuous for the purpose of understanding process dynamics. Identify the goals and constraints for that decision.

1.24. Identify some general software development best practices and discuss how they would apply to system dynamics model development (you may refer to Chapter 2 if not familiar yet with the modeling process).

1.25. Identify significant issues involved in verifying and validating system dynamics models (you may also get some ideas from Chapter 2). Give suggestions on how the issues can be dealt with and overcome so that system dynamics models will be accepted more readily by practitioners and researchers.

1.26. Suggest modifications to the simple project feedback model to make it more realistic.

1.27. Suggest modifications to the Brooks's Law model to make it more realistic.

1.28. The Brooks's Law model only varied the number of new personnel, but the time of adding new people is another dimension to the problem. What other factors might come into play in terms of optimizing the schedule finish? Might there be more than one local maximum across the different dimensions?

   a) Define an experiment for future implementation to find the optimal solutions in Brooks's Law situations.

   b) Sketch the multidimensional space of optimization and make conjectures as to the shape of the optimization curves.

1.29. Do some research and write a report on quantitative software process modeling that occurred before Abdel-Hamid's work. How much of it is still being (re)used? What has been the impact? Have any good practices gone unnoticed?

1.30. Perform a research study on the effects of implementing CMM, CMM-I, ISO, Six Sigma, or other process frameworks. What are the quantitative impacts to the software process?

1.31. Explain any relationships between the iterative activities in Figure 1.12 and the dynamics in Figure 1.15.

1.32. Read *Software Quality Management, Volume 1, Systems Thinking* by Weinberg and write a report on the applicability of the feedback examples in your environment.

1.33. Read *The Fifth Discipline* by Peter Senge and write a report on the applicability to software process improvement. Do any of the system archetypes apply to software processes? Explain.

1.34. Expand on the section regarding challenges for the software industry.

2

THE MODELING PROCESS
WITH SYSTEM DYNAMICS

This chapter provides a foundation for undertaking modeling projects. It describes an end-to-end modeling process (or life cycle) using the technique of system dynamics. Modeling concepts are elaborated with working examples progressively introduced during the steps. Besides "how-to" information, important material on general system behaviors and structural patterns are also presented, which is particularly useful for both developing and understanding modeling results. If you are already familiar with system modeling and/or your purpose is to quickly learn the practical aspects of coding executable models, start with Section 2.6, Model Formulation.

The purpose of modeling is to be better informed about the dynamic consequences of process and policy decisions. This chapter will help illustrate that the scope and process of modeling is driven by the purpose. It contains content regarding general modeling principles drawn from the classic sources [Richardson, Pugh 1981] and [Forrester 1968]. Some additional modeling guidelines come from [Richmond et al. 1990] and various publications from the annual ProSim workshops. Another good reference on the modeling process with system dynamics is [Sterman 2000], which is oriented towards business applications but the same principles hold.

Fortunately, many modeling concepts are similar to those used in software development. Process modeling and simulation is a form of software development after all, and this description of the process is tailored to the software engineering professional in terms of the assumed skillset and application examples used. The software engineer

Software Process Dynamics. By Raymond J. Madachy
Copyright © 2008 the Institute of Electrical and Electronics Engineers, Inc.

is particularly well suited for applying system dynamics to his/her domain compared to practically all other disciplines.

The building of a model essentially involves defining the requirements for and developing a software application. A systems engineer may be more trained at system conceptualization, but a software engineer has the immediate skills to implement complex models. Many activities and applicable heuristics used in system dynamics modeling are identical or very similar to those used in software development. Some concerns are unique to simulation projects, such as during model validation.

If the modeling process is done well, some major benefits achieved include:

- Development of stakeholder consensus and client ownership, leading to shared commitment to decision making
- Becoming a learning organization
- Better decision making based on improved information from the models
- Improved project execution with lessened risk

Next is a brief overview of the system dynamics technique. After this section is a description of general system behaviors to gain an understanding of time patterns with elemental structures that produce them. Following that are detailed descriptions of modeling activities and model elements. The latter part of the chapter addresses important considerations for software metrics, management guidelines for modeling projects, and tool discussions.

2.1 SYSTEM DYNAMICS BACKGROUND

System dynamics refers to the simulation methodology pioneered by Jay Forrester, which was developed to model complex continuous systems for improving management policies and organizational structures [Forrester 1961, Forrester 1968]. Improvement comes from model-based understandings. This paradigm has been applied to managerial systems for many years, but only recently has software engineering started realizing its potential. This may be due to the fact that the field is still young, and much effort to date has gone into first codifying the software engineering field. Now that many aspects are better defined, it is easier to delve into the processes, model them, and explore alternatives.

System dynamics provides a very rich modeling environment. It can incorporate many formulations including equations, graphs, and tabular data. Models are formulated using continuous quantities interconnected in loops of information feedback and circular causality. The quantities are expressed as levels (also called stocks or accumulations), rates (also called flows), and information links representing the feedback loops.

The system dynamics approach involves the following concepts [Richardson 1991]:

- Defining problems dynamically, in terms of graphs over time
- Striving for an endogenous ("caused within") behavioral view of the significant dynamics of a system

- Thinking of all real systems concepts as continuous quantities interconnected in information feedback loops with circular causality
- Identifying independent levels in the system and their inflow and outflow rates
- Formulating a model capable of reproducing the dynamic problem of concern by itself
- Deriving understandings and applicable policy insights from the resulting model
- Ultimately implementing changes resulting from model-based understandings and insights, which was Forrester's overall goal

A major principle is that the dynamic behavior of a system is a consequence of its own structure. Given this, the structure of a system can be focused on in order to effect different behavior. Improvement of a process thus entails an understanding and modification of its structure. The structures of the as-is and to-be processes are represented in models.

The existence of process feedback is another underlying principle. Elements of a system dynamics model can interact through feedback loops, where a change in one variable affects other variables over time, which in turn affect the original variable. Understanding and taking advantage of feedback effects can provide high leverage.

2.1.1 Conserved Flows Versus Nonconserved Information

In the system dynamics worldview, process entities are represented as aggregated flows over time. The units of these rates are entities flowing per unit of time. These flows are considered material or physical flows that must be conserved within a flow chain. Information connections are not conserved flows, on the other hand. Although the artifacts of software development are information in one form or another, they constitute physical entities in system dynamics models and should not be confused with nonconserved information links.

Information links only provide data from auxiliaries or levels to rates or other auxiliaries. Nothing is lost or gained in the transfer. So whereas software tasks are conserved as they transform through life-cycle phases, information on them is not conserved such as a derived indicator like percent of job complete.

A physical example of a real-world level/rate system is a water network, such as a set of holding tanks connected with valved pipes. It is easy to visualize the rise and fall of water levels in the tanks as inflow and outflow rates are varied. The amount of water in the system is conserved within all the reservoirs and readings of current tank levels are signals that can be propagated anywhere.

2.1.2 The Continuous View Versus Discrete Event Modeling

The continuous view does not track individual events; rather, tasks are treated "in the aggregate" and systems can be described through differential equations. There is a sort of blurring effect on discrete events. The focus is not on specific individuals or events, but instead on the patterns of behavior and on average individuals in a population. System dynamics as a simplifying technique does not lose important resolution, since the large number of individual "events" in a typical software project precludes management overview at that granularity level anyway. When called for, this resolution can be handled in system dynamics using a hybrid approach.

Discrete-event approaches model each and every event. Their focus is usually on the flow of discrete entities without having feedback connections and the resulting internal dynamics. These effects can sometimes be implemented with discrete modeling but, generally, discrete simulation packages do not easily support feedback connections. A continuous representation is mechanically easier to achieve, and it is always possible to transform a continuous model into a discrete one.

Before choosing a modeling method for software processes, an important question that should be answered is "What in the software process is continuous and what is truly discrete?" Are there discrete aspects that need to be preserved for the purpose of the study? If so, then a discrete or hybrid modeling approach may be better suited than system dynamics. See later chapters for more discussions of continuous modeling versus discrete modeling; Appendix B also summarizes some hybrid software process modeling work.

2.1.3   Model Elements and Notations

This section expands on the Chapter 1 summary of model elements. They are summarized along with their notations in Table 2-1. These notations are the ones available in the Ithink and Stella toolsets used for almost all of the examples in this book. Notations used for other popular toolsets are nearly identical and shown in Section 2.13.

The descriptions in Table 2-1 are elaborated with more detail in later parts of this chapter, especially in section 2.6 Model Formulation and Construction. Figure 2.1, Figure 2.2 and Figure 2.3, respectively, show simplified examples of levels, rates, and auxiliaries with their next-door neighbors for some typical software process structures. Connections to other model elements from the neighbors are not shown for overall legibility.

Elements can be combined together to form infrastructures. Using common existing infrastructures in models can save a lot of time and headache. Two examples of common infrastructures are shown in Figure 2.4. The first is a simple software production infrastructure and the other is a defect propagation infrastructure. Connections to other model elements are not shown for simplification. An infrastructure can be easily modified or enhanced for different modeling purposes. See Chapter 3 for applied examples of software process infrastructures.

2.1.4   Mathematical Formulation of System Dynamics

The mathematics in this section is for general background, and is not necessary for developing or using system dynamics models. It illustrates the underpinnings of the modeling approach and provides a mathematical framework for it. An elegant aspect of system dynamics tools is that systems can be described visually to a large degree, and there is no need for the user to explicitly write or compute differential equations. The tools do all numerical integration calculations. Users do, however, need to compose

Table 2-1. System dynamics model elements

Element	Notation	Description
Level		A level is an accumulation over time, also called a stock or state variable. It can serve as a storage device for material, energy, or information. Contents move through levels via inflow and outflow rates. Levels represent the state variables in a system and are a function of past accumulation of rates. Some examples are: • Software tasks (function points, SLOC, use cases, modules, COTS components, etc.) • Defect levels • Personnel • Expended effort
Source/Sink		Sources and sinks indicate that flows come from or go to somewhere external to the process. Their presence signifies that real-world accumulations occur outside the boundary of the modeled system. They represent infinite supplies or repositories that are not specified in the model. Examples include: • Source of requirements • Software delivered to customers • Employee hiring sources and attrition sinks
Rate		Rates are also called flows; they are the "actions" in a system. They effect the changes in levels. Rates may represent decisions or policy statements. Rates are computed as a function of levels, constants, and auxiliaries. Examples include: • Software productivity rate • Defect generation • Personnel hiring and deallocation • Learning rate • Financial burn rate
Auxiliary		Auxiliaries are converters of input to output, and help elaborate the detail of stock and flow structures. An auxiliary variable must lie in an information link that connects a level to a rate. Auxiliaries often represent "score-keeping" variables. Example variables include: • Percent of job completion • Quantitative goals or planned values • Constants like average delay times • Defect density

(continued)

Table 2-1. System dynamics model elements *(continued)*

Element	Notation	Description
Information Link	ᘔ	Information linkages are used to represent information flow (as opposed to material flow). Rates, as control mechanisms, often require connectors from other variables (usually levels or auxiliaries) for decision making. Links can represent closed-path feedback loops between elements. Examples of such information include: • Progress and status information for decision making • Knowledge of defect levels to allocate rework resources • Linking process parameters to rates and other variables.

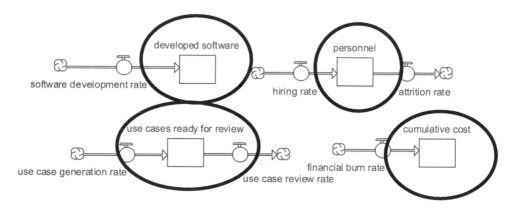

Figure 2.1. Level examples.

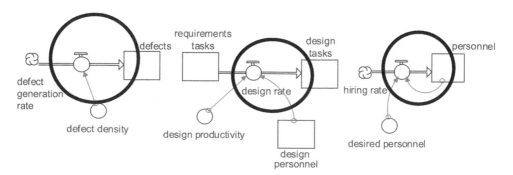

Figure 2.2. Rate examples.

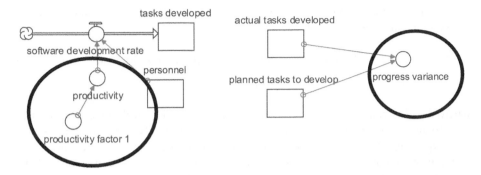

Figure 2.3. Auxiliary examples.

equations for rates and auxiliaries, which can sometimes be described through visual graph relationships.

The mathematical structure of a system dynamics simulation model is a set of coupled, nonlinear, first-order differential equations:

$$\mathbf{x}'(t) = \mathbf{f}(\mathbf{x},\mathbf{p})$$

where $\mathbf{x}$ is a vector of levels, $\mathbf{p}$ a set of parameters and $\mathbf{f}$ is a nonlinear vector-valued function. State variables are represented by the levels. As simulation time advances, all rates are evaluated and integrated to compute the current levels. Runge–Kutta or Euler's numerical integration methods are normally used. These algorithms are described in standard references on numerical analysis methods or provided in technical documentation with system dynamics modeling tools such as [Richmond et al. 1990].

Numerical integration in system dynamics implements the following calculus integral for determining levels at any time t based on their inflow and outflow rates:

$$Level = Level_0 + \int_0^t (\text{inflow} - \text{outflow})\, dt$$

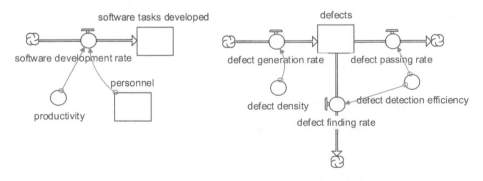

Figure 2.4. Infrastructure examples.

The *dt* parameter corresponds to the chosen time increment for execution. Corresponding system dynamics code for the level calculations would be:

$$Level(\text{time}) = Level(\text{time} - dt) + (inflow - outflow) \cdot dt$$

$$\text{INIT } Level = Level_0$$

where *Level* is computed for any time, $Level_0$ is the initial level value, and the flow rates to and from the level are *inflow* and *outflow*, respectively. Describing the system with equations like the above spares the modeler from integration mechanics. Note that almost all tools also relieve the modeler from constructing the equations; rather, a diagrammatic representation is drawn and the underlying equations are automatically produced. See the following sections for more detail of the model components.

2.1.5 Using Heuristics

One of the ultimate challenges in modeling is dealing with the complexity of the systems under study. Since the systems being modeled are complex, the task of modeling them can also become complex without some simplifying guidelines. Both art and science are called for. Model conceptualization in particular cannot be algorithmically described. It is akin to architecting complex systems that exhibit ambiguity and unboundedness. Dr. Eberhardt Rechtin elucidates the heuristic process used by architects of complex systems in the insightful and entertaining book, *Systems Architecting* [Rechtin 1991], and the follow-on, *The Art of Systems Architecting* [Rechtin, Maier 1997]. Many of the heuristics also apply in simulation modeling.

Heuristics are normally described with short aphorisms. They are used as guidelines or rules of thumb to help simplify the multivariate decision process in the midst of complexity. They help to reduce the search for solutions based on contextual information. Relevant heuristics to deal with the complexities and help simplify the modeling are identified throughout this chapter. An example is,

> Don't try to model the "system."

This heuristic helps reduce modeling complexity by not trying to include everything in a model. It reminds one that a model addresses a particular problem and that irrelevant details should be abstracted out. The heuristics serve as general guidelines for dealing with hard modeling issues and are summarized at the end of this chapter in Section 2.15.1, Summary of Modeling Heuristics.

2.1.6 Potential Pitfalls

Computer models using system dynamics may on occasion exhibit stability problems, system lags and delays, discrete transients, off-nominal behavior problems, saturation effects, and so on. Sound and rigorous modeling can overcome these problems that ultimately stem from specification inadequacies. Methods to avoid some of these problems are described later in the book, and serious modelers may want to consult other system dynamics implementation references for more detail.

Recall that system dynamics is a technique that models continuous variables, so discrete entities lose their individuality and are "blurred" together. This may represent a new change of perspective for some readers. Keep in mind that models are abstractions of reality, and continuous models will compute fractional quantities of things normally thought of as discrete. The results are just as meaningful for an aggregate view as if the quantities were discretized.

2.2 GENERAL SYSTEM BEHAVIORS

This section will review general system behaviors representative of many types of systems, and illustrate them with simple structures. Knowing how systems behave and respond to given inputs is valuable intuition for the modeler. This knowledge can be used during model assessment, such as when evaluating the system response to test inputs used to stimulate the system behavioral modes.

The *order* of a system refers to the number of levels contained. A single-level system cannot oscillate, but a system with at least two levels can oscillate because one part of the system can be in disequilibrium.

2.2.1 Goal-Seeking Behavior

Figure 2.5 shows generic goal-seeking behaviors found in feedback systems, as modified from [Forrester 1968]. Time starts at the beginning of a project, process improvement program, or other goal-attainment activity. Examples of the goal or measurement being tracked could be product quality as measured by defect density trends or average

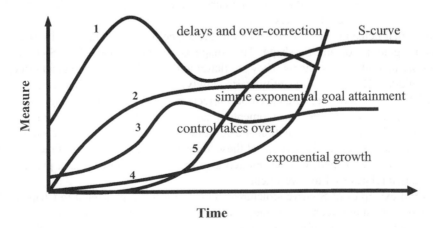

Figure 2.5. Goal-seeking behaviors.

system response time; process performance such as earned value, productivity, or defect yield; organizational hiring; financial goals such as sales; and so on. Rudimentary model structures and inputs that produce these dynamic behaviors are shown in Section 2.2.3.

Curve #1 at the top is the result of excessive delays in the control loop or overcorrections. Consider a shower with sluggish controls that you are getting used to. The water temperature oscillates wildly as you adapt to the internal delays of the temperature control system. In a software process, this would be akin to late metrics feedback. Possibly, signals from the process are not being interpreted properly by management, "an unwise prince who doesn't recognize."

The next curve, #2, is the result of an exponential goal attainment feedback loop (also called negative or balancing feedback). The curve gradually reaches the set point and eventually levels off to the desired quantity. The system reaches equilibrium in a controlled manner. It shows negative feedback for a positive goal. For a zero goal, the curve mirrors itself by approaching from the top and asymptotically approaching the goal. The curve may represent the number of people when hiring toward a desired number. The speed at which the goal is attained depends on the hiring time delay. This will be used as an exercise later to examine the curve sensitivity to varying time delays.

Curve #3 starts out with an early exponential growth pattern until control takes over. From that point, the deviations diminish and the goal is gradually eased into. It is quite possible that a system will not recover and continue to oscillate, such as when there are excessive delays and overcorrecting taking place.

Curve #4 starts at the bottom and is an exponential growth curve that dramatically rises. It is best plotted on logarithmic paper to cover the wide range of values. This type of growth has been observed for defect-fixing costs as the life cycle progresses (whereby fixing overhead accumulates), early growth of new product users or sales, global Internet traffic or online program usage, growth of regional Internet users until the area becomes saturated, early corporate growth, and so on. A market stagnation could cause enterprise-related exponential curves to eventually peak and level off like the third curve when control takes over.

Sigmoidal behavior in curve #5 refers to the shape of a graphed quantity that exhibits a sigmoidal or an "S" shape. This shape is commonly called an S-curve. S-curves are ubiquitous in systems. They are flatter at the beginning and end, and steeper in the middle. The S-curve quantity starts slowly, accelerates, and then tails off. S-shaped progress curves are often seen on projects because cumulative progress starts out slowly, the slope increases as momentum gains, then work tapers off. S-curves are also observed in technology adoption and corporate and sales growth where saturation points are reached (the early portions of these are exponential). The ROI of technology adoption is also S-shaped, whether plotted as a time-based return or as a production function that relates ROI to investment.

Several examples of S-curve structures and behaviors are presented in Chapters 3, 4, 5, and 6, including technology adoption, software virus propagation, sales growth and stagnation, project effort expenditures when staffing approximates a Rayleigh curve, and more.

These curves illustrate that feedback loops must be finely tuned. The right information must be used to effect feedback in the proper manner. A system can go into oscillations if the wrong or poorly timed feedback is used (just like the shower temperature with sluggish controls). Too much positive feedback can produce system oscillation. A system can become overdamped if there is too much negative feedback, because there will be more resistance than is needed.

2.2.2 Information Smoothing

Smoothing of information is used to detect real trends by eliminating random spikes. Decision makers should not interpret a day's jump in a relatively long-term pattern of some quantity as a permanent trend to base decisions on. Therefore, information is averaged over a sufficient time period.

Smoothed variables exponentially seek the input signal. Information smoothing can be modeled as a first-order negative feedback loop. The smoothing curve could represent information on the apparent level of a system as understanding increases toward the true value. There is a time delay associated with the smoothing, and the change toward the final value starts rapidly and decreases as the discrepancy narrows between the present and final values. A graphic example of a smoothed variable that follows an input signal that steps up and down is in Figure 2.6. Example structures and behaviors for information smoothing are shown later in Chapter 3.

2.2.3 Example: Basic Structures for General Behaviors

Now let us observe rudimentary behaviors using simple models. A single rate/level pair will be used to demonstrate the general behaviors. Figure 2.7 shows the rate/level model used for the nonfeedback tests for pulse, step, ramp, and Rayleigh curve rate inputs. The rate represents the net flow in or out of the level. Figure 2.8 shows the simple negative and positive feedback systems for the last two examples in Table 2-2. All of these are first-order systems because only one level is contained in them.

Table 2-2 shows the flow inputs, situations they could model in the software process, and the level response. When the flow type is characterized as a staffing profile, the level corresponds to the cumulative number of staff. When the flow is a defect generation rate, the level represents the cumulative defects, and so on. The positive

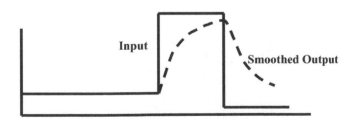

Figure 2.6. Information smoothing.

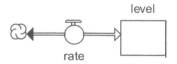

Figure 2.7. Rate/level system (no feedback).

feedback keeps increasing per the growth fraction to represent exponential growth. The negative feedback rate diminishes over time as the level reaches its goal of five (e.g., hiring, quality, or process maturity goals).

Note how a pulse input produces a step increase in the corresponding level. A step input produces a ramp, and a ramp input creates a nonlinear rise in the level. The Rayleigh curve input produces an S-shaped response in the level.

The graph pad format in Figure 2.9 is a handy worksheet for plotting rates and levels manually. It shows the same case as the step input response in Table 2-2. One should be able to calculate a level from rate inputs and, conversely, derive the rate that must have existed to produce indicated changes to a level (at least for linear trends). The units should be derivable also. The interested student should practice this and develop the skill for integrating simple rates. Though simulation software does this for you, it is extremely valuable for modelers to crosscheck and be able to determine expected responses.

2.3 MODELING OVERVIEW

This section contains an overview of the modeling process and lists the basic steps. Much of this section is derived from [Richardson, Pugh 1981] and [Richmond 1994]. The [Richardson, Pugh 1981] reference represents classic, traditional system dynamics in the pre-Graphical User Interface (GUI) Dynamo era, whereas Richmond pioneered visual system dynamics starting with the very early Macintosh models. The differing historical perspectives likely explain the additional manual steps from conceptualization to final model elaboration (such as using causal loop diagrams) in the older approach.

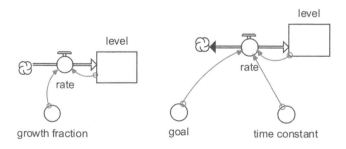

Figure 2.8. Positive and negative feedback systems.

Table 2-2. General behaviors from model structures

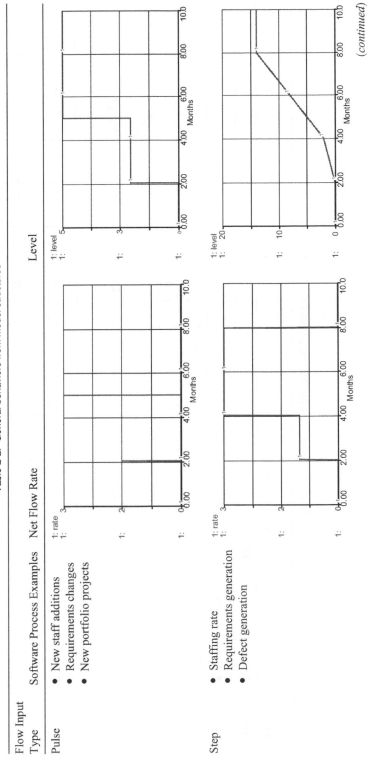

Flow Input Type	Software Process Examples	Net Flow Rate	Level
Pulse	• New staff additions • Requirements changes • New portfolio projects		
Step	• Staffing rate • Requirements generation • Defect generation		

(continued)

Table 2-2. General behaviors from model structures *(continued)*

Flow Input Type	Software Process Examples	Net Flow Rate	Level
Ramp	• Defect generation before unrealistic deadline • Software check-in rate before build deadline • User growth		
Rayleigh Curve	Project effort expenditure • Defect generation • Technology adoption		

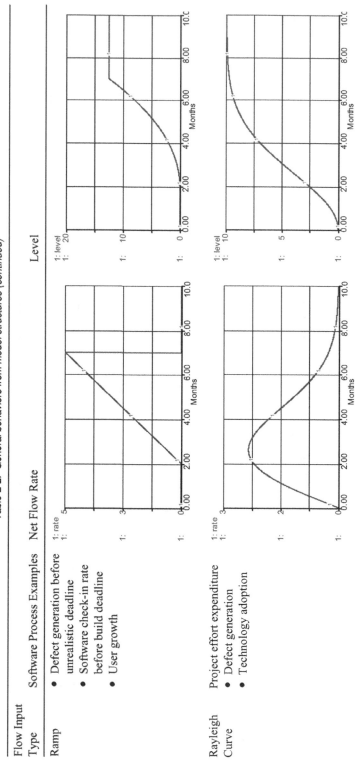

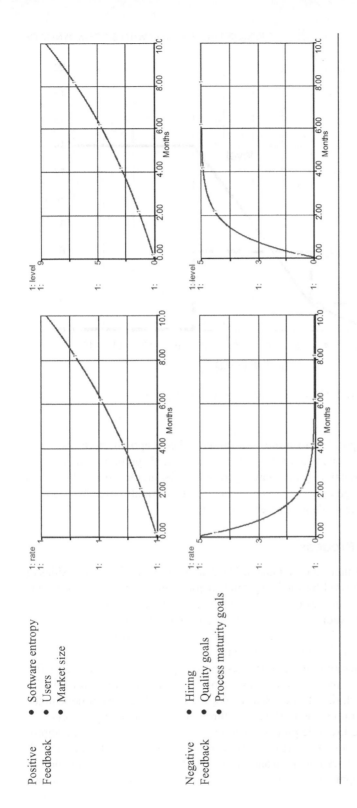

Positive
Feedback
• Software entropy
• Users
• Market size

Negative
Feedback
• Hiring
• Quality goals
• Process maturity goals

67

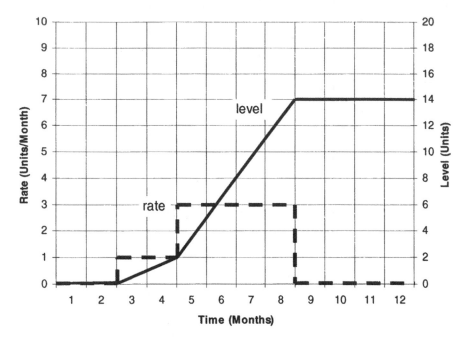

Figure 2.9. Manual graph depiction for step input.

In the early stages of problem identification and model conceptualization, the activities include developing a statement of the problem context and symptoms, articulating the modeling purpose, identifying and drawing reference behavior modes, defining a system boundary, and beginning the system structure of information feedback loops. The purpose will drive the modeling process and scope.

2.3.1 An Iterative Process

Modeling with system dynamics is an inherently iterative process. The complexities of the problems being addressed by modeling tend to force an iterative approach. One passes through several sequences of conceptualization, formulation, simulation, validation, and reconceptualization as a model is elaborated and refined over time. Even if a model can be fully specified at once, it is highly recommended to assemble it in pieces and test the model as it continues to be integrated.

The process is also iterative in that one does not complete a step, consider it finished, then set it aside and move onto the next step. You arrive at an interim completion of the first step, and during the next step you return to clarify the work done in the first step. Revisiting your previous work repeats throughout the modeling process.

The iterative software lifecycle process overviewed in Chapter 1 is also an appropriate general framework for modeling projects. Variants of the system dynamics modeling process have always been iterative and cyclic, similar to evolutionary and nonsequential software development. A mapping of the generic phases used in traditional software development processes (as described in Chapter 1) to the specific modeling steps is shown in Table 2-3.

The process shown in Figure 2.10 is adapted from [Richardson, Pugh 1981]. It starts with problem definition and progresses clockwise through the phases. System understanding can be enhanced at different stages of the modeling process (indicated by the nonsequential connections back to system undertstandings), and the improved understanding helps further the modeling. The overall process may be repeated as software policies improve.

Figure 2.11 shows the modeling stages and their respective concerns adapted from [Richardson, Pugh 1981]. There is a large overlap of concerns between the stages. This again indicates some of the nonsequential aspects of modeling. Minicycles may occur at anytime, and cycles can be going on in parallel, as in the spiral model for software development.

The process has distinct similarities to the spiral model of software development with WinWin extensions. Both start with an evolutionary premise and rely on successive improvement cycles interlaced with mission redefinition based on usage of the preceding product. Defining the model purpose is essentially the same as defining stakeholders and their win conditions, and should be considered just as critical to modeling success. The product of a system dynamics analysis could be the resulting knowledge (estimate, new insight, process improvement action item) gleaned from a working model as well as the model (tool) itself.

Figure 2.12 shows a first-order mapping between the WinWin spiral model and the traditional modeling phases. System understanding is not shown because it is continuous throughout. The inner core shows the WinWin spiral model and the outer layer shows the process modeling activities. Realizing that this is a simplification, there may be additional cycles between some of the steps to reduce risk (such as going from concept to model formulation). There is a high degree of correlation between the life-cycle models, particularly when one explores the details of the steps.

The similarities indicate that the iterative spiral model is a good fit to simulation model development in addition to other types of software. Some of the activities for modeling are unique, of course, such as the extensive nature of model validation. Additionally, simulation models frequently have a smaller user base and time horizon compared to other software. They are sometimes used just long enough to determine that a process improvement is necessary, and they become outdated or irrelevant once

Table 2-3. Mapping of software life-cycle process phases to modeling steps

Generic Software Life-cycle Phase	Modeling Steps
Inception	Problem Definition
Elaboration	Model Conceptualization
	Top-Level Model Formulation
Construction	Detailed Model Formulation and Construction
	Simulation
	Model Assessment
Transition	Policy Analysis and Implementation

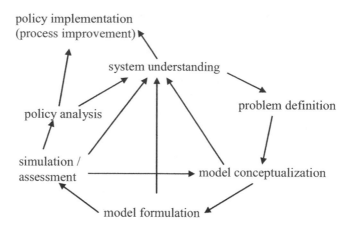

Figure 2.10. Cyclic modeling process.

the process is changed. Sometimes they should still be created to be easily evolvable; it all depends on the intended purposes.

2.3.2 Applying the WinWin Spiral Model

An executable software process dynamics model is a software artifact. Not too surprisingly, then, we have found that good strategic software development processes such as the WinWin Spiral model used by MBASE work well in developing process models.

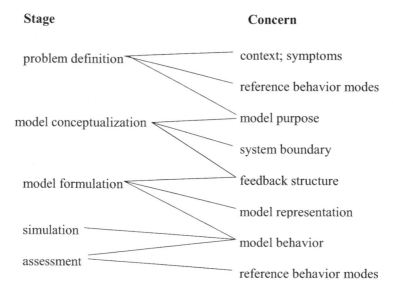

Figure 2.11. Modeling stages and concerns.

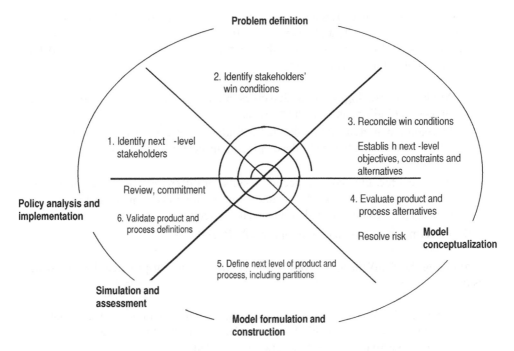

Figure 2.12. WinWin spiral model and process modeling phases.

The WinWin Spiral model approach has the following major strategic steps and guidelines when applied to the modeling process:

1. Use a stakeholder win–win negotiation process to determine the objectives, constraints, and alternative solution approaches for your model.
2. Evaluate the alternative modeling choices for their ability to satisfy the objectives within the constraints.
3. Identify risk areas (e.g., model performance, calibration data, reusability of existing models) in which there is too much uncertainty to evaluate and decide on the choice of model.
4. Buy information to reduce the risk of making the wrong decision via model prototyping, benchmarking, reference checking, or other analyses.
5. Choose the best alternative, or carry two or three along initially if they are different but about equally likely to succeed, based on what you know so far.
6. Within this context, repeat the steps at the next level of detail until your modeling objectives are achieved.

2.3.2.1 Example: Modeling Strategy

Let us see how this works with respect to an example. Suppose you are finding that your normal inspection techniques are not catching as many defects per hour invested when you are inspecting COTS integration glue code, and you would like to model the situation to determine a potentially more cost-effective mix of inspections, benchmarking techniques, and testing techniques that increases your defect detection yield for glue code. Your main alternatives are:

A. Modify an existing systems dynamics model of the inspection and testing process for built-from-scratch software.

B. Develop a new dynamic model that includes the effects of COTS assessment; COTS tailoring; glue code development, inspection and testing; and COTS volatility.

C. Analyze a few glue code inspection results for differences in classes of defects found, and use this to develop a simple, informal nondynamic model of options to best remove late-detected or undetected defects.

D. Perform some combination of options A, B, and C.

Applying the WinWin Spiral Model to this situation might produce the following results:

1. Some of your stakeholders may have significant constraints on the amount of money and time available for the modeling activity. Others may have ambitious objectives for model generality and fidelity.

2., 3. When you evaluate the alternatives with respect to these objectives and constraints, you find that the full form of Alternative B would be an overkill, and that there is insufficient data to assess how much time and effort it would take to modify the existing model (A) to satisfy the stakeholders' generality and fidelity objectives.

4. Analyze a couple of representative glue code inspection and integration processes (a subset of C) to better determine how much modification of the existing model is necessary to achieve various levels of fidelity.

5., 6. If a key stakeholder has a very tight time constraint (e.g., a new-project proposal), choose alternative C to satisfy this near-term need. If other key stakeholders still have strong needs for a dynamic model and model A looks satisfactory to modify, choose to do C, and then do A based on the additional insights gained from doing C. If it is not clear whether A or a subset of B would be preferable, choose to do C followed by another round of the spiral to establish a stronger basis for choosing between A and an appropriate subset of B.

Thus, the WinWin Spiral Model provides strategic guidance with respect to the top-level choices you make, in determining what combinations and sequences of modeling activities to pursue in order to best achieve your stakeholders' objectives. As you elaborate the definition and development of the models, more modeling-specific process guidelines become more important. These modeling steps are now expanded on in the following sections.

2.4 PROBLEM DEFINITION

Problem definition is of primary importance as it sets the stage for subsequent modeling activities. You can make your biggest mistakes in this phase and doom the entire study. At the outset, you define the purpose of the modeling study and its intended audience. Major process stakeholders should be involved from the very beginning to define model purpose. The problem must be important enough to the involved stakeholders to warrant a study. Make explicit what system behavior is of interest and what policies are to be simulated. Consider the type and degree of model implementation; will it be a short exercise that only develops causal diagrams, a several-month model development to test policies, or are you creating an enterprise-wide distributed simulation to be used by many?

Identifying the problem to be addressed requires an unambiguous and explicit definition. The context and symptoms of the problem should be concise and easily verbalized. One informal test of this is called the "elevator test": Can the problem statement be summarized to others well enough to be understood in a minute-long elevator ride?

When defining the problem, you make initial attempts to sketch out system structures and develop reference behavior patterns. These reference behaviors help define the problem dynamically in terms of plots over time. The reference modes can show the problem behavior, desirable to-be system behavior, or observed behavior as a result of previous process policy changes.

2.4.1 Defining the Purpose

A model is created to answer a specific set of questions relating to organizational goals. Defining the goals and deriving questions related to the goals correspond to the first two steps of the Goal–Question–Metric paradigm [Basili 1992], while specific model metrics answering the questions are identified later. The modeling effort strives to improve understanding of the relationships between feedback structure and dynamic system behavior. With this understanding, policies can be developed to improve future process behavior. In some research contexts, a model may be developed to test a theory, but the focus is primarily on modeling for process design and improvement.

The model purpose statement includes identifying the stakeholder audience, the desired set of policies to be simulated, and the type of model implementation. The objectives must be realistic and credible. The degree of implementation can vary across the spectrum. Examples of progressive levels of implementation include:

- Basic consciousness raising via causal loop diagramming, with no executable models developed
- A short modeling exercise to compare policies for an upcoming project decision (like a one-off Brooks's Law analysis)
- Actual adoption of new policies tested by a model and continued policy analysis with the model
- Developing institutional models with dozens of factors for ongoing project estimation and planning

Consider whether the effort will be a one-time adoption of new policies or an ongoing process for continual analysis. The level of implementation clearly will have an important effect on the resulting model content.

Defining the purpose thus includes early consideration of acceptance criteria and process transition planning. Implementation of eventual process changes must be consciously planned from the start. The ability to adapt to change in the organization must be accounted for. The possible side impacts on related processes or other systems should be assessed. Consider what sort of training or reeducation of process participants might be necessary.

Following is a ditty from [Richardson, Pugh 1981] that uses analogy to stress that you need a clear modeling purpose to know where you are going:

> *A model without a purpose is like a ship without a sail,*
> *A boat without a rudder, a hammer without a nail . . .*

Write the purpose down, and be specific. Instead of beginning a study with a top-level goal like "analyze inspections," refine it to something specific and measurable like "What is the dynamic cost profile over time of performing inspections?" or "What is the optimal staffing policy for inspection rework?" Do not try to "model the system" as a goal. A clear, operational purpose is needed or the resulting model will be too big and complex because everything will be included.

The purpose statement should be supplemented with specific behaviors or patterns. These reference behaviors are expressed as graphs of important system variables over time, and described in the next section.

2.4.2   Reference Behavior

Reference behavior patterns help define a problem dynamically; they focus model conceptualization and are used in validation. They are a plot over time of a few variables that best characterize the dynamic phenomenon to be understood. These graphs may include observed and/or desired patterns. They make the purpose statement operational as a graph. They also help specify the time horizon for the model.

The resulting model is tested in subsequent stages of development to see if the reference modes can be reproduced. The ability to do so constitutes an acceptance criterion for the model. Even if this fails, things may be learned that still contribute to an overall successful modeling effort. One possible outcome is that the initial reference modes were not appropriate or misleading.

Reference behaviors are ideally based on actual data. When data is lacking, some of the graphs may need to be inferred and/or drawn on relative scales. Even with good data, it is often advantageous to normalize a variable used in a reference behavior pattern. Absolute quantities may need to be carefully bounded, whereas relative measures are often easier to interpret and are more forgiving since they are valid across a wider range of values, and generally lead to relevant questions about important relationships. Reference behaviors should indicate problematic behavior, not the variables that are causing the behavior.

Not having data for all quantities should not hamper model specification and elaboration. More subjective measures will always be harder to get hard data for, for example, motivation, yet are still important determinants of system behavior. Often, the modeler will have to rely on expert judgment and the intuitions of those closest to the process. Sometimes, other models can be leveraged. Various examples of dealing with missing or incomplete data are described in Chapters 4–7.

2.4.3 Example: Model Purpose and Reference Behavior

Sample goals for the Brooks's Law model may include:

- Understanding the dynamic phenomena behind Brooks's Law
- Improving project execution for a current project
- Improving future project planning

Based on these goals, sample relevant questions to answer are:

- What is the impact on productivity of adding people?
- How much extra communication overhead will result from adding people to a project?
- How much effort will be required to train new people?
- Can people be added to the ongoing project X and can we come out ahead schedule-wise? If so, what is the optimal number of people to add? When is the best time to add them?
- How big should our teams be on future projects?

The implied reference behavior for the Brooks's Law model is an overrunning project. It can be visualized as productivity and personnel over time or planned versus actual progress over time in terms of tasks developed (Figures 2.13 and 2.14).

2.5 MODEL CONCEPTUALIZATION

Conceptualization includes identifying the system boundary to determine what is relevant to the study, and deriving a high-level view of system elements. The boundary must include the parts necessary to generate the behavior of interest, including all relevant policy levers. Some of the process stakeholders should continue their involvement in this stage if they are knowledgeable enough and time should be dedicated to help conceptualize a high-level view of the relevant process(es).

A top-down, iterative approach to model conceptualization generally works best. Compose the model first with small, simple pieces and iteratively broaden it to larger sectors. Build it up using relatively small changes. This way, the gap between iteration versions can be understood and tracked and the model debugged more easily. The same "build a little, test a little" approach also applies during later stages of model formulation.

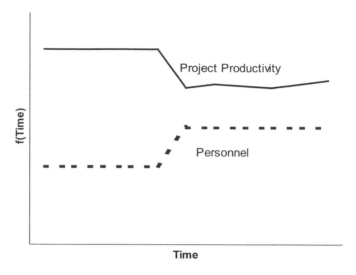

Figure 2.13. Brooks's Law reference behavior—productivity and personnel.

The typical order of conceiving model elements within the boundary is:

1. Develop the physical structure of the system
2. Identify basic information flows
3. Distinguish perceived versus actual information in the system
4. Identify the decisions made by actors in the system resulting from the perceptions

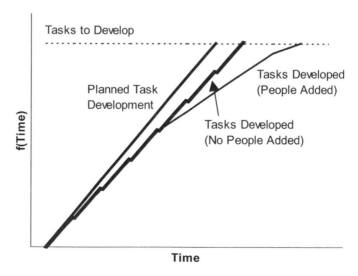

Figure 2.14. Brooks's Law reference behavior—task development.

The perception-based decisions lead to pressures that change the system behavior somehow.

First, develop a system diagram using a high-level depiction of key sectors within a model whose interplay is thought to generate the reference behavior. This focuses on the structural aspects of the system. For software, the physical structure reflects the organization and its processes for developing and transforming software artifacts. Example sectors would be project planning, software construction, and so on. Differentiate physical exchanges (conserved flows) from information connections (that are nonconserved "data links"). Later, the sectors will be elaborated to identify flow chains. At this stage, it is best to concentrate on the system as is, since the desired to-be system will eventually have to be implemented on top of what currently exists anyway.

The decisions represented in the system may consist of the following elements: an actual system state, a perceived state, a desired state, pressures to close the gap and achieve the desired state, and resultant action to change the state and thus close the feedback loop. Often, the delineation of perceived versus actual information gets to the heart of the problematic system behavior. Only that information actually used by actors in the process for decision making should be included. Reflecting this reality, all variables cannot be directly linked in a model if they are not so in the real world.

Early on, a dynamic hypothesis about the feedback structures thought to cause the problem behavior should be attempted. The statement can be verbal or graphic. It may include possible causes of the problem behavior. Keep in mind that such hypotheses are refined throughout the modeling process. It is quite possible that a succinct, well-focused, and consistent hypothesis statement will be realized only after many modeling iterations of conceptualization, formulation, simulation, and evaluation.

One must aggregate and abstract factors to the appropriate degree, though it is a bit of a practiced art to make all model elements relevant to general stakeholders. How much aggregation versus "drilling down" into the process should one undertake? Initially, aggregate things until the level of aggregation obfuscates entities or factors deemed important to the study. Decompose factors only when the problem calls for it.

Always try to match the level of detail to the audience. Represent the system at a level of abstraction that is meaningful to the stakeholders and matches their mindset. Different levels of an organization will expect different degrees of roll-up or data aggregation. Also address the problem statement commensurate with the current stage of model elaboration. The measures of effectiveness in the model and the result variables must be consistent with real-world measures of process performance.

The KISS principle (keep it simple, stupid) should always be kept in mind during model conceptualization and formulation. Do not bite off more than you can chew and strive to minimize the model complexity. The resulting model will be easier to develop and be understood by others.

The following concepts in the Brooks's Law model would be identified at this stage:

- Task flows and personnel flows should be covered
- Effects of adding more people must be included in the formulation
- A schedule completion date must be calculable in the model

2.5.1   Identification of System Boundary

A boundary is the imaginary line delineating what is considered inside and outside the system for modeling purposes. Within the boundary are concepts and quantities thought to be significant to the dynamics of the problem being addressed. Without a relevant boundary, "analysis paralysis" becomes a risk since too many factors keep being considered.

Where exactly does one draw the boundary line between systems and subsystems? Since systems exist on many interacting levels, it is a modeling challenge to cleanly isolate the elements of study. The naturalist John Muir illustrated this conundrum of systems as follows: "When we try to pick out anything by itself, we find it hitched to everything else in the universe."[1]

Defining the boundary of the system is of utmost importance to isolate exactly what parts of the system are necessary to generate the behavior of interest. The boundary must be wide enough to include information feedback loops that help cause system behavior, applicable policy levers, and variables used to evaluate the process in response to new policies. The variables used to assess process changes based on new policies are sometimes called "result variables," as described in Chapter 1.

The policy levers to be included are intervention points that represent leverage in the system, that is, the places where system impacts can be made in the real world and first tested in a model. System components not relevant to the problem should be excluded. When in doubt, recall that the focus is on a problem, not "the system." Otherwise, it is tempting to include too many factors.

It is impossible to define a boundary without a model purpose. When the questions of the modeling study are known, then the importance of factors to include or exclude from the system can be judged. One distinguishes what is explicitly inside, what is implicitly represented inside through aggregation and interpretation of system variables, and what is explicitly outside.

A boundary should be drawn that encloses the smallest number of possible elements. Do not ask whether a piece is in the system or not but, rather, consider whether the behavior of interest will disappear or be erroneously modeled if the piece is excluded. If a component can be easily removed without defeating the purpose, then take it out. It is useful to keep in result variables since they are indicators to assess process performance and measure the relative gains of new or revised policies.

Other questions to consider when defining the boundary are the following:

- What are the physical processes in the system relevant to the problem?
- What are the perceptions of those processes to those in the system and how are those perceptions formed?

---

[1] John Muir, *My First Summer in the Sierra*, 1911. Interestingly, a connection of natural forces and software processes occurred in Los Angeles in the 1994 Northridge earthquake. Some of us were intimate with software projects that had official schedule reprieves due to facility cleanup and employee situations dealing with serious home damage. The lingering project effects of the earthquake lasted for many months thereafter.

- How do the perceptions help create pressures that influence the physical processes?

Answering these questions will set the stage for model conceptualization.

The physical processes in the Brooks's Law model include software task development (implying a flow chain from required tasks to completed tasks), people coming on board the project, added communication, and training. A perception of project lateness is necessary for a decision to be made to add people, as realized by the amount of software developed to date compared to a desired amount. At some "breaking point," whereby the gap becomes large enough for action, the project takes on more people.

2.5.1.1 *The Endogenous View*

It is instructive to consider an important aspect of system dynamics modeling—the endogenous point of view. This perspective says that all components necessary to generate problem behavior are contained within the system boundary. Hence, the focus is internal, not looking for external blame. The contrasting internal and external views are frequently a source of controversy to be resolved. The external view is often event oriented, considering the system to be at the mercy of outside forces. Rather, events should be seen in the context of patterns, and structural reasons for the patterns searched for. System behavior is the consequence of its structure.

The internal view is essentially an axiom. Internally looking for behavior patterns from system structure is thought to have much more explanatory power than the external view. The focus of modeling is inward once the boundary is drawn. The existence of feedback loops within the boundary is essential. Without them, causal links would be externally connected and the causes of behavior would be traced to outside forces. This is not to deny that external influences can have important impact on a system. Sometimes, these external forces may be a focus of study, but in that case the system boundary has been redefined to include them.

2.5.2 Causal Loop Diagrams

Causal loop diagrams (also called "causal diagrams") are simple diagrams with words and arrows that help portray cause and effect relationships and information feedback in a system. A loop refers to a closed chain of cause and effect. Used carefully, these diagrams can be very effective in explaining how dynamic behavior patterns are generated. The usage of causal loop diagrams is sometimes debated, but ultimately their effectiveness depends on the context. They may be very useful or they may be practically superfluous, depending on the goals, constraints, and participants of a study. They are generally valuable during the top-level formulation of a fuzzy system concept, but elaborated stock and flow models show additional concepts and are more precise. The primary drawback is that causal diagrams obscure the stock and flow structure of systems and lose the crucial concept of accumulation.

Causal diagrams can be misleading due to the lack of accumulations and flows. Causal diagrams make no distinction between information links and rate-to-level links (conserved flows). When there are rate-to-level links, this simplification causes false characterizations of positive and negative polarities in causal loops. Even experienced modelers can easily come up with different (and erroneous) behaviors from the same causal diagram. Using a stock and flow structure will increase the number of correct interpretations of system behavior. Caution should be used since causal diagrams can be easily abused.

In early system dynamics, feedback structure was portrayed with equations and stock and flow diagrams. These representations are natural for engineers, but causal loop diagrams were created to serve a wider range of people and have become popular since then. Causal diagrams support free-form, creative thinking, whereas stock and flow diagrams are more explicit and support analytical thinking. Causal diagrams are often appropriate to begin group modeling exercises. Others use causal diagrams after the fact to illustrate the high-level concepts of an elaborated stock and flow model.

With modern visual programming utilities for system dynamics models, experience has shown that causal diagrams have limited staying power when elaborated, executable models are desired. They quickly lose relevance when more detailed concepts and equations start being fleshed out since there is no distinction between levels, rates, auxiliaries, and so on. Elaborated stock and flow models show more than what causal diagrams can, so they are more powerful to communicate with if the audience understands them. Frequently, the model elaboration process shows that the initial causal diagrams were too simplistic or incomplete to explain a system and its behavior. In many situations, causal diagrams can be bypassed and an elaborated stock and flow model can be started immediately.

On the other hand, some studies will entail only causal diagrams, with no need for further model elaboration. If they satisfy the goals of a study then it is certainly valid to stop there. Despite their drawbacks, people at all levels will probably continue to rely on causal diagrams to communicate feedback structure. Their most appropriate role appears to be for public consumption. A classic article on causal diagram issues is George Richardson's "Problems with Causal-loop Diagrams" [Richardson 1986].

2.5.2.1 Diagramming Conventions

There are several similar conventions for drawing causal loop diagrams. They all use words and arrows to identify system entities and causal connections. Symbols denote the polarity of the connections and the types of feedback loops created (i.e., positive or negative loops). The following outline for creating causal loop diagrams describes a basic method with minor variants. This method is illustrated in the following steps that lead up to an enhanced causal diagram for Brooks's Law.

Step 1. Use words to represent the variables in the system that you wish to interrelate. Use nouns and avoid using verbs or action phrases that indicate a direction of change, such as "increasing" or "decrease in . . ." Arrows will convey the actions and their signs will indicate whether variables increase or decrease relative to each other. Figure 2.15 shows a couple of simple causal relations.

Try to use the more positive sense of a variable name so that relationships are clearer. Take, for example, the aspect of increasing project overhead due to added person-

Figure 2.15. Simple causal relations.

nel per Brooks's Law. The term "project overhead" is preferable to "increasing project overhead" because a decrease in "increasing project overhead" is confusing (see Figure 2.16). Or if "motivation" goes up or down, it is easier to convey an increase or decrease in "lack of motivation."

For every action included in the diagram, try to think of unintended consequences as well as expected outcomes. For example, "schedule pressure" may increase productive time on the job but also induce more errors. It does not matter at this point whether the variables are levels, flows, or auxiliaries. But they should represent quantities that can change over time.

Distinguish between perceived and actual states, such as "perceived quality" versus "actual quality." Perceptions often change slower than reality does, and mistaking the perceived status for current reality can be misleading and create undesirable results. For example, determining if a software product is ready to release may be erroneous if defect reports are not being written or there are substantial reporting delays. The decision maker assumes that there are few defects when the reality is that there are many defects that he is not aware of.

If a variable has multiple consequences, aggregate them first by lumping them into one term while completing the rest of the loop. For example, we started illustrating an aspect of Brooks's Law in Figure 2.16 by showing that added people cause a change in "project overhead." Next we can add the causal effect of project overhead on productivity by adding a positive sense arrow from project overhead to productivity.

In order to represent the different aspects of project overhead, we split it into communication overhead and training overhead. Figure 2.17 shows this disaggregation with both of the effects on productivity.

Step 2. Arrows stand for causal connections between the variables. Draw arrows that point from causes to effects, completing loops wherever possible. In some conventions, a "//" is used to interrupt any arrow that represents a process that contains a significant delay. Some methods distinguish between long-term and short-term consequences of actions. Larger loops are used as the consequences progress from short-term to long-term processes.

Figure 2.16. Causal relation using positive sense for personnel project overhead.

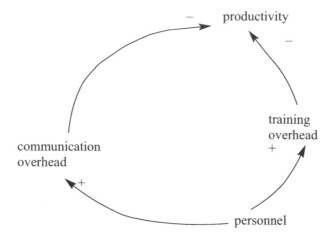

Figure 2.17. Disaggregating project overhead causal effects on productivity.

Step 3. Label the connection polarities at the arrow tips. To determine the polarity for each arrow, either increase or decrease the cause (i.e., the variable at the tail of an arrow). Then, determine whether the effect (i.e., the variable to which the arrow is pointing) moves in the same or opposite direction. If the effect moves in the same direction, use a "+" sign to indicate a positive polarity. If the effect moves in the opposite direction, adorn the arrowhead with a "−" sign.

Note that some diagramming conventions use different pairs of polarity signals. One convention uses the letter "s" to indicate "same" and an "o" to denote an "opposite" effect of one variable relative to another. Sometimes, a positive connection has a blank label and a negative one denoted by a U-turn symbol. The advantage of the latter approach is that the diagrams are less daunting with one-half as many polarity signals. The U-turn symbol is also more recognizable for the inverting concept.

If a link between two terms requires a lot of explanation to be clear, redefine the variables or insert an intermediate term. For example, the relationship between "market window" and "defects" may be more obvious when "schedule pressure" is inserted between them. A decreasing market window increases schedule pressure, which causes more defects (and thus lower quality).

Step 4. Trace the direction of change around each loop in the diagram, beginning with any variable in it. If, after cycling around the loop, the direction of change of the starting point variable is in the same direction as the initial direction of change for this variable, place a (+) in the loop center to indicate a positive (or reinforcing) feedback loop. If, after propagating around the loop, the direction of change of the starting point variable is opposite to the initial direction of change, place a (−) in the center to indicate a negative (or balancing) loop.

There is a shortcut for determining whether a loop is positive or negative. Count the number of negative signs (or "o"s) in the loop. An odd number of negative signs indicates a negative or balancing loop (i.e., an odd number of U-turns keeps you headed in the opposite direction). An even number of negative signs means it is a positive, reinforcing loop. After labeling the loop, you should always read through it again to make sure the story agrees with the loop type label.

Negative feedback loops are goal-seeking processes (hence they are also called balancing loops). Try to make explicit the goals driving the loop. In the Brooks's Law situation, by identifying "planned software" as the goal, we see that the "schedule gap" (which is reflected in the delta between planned and actual developed software) is really driving actions to add people. Figure 2.18 is an enhanced causal loop diagram of Brooks's Law effects with a goal-seeking feedback loop to close the schedule gap.

There are many more elaborate treatments of causal loop diagramming in the system dynamics literature. Hart describes a method in [Hart 2004] with different software process examples.

2.6   MODEL FORMULATION AND CONSTRUCTION

Model formulation elaborates the conceptual system structure into detailed equations for simulation. The system of interest is described in a model consisting of levels, rates, auxiliary variables, and feedback connections. This transformation to a more precise and quantitative state forces a clarity of thinking that continuously improves understanding of the system under study. Formulation and construction of a model involves iterative elaboration, construction, and simulation activities. This section will describe detailed model development in which the pieces are put together, whereas Section 2.7 focuses on executing the progressively complex constructed models.

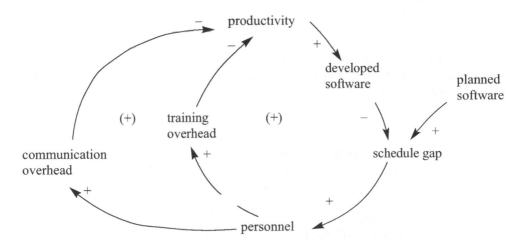

Figure 2.18. Brooks's Law causal loop diagram with goal-seeking feedback.

Just as a group of minds is used to conceptualize a model in the beginning, other participants are also needed during model formulation to describe the current or desired processes. This continuation of the stakeholder communications started during problem definition and model conceptualization often involves people in different roles than those first engaged. Conduct interviews and meetings with those executing the processes. An important heuristic to keep in mind is, *Don't model in isolation; try to involve those being modeled.*

2.6.1   Top-Level Formulation

The top-level formulation activities continue model conceptualization and overlap it to some extent. Conceptualization and top-level model formulation are the iterative elaboration activities before detailed model construction and assessment. Top-level structures serve as an intermediate design bridge between conceptualization and detailed construction. In system dynamics, this intermediate artifact is often represented in an executable model with appropriate stubs and initial approximations.

A high-level mapping of the system is the desired result in this stage. Things should be kept relatively simple. The formulation process can be started by looking for a main chain in the system, which is a sequence of stocks connected by conserved flows. As systems are composed of flows and their accumulations, ask the question, What is accumulating in the system?

2.6.1.1   Identify Major Flow Chains and Model Sectors

Identify the single most important accumulation (i.e., stock or level) in the system. Is it software artifacts? Is it people, defects, effort, or something else? Then define the flows associated with the accumulation(s). Look at each flow in isolation. Ask, What is the nature of the activity generating the flow?

Tasks and people accumulate in the Brooks's Law situation. Since tasks and people are quite distinct entities, they should be modeled as separate flow chains. The two flow chains constitute the backbone of the Brook's Law model upon which specific rate equations and auxiliaries are built on top of.

If a main chain is not apparent, one method that can help is to focus on the key actors in the system. Identify a small set of actors (not always human) that constitute a class of individual elements. These are high-level model sectors. Sectors often correspond to functional areas within a business enterprise, and the key actors are the process stakeholders in those areas. For each actor, try to assess the following:

- What conditions does this actor monitor?
- What actions are taken when conditions need to be adjusted?
- What resources are used when the actions are taken?

The conditions may eventually be elaborated into levels, actions will become flows in the system, and resources will also translate into levels.

Sometimes, pictures can be used to illustrate important model sectors or key actors. These pictures will help in the overall model understanding. It is fruitful to see how various stakeholders view the system differently. The visualizations can be important to help understand and reconcile differences between stakeholders.

Examples of model sectors for the software process include software development, quality assurance, and planning and control. The software development sector works off of project goals and constraints. Planning and control monitors the output of software development, and may revise project goals and constraints (e.g., new deadlines) and assign more resources. Quality assurance monitors the products of software development and makes adjustments by spending more or less time on artifact review. All sectors use personnel labor resources.

Generally, you do not want to include each and every key actor or sector in the initial formulation. Typically, the sectors represent aggregations of smaller elements. As you continue to elaborate the model formulation, you see how far the initial aggregations and characterizations take you.

2.6.1.2 Layout Plumbing and Generic Flows

Try to "lay out the plumbing" of the system in terms of putting down stocks and flows without extraneous connectors. You lay out the core infrastructure upon which further details are added later. After each stock is deposited into the system, ask what are its respective inflows and outflows. When possible, use generic infrastructures like those discussed in Chapter 3. Using existing structures that fit the system is cost efficient reuse. The core structures will be used to define relationships that are thought to be causing the dynamic phenomena under study.

The basic plumbing connections are then elaborated into more detail. The flows should be characterized and information loops should be closed. For each flow in the system consider the following:

1. What is the nature of the process?
2. How does the process really work?
3. How are decisions made?

Do not focus on "what are the inputs to the process"; instead consider how you would actually make a decision yourself.

Generic flow processes (provided in Chapter 3) should be considered for each flow. It is very rare to have a structural element that has not been modeled before. When using a generic flow process, try to not violate its integrity. Other inputs can be brought into the structure of an existing generic process. Ensure that the units of each flow match its associated levels divided by time. Use real-world variables instead of creating conversion factors for the equations to match.

The last step of fleshing out the plumbing is to close loops. Examine any converters that do not have connections to them. Determine whether they should be in a feedback loop or not. Make sure that outflows from a level are linked to that level with a connector chain that does not pass through other levels. Such a connection could allow a level to go negative.

Model elements consisting of levels (stocks), rates (flows), sources and sinks, auxiliaries, and feedback connections were introduced in Chapter 1. The following subsections provide more detail to interpret and apply these elements during model formulation.

2.6.1.3 Levels

A level is an accumulation over time, also called a stock or state variable. It can serve as a storage device for material, energy, or information. Just as the instantaneous level of water in a storage tank measures the time accumulation of its inflow and outflow rates, the level of software waiting to be tested is the accumulation of developed software minus that already incorporated into system testing.

Levels exist in conservative subsystems since they store conserved quantities of flowing entities. They can be changed in quantity only by moving the contents between levels, or to a sink or from a source. Contents move through levels via inflows and outflows. A level can have multiple inflows and outflows. These flows are the *rates* described in the next major section. All levels must, therefore, have rates associated with them.

Levels represent the states since they are the only parameters needed to describe a system at a point in time. They are a function of past accumulation of rates, and exist at system rest. They must be initialized with a value.

A level can easily transform the pattern of behavior coming into it. Suppose the inflow to a level is constant. With no outflows, the level will show a rising pattern in a straight line. The slope of the line equals the constant inflow rate. If the inflow is rising in a straight-line pattern, the level with no outflows curves up like a parabola. Both of these are seen in the general behaviors in Table 2-2. Oscillating inputs to levels cause similar oscillating outputs that are shifted in time.

In contrast to a level, if the inputs to an auxiliary equation are constant then the auxiliary is too. If the auxiliary inputs oscillate, so will the auxiliary itself but it will not be shifted in time like a level. There are no delays when quantities change for auxiliaries (or rates).

There are some modeling implications for tightly linked variables. If variables in a causal loop are tightly linked in their behavior, they may be modeled as auxiliaries. If one of the variables can exhibit a different dynamic behavior, then a level variable is indicated somewhere in the chain. It will decouple the ends of the auxiliary chain and allow them independent behavior.

A level also serves to decouple rates. Consider the purpose of inventory: it is a buffer, or decoupler, between production and orders so that if one of them fluctuates the other can stay relatively smooth. By decoupling production and shipment rates, they can vary independently over time.

All level variables with inflows and outflows have the capability to decouple rates. By rising and declining when necessary, the level absorbs the differences between the inflows and outflows.

2.6.1.3.1 MULTIPLE LEVELS AND OSCILLATION. Levels can also cause states of disequilibria. Previously, it was noted that levels can be fluid couplers between causal chains or decouplers of inflow and outflow rates. Because of these characteristics, adding a level can cause disequilibrium in the system. Equilibrium is when inflows are balanced with outflows in a dynamic system. Since levels can decouple, then adding a level makes it possible for inequalities to exist.

Suppose a model has a single level. It stops changing when its inflows and outflows are equal. With no other levels, all the variables in the model are traceable to the level and they remain constant from the point at which the flows are made equal. If another level is added, then both sets of inflows and outflows must be balanced for total system equilibrium. Otherwise, there could be oscillations as the second level perturbs the equilibrium.

Thus, a model with a single level cannot oscillate, but a model with two or more levels can. This is because a second level provides an opportunity for one part of the system to be in disequilibrium. For example, suppose there are separate personnel levels to represent different projects and proposal activities. When new projects come on board and hot proposals request people from projects, there is a distinct possibility of volatile staff levels continuously rising and falling to address the perceived needs. New project staffing needs are not balanced in conjunction with other activities—a policy of poor communication. Chapter 3 shows applied examples of oscillating systems.

2.6.1.4 Time Horizon Considerations

There is a conceptual connection between the model time horizon and the time for which different variables actually change. Something may be well represented as constant when it is essentially fixed for the simulation time horizon, but it may change during a longer time frame. Quantities are modeled as constant when they do not change for the applicable time horizon, not because it never changes. Some constants represent accumulations that are changing too slowly to be significant. Conversely, an accumulation that is very fast for the time horizon can be modeled as an auxiliary (if saving computations is important).

It has been stated that all levels represent accumulations, but the converse is not always true. Some concepts may be better suited as constants or auxiliaries rather than levels. The "snapshot test" described next may provide guidance for deciding what to model as a level.

2.6.1.4.1 SNAPSHOT TEST. Pretend to take a snapshot of the actual system under study. Stop time and freeze flows in the system as if you took a photograph. Again, it is useful to consider a water analogy of a running stream and intermittent pools. One could measure the height of pools in a static photograph but not the rate of water flow between them. Level variables are those that still exist and have meaning in the snapshot; the accumulations can be measured.

If time were frozen on a software process, production rates could not be measured but the number of produced artifacts could be determined. This signifies that the number of developed artifacts is suitable to be modeled as a level, with the artifact production rate being an inflow to it.

Suppose a snapshot is taken during the middle of software construction. Software coding rates would cease, but a measure like average productivity would continue to exist and could be determined. With units of function points/person-month, the variable seems more like a rate. But averaging involves accumulation over time. Thus, units are not always helpful for selecting level variables. The snapshot test may be difficult to apply in averaging or perceiving situations. The time constant associated with the accumulation is also considered, to ensure that the accumulation is not changing too fast or too slow to be modeled with something other than a level variable.

Not all quantities that continue to exist in a snapshot should be modeled as levels. Suppose one has a constant workforce that will not change during the time horizon. Even though the workforce was put into place and accumulated through hiring and attrition, it can safely be modeled as a constant if the determination is made that it effectively will not vary for the purposes of the study. One example is a very short project with a fixed staff size in an organization with very low attrition.

2.6.1.4.1.1   Example: Snapshot Test. Suppose we take a snapshot of a running project for the Brooks's Law model. The following elements can be measured and are eligible to be levels (accumulations):

- The amount of software still to be developed
- The amount of software already developed
- The number of people working on the job, both new and experienced

It is important to account for different experience levels, so both new and experienced personnel warrant separate levels. If they are combined into one, then important effects for learning and training cannot be handled.

Model elements that cannot be measured at an instant of time and are best modeled as rates are:

- The current productivity rate, or "project velocity"
- The rate of new people coming on board the project
- The rate of people becoming experienced

2.6.1.5   Sources and Sinks

Sources and sinks indicate that flows come from or go to somewhere outside of the model. Their presence signifies that real-world accumulations occur outside the boundary of the modeled system. They represent infinite supplies or repositories that are not specified in the model. The concept of a system boundary is crucial to all system modeling—it must be unambiguously defined and it drives modeling decisions. Sources and sinks must, therefore, be carefully considered and revisited throughout the modeling process. The implications of replacing them with levels should be given careful thought. See Section 2.5.1 for guidance on identifying system boundaries.

2.6.1.6 Rates

Rates are also called flows—the "actions" in a system. They effect the changes in levels and are thus inseparable from levels. They must occur together. Rates are computed as a function of levels, constants, and auxiliaries. Rates may be bidirectional. Levels and rates are both necessary to model a system. Rates only interact through their influence on system levels.

Rates represent decisions (for action and change) or policy statements. They are based only on available or apparent information. This information may be delayed in the real world, since levels changes often occur before information on them is available for decision making. You must distinguish between desired and actual conditions, as well as between actual and perceived conditions, since decisions are made relative to perceived conditions. Thus, rate equations for making decisions must account for perception delays and other biases that exist in the real system. All rate equations should make sense even under extreme or unlikely conditions.

To a large degree, the essence of system dynamics modeling is defining levels and rates, and then developing the rate equations. It is from the rates and initial values of levels that everything else is calculated. In some studies, it may become difficult to differentiate level and rate variables in systems. The snapshot test previously described is often useful for identifying rates versus levels.

2.6.1.7 Auxiliaries

An auxiliary variable signifies information in the system. As model elements, they make relevant information accessible. Though it may be possible to develop a system dynamics model without auxiliaries, since all information is traceable to levels and rates could be formulated with constants and rates, the resulting model would be unreadable and hard to follow. Important system information is captured in auxiliaries that help in the formulation of rate equations. They can take on a wide range of meanings.

Auxiliaries are converters of input to output, and help elaborate the detail of stock and flow structures. An auxiliary variable must lie in an information link that connects a level to a rate. Auxiliaries often represent "score-keeping" variables, such as the percent of job completion.

Auxiliary equations represent algebraic computations like rates, and have no standard form. Depending on the functional relationship, an auxiliary can be computed from constants, levels, rates, or other auxiliaries.

When translating a system concept into quantitative terms, deciding on levels and their affecting rates is a first step. The remaining concepts are typically formulated as auxiliaries. To do this, identify the units of the concept. Understand what it means if it rises or falls. Next, identify the units of the variables that will determine the concept. Sometimes, looking ahead in the model will help identify the units. It is important to note the distinction between a quantity and its effects in the system. The variable should be formulated before trying to quantify its effects.

If an auxiliary is a function of one or more quantities and their units match, then an additive or subtractive formula is a good bet. If the units of an auxiliary are different than those of the variable that determine it, then multiplication or division is likely. Examples of these different auxiliary formulations are shown in Chapter 3.

2.6.1.8 Connectors and Feedback Loops

Information linkages are used to represent information flow (as opposed to material flow). Rates, as control mechanisms, often require connectors from other variables (usually levels or auxiliaries) for decision making. For example, knowledge of the progress of tasks tested may influence a decision represented in a controlling rate (e.g., to move resources from a less critical path to testing). Information links are the only inputs to rate equations.

A feedback loop is a closed path connecting an action decision that affects a level and information on the level being returned to the decision-making point to act on. Such a loop exists if a rate connection represents information based on previous decisions. The elements of a feedback loop are a decision (or action or rate), an affected level, and an information path connecting the level to the action. See Figure 2.19 for an example.

The example in Figure 2.19 is the simplest form of feedback without additional delays, information distortions, or interconnected feedback loops. It is important to realize that only available, *apparent* information is used for a decision basis. Feedback data may be late or erroneous. Such imperfections can lead to poor decisions and project downfalls, as will be detailed in later sections.

Feedback mechanisms whereby decisions made at one point in the process impact others in complex or indirect ways must be accounted for. In a software development process, the decision to hire a new employee has multiple impacts and implications over the entire course of the project. The decision to inspect requirements or not also has many implications. For complex feedback or feedforward systems, an analytic solution may not be feasible, so simulation enables a more useful alternative.

2.6.2 Basic Patterns and Rate Equations

Formulating rate equations is a primary focus of model formulation. All system variables (except constants) are ultimately calculated from rates integrated over time in the simulation tools. Rate equations translate system pressures such as planning policy into actions that alter the system state. Typical rate formulations, or patterns, are described in this section.

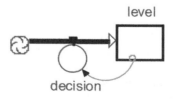

Figure 2.19. Feedback loop.

2.6.2.1 Constant Rate with a Level

The basic rate equation below multiplies a constant and a level:

$$\text{rate} = \text{constant} \cdot \text{level}$$

The constant may take on several interpretations that impact the resulting dynamic system behavior. This equation is suitable for modeling a simple production function as follows:

$$\text{software development rate} = \text{productivity} \cdot \text{personnel}$$

An example is the production structure shown in Figure 2.20 that connects a task and personnel chain.

This is one of the basic infrastructures presented in Chapter 3 and is the core of the Brooks's Law model software development rate formulation. Progressing beyond the assumption of static productivity, the constant is replaced with a variable function such as in the Brooks's Law model. The modeling goals and constraints will dictate the level of detail in formulating the rate.

2.6.2.2 Variable Rate with a Level

An extension of the constant rate equation is to replace the constant with an auxiliary variable:

$$\text{rate} = \text{auxiliary} \cdot \text{level}$$

This structure will model more realistic situations, such as when productivity is not constant over time. The initial Brooks's model is a good example. An auxiliary variable is needed to adjust the overall productivity for communication overhead, training, and learning. Even without complicating project factors like new hires, a learning curve applies in most situations. Learning curves are addressed further in Chapters 3 and 4.

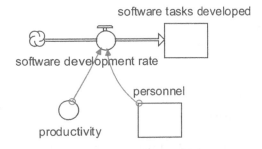

Figure 2.20. Example software production structure.

2.6.2.3 *Positive (Reinforcing) Feedback Growth or Decline*

Positive feedback is reinforcing feedback that tends to amplify movement in a given direction. Positive feedback often produces a growth or decline process, such as population growth. A simple modification of the linear rate equation uses feedback from a level to its inflow rate to produce positive exponential growth or decline. Positive feedback can be formulated with the following equation:

$$\text{rate} = \text{growth fraction} \cdot \text{level}$$

The structures shown in Figure 2.21 produce exponential growth behavior.

This structure produces exponential growth over time, as seen previously in Table 2-2, which shows general model behaviors. Compared to a standard linear rate equation, the constant now represents a growth fraction and its value determines the dynamic behavior. This formulation fits when the real-world process exhibits a rate that increases in proportion to its level.

Using population growth as an example, the birth rate depends on the current population. The number of births increases as population increases. A birth rate increase leads to more population. If population declines for some reason, the opposite occurs. The up or down direction is reinforced. The term positive feedback can sometimes be confusing since it can produce a negative trend, so reinforcing feedback is often used instead. There are analogous positive feedback growth situations in the software industry. See Chapter 3 for specific software process examples.

Positive feedback is analytically formulated per the following formulas. Exponential growth is represented as $\text{level} = \text{level}_0 e^{at}$. Exponential decay is written as $\text{level} = \text{level}_0 e^{-t/TC}$. The doubling time for exponential growth is $0.69/a$ and the half life for exponential decay is $0.69 \cdot TC$, where TC is the time constant.

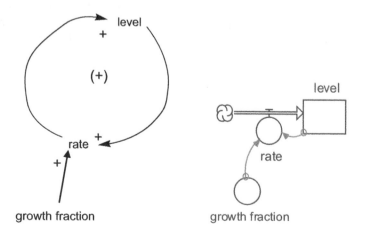

Figure 2.21. Exponential growth structures.

2.6.2.4   Delays

Time delays are ubiquitous in processes, and are important structural components of feedback systems. Examples include delays associated with any complex activity (or life-cycle process step) performed by resource-limited teams, hiring delays, problem resolutions, change approvals, and so on.

The world has a lot of situations in which a delayed outflow from a level can be represented by

$$\text{rate} = \text{level/delay time}$$

Figure 2.22 shows the delay structure. The delay time is the average lifetime an entity stays at the level. It may signify the average time an order is in backlog before being shipped, or the average time that a software module remains in the design stage. The delay constant thus has real-world meaning. Another advantage of this formulation is that an outflow rate cannot cause its level to go negative, which is another appropriate model of reality.

As an example, the formulation for new hire assimilation in the Brooks's Law model uses this simple delay structure. The average time for assimilation (20 days) becomes the delay time, so that the number of people transitioning to experienced in a time interval is 1/20 of the current level.

The delay time constant may be replaced with an auxiliary variable, just as the first rate equation in Section 2.6.2.1 used a constant and was elaborated into a variable in Section 2.6.2.2. Thus, the variable delay equation takes on the form

$$\text{rate} = \text{level/auxiliary}$$

where the auxiliary now represents variable delays, lifetimes, and so on.

Delays are parent objects for a number of other structures including decays, exponential decays, and cascaded (compounded) delays. They are common components of other substructures, including goal-seeking feedback. See Chapter 3 for more discus-

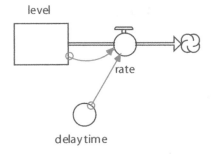

Figure 2.22.   Delay structure.

sion of delays, infrastructures that contain them, and real-world interpretations of the delay time constant.

2.6.2.5 Negative (Balancing) Feedback

Negative feedback is probably the most classic feedback loop in human systems. It is a structure that strives to bring the system state closer to a desired goal:

$$\text{rate} = (\text{goal} - \text{present level})/\text{adjustment time}$$

The adjustment time is a time constant representing the period over which the rate tries to close the gap. Negative feedback exhibits goal-seeking behavior in which the change is more rapid at first and slows down as the discrepancy between desired and perceived decreases. Goal-seeking negative feedback systems abound, so the above structure is a powerful general pattern for many rate equations. Figure 2.23 shows a negative feedback structure with both a causal loop diagram and a level/rate model. The analytic expression for this negative feedback is

$$\text{level} = \text{goal} + (\text{level}_0 - \text{goal})e^{-t/TC}$$

where level_0 is the initial level value and TC is the time constant or adjustment time. Negative feedback is balancing feedback that tends to offset or balance movement in a given direction, often described as a goal-seeking loop or control process. Common examples are heating systems or other homeostatic devices (such as the governor on a bus or lawnmower). When balancing feedback is present, the signal or information that is fed back is opposite in sign, such that it tends to cause the system to resist the change. Sometimes, the term negative feedback can be misleading, so balancing feedback is more precise. Chapter 3 has software process examples.

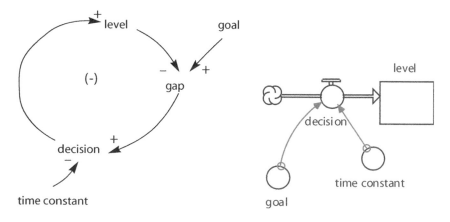

Figure 2.23. Negative feedback structures.

The previous rate pattern, rate = level/delay, is a special case of the net rate pattern for negative feedback. The difference is that the "goal" in the delayed outflow example is zero level. Table 2-2 shows behavior for negative feedback with a positive goal. For a zero goal, the graph is flipped upside down as the level starts high and approaches zero.

2.6.2.6 *Addition and Multiplication of Effects*

The rate patterns described above are the building blocks for more detailed equations. Two more complications arise when a rate is adjusted by the addition of more effects or when it is multiplied. The addition rate is

$$\text{rate} = \text{normal rate} + \text{additional rate(s)}$$

The terms added together must represent well-understood process concepts that are truly additive. A simple case is a personnel hiring rate accounting for both the natural quit rate and the rate of adjusting the workforce to a desired level to meet project demands:

$$\text{hiring rate} = \text{average quit rate} + (\text{desired staff} - \text{staff})/\text{hiring delay}$$

A multiplicative effect is modeled with

$$\text{rate} = \text{normal rate} \cdot \text{multiplier}$$

This structure is valuable for modeling a good number of situations in which a normal flow rate is multiplied by one or more factors. The multiplier is easily conceptualized, understood, and handy if it represents a percentage change. For example, effort multipliers are well known in other modeling situations like static cost models. Linear factors are used that use unity as a nominal or reference value.

A value of one for the multiplier represents the normal situation. A value of 0.8 for example signifies a 20% reduction in the rate, and 1.5 represents 50% additional flow. The basic formula can be made more complicated with additional factors. When such factors are truly multiplicative, a cascade of factors can be used to represent the situation:

$$\text{rate} = \text{normal rate} \cdot \text{multiplier } 1 \cdot \text{multiplier } 2 \cdot \ldots \text{multiplier } n$$

The Brooks's Law model has this type of formulation for the software development rate. The rate is adjusted multiplicatively with factors for communication overhead, weights for personnel mix, and an adjustment for the effective number of personnel.

When formulating additive or multiplicative rate equations, some principles should be kept in mind. Multiplication can shut off a flow rate completely if a multiplier takes on a zero value. Addition will not zero out a rate except when the added terms are negatives of each other. Addition can be thought of as cooperating or contributing to a rate determination. Multiplication can, however, be dominating in its influence. If one is trying to decide between the two, consider whether the different combining influences cooperate or whether one dominates the other. If an effect can dominate, then it should be modeled with multiplication.

2.6.2.7 Coincident Flows (Coflows)

Coincident flows (coflows) occur simultaneously (in parallel) through a type of slave relationship. An information connection is used to model one flow driving another. A general equation for a coflow is

$$\text{rate 2} = \text{rate 1} \cdot \text{conversion coefficient}$$

A prime example in the software process is defects being generated in unison with software development. A convenient way of expressing the defect generation rate is multiplying the defect density (the number of defects normalized by size) by the production rate, such as in the example for software design in Figure 2.24. The design defect generation rate is slaved to the design rate per the design defect density.

The equation for this coflow is

$$\text{design error generation rate} = \text{design rate} \cdot \text{design error density}$$

2.6.3 Graph and Table Functions

A graph or table function is a simple and convenient way to specify variable relationships. The graphical version is easy to understand through its visualization. The slope, shape, anchor points, and reference lines in a graph require careful consideration. Some guidelines for formulating graphical functions or their table equivalents are discussed below.

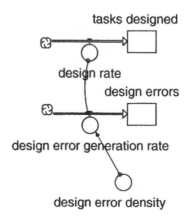

Figure 2.24. Example defect generation coflow.

Set the slope of the relationship to the polarity of the effect it represents. A negative effect should inspire a negative slope, and a positive slope denotes a positive relationship between variables. The shape of the curve should be evaluated in terms of the slope and curvature at the middle and extremes. The flattening of a function corresponds to a weakening or saturating effect. An example of this is the tail of an S-curve representing a saturation point, like a saturated market. Steepening a curve represents the strengthening of an effect.

It is highly recommended to normalize or make the graph relative by formulating it as a function of the ratio of the input to its reference value. The nominal reference point is then clearly indicated where it equals one.

Sometimes, when quantifying information in feedback loops, the modeler must mentally shift from conceptual thinking to algebraic thinking. Considering the units of the quantities involved can help lead the way. Dimensional analysis, which is the manipulation of units as if they were algebraic quantities, is a valuable skill for this.

Graph and table functions are highly useful for formulating nonlinear pressures and effects. All they require are determination of the slope, the general shape, a couple of reference lines, and points to define a function. Normalize the inputs to table or graphical functions. Try to pick meaningful lower and upper bounds for the range, then pass smooth monotonic curves through the range.

2.6.3.1   Example: Overtime Multiplier Function

This example will create a normalized graph function for an overtime effect. It is an approximation with a limited range that will be extended further in Chapter 5. Suppose that management pushes for overtime in order to catch up on schedule, and that the management edict can be expressed in terms of desired output to normal output. We wish to model an effective overtime multiplier for productivity. How should this relationship be modeled? Limits exist such that people will not continue to increase their overtime past their saturation thresholds. Thus, there is a value of desired output beyond which no further overtime will be worked. Studies have shown that a small amount of aggressive scheduling will tend to motivate people to produce more, but highly unreasonable goals will have the opposite effect.

A few people might work 80 hour weeks and even longer, but a more reasonable limit might be a 60 hour workweek for most industry segments. This puts an upper bound of $60/40 = 1.5$ on the overtime factor. We will model the response of the aggregate system as a smooth curve (realizing that different individuals will have varying responses).

Recall that such functions are best done in terms of normalized variables, so the independent variable will be the desired/normal output. The relationship in Figure 2.25 was adapted from [Richardson, Pugh 1981], and shows the productivity overtime multiplier as a function of desired/normal output. This graph function is handy and easily used in a system dynamics model to relate variables. Moreover it is a relative relationship that does not need rescaling to fit different situations (though the desired output ratio range can be extended per an example in Chapter 4).

The relationship is captured in a model auxiliary variable either graphically or by specifying table values. Figure 2.26 shows a model representation for the auxiliary

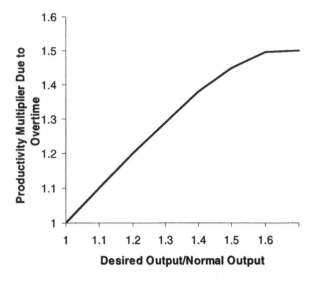

Figure 2.25. Graph function for productivity due to overtime.

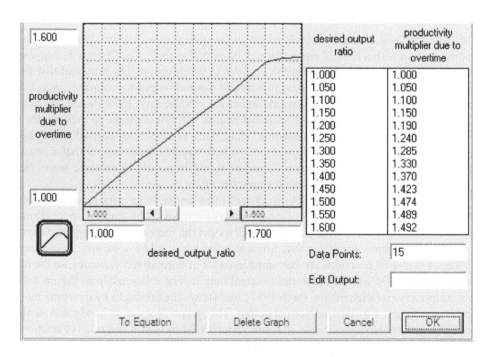

Figure 2.26. Model graph function for productivity multiplier due to overtime.

variable, which can be drawn and/or specified numerically. Its input is shown as the desired output ratio, but it could have two inputs for the desired and normal output. In that case the graph x-axis would be specified as the ratio of the inputs. Most subsequent illustrations of auxiliary relationships in this book will only show the graph with the table values cropped out.

2.6.4   Assigning Parameter Values

Values must be assigned to constants, graphs, table functions, and levels before a simulation can be executed. All level variables must be initialized. Rates and auxiliaries are computed from levels and constants and do not need initialization. There are several types of parameters, including constant measures, conversion factors, growth factors, delays, and adjustment times.

Every parameter and variable should have a meaningful interpretation or real-world counterpart. Parameters should have recognizable meanings to personnel familiar with the system. All parameters and variables in a model should clearly correspond to a real-world quantity (or commonly understood concept). If they are not directly observable, they should at least be intuitable to the model audience. Being careful to specify units properly will help assure that quantities are real and observable, as opposed to a parameter with contrived units. Selecting parameters is easier when they are held to standards of realism and observability.

2.6.4.1   Accuracy

The parameter values should be estimated only to the degree of accuracy called out by the study. There may be many possible purposes and ranges of accuracies required. The question to be answered is, accuracy for what purpose? Since policy analysis is generally the purpose of most studies, the parameters do not need to be estimated any more accurately than when they have no further influence on the policy. If the policy implications do not change when model parameters are varied by a certain percentage, then the parameters are precise enough for the study. Different kinds of parameters and estimates are discussed below.

Some sources for parameter estimates include:

- Firsthand process knowledge
- Quantitative relationship data that has been collected
- Quantitative data on the system behavior
- Statistical based estimates

Parameters representing measurements are usually simple to estimate because they are easily known. They can be obtained through data sources, direct observation, or knowledgeable people. One must be careful that the data used is congruent with the meaning used in the model. For example, if external defect data is used, make sure that it is reported using the same definition relevant in the model. The way quantities are used in a model will dictate how data is collected, interpreted, and estimated for the modeling.

Conversion factors translate from one unit to another (e.g., function point backfiring values convert from function points to lines of code). Normal or reference parameters require knowledge of individual relationships, such as the effect on effort of multiplicative cost drivers (e.g., product or personnel factors). These quantitative relationships may be borrowed from other types of models. As an example, the simple Brooks's Law model used multiplicative factors from static cost models to weight productivity for experience levels (in particular, the adjustment factors of 0.8 and 1.2 to account, respectively, for differing productivities of new and experienced personnel).

Some of the harder parameters to estimate include delays and adjustment times. These require cognitive thinking about the time taken to adjust perceptions, habits, and so on. Time constants are not directly observable from idealized inputs and often require mental experimentation.

2.6.4.2 Bounds

If data is lacking, the upper and lower bounds of a parameter can often be estimated. Parameter values can be estimated from detailed knowledge of a process that is modeled in aggregate, or the overall behavior of a model piece can be used. One may use aggregate data to calibrate a parameter that represents an aggregate. This involves estimating a parameter from knowledge of behavior instead of detailed knowledge of underlying processes. The bounds can also be estimated from process and behavior, and an initial trial value can be picked in the middle of the spread.

2.6.4.3 Parameters and Validity

It is always preferable (when feasible) to estimate parameters below the level of aggregation in a model, such as when using detailed knowledge of a process. When estimating from behavior though, there are potential pitfalls. One must make assumptions about equations in the model, and more assumptions means a higher probability of error. Also, estimating from behavior impacts model validity testing. This is because an ideal model will generate reference behaviors on its own, rather than using parameters made to fit the desired reference behavior. Thus, no additional confidence can be had with a good fit made this way.

Alternatively, if parameters are individually estimated from knowledge of the underlying processes and the resulting integrated model generates reference behavior, then more confidence can be placed in the model.

It is tempting to use a traditional statistical technique like correlation to estimate parameters. But one should always be wary when interpreting correlational data, as a correlation coefficient can imply the wrong polarity of a connection between parameters. This may be due to everything else not being held constant when the data is collected. The same pitfall is possible when doing multiple regression. As model behavior is more tied to its structure than parameter values, it behooves a modeler to be adept at conceptualization and formulation. These skills are more valuable than knowing sophisticated mathematical techniques for statistical estimation. Blind usage of such techniques can usurp intuition. It is also more important to have good data to begin with.

2.6.4.4 *Level Initialization and Equilibrium*

Levels must be initialized with beginning values. The values can be matched to historical data, numbers can be chosen to initialize the model in equilibrium, or they can be purposely set to put a model on a path of growth or decline. An important skill is knowing how to start a model in equilibrium. A good understanding of many models can be had by disturbing them from a state of equilibrium and observing the generated dynamics.

A model in a state of equilibrium means the inflows and outflows of each level match or are in balance. The levels will remain unchanged and related model variables will stay constant. Things are still flowing in the system but there is no net change to the levels. During the course of model development, selected sectors may be put into equilibrium as part of the iterative process.

Analytic procedures can be used to determine the balancing inflow and outflow values. When models become too complex, however, the procedures may become intractable. In that case, a model can be run until a state of equilibrium exists, and the appropriate flow values read from the run for subsequent value setting.

Sometimes, models should be initialized for growth. An example would be the increasing size of a system being enhanced over time or any number of Internet usage patterns. In this case, parameters should be set to start a linear or exponential growth trajectory.

2.6.5 Model Building Principles

This section will highlight and review some of the important principles of model building. Both the structure of models and the process of creating them are addressed. The principles are aids for modeling, not rigid prescriptions. Some identify pitfalls, some restate modeling philosophy, and some can even be violated under certain conditions. The experienced modeler will understand the context and be able to justify any violation of principles.

2.6.5.1 *Structure*

Physical quantities must be conserved in a system dynamics model. A conserved subsystem is the flow of only a single type of entity together with rates that control the flow and the levels that it accumulates in. The rates and levels must alternate in any conserved subsystem.

Conserved flows and information links are distinctly different, however. Information is not a conserved flow because it can be transmitted to other parts of the system without diminishing the source. Information to rates and auxiliary variables is not conserved through time like levels are.

Only information links can connect between conservative subsystems. The flow rates of subsystems cannot be affected directly by flows from levels in other subsystems, since material flows stay within a conserved subsystem. Rather, they can be controlled only by *information* on levels in other subsystems.

Levels can be changed only by rates. No level directly affects the value of another level. The current value of a level can be computed without the present or previous values of other levels, since a level is computed from its own past value and the flow rates affecting it over a given time interval. Every feedback loop in a model must contain at least one level. Levels completely describe the system condition at any point in time; hence, they are called *state variables.*

Rates depend only on levels and constants. Rate inputs are information links that are traceable to levels and system parameters. In some exceptions, a model may contain rate-to-rate connections where a physical rate directly determines the rate of change of a paper quantity or when the time constant of intervening levels are very small relative to other time constants. When used as information affecting other subsystems, flow rates should be averaged over a given period of time.

The units of measure must be consistent in all model equations. Any terms that are added or subtracted must, of course, have the same units. Dimensional analysis cannot prove that an equation is correct, but it can show when some equations are incorrect. Levels and rates cannot be distinguished by their measurement units alone. There are many diverse units that can be used. Within any conserved subsystem of flows, all levels have the same units of measure and all rates are measured in the same units divided by time.

Normalize measures and relationships whenever possible to make them relative. This makes things easier in the long run; the model is more scalable and easier to judge than with absolute numbers. Graphs are convenient for describing relative relationships, including normalization.

2.6.5.2 Process

Iteratively refine and slowly add relationships to a model. Do not try to enumerate all the influencing factors at first, as they quickly become unwieldy. Considering simulation model development as a type of software development, an iterative approach makes much sense. Small iterations are much easier to handle when adding model elements.

Strive for a top-down approach instead of focusing on event details. Be selective in choosing what to add to a model. Try to lump things together in classes, then slowly add new relationships. Start with aggregated patterns of behavior and add more detail when ready. Keep things simple for maximum understanding.

Do not stray too far from a simulatable model. Refrain from adding too many elements before specifying their logic and testing them. Use small incremental changes whereby only a few elements are added to the model before resimulating. A rule-of-thumb is to try to keep the number of added elements to approximately five or less. From a time perspective, do not be more than 30 minutes away from a simulatable model. Figure 2.27 from [Richmond et al. 1990] shows an empirically derived relationship between the probability of losing control of the simulation versus the number of elements added to the model before simulating.

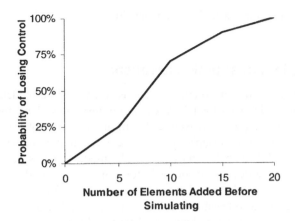

Figure 2.27. Probability of losing control of simulation.

Once you try adding about 10 elements or more, you are asking for serious trouble, and at 20 elements there is a virtual certainty of losing control. This author can personally vouch for this principle. It is like software product integration, whereby it is desired to minimize the number of changed elements being integrated together. Problems are much more tractable when an area of change can be isolated.

Before simulating, ensure that the model mechanics are finalized. Close feedback loops. Make connections between existing elements. Specify the algebra and elaborate the equations. Check the dimensional balance of equations. Ensure that all parameter values, constants, initial values, and graphical functions are set.

2.6.6 Model Integration

When integrating different sectors in an elaborate model, each sector should be tested in isolation before being combined with other sectors. As always, a steady-state situation should first be created for testing a sector. This often implies setting constants for what would normally be variable entities. There may be ghost variables (aliases) from other sectors that should be initialized to an appropriate value to simulate running the entire model. They will not change during the test simulations of isolated portions, but will vary over time when the full model is integrated.

The tests are important to make sure things are working right and to give the modeler better understanding. Yet the isolated tests are tentative in the sense that set parameters may be affected by the dynamics of the global model when it is completely put together.

Consider the two flow chains in the Brooks's Law model: tasks and personnel. The common link between the two chains is the number of personnel. The task chain can be developed in isolation if a variable for number of personnel (or two variables to denote new and experienced personnel) is used. When the two chains are working independently from each other, then they can be combined by eliminating the ghost vari-

able(s) for personnel in the task chain and substituting the actual levels in the personnel chain.

2.6.7   Example: Construction Iterations

This example sequence of construction iterations illustrates the modeling process for
the Brooks's Law model in Chapter 1. At each step, just a few elements are added and
the model retested to keep its increasing elaboration under control. By adhering to the
"code a little, test a little" philosophy, confidence is retained in the model because interim versions are validated before moving on. The model remains stable as it evolves.
Expected behaviors are developed for each iteration and the model outputs assessed
against them. Iterations of the model are shown in Figures 2.28–2.34.

Other sequences are also feasible to achieve the same end result. This approach lays
down the flow chains for tasks and personnel first and then adds auxiliaries to adjust
the software development rate for experience, training, and communication effect. It is
also possible add some of the overhead effects to a partial personnel chain first and
then complete the flow chain.

Construction Iteration #1 (Figure 2.28). Create a flow chain for software development tasks. The requirements level will be initialized, a constant value will be assigned
to the software development rate, and the level of developed software starts empty. The
sample project will be sized to 500 function points (the initial value of requirements) and
employ 20 people for the duration. For initial testing of the software development rate,
assume a mid-range value of 0.1 function points/person-day. This value is inline with
published data sources and other models. The software development rate is set as such:

$$\text{software development rate} = (0.1 \text{ function points/person-day}) \cdot (20 \text{ people})$$

$$= 2 \text{ function points/day}$$

With this formula, the rate will be constant throughout the simulation, the developed
software will rise linearly, and the project completion time can be calculated as:

$$\text{completion time} = (500 \text{ function points})/(2 \text{ function points/day}) = 250 \text{ days}$$

The simulation is run and checked against the above calculation.

Construction Iteration #2 (Figure 2.29). Begin creating a personnel flow chain
and add an auxiliary variable for nominal productivity to create a parameterized soft-

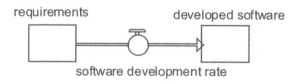

Figure 2.28. Iteration #1 structure.

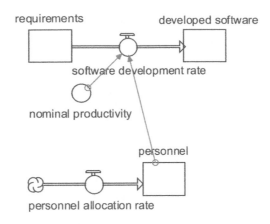

Figure 2.29. Iteration #2 structure.

ware production structure. The software development rate will depend on the number of personnel and the nominal productivity. No adjustments are made to productivity in this iteration. The personnel chain consists of a single level and inflow rate. The inflow to personnel termed "personnel allocation rate" will be used to simulate the addition of people to the project when we finally test Brooks's Law. Other optional structures that could have been used as a placeholder for personnel, including an auxiliary variable set to a constant value or a single level with no inflows or outflows, could be initialized with a value. Either of these options would eventually have to be replaced with a stock and flow structure in a subsequent iteration.

The nominal productivity will be set to the same value of 0.1 function points/person-day and the rate equation rewritten as:

$$\text{software development rate} = \text{nominal productivity} \cdot \text{personnel}$$

Construction Iteration #3 (Figure 2.30). Complete the personnel flow chain. Another level is added to differentiate experienced personnel from new personnel. An intermediary flow between the levels is added to represent the assimilation of new people into the pool of experienced people. In this iteration, the personnel chain will be set to steady state so that there are no flows. All people will reside in the experienced personnel pool, and there will be no new project personnel. The experienced personnel pool best represents the project before new people are added. Keeping everyone in a single level will also simplify testing of the new structure and ensure that the software development rate works with no differentiation for experience levels. In the next iteration, provisions will be made for the different productivities of new and experienced people.

Construction Iteration #4 (Figure 2.31). Elaborate the productivity rate to account for the effect of personnel experience. The software development rate is linked to both levels for new and experienced personnel. This capability is first tested with the per-

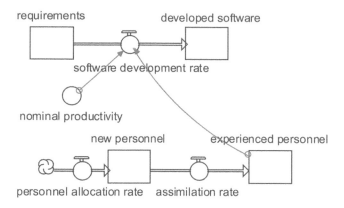

Figure 2.30. Iteration #3 structure.

sonnel chain in steady state with no flow. The portion of new to experienced personnel is varied in multiple runs to test the revised software development rate formula. A sequence of test runs could be:

1. 20 new personnel, 0 experienced personnel
2. 0 new personnel, 20 experienced personnel
3. 10 new personnel, 10 experienced personnel
4. 5 new personnel, 15 experienced personnel
5. And so on

The above values are used to initialize the levels. In steady state, they will remain at those values because the rates will be zeroed out. We will use productivity adjustment

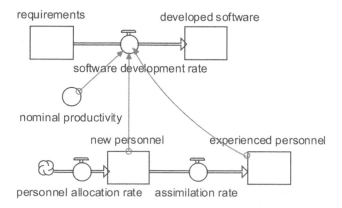

Figure 2.31. Iteration #4 structure.

factors of 0.8 and 1.2 as weights, which are in line with numerous static cost models such as COCOMO II. The equation becomes:

software development rate = nominal productivity · (0.8 · new personnel

+ 1.2 · experienced personnel)

The resulting productivity rate and completion time are computed independently outside the simulation and compared to simulation output for the test cases. The variables to evaluate in these runs include productivity and personnel levels (to ensure that they stay at their initial values with no personnel flow).

The productivity should remain constant throughout each simulation run because the different levels of personnel remain constant, and the accumulation of developed software representing progress will rise linearly accordingly.

Construction Iteration #5 (Figure 2.32). Make the personnel chain dynamic by allowing new personnel to assimilate into the experienced personnel pool. This will test the assimilation delay structure, ensure that the personnel chain flows are as expected, and make the productivity rate dynamic. The same set of initial values used in the test runs in iteration #4 could be used in this iteration. The same variables are tracked, paying close attention to the varying levels of personnel. A standard assimilation delay of 20 days will be used. The assimilation rate will assume this average value and be written as

assimilation rate (persons/day) = new project personnel/20

The first test run initialized with all new personnel will be the clearest indicator of whether the 20 day delay works as expected. The productivity rate will now increase over time as new personnel become more productive. The initial values of new vs. experienced will have an impact on the final completion time. In order to regression test

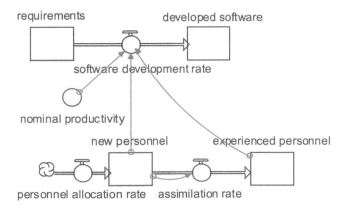

Figure 2.32. Iteration #5 structure.

and make sure previous simulation results still hold, the delay time could be made inordinately long.

Note that the addition of the delay could have been included in the previous iteration #4, but two distinct sets of iterative test cases would still have been required. The first set would revolve around testing different combinations of new and experienced (with the delay neutralized somehow), and the second set would test the delay structure.

Construction Iteration #6 (Figure 2.33). Add an effect for training of new personnel. An auxiliary is created for the equivalent number of experienced personnel needed for training. It is calculated from the number of new personnel and a parameter for the training overhead percentage. The software development rate is refined again to reduce the effective number of experienced people working directly on development with the new auxiliary:

software development rate = nominal productivity · [0.8 · new personnel + 1.2

· (experienced personnel − experienced personnel needed for training)]

Based on studies [Stutzke 1994] and personal experience, 25% of a full-time experienced person's time is initially used for training of new hires. The portion of time expended on training is "released back" once the new people assimilate and become experienced.

First, this formula should be tested with the personnel chain in steady state, which again can be effected by zeroing the assimilation rate or making the delay time inordi-

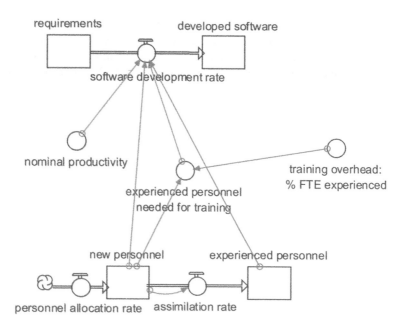

Figure 2.33. Iteration #6 structure.

nately long. The effect is verified in a static situation, assimilation is allowed again, and the results tracked against expected values.

Construction Iteration #7 (Figure 2.34). Account for communication overhead and add the feedback loop to add personnel. A function is defined for communication overhead percentage and used to modify the software development rate. The formula used in the Abdel-Hamid model [Abdel-Hamid, Madnick 1991] is converted into a graph that displays overhead percentage as a function of the number of total personnel. Abdel-Hamid provides references for his formulation, but it is important to note that it only covers a specific region of personnel size (which happens to match our current situation). The lack of scalability will be discussed as a constraint on the model that impacts overall assumptions of team size phenomena. This is due to team repartitioning that occurs when the overall staff increases substantially beyond the nominal size for a single team.

The final software development rate formula adjusts the nominal productivity for communication overhead and becomes

software development rate = nominal productivity · (1 − communication overhead %)

· [0.8 · new personnel + 1.2 · (experienced personnel

− experienced personnel needed for training)]

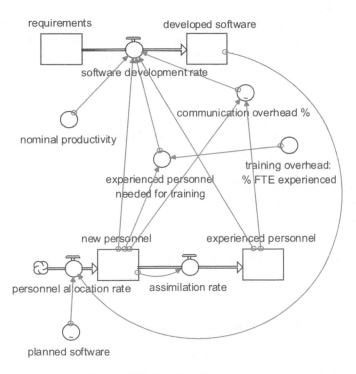

Figure 2.34. Iteration #7 structure.

Like the previous three iterations, this one can be tested first with the personnel chain in steady state before allowing personnel to flow, but in this case the communication overhead percentage should remain the same constant value between runs if the total number of people are equal. The relative proportions of new to experienced personnel do not matter for this effect. The feedback loop should be deactivated at first to keep the personnel chain in steady state, then activate it to induce the dynamics from adding people.

2.7 SIMULATION

Simulation means executing the computer model; some testing also occurs. Run-time parameters must be set, such as the time horizon and any sensitivity parameters. Other run-time options may include whether the model runs in interactive mode or not, plotting and tabulation parameters, the selection of DT (the time step), the form of numerical integration used for internal calculations, and use of input files. When all is ready, you simply start the simulation and let it progress. It will compute the equations as time advances and stop when the time horizon is up or, alternatively, at a user intervention point.

As part of the iterative model building process, it is quite possible (and recommended) to have already simulated early versions of the model during formation. The iterative simulations continue, leading up to fuller validation tests against the progressively complete model.

Simulation inherently entails a certain amount of white-box and other verification testing (just like unit testing is part of coding). Hence, there is some overlap with Section 2.8, Model Assessment. The white-box testing addresses the specific structural components and equations of an elaborated model. Section 2.8 describes further validation tests, many of which resemble black-box testing, whereby the model at large is assessed against the goals of the study, real-world policies, and insights. That assessment builds upon the testing performed in this stage.

Steps in verification testing during initial simulation and subsequent assessment include:

- Eliminating mechanical mistakes
- Ensuring steady-state behavior
- Initial robustness testing with idealized test inputs
- Trying to recreate reference behavior patterns
- Assessing the sensitivity of the base case run to parameter values
- Assessing the model sensitivity against structural and policy changes

In the previous stage of model construction, you should have already verified the dimensional balance of all equations so that units match on both sides. Flows should have the same units of measure as the levels they are attached to with the addition of "per time." Other questionable model elements should also be resolved before simulation testing begins.

During simulation testing, you attempt to ferret out mechanical mistakes. Problems may be due to coding or logic errors. Possible sources include numerical data errors, unexpected random variates (see Appendix A), inconsistent units, entity flow problems (e.g., levels going negative), or incorrect statistics specifications. Some error detection and prevention approaches include:

- Modular validation of the model
- Well-commented and legible model equations
- Trying alternative approaches to crosscheck the results, such as spreadsheets or manual numerical evaluations
- Use of outside analysts to assess the model
- Inducing infrequent events to uncover "hidden" model areas
- Using animations available in simulation tools to visualize the changing rates, levels, and other functions

You should make short model runs, look for anomalous values, and identify mistakes. It is wise to instrument all variables in the model during the formative stages. An example first-level bug at this stage might be that a stock goes negative. Make the process highly iterative by adding a little to the model each time to fix it; keep it "top-down and iterative" as explained in model conceptualization.

During testing, parameter values should be specified with simple, internally consistent numbers instead of spending much effort collecting numerical data. Try to quantify qualitative variables using a consistent scale. A relative scale of 0–1 is extremely useful in this context also. Choose initial numbers so the system can reach a steady-state condition.

Start testing activities with basic debugging of a very short simulation, like for a single DT timestep. Check out and fix any aberrations that you observe. Debugging can be performed in several ways. Anomalous variables and their inputs can be put into a table (or a graph used for debugging). Printing these values in a table at every DT can help identify bugs in the model formulation. Eyeball the results to see which variable might be causing the problem. Repeat these steps until the mechanical mistakes are fixed. Always make notes and save each model run until the debugging stage is over. As is well known in the software process, defects have a way of producing more defects. It is prudent to keep track of the defects found.

One common bug is using too large a value for the DT. Normally, a value of less than one-half of the smallest time constant will ensure that the DT does not influence the model outputs. To be even safer, the DT should be less than one-third of the smallest time constant. If too large of a DT value is used, the behavior may exhibit oscillations, the oscillations may increase over time, or other jerky behavior may be observed.

A long solution interval generates numerical instability. If the interval is too short, unnecessary computations take place that slow it down (this is becoming less of a hindrance as computing power increases).

Validation begins during simulation. Ensure robustness first by attaining steady state, putting in idealized test inputs, and looking at key variables. Determine if the behavior is plausible; fix and iterate. After the initial verification, you graduate to more sophisticated tests described in later sections:

- *Robustness testing*—torture the model to see where it breaks down, such as using steps and pulse inputs to see how well the model regulates itself.
- *Reference behavior testing*—does the model generate reference behaviors and how robust is the pattern to changes in model parameters.
- *Sensitivity analysis testing*—determine how sensitive and robust policy recommendations are to variations in parameters.
- *Scenario analysis testing*—vary the external environment and see if policy recommendations remain robust.
- *Model boundary testing*—challenge the sinks and sources by assessing if policy recommendations would change if the clouds were replaced by levels, and challenge converters by assessing what would happen if they were replaced with levels.

2.7.1   Steady-State Conditions

Ensure steady-state conditions before controlled experiments. For a model to be in steady-state equilibrium, the inflows and outflows must be balanced for each level such that the net of all flows across a level is zero. Two important reasons for steady-state initialization are:

1. Ensuring that model parameters are internally consistent.
2. After achieving steady state, then controlled experiments can be run to further test robustness and policies.

A base steady-state simulation run should be completed before making conclusions about nonsteady-state behavior. The same debugging techniques described in the previous section can also be useful in steady-state testing. Here you determine if any stock values change and find the culprits.

Sometimes, only portions of a model are put into steady state during a particular testing stage. In the Brooks's Law model, for example, we focus on putting the personnel chain into steady-state conditions. If the task development chain was in steady state then no project progress would be made. The main chain for software tasks must flow properly with the personnel chain in steady state (i.e., no personnel changes) before other tests are made.

On the first steady-state run, choose numbers that are simple and make sense with each other. Internally consistent numbers will help put a model into steady state. Sometimes, one can use algebraic initialization to derive initial values for levels. One should be able to calculate equilibrium levels independent of any simulation tools, at least as a crosscheck of steady-state conditions.

Determine how much latitude there is for specifying flow values. Smaller numbers with few digits are easier to understand when assessing the model. It is possible that you will need to modify numbers from an actual system to achieve steady state, because few real systems are in steady state. You can incorporate other real-world data on subsequent passes as appropriate.

2.7.1.1 Example: Steady-State Behavior

A base equilibrium run of the Brooks's Law model is first needed to start assessing its behavior. Complete steady state is achieved when neither software tasks nor personnel are flowing. This is a degenerate case that shows nothing is changing in the model, and is not shown. Steady state conditions relative to personnel levels are present when no additional people are added. These conditions are necessary to validate a model before adding perturbations. Figure 2.35 shows the steady-state behavior relative to personnel for developing 500 initially required function points with a constant staff of 20 experienced personnel. This represents the project with no hiring adjustments.

The final completion time with the default parameters and no additional hiring is 274 days. The graphic results are not very interesting but do provide confidence that the model behaves as expected and perturbations can now be introduced.

2.7.2 Test Functions

Models are tested through controlled experimentation with idealized test inputs to understand their inner workings. Test functions are used to exercise models by introducing disturbances such as a sudden variable increase, a constant signal, a steady decline, oscillation, or randomness. Commonly used test inputs include the pulse, step func-

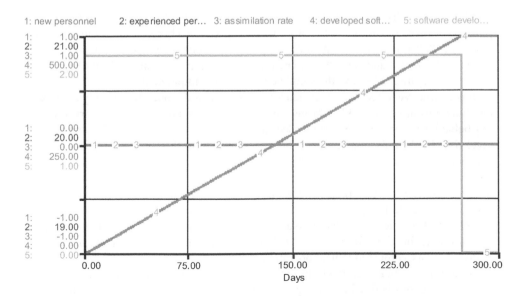

Figure 2.35. Steady-state behavior of Brooks's Law model (personnel in steady state).

tion, and a ramp function. These functions help to expose model relationships and enable understanding of the model and the system it represents. Behavior of pieces of the model can be understood.

Graph the response of key variables to assess how they respond to the disturbances that knock them out of steady state. Determine if the model is showing unreasonable behavior, such as levels going negative, levels continuing to grow, too short of a response time, and so on. You may want to trace the paths through the model to help understand the results. Sometimes, a feedback loop is missing or it is too strong or too weak. A high-frequency oscillation might be caused from using too large a value for DT. A smooth but expanding oscillation pattern might be due to the integration method, and can be fixed by using the Runge–Kutta method instead of Euler's (an option set in the simulation software).

The pulse provides an instantaneous, isolated change in a variable and resembles a spike. The variable returns to its previous value after the momentary change. A pulse was used in the initial Brooks's Law model to effect the abrupt addition of new personnel. In simulation, a pulse occurs over a DT time interval, which is the closest approximation to an instant of time. The change produced in a level by a pulse is the height of the pulse multiplied by the DT value.

The step function changes a quantity abruptly at some point in time and it stays at the new constant level. A combination of step functions can be used to add or subtract constant signals to produce rectangular shapes for variables. A step is useful for idealized testing, such as a first approximation of a staffing profile to understand the steady-state characteristics of a process model.

A ramp is a linear function of time that continuously grows or declines with a specified slope. It can be used to model a gradual increase or decrease in some system variable.

The three idealized test inputs are shown in Figure 2.36. The pulse is set to an impulse quantity of 100 at time = 5. It appears as a spike to 40 because the simulation DT interval is 0.25 time units, so 100/0.25 = 40. The step function begins at time = 10, rises to a value of 10, and stays there. The ramp function has a slope of 1 and begins at time = 15. Figure 2.37 shows the simple equations that implement these.

It is instructive to see how levels react to these standard inputs. If we apply the three test functions in Figure 2.37 as hiring-rate inputs to personnel levels, the corresponding behavior in Figure 2.38 results. See model file *test functions.itm*. The personnel level rises by the pulse magnitude, it linearly increases to the constant step input, and shows exponential growth to the ramp input. These same test inputs could have been used to model behavior of other process variables, such as the influx of software requirements. The level of requirements to be implemented would react in the same fashion to the generic inputs.

Other test functions are readily available in simulation packages such as standard trigonometric functions for oscillating behavior, random number generators, probability distributions, combined logical operations, and more.

As a model is built iteratively in pieces, submodels are constructed and perturbed with test functions before being integrated together. Care must be used when deciding which submodel variables to perturb with test functions and the choice of tests. The

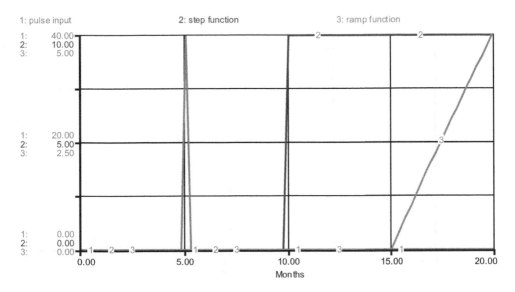

Figure 2.36. Test input functions.

test inputs should go into equations that represent inputs from other model sectors or from outside the model boundary. Common choices for test inputs are rate equations or the auxiliary equations that feed into rates.

2.7.3 Reference Behavior

A model should eventually be checked against reference behavior patterns after assuring that it is free of mechanical bugs and responds to idealized test inputs as expected. Only look for qualitative similarity on the first pass. Eventually, you will want to replicate reference behavior using real-world numbers and check the resulting behavior similarly using historical real-world data.

The introductory graph for productivity from the Brooks's Law model in Chapter 1 compares favorably with the conceptualized Figure 2.13, and Figure 2.39 demonstrates task progress against the reference behavior from Figure 2.14. More applied examples of model reference behavior evaluation are shown in Chapters 4 through 6.

⏱ ramp_function = ramp(1,15)
  DOCUMENT: Produce a ramp signal of slope 1 beginning at time=15.
⏱ pulse_input = pulse(10,5,999)
  DOCUMENT: Inject a single pulse input of magnitude 10 at time=5 (999 denotes the pulse interval)
⏱ step_function = step(10, 10)
  DOCUMENT: Generate a step function of size 10 starting at time=10.

Figure 2.37. Test input equations.

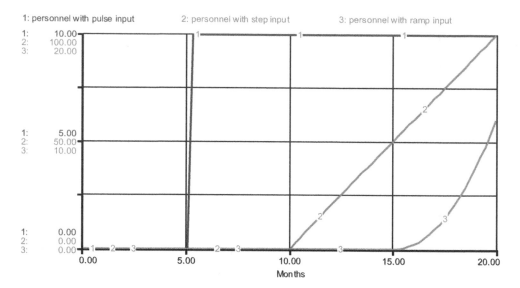

Figure 2.38. Using test inputs as hiring rates to personnel levels.

2.8 MODEL ASSESSMENT

Model assessment is a collection of verification and validation processes, whereby models are iteratively evaluated from several perspectives. During verification, you determine whether the model implementation is error free and properly represents the intended logical behavior (this was largely addressed in the previous section). In validation, you assess if the model helps solve the end user's problem. As always, this must be considered within the context of the study purpose.

Simulation runs should be designed to gain the most insight and understanding from a model. These runs constitute simulation experiments, and a model is essentially a laboratory tool. Plan a sequence of runs that focus on particular structural elements. A hypothesis should be formed before each run. Unexpected results should be thoroughly analyzed. Like other experimental scenarios, a notebook should be kept to record details of model structure, hypotheses, observations, and analysis. Reproducibility of results is required as for other scientific disciplines.

The behavior of each run should be evaluated and reasoned through in terms of the real-world system it represents. A narrative story that sequences through the behavioral dynamics of a run and ties results to the real world is useful for this. Such a story helps bridge the gap between model and reality when real-world terminology is supplemented with model understandings. Explaining model behavior relative to the real world fulfills a goal of modeling—to gain insight and understanding. Ultimately, these insights should increase the probability that improved policies for the real system will be identified and implemented.

Model structure and behavior can be assessed by exploring the behavior due to individual and combined feedback loops. Experiments can be devised to isolate the effects

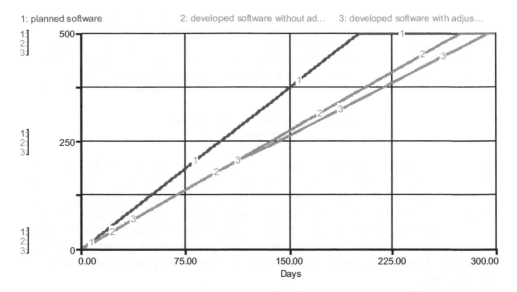

Figure 2.39. Brook's Law model task progress reference behavior.

of specific factors and pinpoint structures responsible for certain behaviors. Due to feedback and circular causality, the notion of linear cause and effect is not very relevant. Thus, feedback structures are sought to explain model behavior as opposed to isolated variables or parameters. Guidance will be given in this section to change parameters and functions, which effectively deactivate chosen feedback loops. With this, the role of a feedback loop can be inferred by analyzing the model behavior with and without the loop.

One method to effectively deactivate loops is to provide extreme parameter values. For example, a rate involving an adjustment time or delay can be zeroed by providing a very large time constant. Consider a general rate equation for goal seeking of the form

$$rate = (goal - level)/adjustment\ time$$

The rate will be essentially zero when a large enough adjustment time is provided. The feedback loops associated with that rate will be effectively broken. With this type of modification, the structures responsible for behavioral modes can be ascertained by comparing runs in which overlapping model portions are neutralized.

Another way to interrupt the effects of feedback loops is to replace variables, graphs, or table functions with constants so that dynamic relationships are made constant and it is easier to isolate their effects or even break causal relationships.

2.8.1 Model Validation

There is nothing in either the physical or social sciences about which we have perfect information. We can never prove that a model is an exact representation of "reality." Conversely, among those things of which we are aware, there is nothing of which we know absolutely nothing. So we always deal with information which is of intermediate quality—it is better than nothing and short of perfection. Models are then to be judged, not on an absolute scale that condemns them for failure to be perfect, but on a relative scale that approves them if they succeed in clarifying our knowledge and our insights into systems.

Jay Forrester [Forrester 1968]

All models are wrong, but some are useful.
George Box [Box 1979]

Stakeholders want to know how much trust can be placed in a model. Model validation is the collection of processes that inspire trust and confidence in a model. The amount of trust involves two issues: (1) what question do we want the model to answer, and (2) how accurate must that answer be? Resolution of these issues ultimately rests on human judgment. By definition, no model is perfect, nor should we expect it to be. As in other scientific disciplines, we cannot guarantee to prove truth but attempt to disprove false hypotheses. The absence of suitability and consistency is probably easier to demonstrate.

Model validity is a relative matter. The usefulness of a mathematical simulation model should be judged in comparison with the mental image or other abstract model that would be used instead [Forrester 1968]. Models are successful if they clarify our knowledge and insights into systems.

Keep in mind that a simulation model addresses a problem not a system, as defined by the set of questions being answered. Only those questions are relevant when placing confidence in a model. The statements of model purpose focus the modeling study and aid in judging the validity of the model results. Thus, they also serve as acceptance criteria. At the end, we seek a shared vision and consensus about the model suitability and consistency. Assuming that the model purpose is improved policy, then the modeler and other stakeholders must create a consensus together.

There is a wide range of model precision in the field. Some models are tightly calibrated to real data, whereas some are not much more than qualitative conjecture, depending on the modeling goals and questions. The nature of the field is that models are produced with varying precision due to diverse modeling purposes.

No single test is enough to validate a system dynamics model. Rather, validation is an ongoing mix of activities in the modeling process with a combination of tests. Approaches for checking validity include parameter and relationship testing, structural and boundary testing, sensitivity analysis, and testing extreme or absurd conditions. This section discusses the multiperspective validation of system dynamics models. Validation is performed with carefully designed test cases, simulation results are compared to existing data, and demonstration of the models for specific purposes should be performed. This includes a number of objective tests. Eventually, insights should be provided by experimenting with the models.

Model validation has been a controversial issue in the software engineering community as system dynamics extends quantitative validation with an extensive range and depth of qualitative criteria. It is akin to a combination of structural and functional testing, and supplemented with multiple quality criteria. The multiple perspectives of quantitative and qualitative validation need to be better understood and accepted by the community. This acceptance can be partially aided by improvements in metrics collection, but software engineers should also gain an appreciation of qualitative validation. The qualitative aspects are sometimes viewed as "soft" validation, but software designers can learn some lessons about judging system quality and ensuring robustness from the system dynamics camp.

There is often confusion with point prediction versus "understanding." In terms of validation, it depends on whether the model purpose is point prediction or behavioral understanding. In many contexts, relative results are more than sufficient as opposed to absolute point predictions of state variables. Knowing the relative differences between policy options is often good enough. Being able to predict absolute quantities is frequently irrelevant.

The emphasis during validation is on building confidence in the suitability of the model for its intended purposes and its consistency with observed reality [Richardson 1991]. Model structure and behavior over time are both examined. A summary of validation tests is shown in Table 2-4, Table 2-5, and Table 2-6, adapted from [Richardson 1981] and [Forrester, Senge 1980]. The passing criteria are identified for each test. The criteria for a valid model consist of the tests in this table and associated subtests. Each individual test is insufficient alone to validate a model, but taken together they provide a robust means of filtering out weak models.

Table 2-4. Model validation tests—suitability for purpose

Focus	Test	Passing Criteria
Structure	Dimensional consistency	Variable dimensions agree with the computation using right units, ensuring that the model is properly balanced
	Extreme conditions in equations	Model equations make sense using extreme values
	Boundary adequacy Important variables Policy levers	Model structure contains variables and feedback effects for purpose of study
Behavior	Parameter (in)sensitivity Behavior characteristics	Model behavior sensitive to reasonable variations in parameters
	Policy conclusions	Policy conclusions sensitive to reasonable variations in parameters
	Structural (in)sensitivity Behavior characteristics	Model behavior sensitive to reasonable alternative structures
	Policy conclusions	Policy conclusions sensitive to reasonable alternative structures

Table 2-5. Model validation tests—consistency with reality

Focus	Test	Passing Criteria
Structure	Face validity Rates and levels Information feedback Delays	Model structure resembles real system to persons familiar with system
	Parameter values Conceptual fit Numerical fit	Parameters recognizable in real system and values are consistent with best available information about real system
Behavior	Replication of reference modes (boundary adequacy for behavior) Problem behavior Past policies Anticipated behavior	Model endogenously reproduces reference behavior modes that initially defined the study, including problematic behavior, observed responses to past policies and conceptually anticipated behavior
	Surprise behavior	Model produces unexpected behavior under certain test conditions: (1) model identifies possible behavior, (2) model is incorrect and must be revised
	Extreme condition simulations	Model behaves well under extreme conditions or policies, showing that formulation is sensible
	Statistical tests Time series analyses Correlation and regression	Model output behaves statistically with real system data; shows same characteristics

The battery of tests in Table 2-4, Table 2-5, and Table 2-6 consider the model's suitability for purpose, consistency with reality, and utility and effectiveness from both structural and behavioral perspectives. For the latter criteria, consider how effective the model is in achieving the purposes of the study. Can the model and its results be used?

Specific modeling objectives should be identified for individual models dependent on the specific application. Simulation test case results are to compared against collected data and other published data, existing theory, and other prediction models. Testing includes examining the ability of the model to generate proper reference behavior, which consists of time histories for all model variables.

When assessing the model consistency to reality (see Table 2-5), it may be a struggle to obtain good metrics representing observed data. This should not be a showstopper unless the expressed purpose is to reproduce past data with a great degree of accuracy and precision. As with other modeling techniques, relative results are often good enough to base decisions on. If desirable, statistical measures like root mean square error (RMSE), relative prediction error, and so on can be applied to the point predictions of simulation models. It should also be pointed out that surprise behavior by a model (see Table 2-6) is not necessarily a bad sign. Counterintuitive results could reveal a new insight and indicate that learning is taking place; old notions are shattered.

The results of judging a model against these individual criteria should be summa-

Table 2-6. Model validation tests—utility and effectiveness of a suitable model

Focus	Test	Passing Criteria
Structure	Appropriateness of model characteristics for audience Size Simplicity/complexity Aggregation/detail	Model simplicity, complexity and size is appropriate for audience
Behavior	Counterintuitive behavior	Model exhibits seemingly counterintuitive behavior in response to some policies, but is eventually seen as implication of real system structure
	Generation of insights	Model is capable of generating new insights about system

rized in appropriate documentation. A good supplemental reference that uses this same framework for verification and validation is [Sterman 2000]. He also provides additional procedures and worked out examples with statistical techniques.

2.8.2 Model Sensitivity Analysis

A model is numerically sensitive if a parameter or structural change results in changes to calculated parameters in a simulation run. Sensitivity analysis is useful in model development, validation, and communicating to others. It helps to build confidence in a model by evaluating its uncertainties. Stakeholders must know the degree to which model analyses and policy recommendations might change with respect to alternative assumptions. For example, if minor and reasonable variations in the model impact conclusions about the real world, then those conclusions are probably not warranted.

Sensitivity analysis also allows the determination of the level of accuracy needed in a parameter for a model to be useful. If a model is found to be insensitive to a chosen parameter, then the modeler knows that an estimate may be used instead of trying to achieve maximum precision. All too often, parameters are difficult or even impossible to measure in a real software process.

Sensitivity analysis will also help determine which parameter values are reasonable to use. If model behavior matches real-world observations, then the values used may reflect real-world data. Sensitivity tests also support system understanding, since experimentation can provide insights into system behavior under extreme conditions. Ultimately, it is desired to determine the high-leverage parameters for which the system is highly sensitive to. Those parameters that significantly influence system behavior represent leverage points in the real system.

There are different types of sensitivity analysis applied to simulation models:

- *Numerical.* The sensitivity of computed numerical values to changes in parameters or structural model changes.
- *Behavioral.* The degree to which model behavior changes when a parameter is changed or an alternate formulation is used.

- *Policy.* The degree to which policy conclusions change with respect to reasonable model changes across a range of reasonable values.

Numerical or parameter sensitivity analysis looks at factor setting, which includes varying a constant between runs. Graphs and table functions can also be modified over a range of meaningful alternative formulations to test sensitivity. The effects of different functions should be evaluated just like the effects of parameter changes. Structural sensitivity analysis looks at model structures—the linking of rates, levels, and loops. For example, should a flowing entity be represented with a single aggregate level or with more intermediate levels. Behavioral sensitivity is observed when the graphs over time change with parameter changes. Policy sensitivity is potentially the most damaging sensitivity because policies are the desired end result of a modeling study. Ultimately, policy insensitivity is the type that really counts.

If the assumptions about structure change, then the conclusions from the model will almost certainly change. Drastic structural changes include redefining the model boundary. Parameter values generally do not have as much of an effect on behavior as do feedback loops, rates, and level structures. This is one characteristic of system dynamics models with dominant feedback loops that are primarily responsible for model behavior. Another reason that such multiloop models often exhibit parameter insensitivity is due to compensating feedback loops. While one feedback loop gets stronger or weaker with a parameter change, other loops in the overall system may strengthen or diminish to compensate.

The compensating feedback is typical of man-made systems that were expressly designed to be insensitive to parameter changes (consider a governor device or car cruise control that maintains a constant speed with changing conditions). It is also instructive to realize that societal systems like software project environments have "built-in" compensating feedback that tends to resist policies designed to improve behavior. This is frequently seen in backlash behavior to process improvement inititiatives.

Sometimes, parameters will have negligible effect on behavior or none at all. Also, given that *relative* results from a model are frequently sufficient for policy conclusions, then precise parameter assignations are not always worth the extra effort. If the patterns remain consistent as a parameter changes over a feasible range, then that is often enough to know without having to be more precise with the parameter values.

Improved policies are ultimately desired. If policies are sensitive, investigations should be made to determine if the sensitivity is an artifact of the model or an accurate reflection of the real system being studied. If the model structure is deemed to be consistent with the real system, then the parameter that causes the sensitivity should be estimated as accurately as possible. It might also be wise to seek other advantageous policies that do not depend so heavily on the value of a particular parameter.

Conversely, if policy conclusions remain solid as parameters are varied over reasonable ranges, then those parameters do not need to be estimated with any more accuracy than the variable ranges used.

2.8.2.1   *Example: Sensitivity Analysis*

This section demonstrates sensitivity analysis applied to the simple Brooks's Law model. It will explore the effects of various parameter changes, initial value changes, and minor structural changes on the system behavior. The sensitivity of the model to different changes is evaluated by running a series of tests.

The first parameter change is the personnel allocation rate. Figure 2.40 (shown previously in Chapter 1) shows the effect on software development rate of adding five and ten people instantaneously at time = 110 days. The graph shows reasonable behavior for the model.

What if hiring takes the form of a step increase rather than a pulse? Figure 2.41 shows the model runs for step increases of 1 person for 10 days and 0.5 persons for 20 days (anything shorter will largely resemble the pulse). The first trendline is the pulse of 10 people, the second is the 10 day step increase, and the third is the 20 day step increase.

Another parameter to vary is the assimilation rate. Values of 20, 40, and 60 days will be used (these represent 1, 2, and 3 working months, respectively). Since the base run has no personnel allocation, these changes will have no impact to it. The case of allocating 10 more people at day 110 with an instant pulse will be used to examine the impact. Figure 2.42 shows sensitivity results.

The behavior is as expected when the training assimilation takes longer. The schedule time varies slightly from 271 days to 276 days when the assimilation increases from 20 to 60 days. Thus, the schedule time is relatively insensitive to these changes.

In conclusion, there are several possible responses when a model is shown to be sensitive. If parameters or graph functions have significant impact, then they should be

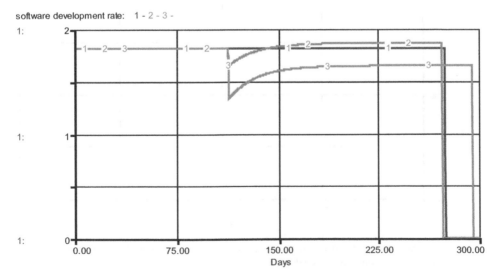

Figure 2.40. Sensitivity of software development rate to personnel allocation pulses (1: no extra hiring, 2: add 5 people on 110th day, 3: add 10 people on 110th day).

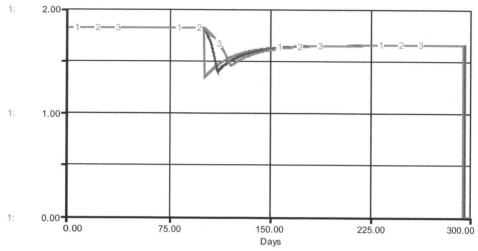

Figure 2.41. Sensitivity of software development rate to personnel allocation steps (1: add 10 people on 110th day, 2: step of 1 new person for 10 days, 3: step of 0.5 new person for 20 days).

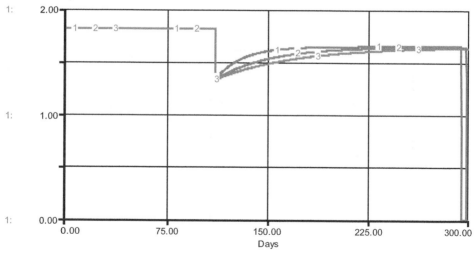

Figure 2.42. Sensitivity of software development rate to different assimilation times (1: assimilation = 20 days, 2: assimilation = 40 days, 3: assimilation = 60 days).

estimated with much care. Another response is to disaggregate and reformulate the model with more detail. Possibly, a parameter or graph covers multiple effects that should be broken out separately. Finally, the sensitivity can be interpreted to identify an important leverage point in the system. Thus, intervention in the real process will truly have a significant impact.

2.8.3 Monte Carlo Analysis

Monte Carlo analysis is a "game of chance" technique used to assess model outcome ranges by applying random sampling. Samples are taken from known input probability distributions to create output distributions. It estimates the likely range of outcomes from a complex random process by simulating the process a large number of times. The following steps are performed for n iterations in a Monte Carlo analysis, where an iteration refers to a single simulation run:

1. For each random variable, take a sample from its probability distribution function and calculate its value.
2. Run a simulation using the random input samples and compute the corresponding simulation outputs.
3. Repeat the above steps until n simulation runs are performed.
4. Determine the output probability distributions of selected dependent variables using the n values from the runs.

See Appendix A for additional details on Monte Carlo analysis, including the following example, which is a shortened version from the appendix.

2.8.3.1 Example: Monte Carlo Analysis

This example will simulate the randomness of the size input to a dynamic effort model, and quantify the resulting output in probabilistic terms. Assume that the likely values for size can be represented with a normal probability distribution with a mean of 50 KSLOC and a standard deviation of 10 KSLOC.

To implement Monte Carlo analysis, a small set of $n = 16$ random samples will be generated for size input to the Dynamic COCOMO model. In actual practice, 16 would be a very low number (except for very large and expensive simulation iterations). Generally 50–100 iterations should be considered as a minimum for filling out distributions, and up to 1000 iterations will give good results in many situations.

First, 16 random numbers between 0 and 1 are generated. The inverse transform technique is then used to determine size by mapping the random numbers onto the cumulative distribution function. Appendix A shows full details of this example, including the set of 16 random numbers (r_i) and the generated size values $F^{-1}(r_i)$, and graphically illustrates the inverse transform technique using the same numbers to determine size 16 times via the cumulative distribution function.

Dynamic COCOMO is then run 16 times with the respective size inputs. The simulation outputs for the personnel staffing curve in Figure 2.43 demonstrate the model

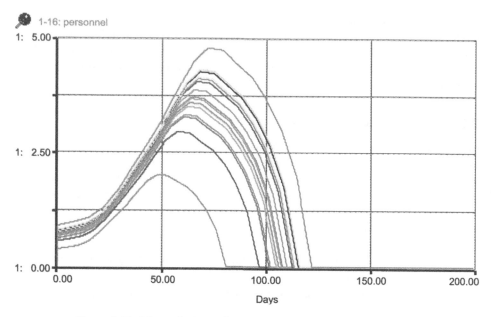

Figure 2.43. Monte Carlo results: personnel staffing curves for 16 runs.

sensitivity to the size samples. Project effort is the area under a staffing curve. Figure 2.44 shows the Monte Carlo results in terms of an effort distribution histogram and its continuous representation. It stacks up the 16 simulation outputs for the total project effort into respective effort bins. A smoother distribution would be seen to be filled out if more iterations were run and plotted beyond the small sample size of 16.

2.9 POLICY ANALYSIS

Policy analysis is the model-based evaluation of process change options, that is, process improvement initiatives. In this stage, we seek to understand what process changes work and why. Investigations are undertaken to determine why particular policies have the effects they do, and to identify policies that can be implemented to improve the real system or process.

Testing of policies and their sensitivities in different scenarios is critical in model evaluation. You alter one parameter at a time at first. Always be conscious of reality constraints on the numbers and policies. Use sensitivity results to identify worthwhile policy initiatives, test the robustness of each policy in isolation, then explore with other parameter changes. Test the policies under different scenarios. Finally, the eventual goal is to update the software process policies based on the analysis results.

However, recommendations from a well-done study should also be explainable and defendable without resorting to a formal model. The final recommendations come from not only manipulating the model but from additional understanding about the real

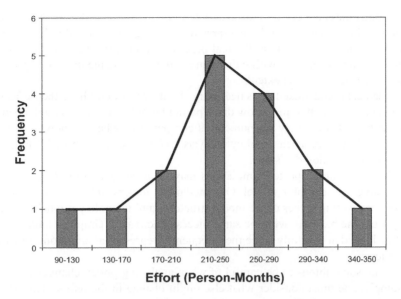

Figure 2.44. Monte Carlo results: effort distribution.

system that was gained during the modeling exercise iterations. The final result of policy analysis is identifying policies that are actually implemented on projects.

The term *policy analysis* has long been used in the system dynamics community. In software process improvement, processes are typically defined by a combination of policies, procedures, guidelines, and standards. A policy in this context generally states what *has* to be done, and the rest of the artifacts provide details of *how*. For this section, these process artifacts are lumped under the umbrella of "policies."

A policy represents a decision on how organizational processes should be executed. An example process policy is that peer reviews must be performed. This policy can be revised and elaborated from modeling insights in terms of what types of peer reviews work best, how frequently, on what artifacts, and so on.

Policy alternatives in the real world correspond to either model parameter changes or structural changes. One always should look for high-leverage change opportunities. Policy parameters with high sensitivity suggest points of leverage in the real system. Changes involving new feedback structure suggest new ways of manipulating information in the real system to improve behavior. The following sections derived from [Richardson, Pugh 1981] discuss parameter changes and structural changes as they relate to policy analysis.

2.9.1 Policy Parameter Changes

Policy changes are often reflected as model parameter changes. Testing a parameter's sensitivity involves making a base run, changing the parameter value, rerunning the simulation, and comparing the resulting model behavior with the base run. Parameters are also sometimes changed in midrun to determine their effects during the course of a simulation. These changes can be interpreted as testing a real-world policy change as long as the change is feasible in the real process. Parameters are classified as policy parameters if their values are within the span of control of people in the real process, or at least controllable to some extent.

A fundamental understanding is necessary about *why* policies have their effects, because it is not sufficient to just know that a particular policy improves model behavior. Understanding of the policy phenomena is compared to what is known or believed about the real system. Then a policy analysis has a better chance of leading to real process implementation decisions.

Much thought and repeated simulations may be necessary to produce a complete understanding in a complex model. One method to understand policy improvements involves deactivating pieces of the model structure until the policy run behaves no differently from the base run with the same pieces deactivated. Graph or table functions should be looked at carefully since they frequently represent assumptions about existing policies.

There are some things to be careful of when analyzing policy changes in a model. For example, one must consider what else might change in the real system when the policy is implemented. There may be other dynamic consequences not yet accounted for. The essence of the real-world policy must be accurately interpreted in terms of the model, to the extent that model aggregation allows. In a sense, the modeler becomes part of the system to accurately simulate a policy change. He/she acts as missing feedback links to manually change other parameters to simulate the side effects of the primary policy change under investigation.

One should also be careful to consider the real limits on policy parameters. A combination of policy parameter changes that work well in a model may be impossible to implement in the real system. The modeler must try to keep policy parameter changes within achievable and realistic bounds (except when testing extreme conditions to gain model insight). Keep in mind that a model does not test what can be implemented, only what is likely to happen if a policy is implemented.

Sensitive policy parameters should be identified, as they indicate possible leverage points in the process. Intimate familiarity with model behavior under different scenarios is critical to locate sensitive parameters. Also important is the location of feedback loops which dominate behavior at various times. Behavior is unlikely to be sensitive to a parameter that has no influence on any dominant loops. Identifying parameters that influence positive loops may also be very useful because such loops are usually destabilizing.

Feedback systems tend to compensate internally for parameter changes, so model behavior in general is insensitive to such changes. So policies represented as parameter changes frequently are not very effective in system dynamics analyses. More dramatic results are usually observed with changes in the policy structure as opposed to parameters.

2.9.2 Policy Structural Changes

New policies often alter or extend the system's feedback structure. The structure of a system with feedback tends to be the strongest single determinant of its time-based behavior. Thus, improvements frequently involve adding new feedback links representing new, beneficial ways of manipulating information about the system.

A simple example of a policy that adds feedback in the process is having to use past project performance and costs to calibrate a new project estimate. Without the usage of historical data to calibrate cost estimation, there is no connection to past performance and, thus, project planning runs open loop. The policy decision to use past data will likely improve the accuracy of new estimates and lead to reduced project overruns.

The main guidance for discovering high-leverage structural changes comes from familiarity with the real system and model. Other principles to keep in mind are that adding a positive feedback loop could have a strong destabilizing influence, and negative loops can add stability. Recall that a negative loop in an oscillatory structure has a damping effect.

A good policy set will be a mix of policies that work in harmony, counteracting the tendencies of undesirable system behavior. Advantageous policies will come to light via intimate knowledge of the system being studied, by insights gleaned from the modeling process, and by considerations of what is possible to implement in the real system.

2.9.3 Policy Validity and Robustness

The ultimate goal of modeling is the application of insights to real-world problems, in such a way that model building will help people manage software processes better. Improved decisions can be made when the dynamic consequences are known. The policy analysis effort and inherent uncertainty of prediction forces one to address the validity of the recommendations and how implementable they are. But people may differ about what constitutes process improvement.

It is the nature of feedback systems, or any complex man-made system, that trade-offs are made. One well-known example in software development is the trade-off of increased cost to accelerate schedule. But how are such trade-offs evaluated? A system dynamics model does not set or evaluate the criteria of improved system behavior. Only people can make such value judgments. A model cannot determine a desirable scenario, but supports people in their weighing of alternatives.

Policy recommendations, like models themselves, are subject to validity and robustness questions. Even if a model has successfully passed all validation tests, how much confidence should be placed in the policy recommendations derived from it?

Robustness refers to the extent to which the real system can deviate from the model assumptions without invalidating policy recommendations based upon it. A recommendation is robust only if it remains advantageous in spite of parameter variations, different exogenous conditions, and reasonable alternatives in model formulation. A policy that is sensitive to such variations is suspect.

Since the real problem will always have aspects that are not captured by a model, a policy must be robust to have real-world effects similar to its effects in a model. For example, few practitioners would trust a policy that flip-flops as a parameter varies over a reasonable range. All policy recommendations should pass rigorous sensitivity tests before being passed on for implementation.

The success of a particular policy should also be tested under a variety of external circumstances. In summary, to build a robust set of policies one must spend considerable effort trying to prove they are not robust. This is like attempting to disprove a proposed theory to see if it still stands up under scrutiny.

2.9.4 Policy Suitability and Feasibility

Robustness is one aspect of policy validity; another is the adequacy of the model to support the recommendations based upon it. Recall that long before policy analysis, it is extremely important to set the model boundary appropriately for the problem being addressed and the questions being asked. During policy analysis, these same boundary questions are addressed. It should be asked whether the factors initially left outside of the boundary could invalidate the model-based analyses.

An important consideration before implementation is whether those responsible for policy in the real system can be convinced of the value of the model-based recommendations. Another is how is the real system likely to respond to the process of implementation?

People responsible for managing complex human systems base their policies on their own mental models. Thus, the policy recommendations must be formulated and argued so as to fit into their mental models. The reasons behind model behavior must be made plain and clear to the process owners.

This is more justification that all stakeholders be integral to the modeling process, and that the WinWin spiral lifecycle is a good fit for modeling. Insights are more likely to come out of the process rather than the deliverable reports of a modeling study. The likelihood of results being implemented are seriously diminished if the process participants are not involved.

In summary, successful implementation of new processes depends on good policies, acceptance by managers and process owners, as well as a sensitively planned transition path to the new process(es). It should also be pointed out that the process of implementing policy change is a feedback problem in and of itself. This problem is left as research for interested readers.

2.9.5 Example: Policy Analysis

Policies contained in the Brooks's Law model must be evaluated with respect to project goals and constraints. Since this is a hypothetical example, we will just list some alternative policies. Options to consider include

- Changing the personnel allocation control rules
- Different timing for adding new people
- The way they are added
- The type of people added
- The team makeup

The correction could take place earlier and/or be a more gradual and continuous approach. Personnel do not have to be added in a single pulse (see the preceding sensitivity tests for this) and, in fact, a pulse was used just for simplicity's sake. More than likely, a real project would ramp up the staff incrementally. The people added do not necessarily have to be new, or they can be able to assimilate faster. Possibly, one could devote support people to training instead of having experienced job performers do the training, which would lessen the training overhead impact. Lastly, the team does not have to stay as a single team, as it could optionally be partitioned.

There might be other organizational considerations to be addressed. Despite the lessened project execution capability, adding people to a project could be a desired policy for other reasons. For example, if training of new hires is important, that alone might be sufficient justification to add people. Possibly, the next project is more critical than the current, and it's more important to be prepared for the upcoming project instead of saving a few days of schedule on the current one.

2.10 CONTINUOUS MODEL IMPROVEMENT

Model reassessment and improvement should be ongoing as part of the iterative development process. Parts of a model are reformulated and refined (sometimes deleted), and new parts added during iteration. The iteration will help ensure that the model is consistent with reality, suited well for its expressed purposes, and understood. Sometimes, constants are reformulated into variables, levels are disaggregated into more levels, new feedback structure is added, or even new hypotheses about dynamic behavior are developed. This section will discuss various issues in the ongoing refinement process.

Continually challenge the work you have already done during the course of a modeling project. It is possible that the original problem will have morphed and/or some of the underlying assumptions do not hold anymore. Take a fresh critical look at the model, and iterate the entire process. Sit back, ponder, and do sanity checks against the known reality. Some starting points to investigate include:

- Challenge what has been left out. Look at sources and sinks at the beginning and end of chains, and consider feedback and policy implications of replacing them with levels.
- Challenge what has been put in. Is it too much or too little detail? It all depends on the purpose. Look at the levels and converters to see if they are commensurate with the model purpose and available data.
- Does the model contain the measures of policy effectiveness that are used in the real process? If not, then these important measurement criteria commensurate with real decision making should be included.

If a full cycle has been completed through policy analysis and implementation, then it is time to plan the next cycle of model improvement. Per the WinWin spiral model, review the previous model development and decide on the commitment for the next phase based on the latest objectives, constraints, and alternatives.

2.10.1   Disaggregation

Sometimes, levels should be disaggregated into more than one level. The decision to do so should be based on policy analysis and/or model behavior. Disaggregation is called for if a policy issue cannot be addressed otherwise. For example, if staffing considerations must account for the different levels of new and experienced workers, then a single aggregate level for personnel should be split. Another reason is when disaggregation will significantly change the behavior of a model. In the Brooks's Law model, for example, we would not get the same dynamic behavior if new and experienced personnel were not tracked separately. The differing productivities and training overhead would not come into play.

In the Brooks's Law model and other studies involving personnel training or skill development, new policy levers are available when multiple personnel levels are used to represent different experience or skill levels. Implementation-wise, splitting a level into two may frequently double the number of equations associated with the original level. This is a potential pitfall to be aware of.

It should be stressed that disaggregating just to better model the real system is not always warranted. It should be done only if the resulting behavior change is important and particularly if policy conclusions depend on it. Otherwise, adding more levels than required is distracting (visually and conceptually) and can make a model harder to understand.

2.10.2   Feedback Loops

Each refinement to a model complicates things. If additional feedback loops are to be added to an existing model, it is highly advisable to add them sequentially instead of all at once. Otherwise, a compounding of changes may lead to loss of model control. By adding one new feedback link at a time, it is easier to identify and fix model defects (like the "code a little, test a little" mantra).

2.10.3   Hypotheses

With a simulation model, one can incorporate more than one hypothesis and compare their potential to recreate system behavior. As part of the iterative approach, a single dynamic hypothesis in the beginning will simplify things. After assessing the model against the original hypothesis, in subsequent iterations alternates can be added that may also be responsible for behavior.

When refining a model, the same techniques are used as during the original model development. Plot a lot and study the outputs. Make sure important key variables and feedback effects are included on the plots. The plots should be kept fairly simple without too many variables on one graph. Here the rule of "7 ± 2" also holds. Often, the scale of plots can be fixed so to that multiple runs can be easily compared to each other. Sometimes, tabular outputs are helpful to read more detail.

2.10.4 When to Stop?

There are no definitive rules about precisely when to stop ongoing model refinement. Generally, you can stop if the model has reached a point at which it is well suited for its stated purpose(s) and consistent with reality. As with many processes, a point of diminishing returns usually exists. If the extra benefits of more refinements are outweighed by the additional costs of further refinement, then a point of diminishing returns has been reached and the exercise should be stopped. If the present model is useful for people to generate insights about the problem, then stop. If, on the other hand, the model has increased in size and complexity so that it is hard or impossible to understand, then some retrenchment might be in order. It is quite possible that you have gone further or faster than necessary, so drop back a little.

Knowing when to stop thus requires some intuition and wisdom. It is certainly tempting to keep going, but always keep in mind that no model is 100% complete and perfect. The point of stopping is also tied to the question of model validity described in Section 2.8.1.

2.10.5 Example: Model Improvement Next Steps

The Brooks's Law model described so far is based on simplified assumptions and has certain limitations. The following enhancements would improve usage of the model:

- Add a stop to the simulation when all requirements are developed. This will prevent the model from running overtime.
- Make the model scalable for larger team sizes up to 60 people to overcome the current restriction on maximum team size.
- Make a continuous personnel allocation instead of a one-time correction.
- Add the effects of team partitioning.

Figure 2.45 shows the default function for communication overhead that stops at 30 people. This auxiliary relates "communication overhead" to the total number of personnel. If we blindly continue with the formula,

$$\text{communication overhead} = 0.06 \cdot \text{team size}$$

then the equation quickly becomes greater than 100%. What is wrong with this? It does not account for partitioning into more teams as the total number of people grows. It assumes that a single team will remain and continue to grow indefinitely in size without breaking into more teams.

Brooks stated that adding people to a software project increases the effort in three ways: training new people, added intercommunication, and the work and disruption of

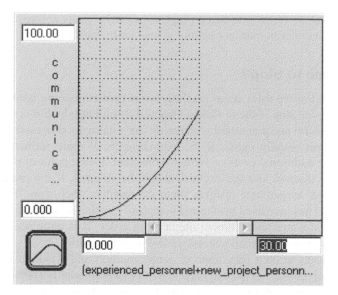

Figure 2.45. Default communication overhead function (communication overhead % versus experienced personnel + new personnel).

team partitioning. We purposely did not address partitioning yet due to its difficult complexities. See Chapter 5 for exercises to enhance the Brooks's Law model to include the effects of partitioning.

2.11 SOFTWARE METRICS CONSIDERATIONS

Process modeling may involve a good deal of metrics collection and analysis, depending on the goals and constraints. When feasible, models should be bolstered by empirical data to reflect reality as closely as possible. However, detailed metrics data is not always warranted or immediately available. The following two sections discuss data collection and describe a useful metrics framework for modeling.

2.11.1 Data Collection

A mathematical model should be based on the best information that is readily available, but the design of a model should not be postponed until all pertinent parameters have been accurately measured. That day will never come.

Jay W. Forrester, *Industrial Dynamics* [Forrester 1968]

Existing data often does not completely match the requirements for a new modeling effort. Comprehensive process models cover a number of different aspects, and these models are best quantified using a single data source commensurate with the comprehensive nature of the model. However, very few published empirical investigations cover a wide range of process aspects with solid statistics. Studies usually have a narrower focus. Fine-grained models should have commensurately detailed data for parameterization. To ensure that the data fits the model, the metrics defined for data collection should be the same as those used in the model.

Having quality data to support modeling efforts is one of the most difficult aspects. Accurate simulation results depend on accurate parameter values, and calibration depends on accurate measurements from the process. Whenever possible, available metrics should be used to quantify relationships between factors. However, not having data at hand should not seriously impair model development. There may be a use for judgmental data and management opinion to estimate parameters for "soft variables" for which numerical data is lacking. Experts can make educated guesses.

Some ways to cope with lack of data from [Kellner, Raffo 1997] include:

- Adjust existing values to approximate desired variables
- Construct values from other detailed records
- Obtain estimates from personnel involved
- Use typical values taken from the literature

One must often go on an archeological data dig. For example, obtaining original inspection data sheets may provide critical data details not available from summary records. Field data to drive models can also sometimes be artificially generated.

The rigor used for collecting data should tie back to the modeling goals. Not every study needs highly precise, validated metrics. Often, qualitative or relative results are good enough for the purpose of a study. The level of rigor depends on how the data is going to be used. A goal-directed technique described next is valuable for defining measurements to be used in modeling efforts.

2.11.2   Goal–Question–Metric Framework

The Goal–Question–Metric (GQM) framework [Basili 1992] for conducting metric analyses can be highly useful for simulation modeling. It provides a framework for developing a metrics program and helps ensure that software metrics are mapped to goals. Organizational goals are identified, questions are developed to determine whether the goals are being met, and metrics are identified that can help answer the questions. The framework was developed at the University of Maryland as a mechanism for formalizing the tasks of characterization, planning, construction, analysis, learning, and feedback. The GQM paradigm was developed for all types of studies, particularly studies concerned with improvement issues. The paradigm does not provide specific goals but rather a framework for stating goals and refining them into questions to provide a specification for the data needed to help achieve the goals.

GQM consists of three primary steps:

1. Generate a set of organizational goals.
2. Derive a set of questions relating to the goals.
3. Develop a set of metrics needed to answer the questions.

The goals are based upon the needs of the organization, and they help in determining whether or not you improved what you wanted to. Goals are defined in terms of purpose, perspective, and environment using the generic templates as follows:

Purpose. {To characterize, evaluate, predict, or motivate} {the process, product, model, or metric} in order to {understand, assess, manage, engineer, learn, or improve it}.

Perspective. Examine the {cost, effectiveness, correctness, defects, changes, product metrics, or reliability} from the point of view of the {developer, manager, customer, or corporate perspective}.

Environment. The environment consists of the following: process factors, people factors, problem factors, methods, tools, and constraints

The questions quantify the goals as completely as possible within the context of the development environment. Questions are classified as product-related or process-related and provide feedback from the quality perspective. Product-related questions define the product and the evaluation of the product with respect to a particular quality (e.g., reliability, user satisfaction). Process-related questions include the quality of use, domain of use, effort of use, effect of use, and feedback from use.

Finally, a set of metrics is developed that provides the information to answer the questions. The actual data needed to answer the questions are identified and associated with each of the questions. As data items are identified, it must be understood how valid the data item will be with respect to accuracy and how well it responds to the specific question. The metrics should have interpretation guidelines, that is, what value of the metric specifies the product's higher quality. Generally, a single metric will not answer a question; a combination of metrics is needed. Figure 2.46 is sample GQM analysis from [Madachy 1995a] for analyzing the inspection process.

2.11.3 Integrated Measurement and Simulation

Measurement efforts and process simulation should be tightly integrated; otherwise, there is a risk of existing data not being commensurate with model constructs (granularity, abstraction level, etc.). There may be unnecessary effort in generation, collection, and possible reformatting of data for simulation models. Effort to locate and assess relevance of empirical data from external sources may be prohibitive.

The GQM framework can help alleviate some of the problems with empirical data. The risk-driven WinWin Spiral model (traditionally used for software projects) is an-

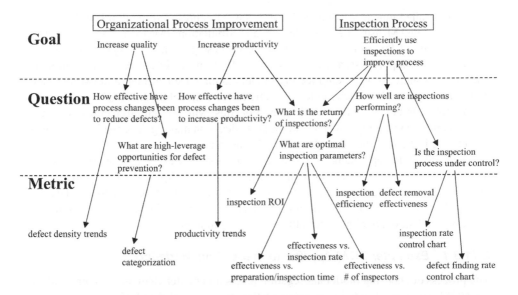

Figure 2.46. GQM applied to inspection analysis.

other framework applicable to modeling studies and measurement experiments. For example, based on modeling risk considerations, a spiral cycle might be dedicated to a measurement exercise before further elaboration of a software process model (see the example earlier in this chapter).

For a simulation study, the GQM goals must match those of the model stakeholders. The metrics are the key variables that the model will output in order to answer the questions. System dynamics may impose data collection requirements and the GQM software metrics may be used to define reference modes for simulation models. Pfahl and Ruhe have developed some integrated approaches in which the GQM method has been interpreted specifically for the context of process simulation [Pfahl 2001], [Pfahl et al. 2003], [Pfahl, Ruhe 2005].

Goal-oriented measurement plus system dynamics are described as complementary approaches in [Pfahl, Ruhe 2005]. "Dynamic GQM" is an evolutionary and learning-based approach for process modeling. The different process steps in GQM and the system dynamics method are multiplexed together in various ways for different purposes. For example, GQM-based measurement can be used at various stages of the system dynamics modeling process.

Dynamic GQM has several advantages. Whereas GQM is local when one goal is looked at in isolation, system dynamics can capture effects on a global level. GQM is static and does not reflect changes over time. Dynamic GQM integrates and synchronizes individual GQM models from a global system perspective. It incrementally increases the validity of both GQM and system dynamics models by mutually reusing and validating the models. Finally, it is a means to integrate real-world empirical results with simulation experiments.

More detailed guidance beyond Dynamic GQM is provided in [Pfahl, Ruhe 2005] where Integrated Measurement, Modelling, and Simulation (IMMoS) is described. The primary goals of IMMoS are to (1) improve process guidance for system dynamics modeling, (2) support system dynamics goal definition, (3) integrate dynamic models and existing static software engineering models to enhance learning, and (4) integrate methods of system dynamics modeling, static process modeling and GQM.

IMMoS combines static modeling approaches with system dynamics, extends process improvement approaches, and supports decision making. The reader is encouraged to read [Pfahl, Ruhe 2005] for detailed examples.

These integrated approaches are showing promise. However, more work is needed to define and implement methods that better combine empirical measurement and process simulation. Further experiments and case studies are necessary to validate the approaches. This will take an alignment of diverse efforts for experimentation and process simulation modeling across the software community.

2.11.3.1 Example: GQM Applied to Inspection Modeling

The process of choosing model aggregation levels and model elements is supported by the GQM paradigm. Modeling goals drive the structure and detail of models. For example, a simplified GQM comparison of the differences between two major models for inspections ([Madachy 1994b] and [Tvedt 1995]) are highlighted in Table 2-7. The different models reflect their respective research goals.

Their different goals result in different levels of inspection process detail. The purpose of the Madachy inspection model is a top-level perspective regarding when and how frequently inspections should be used. The Tvedt model focuses on optimizing the inspection process itself. In the former, the overall project effects of incorporating inspections are investigated, resulting in a more aggregated model than the latter's focus. This example will be elaborated with more detail in Chapter 3.

2.12 PROJECT MANAGEMENT CONSIDERATIONS

A modeling and simulation effort should be managed as any other software project. The average model development is relatively small compared to most software pro-

Table 2-7. Illustration of GQM applied to software inspection modeling

Model	Goal	Questions	Metrics (Model-realized Level Instances)
Madachy 1994b	Improve overall software process performance	What are the dynamic project effects of incorporating inspections?	Levels before and after inspection
Tvedt 1995	Improve the inspection process	What are optimal inspection parameter values?	Levels for each inspection activity

jects, but that does not subvert the need for best practices. Focusing on people, addressing risk, and overall diligence should be practiced nonetheless.

2.12.1 Modeling Communication and Team Issues

Communication is vitally important in modeling just like it is on software development projects. Always seek involvement from the front end per the WinWin spiral, or modeling efforts will not succeed. Make sure to identify the stakeholders and their win conditions, and consider them from the outset. Developing buy-in to the model is usually more important than the model itself. Otherwise, the results will never be used.

Modelers should be constantly talking to the organizational teams that both support and underwrite the modeling, as well as those being modeled. They need to know what is being done, their expectations might need to be managed, and they will cooperate and be much more proactive when they realize how they will gain from the process modeling. Always keep in mind that modeling in industry must be very applied and have demonstrable value. Oftentimes, a business case for the modeling should be developed beforehand.

Everyone comes with his or her own preconceived mental models and success criteria. Open communication will go far to elucidate those models and identify the clashes between stakeholders' visions of success. Eliminating the clashes between peoples' internal models is a major premise of the MBASE philosophy.

Be aware of the different perspectives of your audience. Typically, executives and those being exposed to system dynamics for the first time do not need or want to see a fully elaborated model. The model could easily alienate if they are not familiar with the notations. Always use simple diagrams to communicate with others until they seek more detail. Sometimes, a causal diagram is useful for high-level explanations. Communicate structure with simplified system diagrams, loop diagrams, and submodels. Try to facilitate interaction with the model. This will go a long way toward getting support and having the model used by others. It is also an important part of the modeling process to have experts validate the model results.

The form of the model itself can be crucial in communication. When possible, a control panel interface is useful for others to be able to view key inputs and outputs. Cluster the controls into related groups. Try to use pictures to illustrate and delineate model sections. Sometimes, a hierarchy of pictures helps to explain the relationships between model sectors.

All models contain hidden assumptions. It is, therefore, critical to present and document assumptions in a model to eliminate confusion and force clarity. Results should be qualified relative to the assumptions built into the model. Equations should have comments describing the assumptions and rationale used in their formulation.

Simple causal loop diagrams (CLDs) are sometimes better for describing a model than a fully elaborated, executable version. This is particularly important when key stakeholders do not have the skillset and/or time to comprehend model details. Often a causal loop diagram that shows the basic feedback loops of a system will get the important points across.

Documentation is an important part of communication, particularly when it is the primary form of imparting information to a group. Not everyone can attend briefings, and many times reading is necessary to understand low-level details. One should clearly describe the problem, study objectives, assumptions, simulation activities, and describe the final recommendations and their organizational impacts. See Section 2.12.3 for more details on documenting modeling projects.

As Barry Boehm said, "The models are just there to help, not to make your management decisions for you" [Boehm 1981]. A model alone is not going to make a decision. Remember that a model is not reality. It is only an aid to be used with other resources before committing to a decision. A team of people should use a model in this proper context. If the model indicates an action that totally flies in the face of realism and practicality, then you must listen to the collective intuition of the team.

Model building, understanding, and application should be a team effort for maximum leverage. Personnel who are not schooled in analytical methods and modeling approaches nevertheless should be effective participants in modeling and simulation. There is a gap between analytical specialists familiar with modeling techniques and tools and others in an organization with little or no modeling background. The quality and depth of team participation should be increased; otherwise, the modeling efforts may fail to have impact. People outside of the modeling loop often feel no ownership of the models and place little meaning or importance to the models.

People should be able to construct meaning from models through active engagement with model building (not just data collection and reporting) and model interpretation. There should be time made available for consideration of, reflection on, and communication about the models. Useful meaning is not inherent in models, but must be constructed by the model's users, that is, the entire team. Issues that must be addressed include collaboration between disparate groups, development of shared understanding, and usability of tools and approaches.

In order to address these issues at Litton, we would begin modeling efforts with a kick-off meeting for everybody with a stake in the models. This includes anyone who provides data or insight, those whose working processes are being modeled, other process "owners" as appropriate, those who need to understand modeling results for planning or management concerns, and the modelers and their sponsors (typically executives funding the effort). Brainstorming and data interpretation sessions are scheduled with those who can contribute, and all stakeholders are kept apprised of the ongoing results. It is vitally important that the model insights be demonstrated and resulting process changes discussed by those impacted.

2.12.2 Risk Management of Modeling Projects

An organizational effort that is not bought into by or relayed to others will be a lost cause and will doom future attempts. Conversely, the possible rewards of group collaboration and modeling are tremendous for process improvement. Table 2-8 shows some common modeling risks and actions that can be taken.

Table 2-8. Modeling risks and mitigation techniques

Risk	Mitigation Techniques
Not involving the right people to achieve buy-in	Work proactively with all stakeholders across organization: executive management, modeling project sponsors, process owners and champions, and other identified stakeholders.
Constantly evolving processes make the model irrelevant in the future	Parameterize the model so its subparts and parameters can be easily updated. Develop and implement a process for periodic model evaluation and updates. Train personnel.
Overly complex model attempting to capture too much or, conversely, an overly simplistic model not capturing important attributes	Balance user friendliness with model prediction figures of merit. Use surveys, workshops, and other user feedback and interface measures to gauge usability. Quantify predictability measures for different model options.
Not having right resources	Renegotiate goals and resources to be compatible.

2.12.3 Modeling Documentation and Presentation

Documenting a simulation study is crucial if others are to understand and apply the results. A model should be made as accessible as possible. Documentation is particularly important to communicate to others who were not directly involved in the study. A report should address the following items at a minimum: clearly describe the real-world problem, identify the objectives of the study, identify all assumptions, describe the simulation process activities, provide details on the resulting model and its testing, and include conclusions and final recommendations for the user/reader. If applicable, transition to other users and model maintenance should also be considered in the report.

All modeling projects and homework exercises, regardless of size, should keep the following in mind:

- Always show equations
- Liberally include comments with equations
- Identify assumptions used
- Provide rationale for numeric values and calibrations
- Show outputs for different simulation cases
- Discuss the results

Early project briefings or reviews should address the following items:

- Describe problem and background
    What will result from your study
- Show system boundary

- How will a user interact?

  Inputs and outputs

  A prototype of input and output is very useful
- Reference behaviors and other methods of verification
- Other material as appropriate (see sample report in Table 2-9)

A good report will be clear, complete, and demonstrate an organized approach to model building. The described model should also be complete and validated, or at least explain the extent of validation. It is critical that all modeling assumptions be made clear, with appropriate rationale for deriving constants and parameter values. The report will thoroughly explain sensitivity analysis and controlled experimentation to verify the model. It will include discussions of model expectations, lessons learned, conclusions, and potential improvements.

Table 2-9 provides a sample report outline that can and should be tailored for particular situations. The size of the report depends on the scope and nature of the study.

2.12.4   Modeling Work Breakdown Structure

The process steps contained in this chapter may serve as the basis for a work breakdown structure for a modeling project. The granularity of activities should depend on the nature of the study, where effort is focused, and the number of people involved. Alternatively, the SEI came up with a preliminary work breakdown structure with two major divisions: managing the modeling work and modeling the process.

Table 2-10 shows an activity decomposition elaborated from unpublished SEI work on a process guide for descriptive modeling. There is a large focus on organizational issues with little detail of model construction activities, and it should be modified for specific situations.

2.13   MODELING TOOLS

Modeling with system dynamics requires a computer simulation tool. It is highly recommended that you use an existing, proven simulation tool rather than creating your own. It will be more flexible, stable, robust, understandable, and save much time. You gain the leverage of high-level commands and an overall modeling framework.

Since the architecture for a simulation software package probably will not change during the usage of a specific model, worries about fragile demonstration prototypes are minimized. Small prototype models can be used as the foundations for enhanced, complex models without the overall architecture breaking (though the model formulation may need revamping).

It is worthwhile to mention specific commercial tools. The history of the field is linked to evolving computing paradigms as reflected in the toolsets. Dynamo was the pioneering system dynamics tool and has been around for decades [Forrester 1961], [Richardson, Pugh 1981]. It is still based on writing source equations and lacks a modern graphical user interface, but many classical references are based on it.

Table 2-9. Sample simulation report outline

Simulation Report

1. Introduction
   - Problem statement and description—extent and history of the problem, causes of the problem; possible solutions and their obstacles
   - Purpose of study
   - Purpose of model building
   - Executive summary of key results
2. Background
   - System description—include diagrams that illustrate the system configuration
   - System reference behavior—narrative description, tabular data, graphs
   - Assumptions and the underlying rationale for each
3. Model Development
   - Modeling process—include modeling approach and sequence of events
   - Model evolution
   - Data acquisition—source of data, method of collection, problems, solutions, analysis, etc.
4. Model Description
   - Timeframe, spatial boundaries, entities, attributes, key assumptions
   - Process flow and model structure—flowcharts, model diagrams, etc.
   - Key logic and equations, sources of uncertainty, probability distributions, etc.
   - Model overview—include related flowcharts, flow networks, block diagrams, etc.
   - Assumptions and other model details
   - Approach for verification and validation
5. Model Verification and Validation
   - Testing results, extreme values, sensitivity analysis
   - Comparison to reference behavior, expert review, etc.
   - Statistical analyses
   - Other testing and V&V methods
6. Model Application and Transition
   - Experimentation and analysis of results—include tabulated data, plots, bar graphs, histograms, pie charts, statistical analyses and other reports, etc.
   - Interpretation of model results
   - Limitations of the model and future enhancements
   - Next steps
   - Model transfer issues
7. Conclusions and Recommendations
   - About the real world system—including policy suggestions
   - About the model
   - About the modeling process
   - About the modeling tool(s) and platform used
   - Process improvement scenarios
   - Future research
8. Appendices (if necessary)
   - Supplementary model details
   - Model run output
   - Selected computer outputs, related letters, technical articles, etc.
   - Additional data analysis as needed

Table 2-10. Modeling activity work breakdown structure

Manage the Modeling Work	
Plan	Establish the objectives of the modeling product and
Plan the product	establish commitment to a specific plan for developing that
Plan the project	product.
Develop the team	Train personnel to be able to participate in the modeling process as a cohesive group.
Contract with management	Ensure management support for the descriptive modeling process. In addition, project issues and their resolutions are identified.
Model the Process	
Conduct process familiarization	Establish a modeling frame of reference by translating
Gather initial data	existing process documentation to an initial model.
Construct initial model	
Collect data	Gathering and assembling interview and other data for use
Prepare for interviews	in building the process model.
Conduct interviews	
Gather other data	
Analyze data	
Construct model	Produce and accurate and appropriate representation of the
Build model	collected interview data in a process model.
Verify model	
Review model	Allow process experts to review and validate the process model.
Documentation	Produce documentation report and presentations.

Current popular toolsets include Extend [Imagine 2006], iThink/Stella [isee 2006], Powersim [Powersim 2006] and Vensim [Ventana 2006]. Collectively, all of them are represented in the work described in this book. These tools are visual applications whereby models can be constructed by drawing them. Some also provide additional programming utilities or access to source code for custom development.

Modeling tools are continuously improving and adapting to new technologies. One of the important new directions is for distributed and networked simulations on the Internet or an intranet. Usage of the Internet has spawned a variety of distributed and collaborative simulation features. Most of the tool vendors are still improving their networking capabilities. Another improvement is for model conversion between tools. Utilities exist for transforming a model created with one tool into a format to be used in a different modeling tool.

Notations used for system dynamics/systems thinking tools are shown in Table 2-11 for the most popular toolsets. The table can be used to help understand system dynamics diagrams generated by unfamiliar tools. A user should consider price, documentation, training, support and maintenance, computer platform, and user familiarity

Table 2-11. Tool notations

	Element				
Implementation	Level	Source/Sink	Rate	Auxiliary	Information Link
Traditional manual drawing (e.g. for Dynamo[1])					
Extend[2]					
iThink/Stella[3]					
Powersim	Level	Cloud	Flow / Flow-with-rate	Auxiliary / Constant	Information link / Cloud / Delayed info-link / Initialization link
Vensim				Variable name (no symbol)	

[1]There is no tool support for diagrams in Dynamo, hence, they are usually drawn manually using traditional system dynamics notation. Newer versions may include limited diagramming capabilities.
[2]Extend allows the substitution of custom graphics for model elements.
[3]iThink diagrams are used throughout this text. Stella is the same product for academic environments.

before committing to a specific tool. Further details on tools and their vendors are provided in Appendix B.

2.14 MAJOR REFERENCES

[Forrester 1968] Forrester J. W., *Principles of Systems.* Cambridge, MA: MIT Press, 1968.

[Forrester, Senge 1980] Forrester J. W. and Senge P., "Tests for building confidence in system dynamics models," in A. Legasto et al. (Eds.), *TIMS Studies in the Management Sciences (System Dynamics),* The Netherlands: North-Holland, 1980, pp. 209–228.

[Rechtin 1991] Rechtin E., *Systems Architecting,* Englewood Cliffs, NJ: Prentice-Hall, 1991.

[Richardson, Pugh 1981] Richardson G. P. and Pugh A., *Introduction to System Dynamics Modeling with DYNAMO,* Cambridge, MA: MIT Press, 1981.

[Richmond et al. 1990] Richmond B. and others, *Ithink User's Guide and Technical Documentation,* High Performance Systems Inc., Hanover, NH, 1990.

[Sterman 2000] Sterman J., *Business Dynamics: Systems Thinking and Modeling for a Complex World,* New York: Irwin McGraw-Hill, 2000.

2.15   CHAPTER 2 SUMMARY

Creating simulation models to understand process dynamics has much in common with other types of software development. The approach described uses system dynamics as a rich, elegant technique for modeling complex dynamic systems. A main premise of the technique is that the behavior of a system over time is a result of its own structure. Another fundamental is that system elements interact through feedback loops, where a change in one variable affects other variables over time, which in turn affects the original variable. When modeling and understanding these effects, we gain leverage to improve processes by being better informed about the dynamic results of our decisions.

System dynamics treats process entities as aggregated flows over time. This assumption greatly simplifies system modeling and makes it easier to handle interconnected factors. However, discrete-event modeling and hybrid approaches also have a place in software process modeling. There are various trade-offs between the methods and system dynamics is generally better suited for macro-level studies.

General system behaviors observed in many types of processes include goal seeking behavior, exponential growth, S-shaped growth, oscillating behavior, and combined behaviors. Information smoothing may also modulate the perception of behavior (i.e., a system actor cannot always observe true, real-time conditions). Common structures are available in system dynamics that mirror real processes and cause these observed behaviors.

A top-down iterative approach to modeling will make it easier in the long run. A risk-driven approach using the WinWin Spiral life cycle works well to help structure the modeling activities and mitigate risks. One cycles through problem definition, model conceptualization, formulation, simulation, assessment, and policy analysis. Once again, the purpose is to better understand decision consequences that drives the scope of study and the subsequent modeling process.

Problem definition sets the stage for modeling. You explicitly define a purpose that addresses organizational goals and is important to other stakeholders. The degree of implementation is also addressed in terms of model form and detail, rigor used, and institutionalization of new process policies. Reference behaviors, which are plots of key variables over time, are generated during problem definition. These behaviors help to gel ideas and are used later during validation of the resulting model.

During model conceptualization the system boundary is defined and a top-level view of system elements is created. Be extremely careful in selecting the portion of reality to model so that it does not include too much or too little. Then you identify physical structures and information flows, distinguish perceived from actual information, and identify decisions made by system actors. Causal loop diagrams can be handy at this stage to portray cause and effect relationships and feedback loops. In some studies, this might be all that is necessary in order to increase understanding.

In model formulation and construction, the high-level concepts are elaborated into detailed equations. The system is described in terms of levels, rates, auxiliaries, and feedback loops. Levels (stocks) represent accumulations in a system. They can change the shape of an input over time and potentially decouple inflow and outflow rates to allow independence, and, as a result, can also induce disequilibrium behavior. A single-level system cannot oscillate, but a system with at least two levels can oscillate because one part of the system can be in disequilibrium. Choosing to model a concept as a level or not depends on if it can be perceived as a stock or accumulation over time. The snapshot test can be handy for determining this.

Rates are the flows that occur in conjunction with levels. They are not instantaneously measurable, and can only be averaged over time. No rate can control another rate without an intervening level variable. Rates may have constant, variable, additive, and/or multiplicative formulations. Rates are essential components in delays, positive feedback loops, and negative feedback loops. System information is captured in auxiliary variables to help elaborate the stock and flow structures, such as containing score-keeping information for rate decisions.

Time delays are found everywhere in processes. Common examples include first-order delays, third-order delays, and pipeline delays. Delayed outflows account for the average time that entities remain in a level and can model artifact transformations or assimilation processes. Negative feedback exhibits goal-seeking behavior and may cause system instability. Positive feedback produces a reinforcing growth or decline process.

During simulation and assessment, a model is verified to be free of defects and validated by running it under different conditions. Many aspects of structure and behavior are evaluated with a wide range of tests. First, the model is put into steady state, test inputs are used, parameter sensitivity, structural sensitivity, and robustness tests are run. You assess whether the model is suitable for its expressed purpose, its consistency with reality, and its overall utility and effectiveness for the end user.

A policy represents a decision on how processes should be performed. During policy analysis, we seek to understand the real-world impact of process changes. Similar to the wide range of tests during model validation, we experiment with changes to policy parameters and structures to assess policy validity, robustness, suitability, and feasibility. Familiarity and insight into real-world problems is critical to judge policies. Human value judgments must be made in order to understand policy trade-offs and determine the most desirable policies.

In the spirit of continuous process improvement, models should be continually rechallenged, assessed for relevancy, and refined. Upon further inspection, model shortcomings may come to light that should be addressed. It is also possible that the goals, constraints, and objectives of the organization may have changed as well as the process environment being modeled.

Quantitative modeling depends on having data, but the lack of good data should not hold up modeling efforts. Techniques are available to cope with missing data. GQM is a valuable framework for many aspects of data collection and modeling. By identifying goals and deriving relevant questions and metrics, GQM ensures that whatever you do can be mapped back to organizational goals and that you are focusing on important metrics data.

Project management of modeling and simulation projects is an important consideration. Concentrating on people, communication, and risk management are some best practices to keep in mind. Documentation is important just like for other software development and evolution projects.

2.15.1   Summary of Modeling Heuristics

Most of the following heuristics were discussed in greater detail in preceding sections. They have been identified for system dynamics modeling, but almost all of them also apply to other modeling methods. As with all guidelines, these generally apply in most situations but the modeler must always interpret them in the context at hand. Some may even conflict with each other in given situations.

Note that these heuristics do not repeat the essential mechanical steps such as "develop a reference behavior," "generate test inputs," "do sensitivity analyses," and so on. Rather, these are guidelines that help in structuring a solution.

General Modeling
   No model is perfect.
   All models are incomplete.
   A model is not reality.
   It is possible to build many different models of a single process.
   All models contain hidden assumptions.
   Continually challenge the model.
   The models are just there to help, not to make your management decisions for you.
Problem Identification
   A model is created to answer specific questions.
   Consider the audience, desired policy set, and level of implementation when defining the model purpose.
   Define the problem dynamically in terms of reference behaviors, even if hard data is missing.
   Strive for relative measures in the reference behaviors.
Model Conceptualization
   Define a clear, operational purpose of the model.
   Within the system boundary, include the parts necessary to generate the behavior of interest.
   Do not try to model the "system."
   Aggregate and abstract to the appropriate degree.
   Use a top-down iterative approach.
   KISS (keep it simple, stupid).
Model Formulation and Development
   Do not enumerate all factors at first.

Iteratively refine and slowly add relationships to model.

Normalize when possible.

Use relative measures.

Do not stray too far from a simulatable model.

Do not model in isolation; try to involve those being modeled.

Model Validation

Look for qualitative similarity on the first pass.

Alter one parameter at a time at first.

Be conscious of reality constraints.

Model validity is a relative matter.

Data Collection

Model design should not be postponed until all pertinent parameters have been accurately measured.

Communication

Use simple diagrams to communicate with others until they seek more detail.

2.16 EXERCISES

2.1. What are the model implications, in terms of sinks and sources, as model boundaries change when focusing on different software engineering activities such as requirements, design, coding, and testing?

2.2. What are the model implications, in terms of sinks and sources, as model boundaries change for progressively larger organizational entities such as project, project portfolio, department, region, and organization? You can choose your own environment or that of another specific organization.

2.3. Provide more specific examples of the general system behaviors observed in software or systems processes.

2.4. Create your own software process domain examples of a first-order delay, negative feedback, and positive feedback.

2.5. Create your own examples of each of the basic rate equation patterns in the software process domain.

2.6. Create a simple example system that demonstrates a coincident flow ("coflow").

2.7. Create a graph function. Choose an important relationship between software process factors that can be modeled with relative scales. Describe the rationale behind the endpoints and slopes.

2.8. Explain why and in what situations you would use a graph function instead of an analytic equation.

2.9. What effects does the smoothing time interval have on information smoothing?

The following three exercises should be done manually without the use of computer simulation. A graph pad is handy for sketching the curves.

2.10. (Do these manually, without a computer.) Given the system diagram below and the following:

- Simulation time is measured in months
- New personnel INIT = 60
- Experienced personnel INIT= 10

a) Identify the units for all model elements.

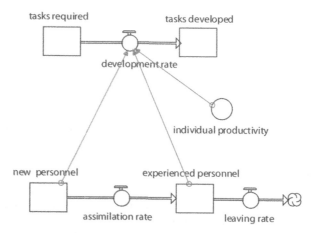

Draw the levels of new and experienced personnel from 0–10 months for the following cases. Clearly label the axes and put numbers on them, so the quantities over time can be easily read.

b) assimilation rate = 5

leaving rate = 0

c) assimilation rate = 6

leaving rate = 2

d) assimilation rate = pulse of 10 at time = 3

leaving rate = 0 for 0 < time < 5, and = 4 for 5 < time < 10

2.11. (Do this manually, without a computer.) Below is a simple hiring model, where the simulation time is measured in months. Identify the units of measurement for each entity in the model. Also sketch the output for staff level for three cases: (1) hiring delay = 0.5, (2) hiring delay = 1, and (3) hiring delay = 3. Your sketches do not have to be exact, but the three cases should be clearly delineated on the chart as best you can draw them. Assign numbers to the y-axis for the plots.

staff(t) = staff(t – dt) + (hiring_rate) * dt
INIT staff = 0
INFLOWS:
hiring_rate = (desired_staff-staff)hiring_delay
desired_staff = 1.0
hiring_delay = 1

Fill in the blank below:

This model is an example of _____ feedback.

2.12. (Do this manually, without a computer.) Below is a software adoption model, in which the simulation time is measured in months. Identify the units of measurement for each entity in the model. Then qualitatively sketch the plot of software users.

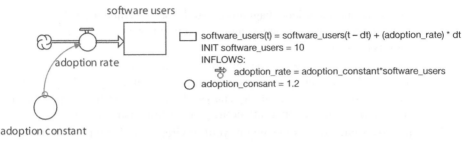

software users

adoption rate

software_users(t) = software_users(t – dt) + (adoption_rate) * dt
INIT software_users = 10
INFLOWS:
  adoption_rate = adoption_constant*software_users
adoption_consant = 1.2

adoption constant

Fill in the blank below:

This model is an example of _____ feedback.

2.13. a)   How would you test a model to determine how sensitive it is to parameters whose true values are unknown?

b)   Identify three aspects of model structure and behavior that should be resolved before such tests are performed.

2.14. Define and demonstrate the differences between exponential growth and goal-oriented growth in terms of rate equations and output graphs.

2.15. Identify a particular problem in your environment and draw causal loop diagrams of the major effects.

2.16. Choose an ongoing software process and perform the snapshot test. Document your conclusions as to what are stocks and flows.

2.17. Explain the importance of test functions in the construction of dynamic models.

2.18. Describe and give examples of three types of model sensitivity analyses.

2.19. In a well-designed model, how do you treat variables that change more slowly or change much more rapidly then the variables of primary interest in the system?

2.20. If you have never run a simulation, choose some of the provided models and begin using them to get familiar with simulation operations.

2.21. If you have never modified a simulation model, choose one or more of the provided models and make some simple changes. Rerun them to see the effect of your changes.

2.22. Create a set of concise models that produce the different general behaviors. Parameterize them so the output shapes can be experimented with.

2.23. Create a set of concise models that implement the different rate patterns, delays, and negative and positive feedback.

2.24. Undertake some of the Brooks's Law model improvements noted in the text (beware of partitioning because of its difficulties), or improve some other aspect of it. Also see the Brooks's Law model exercise in Chapter 6.

2.25. Choose any of the software process feedback examples in [Weinberg 1992] and draw causal loop diagrams to represent them.

Advanced Exercises

2.26. Elaborate the causal loop diagrams created from [Weinberg 1992] in the previous exercise into simulation models. Run experiments and document the lessons learned.

2.27. Create a simple model of your environment to evaluate the attainment of a measurable corporate goal. Does your output resemble any of the generic behaviors? Also perform sensitivity analysis by varying the process parameters. How do the different inputs affect the goal-seeking behavior curve?

2.28. Identify some policies to study in your environment that will form the basis for a simulation term project. Start the report using the documentation outline.

2.29. Identify a software process topic that will form the basis for a simulation term project. Start the report using the documentation outline.

2.30. Identify a research problem and apply GQM to determine what relevant measurements a process model should include.

2.31. Identify a software process research problem and find or develop reference behaviors for it.

2.32. Identify a major research problem that you will address beyond the scope of a course term project. Start writing down the description using the provided documentation outline or your own format.

2.33. Choose a policy addressed in one of the provided elaborate models. Use the model to go through the steps of policy analysis. Document your process and conclusions.

2.34. Model a feedback process for implementing new policies.

2.35. Choose one of the provided small-scale models and put it into steady state.

2.36. Study the Abdel-Hamid project model (or one of the other provided elaborate models), describe how to put it into steady state, and suggest validation tests.

2.37. Draw a rough reference behavior for one or more of the following trends for a given environment. Do not refer to any source except your own insight. Qualify the context of your graph. Is the behavior for the last, current, or a hypothetical project? Does it represent an organizational trend for multiple projects?
   • Requirements changes over time
   • Estimated size over time
   • Staffing profile over time
   • Defect fixing cost over time
   • Defect density over time

- Productivity over time
- Schedule performance index (SPI)
- Cost performance index (CPI)

The following refer to multiproject organizational trends:

- % reuse over time
- % COTS over time
- Defect detection efficiency over time
- Estimation quality factor over time

2.38. In a sort of reverse Brooks's Law, model the effect of extra work required when someone leaves a project. There is often additional coordination work needed to sort out the lost person's tasks. Since there are fewer workers and the project has slowed down, management may increase the pressure. This may then lead to others leaving.

2.39. Choose one or more of the following general process/product measures, perform the necessary research and analysis to assign them reasonable numeric values to use in a model (or for the purpose of evaluating a model that calculates them). Either use average values, define a reasonable range, or develop a factor relationship (e.g., average productivity as a function of size). Consider the metrics within the context of a particular organization or a defined meta-group (e.g. a country or type of company), and make them process specific. For example, productivity can be defined as overall productivity, design productivity, testing productivity, and so on.

Qualify your values, describe your analysis, and optionally show the background data used. Is the measurement context for your last, current, or next project? An organizational average? For an upcoming model of your process?

- Productivity
- Defect density
- Defect detection efficiency (yield)
- Defect finding and fixing effort
- % of effort on rework
- Assimilation delay
- Hiring delay
- Learning curve rate

- % effort on requirements
- % effort on design
- % effort on programming
- % effort on testing
- % effort on system engineering
- % effort on quality assurance
- % effort on peer reviews
- % effort on software process improvement
- % effort on transition activities

- Cost drivers from COCOMO II or other software cost model
- Defect prediction factors from a defect model
- % requirements evolution and volatility
- % reuse
- % COTS
- % modification
- Financial overhead percentage
- Other measures relevant to your concerns

2.40. Go through each of the validation tests and assess the Brooks's Law model. Create a validation report using the test matrix as an outline. You will need to create and run your own tests.

2.41. Begin a study to compare different software process life cycles, such as the iterative versus the waterfall. Chapter 1 provides a nominal progress reference behavior for that comparison. Other possibilities include a comparison of agile methods, transformational approaches (e.g., fourth-generation languages), or any defined life cycle being used. Examine the different processes in terms of what accumulates and flows, and identify structural differences in their main chains. When devising a comparison model, strive to keep all project factors equal except for the life-cycle process. It is also suggested to compare only two life cycles at a time to simplify the project. Branch out into more life cycles after initial success with comparing two.

2.42. Take one or more of the modeling risks and expand on their description(s) and specifics as to how the mitigation activities might work or not. Or identify your own modeling risk(s) and develop detailed mitigation plans.

2.43. Identify more modeling heuristics; explain their usage and significance.

2.44. Take a modeling heuristic and study it in more detail. Examine and write up its nuances. Provide detailed rationale for specific situations in which it is applicable, or counterconditions in which it may not be. Modify the heuristic accordingly for different contexts.

MODEL STRUCTURES AND BEHAVIORS FOR SOFTWARE PROCESSES

3.1 INTRODUCTION

This chapter presents model structures for software processes starting with a review of elemental components, incorporating them into basic flow structures and building up to larger infrastructures. The structures and their behaviors are process patterns that frequently occur. The recurring structures are model "building blocks" that can be reused. They provide a framework for understanding, modifying, and creating system dynamics models regardless of modeling experience. With access to reusable formulations that have been repeatedly proven, previous work can be understood easier and the structures incorporated into new models with minimal modification.

Below is an overview of terminology related to model structures and behavior:

- *Elements* are the smallest individual pieces in a system dynamics model: levels, rates, sources/sinks, auxiliaries, and feedback connections.
- *Generic flow processes* are small microstructures and their variations comprised of a few elements, and are sometimes called *modeling molecules* [Hines 2000]. They are the building blocks, or substructures from which larger structures are created and usually contain approximately two to five elements. They produce characteristic behaviors.
- *Infrastructures* refer to larger structures that are composed of several microstructures, typically producing more complex behaviors.

Software Process Dynamics. By Raymond J. Madachy
Copyright © 2008 the Institute of Electrical and Electronics Engineers, Inc.

- *Flow chains* are infrastructures consisting of a sequence of levels and rates (stocks and flows) that often form a backbone of a model portion. They house the process entities that flow and accumulate over time, and have information connections to other model components through the rates.

Not discussed explicitly in this chapter are *archetypes*. They present lessons learned from dynamic systems with specific structures that produce characteristic modes of behavior. The structures and their resultant dynamic behaviors are also called patterns. Whereas molecules and larger structures are the model building blocks, archetypes interpret the generic structures and draw dynamic lessons from them. Senge discusses organizational archetypes based on simple causal loop diagrams in *The Fifth Discipline* [Senge 1990].

An object-oriented software framework is convenient for understanding the model building blocks and their inheritance relationships described in this chapter. Consider a class or object to be a collection of model elements wired in a way that produces characteristic behavior. Figure 3.1 shows the model structures in a class hierarchy with inheritance. Object instances of these generic classes are the specific structures used for software process modeling (e.g., software artifact flows, project management policies, personnel chains, etc.).

The specific structures and their respective dynamic behaviors are the inherited attributes and operations (likened to services or methods). The hierarchy in Figure 3.1 also shows multiple inheritance since some infrastructures combine structure and behavior from multiple generic classes. Not shown are the lower levels of the hierarchy consisting of specific software process instances that all inherit from this tree.

The simplest system is the rate and level combination, whereby the level accumulates the net flow rate (via integration over time). It can be considered the super class.

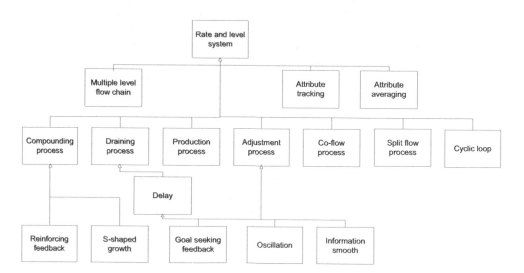

Figure 3.1. Class hierarchy for model structures.

The next level of structures include the generic flow processes, which are all slight variants on the rate and level system. Each of them adds some structure and produces unique characteristic behavior. For example, the compounding process adds a feedback loop from the level to the rate with an auxiliary variable that sets the rate of growth. The new behavior derived from this structure is an exponential growth pattern.

This hierarchy only includes systems explicitly containing rates and levels. There are also structures using auxiliary variables instead of levels that can produce similar dynamics. One example is the adjustment process to reach a goal that could operate without levels. These instances will be identified in their respective sections, and there are also some stand-alone infrastructures presented without levels at all. Normally, these structures would be enhanced with levels and rates in full models. Only the simplest of software process models would not contain any levels and would be of very limited use in assessing dynamic behavior.

Simulation toolsets and this book provide modeling molecules, infrastructures, and whole models that can be reused and modified. The modeler is encouraged to leverage these opportunities, as applicable, for potentially quicker development. For more on how the object-oriented modeling concept can be extended and automated for modelers, see the exercises at the end of this chapter and further discussion in Chapter 7.

A related technique is *metamodeling* [Barros et al. 2006a], which is a domain-specific methodology for creating software process structures. They are system dynamics extensions providing a high-level representation of application domain models for model developers. See [Barros et al. 2006b] for examples of metamodels created specifically for software process modeling, and the annotated bibliography for more references.

Next in this chapter is a review of the basic model elements. Then generic flows and infrastructures will be described. Specific structures for software process models and some behavioral examples will be presented. Virtually all of the structures are derived from one or more generic structures. Each structure will be presented with a diagram, summary of critical equations, and optionally behavioral output if it is new or unique.

3.2 MODEL ELEMENTS

The basic elements of system dynamics models previously described in Chapters 1 and 2 are levels, flows, sources/sinks, auxiliaries, and connectors. These are briefly reviewed below with lists of sample instantiations for software processes.

3.2.1 Levels (Stocks)

Levels are the state variables representing system accumulations. Typical state variables are software work artifacts, defect levels, personnel levels, or effort expenditure. Examples of software process level instances include:

- Work artifacts like tasks, objects, requirements, design, lines of code, test procedures, reuse library components, or documentation pages—these can be new, reused, planned, actual, and so on. Sublevels like high-level design could be differentiated from low-level design.

- Defect levels—these can be per phase, activity, severity, priority or other discriminators. Note that the term "error" is sometimes used in models instead of defect; the terms are interchangeable unless clarified otherwise for a particular application.
- Personnel levels—often segregated into different experience or knowledge pools (e.g., junior and senior engineers)
- Effort and cost expenditures
- Schedule dates
- Personnel attributes such as motivation, staff exhaustion, or burnout levels
- Process maturity
- Key process areas
- Process changes
- Others

Other accumulations include financial and other business measures for a project (or ongoing organizational process). Relevant levels may include:

- Revenue
- Cumulative sales
- Market share
- Customers
- Orders
- Inventory
- Others

However, the value of software does not always reduce to monetary-related figures. In some instances, the value is derived from other measures such as in military systems where threat deterrence or strike capability is desired. Product value attributes such as quality, dependability, reliability, security, and privacy come into play. Thus, there are many more potential level instances that may play a part in value-based software engineering applications.

If one considers what tangible level items can be actually counted in a software process, levels are naturally aligned with artifacts available in files, libraries, databases, controlled repositories, and so on. Applying the snapshot test from Chapter 2 would lead to the identification of these artifact collections as levels. A process that employs configured baselines for holding requirements, design, code, and so on provides low-hanging fruit (process and project data) for model calibration and validation. Similarly, a trouble report database provides time trends on the levels of found defects. Thus, standard software metrics practices conveniently support system dynamics modeling. Refer to the GQM discussions in Chapter 2 to better align the metrics and modeling processes.

3.2.1.1 *Sources and Sinks*

Recall that sources and sinks represent levels or accumulations outside the boundary of the modeled system. Sources are infinite supplies of entities and sinks are repositories for entities leaving the model boundary. Typical examples of software process sources could be requirements originating externally or outsourced hiring pools. Sinks could represent delivered software leaving the process boundary or personnel attrition repositories for those leaving the organization. More examples include:

- Sources of requirements or change requests (product and process)
- Software delivered to customers and the market in general
- Software artifacts handed off to other organizations for integration or further development
- Employee hiring sources and attrition sinks
- Others

3.2.2 Rates (Flows)

Rates in the software process are necessarily tied to the levels. Levels do not change unless there are flow rates associated with them. Each of the level instances previously identified would have corresponding inflow and outflow rates. Their units are their corresponding level unit divided by time. A short list of examples include:

- Software productivity rate
- Software change rate
- Requirements evolution
- Defect generation
- Personnel hiring and deallocation
- Learning rate
- Process change rate
- Perception change
- Financial burn rate
- Others

3.2.3 Auxiliaries

Auxiliaries describe relationships between variables and often represent "score-keeping" measures. Examples include communication overhead as a function of people, or tracking measures such as progress (percent of job completion), percent of tasks in certain states, calculated defect density, other ratios, or percentages used as independent variables in dynamic relationships. Example variables include:

- Overhead functions
- Percent of job completion

- Quantitative goals or planned values
- Constants like average delay times
- Defect density
- Smoothed averages
- Others

3.2.4   Connectors and Feedback Loops

Information linkages can be used for many different purposes in a software process model. They are needed to connect rates to levels and auxiliaries. They are used to set the rates and provide inputs for decision making. Rates and decision functions, as control mechanisms, often require feedback connectors from other variables (usually levels or auxiliaries) for decision making. Examples of such information include:

- Progress and status information for decision making
- Knowledge of defect levels to allocate rework resources
- Conditions and pressures for adjusting processes
- Linking process parameters to rates and other variables (e.g., available resources and productivity to calculate the development rate)
- Others

Feedback in the software process can be in various forms across different boundaries. Learning loops, project artifacts, informal hall meetings, peer review reports, project status metrics, meetings and their reports, customer calls, newsletters, outside publications, and so on can provide constructive or destructive feedback opportunities. The feedback can be within projects, between projects, between organizations, and with other various communities.

3.3   GENERIC FLOW PROCESSES

Generic flow processes are the smallest essential structures based on a rate/level system that model common situations and produce characteristic behaviors. They consist of levels, flows, sources/sinks, auxiliaries, and, sometimes, feedback loops. Most of the generic processes in this section were previously introduced and some were shown as examples in Chapter 2. Each generic process can be used for multiple types of applications.

This section highlights the elemental structures and basic equations for each generic process. They are elaborated with specific details and integrated with other structures during model development. The inflow and outflow rates in the simplified equations represent summary flows when there are more than one inflow or outflow.

3.3.1   Rate and Level System

The simple rate and level system (also called stock and flow) is shown in Figure 3.2 and was first introduced in Chapter 2. It is a flow process from which all of the prima-

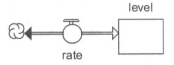

Figure 3.2. Rate and level system.

ry structures are derived. This system has a single level and a bidirectional flow that can fill or drain the level. It can be considered a super class for subsequent structures in this chapter, because each one builds on top of this basic structure with additional detail and characteristic behavior.

This system can also be represented with separate inflows and outflows, and very frequently in a modeling application it is best to consider the flows separately. However, they can always be algebraically combined into a single net flow for the simplest representation and, thus, the generic structure here is shown with a single flow.

The equations for this system are the standard-level integration equations automatically produced by the simulation software when the level and rate are laid down. As a review, the generated equation that applies for any such level is the following:

$$\text{level(time)} = \text{level(time} - dt) + \text{rate} \cdot dt$$

When there are separate inflows and outflows the equation becomes

$$\text{level(time)} = \text{level(time} - dt) + (\text{inflow rate} - \text{outflow rate}) \cdot dt$$

The inflow and outflow rates in the above equation represent summary flows if there are more than one inflow or outflow. No specific behavior is produced except that that level accumulates the net flow over time. The behavior of interest comes after specifying the details of the rate equation(s) and potential connections to other model components as shown in the rest of the generic flow processes.

3.3.2 Flow Chain with Multiple Rates and Levels

The single rate and level system can be expanded into a flow chain incorporating multiple levels and rates. It can be used to model a process that accumulates at several points instead of one, and is also called a cascaded level system. Figure 3.3 shows an example. The levels and rates always alternate. One level's outflow is the inflow to an-

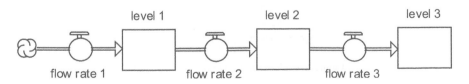

Figure 3.3. Flow chain.

other level, and so on down the chain. Each additional level in a system requires at least one more rate to be added accordingly between successive levels. The number of contained levels determines the order of a system. The dynamics get far more complex as the system order increases.

The end of a multiple level flow chain may also empty into a sink instead of having an end accumulation, and each end flow can also be bidirectional. A generic flow chain within itself does not produce characteristic behavior, like the single rate and level system. It requires that other structures and relationships be specified first.

The flow chain is a primary infrastructure for software process models. Frequently, it is a core structure laid down before elaborating detailed model relationships. Subsequent sections will show specific flow chains and their variants for software artifacts, personnel, defects, and so on.

Multiple levels and rates can be in conservative or nonconservative chains. Flow chains are normally conservative, such as in Figure 3.3, whereby the flow is conserved within directly connected rates and levels in a single chain. There are also nonconserved flows with separate but connected chains. These may be more appropriate at times and will be described with examples for specific software process chains in later sections.

3.3.3 Compounding Process

The compounding structure is a rate and level system with a feedback loop from the level to an input flow, and an auxiliary variable representing the fractional amount of growth per period, as in Figure 3.4. A compounding process produces positive feedback and exponential growth in the level as previously described in Chapter 2. The growth feeds upon itself. Modeling applications include user bases, market dynamics, software entropy, cost-to-fix trends, interest compounding, social communication patterns (e.g., rumors, panic), and so on. The growth fraction need not be constant and can vary over time. It can become a function of other parameters. When growth declines instead of increasing continuously, an overshoot and collapse or S-shaped growth model can be employed with additional structure (see subsequent sections).

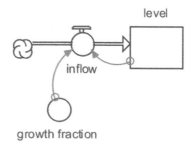

Figure 3.4. Compounding process. Equation:

inflow = level · growth fraction

3.3.4 Draining Process

Draining can be represented similarly as the compounding process, except the feedback from the level is to an outflow rate and the auxiliary variable indicates how much is drained in the level, as in Figure 3.5. The variable may denote the fractional amount drained per period or it might represent a delay time, whereby the equation divides the level by the delay (see Section 3.4.3 on delays). Both representations produce the same behavior.

Draining is a common process that underlies delays and exponential decays. Delayed outflows and various orders of delays were shown in Chapter 2. In exponential decay, the draining fraction is often interpreted as a time constant that the level is divided by. Personnel attrition, promotion through levels, software product retirement, skill loss, and other trends can be modeled as draining processes.

3.3.5 Production Process

A production process represents work being produced at a rate equal to the number of applied resources multiplied by the resource productivity. Figure 3.6 shows the inflow to a level that represents production dependent on another level in an external flow chain representing a resource. Sometimes, the external resource is modeled with an auxiliary variable or fixed constant instead of a level. This software production infrastructure was introduced in Chapter 2. It can also be used for production of other assets such as revenue generation as a function of sales or several others.

3.3.6 Adjustment Process

An adjustment process is an approach to equilibrium. The structure for it contains a goal variable, a rate, level, and adjusting parameter, as in Figure 3.7. The structure models the closing of a gap between the goal and level. The change is more rapid at first and slows down as the gap decreases. The inflow is adjusted to meet the target goal, and the fractional amount of periodic adjustment is modeled with a constant (or possibly a variable).

The adjusting parameter may represent a fraction to be adjusted per time period (as in the figure) or it might represent an adjustment delay time. The only difference is that

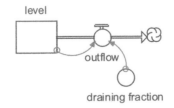

Figure 3.5. Draining process. Equation:

outflow = level · draining fraction

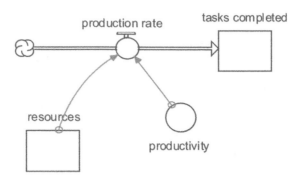

Figure 3.6. Production process. Equation:

production rate = resources · productivity

in the rate equation the goal gap is multiplied by an adjustment fraction or it is divided by an adjustment delay time.

This basic structure is at the heart of many policies and other behaviors. It can be used to represent goal-seeking behavior such as hiring and other goal-seeking negative feedback introduced in Chapter 2. The time constant in negative feedback is the reciprocal of the adjustment fraction (similar to the reciprocal of the draining process fraction parameter becoming the time constant for exponential decay). The structures can also model perceptions of quantities such as progress, quality, or reputation. The time constant (adjustment fraction reciprocal) represents the information delay in forming the perception.

Note that the most fundamental adjustment structure to close a goal gap does not require a level as in the figure. The current value of what is being controlled to meet a goal can be another variable instead of a level.

3.3.7 Coflow Process

A Coflow is a shortened name for a coincident flow, a flow that occurs simultaneously through a type of slave relationship. The coflow process has a flow rate synchronized

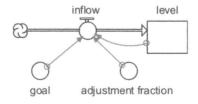

Figure 3.7. Adjustment process. Equation:

inflow = (goal – level) · adjustment fraction

or

inflow = (goal – level)/adjustment delay time

with another host flow rate, and normally has a conversion parameter between them as shown in Figure 3.8. This process can model the coflows of software artifacts and defects. It can also be used for personnel applications such as learning or frustration, resource tracking such as effort expenditure, or tracking revenue as a function of sales.

3.3.8 Split Flow Process

The split flow process in Figure 3.9 represents a flow being divided into multiple subflows or disaggregated streams. It contains an input level, more than one output flow, and typically has another variable to determine the split portions. It is also possible that the split fractions may be otherwise embedded in the rate equations.

The outflows may be modeled as delays (not shown in this figure) or they may be functions of other rates and variables. The operative equations must conserve the entire flow. Sometimes, the split flows can start from external sources instead of the original input level. Applications include defect detection chains to differentiate found versus escaped defects (i.e., defect filters), or personnel flows to model dynamic project resource allocation at given organizational levels.

3.3.9 Cyclic Loop

A cyclic loop representing entities flowing back through a loop is shown in Figure 3.10. The difference from nonclosed chains is that a portion of flow goes back into an originating level. The rate determining the amount of entities flowing back can take on any form, but must not violate flow physics, such as making the level go negative. This structure is appropriate to represent iterative software development processes, artifact rework, software evolution, and other phenomena.

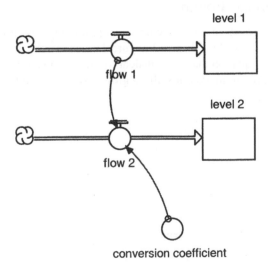

Figure 3.8. Coflow process. Equation:

flow 2 = flow 1 · conversion coefficient

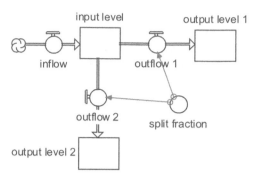

Figure 3.9. Split flow process. Equation:

outflow $1 = f$(split fraction)

outflow $2 = f(1 -$ split fraction)

3.4   INFRASTRUCTURES AND BEHAVIORS

The infrastructures in this section are based on one or more of the generic flow types with additional structural details. The additional structure typically leads to characteristic dynamic behaviors. A few of the structures herein do not cause specific dynamic behaviors, but instead are used for intermediate calculations, converters, or instrumentation of some kind. This section also builds on the introduction to general system behaviors from Chapter 2 and provides some software process examples.

3.4.1   Exponential Growth

Growth structures are based on the generic compounding flow process. Exponential growth was also introduced in Chapter 2. Figure 3.11 shows the exponential growth infrastructure and the equation that is equivalent to the compounding process. Exponential growth may represent market or staffing growth (up to a point usually representing

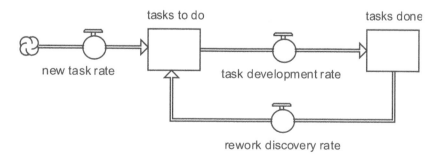

Figure 3.10. Cyclic loop process. The backflow rate formula has no special restrictions.

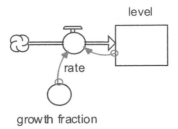

Figure 3.11. Exponential growth infrastructure. Equation:

rate = level · growth fraction

saturation), software entropy, the steep rise of user populations, Internet traffic, defect fixing costs over time, computer virus infection levels, and so on.

As an example, exponential growth can model the user base of new innovative programs. The rate of new users depends on word-of-mouth reports from current users, the Internet, and other media channels. As the user base increases, so does the word-of-mouth and other communication of the new software capabilities. The amount of new users keeps building and the cycle continues. This was observed with the debuts of Web browsers and peer-to-peer file sharing programs.

Generally there are limits to growth. A system starts out with exponential growth and normally levels out. This is seen in the sales growth of a software product that early on shoots off like a rocket, but eventually stagnates due to satisfied market demand, competition, or declining product quality. The limits to growth for a user base are the available people in a population. For instance, exponential growth of Internet users has slowed in the United States but is still rising in less developed countries. An S-curve is a good representation of exponential growth leveling out. After the following examples of exponential growth, S-curves are discussed in the next section, 3.4.2.

3.4.1.1 Example: Exponential Growth in Cost to Fix

The structure in Figure 3.12 models exponentially increasing cost to fix a defect (or, similarly, the cost to incorporate a requirements change) later in a project lifecycle. It uses a relative measure of cost that starts at unity. The growth fraction used for the output in Figure 3.13 is 85% per year. The same structure can be used to model software entropy growth over time, where entropy is also a dimensionless ratio parameter.

3.4.2 S-shaped Growth and S-Curves

An S-shaped growth structure contains at least one level and provisions for a dynamic trend that rises and another that falls. There are various representations because S-curves may result from several types of process structures representing the rise and fall trends. The structure in Figure 3.14 contains elements of both the compounding process and draining process, for example. It does not necessarily have to contain both

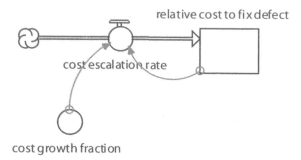

Figure 3.12. Cost-to-fix exponential growth structure.

of these structures, but there must be some opposing trends in the model to account for both the growth and declining portions of the S-curve dynamics. Frequently, there is gap closing that declines over time.

Sigmoidal curves are the result of growth that starts out small, increases, and then decreases again. This is reflected in its shape, which is flatter at the beginning and ends, and steeper in the middle. Frequently, there is a saturation effect in the system that eventually limits the growth rate. This may model technology adoption, staffing and resource usage dynamics, progress, knowledge diffusion, production functions over time, and so on.

An S-curve is seen in the graphic display of a quantity like progress or cumulative effort plotted against time that is S-shaped. S-shaped progress curves are often seen on

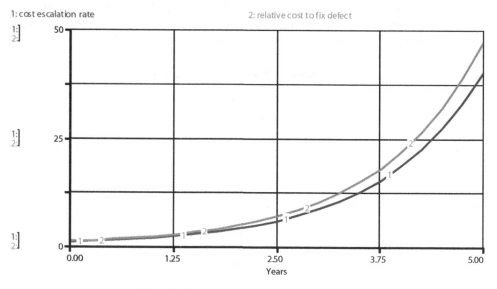

Figure 3.13. Exponential cost-to-fix behavior.

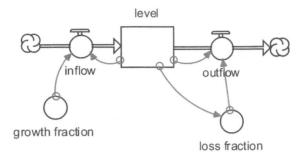

Figure 3.14. S-shaped growth infrastructure. Equations:

inflow = level · growth fraction

outflow = level · loss fraction

loss fraction = graph(level)

projects because cumulative progress starts out slowly, the slope increases as momentum gains, then work tapers off. The cumulative quantity starts slowly, accelerates, and then tails off. See the Rayleigh curve example in Section 3.4.10 that produces an S-curve for cumulative effort expenditure.

S-curves are also observed in technology adoption and sales growth. The ROI of technology adoption is also S-shaped, whether plotted as a time-based return or as a production function that relates ROI to investment. See the exercise in this chapter for technology adoption.

S-curves are also seen in other types of software phenomena. For example, a new computer virus often infects computers according to an S-curve shape. The number of infected computers is small at first, and the rate increases exponentially until steps are taken to eliminate its propagation (or it reaches a saturation point). Applications in Chapters 4–6 show many examples of S-curves in cumulative effort, progress, sales growth, and other quantities.

3.4.2.1 *Example: Knowledge Diffusion*

The model in Figure 3.15 accounts for new knowledge transfer across an organization. It is a variant of the previous S-curve structure with two levels and a single rate that embodies growth and decline processes. It employs a word-of-mouth factor to represent the fractional growth, and a gap representing how many people are left to learn. The diminishing gap models saturation. The S-curve trends are shown in Figure 3.16. The infusion rate peaks at the steepest portion of the cumulative S-curve.

3.4.3 Delays

Delays are based on the generic draining process. Time delays were introduced in Chapter 2 as being present in countless types of systems. Figure 3.17 shows a simple

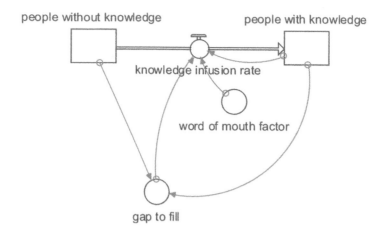

Figure 3.15. Knowledge diffusion structure. Equations:

knowledge infusion rate = (word-of-mouth factor · people with knowledge) · gap to fill

gap to fill = (people with knowledge + people without knowledge) − people with knowledge

word of mouth factor = 0.02

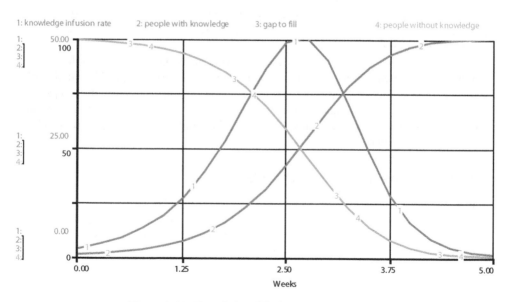

Figure 3.16. Knowledge diffusion S-curve behavior.

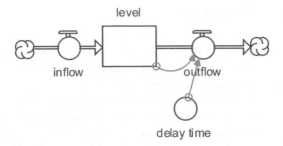

Figure 3.17. Delay structure. Equation:

outflow = level/delay time

delay structure. Hiring delays are one such common phenomenon in software development. A personnel requisition does not result in the immediate coming onboard of a new hire. There are often delays of weeks or months that should be accounted for (see Chapter 4 for suggested values). There are inherent delays in process data used for decision making, and distorted signals might be used. For example a project monitoring system that examines test reports on a monthly basis could miss an important problem spike early in the month, and visibility would come too late to bring the project back on track. Resource limitations can also induce large lags.

Other delays in development could occur at any manual step, including problem resolution, change approvals, signature cycles (the delay time is said to increase exponentially by 2^n, where n is the number of required signatures), and peer review artifact routing and handoffs. Even the existence of social networks within companies introduces delays, distorted signals, and even dropped information. Some employees act as bottlenecks of information, often knowingly for personal gain, whereas others willingly communicate vital information. Reorganizations and employee attrition also impact information transfer delays.

Communication delay also depends on the number of people. It takes much longer to disseminate information on large teams compared to small teams. This could have a profound impact on project startup, since the vision takes much longer to spread on a large team.

Overcorrection can result from excessive time delays in feedback loops and trying to fix a discrepancy between a goal and the apparent system state. Sometimes, test results or other crucial software assessment feedback comes very late, and often causes unnecessary and expensive rework.

At a detailed level, delays even exhibit seasonal behavior. For example, work is often left unattended on desks during peak vacation months. The month of December is typically a low-production month with reduced communication in many environments, as people take more slack time tending to their holiday plans. These seasonal effects are not usually modeled, but might be very important in some industries (e.g., a model for FedEx accounts for its annual December spike in IT work related to holiday shipping [Williford, Chang 1999]).

3.4.3.1 Example: Hiring Delay

Delays associated with hiring (or firing) are an aggregate of lags including realizing that a different number of people are needed, communicating the need, authorizing the hire, advertising and interviewing for positions, and bringing them on board. Then there are the delays associated with coming up to speed.

A first-order delay is shown in Figure 3.18 using personnel hiring as an example. The average hiring delay represents the time that a personnel requisition remains open before a new hire comes onboard. This example models a project that needs to ramp up from 0 to 10 people, with an average hiring delay of two months. This also entails balancing, or negative feedback, where the system is trying to reach the goal of the desired staffing level.

3.4.3.2 Exponential Decay

Exponential decay results when the outflow constant represents a time constant from a level that has no inflows. The decay declines exponentially toward zero. Both the level and outflow exhibit the trends. An old batch of defects that needs to be worked off is an example situation of decay dynamics. See Figure 3.20 for the structure and equation. It uses the same formula type as for delayed outflow. The graph of this system is a mirror of exponential growth that declines rapidly at first and slowly reaches zero.

Knowledge of time constant phenomena can be useful for estimating constants from real data, such as inferring values from tables or graphs. There are several interpretations of the time constant:

- The average lifetime of an item in a level
- An exponential time constant representing a decay pattern
- The time it would take to deplete a level if the initial outflow rate were constant

The time constant may represent things like the average time to fix a defect, delivery delay, average product lifetime, a reciprocal interest rate, and so on.

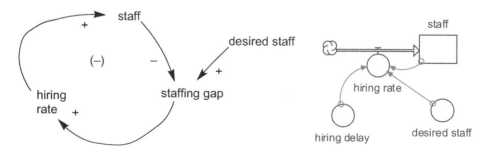

Figure 3.18. Goal-seeking hiring delay structure. Equation:

hiring rate = (desired staff – staff)/hiring delay

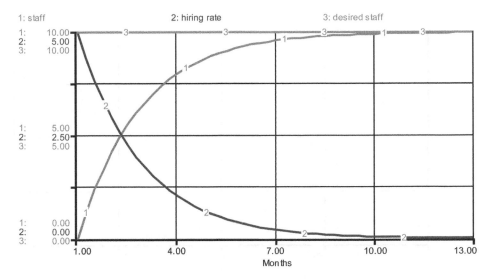

Figure 3.19. First-order hiring delay behavior.

3.4.3.3 *Higher-Order (Cascaded) Delays*

A higher-order delay behaves like a connected series of first-order delays. For example, a third-order delay can be visualized as the fluid mechanics of three water tanks in series. The first one flows into the second that flows into the third that empties into a sink. The first tank starts out full and the others empty when all the valves are opened. The dynamic level of the first tank is a first-order delay, the second tank level exhibits a second-order delay, and the third tank shows a third-order delay as they empty out.

Figure 3.21 shows the first-, second-, third-, and infinite-order delay responses to a pulse input, and Figure 3.22 shows the responses to a step input. The signals are applied at time = 1 day, and the delays are all 10 days. Figure 3.23 summarizes these delays in a generalized format.

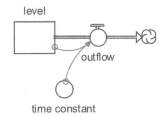

Figure 3.20. Exponential decay. Equation:

rate = level/time constant

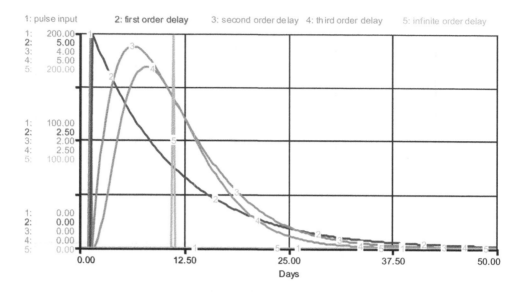

Figure 3.21. Delay responses to impulse.

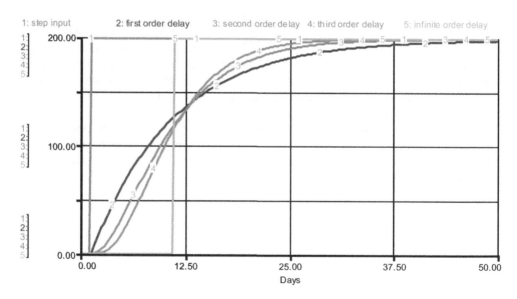

Figure 3.22. Delay responses to step input.

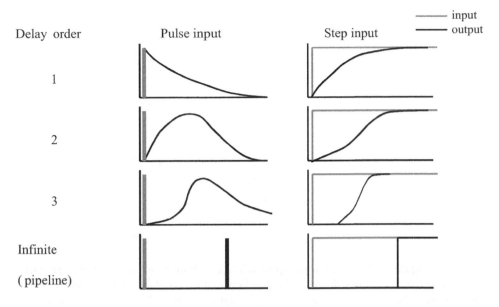

Figure 3.23. Delay summary.

Note that an infinite-order delay (pipeline) replicates the input signal (here a fortieth-order delay was sufficient for demonstration purposes). It is called a pipeline delay because it reproduces the input signal but is shifted by the delay time. Information delays are not conservative like material delays.

In most situations, a first- or third-order delay is sufficient to model real processes. A third-order delay is often quite suitable for many processes, and delays beyond the third order are hardly ever used. For example, note that the third-order delay response looks like a Rayleigh curve. The staffing curve with a characteristic Rayleigh shape can be considered the system response to a pulse representing the beginning of a project (the "turn-on" signal or the allocated batch of funds that commences a project).

A cascaded delay is a flow chain with delay structures between the levels, such as in Figure 3.24. It is sometimes called an aging chain. It drains an initial level with a chain such that the final outflow appears different depending on the number of intervening delays (see Figure 3.21). With more levels, the outflow will be concentrated in the peak. Normally, having more than three levels in a cascaded delay will not dramatically change the resulting dynamics. This structure is frequently used to represent a workforce gaining experience.

3.4.4 Balancing Feedback

Balancing feedback (also called negative feedback) occurs when a system is trying to attain a goal, as introduced in Chapter 2. The basic structure and equation are repro-

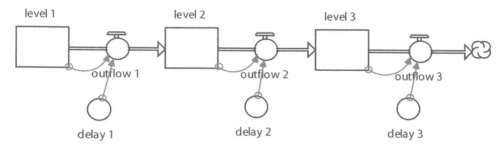

Figure 3.24. Cascaded delay (third order). Equations:

outflow 1 = level 1/delay 1

outflow 2 = level 2/delay 2

outflow 3 = level 3/delay 3

duced in Figure 3.25. It is a simple approach to equilibrium wherein the change starts rapidly at first and slows down as the gap between the goal and actual state decreases. Figure 3.26 shows the response for a positive goal and Figure 3.27 for a zero goal.

Balancing feedback could represent hiring increases. A simple example of balancing feedback is the classic case of hiring against a desired staff level. See the example in Section 3.4.3.1 for a hiring adjustment process, which is also a first-order delay system. Balancing feedback is also a good trend for residual defect levels during testing, when defects are found and fixed; in this case, the goal is zero instead of a positive quantity.

There are different orders of negative feedback and sometimes it exhibits instability. The examples so far show first-order negative feedback. Figure 3.28 shows a notional second-order system response with oscillations. The oscillating behavior may start out with exponential growth and level out. We next discuss some models that produce oscillation.

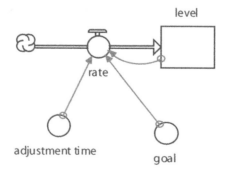

Figure 3.25. Balancing feedback structure. Equation:

rate = (goal − level)/adjustment time

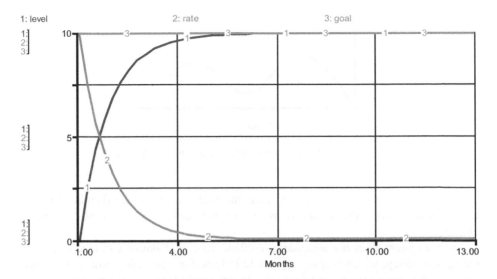

Figure 3.26. Goal-seeking balancing feedback (positive goal).

3.4.5 Oscillation

Oscillating behavior may result when there are at least two levels in a system. A system cannot oscillate otherwise. A generic infrastructure for oscillation is shown in Figure 3.29. The rate 1 and rate 2 factors are aggregates that may represent multiple factors. Normally, there is a parameter for a target goal that the system is trying to reach,

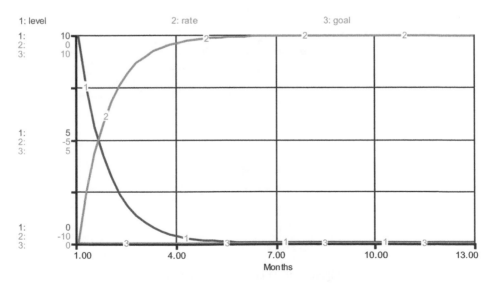

Figure 3.27. Goal-seeking balancing feedback (zero goal).

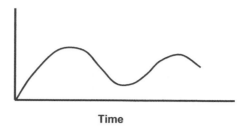

Time

Figure 3.28. Second-order balancing feedback response.

and the system is unstable as it tries to attain the goal. Unsynchronized and/or long delays frequently cause the instability as the gap between actual and desired is being
closed.

Such a system does not necessarily oscillate forever. Control can take over with
changes in policy, which may or may not be reflected in a modified process structure.
For example, there may be instability due to iteratively increasing demands, so management has to descope the demands. The oscillations will dampen and the system
eventually level out when control takes over.

There are many different forms that the equations can take. Examples related to
software production and hiring are shown below with their equations.

3.4.5.1   Example: Oscillating Personnel Systems

Instability may result when demand and resources to fill the demand are not synchronized. Figure 3.30 shows a simplified structure to model oscillating production and
hiring trends. Figure 3.31 shows an oscillating system with more detail, demonstrating

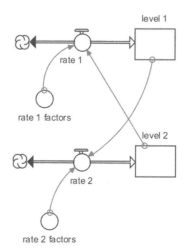

Figure 3.29. Oscillating infrastructure.

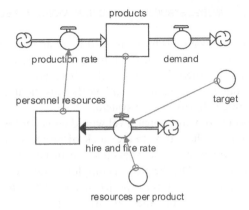

Figure 3.30. Oscillating production and hiring—simplified. Equation:

hire and fire rate = (target – products) · resources per product

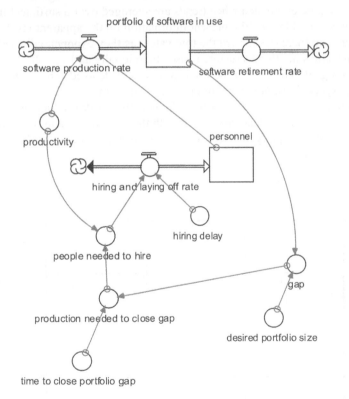

Figure 3.31. Oscillating production and hiring. Equations:

software production rate = personnel · productivity

hiring and laying off rate = people needed to hire/hiring delay

production needed to close gap = gap/time to close portfolio gap

people needed to hire = production needed to close gap/productivity

179

hiring instability. An organization is trying to staff to an appropriate level to meet current demands for creating software to be used. If the gap for new software becomes too large, then new hiring is called for. Conversely, there are times when there is not enough work to go around and organizational layoffs must be undertaken. Figure 3.32 shows resulting dynamic behavior for the system.

A similar system at the organizational level would consider the number of software projects being undertaken. The inflow to the stock of projects would be the new project rate representing the approval and/or acquisition of new projects chartered to be undertaken. The outflow would be the project completion rate. Unstable oscillating behavior could result from trying to staff the projects. This chain could also be connected to the one in Figure 3.31 representing the software itself.

3.4.6 Smoothing

Information smoothing was introduced in Chapter 2 as an averaging over time. Random spikes will be eliminated when trends are averaged over a sufficient time period. The smoothed variables could represent information on the apparent level of a system as understanding increases toward the true value, as they exponentially seek the input signal. A generic smoothing structure is used to gradually and smoothly move a quantity toward a goal. Thus, it can be used to represent delayed information, perceived quantities, expectations, or general information smoothing.

Smoothing can be modeled as a first-order negative feedback loop as shown in Figure 3.33. There is a time delay associated with the smoothing, and the change toward the final value starts rapidly and decreases as the discrepancy narrows between the present and final values.

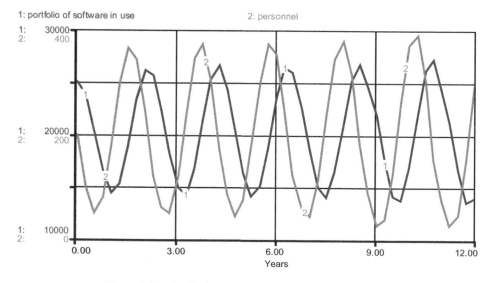

Figure 3.32. Oscillating portfolio and personnel dynamics.

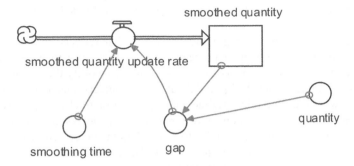

Figure 3.33. Information smoothing structure. Equations:

smoothed quantity update rate = gap/smoothing time

gap = quantity – smoothed quantity

The smoothed quantity update rate closes the gap over time. The gap is the difference between a goal and the smoothed quantity. There are performance trade-offs with the choice of smoothing interval. A long interval produces a smoother signal but with a delay. A very short interval reduces the information delay, but if too short it will just mirror the original signal with all the fluctuations.

3.4.6.1 Example: Perceived Quality

An example structure for information smoothing is shown in Figure 3.34, which models the perceived quality of a system. The same structure can be used to model other perceived quantities as smoothed variables. The operative rate equation for smoothing of quality information expresses the change in perceived quality as the difference be-

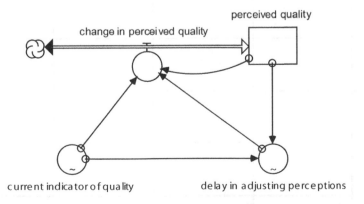

Figure 3.34. Perceived quality information smoothing. Equation:

change in perceived quality = (current indicator of quality-perceived quality)/delay in adjusting perceptions

tween current perceived quality and the actual quantity divided by a smoothing delay time.

The delay relationship is a graphical function that reflects an assumption about asymmetry in the adjustment of perceptions. It is very easy to modify perceptions downward, but far harder and more time-consuming to modify them upward. If a software product suddenly gets bad press about serious defects, then even if the problems are fixed it will take a long time for the public perception to change positively.

The graph in Figure 3.35 shows how the asymmetric delays impact the quality perception. When the actual quality indicator falls, then the perceived quality closely follows it with a short delay (bad news travels fast). But it is much harder to change the bad perception to a good one. It is seen that the delay is much greater when the actual quality improves, as it takes substantially longer time for the revised perception to take place.

3.4.7 Production and Rework

The classic production and rework structure in Figure 3.36 accounts for incorrect task production and its rework. Work is performed, and the percentage done incorrectly flows into undiscovered rework. Rework occurs to fix the problems at a specified rate. The work may cycle through many times. This structure is also related to the cyclic loop, except this variant has separate sources and sinks instead of directly connected flow chains. This is an important structure used in many models, including Abdel-Hamid's integrated project model.

A number of other structures can be combined with this, such as using the production structure for the task development rate. The rate for discovering task rework and the fraction correct can be calculated from other submodels as well. Another variation

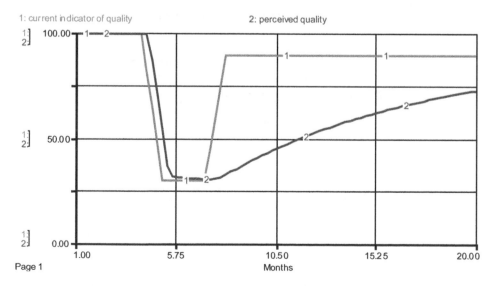

Figure 3.35. Output of perceived quality information smoothing.

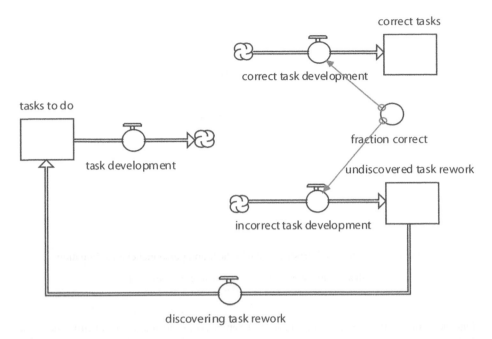

Figure 3.36. Production and rework structure. Equations:

correct task development = task development · fraction correct

incorrect task development = task development · (1 – fraction correct)

would have discovered rework flow into a separate level than the originating one. This would allow for the differentiation of productivity and quality from the original tasks. A number of other variations are also possible. Structures for working off defects specifically (instead of tasks) are provided in later sections.

3.4.8 Integrated Production Structure

The infrastructure in Figure 3.37 combines elements of the task production and human resources personnel chains. Production is constrained by both productivity and the applied personnel resources external to the product chain. The software development rate equation is typically equivalent to the standard equation shown for the production generic flow process. As shown earlier in Figure 3.6, the level of personnel available is multiplied by a productivity rate.

3.4.9 Personnel Learning Curve

The continuously varying effect of learning is an ideal application for system dynamics. Figure 3.38 shows a classic feedback loop between the completed tasks and productivity.

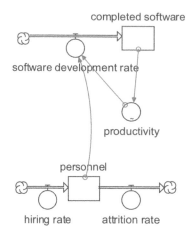

Figure 3.37. Production infrastructure with task and personnel chains. Equation:

software development rate = personnel · productivity

One becomes more proficient at a task after repeated iterations of performing that task. This figure shows a representation in which the learning is a function of the percent of job completion. The learning curve can be handily expressed as a graph or table function.

Another formulation would eliminate the auxiliary for percentage complete and have a direct link between tasks completed and the learning curve. The learning would be expressed as a function of the volume of tasks completed. The learning curve is a

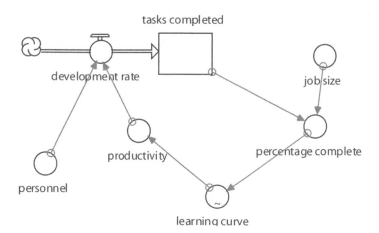

Figure 3.38. Learning curve. Equations:

learning curve = ƒ(percentage complete)

productivity = ƒ(learning curve)

complex area of research in itself. See Chapter 4 for a more detailed look at modeling this phenomenon and alternative formulations.

The learning curve function for this model is a graph relationship in Figure 3.39. It is expressed as a unitless multiplier to productivity as a function of project progress. It exhibits the typical S-curve shape whereby learning starts slow and the rate of learning increases and then drops off when reaching its peak near the end.

3.4.10 Rayleigh Curve Generator

The Rayleigh generator in Figure 3.40 produces a Rayleigh staffing curve. It contains essential feedback that accounts for the work already done and the current level of elaboration on a project. The output components of the Rayleigh generator are in Figure 3.41. The familiar hump-shaped curve for the staffing profile is the one for effort rate. The manpower buildup parameter sets the shape of the Rayleigh curve. Note also how cumulative effort is an S-shape curve. Since it integrates the effort rate, the steepest portion of the cumulative effort is the peak of the staffing curve.

This modeling molecule can be extended for many software development situations. The generator can be modified to produce various types of staffing curves, including those for constrained staffing situations, well-known problems, and incremental development. The Rayleigh curve is also frequently used to model defect levels. The defect generation and removal rates take on the same general shape as the effort rate curve. The Rayleigh curve and its components are further elaborated and used in Chapters 5 for defect modeling and in Chapter 6 for project staffing.

The standard Rayleigh curve in this section can be modified in several ways, as shown later in this book. It can become nearly flat or highly peaked per the buildup parameter, it can be scaled for specific time spans, clipped above zero on the beginning

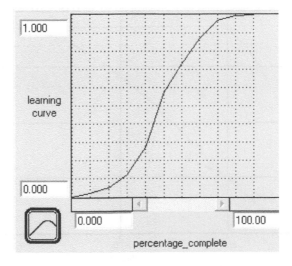

Figure 3.39. Learning curve function.

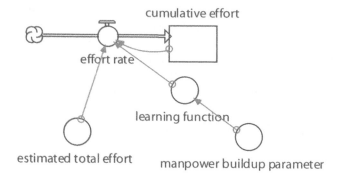

Figure 3.40. Rayleigh curve generator. Equations:

effort rate = learning function · (estimated total effort − cumulative effort)

learning function = manpower buildup parameter · time

or end of the curve, offset by time, or superimposed with other Rayleigh curves. Applications in Chapters 5 and 6 illustrate some of these modifications.

3.4.11 Attribute Tracking

Important attributes to track are frequently calculated from levels. The structure in Figure 3.42 is used to track an attribute associated with level information (i.e., the state variables). This example calculates the normalized measure defect density by dividing

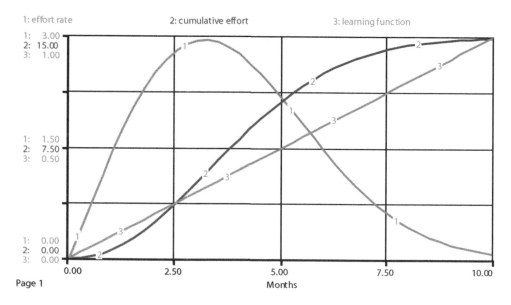

Figure 3.41. Rayleigh curve outputs.

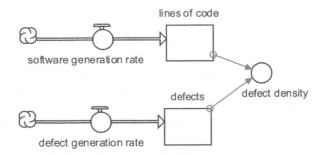

Figure 3.42. Attribute tracking infrastructure (defect density example). Equation:

defect density = defects/lines of code

the software size by the total number of defects. The defect density attribute can be used as an input to other model portions, such as a decision structure.

3.4.12 Attribute Averaging

A structure for attribute averaging (similar to attribute tracking) is shown in Figure 3.43. It calculates a weighted average of an attribute associated with two or more levels. This example calculates the weighted average of productivity for two pools of personnel. It can be easily extended for more entities to average across and for different weighting schemes.

3.4.13 Effort Expenditure Instrumentation

Effort or cost expenditures are coflows that can be used whenever effort or labor cost is a consideration. Frequently, this coflow structure serves as instrumentation only to

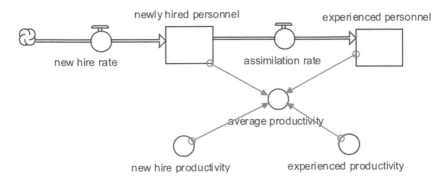

Figure 3.43. Attribute averaging infrastructure (software productivity example). Equation:

average productivity = [(newly hired personnel · new hire productivity) + (experienced personnel · experienced productivity)]/(newly hired personnel + experienced personnel)

obtain cumulative effort and does not play a role in the dynamics of the system. It could be used for decision making in some contexts. In Figure 3.44, the task production rate represents an alias computed in another part of the model. Using an alias is convenient for isolating the instrumentation, or the variable can be directly connected, depending on the visual diagram complexity. Effort accumulation rates can be calibrated against productivity for every activity modeled. Cost accumulation is easily calculated with labor rates.

If the number of people is represented as a level (set of levels) or another variable, then the effort expenditure rate (same as manpower rate) will be the current number of people per time period, as shown in Figure 3.45. The accumulated effort is contained in the level. In this example, the traditional units are difficult to interpret, as the rate takes on the value of the current personnel level. The rate unit still works out to effort per time.

3.4.14   Decision Structures

Example infrastructures for some important decision policies are described in this section.

3.4.14.1   Desired Staff

The structure in Figure 3.46 determines how many people are needed in order to meet a scheduled completion date. It is useful in project models where there is a fixed schedule and staffing decisions to be made. It takes into account the work remaining, allowable time to complete, and the current productivity. It then computes the desired project velocity to complete the project on time and how many people are needed for it. Desired project velocity has the units of tasks per time, such as use cases per week. This structure can be easily modified to determine the number of people to meet other quantitative goals besides schedule.

This is similar to a reverse of the production structure in that it figures out the desired productivity and staff level. This particular structure contains no levels, but levels could be used in place of some of the parameters. The maximum function for remaining dura-

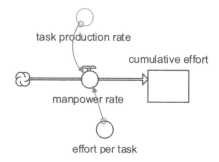

Figure 3.44. Effort expenditure coflow. Equation:

manpower rate = task production rate · effort per task

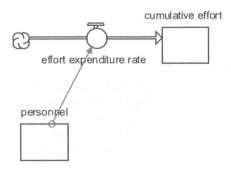

Figure 3.45. Effort expenditure linked to personnel level. Equation:

effort expenditure rate = personnel

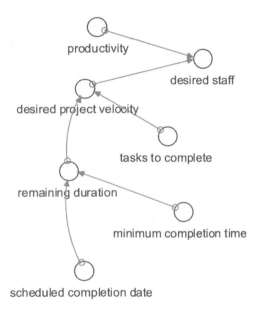

Figure 3.46. Desired staff structure. Equations:

desired staff = desired project velocity/productivity

desired project velocity = tasks to complete/remaining duration

remaining duration = maximum (minimum completion duration,
scheduled completion date – time)

tion ensures that time does not become so small that the desired staff becomes unreasonably large. A perceived productivity could also be used in place of actual productivity.

3.4.14.2 Resource Allocation

Project and organizational management need to allocate personnel resources based on relative needs. The infrastructure in Figure 3.47 supports that decision making. Tasks with the greatest backlog receive proportionally greater resources ("the squeaky wheel gets the grease"). This structure will adjust dynamically as work gets accomplished, backlogs change, and productivity varies. Many variations on the structure are possible (see the chapter exercises).

3.4.14.3 Scheduled Completion Date

The structure in Figure 3.48 represents the process of setting a project completion date, and it can be easily modified to adjust other goals/estimates. A smoothing is used to

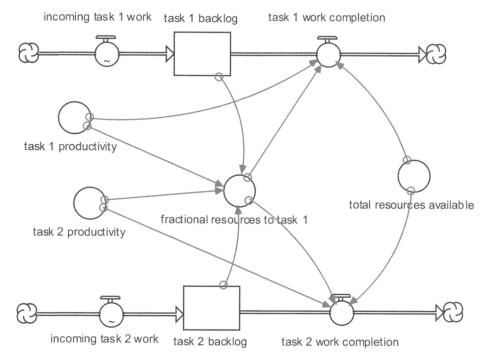

Figure 3.47. Resource allocation infrastructure. Equations:

fractional resources to task 1 = (task 1 backlog/task 1 productivity)/
  [(task 1 backlog/task 1 productivity) + (task 2 backlog/task 2 productivity)]

task 1 work completion = (total resources available · fractional resources to task 1)
  · task 1 productivity

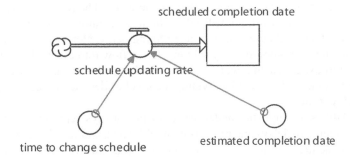

Figure 3.48. Scheduled completion date. Equation:

schedule updating rate = (estimated completion date
   – scheduled completion date)/time to change schedule

adjust the scheduled completion date toward the estimated completion date. The estimated date could be calculated elsewhere in a model.

3.4.14.4 Defect Rework Policies

The capability to assess cost/quality trade-offs is inherent in system dynamics models that represent defects as levels, and include the associated variable effort for rework and testing as a function of those levels. Figure 3.49 shows an example with an implic-

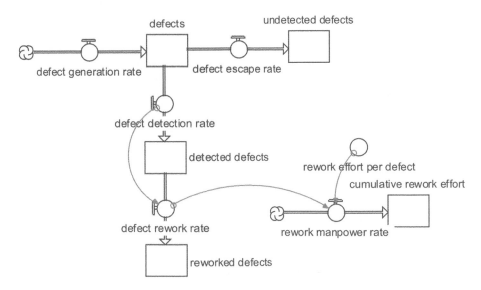

Figure 3.49. Rework all defects right away structure. Equation:

rework manpower rate = defect rework rate · rework effort per defect

it policy to rework all errors as soon as they are detected. The resources are assumed to be available to start the work immediately with no constraints. The rework rate drains the detected defect level based on an average fixing delay. Not shown is a detection efficiency parameter to proportionally split the defect flow into escaped and detected errors. The effort expended on rework is also tracked with this infrastructure. An alternative would be to model the rate by dividing the level of detected defects by an average rework (delay) time.

Figure 3.49 is a simplistic model that does not always represent actual practice. More often, there are delays and prioritization of defects, and/or schedule tradeoffs. An alternative structure is to have the rework rate constrained by the personnel resources allocated to it, as shown in Figure 3.50. More defect examples are shown in Chapter 5.

There are usually staffing constraints, even when the policy is to rework all defects immediately. In this case the resource constraints have to be modeled. The structure in Figure 3.49 has a level for the available personnel.

3.5 SOFTWARE PROCESS CHAIN INFRASTRUCTURES

This section provides flow chain infrastructures related to software processes consisting mostly of cascaded levels for software tasks, defects, people, and so on. These in-

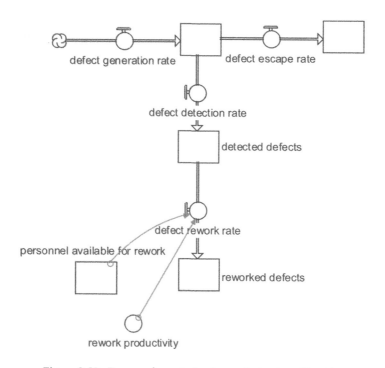

Figure 3.50. Personnel-constrained rework structure. Equation:

defect rework rate = personnel available for rework · rework productivity

frastructures can be used as pieces in a comprehensive software process model, or could serve as standalone base structures for isolated experimentation. The modeling challenge lies in balancing simplicity with the complexity imposed by integrating infrastructures into a meaningful whole.

Basic flows pervasive in software processes are discussed in the following sections. When applying system dynamics, the question must be asked, What is flowing? Determination of what kinds of entities flow through a software process is of primary importance, and this section will provide applied examples. For simplicity and conciseness, the flow chains in this section do not show all the information links that can represent feedback or other variable connections.

The applied examples include actual implementations of main process chains from some major models. The chains shown are isolated from their encompassing models to ease their conceptual understanding, and are idealized in the sense that levels with corresponding inflow and outflow rates are shown without information links. (The variable names shown in these examples are largely left intact from the original authors with some very slight changes to enhance understanding.) The connections would likely distract focus away from the main chains. Comparison of the chains for products, personnel, and defects illustrates specific model focuses and varying aggregation levels. The structures of the different models reflect their respective goals.

A number of executable models are also identified and provided for use. They may be experimented with as is or be modified for particular purposes. Before running a new or revised model, all input and output flow rates must be specified and initial values of the levels are also needed.

3.5.1 Software Products

Software development is a transformational process. The conserved chain in Figure 3.51 shows a typical sequential transformation pass from software requirements to design to code to tested software. Each level represents an accumulation of software artifacts. The chain could be broken up for more detail or aggregated to be less granular.

The tasks are abstracted to be atomic units of work uniform in size. Note that the unit of tasks stays the same throughout the chain, and this simplification is reasonable for many modeling purposes. In reality, the task artifacts take on different forms (e.g., textual requirements specifications such as use case descriptions to UML design notation to software code). Operationally, a task simply represents an average size module in many models.

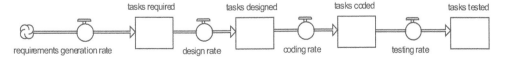

Figure 3.51. Product transformation chain.

3.5.1.1 *Conserved Versus Nonconserved Product Flow*

Software artifact sequences can be modeled as conserved flows, where each level has the same unit, or in nonconserved flow chains where product transformation steps are modeled using distinct artifact types. Each level in the process has different units in nonconserved chains. One of the elegant aspects of system dynamics is the simplification of using conserved flows. Hence, many models employ a generic "software task" per the examples shown above.

However, the process and modeling goals may dictate that sequential artifacts be modeled in their respective units. For example an agile process may be modeled with the nonconserved and simplified product transformation as in Figure 3.52. This structure only represents a single cycle or iteration. Additional structure, like that of a cyclic loop, is needed to handle multiple passes through the chain. Other variations might have use cases instead of user stories or classes implemented instead of software code; the acceptance tests could have been converted from user stories instead of code, and so on.

The conversion between artifact types may be modeled as an average transformation constant. For example, the parameter *user story to design task conversion* could be set to three design tasks per user story. A variable function could also be used in the conversion. A discrete model may even use individual values for each software artifact, whereby each user story entity is associated with a specific number of design tasks.

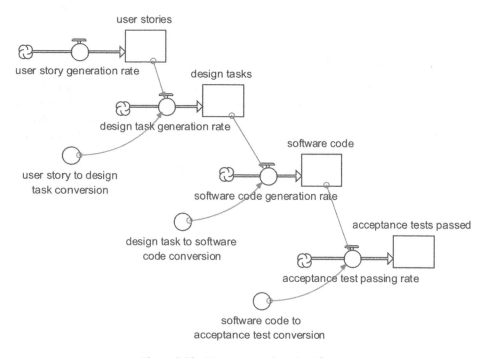

Figure 3.52. Nonconserved product flow.

3.5.1.2 Example Software Product Chains

The following three examples of software product chains illustrate successive "boring in" to the process. The different levels of detail correspond to the goals of the particular models, and are reflected in the different number of levels modeled. First is a highly aggregated chain of three levels representing software tasks in a general project model. Second is a chain of six levels to account for individual project phases and inspection points. Finally, a chain of eight intraphase levels is used to investigate even further down into the inspection process itself.

Abdel-Hamid's integrated project model [Abdel-Hamid, Madnick 1991] represents software tasks at a top-level, highly aggregated view. Figure 3.53 shows only three levels being used. The software development rate covers both design and coding. More information on the surrounding information connections and the rest of the Abdel-Hamid model are provided in Chapters 4–6 with associated models. The skeleton product chain in Figure 3.53 is elaborated in Chapter 5.

The product chain from [Madachy 1994b] in Figure 3.54 includes more detailed phases for the purpose of evaluating inspections throughout the lifecycle. The more aggregated view in the Abdel-Hamid model (Figure 3.53) combining design and coding and with no requirements stage, would not provide requisite visibility into how inspections effect process performance in each phase. The inspection model from [Madachy 1994b] is detailed in Chapter 5.

The detailed chain from [Tvedt 1995] in Figure 3.55 includes the subphases of the inspection process. Each of the primary phases in Figure 3.54 could be broken down to this level of detail. The purpose of this disaggregation is to explore the steps of the inspection process itself in order to optimize inspections.

The comparison of the Madachy and Tvedt chains for inspection modeling reflects the different modeling goals. Per the GQM example in Chapter 2, the different goals result in different levels of inspection process detail in the Madachy model versus the Tvedt model. The top-level view of the Madachy model to investigate the overall project effects of incorporating inspections results in more aggregation than Tvedt's detailed focus on optimizing the inspection process. Tvedt's model is another layer down within the inspection process, i.e. a reduced level of abstraction compared to the Madachy model. There is finer detail of levels within the product chain.

Inspection parameters in the Madachy model were used and calibrated at an aggregate level. For example, an auxiliary variable, *inspection efficiency* (the percentage of defects found during an inspection), represents a net effect handled by several components in the detailed Tvedt inspection model. The Madachy model assumes a given

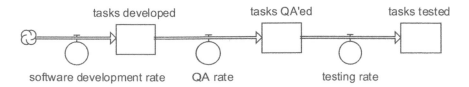

Figure 3.53. Product chain from [Abdel-Hamid, Madnick 1991].

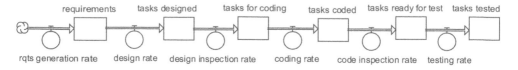

Figure 3.54. Product chain from [Madachy 1994b].

value for each run, whereas the Tvedt model produces it as a major output. A possible integration of the two models would involve augmentation of the Madachy model by inserting the Tvedt model subsystem where *inspection efficiency* is calculated.

3.5.2 Defects

This section shows ways to represent defects, including their generation, propagation, detection, and rework. Defects are the primary focus but are inextricably tied to other process aspects such as task production, quality practices, process policies to constrain effort expenditure, various product and value attributes, and so on.

3.5.2.1 Defect Generation

Below are several ways to model the generation of defects. They can be tied directly to software development or modeled independently.

3.5.2.1.1 DEFECT COFLOWS.   An obvious example of coflows in the software process is related to one of our common traits per the aphorism "to err is human." People make errors while performing their work. Defects can originate in any software phase. They are simultaneously introduced as software is conceived, designed, coded,

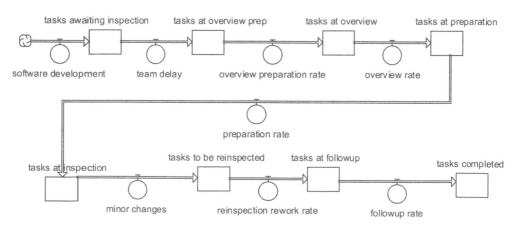

Figure 3.55. Product chain from [Tvedt 1995].

integrated etc.* Defects can also be created during testing or other assessment activities, such as a test case defect that leads to erroneous testing results.

A convenient way of expressing the defect generation rate multiplies the defect density, or the number of defects normalized by size (defects/SLOC, defects/function point, etc.), by the production rate, such as in Figure 3.56. With this, the defect generation rate is associated with the software development rate. The defect density used in this example could be constant or variable. This structure can be applied to any process subactivity; for example, design defect generation tied to a design rate or code defect generation as a function of the coding rate. Modeling the dynamic generation or detection of defects over time provides far greater visibility than static approaches, by which defect levels are described as the final resulting defect density.

3.5.2.1.2 RAYLEIGH DEFECT GENERATION. The generation of defects can also be modeled independently of task production. The Rayleigh curve is one traditional method of doing so. See Section 3.4.10 for a Rayleigh curve generator that can be modified for defects (and the corresponding chapter exercise).

3.5.2.2 Defect Detection (Filters)

It is instructive to consider the flow of defects throughout life-cycle phases with each potential method of detection as a filter mechanism. Reviews and testing are filters used to find defects. Some defects are stopped and some get through. The split-flow generic process is a perfect representation of filtering and easy to understand.

A natural way to model the detection of defects is to introduce *defect detection efficiency,* which is a dimensionless parameter that quantifies the fraction of total defects found. Figure 3.57 shows the defect chain split into detected and undetected subchains. Conservation of flow dictates that the overall incoming flow must be preserved among the two outflows from the initial defect level.

Process defect detection efficiencies (also called *yields*) should be readily available in organizations that have good software defect and review metrics across the life cycle. Typically, these may vary from about 50% to 90%. See Chapter 5 for additional references and nominal detection efficiencies, which can be used if no other relevant data is available.

3.5.2.3 Defect Detection and Rework

The high-level infrastructure in Figure 3.58 adds the rework step after detection. This infrastructure represents a single phase or activity in a larger process and could be part of an overall defect flow chain. The defect generation rate could be expressed as a coflow with software artifact development. The split in the chain again represents that some defects are found and fixed at the detection juncture, while the others are passed on and linger in the undetected level. Those that are detected are then reworked.

---

*The cleanroom process philosophy (i.e., "you can be defect free") is not incongruent with this assumption. Defects are still introduced by imperfect humans, but cleanroom methods attempt to detect all of them before system deployment.

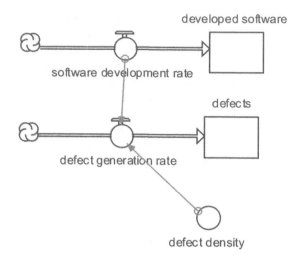

Figure 3.56. Defect generation coflow. Equation:

defect generation rate = software development rate · defect density

This structure only shows defects being reworked a single time, whereas they may actually recycle through more than once. Another way to model defect rework is to use a variant of the production and rework structure in Figure 3.36, or a cyclic loop flow can be used to model the cycling through of defects. Another addition would model bad fixes, whereby new defects would be generated when old defects were being fixed. Figure 3.58 only shows the detection and rework for part of a defect chain. The defects may also be passed on or amplified as described next.

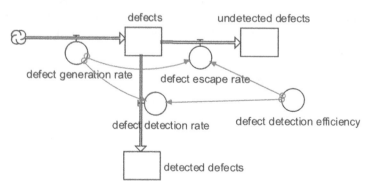

Figure 3.57. Defect detection structure. Equations:

defect escape rate = (1 − defect detection efficiency) · defect generation rate

defect detection rate = defect detection efficiency · defect generation rate

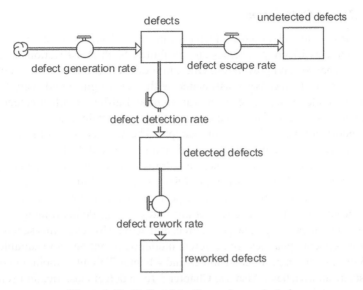

Figure 3.58. Defect detection and rework chain.

3.5.2.4   Defect Amplification

Defects may be passed between phases (corresponding to sequential activities) or possibly amplified, depending on the nature of elaboration. The structure in Figure 3.59 shows an example defect amplification (multiplication) structure from the Madachy inspection model that uses an amplification factor. Abdel-Hamid's project model used a different approach for error amplification described later in Chapter 5.

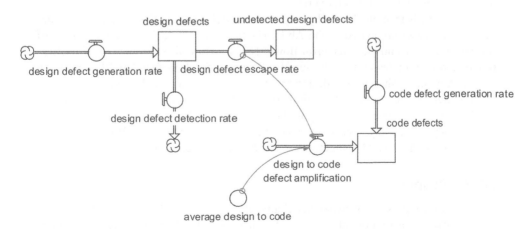

Figure 3.59. Defect amplification structure.

3.5.2.5 Defect Categories

There are many defect taxonomies. Defects can be modeled, assessed, and prevented using different classification schemes and attributes. Such classifications can be critical for defect analysis and prevention. One can model different severities such as low, medium, and high. Defect types associated with their origin could include requirements, design, code, or test defects. A way to model different defect categories is to have separate flow chains for the categories. One flow chain could be for minor defects and another for major defects, for example. The next section will show structures to separately track discovered, undiscovered, and reworked defects.

Figure 3.60 shows an example structure to track different requirements defect types per the Orthogonal Defect Classification (ODC) scheme [Chillarege et al., 2002]. For simplicity, it only shows their generation aspect and not their detection and removal. It could also be enhanced to include further attributes such as defect finding triggers, defect removal activities, impact, target, source, and so on. However, this scheme can get difficult with system dynamics, and discrete modeling might be more suitable (see the Chapter 5 discussion on product attributes and Chapter 7 about combining continuous versus discrete approaches). Also see Chapter 5 for a defect classification scheme and examples of modeling applications for detailed product attributes.

This simplistic scheme decomposes generic requirements defects into subcategories according to their respective fractions. A more detailed model would use unique factors to model the introduction and detection of each type of defect. The timing and shape of the defect curves is another consideration. See the example model in Chapter 6 on defect removal techniques and ODC that uses modified Rayleigh curves.

3.5.2.6 Example Defect Chains

Example defect chains from major models are shown here without connections to external parameters used in the rate formulas. Figure 3.61 shows two separate, unlinked defect propagation chains from the Abdel-Hamid project model. Active errors are those that can multiply into more errors.

Figure 3.62 is from the Madachy inspection model. Note the finer granularity of development phases compared to the Abdel-Hamid project model. The chain splits off for detected versus nondetected error flows. This structure also accounts for amplification of errors from design to code (see also Section 3.5.2.4, Defect Amplification). An information link is shown from design error escape rate to denote this, but not shown is a parameter for the amount of amplification. The code error generation rate refers to newly generated code errors, as opposed to design errors that escape and turn into code errors. They collectively contribute to the overall level of code errors. Without amplification, the chains would be directly connected as conserved flows.

3.5.3 People

Structures for representing personnel chains are provided in this section. These conserved-flow chains traditionally account for successive levels of experience or skill as people transition over time. Levels representing the number of personnel at each stage are mainstays of models that account for human labor. In simplistic models in which

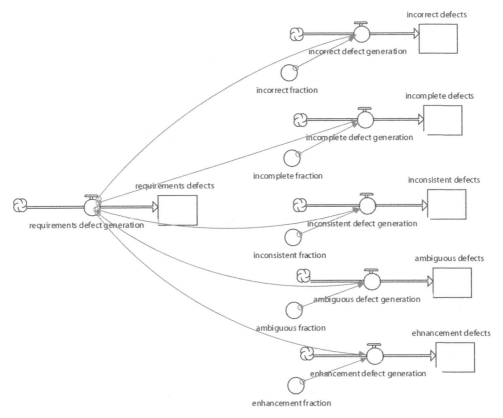

Figure 3.60. Example streams for ODC requirements defects. Equations:

incorrect defect generation = incorrect fraction · requirements defect generation

incomplete defect generation = incomplete fraction · requirements defect generation

inconsistent defect generation = inconsistent fraction · requirements defect generation

ambiguous defect generation = ambiguous fraction · requirements defect generation

enhancement defect generation = enhancement fraction · requirements defect generation

dynamic staff levels are not of concern, one can get by with auxiliary variables to represent the staff sizes. More complex analysis of personnel attributes corresponding to different skillsets, experience, performance, other personnel differentiators, and non-monotonic trends requires more detail than auxiliaries or single levels can provide.

3.5.3.1 *Personnel Pools*

Each level in a personnel chain represents a pool of people. Figure 3.63 shows a three-level model of experience. The sources and sinks denote that the pools for entry-level recruiting and cumulative attrition are not of concern; they are outside the effective organizational boundary for analysis. Varying degrees of detail and enhancements to the

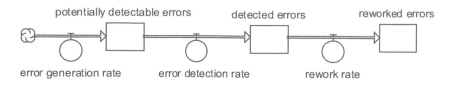

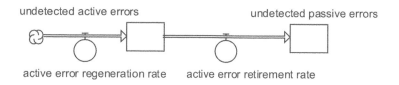

Figure 3.61. Defect chains from [Abdel-Hamid, Madnick 1991].

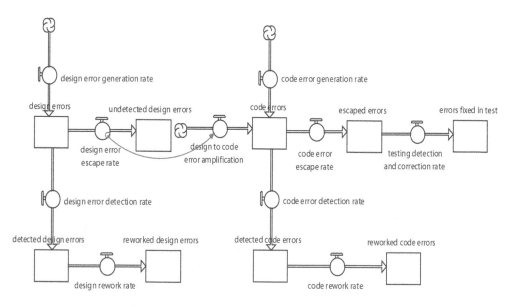

Figure 3.62. Defect chains from [Madachy 1994b].

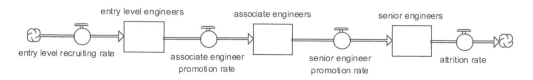

Figure 3.63. Personnel chain (three levels).

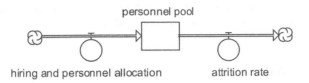

Figure 3.64. Personnel pool from [Madachy 1994b].

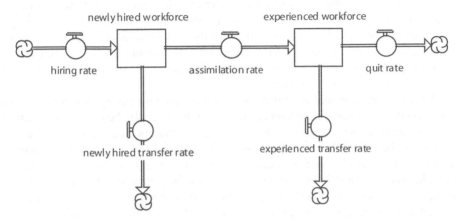

Figure 3.65. Personnel pool from [Abdel-Hamid, Madnick 1991].

personnel pool chain are possible, such as adding chain splits for attrition to occur from any experience level.

3.5.3.2 Example Personnel Chains

The single-level representation in Figure 3.64 is from [Madachy 1994b]. Since the effects of personnel mix were not germaine to the study, a single aggregation was sufficient. It can be augmented to handle multiple experience levels, but doing so adds additional overhead for data calibration and model validation.

The two-level chain in Figure 3.65 is from the Abdel-Hamid model. Two levels are used for some considerations such as overhead for rookies and differing error injection rates. This chain has been used as a traditional system dynamics example for many years outside of software engineering.

MAJOR REFERENCES

[Forrester 1968] Forrester J. W., *Principles of Systems.* Cambridge, MA: MIT Press, 1968.

[Hines 2000] Hines J., *Molecules of Structure Version 1.4,* LeapTec and Ventana Systems, Inc., 2000.

[Richmond et al. 1990] Richmond B., and others, *Ithink User's Guide and Technical Documentation,* High Performance Systems Inc., Hanover, NH, 1990.

CHAPTER 3 SUMMARY

Models are composed of building blocks, many of which are generic and can be reused. Model elements can be combined into increasingly complex structures that can be incorporated into specific applications. Generic flow processes, flow chains, and larger infrastructures are examples of recurring structures. Archetypes refer to generic structures that provide "lessons learned" with their characteristic behaviors (and will be addressed in subsequent chapters). There are few structures that have not already been considered for system dynamics models, and modelers can save time by leveraging existing and well-known patterns.

The hierarchy of model structures and software process examples can be likened, respectively, to classes and instantiated objects. Characteristic behaviors are encapsulated in the objects since their structures cause the behaviors. The simple rate and level system can be considered the superclass from which all other structures are derived. Additional rates and levels can be added to form flow chains. Generic flow processes add additional structural detail to model compounding, draining, production, adjustment, coflows, splits, and cyclic loops. Some of their typical behaviors were first described in Chapter 2, such as growth, decline, and goal-seeking behavior. The structures all have multiple instantiations or applications for software processes.

The generic structures can be combined in different ways and detail added to create larger infrastructures and complex models. The production infrastructure is a classic example that combines the generic flow for production with a personnel chain. Other structures and applied examples were shown for growth and S-curves, information smoothing, delays, balancing feedback, oscillation, smoothing, learning, staffing profiles, and others. The structures for attribute averaging, attribute tracking, and effort instrumentation produce no specific behavior and are used for calculations.

Some decision structures relevant to software projects were shown, including policies to allocate staff, adjust project goals/estimates as a project progresses, and defect rework policies. All of these structures can be reinterpreted to simulate policies for different decision contexts.

Finally, main chain infrastructures for software processes were illustrated. Some common infrastructures include product transformation, defect generation, defect detection and rework, personnel flow chains, and more. Applied examples of these chains from past modeling applications were highlighted to illustrate the concepts. The level of aggregation used in the chains depend on the modeling goals and desired level of process visibility.

3.8 EXERCISES

Exercises 3.1–3.8 should be done without the use of a computer.

3.1. Below is the personnel structure from the Abdel-Hamid project model. Identify and trace out an example of a feedback loop in it. Each involved entity and connection must be identified.

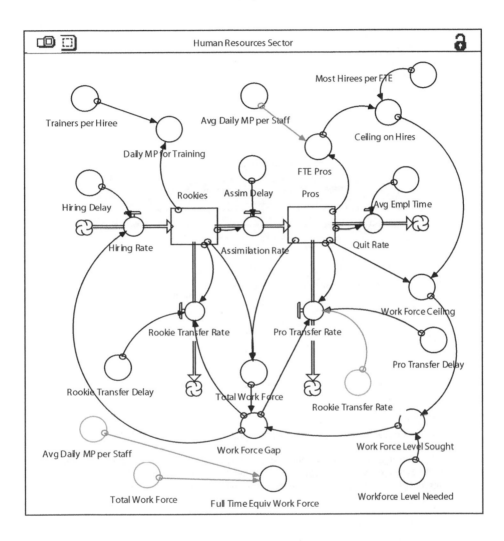

3.2. Identify the units of measurement for each entity in the system below and sketch the graphic results of a simulation run for the named variables.

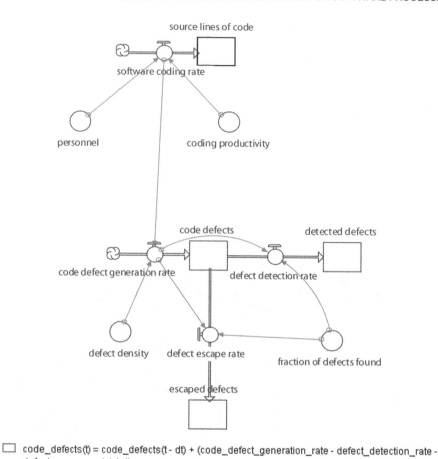

☐ code_defects(t) = code_defects(t - dt) + (code_defect_generation_rate - defect_detection_rate - defect_escape_rate) * dt
INIT code_defects = 0
INFLOWS:
   ♒ code_defect_generation_rate = software_coding_rate*defect_density
OUTFLOWS:
   ♒ defect_detection_rate = code_defect_generation_rate*fraction_of_defects_found
   ♒ defect_escape_rate = code_defect_generation_rate*(1-fraction_of_defects_found)
☐ detected_defects(t) = detected_defects(t - dt) + (defect_detection_rate) * dt
INIT detected_defects = 0
INFLOWS:
   ♒ defect_detection_rate = code_defect_generation_rate*fraction_of_defects_found
☐ escaped_defects(t) = escaped_defects(t - dt) + (defect_escape_rate) * dt
INIT escaped_defects = 0
INFLOWS:
   ♒ defect_escape_rate = code_defect_generation_rate*(1-fraction_of_defects_found)
☐ source_lines_of_code(t) = source_lines_of_code(t - dt) + (software_coding_rate) * dt
INIT source_lines_of_code = 0
INFLOWS:
   ♒ software_coding_rate = coding_productivity*personnel
○ coding_productivity = 200
○ defect_density = .05
○ fraction_of_defects_found = .5
○ personnel = 10

1: source lines of code

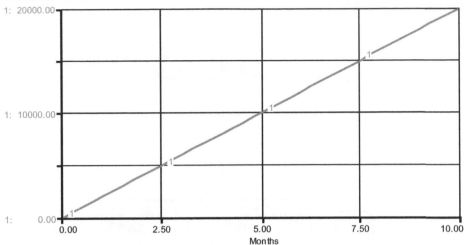

Months

Sketch the three graphs of code defects, defect detection rate, and detected defects.

3.3. Below is a model of customer trends, in which the simulation time is measured in months. Identify the units of measurement for each entity in the model and sketch the trend for customers. If an entity has no units, then write "dimensionless." Be as accurate as possible drawing the shape of the customer graph, and be sure to assign numbers to the y-axis for it.

potential customers   customer capturing rate   customers

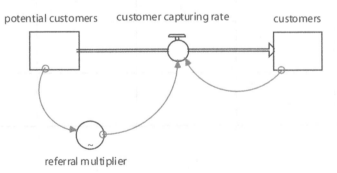

referral multiplier

☐ customers(t) = customers(t - dt) + (customer_capturing_rate) * dt
   INIT customers = 1
   INFLOWS:
      ☷ customer_capturing_rate = customers*referral_multiplier
☐ potential_customers(t) = potential_customers(t - dt) + (- customer_capturing_rate) * dt
   INIT potential_customers = 99
   OUTFLOWS:
      ☷ customer_capturing_rate = customers*referral_multiplier
⊘ referral_multiplier = GRAPH(potential_customers)
   (0.00, 0.005), (10.0, 0.045), (20.0, 0.08), (30.0, 0.105), (40.0, 0.135), (50.0, 0.175), (60.0, 0.215), (70.0, 0.24), (80.0, 0.265), (90.0, 0.31), (100, 0.36)

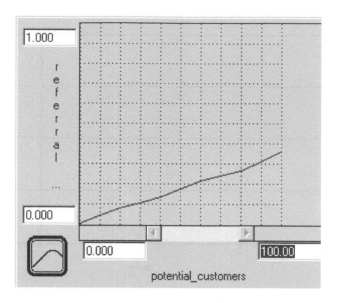

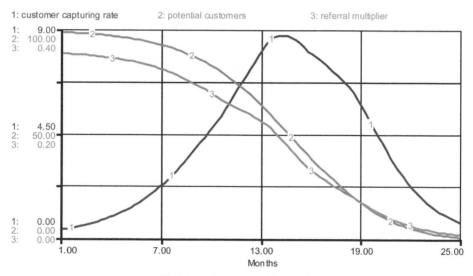

1: customer capturing rate   2: potential customers   3: referral multiplier

Sketch *customers* on this graph.

3.4. Create a comprehensive list of software process measures that the attribute tracking and attribute averaging structures can be used to calculate. What types of decisions and other submodels could those measures be used in?

3.5. What other important cumulative quantities in the software process can be instrumented like effort, and for what purposes? These measures are process indicators but do not necessarily add to the dynamics. They must provide visibility into some aspect of software process performance.

Advanced Exercises

3.6. Create some new infrastructures by combining generic flow processes. What do they model and how could they be used?

3.7. a. Parameterize the Rayleigh curve model for different staffing shapes. Enable the user to specify the shape through its ramp-up characteristics.

b. Modify and parameterize the Rayleigh curve to be consistent with the appropriate schedule span for a project. It should retain the same effort/schedule ratio as an accepted cost model.

3.8. Add the following extensions to the squeaky wheel resource allocation structure:

a. Enhance the structure to include additional tasks.

b. Vary the productivities.

c. Put additional weighting factors into the allocation such as effort multipliers for unique project factors.

d. Add a feedback loop so that the resource acquisition rate changes in response to the perceived need for additional resources.

3.9. Modify the scheduled completion date structure for effort and quality goals.

3.10. Below is a technology adoption curve observed at Litton Systems for a new Web-based problem reporting system.

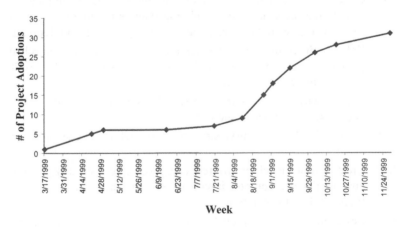

Create a simple S-curve technology adoption model, and calibrate it as best as possible to the time dynamics of this figure.

3.11. Create a model of software entropy that exhibits code decaying over time as the result of ongoing changes to a system. The average cost to fix a defect or implement a new feature should increase over time. The time horizon for this model should be lengthy, on the order of years. Evaluate some of the code decay measures from [Eick et al. 2001] and experiment by testing some of their suggestions (or your own) to reduce code decay effects. Validate the model against actual change data.

3.12. Modify a learning curve model so that the learning is a function of completed tasks rather than the percent of job completion. Optionally, calibrate the learning curve function to actual data, or other models of experience and learning.

3.13. Create a model for information smoothing of trends used for decisions and combine it with one of the decision structures. For example, suppose software change requests are received with many fluctuations over time. Smooth the input in order to determine the desired staff. Justify your smoothing interval time.

3.14. The example behaviors early in this chapter are shown for unperturbed systems, in order to demonstrate the "pure" response characteristics. Do the following and assess the resulting behaviors:

a. Modify the goal for the hiring delay example to vary over time instead of being constant. A graph function can be used to draw the goal over time. Also vary the hiring delay time.

b. Take an exponential growth or S-curve growth model and vary the growth factors over time.

c. Evaluate how the desired staff model responds to dynamic changes to the scheduled completion date and the tasks to be completed.

d. Choose your own structure or model and perturb it in ways that mimic the real world.

3.15. Combine the desired staff structure and the scheduled completion date structure. Using the scheduled completion date as the interfacing parameter, assess how the desired staff responds to changes in the completion date.

3.16. Enhance the combined model above for the desired staff and scheduled completion date to include hiring delays. Experiment with the resulting model and determine if it can oscillate. Explain the results.

3.17. Explain why two levels are necessary for system oscillation and demonstrate your answer with one or more models.

3.18. Modify the Rayleigh curve structure to model defect generation and removal patterns.

3.19. Create a flow model for different categories of defects using your own taxonomy. Optionally, combine it with a Rayleigh curve function to create the profile(s) of defect generation.

3.20. Research the work on global software evolution by Manny Lehman and colleagues (see Appendix B). Modify the cyclic loop structure for a simple model of software evolution.

3.21. Integrate the provided Madachy and Tvedt inspection models to create a model of both high-level inspection effects and the detailed inspection steps. Reparameterize the model with your own or some public data. Experiment with the detailed process to optimize the overall return from inspections.

3.22. If you already have a modeling research project in mind, identify potential structures that may be suitable for your application. Start modifying and integrating them when your project is well defined enough.

Part 2

APPLICATIONS AND FUTURE DIRECTIONS

INTRODUCTION TO APPLICATIONS CHAPTERS

Overview

People use **processes** to create **products** for **people** to meet **project** and **organization** goals.* This statement positions the application chapters by illustrating the primary dependencies between the taxonomy areas:

- People applications
- Process and product applications
- Project and organization applications.

These aspects are distinct yet an integrated whole with many connections. For instance, there are application examples that are referenced in multiple chapters. Applications that are split across the areas are identified, and pointers given to related sections.

---

*This statement is a simplification expressing the ideal. For example, some "processes" are debatable, the more ad hoc they appear. With respect to satisfying goals, it must be recognized that goals are not always completely satisfied or even explicitly stated. There may be constraints to deal with that affect goal attainment. Additionally, other goals unrelated to projects or organizations may come into play when it comes to people. Personal win conditions fall in this category (which organizations should explicitly consider and attempt to reconcile for mutual benefit). Additionally, organizations may include informal groups such as open-source communities. Though this statement is a simplification, it does express the basic intent of software development and evolution.

Different classification schemes for the applications are possible, but this one is the most meaningful and feasible division of topics in terms of model state variables. A way to differentiate the areas is by their most important state variables—the levels (accumulations) in the main chains of primary focus. People applications quantify personnel levels and characteristics. Process and product applications are centered around software artifacts, their transformations, and attributes through the process stages. Project and organization applications frequently integrate the other structures to monitor activity status against plans; acquire people and other resources; make policy decisions regarding people, processes, and products; track expenditures and business value measures; and so on. These actions may apply on a single project or a portfolio of projects.

Processes and products are difficult to extricate, considering that software artifact quantities and their attributes are primary state variables for both. Their flow chains are often identical. Project and organization considerations are tightly congruent with each other and their entities are similar in structure and behavior.

The next three chapters include historical overviews of applications and research, more detailed descriptions of selected example implementations with system dynamics, and some critiques of the various works. Each chapter begins with an introduction to the application areas, identifies the major opportunities to improve practices in each area, and briefly overviews the applications to be covered.

Structures called opportunity trees are shown at the beginning of each chapter to help visualize the different ways of improving in the areas. Opportunity trees were first shown in [Boehm 1987] for improving software productivity. They are hierarchical taxonomies of opportunities for achieving objectives. They can serve as a guide to understand the options and can be referred to when traversing through the material. The opportunities also represent potential modeling application areas and, indeed, each chapter addresses some of the important opportunities listed in the trees.

A notional top-level view of the highly connected opportunity trees is shown in Figure 1. The four application areas are starting nodes in their respective trees in each chapter. The multiple leaves from each branch in Figure 1 represent the many subbranches of opportunities. There are many connections between the branches, both within and between areas. Sample overlaps are shown for visual simplicity, but all branches could potentially connect.

A number of opportunities show up more than once on different trees in the chapters. The opportunity trees in Chapters 5 and 6 combine different perspectives and show some major overlaps. Other subtler interconnections can be seen when comparing the end leaves on different trees.

The trees help illustrate the significant overlap and synergies between people, process, product, project, and organization opportunities. For example, better trained and motivated people will tend to create improved processes and better products, process improvement programs will impact product quality, or employing reuse may improve both process performance and product capability simultaneously. Likewise, opportunities may show up more than once on the same tree. The placement depends on the perspective of a tree.

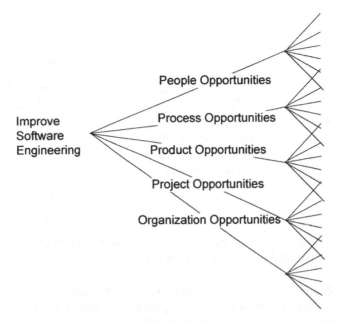

Figure 1. Software engineering opportunity tree (notional top-level view).

Terminology and Process Performance

Why is this book titled "Software *Process* Dynamics," given the different application areas (people, process, product, project, and organization) and their interactions? Though the title might seem limiting, consider that *process* is central to the other elements when considering process performance. By convention, *process performance* refers to the achieved results from executing a process such as expended effort, schedule, or final product quality. So the performance of a process depends on the interactions between people, processes, products, projects, organizations, and so on. They collectively form the context for *measurable* process performance per Figure 2.

Figure 2 combines the application areas with the control system depicted in Chapter 1, without the feedback connections (it is also a standard Input–Process–Output (IPO) format). The process is the system in the middle with inputs from people, projects, and organizations, and software artifacts as outputs representing the product. All process performance measures are indicators based on the inputs and outputs of the process; therefore, people, project, organization, and product measures are involved in an executed process.

Organization of Topics

Topical subareas in each chapter begin with a brief review of the phenomenology, then modeling examples are shown with sample insights. Not every past application is covered, and the reader should refer to the annotated bibliography for a complete list of all

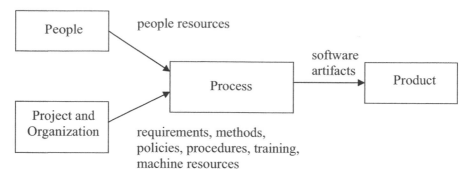

Figure 2. Process performance context.

previous work in the field. Unfortunately, some of the best simulation work occurs in industry behind closed doors. Much of it remains proprietary and, thus, cannot even be published.

Table 1 shows the top-level topics contained in each chapter. The list is not definitive or complete for any given area with respect to all potential applications. The sample topics are those that have been studied and allowed to be published, or, in some cases, important areas already identified for future work. Rigorous studies like Ph.D. dissertations or major funded modeling initiatives are heavily covered. Since there are few people-oriented models in the literature, Chapter 4, People Applications, contains a number of sections for which there are no example models yet.

The degree of detail per topic also varies in order to showcase certain valuable aspects, or it may be a reflection of the available information on a topic. The unique value to the reader is frequently found in the lessons learned and model formulations, but may also be the method of research, data collection and analysis, project management techniques, or other aspects. Substantial space is dedicated to new and previously un-

Table 1. Application topics

People	Process and Product	Project and Organization
• Workforce Modeling • Exhaustion and Burnout • Learning • Team Composition • Motivation • Slack Time • Personnel Hiring and Retention • Skills and Capabilities • Communication, Negotiation, and Collaboration • Simulation for Personnel Training	• Peer Reviews • Global Process Feedback • Software Reuse • Commercial Off-The-Shelf Software (COTS)-Based Systems • Software Architecting • Quality and Defects • Requirements Volatility • Software Process Improvement	• Integrated Project Modeling • Software Business Case Analysis • Personnel Resource Allocation • Staffing • Earned Value

Table 2. Key to model summary tables with examples from Brooks's Law model

Purpose: Training and Learning, Planning
Scope: Development Project

Inputs and Parameters	Levels	Major Relationships	Outputs

Inputs that a user changes for each run, plus additional model parameters that may be set. These include constants and functions. Simple conversion factors are not shown, nor level initialization values when zero.
 • Number of people to add
 • Pulse time
 • Nominal productivity
 • Training overhead portion
 •Communication overhead multiplier
 • Planned software
 • New personnel
 • Experienced personnel
	Levels comprising the system; the stocks or state variables (which could be measured on an actual process). Levels used purely for instrumentation are not shown.
	 • Software
	    Required
	    Developed
	 • Personnel
	    New
	    Experienced
		These include important trade-off relationships, multiplier functions, rates, or policy equations germane to the model. Simple linear rates are not listed.
		 • Assimilation delay
		 • Communication overhead
		 • Training losses
			Primary outputs or result variables used in the model studies. Many outputs may be available but only the most important ones are shown.
			 • Schedule time
			 • Productivity trend

published original work. There are undoubtedly more unlisted areas that people will work on, and some of them will be included in the next book version.

The major models are introduced with a standard summary table, as explained in Table 2 with example items listed for the simple Brooks's Law model. First shown are the purpose(s) and scope per the process model characterization matrix in Chapter 1. Then the format follows an IPO convention. The inputs needed for running the model are listed in the left column, then the levels and major relationships used in the model are shown, then the primary outputs. As described, not all elements are shown and sometimes the items are abstractions. Sometimes, the names of model elements are revised for clarity and the naming differences will be evident when the models are studied.

4

PEOPLE APPLICATIONS

4.1 INTRODUCTION

People offer the highest leverage opportunity to improve process performance and increase the chance of project success. Software processes will always be sociotechnical by nature, and due attention should be paid to the human aspects. Unfortunately, people issues have been less represented in process modeling and simulation compared to technical aspects. Abdel-Hamid's model had a large portion dedicated to people aspects [Abdel-Hamid, Madnick 1991] and other models have stocks for personnel staffing levels, but only a few other efforts referenced in this chapter explicitly assess people attributes and trade-offs.

Many proposed "silver bullets" for software engineering focus on technical solutions while ignoring the people dynamics. People must be available. They should have requisite skills and experience for their jobs, the ability to work well with others, and they should be adequately motivated to perform, have necessary resources, and have a good working environment that fosters creativity and learning. The best designed processes and latest technology will not help a project without human cooperation. Agile approaches recognize that processes are ultimately executed by people. No process will work without people and, therefore, "people trump process" [Cockburn, Highsmith 2001].

The focus of this applications chapter is on phenomena directly related to people. Constructs are shown for important people aspects including motivation, exhaustion, experience and learning curves, skill development, training, hiring and retention, com-

Software Process Dynamics. By Raymond J. Madachy
Copyright © 2008 the Institute of Electrical and Electronics Engineers, Inc.

munication, stakeholder collaboration, and workforce dynamics at the project and macro levels. Even though many of the people attributes are considered "soft factors," it is feasible and meaningful to model them. One strength of system dynamics is the ability to model soft factors and easily integrate them with hard factors.

Due to the relative scarcity of people-oriented models, this chapter includes a few areas for which there are currently no example models. These are important topics and it is expected that relevant models will be created in the future.

It can be argued that virtually all process, product, and organizational phenomena are impacted by human actions to some degree. However, this chapter will overview applications and research centered on people issues. When the work also involves more than people concerns, only relevant portions will be described in this chapter, with references to the rest of the nonpeople aspects.

One view of system dynamics is that the purpose of all models is to provide understanding to people. Thus, all models can be considered training applications, but the model topics have to be compartmentalized for the sake of organization. However, there are applications purposely created for education and training and they are covered in a corresponding section. These simulation applications were explicitly devised for classroom and other teaching venues, and typically use hypothetical project scenarios for analysis and making decisions instead of actual "live" or "to-be" projects (though they could also use them). Education and training applications have enormous potential to be tapped.

How important are people characteristics relative to other factors? Our COCOMO II research in [Boehm et al. 2000] provides quantitative relationships for major software project factors. Data shows that the combined people-related factors provide for the widest range of software productivity impact against all other cost factor types (process, product, project, and organizational).

Figure 4.1 shows the linear range of variation for software productivity due to factors directly related to people. For example, the range of 1.76 for *Programmer Capability* indicates that productivity may vary by 176% between the lowest and highest ratings. Note that the factor for *Team Cohesion* covers stakeholder negotiation and collaboration between people (an application discussed in this chapter). The total productivity variation due to direct people factors in the figure is 2008%, including 302% for the combined experience factors and 353% variation due to capability factors. The entire set of factors and their productivity ranges are listed in Appendix E and further described in [Boehm et al. 2000].

Keep in mind that the COCOMO II multipliers are from a macro, static model essentially based on regression techniques. The challenge of dynamic modeling is to move away from a static representation and consider the underlying mechanics of how these phenomena work together and the associated nonlinearities. Additionally, the COCOMO II data is from mature organizations from which data is collected; good management is assumed and, likewise, good motivation. Unfortunately, these are not always the case so nonlinear, fringe conditions also need to be considered. A more holistic view of dynamic interactions will enable better insight and decision making.

Communication overhead is another important factor due to people, but is not included in these calculations because it is represented in the size penalty in the

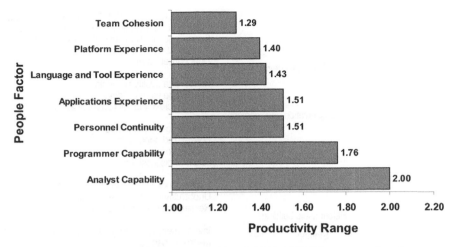

Figure 4.1. People factor impacts from COCOMO II. What causes these?

COCOMO model. Other scale factors in COCOMO II attributable to people in lesser degrees include *Architecture/Risk Resolution,* which depends on top architect availability, and *Precedentedness,* which has an experience component. Many of the other COCOMO factors are also influenced by human actions, so the overall variation due to people is actually greater than 2008%. Other static cost models include additional people factors such as management experience and capability, office ergonomics, team assignment, fragmentation, intensity, and more (see [Cost Xpert 2003], for example).

However, COCOMO assumes that people are reasonably well motivated (a corollary of the assumption that projects are reasonably well managed) and that other soft factors can be treated as invariant across projects. These assumptions do not hold true in many instances, so some people factors not currently represented in COCOMO will be addressed in this chapter. Most of these represent measures that are harder to define and collect in the COCOMO context, so some means of quantification will be shown.

An opportunity tree for people-related improvements is shown in Figure 4.2. The tree is based on our USC course notes for software engineering economics in [USC 2004] and includes some enhancements from [Bhatnagar 2004]. The tree amply shows the necessity of organizational commitment to employee growth and development. These people strategies are all areas that can be explored more through modeling and simulation, and some are reviewed in this chapter.

This chapter primarily deals with past work, and there are critical people areas that have not yet been covered in the simulation literature. Thus, the reader should be aware of some important and classic references on people considerations for software processes that do not deal explicitly with modeling and simulation. *Peopleware, Productive Projects and Teams,* by Tom DeMarco and Tim Lister [Demarco, Lister 1999] is an insightful book for those wanting to understand how to improve productivity in people. We require this book as a text for our graduate software engineering courses at USC. One of highest leverage improvements that DeMarco and Lister identify is office

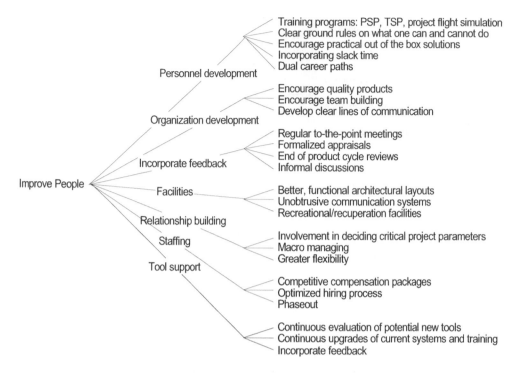

Figure 4.2. People opportunity tree.

ergonomics, but ergonomic factors have not even been modeled yet for software processes.

The 1971 classic *The Psychology of Computer Programming* by Gerry Weinberg was updated in 1998 [Weinberg 1998]. This is the first and still most comprehensive treatment of the psychological aspects of people who develop software and sheds light on what makes them tick. Weinberg describes the inner workings of programmers, but these phenomena also have not been addressed in models to date.

Another valuable reference for managers is *Managing Technical People* by Watts Humphrey [Humphrey 1997]. It is an insightful guide for leading technical software professionals using sound management principles. Humphrey gives advice on how to identify, motivate, and organize innovative people. People must be understood and re-spected in order to be fully dedicated. Though there are special challenges with techni-cal people, taking the right steps can improve efficiency and quality. The resounding message is that people are the overriding important factor for software project success.

The People Capability Maturity Model [Curtis et al. 2001] complements and ex-pands on [Humphrey 1997] by providing a structured maturity model for getting the best out of people. It also complements the software CMM and CMMI because it ad-dresses the workforce practices for continuous improvement. This compilation out-lines tangible actions that an organization can take to assess and improve their people maturity.

The handbook, *A Software Process Model Handbook for Incorporating People's Capabilities* [Acuña et al. 2005] is a valuable contribution on people-related aspects. The focus is on extending software process definitions to more explicitly address people-related considerations. It provides a capabilities-oriented software process model formalized in UML and implemented as a tool.

The guidelines in these classic books and subsequent references help to understand people dynamics and provide substantial fodder for future modeling and simulation applications. Discrete models might be suitable for some of these people effects in addition to system dynamics. The reader is encouraged to study these references and examine the chapter exercises based on them.

4.2 OVERVIEW OF APPLICATIONS

This chapter starts with a review of the detailed human resources sector in the Abdel-Hamid integrated project model from [Abdel-Hamid, Madnick 1991]. It is historically significant and covers some classic phenomena with structures for hiring, assimilation, training, and transferring of people on a project.

Exhaustion and burnout have large effects on productivity and are intimately related to motivation. These are vital people factors to be concerned about, but are rarely considered on projects. Some example models are shown, including one that is part of the Abdel-Hamid integrated model.

Learning is a broad topic that is addressed from the perspective of continuous modeling. Models to implement experience and learning curves in the context of software development are described. They are also contrasted with alternate learning curves and experience impact models.

One of the people issues for hybrid processes is how to compose the teams in terms of skill sets and responsibilities. The next section describes a model to find the optimum number of agile people to match anticipated change traffic on a very large project.

Next is a section on critical people-related areas, yet uncovered with full models. The all-important aspect of motivation is included. The effect of motivation may overwhelm any other attempt to improve process performance. Motivation is a classic case of a "soft" factor and some ways are shown to model related phenomena.

The next topics include personnel attributes such as skills, team communication, stakeholder negotiation, and collaboration factors. These application areas are described in general with few supporting models, though the references will contain some.

Understanding the dynamics of hiring and retention is necessary to maintain a ready organization. Standard modeling constructs and integrated models for assembling and maintaining teams are described. Issues of workforce dynamics at the macro level are also covered.

Simulation for personnel training is a different class of application. Experiences and research into the effectiveness of using simulation for personnel training are summarized from several studies. For more on this topic, the reader is encouraged to read the references in that section, and to look ahead to Chapter 7.

4.3　PROJECT WORKFORCE MODELING

Workforce modeling quantifies personnel resources over time. Separate levels are frequently used to represent different experience or skill pools. The number of levels used to represent different classes of people will depend on the environment and modeling goals.

4.3.1　Example: Personnel Sector Model

The personnel sector of the Abdel-Hamid model covers personnel hiring, assimilation, training, quitting, and transferring of people onto or off the project. It is summarized in Table 4.1.

Figure 4.3 shows the structure of the personnel sector from the Abdel-Hamid integrated project model. It is driven by the number of people sought with hiring and transferring controlled by personnel decision policies. The gap between *total workforce* and *workforce level sought* is used to control hiring and transfer rates considering schedule completion time, workforce stability, and training requirements.

New and experienced people are differentiated as separate levels for a couple of reasons. Productivity differences between new and experienced people are modeled this way. Another important factor is that experienced people are involved in training new hires. The training overhead on the part of the experienced people gives them less time to devote to other development tasks, and providing two levels allows the differentiation of which resources are consumed in training. Experienced people may work on multiple

Table 4.1. Personnel sector model overview

Purpose: Planning
Scope: Development Project

Inputs and Parameters	Levels	Major Relationships	Outputs
• Hiring delay • New hire transfer delay • Experienced transfer delay • Assimilation delay • Trainers per hiree • Average daily manpower per staff • Workforce level needed (from planning sector) • Maximum hirees per staff • Average employment time	• Workforce 　Newly hired 　Experienced	• Workforce level sought • Delays • Hiring constraints • Training effects	• Staffing profiles per workforce type • Workforce gap

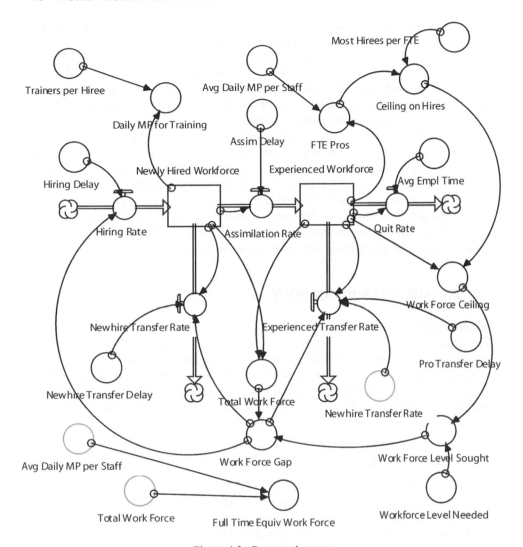

Figure 4.3. Personnel sector.

projects at once, so they may be diverted from the project in addition to training new hires. Both the assimilation rate between new hires and experienced workforce, and the quit rate representing turnover are modeled as first-order exponential delays.

Policies represented in closing the work gap via hiring and transferring decisions are important dynamic drivers of this sector. The *workforce level needed* parameter represents the decision on how many people are currently required for the project. It is calculated in the planning sector based on the current schedule completion date and perceived tasks remaining. However, the needed workforce is not always the hiring goal due to concerns for stability and the ability to take on more people. See Chapter 6 in the section on the integrated Abdel-Hamid model for the specific policy formulations in the planning sector used to make decisions based on workforce stability and the pressure to change the workforce.

Competing desires for workforce stability and schedule attainment change through the project. Towards the end of the project it would take too much time to integrate new people into the team. The number of personnel is limited partly on the ability to assimilate new people onto the project via the constraint *ceiling on new hires*.

There is also a *workforce level sought* parameter, which is used in conjunction with the *workforce level needed* parameter. The maximum number of personnel is the sum of the *ceiling on new hires* and the *ceiling on total workforce*. It is then determined whether new employees will be hired or if people are to be transferred off the project. New hires and transfers all entail delays that are modeled as first-order exponential delays.

In addition to this workforce dynamics structure, the Abdel-Hamid model also has provisions for human characteristics that impact productivity. These important factors include exhaustion and burnout, which are reviewed in the next section.

4.4 EXHAUSTION AND BURNOUT

Human nature dictates that the increased productivity effects of overtime can only be temporary, because everyone needs to "de-exhaust" at some point. This has been observed across all industries. It even held true during the Internet boom of the late 1990s in some of the hottest start-up companies. People start working a little harder with some schedule pressure, but after several weeks fatigue sets in and productivity drops dramatically. Then there is a recovery period during which people insert their own slack time until they are ready to work at a normal rate again.

4.4.1 Example: Exhaustion Model

This example models the phenomenon of exhaustion due to overwork. The representation is based on the Abdel-Hamid integrated project model. A high-level summary of the model is in Table 4.2.

The underlying assumptions of this exhaustion model are:

- Workers increase their effective hours by decreasing slack time or working overtime.
- The maximum shortage that can be handled varies.
- Workers are less willing to work hard if deadline pressures persist for a long time.
- The overwork duration threshold increases or decreases as people become more or less exhausted.
- The exhaustion level also increases with overwork.
- The multiplier for exhaustion level is 1 when people work full 8 hour days, and goes over 1 with overtime. The exhaustion increases at a greater rate in overtime mode up to the maximum tolerable exhaustion.

Table 4.2. Exhaustion model overview

Purpose: Planning, Training
Scope: Development Project

Inputs and Parameters	Levels	Major Relationships	Outputs
• Nominal fraction of daily effort for project • Exhaustion depletion delay • Maximum tolerable exhaustion • Overwork duration multiplier	• Fraction of daily effort for project • Exhaustion	• Exhaustion flow • Overwork duration threshold	• Fraction of daily effort for project • Exhaustion • Overwork threshold • Software productivity (indirectly)

- The exhaustion level slowly decreases with an exhaustion depletion delay when the threshold is reached or deadline pressures stop.
- During this time, workers do not go into overwork mode again until the exhaustion level is fully depleted.

Figure 4.4 shows the exhaustion model structure, which is a portion of the overall Abdel-Hamid project model. Figure 4.5 shows the graph function for exhaustion flow and Figure 4.6 shows the function for the multiplier to overwork duration threshold. See the equations in the provided model for a full description.

People naturally exhibit different breaking points and rest times. Table 4.3 shows typical maximum workweeks for different environments, though thresholds obviously differ by individuals. A serious workaholic may be able to put in 80-hour weeks for a few months and only need a few days rest between projects, whereas someone else might need a three-week vacation. This model used the following average values to describe an aggregate project situation:

- Exhaustion depletion delay time = 20 days
- Maximum tolerable exhaustion = 50 days
- Nominal fraction of man-days for the project = 0.6

The burnout parameters also vary by software development class (e.g., mainstream, civil service, start-up) similar to the differences in motivation. The values in this example approximate a mainstream situation. The aggregate parameters should be carefully reviewed for a given class of software development, such as the maximum tolerable exhaustion. The tolerable exhaustion is correlated to the productivity multipliers shown in Figure 4.26.

A run of the exhaustion model is shown in Figure 4.7 using these inputs and other default parameters from the Abdel-Hamid integrated project model. It clearly shows increasing exhaustion up to a breaking point. The actual fraction of man-days for the

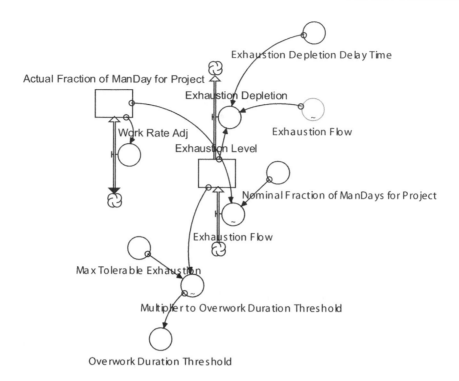

Figure 4.4. Exhaustion model structure.

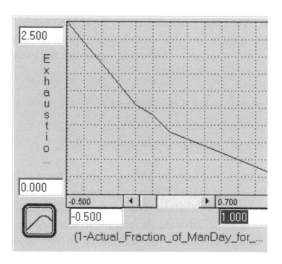

Figure 4.5. Exhaustion flow [exhaustion flow vs. (1 – actual fraction of mandays for project)/(1 – nominal fraction of mandays for project)].

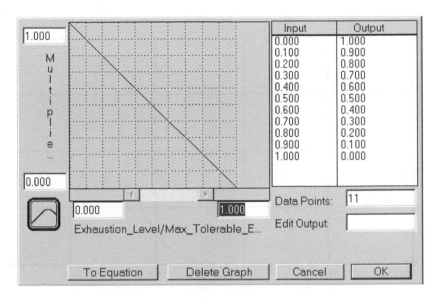

Figure 4.6. Multiplier to overwork duration threshold (multiplier to overwork duration threshold vs. exhaustion level/max tolerable exhaustion).

project rises from 0.6 to over 1 as the project falls behind schedule, which means that people have less and less slack time during their day. The fraction increases as the work rate adjustment kicks in. As the exhaustion level accumulates, it affects the overwork duration threshold such that the number of days people will work overtime starts to decrease.

These general trends continue and productivity is increased nearing the point of maximum exhaustion. When the overwork duration threshold reaches zero, the team cannot continue at the same pace, so the de-exhausting cycle starts. The actual fraction of man-days for the project and the exhaustion level both slowly decrease. The fraction of man-days decreases faster because people suddenly stop overworking. The overwork duration threshold begins to increase again, but a new overwork cycle will not start until the exhaustion level reaches zero.

The de-exhausting phenomenon is related to the concept of slack described in [De-Marco 2001] (see Section 4.7.1.2). Rest time is needed for people to gain energy and think creatively. Alternative model formulations for burnout dynamics have been created by High Performance Systems [Richmond et al. 1990] and Pugh [Richardson, Pugh 1981]. See the model *burnout.itm* as an example.

4.5 LEARNING

Learning is the act of acquiring skill or knowledge through study, instruction, or experience. In the context of a software process, developers become more productive over

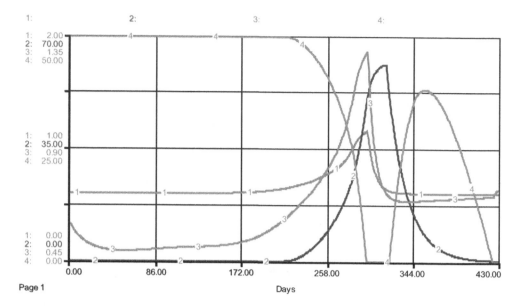

Figure 4.7. Exhaustion model behavior (1: actual fraction of man-days for project, 2: exhaustion level, 3: software development productivity, 4: overwork duration threshold).

the long term due to their accumulated experience. The increase in productivity occurs indefinitely, and a *learning curve* describes the pattern of improvement over time.

Many people are familiar with the general shape of a learning curve as expressed by a productivity function over time, such as in Figure 4.8. The curve shows an initial period of slow learning in which the development process is being learned, then a middle period of fast learning, followed by a decreasing-slope portion that nearly levels out (the form of a typical S-curve). The reduced learning portion is due to other constraints on productivity that are reached, such as machine limitations. There are always parts of

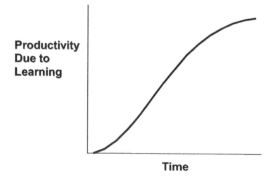

Figure 4.8. Learning as productivity over time.

the process that are constrained by machine-paced tasks such as waiting for compiles, print jobs, computer downtime, network access, and so on. Calibration of this curve for software development is treated later in this section.

The implications of learning while executing software processes can be substantial when trying to plan effort and staffing profiles. Unfortunately, few planning techniques used in software development account for learning over the duration of a project. The standard usage of COCOMO, for example, assumes static values for experience factors on a project. But learning is a very real consideration that can be easily handled with system dynamics. This section will describe techniques for expressing learning curves over time.

Learning curves are a family of equations. They have been treated in detail in many industrial applications, but have received scant attention in the software process literature. The most comprehensive treatment of learning curves in software engineering to date is an article by Raccoon [Raccoon 1996]. He ties together concepts of process stability and improvement with learning curves. For example, he points out that disruptions in the process affect learning curve offsets but not the overall slope. Some of the formulaic discussion of learning in this section is derived from his paper.

The existence of learning conflicts with some approaches to process stability. For example, a stable process is normally assumed to have a constant productivity over time. Calibration of cost models is usually performed against past project data, assuming that the calibration holds for future projects. Note, however, that some models such as COCOMO II have a provision for learning in experience cost drivers. In particular, COCOMO II has cost drivers for applications experience, platform experience, and language/toolset experience. These cost drivers provide effort multipliers for coarse ranges of experience.

Learning curves are used in several of the models throughout this book. Some of the Litton Systems case studies embody learning curves to model the effects of major process disruptions. It should also be noted that the standard Rayleigh curve that describes staffing profiles embodies the notion of a linear learning function.

At first glance, learning curves may be easily expressed as graphs over time, but this simple depiction will only be accurate when time correlates with cumulative output. As Raccoon discusses, there are biases that mask learning curves. For example, the output of a software process (whether a line of code, a function point, or an object measure) represents a different cost and work in different project phases. Growth biases also affect learning curves, such as the rapid escalation in staff that confuses underlying individual productivities.

There are also process disruptions for periods of time that affect productivity. These can be after a long break (vacation, sickness, holidays, etc.) or other work disruptions. This author distinctly remembers his days in the software development trenches when the first days back after long holiday breaks were spent relearning operating system commands, the keyboard to an extent, and the problem at hand. It definitely took some time to get back to previous levels of productivity. Process bottlenecks may also delay learning, such as when machines pace the work. As Raccoon states: "When biases affect measurement and time does not correlate with cumulative output, then the units of measurement on the x axis must be translated to cumulative output" [Raccoon 1996].

Learning curves are traditionally formulated in terms of the unit costs of production. The most widely used representation for learning curves is called the log-linear learning curve expressed by

$$y = ax^n$$

where a is the cost of the first unit, x is the cumulative output, and n is the learning curve slope. Figure 4.9 shows this relationship. Compare this with Figure 4.8; they are inverse relationships (excepting for the S-shape characteristic) since productivity = 1/unit cost. The slope of a learning curve is related to the learning rate, which describes the scaling of unit cost for every doubling of cumulative output. For example, a learning rate of 75% indicates that the unit cost scales by 75% every doubling of cumulative output. If the unit cost of the 1000th line of code is 60 minutes, then the cost of the 2000th line would be 0.75(60) = 45 minutes. The slope of a learning curve is equivalent to $\log_2$(learning rate). If plotted on a log-log scale, the slope would be directly measurable since the unit cost function would be a line.

Other important learning curve equations per [Raccoon 1996] are:

- Stanford-B: $y = a (x + b)^n$
- DeJong: $y = a + bx^n$
- S-curve: $y = a + b (x + c)^n$

The log-linear equation is the simplest and most common equation and it applies to a wide variety of processes. It has been shown to model future productivity very effectively. The log-linear curve models the middle portion of the typical learning curve in Figure 4.8 fairly well, but does not account for the beginning and end segments with much accuracy.

In some cases, the DeJong and Stanford-B equations work better. The Stanford-B equation is used to model processes in which experience carries over from one production run to another, so workers start out more productively than the asymptote predicts.

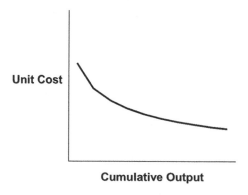

Figure 4.9. Log-linear unit cost function.

The DeJong equation is used to model processes in which a portion of the process cannot improve.

The S-curve equation combines the Stanford-B and DeJong equations to model processes in which both experience carries over from one production run to the next and a portion of the process cannot improve. The S-curve equation often models past productivity more accurately but usually models future productivity less accurately than the other equations. See [Raccoon 1996] for more details.

As it is desirable to maximize learning in an organization, training methods and modes of education come into play. Little or poor training will not provide opportunities to maximize the learning. See the Section 4.7.6, Simulation for Personnel Training, on how simulation itself can be a cost-effective training solution.

4.5.1 Example: Learning Curve Models

Now let us apply some of these learning curve concepts and implement the formulas in system dynamics feedback structures. A summary of these models is in Table 4.3. A demonstration set of learning curve models is provided in *learning curves.itm*. The model in Figure 4.10 uses a log-linear learning curve with a learning factor of 80%. This is the factor for software development estimated by Raccoon, and will be compared later to other data and formulations.

The output for this model shows a 6:1 range in productivity over 500 days (Figure 4.11), which is much greater than intuition and experience dictates. This indicates that some scaling and/or an offset should be employed, but the general shape is reasonable for a learning curve.

The next section shows how this learning function and similar formulations compare to the COCOMO static model experience factors. It also shows a way to mimic the COCOMO multipliers directly using a fixed learning curve as an alternative to the dynamic learning approach described above.

4.5.1.1 *Learning Curve Comparison with COCOMO Experience Data*

It is best to use empirical data for comparison when assessing the learning curve for software processes. One source of data for this is the COCOMO II project. There are several experience factors in the model. The effort multipliers for these factors are derived from Bayesian statistical analysis of actual reported project data. Some of the

Table 4.3. Learning curve models overview

Purpose: Planning, Training			
Scope: Development Project			
Inputs and Parameters	Levels	Major Relationships	Outputs

• Learning factor
• First unit cost
• (or) Productivity curve
	• Tasks completed	• Unit cost or
		  productivity
			• Productivity or
			  productivity
			  multipliers

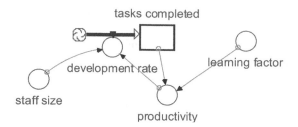

Figure 4.10. Model of log-linear learning curve (learning factor = 0.8).

learning curve formulations will be compared with COCOMO multipliers derived from this data.

Figure 4.12 shows a comparison of the log-linear learning curve with COCOMO experience multipliers using hours of experience as the common unit. There is a mild disparity between the COCOMO points and the continuous learning curve. The CO-COMO multipliers exhibit a learning factor of about 0.7 for the first year, 0.8 for the next couple of years, and about 0.82 after three years of experience.

The graph shows reasonable agreement with Raccoon's estimate of an 80% learning rate for software development. The COCOMO multipliers exhibit an S-shaped curve, however, whereby learning is quicker in the beginning (a smaller learning rate) and not as great after several years (e.g., the approximate learning rate of 82%). The S-curve described by $y = a + b(x + c)^n$ can also be fitted to the COCOMO S-shape. This

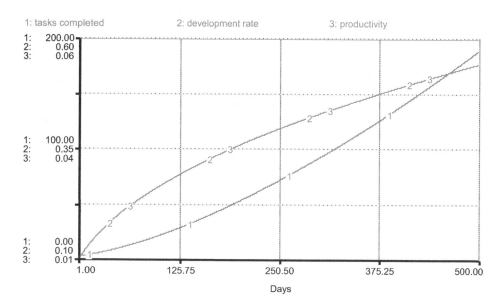

Figure 4.11. Output of log-linear learning curve model.

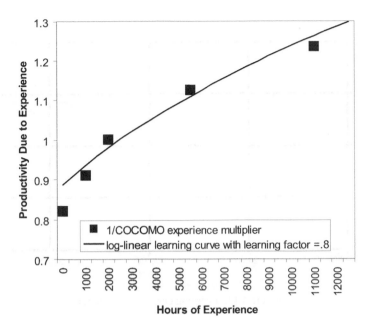

Figure 4.12. Comparison of log-linear learning curve with COCOMO experience multipliers.

mathematical exercise is beyond the scope of this book and is left as an exercise for the interested student.

The modeling implications are that a learning rate of 80% with an initial offset for experience is a fairly good approximation to real data, and that a learning curve is a straightforward formulation for a system dynamics model. The modeler must be aware, though, of the S-shaped characteristics that would produce relatively larger errors in the short term (about one year) and very long term (beyond about 6 years). If only those time portions are of interest, then use the appropriate learning rates instead. For example, use a 70% learning rate if the time horizon is a year or less.

After applying an offset for accumulated experience to the log-linear learning curve model in Figure 4.10, its new corresponding output is in Figure 4.13. The shape is valid for a learning curve and covers the expected region of productivity.

These results against the COCOMO experience factors with learning curves have been corroborated by others. In [Eickelman et al. 2002] the authors used simulation and benchmarking for quantitative control of process changes, and explored productivity issues. Different productivity learning curves were evaluated and compared to CO-COMO II factors. They also found that a curve with an 80% learning rate is the best match to COCOMO data. The regions in which the curves diverged were the same as the results above. They found that using a learning curve helped in benchmarking from year to year and in evaluating longer-term trends and cumulative effects of training and new technologies. A simulation model was useful for evaluating short-term impacts to productivity in a 2 months to 6 year time horizon.

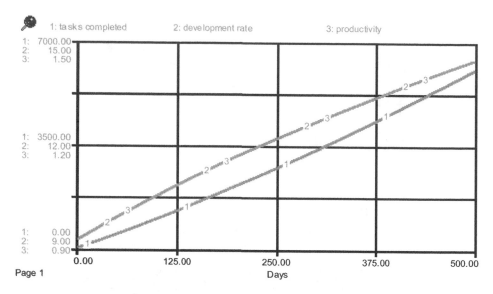

Figure 4.13. Learning curve model output.

4.5.1.2 *Fixed Learning Functions*

Alternatively, a table function could be generated to mimic the COCOMO multipliers. Figure 4.14 shows a function that embodies a productivity multiplier equal to the inverse of the COCOMO effort multipliers. The modeler must be aware, though, of the uncovered region for large time values, as opposed to the log-linear formulation that holds for all time.

A fixed learning curve was used in early system dynamics modeling of software processes at NASA Jet Propulsion Laboratories (JPL) [Lin et al. 1997]. It was one of the first projects to enhance the Abdel-Hamid model, and Chi Lin led the modeling. They employed a fixed learning curve that was calibrated to their typical project length of approximately two years. Figure 4.15 shows the resulting curve as a simple multiplier of productivity. It assumes full-time dedication to the project and approximates the aggregation of COCOMO experience factors. Such a curve will not be the same for a 3-month development project as for a 2-year project. It should be used with caution and recalibrated for different environments.

Learning curves are represented in several other applications in this book. A good example is the use of different learning curves for new language training (see the Chapter 5 modeling example on reuse and high-level languages).

4.6 TEAM COMPOSITION

A hybrid process involves elements of both agile and plan-driven approaches. One of the people issues for hybrid processes is how to compose the teams in terms of skill

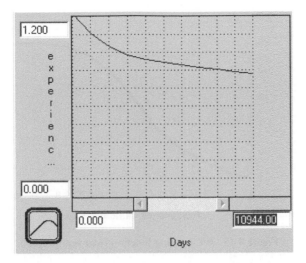

Figure 4.14. Table function for productivity multiplier based on COCOMO experience factor (experience multiplier vs. days).

sets and responsibilities. The following section is based on [Madachy et al. 2007], where simulation is used to find the optimum number of agile people to match anticipated change traffic.*

4.6.1 Example: Assessing Agile Team Size for a Hybrid Process

New processes are being assessed to address modern challenges for Software-Intensive Systems of Systems (SISOS), such as coping with rapid change while simultaneously assuring high dependability. A hybrid agile and plan-driven process based on the spiral life cycle has been outlined to address these conflicting challenges by rapidly fielding incremental capabilities in a value-based framework. A system dynamics model has been developed to assess the incremental hybrid process and support project decision making. It estimates cost and schedule for multiple increments of a hybrid process that uses three specialized teams, and also considers the mission value of software capabilities. It considers changes due to external volatility and feedback from user-driven change requests, and dynamically reestimates and allocates resources in response to the volatility. Deferral policies and team sizes can be experimented with, and it includes trade-off functions between cost and the timing of changes within and across increments, length of deferral delays, and others. We illustrate how the model can be used to determine optimal agile team size to handle changes. Both the hybrid

---

*This is classified as a people application instead of a project application because the primary state variables of interest are the number of people, especially the agile team. Project staffing applications in Chapter 7 use tasks, effort, or other state variables, and staffing needs are derived from those (though there is strong overlap between staffing and people applications).

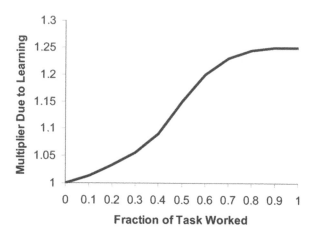

Figure 4.15. JPL learning function (two-year project).

process and simulation model are being evolved on a very large-scale incremental SISOS project and other potential pilots. See Table 4.4 for a summary of the model.

4.6.1.1 Introduction and Background

Our experiences in helping to define, acquire, develop, and assess 21st century SISOS have taught us that traditional acquisition and development processes do not work well on such systems [Boehm et al. 2004, Boehm 2005]. At the University of Southern California (USC) Center for Systems and Software Engineering (CSSE) we are using simulation modeling to help formulate and assess new processes to meet the challenges of these systems.

The systems face ever-increasing demands to provide safe, secure, and reliable systems; to provide competitive discriminators in the marketplace; to support the coordination of multicultural global enterprises; to enable rapid adaptation to change; and to help people cope with complex masses of data and information. These demands will cause major differences in current processes [Boehm 2005].

The USC team and others have been developing, applying, and evolving new processes to address SISOS challenges. These include extensions to the risk-driven spiral model to cover broad (many systems), deep (many supplier levels), and long (many increments) acquisitions needing rapid fielding, high assurance, adaptability to high change traffic, and complex interactions with evolving commercial off-the-shelf (COTS) products, legacy systems, and external systems.

The distinguishing features of an SOS are not only that it integrates multiple independently developed systems, but also that it is very large, dynamically evolving, and unprecedented, with emergent requirements and behaviors and complex sociotechnical issues to address. Thus, we have developed a system dynamics model because the methodology is well suited to modeling these dynamic phenomena and their interactions.

Table 4.4. Hybrid incremental process model overview

| Purpose: Planning, Process Improvement | | | |
| Scope: Multiple, Concurrent Increments | | | |

Inputs and Parameters	Levels	Major Relationships	Outputs

• Increments
• Increment overlap
• Baseline capabilities
  per increment
• Agile team size
• Change policies
• Volatility profile
• Capability flags
• Volatility multiplier
• Life-cycle timing
  multiplier
• Change analysis effort
• Construction effort
  distribution
• Increment values
• Field issue metrics
• Schedule per increment
• Overall costs per
  increment
	• Team sizes
	  Agile team
	  Developer team
	  V&V team
	• Software capabilities
	  per increment
	  Changes
	  Required
	  Developed
	  V&V'ed
	• Effort per increment
		• Volatility tradeoffs
		• Change analysis
		  dynamics
		• Effort and schedule
		  algorithms
		• Staffing change
		  algorithms
			• Staffing profiles
			  per team per
			  increment

4.6.1.1.1 PREVIOUS SIMULATION WORK. No previous work in software process modeling has focused on hybrid processes for SISOS development. A few efforts have addressed incremental (or iterative) development and the effects of requirements changes. Software requirements volatility and change control dynamics was investigated in [Ferreira 2002] and [Ferreira et al. 2003]. Data in that research showed an average of 32% requirements volatility in over 200 projects, which was captured in their model. Iteration management as a way to reduce cycle time in the midst of change was addressed in [Ford, Sterman 2003], who modeled the 90% syndrome and impact of concealing requirements changes. The use of fire-fighting techniques to handle late changes is described in [Repenning 2001], which illustrates how late rework leads to perpetual firefighting in a multiproject development environment. Both [Ford, Sterman 2003] and [Repenning 2001] addressed high technology applications, but not in the specific context of software projects.

A few efforts have simulated incremental or iterative software development. The research in [Tvedt 1996] modeled concurrent incremental development and the impact of inspections. The cost and schedule impacts of different increment options were assessed with the model. Another incremental development model to assess cost and schedule was developed in [Sycamore 1995], though both of these models were limited in their cycle variability since they used replicated structures to represent the different increments. Iterative development was modeled with system dynamics in [Powell et al. 1999] and [Powell 2001] to assess both concurrent software engineering and staged delivery as methods to improve cycle time. Requirements changes were included in the iterative model in [Powell 2001] and were based on substantial empirical data. However, none of these efforts considered personnel makeup to best handle changes.

A qualitative model of agile processes is described in [Fernández-Ramil et al. 2005] but this is the first known instance of modeling with system dynamics applied to either hybrid or agile processes.

The model presented here builds on the concepts of requirements volatility and incremental or iterative development in previous research, but it goes a step further by showing the effects of a hybrid process used in incremental development to move away from firefighting to a more controlled process for accommodating changes quickly while balancing software cost, schedule, and value issues.

4.6.1.1.2 THE SCALABLE SPIRAL MODEL.

The outlines of a hybrid plan-driven/agile process for developing an SISOS product architecture are emerging. It is a risk-driven balance of agility and discipline [Boehm, Turner 2004]. In order to keep SISOS developments from becoming destabilized due to large amounts of change traffic, it is important to organize development into plan-driven increments in which the suppliers develop to interface specs that are kept stable by deferring changes, so that the systems can plug and play at the end of the increment. But for the next increment to hit the ground running, an extremely agile team needs to be concurrently and continuously monitoring the market, competition, and technology, doing change impact analysis, refreshing COTS, and renegotiating the next increment's prioritized content and the interfaces between the suppliers' next-increment interface specs.

The spiral model was introduced in 1986 and later elaborated for WinWin extensions [Boehm et al., 1998]. It has continued to evolve to meet the needs of evolving development processes. We have been converging on a scalable spiral process model for SISOS that, for partial implementations to date, has scaled well from small e-services applications to super-large defense systems of systems and multienterprise supply chain management systems.

Figure 4.16 shows a single increment of the development and evolution portion of the model. It assumes that the organization has developed:

- A best-effort definition of the system's steady-state capability
- An incremental sequence of prioritized capabilities culminating in the steady-state capability
- A feasibility rationale providing sufficient evidence that the system architecture will support the incremental capabilities, that each increment can be developed within its available budget and schedule, and that the series of increments create a satisfactory return on investment for the organization and mutually satisfactory outcomes for the success-critical stakeholders

As seen in Figure 4.16, the model is organized to simultaneously address the conflicting challenges of rapid change and high assurance of dependability. It also addresses

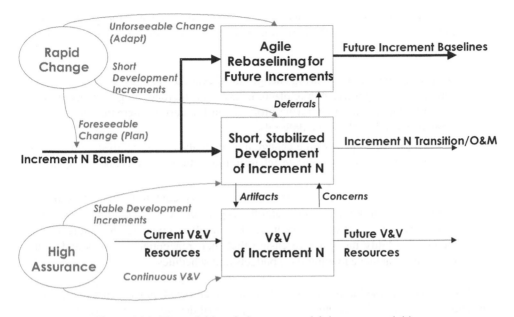

Figure 4.16. The scalable spiral process model: increment activities.

the need for rapid fielding of incremental capabilities with a minimum of rework, and the other trends involving integration of systems and software engineering, COTS components, legacy systems, globalization, and user value considerations.

The hybrid process uses a three-team cycle (lean, plan-driven, stabilized developers; thorough V&Vers; and agile, proactive rebaseliners) that plays out from one increment to the next.

The need to deliver high-assurance incremental capabilities on short fixed schedules means that each increment needs to be kept as stable as possible. This is particularly the case for very large systems of systems with deep supplier hierarchies in which a high level of rebaselining traffic can easily lead to chaos. The risks of destabilizing the development process make this portion of the project into a waterfall-like, build-to-specification subset of the spiral model activities. The need for high assurance of each increment also makes it cost-effective to invest in a team of appropriately skilled personnel to continuously verify and validate the increment as it is being developed.

However, "deferring the change traffic" does not imply deferring its change impact analysis, change negotiation, and rebaselining until the beginning of the next increment. With a single development team and rapid rates of change, this would require a team optimized to develop to stable plans and specifications to spend much of the next increment's scarce calendar time performing tasks much better suited to agile teams.

The appropriate metaphor for addressing rapid change is not a build-to-specification metaphor or a purchasing-agent metaphor but an adaptive "command–control–intelligence–surveillance–reconnaissance" (C2ISR) metaphor. It involves an agile team performing the first three activities of the C2ISR "Observe, Orient, Decide, Act"

(OODA) loop for the next increments, while the plan-driven development team is performing the "Act" activity for the current increment. These agile activities are summarized below:

- Observing involves monitoring changes in relevant technology and COTS products, in the competitive marketplace, in external interoperating systems, and in the environment; and monitoring progress on the current increment to identify slowdowns and likely scope deferrals.
- Orienting involves performing change impact analyses, risk analyses, and trade-off analyses to assess candidate rebaselining options for the upcoming increments.
- Deciding involves stakeholder renegotiation of the content of upcoming increments, architecture rebaselining, and the degree of COTS upgrading to be done to prepare for the next increment. It also involves updating the future increments' feasibility rationales to ensure that their renegotiated scopes and solutions can be achieved within their budgets and schedules.

A successful rebaseline means that the plan-driven development team can hit the ground running at the beginning of the "Act" phase of developing the next increment, and the agile team can hit the ground running on rebaselining definitions of the increments beyond.

As much as possible, usage feedback from the previous increment is not allowed to destabilize the current increment, but is fed into the definition of the following increment. Of course, some level of mission-critical updates will need to be fed into the current increment, but only when the risk of not doing so is greater that the risk of destabilizing the current increment.

4.6.1.2 Model Overview

The primary portion of the system dynamics model diagram showing increment activities and the teams is in Figure 4.17. It is built around a cyclic flow chain for capabilities and uses arrays to model multiple increments. The flow chains for the increment activities show multiple layers of levels and rates; these identify array elements that correspond to the increments. Thus, the flow chain and its equations are arrays of five to model five increments (this preset number can be changed to model more or fewer increments). Note that multiple flows that appear to be flowing into the same level may be flowing into different levels with different array indices, depending on the logic of the increment allocation of capabilities.

Unanticipated changes arrive as aperiodic pulses via the *volatility trends* parameter. This is how they actually come on the projects as opposed to a constant level of volatility over time. The user can specify the pulses graphically (see the input for volatility profile in Figure 4.18) or use formulas. The *capability volatility rate* will flow the changes into the corresponding increment for the current time. From there they arrive in the level for *capability changes* and are then processed by the agile rebaselining team. They analyze the changes per the *average change analysis effort* parameter.

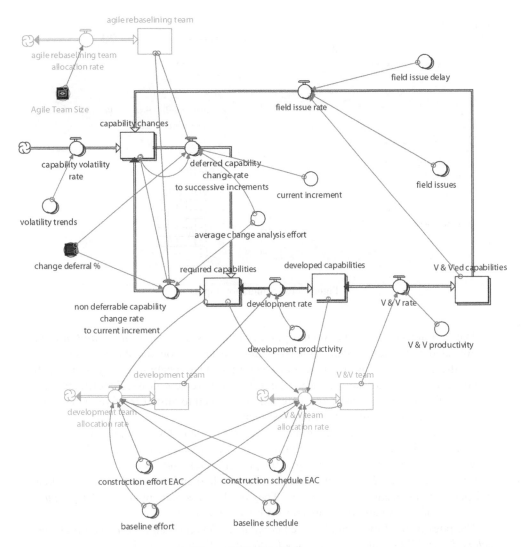

Figure 4.17. Model diagram.

Their overall productivity is a function of the *agile team size* (as specified by the user in Figure 4.18) and the average analysis effort.

The *change deferral %* is a policy parameter used to specify the percentage of changes that must be deferred to later increments via the *deferred capability change rate to succeeding increments* to the *required capabilities* for the appropriate increments. The remaining ones are nondeferrables that flow into the *required capabilities* for the current increment via the rate *non deferrable capability rate change to current increment.* The deferral policy parameter is also shown in the inputs in Figure 4.18.

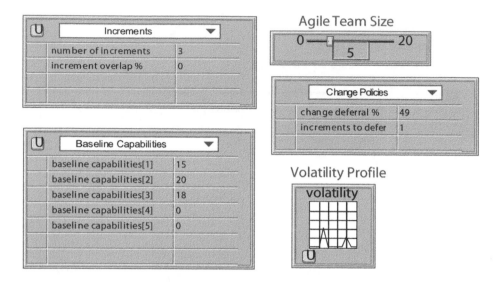

Figure 4.18. Simulation inputs.

The two arrayed flows between *capability changes* and *required capabilities* are complicated multiplexers that cannot be fully visualized on the diagram. On both paths, there are five flows (or pipes) between them that capabilities may go through and the capabilities can move between the different increment flows. For different reasons, capabilities may be assigned, deferred, or delayed to any of the five increments, and the full set of possible paths cannot be seen.

When an increment starts, the *required capabilities* are developed by the development team at the *development rate* and flow into *developed capabilities* (all using the flow chain array index corresponding to the proper increment).

Similarly, the *developed capabilities* are then picked up by the V&V team for their independent verification and validation. They do their assessment at the *V&V productivity rate* and the capabilities flow into *V&V'ed capabilities*.

The rates in the flow chain between *capability changes, required capabilities, developed capabilities,* and *V&V'ed capabilities* are all bidirectional. There is a provision for capabilities to be "kicked back" or rejected by the various teams and sent back up the chain. For example, there are times when the developers have major concerns about a new capability and send it back to the rebaselining team. Likewise, the V&V team might find some serious defects that must be reworked by the developers.

Finally there are user-driven changes based on field experience with the system. These are identified as *field issues* that flow back into the *capability changes* per the *field issue rate* at a constant *field issue delay* time. The *field issues* parameter represents the amount of concern with the fielded system and accounts for a primary feedback loop.

The agile baselining team is shown in the top left of the diagram. The size of the team can be specified as a constant size or a varying number of people over time via the inputs in Figure 4.18. The *agile rebaselining team allocation rate* flows people in or out of the team to match the specified team size over time.

The development and V&V teams are shown at the bottom. Their allocation rates are based on the construction effort and schedule for the required capabilities known to date. Currently, the productivities and team sizes for development and V&V are calculated with a Dynamic COCOMO [Boehm et al. 2000] variant. They are equivalent to COCOMO for a static project (the converse situation of this model context) and are continuously recalculated for changes. However, this aspect of the model whereby the team sizes are parametrically determined from size and effort multipliers will be refined so that constraints can be put on the development and V&V staff sizes. See Section 4.6.1.2.2 for more details on the staffing algorithms.

4.6.1.2.1   TRADE-OFF FUNCTIONS.   There are several functional relationships in the model that effect trade-offs between deferral times and cost/schedule. For one, it is costlier to develop software when there is a lot of volatility during the development. If required capabilities are added to an increment being developed, the overall effort increases due to the extra scope as well as the added volatility. The effort multiplier in Figure 4.19 is used to calculate the construction effort and schedule based on a volatility ratio of total required capabilities to the baseline capabilities. This example shows a simple linear relationship, though the graphical construct allows it to be user defined and become nonlinear (as in Figure 4.20 described next).

The volatility factor in Figure 4.19 is an aggregate multiplier for volatility from different sources. It works similarly to the platform volatility multiplier in COCOMO II, the USC CSSE software cost estimation model. The difference in this context is that there may be many more sources of volatility (e.g., COTS, mission, etc.). This multiplier effect only holds for an increment when changes arrive midstream. If new

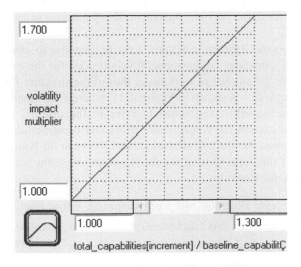

Figure 4.19. Volatility effort multiplier.

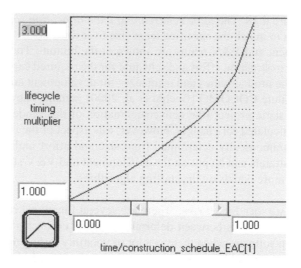

Figure 4.20. Life-cycle timing effort multiplier.

changes are already in the required capabilities when an increment starts, then it has no effect.

Additionally, the later a new capability comes in during construction, the higher the cost to develop it. This is very similar to the cost-to-fix defects, for which the costs increases exponentially. Figure 4.20 shows the life-cycle timing multiplier based on a ratio of the current time to the entire increment schedule.

Under normal circumstances, there is an additional cost of delaying capabilities to future increments because there is more of a software base to be dealt with and integrated into. Therefore, we increase the cost of deferring to future increments by an additional 25% relative to the previous increment (this parameter is easily changed).

4.6.1.2.2 DYNAMIC RESOURCE ALLOCATION. In response to changes in the capabilities, the model calculates the personnel levels needed for the new increment size and interpolates for the amount of work done. Part of the structure for continuous calculation of staffing levels is shown in Figure 4.21, where EAC stands for "estimate at completion." Baseline effort and schedule refer to the original plan without any volatility. The parameters for construction effort and construction schedule are the ones used to determine the staffing allocation rates shown at the bottom of Figure 4.17.

An example of the delta staffing for the development team when new capability changes come into the system is:

development team allocation rate = (development_effort_fraction

· construction_effort_EAC(increment)/development_schedule_fraction

· construction_schedule_EAC(increment)) – development_effort_fraction

· baseline_effort(increment)/(development_schedule_fraction

· baseline_schedule(increment)

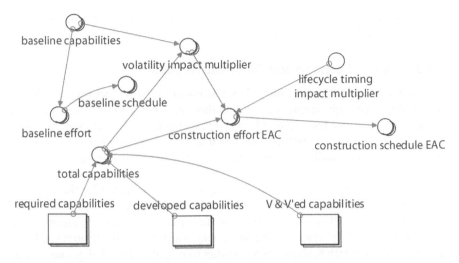

Figure 4.21. Staffing calculation parameters.

The development effort and schedule fractions are the calibrated portions of effort and schedule for development with respect to all of construction, and the V&V allocation algorithm works similarly. If the increment has just started, then the interpolated staffing level will be closer to the higher level needed for the new EAC. If the increment is mostly done, then it does not make sense to increase staff to the EAC level because almost all the work is done anyway.

On the SISOS project we are primarily applying the model to, there are already over 2000 software development people on board, and most contractors have already hired their steady-state levels of personnel. Thus, it is reasonable to assume a nearly constant level of construction staffing with no major ramp-ups, and a step-function staffing profile that approximates labor with average levels and nonoverlapping phases.

The step-function staffing profile is improved with a Rayleigh curve staffing version of the model that intrinsically changes the staffing when changes occur, with no interpolation necessary. It also assumes overlap of activities, and the starting point of V&V can be specified with respect to development. For illustration here, we will continue to use the step-function version since the results are generally easier to follow and interpret.

4.6.1.2.3 PARAMETERIZATIONS. Since this is a macro model for very large systems, a capability is a "sky level" requirement measure. It is defined as a very high-level requirement that we have made equivalent to 10 KSLOC for the purpose of estimation. The construction effort and schedule is currently calculated with a Dynamic COCOMO approach using the COCOMO II.2000 calibration [Boehm et al. 2000].

The volatility impact multiplier is an extension of COCOMO for the SISOS situation. It is extrapolated from the current model and partially based on expert judgment. Other parameterizations relying on expert judgment include the average change analysis effort, life-cycle timing multiplier, and amount of field issues. They will be updated based on empirical data we are collecting.

4.6.1.3 Sample Scenario and Test Case Results

We have put the model through multiple scenarios to assess project options. Here, we demonstrate a seemingly simple scenario and show how it plays out to be a rather complex trade-off situation. The scenario being demonstrated is for developing two successive increments of 15 capabilities each, with a nondeferrable change coming midstream that has to be handled. The agile team size is varied from two to twenty people in the test cases.

A capability change comes in at month eight and is processed by the agile team. The change is nondeferrable as it needs to be in Increment 1. An illustration of how the system responds to such a volatility pulse in Increment 1 is shown in Figure 4.22. In the figure legend, "[1]' refers to the increment number 1. An unanticipated set of changes occurs at month 8, shown as a *volatility trend* pulse. The changes immediately flow into the level for *capability changes,* which then starts declining to zero as an agile team works it off per the average change analysis effort of four person-months. The change is nondeferrable and it becomes incorporated into Increment 1, so the *total capabilities* for the increment increases. As the new capabilities become required for Increment 1, the development staffing responds to the increased scope by dynamically adjusting the team size to a new level.

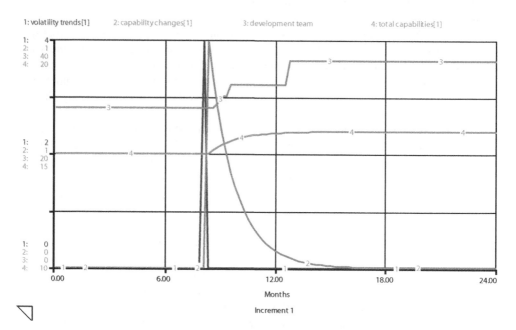

Figure 4.22. System response to volatility—Increment 1.

However, the different team sizes will analyze the change at different rates. Figures 4.23–4.25 show the test cases results for varying the agile team size. If the team size is too small, then it will not even make it into Increment 1. The agile team cannot even process the change in time for Increment 1 with two to four people. In these cases, the new capability for Increment 1 is processed too late and goes into Increment 2 instead. But with six people on the agile team it can make it in time. The larger team size will process the change and incorporate it faster; hence, the effort and schedule for Increment 1 improves with an agile team size of six or higher.

A summary of the resulting dynamics for these cases are:

- Two agile people take the longest time to process the change. The capability is ready for implementation late in Increment 2 and incurs a substantial effort penalty per the lifecycle timing effort multiplier. Its cost is greater than if the capability were ready at the start of Increment 2. Increment 2 also incurs the volatility multiplier effect and costs more than its original baseline. Increment 1 executes to its baseline plan.

- Four agile people process the change faster, but still not in time for Increment 1. The Increment 2 life-cycle timing impact is not as great as the case for two people. Increment 1 again matches its original baseline plan.

- Six people can process the change fast enough to get it into Increment 1, but it comes in late and incurs the late life-cycle timing effort multiplier. Increment 2 does not vary from its baseline

- Eight people are faster than six, so the Increment 1 losses are reduced and Increment 2 is still at its baseline.

- Ten people similarly improve upon the team of eight. Increment 1 construction effort is reduced relative to the team of eight because the change comes in sooner. Increment 2 remains unchanged.

- As the agile team grows from ten to twenty people, the impact of late life-cycle changes decreases less than the added effort due to more agile people. With larger agile team sizes, the effect of the life-cycle timing effort multiplier in Figure 4.20 moves from the steep portion at the top down to the shallow part where changes come early in the increment.

Figure 4.23 shows the components of effort as a function of the agile team size. The effort for the constant-size agile team increases linearly as its size grows. It is the smallest relative component of effort when under ten people. The Increment 1 construction effort (development + V&V) at two and four agile people is the baseline effort since the capability change did not reach it. It is highest cost at six people due to the late life-cycle effort multiplier effect, and that penalty is reduced at eight and ten people since it comes in sooner. Above ten people, the total cost rises slowly due to the agile team size increasing and impact of lateness decreasing, as previously described.

Roughly converse effects are shown in the effort function for Increment 2. At two and four people, the cost of Increment 2 is very high because the small agile team takes a long time to analyze the change. It comes in latest with the smallest team incurring a

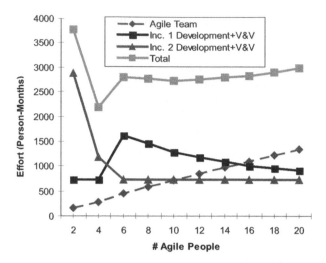

Figure 4.23. Effort versus agile team size.

very high penalty for being late in the life cycle. Six through twenty people can process the change before Increment 2 starts, so the effort is the same for those cases. The Increment 2 effort exceeds its original baseline due to the added volatility of the single capability.

Figure 4.24 shows the test case schedule results for both increments and overall. They are analogous to the effort functions shown in Figure 4.23 for the two increments. Their shape mirrors the effort curves at approximately the 1/3 power. This em-

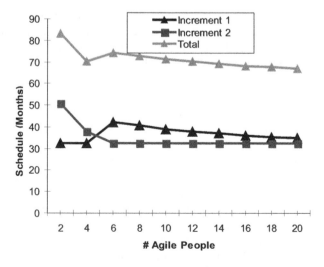

Figure 4.24. Schedule versus agile team size.

pirical correlation between software effort and schedule is described in [Boehm et al. 2000].

Investigating Figure 4.23 and Figure 4.24 may lead to the erroneous conclusion that four people is the optimum since that produces the least overall cost and schedule. The total effort for four agile people may look promising since the change was effectively deferred and did not incur life-cycle timing losses. However, the bigger picture must consider the mission value losses incurred by the smaller teams.

4.6.1.3.1 SOFTWARE VALUE CONSIDERATIONS. These results are incomplete without casting them in a value-based framework. The model outputs described so far cover development cost and schedule impacts, but not the mission value of the software intended for the increments. Our project context of an extremely large government defense project places value on the utility of mission capabilities in terms of war-time performance measures. However, the value-based technique also is applicable to commercial projects where the software utility is more directly quantified in terms of monetary return on investment (ROI). See the business case model in Chapter 5 for process and product decisions using business value measures such as market share, sales, and ROI.

The mission capability values will be simplified using the conservative assumption that they are at least equivalent to their cost of development. Presumably in any software venture, the desired capabilities are worth at least their cost, otherwise there is no reason to take on the project, though there are exceptions to knowingly lose money on development as an investment to gain better chances for larger future gains (e.g., internal product research and development for a potentially large external market).

In our project case, the required capabilities are direly needed to address real battle threats, and they are carefully planned out in time. Real mission value will be lost if they are not delivered on time. Our assumption of their value being equal to development cost is unquestionably very conservative; in reality, their utility values are judged to be several times more. Their utility does not expire 100% at the planned time of delivery, but for simplification we will assume so in our analysis and still demonstrate a valid picture of the situation. Our two simplifying assumptions also balance out each other a bit, by underestimating the mission value and possibly overestimating the full discrete loss at intended delivery time. Now we have accounted for a discrete mission value loss in Increment 1, but there are even more time-dependent losses to account for since Increment 2 stretches out. This analysis can be further refined to account for the loss of value as a diminishing function over time, and the results will vary a bit.

Figure 4.25 shows the value-based analysis for handling the capability change in terms of all costs, and can be considered a minimum view of the actual value loss per our conservative assumption previously described. With a more global value consideration, it is evident that four people are no longer the optimum. According to these results, a larger team size is optimum and the losses decrease very slightly when increasing the team size up to ten people. The region of slightly rising effort between ten and twenty people produces the sweet spot cost minimum at ten people.

These results account for the life-cycle timing multiplier, volatility multiplier, increment delay losses, and a quantification of software capability value. The model

Figure 4.25. Cost versus agile team size.

shows that a sufficient level of agile rebaseliners is necessary, or the cost and schedule for the project increases substantially. The losses are even worse when considering the mission value. Enough people must be on board and productive enough to analyze the changes in a timely manner. Otherwise, there could be a backlog of work to worry about at the beginning of a later increment that could have been resolved earlier by the agile team, or there are other losses. If we further refine upward our conservative estimate of the mission value, the results will lead to the same decision.

Without explanation of these dynamic effects across increments, this apparently simple case of a single change may seem confounding at first with the multiple maxima and minima in the results. When adding the consideration of mission value, the results become even more cogent, explainable, and grounded in practicality. Another corresponding example is to show the results for a single change destined for Increment 2 while holding all the experimental parameters the same. The results are similarly complex, and we are going forward with scenario permutations consisting of multiple capability changes.

4.6.1.4   Conclusions and Future Work

Processes need to be rethought for current and upcoming SISOS, and the outlined hybrid process based on the scalable spiral model appears to be an attractive option. The dynamic model will help to further refine the hybrid process and determine optimized variants for different situations.

Traditionally, it has been thought that agile processes are not suitable for very large software development projects, particularly ones with high dependability requirements. However, this approach addresses concerns by retaining large pockets of stability on the construction teams for development and V&V. We believe this hybrid approach would be applicable to programs across the size spectrum from small to very large. This is another aspect that we can eventually address with the model by descaling the simulated project and even changing its domain context.

This second major iteration of the model provides interesting results. It shows that if the agile team does not do their work rapidly enough, then developers will have to do it at a higher cost due to changes late in the life cycle, and mission losses may also occur. Further experiments are underway to vary the deferral percentages and perturbation smoothing policies, include rework, and constrain the staff sizes for development and V&V.

Both the hybrid process and the model will be further analyzed and evolved. Various improvements in the model have already been identified and are briefly discussed below, but further changes will come from users of the model and additional empirical data will be used to calibrate and parameterize the model.

The set of test cases we demonstrated varied agile team size, but other dimensions to vary are the deferral percentage and perturbation smoothing policies. Additionally, we are simulating all five increments with volatility occurring in more than one increment in experiments.

This version of the model uses step function staffing profiles that adjust dynamically to changes. Another version uses Rayleigh curves for more realistic staffing patterns that adjust on the fly to midstream changes. These models will be integrated to allow the user to specify the type of staffing.

In the current test cases, only the optimum personnel levels are used for development and V&V but, in reality, there may be staffing constraints. The model will be refined so users can constrain the development and V&V staff sizes. Another set of tests will compare trade-offs between different agile team staffing policies (e.g., level of effort vs. demand driven).

Patterns of changes and change policies will be experimented with. We will vary the volatility profiles across increments and demonstrate kickback cases for capabilities flowing back up the chain from the developers or V&V'ers. Additionally we will model more flexible deferral policies across increments to replace the current binary simplification of allocating changes to the current or next increment.

We are implementing an increment "balancing policy" so that large perturbations for an increment can be optionally spread across increments. The user can specify the number of increments and the relative weighting of capability across them. This balancing policy will tend to smooth large fluctuations in staffing and minimize costly ramp-ups (but always traded off against lost mission value).

Value-based considerations should be part of the overall process analysis. We showed that accounting for the mission/business value of software capabilities made the results more practical, coherent, and explainable in terms of finding trade-off sweet spots. We will refine the value-based considerations to quantify the time-specific value of capabilities instead of assuming full discrete losses.

Parts of the model have been parameterized based on actual empirical data, but not the change traffic. We will be getting actual data on volatility, change traffic trends, and field issue rates from our USC affiliates and other users of the model. Data for the change analysis effort and volatility cost functions will also be analyzed.

After we get change data to populate the model and make other indicated improvements, we plan to use it to assess increment risk for a very large-scale SISOS program. It will also be used by contractors on the program in addition to our own independent usage to assess process options.

We also plan to apply it to other projects we are involved with, and the model will be supplied to our USC-CSSE industrial affiliates for assessing and improving their processes. Some of these users will also provide us with additional empirical data for parameterizing the model.

4.7 OTHER APPLICATION AREAS

This section is a special case for the applications chapters. There are many important areas of people issues not covered by examples earlier in this chapter. Some of these are addressed below to help "prime the pump" and overview areas for which no major models were available or only preliminary efforts have been made. Therefore, these sections are not supported with specific models except for some small demonstrations and/or causal loops. All of them provide fodder for future people-modeling applications.

4.7.1 Motivation

Motivation can have tremendously varying impact over time. It may even eclipse the effects of skill and experience on projects. Motivation may wax and wane due to a multitude of factors and impact productivity either way. A developer may or may not be interested in the application, he/she may have a very good or poor relationship with superiors, and management might be responsible for creating conditions for high or low motivation. For example, if a project is perceived to be not particularly important to the company, then developers will likewise not place too much emphasis on their performance. If there are impending organizational changes or just rumors to that effect, then some people will go into a "wait-and-see" mode and not produce much until their place in the organization is known. On the other hand, if there is a competitive chance that one's career trajectory might hinge on one's short-term performance, then that person will probably work very hard. These events may go on throughout a project's lifetime, and people will traverse through several up or down motivational phases during a project. Sometimes, the degree of staff motivation is obvious and can be modeled with relative certainty.

It is well known that people may use some time during the day to catch up on personal errands or do other nonproductive activities. Several studies have indicated that usually only about 60% of a person's time is actually spent producing (reference the exhaustion model preceding this section). This is related to Parkinson's Law, which holds that work expands to fill up the available time.

Motivation is clearly a decisive factor in successful companies. The following passages from [Yamamura 1999] are from the article *Process Improvement Satisfies Employees* that describes experiences in an early Boeing CMM Level 5 organization:

An inspired employee's performance is a powerful tool for an organization. Motivated employees work with unbounded energy, create innovative solutions, and, most importantly, have great attitudes. They are always looking for better ways to do their job, and they feel comfortable volunteering for special assignments. In addition, management and the employees have a sense of trust.

Satisfied employees lead to successful programs. People that are well trained, fit the job, have the right skills, are motivated, and execute their tasks with passion are the most likely to help a project succeed. Management can promote employee satisfaction with a project with good planning, a disciplined development environment, growth opportunities, special assignments, mentoring, and a focus on process improvements. Management should not overlook one of the most powerful tools they have—the highly satisfied and motivated employee.

There are various incentive schemes that companies can offer to improve motivation. These may be in the form of career planning and guidance, training and mentoring programs, an open environment for proactive improvements, financial bonuses, awards, recreational facilities and activities, extracurricular events, and so on.

A recent article by [Humphrey, Konrad 2005] discusses motivation and process improvement. It discusses people issues in a broader context than just developers and their capabilities and motivations. Many people in an organization affect the work. They show how the attitudes and concerns of people in the entire integrated community can help or hurt the work of developing, supporting, and enhancing software.

4.7.1.1 Overtime

Pressure to work overtime can greatly influence motivation and overall productivity. Studies have indicated that a small amount of aggressive scheduling will tend to motivate people to produce more, but highly unreasonable goals will have the opposite effect. The management challenge is to strike the right balance. The following example picks up from Chapter 2, where an overtime productivity function was formulated. We will elaborate the function for additional effects and organizational variants.

The overtime function in Chapter 2 represents the dynamics in a typical company, but in reality different classes of organizations exhibit varying productivity multiplier curves. Overtime rates, like other dynamic effects, often depend on the type of industry. Compensation is a primary motivation factor in most cases, and the degree of pioneering work is also of importance. People who have large financial incentives (such as the stock options in start-up companies) tend to work much longer hours. For example, people in an entrepreneurial start-up situation are going to be much more willing to put in overtime as opposed to those in a civil servant position. They are expected to do so and generally are motivated by the chance to make an impact and a windfall of money if the start-up is successful. Civil service employees have no such motivation and may, in fact, expect job security even if they do not consistently work hard.

Table 4.5 shows typical maximum workweeks for representative software development environments. These may also be adjusted higher depending on whether standard pay or extra overtime pay is given beyond 40 hours. Except for the civil service sector,

Table 4.5. Representative maximum workweeks

Industry Type	Typical Maximum Workweek (Hours)
Civil service	40
Fortune 500 aerospace/defense	50–60
Fortune 500 commercial software (e.g., telecommunications, enterprise software)	50–70
High-technology start-ups with stock options	80–100

these workweeks may become even longer during schedule crunch periods immediately preceding product delivery dates.

Figure 4.26 shows a representative family of curves for these extreme situations. Any organization modeling the overtime factor should calibrate as best as possible for their own environment and culture. Different organizational behaviors varying by industry or domain are seen for many phenomena. See the previous section for representative workweeks and later sections on attrition rates for selected industries.

The curves shown level off, and when extrapolated further into the oversaturated zone they eventually show degraded productivity as the expectation is set too high. For many individuals, the overtime productivity curve will exhibit a downward trend after a point, representing a retrenchment or purposeful backlash against (unreasonable) management policy. They may feel they have already paid their dues of heavy

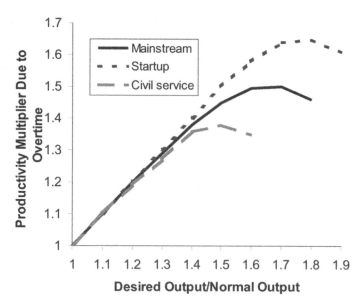

Figure 4.26. Family of curves for productivity due to overtime.

overtime and no matter what, they are going to take care of things other than work.

The deleterious effects of overly aggressive schedules are realized in other ways such as increased error generation (see the Abdel-Hamid project model for example) and personnel attrition. Too high pressure will cause more turnover, so the new learning curves and ramping up for the replacements have to be accounted for.

Mandatory overtime can also lead to the destruction of well-working teams as described in [DeMarco, Lister 1999]. Since not everyone can participate equally in overtime due to outside responsibilities, a divide widens on the team and it can eventually lead to total team breakdown. These are some of the ways that aggressive and unrealistic scheduling can be cross-purposeful. The indirect costs of overtime can easily outstrip any temporary gains in productivity. Another negative aspect of sustained overwork is modeled in the section on exhaustion and burnout.

4.7.1.2 Slack Time

The near opposite of overtime is slack time. The importance of having slack time is described in Tom DeMarco's book *Slack: Getting Past Burnout, Busywork, and the Myth of Total Efficiency* [DeMarco 2001]. Slack is necessary for people to get inspiration for new ideas and be creative. Running too tight a ship and requiring overtime works against that. Managers should foster environments where slack time is possible.

DeMarco also quantifies the effects of overtime in terms of probability of meeting schedule. Figure 4.27 shows that relationship from [DeMarco 2001]. The effect he is modeling is a schedule-oriented view of the overtime phenomenon modeled in Section 4.7.1.1. In region I, workers respond to pressure by trimming waste and concentrating on the critical path. In region II, they are getting tired and feeling added life pressure, so some undertime is taken. In region III, they have had enough and are looking for other work. This relationship may serve as reference behavior for a simulation project investigating slack time effects.

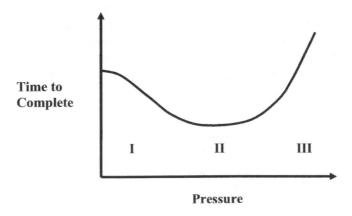

Figure 4.27. Effect of pressure on completion time, from [DeMarco 2001].

4.7.2 Personnel Hiring and Retention

Acquiring good personnel is often very difficult, but is time well spent. Personnel must first be found and identified. Then they have to be sold on a particular job, and negotiations ensue until all parties reach a hiring agreement. But acquisition is only part of the battle. People need to stick around long enough to recoup the investments made in them.

4.7.2.1 Hiring Delays

The time needed to hire new employees depends on the position levels, organizational culture and processes, current market trends, and so on. There are a number of steps in the overall hiring process at which things can slow down. The average hiring delay time for a position increases greatly with the level of experience and specialized knowledge sought. Table 4.6 shows some representative delay times for standard positions that can be used with a model for hiring delays.

The ranges in Table 4.6 account for differences in organizational practices, market conditions, and so on. A nimble, small startup company can accelerate hiring to a fraction of the time needed by a large entrenched organization requiring multiple approvals and background checks. It has been reported that Internet technology has been able to reduce the time for hiring from a 2–3 months to a few short weeks for some companies. The gains are presumably in the candidate location phase and not the resulting interviews, decision making, negotiations, and so on.

The ranges also account for some of the management controllables. For example, there are ways that the hiring process can be accelerated, like allocating enough money up-front for prime candidates to avoid offer iteration, hiring bonuses, or creative ways to lure good prospective employees. The hiring personnel, often human resources, can be given explicit priorities or be motivated otherwise to expedite hiring.

4.7.2.1.1 EXAMPLE: HIRING DELAY MODEL. A simple delay structure is a convenient way to model hiring delays. The delay time refers to the period from when a position is open, normally through a job requisition process, to when a new hire starts work. The hiring delay from model in Chapter 3, also shown in Figure 4.28, is used for sensitivity testing in Figure 4.29. For an entry-level person, the average hiring delay is varied from 1 to 3 months to gauge the effect on the hiring ramp-up. See the model, *hiring delay.itm.*

Table 4.6. Representative software development hiring delays

Position	Typical Hiring Delays
Entry-level programmer	1–3 months
Senior technical person/team lead	2–6 months
Software manager	3–8 months
Software director	6–12 months

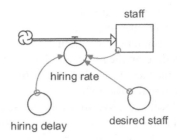

Figure 4.28. Hiring delay structure.

4.7.2.2 Attrition

Attrition should be minimized to reap the benefits of gained experience and to maintain a corporate memory. Employee turnover has been identified in recent years as an important factor in process performance. It is one of the newer factors in the COCOMO II model.

An ACM special interest group undertook a study on factors influencing employee turnover [Palmer et al. 1998]. This article has some good guidelines for those wrestling with retaining employees. It also lists some classic references about employee turnover issues for general industry. It is part of a conference proceedings on computer personnel that discusses several other highly relevant people issues.

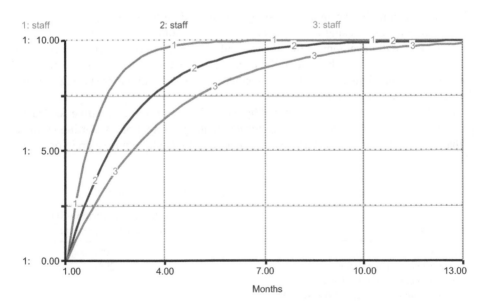

Figure 4.29. Hiring delay sensitivity (1: hiring delay = 1 month, 2: hiring delay = 2 months, 3: hiring delay = 3 months).

Table 4.7 shows typical personnel attrition rates for standard industry working environments. These are aggregate rates that include all ranges of experience. Younger personnel tend to move between jobs more often than senior people, so the rates listed may need adjustment depending on the respective levels of experience within an organization. During periods of business instability, the Fortune 500 companies may exhibit higher attrition by an additional 10%–15%.

Attrition rates are also localized geographically. Most notably, Silicon Valley and other pockets of high-technology start-up companies exhibit much higher attrition rates across all industry types due to the plethora of opportunities available.

These rates could change substantially given different economic conditions. We know that the dynamic pendulum swings ever quicker now; witness the droves of people who left for Internet firms in 1996–2000 and the migration back in the dot com shakeout shortly thereafter.

Some have argued that the type of process itself can lead to more stability in the workforce. Watts Humphrey has reported that the attrition rates observed when following the Team Software Process (TSP) are essentially zero [Humphrey 1999], though this claim should be followed up and analyzed with more samples.

In *Peopleware,* Demarco and Lister explain that there are both visible and not so visible signs of attrition. It is the not so visible signs that can have far greater effects. A visible sign would be manpower expense. A primary not so visible effect is the tendency of people to lean toward a short-term perspective, which becomes destructive.

4.7.2.3 Workforce Shortage

There is a seemingly ever-present shortage of skilled software and IT personnel to meet market needs. Closing the gap entails long-term solutions for university education, ongoing skill development in industry, and worker incentives. Howard Rubin has studied the IT workforce shortage in the United States [Rubin 1997]. One of the problem issues he mentions is a destructive feedback loop whereby labor shortages cause further deterioration in the market.

The degenerative feedback described by Rubin is a reinforcing (positive feedback) process between worker shortages, staff turnover, and job retention. A starting premise is that new people on a project are less productive at first, and require a drain on expe-

Table 4.7. Representative software development attrition rates

Industry Type	Typical Personnel Attrition Rates* (percent attrition per year)
Civil service	5%–10%
Fortune 500 aerospace/defense	5%–20%
Fortune 500 commercial software (e.g., telecommunications, enterprise software)	5%–25%
High-technology start-ups with stock options	20%–50%

*See the discussion above for modifiers due to business instability and geography.

rienced people needed to teach the new hires. The learning curve and training overhead are primary effects already described in the Brooks's Law model. This situation further causes an overall shortage due to the lessened productivity.

Organizations try to alleviate the labor shortage by offering salary increases to attract new hires. As more people job hop for better compensation, the shortage problem is exacerbated because more attrition and shorter job tenures cause lessened productivity. Thus, the market response adds fuel to the destructive feedback loop. The increased compensation to reduce the impact of attrition causes more attrition.

The feedback results in a greater need for people to develop a fixed amount of software, in addition to the overall increased demand for software development in the world market. Considering the larger world picture illustrates interactions between national and global economic trends.

Also see Chapter 7 on global and national workforce shortage issues. The report in [DoD 2000] includes shortages for particular types of software personnel categories, and provides recommendations for long-term solutions.

4.7.2.3.1 EXAMPLE: WORKFORCE SHORTAGE CAUSAL LOOP. Figure 4.30 is a causal loop structure of the labor shortage feedback dynamics. Desired productivity is that required to meet software demands in the market. The difference between desired productivity and actual productivity (on a local or aggregate level) manifests itself as a workforce shortage. The shortage causes aggressive hiring such as providing large starting salaries (or other hiring incentives) to fill the gap. The increased compensation available to workers causes higher attrition rates.

The increased personnel turnover causes learning overhead for new people to come up to speed and training overhead on the part of existing employees needed to train them. Both of these impact productivity negatively, which further exacerbates the workforce shortage. See the chapter exercises for further elaboration of labor shortage dynamics.

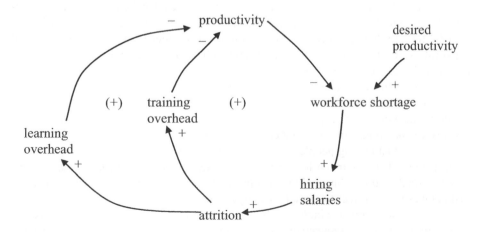

Figure 4.30. Workforce shortage feedback loop.

4.7.3   Skills and Capabilities

There have been very few models that account for specific skills other than aggregate experience and capability. Plekhanova performed research on integrating detailed software personnel skill profiles with simulation. A set-theoretic approach is used to describe the arrays of skills that people possess [Plekhanova 1999]. A number of capability and compatibility metrics were elaborated. With this information, resource-based process constraints scheduling can be determined based on critical human resource variables. Both individual and team characteristics impact the WBS, costs, time, and risks. Plekhanova presents a capability-based approach to stochastic software process modeling using a combination of discrete event simulation and system dynamics. The approach provides detailed process analyses, resource utilization, and how people resources fit a project not only at each discrete point in time, but also for each feedback path in the system.

Other process modeling work on people's competencies and characteristics for software development has been done by Acuña and colleagues. In [Acuña, Juzgado 2004], a capabilities-oriented process model is proposed that includes software process activities, products, techniques, and people, their roles, and capabilities. They define capability-person and capability-role relationships and procedures to determine capabilities and to assign people. The results of experiments confirm that assigning people to roles according to their capabilities improves software development.

A software process model handbook for incorporating people's capabilities [Acuña et al. 2005] covers people aspects. The focus is on extending software process definitions to more explicitly address people-related considerations. The authors developed a capabilities-oriented software process model formalized in UML and implemented in a tool. Also see [Acuña et al. 2006] on emphasizing human capabilities in software development.

4.7.4   Team Communication

Good communication between people is practically necessary for project success. Frequently, it is cited as the most important factor. Personnel capability factors (such as in COCOMO II) inherently account for team dynamics rather than assessing individual capabilities. If a team does not communicate well, then it does not matter how smart and capable the constituents are.

As previewed in the Brooks's Law model in Chapter 1, team size is an important determinant of communication and associated delays. Communication overhead depends on the number of people. The number of communication paths increases proportionally to the square of the number of people communicating. The Brooks's Law model shows that adding people increases communication overhead and may slow the project down. It takes much longer to disseminate information on large teams compared to small teams. This could have a profound impact on project startup, since the vision takes much longer to spread on a large team.

As the overall team size increases, however, team partitioning takes place and communication overhead is reduced on a local scale. Partitioning is not trivial to model and the communication overhead should be reformulated to account for it. See Exercises for Chapters 2 and 6 for further discussion and elaboration of the Brooks's Law model for partitioning.

DeMarco and Lister discuss "teamicide" in *Peopleware,* and identify issues that affect team communication and formation. These include defensive management, bureaucracy, physical separation, fragmentation of people's time, quality reduction, phony deadlines, and clique control.

Additionally, motivational accessories may end up harming team communication. Accessories include award recognition, plaques, and so on. Bad feelings may emerge from competition and jealousy. Overtime can also affect the team chemistry; not everyone will be as willing or able to work longer hours. Other factors that may affect team communication include individual personality traits. Some team members may have dominating personalities, whereas others may be reluctant participants.

4.7.5 Negotiation and Collaboration

Achieving early agreements between project stakeholders is of paramount importance, otherwise it is likely that all stakeholders will not be satisfied and the project becomes a failure. Reaching a common vision between people and identifying their respective win conditions are major precepts of the WinWin process. Negotiation and collaboration processes can be difficult, though, and modeling the social aspects can provide insight. Several models have explored both the social and organizational issues of requirements development.

An early state model of the WinWin requirements negotiation was developed by Lee [Lee 1996]. It was a formal model of the infrastructure and dynamics of requirements collaboration and negotiation. This work established foundations for subsequent WinWin tools that help guide stakeholder involvement and collaboration, including the Easy WinWin process tool mentioned later in this section.

An important application in this area is [Christie, Staley 2000]* that simulates the organizational and social dynamics of a software requirements development process because they are so crucial to project success. The model explores organizational issues of requirements development as well as the social issues to see how the effectiveness of people interactions affects the resulting quality and timeliness of the output.

The model simulates a Joint Application Development (JAD) process [Wood, Silver 1995] that was implemented by the Computer Sciences Corporation for the U.S. Air Force. It was used to provide insights into the behavioral characteristics of a JAD requirements process in terms of resource needs and constraints, cycle times, quality, the effects of feedbacks on the system's dynamics, and the impact of social interactions on organizational dynamics.

JAD was used to identify detailed requirements for a large incremental release of a command and control system. Using the JAD process, system users and engineering specialists worked jointly in an electronic meeting environment and successfully re-

*This work probably would have continued had not Dr. Alan Christie, a highly respected researcher in software process simulation, passed away in 2002.

duced development time and failure risk. The outputs from the JAD sessions were then assessed by two independent reviewers and occasionally upper management became involved in decision making. Nine separate working groups were modeled; each group consisted of people in prescribed roles.

The model covers feedback between the social and organizational components resulting from the interpersonal effectiveness within the nine groups. The quality of the outcome from these groups is dependent on personal and social attributes, and this quality impacts the duration of the review process and how long subsequent corrective action will take. A Monte Carlo approach was used identify the quality value associated with a specified management threshold.

The model has both continuous and discrete modeling components, and a challenge was integrating the aspects. Although the modeling of the organizational processes uses a discrete, event-based approach, the "social" model was based on continuous simulation. The social model gives each individual three characteristics:

1. Technical capability
2. Ability to win over other team members to their point of view (influence)
3. Degree to which they are open to considering the ideas of others (openness).

An important conclusion from the work was that social simulation (i.e., the modeling of the interaction between individuals) needs to play a more important role in modeling software processes. The model showed that the level of commitment or trust escalates (or decreases) in the context of a software project. Commitment toward a course of action does not happen all of a sudden but builds over a period of time. Social phenomena can clearly be key in determining the outcomes of software processes and should be considered for realistic planning.

Another conclusion was that since organizational modeling focuses on "things" (e.g., people and artifacts), discrete simulation is appropriate. On the other hand, since social modeling more often focuses on parameters that vary smoothly, continuous simulation appears to be more appropriate. The Christie JAD model is a potential basis for modeling WinWin negotiations (see the chapter exercises).

Another application using system dynamics to model stakeholder collaboration activities is [Stallinger, Gruenbacher 2001]. They simulated the Easy WinWin requirements negotiation process to assess issues associated with the social and behavioral aspects, and to explore how the outcome is impacted. Easy WinWin attempts to foster stakeholder cooperation and involvement through tool guidance. They revisited the previous work by Christie and Staley and incorporated some of their concepts, including the modeling of an individual's characteristics for technical ability, ability to influence others, and openness to influence from others.

A method called Quantitative WinWin [Ruhe et al. 2003] uses simulation to support trade-off analysis for requirements selection. In this evolutionary approach to requirements negotiation, an analytic hierarchy process is used iteratively to balance stakeholder preferences with respect to classes of requirements. Next, a simulation model, GENSIM, is used to predict and rebalance the impact of effort, time, and quality. Alternative solutions are offered and trade-offs made so that a small number of possible sets of requirements can be selected.

4.7.6 Simulation for Personnel Training

Simulation models are highly effective tools for training and education. Students and working professionals can interact with the simulations instead of learning the hard and expensive way on real projects. Simulation is used in many other fields to reduce risk, but has not been fully utilized in software engineering to date. For example, pilots spend thousands of hours in simulators before flying new planes to hone their decision-making skills. It is cheaper and much less risky compared to flying in a real plane the first time. Software people can also avoid some expensive mistakes on real projects by practicing first via simulation. The analogy to flying is so strong that sometimes the interactive training is referred to as "flight simulation."

Flight simulation is interactively running a model such that parameters can be adjusted midstream during execution. This mode lends itself to interactive decision making, whereby the user can influence the simulation outcome based on how the simulation has already proceeded. Flight simulation is an ideal training environment in which control decisions can be practiced risk-free.

Several efforts have used system dynamics for software process training in industry and academia. Deitmar Pfahl and colleagues have actively researched the usage of system dynamics modeling for training in [Pfahl 1995], [Pfahl et al. 2001] and [Pfahl et al. 2004a]. We have used simulation in a less formal and nonexperimental context at USC and at Litton Systems, as described in [Madachy, Tarbet 2000]. James Collofello at Arizona State University (ASU) has been using simulation for graduate software project management and industrial training [Collofello 2000]. A more general treatment of simulation for training can be found in [Drappa, Ludewig 2000].

A strong example of an empirical study using replicated experiments is [Pfahl et al. 2004b]. The experiments have shown that system-dynamics-based simulations are effective for understanding software project behavior patterns for project management and for learning multicausal thinking. An experimental group used a system dynamics model while the control group used COCOMO for project planning. Students using the simulations gained a better understanding of typical behavior patterns. Simulation models were found to be more advantageous than using static models like COCOMO. Students consistently rate the simulation-based role-play scenario very useful for learning about software project management issues. A recent overview of issues when using system dynamics for learning can be found in [Pfahl et al. 2006b]. After providing industrial examples, it discusses limitations, risks, and proposes future work.

The goal in [Collofello 2000] was to improve software management by having people practice with simulators. Favorable results were obtained using the simulator at Motorola that uses several models developed over the years at ASU. Some of the exercises included comparing life cycles and risk management approaches, and assessing the impact of software inspections, critical path scheduling, planning, and tracking. All participants found the simulator significantly added value to the course. The simulations were also incorporated into a Web-based graduate-level software project management course.

Likewise, we have used system dynamics in the classroom at USC in both process modeling and general software engineering courses to teach concepts such as Brooks's Law, risk management approaches, and earned value management concepts. Many students were stimulated enough to take further classes and undertake research study in software process simulation.

We also had good success in industry at Litton Systems [Madachy, Tarbet 2000] when we introduced simulation in our training curriculum for software managers (see the next section). Some vendor tools have also incorporated system-dynamics-based training modules. Howard Rubin developed a software process flight simulation tool for the commercial market based on an implementation of the Abdel-Hamid integrated project model [Rubin et al. 1995].

Also refer to Chapter 7 for current and future directions of using simulation for training and game playing. The current direction is that interactive simulations are incorporating more intensive graphics and virtual reality to enhance the training experience. Chapter 7 describes how some other modeling techniques are doing this, and how interactive simulation-based training will be integrated with process mission control and analysis facilities.

4.7.6.1 Software Manager Training

Selected process management principles were successfully demonstrated through the use of live classroom simulations at Litton Systems [Madachy, Tarbet 2000]. Software managers and other designated leads received training from the Software Engineering Process Group (SEPG) in project management, software metrics, and other related subjects. Live simulations were used in the training venues for students to better visualize metrics trends and to improve their control techniques via interactive situations.

Use of the dynamic models enlivened the training sessions and stirred thought-provoking discussions. Using the models in real time allows for quick simulation runs to explore issues brought up during discussion. For example, a posed question may be translated into a model input and the simulation run for all to see the outcome. This often happens when presenting managerial subjects, as students propose specific scenarios that can be quickly evaluated through the simulation model.

The first models used for training purposes were an earned-value model, the Brooks's Law model, and a simple estimated productivity model. To teach earned-value techniques and project control, earned-value trends for a project were shown and trainees had to interpret them. Showing the different components of the earned-value algorithms helped them understand the method better. After interpreting the trends, corrective actions were suggested, as necessary. The simulation allowed some of the corrective actions to be modeled in order to see the impacts of their decisions. See Chapter 6 for more information on modeling earned value for training purposes.

The earned-value model at Litton Systems was also used as a basis for actual project control and evaluating the impact of requirements volatility (see Chapter 6). The Brooks's Law model was used to determine optimal staffing for some real projects.

The estimated productivity model helped to identify inconsistencies in some project plans. Using the same models for both training and real projects made the lessons stick much better than just leaving the models in the classroom.

Howard Rubin, Margaret Johnson, and Ed Yourdon also created a flight simulator to help managers understand the dynamics of new processes and technologies before they are introduced [Rubin et al. 1995]. The authors show how the tools can be used for information systems project management.

MAJOR REFERENCES

[Abdel-Hamid, Madnick 1991] Abdel-Hamid T. and Madnick S., *Software Project Dynamics,* Englewood Cliffs, NJ: Prentice-Hall, 1991.

[Acuña et al. 2005] Acuna S., Juristo N., Moreno A., and Mon A., *A Software Process Model Handbook for Incorporating People's Capabilities,* 2005.

[Curtis et al. 2001] Curtis B., Hefley B., and Miller S., *The People Capability Maturity Model,* Reading, MA: Addison Wesley, 2001.

[DeMarco, Lister 1999] DeMarco T. and Lister T., *Peopleware, Productive Projects and Teams,* Nes York: Dorset House Publishing, 1999.

[Humphrey 1997] Humphrey W., *Managing Technical People,* Reading, MA: Addison-Wesley, 1997.

[Raccoon 1996] Raccoon L., "A Learning Curve Primer for Software Engineers," *Software Engineering Notes,* ACM Sigsoft, January 1996.

[Weinberg 1998] Weinberg G., *The Psychology of Computer Programming: Silver Anniversary Edition,* New York: Dorset House Publishing, 1998.

4.9 CHAPTER 4 SUMMARY

People rather than technology provide the best chance to improve processes, increase productivity, and execute successful projects. They are the most important aspect to focus on overall because more can be gained by concentrating on people factors and human relations than technical methods. In this sense, agile approaches have it right. Processes are ultimately executed by people; hence, people can trump processes. The effectiveness of many processes and ultimate project success are dependent on people and their working together.

Motivation is always a key factor to achieve good productivity. It can enable people to work very hard and be creative. Yet people have limits on their amount of hard work and long hours. They can work at increased levels for only so long until burnout inevitably occurs. Then a period of de-exhausting is necessary.

Learning is an S-shaped phenomenon that can be successfully modeled, yet plans usually do not account for individual and team learning curves. The right environment must be in place for learning to occur because people are dependent on machines and usually other human beings for learning. Eventually, machine limitations will curtail the increased productivity due to learning.

Large projects undergoing change have needs for different kinds of people. We showed a simulation model that can be used to optimize the number of agile people on a hybrid process, in order to keep up with anticipated change traffic while still retaining pockets of stability for product dependability.

The right balance has to be struck in order to motivate people enough but not make them work so hard that a backlash occurs. In the end, too much overtime and pressure will negate any short-term gains. Management needs to be very careful about overtime and its converse, slack time.

Workforce issues should be dealt with at the macro level also. There are feedback dynamics that create and sustain a shortage of skilled people across the industry. Without a long-term vision to address the causes, the industry will continue to be plagued with staffing problems. Modeling and simulation can be used to help understand this and other people issues.

Companies should invest in retaining good employees. Personnel attrition can sink organizations. Making up for lost employees takes a lot of effort and entails hiring delays. Too much turnover causes everything to bog down, so whatever organizations can do to keep their (good) people around is worthwhile.

People also must have the appropriate skills at the right time. Those skills must first be defined and then the hard part of finding the right people or imparting new skills to present staff must occur.

Good communication between people is crucial, both within a development team and with external stakeholders. Individual capabilities are not as important as communicating well as a team. Emphasis should be placed on creating an environment for teams to gel.

Team dynamics play a particularly critical role when identifying and negotiating stakeholder win conditions. Teams generally will not work well together without open, honest communication and negotiation of win conditions to reach a shared vision between people. Theory W and WinWin negotiation methods have been shown to be useful for identifying and reconciling peoples' win conditions. For external stakeholders, expectations management is critical to make everyone a winner.

Process simulation is a valuable method for personnel training. It should be part of the training resource arsenal, like other methods of teaching and mentoring. Formal, replicated experiments have consistently shown that system dynamics is a viable and preferred method over static cost modeling in order to learn about complex project behavior patterns.

System dynamics is a good choice for modeling many people aspects. It is appropriate for those factors that tend to vary continuously (frequently, short-term fluctuations can reasonably be ignored) and/or can be considered in aggregate for the purpose of the analysis. The simplicity of system dynamics makes it handy to start modeling aspects that are difficult to model otherwise and thus ignored. Discrete approaches are better suited when it is prudent to model characteristics of individuals in a population and a continuous approximation is insufficient.

We have reviewed just some of the people phenomena that should be better understood and accounted for on software projects. Over time, more human aspects will be addressed by modeling and simulation to help promote people-oriented practices.

4.10　EXERCISES

These application exercises are potentially advanced and extensive projects.

4.1. Experiment with the Abdel-Hamid personnel sector under different staffing gap situations (inspired by [Johnson 1995]). Analyze the model behavior with three scenarios:
   • The workforce is exactly the same the workforce level needed
   • The workforce is less than the workforce level needed
   • The workforce is greater than the workforce level needed

   For the first case, set new hires to 0, experienced personnel to 12, and workforce level needed to 12. Run the simulation for 300 days. For the second scenario, make the gap large by setting new hires to 0, experienced personnel to 8, and workforce level needed to 12. Lastly, set new hires to 8, experienced personnel to 8, and workforce level needed to 12 to model a greater than needed workforce. Describe what happens in each scenario.

4.2. a. Research the literature for modeling human capabilities with system dynamics in other disciplines, or other simulation methods applied to software people. See [Acuña, Juzgado 2004] or [Acuña et al. 2005] for examples with software processes. Can any of the work be adapted for a system dynamics model for software processes?

   b. Based on your research, develop new software process model(s) and carry out simulation experiments.

4.3. Identify some improvements to the Abdel-Hamid personnel sector model for your environment and implement them.

4.4. Develop and compare learning models for software development using both time and work volume as the independent variable. Does either seem most in line with intuition and experience? Why?

4.5. Perform some experiments to test the learning curve theories. Compare the model results to empirical data.

4.6. Extrapolate the overtime productivity curve into the "too high" region where productivity falls. Document the reasons why this happens and justify your values.

4.7. Model the interactions between overtime pressure and personnel attrition, and/or the interactions between overtime pressure and defect generation.

4.8. Read Tom Demarco's *Slack: Getting Past Burnout, Busywork, and the Myth of Total Efficiency* [DeMarco 2001] and create a simulation model for slack time. Integrate the phenomena he describes, some of which are already expressed as notional reference behaviors.

   a. Identify and graph reference behavior(s) that the book describes about your topic.

   b. Create a model, experiment with it, and write a report.

4.9. Read *Peopleware* [DeMarco, Lister 1999] to help define a project for modeling human factors. Some possibilities include Parkinson's Law, the office environment, team jelling dynamics, "teamicide," coding war games, overtime, corporate entropy, turnover, process improvement paradox, change dynamics, staffing dynamics, miscellaneous productivity factors, and more. Slack time concepts can also be included (see previous exercise).

   a. Identify and graph reference behavior(s) that the book describes about your chosen topic.

   b. Create a model, experiment with it, and write a report. Clearly identify what organizational "levers" are available to influence individual and group behavior.

4.10. Read *The Psychology of Computer Programming* [Weinberg 1998] to help define a project for modeling human factors.

   a. Identify and graph reference behavior(s) that the book describes about your chosen topic.

   b. Create a model, experiment with it, and write a report.

4.11. Evaluate the labor shortage degenerative feedback loop with an executable model.

4.12. Which effects in the IT workforce shortage causal loop diagram operate locally, globally (an aggregate of organizations or geographic provinces), or both? Define the system boundaries and enhance the diagram to model interactions between national shortages and global shortages. Develop a corresponding executable model.

4.13. Model collaboration dynamics between stakeholders. See [Christie, Staley 1999] or [Stallinger, Gruenbacher 2001] for some ideas or adapt their models. A review of the Easy WinWin tool used in [Stallinger, Gruenbacher 2001] or a similar groupware tool for negotiating requirements can provide insight on measures to include in the model.

5

PROCESS AND PRODUCT APPLICATIONS

5.1 INTRODUCTION

Process and product modeling applications cover broad and overlapping areas. The importance of good processes was introduced in Chapter 1 as a way to efficiently produce software that is useful to people. The ultimate goal is to provide product utility to users. Applications in this chapter elaborate more on process technology, covering both process life cycle and process improvement aspects along with product modeling. Substantial modeling and simulation work has been done for process applications due to the concentrated focus on process improvement in recent years.

Although software is the product that people actually use to obtain benefits from, there have been fewer software product applications with system dynamics than process applications. Some product attributes are not as amenable to tracking over time in an aggregate fashion. Discrete modeling approaches are more frequently used for product-related attributes than continuous systems modeling, as they allow linking of different attribute measures to individual software entities.

Process and product analysis are often difficult to extricate in many modeling applications, since software artifacts are primary state variables for both. Both types of applications frequently center on software artifacts and their attributes. Processes were defined generally as the life-cycle steps taken to develop software, so modeling life cycles entails the tracking of product artifacts over time. Hence, levels are dedicated to software artifacts, and a view of product characteristics or measurements is intertwined with the process view.

Software Process Dynamics. By Raymond J. Madachy

Two types of processes can be modeled to investigate product phenomena. Development process models mainly address software defect introduction and removal rates. Operational process models address the probability of various classes of product failure during usage (e.g., race conditions or missing real-time deadlines). System dynamics does not lend itself easily to failure mode assessment, so other methods like analytical approaches are frequently used instead.

Process and product factors account for a very significant amount of effort variance between projects. Product size itself has the biggest overall influence on effort (next in influence are the collective people factors; see Chapter 4). The process and product related factors (besides size) in COCOMO II with direct impacts on productivity are shown in Figure 5.1.

Product complexity constitutes several attributes and by itself provides for the largest impact of any single factor in the COCOMO model. Another important product-related factor is *Precedentedness* (with a range of 1.33), but it also has an organizational experience component to it and thus is not shown as a direct product factor. There may be additional business or mission-critical product factors, such as security or safety, that are important and large sources of variance that can also be added to COCOMO.

The life-cycle process for a project is not a source of variance in the COCOMO model, however, because it assumes that processes are well suited and properly tai-

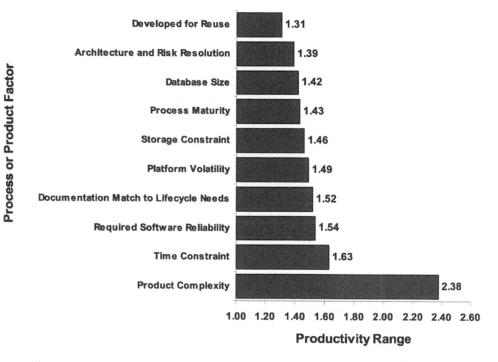

Figure 5.1. Process and product factor impacts from COCOMO II. What causes these?

lored for a project. Since this is not always the case, modeling applications like many in this chapter can be used to assess the impact of life cycles.

A combined process and product opportunity tree is shown in Figure 5.2. The tree demonstrates the many overlaps of concerns shown in the middle branches. There are also some common leaf nodes visible upon further inspection. These opportunities for

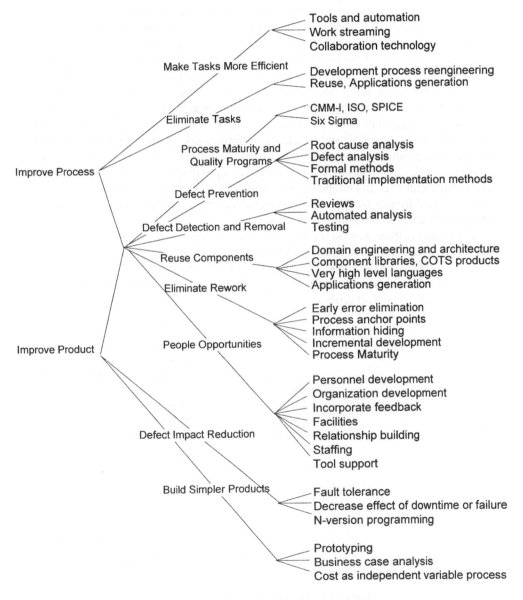

Figure 5.2. Process and product opportunity tree.

improving processes and products also represent opportunities to use modeling and simulation to better understand and leverage the strategies.

Product characteristics are wide-ranging in scope. Desired product attributes, from a user view, usually fall under the general umbrella of "quality." Various aspects of software quality are frequently considered, but the definition of quality depends on who is judging it. Defects are usually modeled to assess quality since they can impact a system with respect to quality attributes.

These quality aspects are frequently termed "ilities" and refer to nonfunctional requirements (usability, dependability, security, etc.). Some representative ilities, or product quality attributes, are shown in Figure 5.3. It is not an exhaustive list. Since quality is in the eyes of the beholder, its definition depends on one's perspective and expectations of utility from the software. The chapter section on quality provides details of using a stakeholder value-based approach for defining quality measurements.

Important relationships between process strategies and products can be exploited, because the impact of different processes and technologies on product attributes can be evaluated through modeling and simulation. A framework for the contribution of modeling to meet product goals is evaluating the effectiveness of the strategy opportunities against specific goals like aspects of quality. The opportunity tree in Figure 5.2 shows that sample strategies and product goals could be related to the attributes in Figure 5.3. Much of the difficulty lies in modeling connections between the strategies, intermediate quantities, and desired product attributes.

For example, three generic process strategies for producing quality software products are to avoid problems (defect prevention), eliminate problems (finding and fixing defects), or to reduce the impact of problems. Modeling the impact of specific types of defects on particular product attributes will help one understand how the defect strategies contribute to product goals.

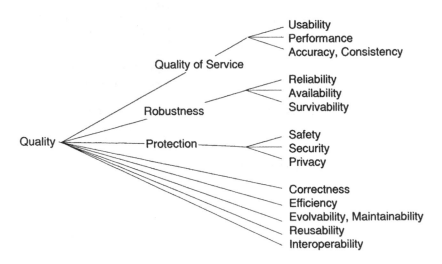

Figure 5.3. Representative quality attributes.

The existence of strong dependencies between product and process was an underlying concept in a simulation model in [Pfahl, Birk 2000]. The purpose of process–product dependency (PPD) models is to focus process improvement actions to be most effective with regard to product quality goals. The work explored how system dynamics models can be used to check the plausibility of achieving product goals when implementing improvements derived from PPD models.

Discrete-event modeling has some advantages for product analysis because different attributes can be attached to individual entities like defects. The attributes may change when system events occur during the simulation (such as a defect-detection or fixing event). Defects can be characterized by their type, severity, detection effort, removal effort, and so on. A hybrid approach combining continuous and discrete-event modeling is very attractive for product applications. It can model the creation of artifacts with attributes, modify those attributes based on system variables, and allow system variables to vary continuously.

A recent book [Acuña, Juristo 2005] contains a number of process and product modeling applications by leading researchers and practitioners. Though it does not focus on system dynamics modeling exclusively, it would serve as a good supplement to this chapter.

5.2 OVERVIEW OF APPLICATIONS

Some primary strategies identified in the opportunity tree are covered in the application sections. The chapter will start with an application for peer reviews, one of most well-known and studied processes for efficiently finding defects and improving product quality. The example from my dissertation on formal inspections [Madachy 1994b] shows substantial detail of the model and its assessment. The last subsection shows examples of using peer review metrics for model calibration.

Global process feedback takes a unique and broader view of the process by accounting for external feedback from the field. Several applications of global process modeling are identified, showing how long-term feedback models of software changes can provide good fidelity. Understanding global feedback can also help address trends such as globalization, COTS, or open-source development. A detailed example model for progressive and anti-regressive work is described in [Ramil et al. 2005].

The related methods of reuse and COTS for improving software productivity are covered next. A study by [Lo 1999] investigates the dynamics of reuse and fourth-generation languages. In the COTS application section, a detailed model of COTS glue-code development and integration is described [Kim, Baik 1999]. Additionally, an example model concept for COTS lifespan dynamics is reviewed.

Software architecting is one of the most success-critical aspects of developing software. An example comprehensive model of iterative architecting activities from [Fakharzadeh, Mehta 1999] is described, that is calibrated to extensive effort data and addresses best practices for architecting.

The next section is dedicated to defects and quality. It covers some issues of defining and modeling quality, and includes applications for defect analysis. The example with defect removal techniques and orthogonal defect classification illustrates how the effectiveness of different methods depends on the type of defect.

Requirements volatility is a seemingly persistent phenomenon on projects. The dynamics behind product volatility are described and investigated with an example modeling application based on [Ferreira et al. 2003]. This doctoral dissertation research included the use of a comprehensive survey to obtain data for the model.

Continuous process improvement is undertaken by organizations to better meet cost, schedule, or functionality goals. Accordingly, extensive coverage of software process improvement is included, based on a comprehensive model. A process improvement model was developed by Burke [Burke 1996] and adapted for use at Xerox [Ho 1999] and other places. The Xerox application demonstrates how a model can be adapted for an organization and modified to be more user friendly. It also provides illustrative detail of defining different test cases and running sensitivity tests.

5.3 PEER REVIEWS

A major goal of software engineering is to produce higher-quality software while keeping effort expenditure and schedule time to a minimum. Peer reviews are a commonly accepted practice to achieve this. Intermediate work products are reviewed to eliminate defects when they are less costly to fix. Peer reviews of software artifacts range from informal reviews to structured walk-throughs to formal inspections. Many variations exist, involving a variety of participants.

Inspections were first devised by Fagan at IBM as a formal, efficient, and economical method of finding errors in design and code [Fagan 1976]. Inspections are carried out in a prescribed series of steps including preparation, having an inspection meeting at which specific roles are executed, and rework of errors discovered by the inspection. Standard roles include moderator, scribe, inspectors, and author.

Since their introduction, the use of inspections has been extended to requirements, testing plans, and more. Thus, an inspection-based process would perform inspections on artifacts throughout system development such as requirements descriptions, design, code, test plans, user guides, or virtually any engineering document.

Inspections are just one method of performing peer reviews, and are more rigorous than other types such as structured walk-throughs. Peer reviews can be included to some degree in virtually all other software life-cycle processes, so peer reviews can be considered a variation within the major life-cycle models.

In general, results have shown that extra effort is required during design and coding for peer reviews and much more is saved during testing and integration, resulting in a reduced overall schedule. By detecting and correcting errors in earlier stages of the process such as design, significant reductions can be made since the rework is much less costly compared to later in the testing and integration phases. Countless authors have corroborated this result over the years, and many references can be found in [Madachy 1994b].

Peer reviews in general are a good idea, but they should not be overdone. There are diminishing returns from peer reviews (see insights from the example inspection model in the next section), and they are not appropriate for finding all classes of software errors.

A number of extensive modeling efforts have focused on peer reviews as a means of finding and fixing defects, including process trade-offs. Several researchers have used system dynamics to investigate the cost, schedule, and quality impact of using formal inspections and other peer reviews on work products [Madachy 1994b, Tvedt 1995], and others have used discrete event modeling [Raffo 1995, Eickelmann et al. 2002].

In [Madachy 1994b], a process model was used to examine the effects of inspection practices on cost, schedule, and quality (defect levels) throughout the life cycle. It used system dynamics to model the interrelated flows of tasks, errors, and personnel throughout different life-cycle phases and was extensively calibrated to industrial data. This application is highlighted in the next section.

A discrete event model for analyzing the effect of inspections was developed in [Raffo 1995]. The quantitative cost/quality trade-offs for performing inspections were very close to those derived from [Madachy 1994b] at the top level. Both studies support the contention that even though inspections may increase effort early on, the overall development costs and schedule are reduced.

The [Tvedt 1995] model allows one to evaluate the impact of process improvements on cycle time. It specifically addresses concurrent incremental software development to assess the impact of software inspections. The model enables controlled experiments to answer questions such as "What kind of cycle time reduction can I expect to see if I implement inspections?" or "How much time should I spend on inspections?" It modeled the specific activities within the inspection process so that one can experiment with effort dedicated to preparation, inspection, rework, and so on.

Recent research on modeling inspections is in [Twaites et al. 2006]. This work uses a system dynamics model to assess the effect of prioritizing the items under inspection when presented with an accelerated schedule. The model is provided with this book and is listed in Appendix C.

5.3.1 Example: Modeling an Inspection-Based Process

In my dissertation, I investigated the dynamic effects of inspections with a simulation model [Madachy 1994b, Madachy 1996b]. It examines the effects of inspection practices on cost, schedule, and quality throughout the life cycle. Quality in this context refers to the absence of defects, where a defect is defined as a flaw in the specification, design, or implementation of a software product. Table 5.3-1 is a high-level summary of the model.

The model demonstrates the effects of performing inspections or not, the effectiveness of varied inspection policies, and the effects of other managerial policies such as manpower allocation. The dynamic project effects and their cumulative measures are investigated by individual phase.

Development of the inspection-based process model drew upon extensive literature search, analysis of industrial data, and expert interviews. The basic reference behavior identified is that extra effort is required during design and coding for inspections and

Table 5.1. Peer review model overview

Purpose: Process Improvement, Planning
Scope: Development Project

Inputs and Parameters	Levels	Major Relationships	Outputs
• Design inspection practice	• Tasks Required	• Staffing rates	• Staffing per activity
• Code inspection practice	Designed For coding	• Defect rates • Schedule tradeoff	• Effort per activity • Schedule per activity
• Job size	Coded		• Errors per type
• Inspection efficiency	Ready for test		
• Design error density	• Errors		
• Code error density	Design		
• Effort constant	Undetected design		
• Schedule constant	Detected design		
• Rework effort per design error	Reworked design Code		
• Rework effort per code error	Detected code Undetected code		
	Reworked code		
	Escaped		
	Fixed in test		

much more is saved during testing and integration, resulting in reduced overall schedule effect. This is shown in [Fagan 1976] and represents a goal of the model; to be able to demonstrate this effect on effort and schedule as a function of inspection practices. The following sections are drawn from [Madachy 1996b], with full detail and complete references in [Madachy 1994b].

5.3.1.1 *Industrial Data Collection and Analysis*

Data collection and analysis for a large project using an inspection-based process was performed at Litton Data Systems. As an application for command and control, the software comprised about 500 thousand lines of code (KSLOC). Over 300 inspection data points were collected and analyzed from the project. Analysis of this and additional projects is documented in [Madachy 1995c]. Some results with important ramifications for a dynamic model include defect density and defect removal effectiveness life-cycle trends and activity distribution of effort. Calibrations are made to match the model to these defect density trends and activity distributions in selected test cases. Additional inspection data was available from JPL to support model analysis and calibration [Kelly, Sherif 1990].

Data for the previous project at Litton in the same product line and having identical environmental factors except for the use of inspections was also collected. It provides several parameters used in calibration of the system dynamics model such as defect density and the average cost to fix a defect found during testing. It also enables a comparison to judge the relative project effects of performing inspections.

Several senior personnel at Litton and international experts were interviewed to obtain data and heuristics for process delays, manpower allocation policies and general project trends relevant to inspection practices.

The model is validated against Litton data such as the proportions of effort for preparation, inspection meeting, rework and other development activities; schedule; and defect profiles. See [Madachy 1995c] for additional analysis of inspection data.

5.3.1.2 Model Overview

The model covers design through testing activities, including inspections of design and code. Figure 5.4 shows the task and error portions of the model. It is assumed that inspections and system testing are the only defect removal activities, as practiced in some organizations. The model also assumes a team trained in inspections, such that inspections can be inserted into the process without associated training costs.

Project behavior is initiated with the influx of requirements. Rates for the different phase activities are constrained by the manpower allocations and current productivity, and are integrated to determine the state variables, or levels of tasks in design, code, inspection, testing, and so on. The tasks are either inspected or not during design or code activities as a function of inspection practices.

Errors are generated as a coflow of design and coding activities, and eventually detected by inspections or passed onto the next phase. The detection of errors is a function of inspection practices and inspection efficiency. All errors detected during inspections are then reworked. Note that escaped design errors are amplified into coding errors. Those errors that still escape code inspections are then detected and corrected during integration and test activities. The effort and schedule for the testing phase is adjusted for the remaining error levels.

Other sectors of the model implement management policies such as allocating personnel resources and defining staffing curves for the different activities. Input to the policy decisions are the job size, productivity, schedule constraints, and resource leveling constraints. Effort is instrumented in a cumulative fashion for all of the defined activities. Learning takes place as a function of the job completion and adjusts the productivity. Schedule compression effects are approximated similar to the COCOMO cost driver effects for relative schedule.

The actual completion time is implemented as a cycle time utility whose final value represents the actual schedule. It instruments the maximum in-process time of the tasks that are time-stamped at requirements generation rate and complete testing.

5.3.1.2.1 MODEL CALIBRATION. To gauge the impact of inspections, effort expenditure was nominally calibrated to the staffing profiles of COCOMO, a widely accepted empirically based model. Correspondence between the dynamic model and COCOMO is illustrated in Figure 5.5. It is based on the phase-level effort and schedule of a 32 KSLOC embedded-mode reference project.

In the nominal case, no inspections are performed, and the manpower allocation policy employs the staffing curves in Figure 5.5 to match the rectangular COCOMO effort profiles as a calibration between the models. Thus, the area under the design

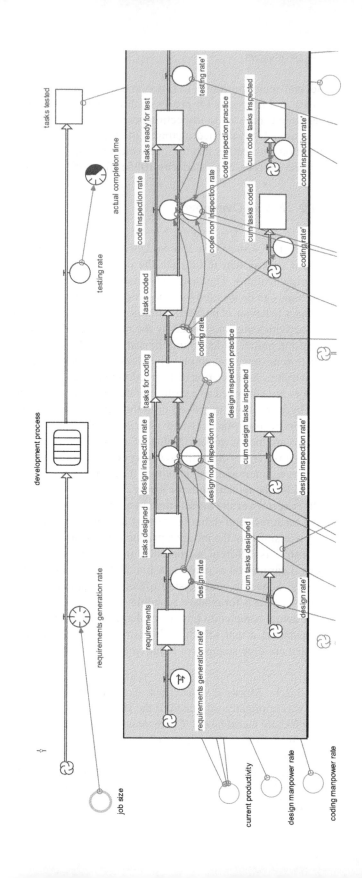

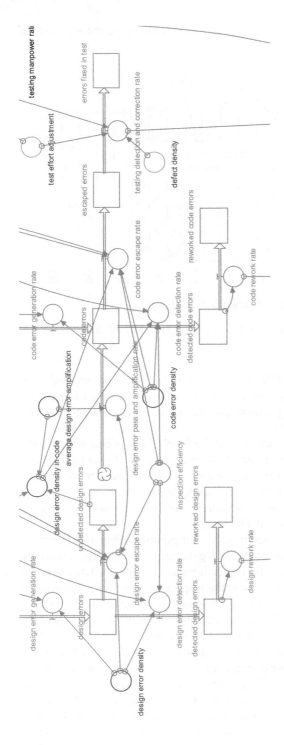

Figure 5.4. Inspection model task and error chains.

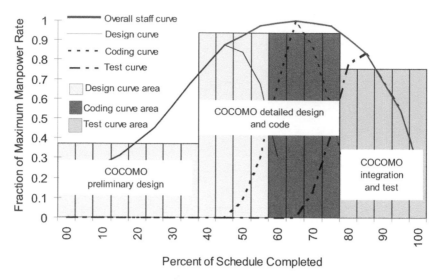

Figure 5.5. Correspondence between dynamic model and COCOMO (no inspections).

curve matches the aggregated COCOMO preliminary and detailed design, and likewise for the coding and testing curves. Unlike COCOMO, however, the staffing curves overlap between phases. The resulting staffing profiles are scaled accordingly for specific job sizes and schedule constraints.

The integration and test phase also depends on the level of errors encountered, and the curve shown is calibrated to an error rate of 50 errors/KSLOC during testing. The testing effort includes both fixed and variable components, where the variable part depends on error levels. When calibrating the model for other parameters, middle regions of published data trends were chosen as calibration points. Some parameters were set to Litton values when no other data was available.

Per the experience at Litton and accordant with other published data, inspection effort that includes preparation, meetings, and rework generally consumes approximately 5–10% of total project effort. Guidelines for inspection rates are always stated as linear with the number of pages (or lines of code), and the inspection effort is set accordingly in the model such that inspection effort does not exhibit diseconomy of scale. The default inspection effort also corresponds to a rate of 250 LOC/hour during preparation and inspection, with an average of four inspectors per meeting [Grady, Caswell 1992].

The rework effort per error is set differently for design and code. Litton data shows that the average cost to rework an error during code is about 1.3 times that for design. The cost to fix errors from [Boehm 1981] shows a relative cost for code of twice that of design. The model is set at this 2:1 ratio since it is based on a larger set of data. The resulting values are also close to the reported ranges of published data from JPL [Kelly, Sherif 1990]. The testing fixing effort per error is set at about 5 hours, which is well within the range of reported metrics. The inspection efficiency is nominally set at 60%, representing the fraction of defects found through inspections.

The utility of the model for a particular organization is dependent on calibrating it accordingly per local data. While model parameters are set with reasonable numbers to investigate inspections in general, the results using the defaults will not necessarily reflect all environments.

Parameters to calibrate for specific environments include productivity, error rates, rework effort parameters, test error fixing effort, inspection efficiency and effort, and documentation sizes.

5.3.1.2.2 COMPARISON TO ABDEL-HAMID INTEGRATED PROJECT MODEL. Using the Abdel-Hamid model as a conceptual reference [Abdel-Hamid, Madnick 1991], this model replaces the software production, quality assurance and system testing sectors. The model excludes schedule pressure effects, personnel mix, and other coding productivity determinants so as to not confound the inspection analysis.

Major departures from the Abdel-Hamid model cover manpower allocation, disaggregation of development activities, and error propagation. In his model, only generic quality-assurance activities are modeled for error detection on an aggregate of design and code. Instead of the Parkinsonian model in [Abdel-Hamid, Madnick 1991] where QA completes its periodic reviews no matter how many tasks are in the queue, resources are allocated to inspections and rework as needed. This organizational behavior is thought to be an indication of a higher maturity level. Instead of suspending or accelerating reviews when under schedule pressure, error detection activities remain under process control.

The other major structural difference is the disaggregation of development phases. The Abdel-Hamid model only has a single rate/level element that represents an aggregate of design and coding. In this formulation, phases are delineated corresponding to those in the classic waterfall model so that design and coding are modeled independently.

5.3.1.3 Model Demonstration and Evaluation

Simulation test case results were compared against collected data and other published data, existing theory, and other prediction models. Testing included examining the ability of the model to generate proper reference behavior, which consists of time histories for all model variables. Specific modeling objectives to test against include the ability to predict design and code effort with or without inspections, preparation and inspection meeting effort, rework effort, testing effort, and schedule and error levels as a function of development phase.

Approximately 80 test cases were designed for model evaluation and experimentation. The reference test case is for a job size of 32 KSLOC, an overall error injection rate of 50 errors per KSLOC split evenly between design and coding, and an error multiplication factor of unity from design to code. Refer to [Madachy 1994b] for complete documentation of the simulation output for this test case and substantiation of the reference behavior.

Other test cases were designed to investigate the following factors: use of inspections, job size, productivity, error generation rates, error multiplication, staffing profiles, schedule compression, use of inspections per phase, and testing effort. The reader is encouraged to read [Madachy 1994b] for complete details on the experimental results.

5.3.1.3.1   REPLICATION OF REFERENCE BEHAVIOR. Inspection effort reference behavior used in problem definition from Michael Fagan's pioneering work [Fagan 1986] is shown in Figure 5.6. The simulation model also provides staffing profiles with and without inspections as shown in Figure 5.7, and the baseline results qualitatively match the generalized effort curves from Fagan.

The net return on investment (ROI) from inspections demonstrated in the reference behavior figures is the test effort saved minus the extra early effort for inspections (visualized as the difference between the curves in the back end minus the difference in the front end). Assessment of detailed quantities is addressed below.

5.3.1.3.2   EFFECTS OF PERFORMING INSPECTIONS. Nine test cases were designed to evaluate the model for job size scalability, ability to be calibrated for productivity in specific environments, and to reproduce the effects of inspections.

Test case results are shown in [Madachy 1994b] consisting of cost, schedule, and error levels per phase. Predictions from COCOMO 1981 [Boehm 1981] are provided as a basis of comparison for effort and schedule. One of the salient features of the system dynamics model is the incorporation of an error model, so comparison with the COCOMO estimate provides an indication of the sensitivity of testing effort to error rates (COCOMO does not explicitly account for error rates). It is seen that the simulation results and COCOMO differ considerably for the testing and integration phases as the process incorporates inspections.

It is not meaningful to compare schedule times for the different phases between COCOMO and the dynamic model because the nonoverlapping step function profiles

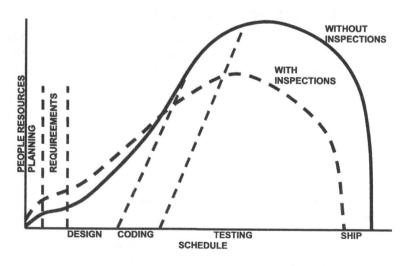

Figure 5.6. Inspection effort reference behavior [Fagan 1986].

1: total manpower rate　　　　　　　　2: total manpower rate

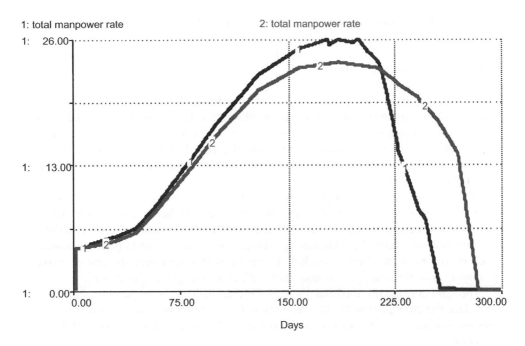

Figure 5.7. Inspection model behavior (1: with inspections, 2: without inspections).

of COCOMO will always be shorter than the overlapping staffing curves of the dynamic model as seen in Figure 5.5.

The remaining error is zero in each test case since ample resources were provided to fix all the errors in testing. If insufficient testing manpower or decreased productivity is modeled, then some errors remain latent and the resultant product is of lower quality.

Another major result is a dynamic comparison of manpower utilization for test cases with and without inspections. The curves demonstrate the extra effort during design and coding, less test effort and reduced overall schedule, much like the reference effect on project effort previously shown by Fagan [Fagan 1976].

Many effects can be gleaned from the results such as the return on investment of performing inspections, relative proportions of inspection effort, schedule performance, defect profiles, and others. It is seen that inspections add approximately 10% effort in the design and coding phases for these representative test cases, and reduce testing and integration effort by about 50%. The schedule for testing can also be brought in substantially to reduce the overall project schedule. These results are corroborated by numerous projects in the literature and verified by experts interviewed during this research.

5.3.1.3.3 ANALYSIS OF INSPECTION POLICIES. The results described above correspond to equal inspection practices in design and code, though an alternate policy is to vary the amounts. The model can be used to investigate the relative cost effectiveness of different strategies.

The model provides insight into the interplay of multiple parameters that determine the threshold at which inspections become worthwhile (i.e., the cost of fixing errors is more expensive than the inspection effort). The following sections provide some results of the multivariate analysis.

5.3.1.3.4   ERROR GENERATION RATES. The effects of varying error generation rates are shown in Figure 5.8 from the results of multiple test cases. The overall defects per KSLOC are split evenly between design and code for the data points in the figure.

It is seen that there are diminishing returns of inspections for low error rates. The breakeven point lies at about 20 defects/KSLOC for the default values of inspection effort, rework, and error fixing.

Although inspection and preparation effort stay fairly constant, the rework and test error fixing effort vary considerably with the defect rates. If there is a low defect density of inspected artifacts, then inspections take more effort per detected error and there are diminishing returns. For this reason, a project may choose not to perform inspections if error rates are already very low. Likewise, it may not always be cost effective to inspect code if the design was inspected well, as seen in [Madachy 1994b].

Though not explicitly modeled, there is a feedback effect of inspections that tends to reduce the error generation rate. As work is reviewed by peers and inspection metrics are publicized, an author becomes more careful before subjecting his work to inspection.

5.3.1.3.5   ERROR MULTIPLICATION. Defect amplification rates vary tremendously with the development process. For example, processes that leverage off of high-level design tools that generate code would amplify errors more than those using a design language that is mapped 1:1 with code.

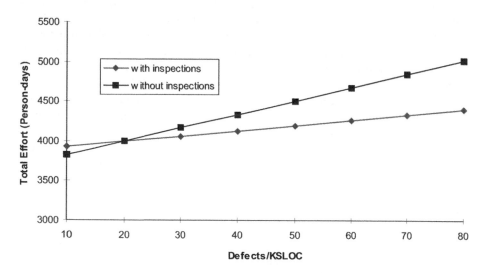

Figure 5.8. Error generation rate effects.

Figure 5.9 shows the effect of design error multiplication rate for performing inspections versus not doing so. It is seen that as the multiplication factor increases, the value of inspections increases dramatically.

The effects of error multiplication must be traded off against error injection rates for different inspected documents. If error multiplication is very high from design to code, then design inspections become relatively more advantageous through multiplication leverage (and code inspections are very important if design inspections are not well performed). Conversely, if error multiplication is low, then inspection of design documents is not as cost-effective compared to high multiplication rates.

5.3.1.3.6 DESIGN VERSUS CODE INSPECTIONS. An organization may opt to inspect a subset of artifacts. The literature suggests that design inspections are more cost-effective than code inspections. The model accounts for several factors that impact a quantitative analysis such as the filtering out of errors in design inspections before they get to code, the defect amplification from design to code, code inspection efficiency, and the cost of fixing errors in test. Experimental results show the policy trade-offs for performing design inspections, code inspections, or both for different values of error multiplication and test error fixing cost [Madachy 1994b].

5.3.1.3.7 SCHEDULE COMPRESSION. The effects of schedule compression are shown in Figure 5.10, where the relative schedule (desired/nominal) is varied from 1 to 0.7. With a reduced schedule, the average personnel level increases and the overall cumulative cost goes up nonlinearly.

5.3.1.4 Derivation of a Detailed COCOMO Cost Driver

As an example of dynamic modeling contributing to static modeling, phase-sensitive effort multipliers for a proposed cost driver, *Use of Inspections,* were experimentally

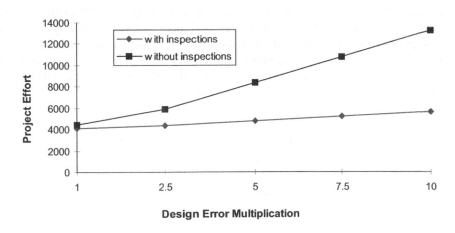

Figure 5.9. Error multiplication rate effects.

1: total manpower rate   2: **total manpower rate**   3: total manpower rate   4: total manpower rate

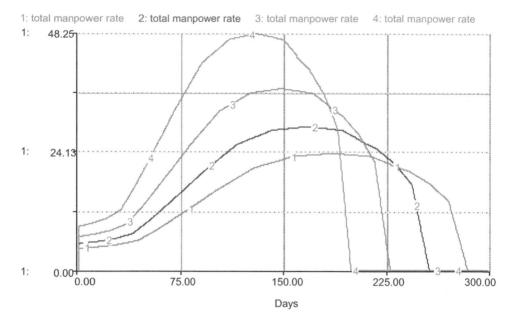

Figure 5.10. Total manpower rate curves for relative schedule (1: relative schedule = 1, 2: relative schedule = 0.9, 3: relative schedule = 0.8, 4: relative schedule = 0.7).

derived. The model parameters *design inspection practice* and *code inspection practice* were mapped into nominal, high, and very high cost driver ratings according to Table 5.2. The dynamic model was calibrated to zero inspection practice being equivalent to standard 1981 COCOMO effort and schedule. This assumption is valid because the project database used for calibrating 1981 COCOMO did not contain any projects that performed formal inspections.

Figure 5.11 shows the model-derived effort multipliers by COCOMO phase. This depiction is a composite of several test cases, and there is actually a family of curves for different error generation and multiplication rates, inspection efficiencies, and costs of fixing defects in test. The effort multiplier for high in the integration and test phase is not necessarily exactly halfway between the other points because there is a fixed amount of testing overhead, whereas half of the error fixing effort is saved.

Table 5.2. Rating guidelines for cost driver, *Use of Inspections*

Simulation Parameters		COCOMO Rating
design inspection practice	*code inspection practice*	for *Use of Inspections*
0	0	Nominal
0.5	0.5	High
1	1	Very High

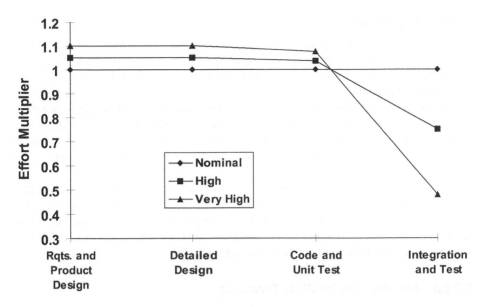

Figure 5.11. Derivation of phase-specific cost driver for *Use of Inspections*.

The results are unique in one regard because no other detailed COCOMO effort multipliers cross the nominal line, and this is the first instance of a cost driver increasing effort in some phases while reducing it in others. The dynamic model can be enhanced for additional COCOMO cost drivers, and investigation of their dynamic effects can be undertaken. Conversely, one can also derive effort multipliers for different COCOMO cost drivers by constructing unique models for investigation. For instance, the model can be used as a platform for varying levels of experience to assist in deriving multiplier weights.

5.3.1.4.1 VALIDATION AGAINST INDUSTRIAL DATA. Many comparisons of model output against specific project data were performed and are described in [Madachy 1994b]. One comparison is for return from inspections during testing, where the return is the test effort saved. The results show that the model is well-balanced to the experience at Litton. Testing effort and schedule performance for the inspection-based project at Litton is also compared against the model. Using both default model parameters and Litton-specific parameters, the model again matches actual project data well.

Another comparison afforded by available data is the ratio of rework effort to preparation and meeting inspection effort. This is done for over 500 data points from Litton and JPL data [Kelly, Sherif 1990]. The model predicts the average amount of rework effort to overall inspection effort for both organizations within 9%. A detailed validation summary of the model, including all time history outputs, is provided in [Madachy 1994b].

5.3.1.5 Conclusions

The model successfully demonstrated several phenomena of software projects, including the effects of inspections and management decision policies. It was also shown that the model is scalable for project size and calibratable for productivity, error generation, and error detection.

The model endogenously illustrates that under nominal conditions, performing inspections slightly increases up-front development effort and returns more in decreased testing effort and schedule. However, the cost-effectiveness of inspections depends on phase error injection rates, error amplification, testing error fixing effort, and inspection efficiency.

Complementary features of dynamic and static models for the software process were also shown. Static models were used to nominally calibrate the dynamic model, and the dynamic model improved on static assumptions. There are many interesting problems and challenging opportunities for extensions of the research. A detailed outline of future directions is provided in [Madachy 1994b].

5.3.1.6 Modification for Walk-Throughs

The inspection model was modified at the Guidance and Control Systems division of Litton to model other types of peer reviews, particularly walk-throughs.

Local walk-through data was used to parameterize the model and scenarios were run to quantify the expected cost and schedule impacts of peer reviews. The experimentation helped to solidify plans for peer reviews on specific projects. On others, it was shown that performing additional formal peer reviews may not be worthwhile. The model has also helped to educate executives and developers alike on the importance of peer reviews, and provided motivation to optimize the peer review processes.

The model is general enough that it required no structural changes to handle other peer review types besides inspections. The following calibration parameters were determined for each project based on existing local baseline data as refined for specific projects:

- Nominal productivity
- Review efficiency
- Design defect density
- Code defect density
- Average design defect amplification

Project-specific parameters include

- Job size
- COCOMO effort parameter
- Schedule constraint

The parameters below represent management decisions regarding scheduled processes for each project:

- Design walk-through practice (percent of design packages reviewed)
- Code walk-through practice (percent of code reviewed)

5.3.2 Example: Inspection Process Data Calibration

Example datasets of inspection data are shown here with respect to model parameter calibration. Table 5.3 shows sample summary data aggregated from inspection data records for each review held on a project. An overall inspection efficiency of 60% on the project denotes that 60% of all defects where found during inspections, and the other defects were found during integration and system testing. The inspection efficiencies directly translate into the model parameters for efficiency (yield %), representing the defect filters. The 60% from this dataset was used as a baseline in the inspection model.

The total inspection effort for this project is distributed as follows: preparation effort, 27%; inspection meeting effort, 39%; and rework effort, 34%. This type of data can also be used to parameterize the model with respect to effort proportions for the life-cycle activities.

An illustration of data used to calibrate the defect introduction rates, detection rates, and review efficiencies for the peer review model in another installation is shown in Figure 5.12 (the data has been sanitized from some actual project data). In this case, defect data came from multiple defect-finding activities corresponding to different

Table 5.3. Example inspection summary statistics

Subject Type	Number of Inspections	Total Defects	Total Majors	Inspection Effort (person-hours)	# Pages	LOC	Defects/ Page	Defect Removal Effectiveness (major defects/ person-hour)
Requirements Description (R0)	21	1243	89	328	552	0	2.25	0.272
Requirements Analysis (R1)	32	2165	177	769	1065	0	2.03	0.230
High Level Design (I0)	41	2398	197	1097	1652	0	1.45	0.180
Low Level Design (I1)	32	1773	131	955	1423	28254	1.25	0.137
Code (I2)	150	7165	772	4612	5047	276422	1.42	0.167
Test Procedure (IT2)	18	1495	121	457	1621	0	0.92	0.265
Change Request	24	824	27	472	1579	340	0.52	0.057
Other	2	57	4	27	31	781	1.84	0.150
Grand total	320	17120	1518	8716	12970	305797	1.32	0.174

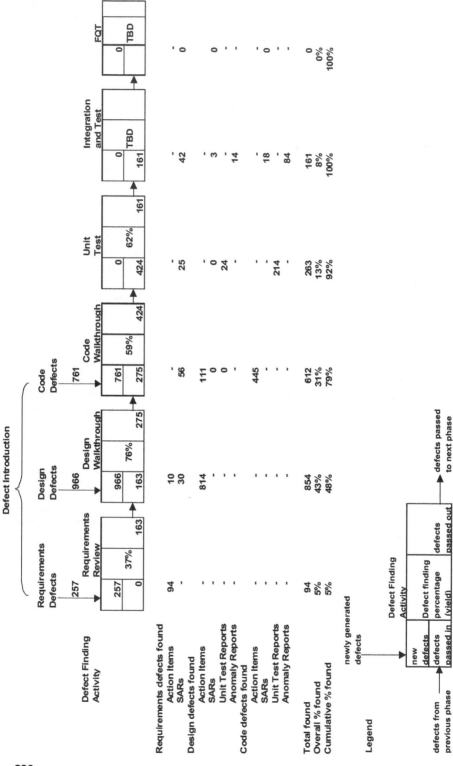

Figure 5.12. Sample defect calibration data.

stages of the process. Data was collected during the defect-finding activities across the top using the reporting mechanisms listed in the left column (an SAR is a software action request), and the review efficiencies are calculated accordingly.

From this type of dataset, a defect flow chain could be calibrated in terms of defect introduction rates and defect detection rates at different junctures of the chain. According to the model structuring principles in Chapter 3, a level would be associated with each step of the process and detection filters would be placed in between them. The introduction rates would be normalized for the project size. All the other values are readily available in the format provided by Figure 5.12.

5.4   GLOBAL PROCESS FEEDBACK (SOFTWARE EVOLUTION)

Global process feedback refers to feedback phenomena associated with the evolution of a fielded software product as it is maintained over time. Software evolution is an iterative process that implements development, adaptation, enhancement, and extension due to changes in application, business, organizational, and technological environments. Changes are initiated, driven, controlled, and evaluated by feedback interactions. Feedback also plays a large role in related organizational business processes.

Why is it natural for global software process feedback and software evolution to occur? A software product encapsulates a model of the real world, but the real world keeps changing. Thus, the rapid pace of change also tends to accelerate software evolution. A need for continual enhancement of functional power is one of the inevitable pressures that emerge when evolving software that addresses real-world problems or automates real-world activities [Lehman, Belady 1985].

Whereas most software process simulation addresses development projects from the beginning through initial delivery, work in the area of software evolution focuses on the entire evolution process and long-term issues associated with feedback from all sources.

Achieving controlled and effective management of such a complex multiloop feedback system and improving its reliability and effectiveness is a major challenge. The problems will become more challenging given current shifts to COTS-intensive systems; distributed development; outsourcing; open-source, multisupplier environments, and so on. Thus work in global feedback is well suited to addressing these new and emerging areas.

Manny Lehman and colleagues have been at the forefront of global feedback modeling for many years [Lehman, Belady 1985, Lehman 1996, Lehman 1998, Wernick, Lehman 1999, Chatters et al. 2000, Lehman, Ramil 2002]. Lehman first observed empirically in 1971 the strong presence of external controlling feedback in the software evolution process [Lehman 1980]. When modeling a software process to assess its performance and improve it, feedback loops and controls that impact process characteristics as observed from outside the process must be included. The process must be modeled at a high enough level such that influences and control aspects of the process, management, marketing, users, and technical personnel can be included.

The earliest studies of evolution and feedback in the software process originated in the 1970s [Riordan 1977], but wide interest in software evolution emerged with formulation of the Feedback, Evolution And Software Technology (FEAST) hypothesis in 1993. The hypothesis of the FEAST project is that the global software process is a complex feedback system, and that major improvement will not be achieved until the process is treated as such. More information can be found at [FEAST 2001]. Per [Lehman 1998],

> It is universal experience that software requires continuing maintenance to, for example, adapt it to changing usage, organizational and technological domains. Such evolution is essential to maintain it satisfactory. Feedback and its management play a major role in driving and controlling this process. The two phenomena are strongly related. The feedback paradigm offers a powerful abstraction whose full potential and the impact it can make remain to be fully investigated.

Because of the very nature of the problem, such investigation requires widespread interdisciplinary collaboration with both industrial and academic involvement. Long-term goals must include the design and management of feedback mechanisms and control and the development and validation of a theoretical framework.

The investigation of software evolution includes the complementary concerns of *how, what,* and *why. How* addresses the achievement and control of software evolution and is considered a verb. *What* and *why* focus on the question of why software evolution occurs, its attributes, characteristics, role, and impact.

A simple example of feedback that contributes to software evolution is when users realize an existing software capability can be improved to solve another problem. Users become empowered when they understand what the software can do for them, and naturally they want more. A similar thing happens with user interfaces. Users will interpret some aspects of an interface design differently than what was intended by the designer and will desire new functionality. This is related to the requirements phenomenon that users do not know what they want until they see it, which is called I'll Know It when I See It (IKIWISI).

One of the earliest efforts applying system dynamics to global feedback processes was [Wernick, Lehman 1999], where good results were obtained from a macro model of global feedback. The model was validated against long-term data from many releases of a large software system over time.

The main structure in their model is reproduced in Figure 5.13. It simulates the software production process, the field testing of the implementation, and changes made to the specification as a result of field trials. The implementation and initial testing is represented as a third-order delay. Then there are feedback paths in the process before field trials. It is found that some units cannot be implemented, so they are eliminated and may be replaced with new or changed equivalents. The completion of a unit may also result in more specification changes.

Other feedback paths occur during field trials. It is found that some specifications need to be re-examined and possibly modified. Others are defective or unnecessary and must be removed from the system. New specifications may also be identified. The

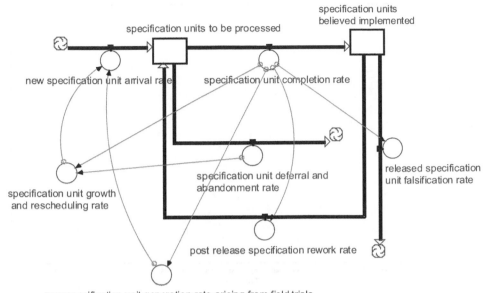

Figure 5.13. Project model with global feedback.

sequence of time trials is simulated as a continuous process, where the interval between trials is progressively reduced in the feedback paths to developers and their completing the work. The model also reflects exogenous changes made to the specifications during the project.

This relatively simple structure only needs to be parameterized with limited, early delivery data from an actual project. A comparison of simulated effort from the model versus actual effort expended on an evolution project is shown in Figure 5.14. It is seen that the model reproduces the actual effort profile well over the long time horizon. Since the model outputs closely simulate actual metrics, it was concluded from this study that external feedback to a software process may significantly influence the process. See [Wernick, Lehman 1999] for further details on the model testing and validation.

This early modeling work in global feedback helped pave the way for many follow-on research studies. The following is a more recent result in global feedback modeling on balancing work activities for optimal evolution from [Ramil et al. 2005].

5.4.1 Example: Software Evolution Progressive and Antiregressive Work

This example presents highlights from [Ramil et al. 2005]. It describes a system dynamics model used to plan and manage long-term software evolution by balancing the allocation of resources to different activities. See the original work for more details and references. Table 5.4 is a high-level summary of the model.

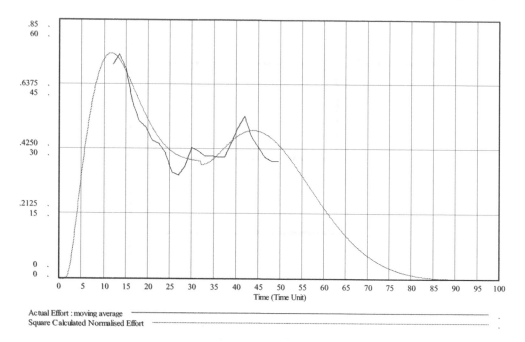

Actual Effort : moving average ————————————————————————————
Square Calculated Normalised Effort --

Figure 5.14. Global feedback model results: actual versus simulated effort.

Table 5.4. Software evolution progressive and antiregressive model overview

Purpose: Planning, Strategic Management, Process Improvement
Scope: Long-term Product Evolution

Inputs and Parameters	Levels	Major Relationships	Outputs
• Percent antiregressive work	• Work Awaiting assignment	• Growth productivity	• Software modules
• Staffing policy	Implemented	• Impact of anti-regressive deficit	• Effort
• Release policy	Validated		
• Domain factors	components		
• Baseline productivity	Outputs		
	Validated elements		
	Standby		
	Completed		
	Released		

5.4.1.1 *Introduction and Background*

Software that is regularly used for real-world problem solving or addressing a real-world application must be continually adapted and enhanced to maintain its fitness to an ever changing real world, its applications, and application domains. This type of activity is termed *progressive*. As evolution continues, the complexity (functional, structural) of the evolving system is likely to increase unless work, termed *antiregressive*, is undertaken to control and even reduce it. However, as progressive and antiregressive work compete for the same pool of resources, management has to estimate the amount of resources applied to each. A systems dynamics model is described that can support decision making regarding the optimal personnel allocation over the system lifetime.

Real-world software must be progressively fixed, adapted, and enhanced, that is, *evolved*, if it is to remain satisfactory to its stakeholders, as evidenced by the universally experienced need for continual software maintenance [Lehman, Belady 1985].

The resources available over some predetermined period or for the development of a new release will be primarily intended for *progressive* activity. This represents activity that adds functionality to the system, enhances performance, and, in general, adds capability to the system as perceived by users and by marketing organizations.

As successive versions of a real-world software system emerge over its long-term evolution, source code is augmented; system size increases and fixes; adaptations, functional, and nonfunctional enhancements get implemented, which are ever more remote from the original conception. The consequence of all these changes and superposition of changes is that the software system *complexity* is likely to increase as the system is evolved. This may bring with it a decline in the *functional growth rate*, as observed in plots of system growth over releases; see, for example, [FEAST 2001]. If this issue is not promptly recognized and addressed, it is likely to lead to decreasing evolvability, increasing maintenance and evolution costs, and even stagnation.

The satisfaction of new or changed needs must not conflict with the need to ensure that the software remains evolvable. The latter is achieved by executing activities such as, for example, restructuring, refactoring, and documentation, termed, in general, *antiregressive* activities. They neutralize or reverse system degradation due to growing structural, functional, and operational complexity.

Antiregressive work is generally not regarded as of high priority in light of other pressures, but a resource trade-off has to be made. A system will degrade if focus is put only on progressive work, but if all activities are antiregressive, then system evolution comes to a halt. Between these limiting situations there must be a division of progressive and antiregressive levels of investment that achieves the best balance between immediate added functional capability and system evolution potential and longevity.

5.4.1.1.1 MODEL OVERVIEW. The model is driven by the observation that each unit of progressive work requires a minimal amount of antiregressive work to forestall accumulation of an antiregressive deficit [Riordan 1977]. As the required but neglected antiregressive effort accumulates over time, its impact on productivity begins to be noticeable. Only restoration to an adequate level can reverse the growth trend and restore productivity. The model provides a tool to determine what is adequate.

The model is shown in Figure 5.15. The outer loops of flows and stocks show the arrival and implementation or rejection of work requests, their validation, and delivery of the product to the field. It is visualized as a process that addresses a continuing flow of work in the form of changes in requirements, functional adaptation, enhancements, and so on.

The inner feedback loop on the bottom is a provision for delaying output of the validation step and for the authorization of rework. Some part of the output will be held, rejected, or recycled.

Parameters for new functions include productivity and staff size to include the assignment of resources to progressive work. To complete the model, there is a subgraph for splitting the effort between progressive and antiregressive work. Antiregressive work is captured as a flow rate. The expressions included in the executable model in the Vensim language are available upon request from the authors.

5.4.1.1.2 CALIBRATION AND EXPERIMENTATION. A calibration process was followed, though not every measure was directly available and attribute surrogates were sometimes use [Ramil et al. 2005]. Nevertheless, the relatively simple model closely approximates real-world patterns of behavior. Figure 5.16 shows how closely the model reproduces the growth trend of an information system over 176 months of its lifetime. As illustrated, the model is able to replicate actual trends even though only a small subset of the model parameters were known. Despite possible refinements to recalibrate for specific processes, the model exemplifies the approach and is sufficient to perform some virtual experiments described next.

One set of experiments concerns the long-term consequences of different levels of antiregressive activity on system growth rate and productivity. Several values of antiregressive work are simulated, expressed in percentage of total human resources available for the evolution of the system. Figure 5.17 and Figure 5.18 permit visualization of the effect of different antiregressive policies.

Figure 5.17 shows several simulated trajectories resulting from alternative fixed-allocation strategies. For the lowest level of antiregressive work, one achieves the highest *initial* accomplishment rates, suggesting initially low antiregressive activity, to maximize initial growth rate.

Figure 5.18 indicates the impact of different levels of fixed antiregressive work on growth–productivity, the number of elements created per unit of total effort applied (where both progressive and antiregressive work are added).

Together, the two experiments suggest that a constant level, in this case approximately 60% of resources allocated to antiregressive work, maximizes long-term growth capability. This number will vary from process to process, but the important lesson is that antiregressive work in excess of some level constitutes resource wastage.

Whether restructuring occurs or not, the experiments suggest that as a system ages one may seek to maintain system growth rate or, equivalently, minimize total effort required to achieve the desired evolution rate and, hence, productivity by adjusting the level of antiregressive activity.

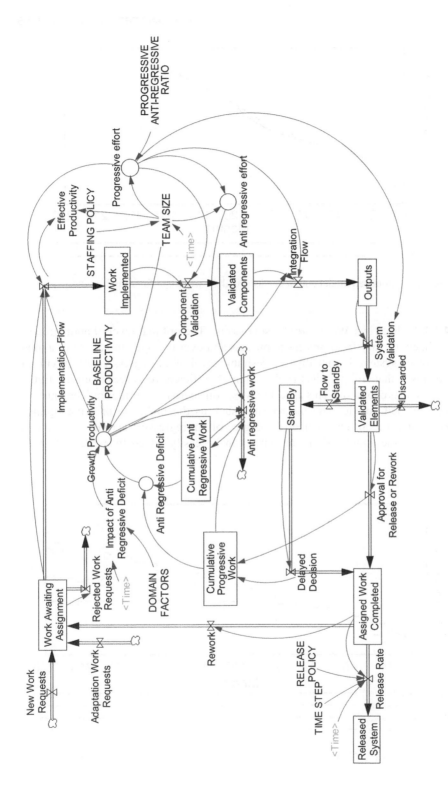

Figure 5.15. Software evolution progressive and antiregressive work model diagram.

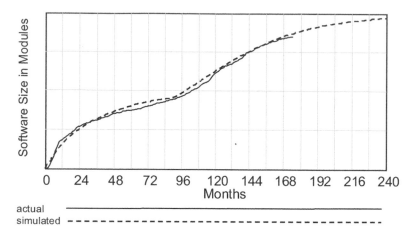

Figure 5.16. Simulated model output versus actual growth trend for an information system.

5.4.1.1.3 FURTHER WORK AND CONCLUSIONS. The optimal level of antiregressive work is likely to vary from process to process and over the operational life of a long-lived software system. Eventually, the desirable level of antiregressive effort will stabilize in a way that still permits the allocation of sufficient resources to ensure further effective system evolution. This aspect may be considered for further refinements.

More detailed policies and mechanisms such as the inclusion of a management feedback control loop that changes the degree of antiregressive activity over time in response to some simulated circumstance can be easily added to explore their impacts.

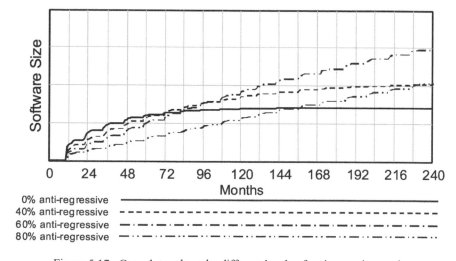

Figure 5.17. Growth trends under different levels of antiregressive work.

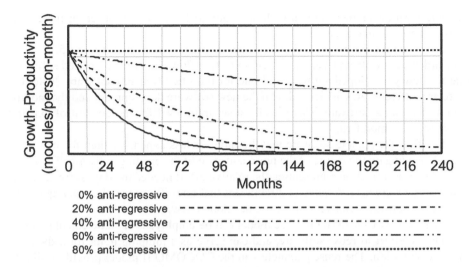

Figure 5.18. Growth–productivity under different policies.

For wider application, the model needs to be refined to accommodate for allocation of work to a wider variety of concerns than antiregressive and progressive work. Extension to more general paradigms, such as component-based and reuse-based processes, and customization of the model to specific process instances is likely to raise issues. These would likely include the need for measures of stakeholder satisfaction and system value.

The described model can serve as the core of a tool to support decisions regarding allocation of personnel to evolution activities over the application lifetime. Process modeling at an aggregated, high level of abstraction can serve as the basis for a tool to assist managers to recognize and control the various influences on long-term behavior. By taking these into account, they may can manage and control complexity to maintain the rate of system evolution at the desired or required level.

Control and mastery of system evolution is vital in a society increasingly reliant on aging software in which increased size, more interdependent functionality, larger numbers of integrated components, more control mechanisms, and a higher level of organizational interdependency are likely to lead to a decrease in evolvability. As society relies increasingly on software, planning and management of complex, dynamic, and ever more widespread and integrated evolution processes is becoming increasingly critical.

5.5 SOFTWARE REUSE

Software reuse was introduced in Chapter 1 under life-cycle models, and will not be repeated here. There are many variants of reuse. Other application areas like COTS, product line strategies (see Chapter 6), and open-source development all employ reuse in some form or another. Virtually all software artifacts can be reused in these contexts, not only source code.

For illustrative purposes, a simple model of reuse is shown in Figure 5.19 using standard structures from Chapter 3. It contains two flows into the completed software: one for newly developed software and one for modified (reused) software. Note that there are different rates associated with the new software development and the modification of existing software. There is also a separate level for the amount of existing software being modified.

The effort for reusing software may be more or less expensive than for new software depending on the nature of the reuse and state of the existing software. The adaptation factor is a fraction representing the relative effort needed to adapt software compared to if it were new. A value of 20% means that one-fifth of the effort is required to modify the software relative to if it were developed new.

The nonlinear COCOMO II reuse model can be employed for static calculations of the relative effort to reuse software, and can serve as a jumping point for a dynamic model elaboration. The reuse parameters in the COCOMO II model provide visibility into some of the important factors and tradeoffs:

- Percent of design modified
- Percent of code modified
- Percent of reintegration required
- Amount of assessment and assimilation

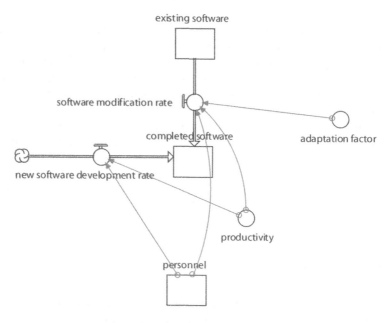

Figure 5.19. Top-level reuse model.

- Degree of software understanding
- Programmer familiarity

These reuse parameters are used to derive an overall adjustment factor. See the CO-COMO II summary appendix for more details of these definitions and the calculations for relative effort.

The resulting effort from a static model like COCOMO can be transformed into a reuse rate. Moreover, the COCOMO II reuse parameters are static approximations that can be reformulated into a dynamic model accounting for feedback interactions. For example, the degree of software understanding is not a static value, but would follow from the amount and type of changes incurred to the software. The following example is a modeling study of reuse and fourth-generation languages that employs a dynamic model of reuse.

5.5.1   Example: Reuse and Fourth-Generation Languages

A USC research study investigated the dynamic effects of reuse and fourth-generation languages (4GLs) [Lo 1999]. The purpose of the modeling project was to study the effects of reuse and very high-level languages (RVHL) in a RAD context for reducing schedule. Using different kinds of programming languages and levels of reuse may affect the schedule and effort, so understanding their effects on the software process will benefit management planning strategy. Table 5.5 is a high-level summary of the model.

5.5.1.1   Background

Different languages have different effort impacts on portions of the development process, such as design, coding, and testing. High-level programming languages typi-

Table 5.5. Reuse and fourth-generation languages model overview

Purpose: Process Improvement, Planning **Scope:** Development Project			
Inputs and Parameters	Levels	Major Relationships	Outputs

• Language level
 • Project size
 • Personnel
 • Hiring delay
 • Attrition rate
 • Reuse percentage
 • Reuse components
 • Decay rate
 • Nominal productivity
 • Learning curve switch
 • Incompressibility factor
	• Personnel
	 • Tasks
	   Required
	   Designed
	   Designed with
	     errors
	   Coded
	   Coded with
	     errors
	   Completed
		• Learning curve
		 • Task approval
		 • Communication
		   overhead
		 • Code adoption rate
		 • Productivity
			• Staffing per activity
			 • Effort per activity
			 • Schedule per activity
			 • Reuse level

cally come with source code libraries, which make code generation and testing more efficient. A higher-level programming language provides similar advantages to reuse because it does automatic code generation. It "reuses" packaged code.

Different language levels affect the error level in each phase because the richer the language, the more you have to test or verify as you build. However, the richer the language, the more training is involved. Reusing assets also reduces human effort and increases productivity in each phase.

5.5.1.2 Model Description

There are four phases represented in the model: requirements, design, coding, and approval phases. By default, each phase uses COCOMO phase effort distributions (see [Lo 1999] for the values). Language effects on effort were also quantified. Effort ratios of 1:6.7 for 3GL to 4GL and a ratio of 1:3 for Assembly to 3GL were used according to [Verner, Tate 1988].

Interviews with language level and reuse experts suggested that high-level languages require more training. A learning curve is used to represent this, with a 90% learning curve for 3GL and an 80% learning curve for 4GL. Both log-linear and De-Jong learning curves are used in the model. A DeJong curve models processes in which a portion of the process cannot improve [Raccoon 1996]. Per interviews, different error rates for the different levels are applied in the design and code phases according to the language level being used.

A reuse structure is in the model that reduces the size of flows into the software development phases. This reduces effort depending on the percentage of reuse on the project. A level for reuse code was added, which can monitor the actual reuse level during the project development. But a reuse policy is not only for code reuse. It also includes pattern reuse, design reuse, test case reuse, and so on. In each case of reuse, there can be different degrees of levels and factors. This model treats reuse as if it reduces the entire software size.

A model of software production provides the personnel staffing profile. A communication overhead factor is also included that reduces productivity. With this, adding an infinite number of people will not finish the project in zero time.

Figure 5.20 presents a causal loop diagram for the model. The causal diagram shows that the language level affects defect density, productivity, and learning curve percentages. Increased language level will decrease defect density and fewer errors occur. Higher language level also increases the productivity. But increased language level will increase the learning curve percentages, which results in a slower learning rate. By increasing the number of human resources, it increases communication overhead and decreases productivity.

With less defects, a certain amount of people and high productivity will increase the design, code, and approved tasks rates. Higher productivity also increases code adoption and increases code reuse. Since design, coding, task approval, and code reuse are all increased, it is more efficient to complete tasks. A higher completed task rate reduces the schedule time.

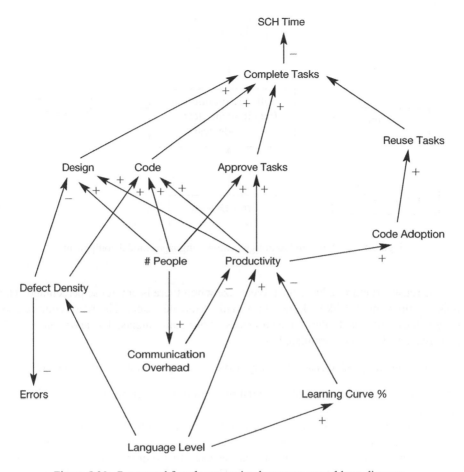

Figure 5.20. Reuse and fourth-generation languages causal loop diagram.

The primary components in the executable model are shown in Figure 5.21. Detailed model components are in Figure 5.22, Figure 5.23, Figure 5.24, and Figure 5.25 with descriptions following the figures.

In the software production structure, development starts with a project-size level and flows into requirements, design, code, and approve phases to complete tasks. The flow rates for each phase are determined by

communication overhead · personnel · productivity/phase effort %

There is error detection used in design and code phases, and rework flows back into the product line. The error rate depends on the defect density, which is controlled by language level.

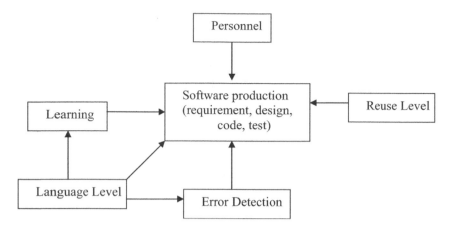

Figure 5.21. Reuse and fourth-generation languages model components.

The reuse structure reduces the project size when there is any reuse percentage. The reuse components act like a library to provide reusable assets. The reuse components have a decay rate due to the change of needs or old components. The adoption rate adjusts reuse tasks and is formulated as

personnel · productivity · learning curve · reuse percentage/adoption factor

The reuse level is used to check the actual reuse in the project where reuse level equals reuse tasks/complete tasks · 100%.

The language level controls the language factor that modifies nominal productivity. The language level also affects the required effort, which is used to calculate the effort for each phase. There are two learning curves used that require a learning percentage, which is also controlled by language level. The original paper [Lo 1999] has more details on the learning curve formulas and parameters.

The personnel staffing component defines the human resources for the project. The hiring rate is affected by a hiring delay, and the attrition rate represents personnel lost. Adding more people will increase communication overhead and may decrease the software development rate.

5.5.1.3 Sample Results and Conclusions

Several types of tests were performed to assess the model and draw phenomenological conclusions. Scenarios were run to verify a nominal case, to test learning curves, the effects of language levels, the effects of varying degrees of reuse, personnel levels, and combined strategies. The detailed inputs and outputs are provided in the original report in [Lo 1999].

Results for varying reuse are shown in Figure 5.26. Reuse will reduce the effective project size, so the effort in all phases and the schedule time are all reduced. A test of language levels that compared 3GL to 4GL with everything else constant is shown in Figure 5.27; 4GL finished first.

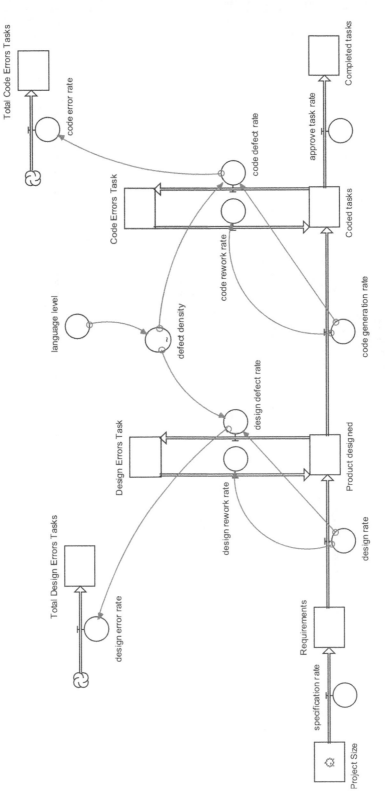

Figure 5.22. Software production phases.

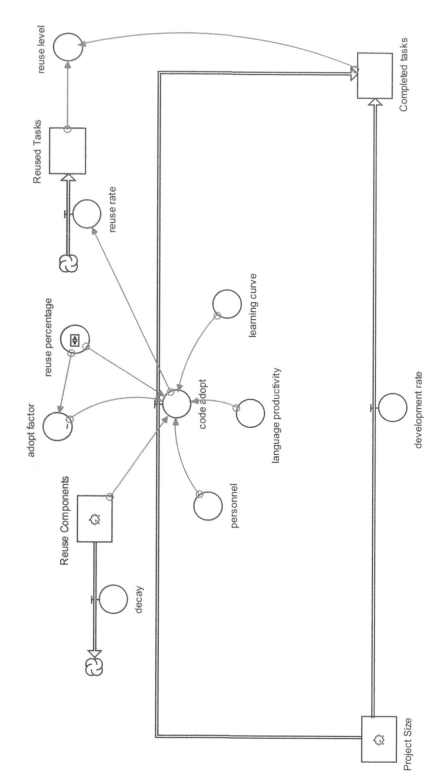

Figure 5.23. Reuse structure.

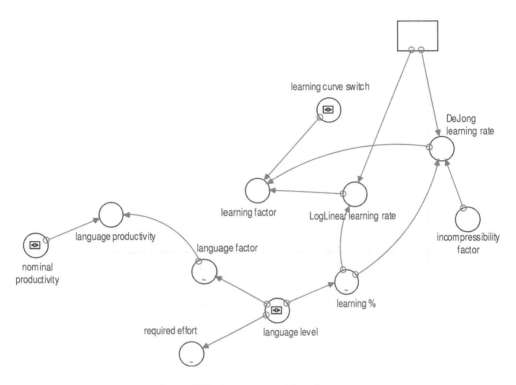

Figure 5.24. Language and learning curve.

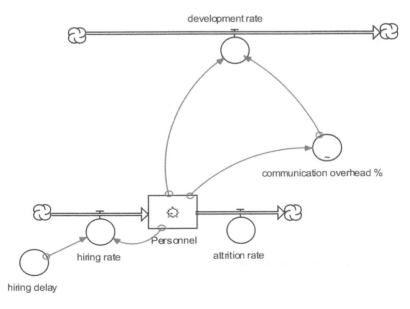

Figure 5.25. Personnel staffing structure.

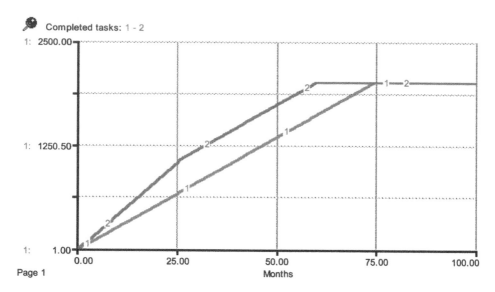

Figure 5.26. Task completion progress for no reuse versus 20% reuse (1: no reuse, 2: 20% reuse).

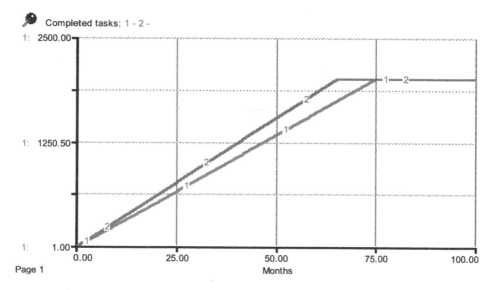

Figure 5.27. Task completion progress for 3GL versus 4GL (1: 3GL, 2: 4GL).

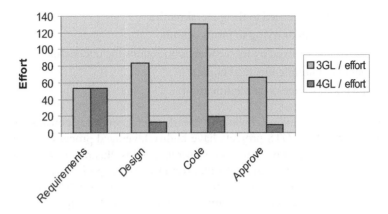

Figure 5.28. Effort distributions for 3GL versus 4GL.

Varying the number of personnel also showed tradeoffs. Optimum staff levels were found that were able to decrease overall schedule time even though communication overhead was slightly increased.

Overall, the model demonstrates that a higher language level reduces the effort on design, code, and approval phases, but it does not reduce effort in the requirements phase (Figure 5.28). With a 4GL, it also reduces the schedule time to finish the project.

5.6 COMMERCIAL OFF-THE-SHELF SOFTWARE (COTS)-BASED SYSTEMS

The use of commercial-off-the-shelf (COTS) products is becoming ever more prevalent in the creation of software systems. COTS software is commercially available as stand-alone products that offer specific functionality needed by a larger system into which they are incorporated. Such systems using COTS are frequently called COTS-based systems (CBSs). Using COTS is not just a somewhat different form of software reuse, but a fundamentally different form of software development and life-cycle management. One purpose of using COTS is to lower overall development costs and development time by taking advantage of existing, market-proven, and vendor-supported products. Shrinking budgets, accelerating rates of COTS enhancement, and expanding system requirements are all driving this process.

The definition of a COTS product per the SEI COTS-Based System Initiative* [Brownsword et al. 2000] is one that is:

---

*The focus of the SEI COTS-Based Systems initiative was to learn, mature, and transition principles, methods, and techniques for creating systems from COTS products. The effort has since been expanded to the creation and sustainment of systems from any set of largely off-the-shelf (rather than only commercial) constituents. The SEI has now formed the Integration of Software-Intensive Systems (ISIS) initiative to address integration and interoperability of systems of systems. The roots of ISIS are in the CBS initiative, where it became apparent that interoperability between many sorts of systems was becoming of paramount importance.

- Sold, leased, or licensed to the general public
- Offered by a vendor trying to profit from it
- Supported and evolved by the vendor, who retains the intellectual property rights
- Available in multiple identical copies
- Used without source code modification

CBSs present new and unique challenges in task interdependency constraints. USC research has shown that COTS projects have highly leveraged process concurrence between phases (see Chapter 6). Process concurrence helps illustrate how CBSs have dynamic work profiles that may quite distinct from traditional project staffing profiles.

One hypothesis about the long-term evolution dynamics of CBSs is that there are diminishing returns in trying to maximize the use of COTS components in a system development [Abts 2000]. Beyond a certain point, an increase in the number of COTS components in a system may actually reduce the system's overall economic life span rather than increase it. With simulation, one can investigate the trade-offs between maintenance costs and the increasing incompatibilities among COTS packages as they evolve to decide when to retire COTS-intensive systems. See the last example in this section on the COTS-Lifespan model for more details.

COTS glue code development presents other complex decision scenarios, and is much different from traditional glue code development. The glue code development process largely depends on factors such as the number of COTS components, volatility of the COTS components, dependability of COTS components, the interfaces provided by the COTS components, and other context factors elaborated in [Abts 2003] and [Baik et al. 2001]. Trend analyses indicate that software developers' time will be increasingly spent on glue code development and integration.

Research at USC investigated the problem of deciding the optimal time to develop glue code and integrate it into the system [Kim, Baik 1999]. This research addressing glue code development and integration processes is highlighted next.

5.6.1   Example: COTS Glue Code Development and COTS Integration

A research project by Wook Kim and Jongmoon Baik at USC sought to understand how the glue code development process and COTS integration process affect each other. They analyzed the effect on schedule and effort throughout a project life cycle of glue code development and the ongoing integration of components into the developing system. The following highlights are mostly taken from their publication [Kim, Baik 1999]. Also see [Baik et al. 2001] for additional related work. Table 5.6 is a high-level summary of the model.

5.6.1.1   Background

One generally has no control over the functionality, performance, and evolution of COTS products due to their black-box nature. Most COTS products are also not designed to interoperate with each other and most COTS vendors do not support glue

Table 5.6. COTS glue code development and COTS integration model overview

Purpose: Process Improvement, Planning
Scope: Development Project

Inputs and Parameters	Levels	Major Relationships	Outputs

• COTS Component factors
• New COTS percent
• Integration starting point
• Glue code design productivity
• Glue code development productivity
• Application design productivity
	• Glue code
	  Required
	  Designed
	  Completed
	• Application software
	  Required
	  Designed
	  Completed
	• Integrated software
		• Design rates
		• Development rates
		• Integration rates
		• Application process concurrence
		• Glue code process concurrence
			• Effort per activity
			• Schedule per activity

code (sometimes called glueware or binding code). Thus, most software development teams that use COTS components have difficulties in estimating effort and schedule for COTS glue code development and integration into application systems.

Glue code for COTS components is defined as the new code needed to get a COTS product integrated into a larger system. It is connected to the COTS component itself, acting more as a "bridge" between the COTS component and the system into which it is being integrated. It can be code needed to connect a COTS component either to higher-level system code, or to other COTS components used in the system.

Glue code is considered as one of following: (1) any code required to facilitate information or data exchange between the COTS component and the application; (2) any code needed to "hook" the COTS component into the application, even though it may not necessarily facilitate data exchange; and (3) any code needed to provide functionality that was originally intended to be provided by the COTS component, and which must interact with that COTS component.

The engineering of COTS-based systems involves significant technical risk in the glue code used to integrate components. This code is often ad hoc and brittle, but it is needed to repair mismatched assumptions that are exhibited by the components being integrated.

Most software development teams also have problems deciding when they should start to develop the glue code and integrate it into the system. It depends on factors such as the number of COTS components, requirement specification, and the availability of COTS components required for the developing system.

5.6.1.2 Model Overview

The model simulates how the integration process is affected by various factors such as the number of COTS, percentage of updated and new COTS, and requirement specification. The developing COCOTS model and data [Abts, Boehm 1998] was used for portions of the model. COCOTS parameters calibrated for the model include COTS Product Maturity, COTS Supplier Product Extension Willingness, COTS Product Interface Complexity, COTS Supplier Product Support, COTS Supplier Provided Training, and Documentation. Data for the simulation was acquired from the COCOTS data collection program at the USC Center for Software Engineering that contained 20 projects at the time.

Staffing levels were analyzed according to concurrency profiles between glue code development and application development (or custom component development). Various starting points of glue code development were simulated to see the effect on system integration process productivity. The impact of parameters such as the ratio of new and updated COTS components, and the number of COTS components were analyzed. With these simulations, several efficient scenarios for glue code development and integration process were suggested.

Reference behavior patterns were first established to characterize the dynamic phenomena, and can be found in [Kim, Baik 1999]. In order to develop the simulation model, the following assumptions were made.

- The simulation model is focused on glue code development and its effect on the integration process, so application development and workforce effort is only briefly simulated.
- For simplicity, the simulation model does not allow feedback to the outside of the system boundary such as reevaluation of the COTS products, feedback to the requirements definition for COTS, or feedback to the COTS product selection process.

Causal loop diagrams were used to clarify the nature of the system before developing an executable model. Figure 5.29 represents a feedback diagram of the simulation model. Complete definitions of the variables in the diagram are in the original report.

Completed Glue Code increases Integrated System and Integrated System increases Glue Code Dev Multiplier. The Glue Code Dev Multipliers affect an increase in Application Design Rate. Increased Application Design Rate also increases Completed Application. Increased Completed Application also increases Integration Rate. Application Dev Rate and Glue Code Dev Rate are promoting each other.

The system dynamics model consists of four submodels: Application Development/Integration, Glue Code Development, COTS Component Factors, and Human Resource models. These are shown in Figure 5.30 with their connections. The first three submodels are highlighted below. The human resource model is not covered because it is not directly germane to the COTS phenomena, but the full details can be found in the original report [Kim, Baik 1999].

5.6.1.2.1 GLUE CODE DEVELOPMENT. This sector represents glue code development in the system. COCOTS parameters for the Glue Code Development submodel are divided into categories. Personnel drivers represent characteristics of COTS integrator personnel. Application/System drivers represent characteristics of the system into which COTS is being integrated. COTS Component drivers are the most important drivers because they represent characteristics of the integrated COTS component

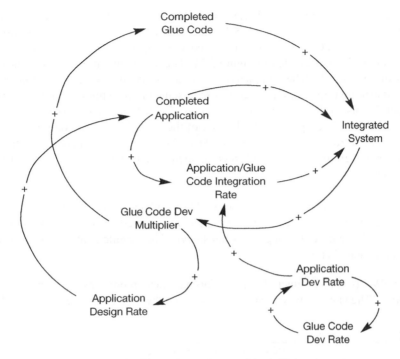

Figure 5.29. Glue code causal loop diagram.

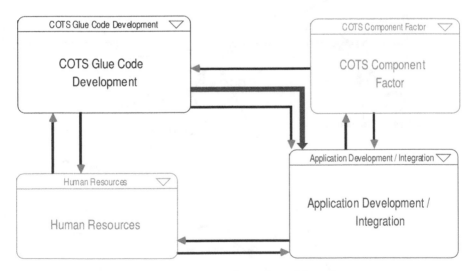

Figure 5.30. COTS glue code model sectors.

itself. These COTS Component drivers are COTS Product Maturity, COTS Supplier Product Extension Willingness, COTS Product Interface Complexity, COTS Supplier Product Support, and COTS Supplier Provided Training and Documentation.

The submodel is represented in Figure 5.31. The development process of glue code consists of three levels. The completed glue code is added to completed application code for integration. Integration process is represented in the application development submodel. In this model, COTS components are divided into new COTS components and upgraded COTS components. In the case of the upgraded COTS components, glue code is modified from a previous version. Thus, glue code development productivity is higher when integrating updated COTS components than when integrating new COTS components.

5.6.1.2.2   COTS COMPONENT FACTORS. This module isolates a number of factors that adjust effort in the model. They are modeled as converters with no levels or rates associated with them, so the diagram is not shown. The module contains the following COTS component factors:

1. ACPMT (COTS Product Maturity). This parameter represents COTS product maturity. The value of this parameter is estimated by time on market of the product.

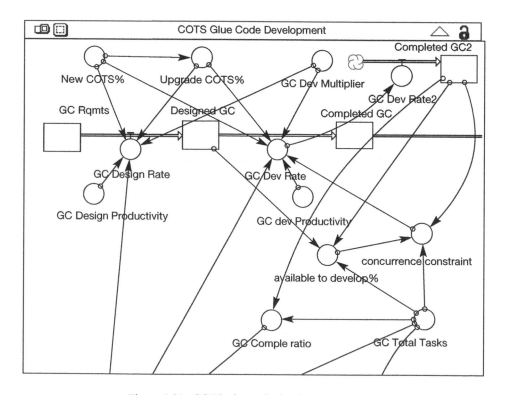

Figure 5.31. COTS glue code development model.

2. ACSEW (COTS Supplier Product Extension). COTS supplier's willingness to change features of COTS components. It is estimated by observing the number of changes the supplier makes to the COTS component and the complexity of the change.

3. APCPX (COTS Product Interface Complexity). Represents the interface complexity of a COTS product. If the interface of the COTS component is complex, it is difficult to integrate it into the application system. The degree of the complexity is calculated using a table.

4. ACPPS (COTS Supplier Product Support). COTS supplier's technical support is represented by this parameter. It includes support for the integration team during the development, either directly from the component suppliers or through third parties.

5. ACPTD (COTS Supplier Provided Training and Documentation). Training and documentation provided from a COTS supplier is enumerated in this factor. It is calculated by estimating the period of training and coverage of COTS products within documentation.

5.6.1.2.3 APPLICATION DEVELOPMENT/INTEGRATION. The submodel in Figure 5.32 represents application development and integration in the system. The application de-

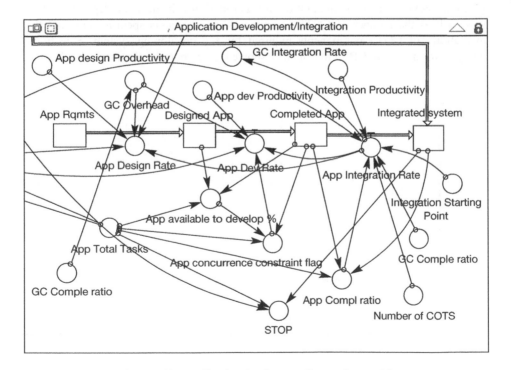

Figure 5.32. Application development/integration model.

velopment model consists of three levels. They are the same as for the glue code development. Completed application flows to the integrated system with the completed glue code. When integrating COTS components, the number of COTS components is an important factor in the integration process. If the number of COTS is higher, then the integration process is slower.

5.6.1.3 Sample Test Results

Data for these simulation results was adapted from a project in the COCOTS database. According to the graphs in Figure 5.33 and Figure 5.34, glue code development is started when parts of the application are ready to complete. There is concurrency in the design and implementation phases. The integration process starts as glue code is completed. The integration graph is S-shaped. As for personnel allocation, the staffing pattern is affected in each development phase.

According to Figure 5.33 and Figure 5.34, integration is started although glue code development is not finished. So integration can be finished just after glue code development is finished. The application development rate is reduced when the glue code development is processed because staff moves to the glue code development.

5.6.1.4 Conclusions and Future Work

One of the important results of the simulation was determining the starting point of glue code development and integration. It was found that the decision depends on factors such as the number of COTS components, requirements specification, and the availability of COTS components required for the developing system. Sensitivity analysis for a sample CBS environment showed glue code development should start

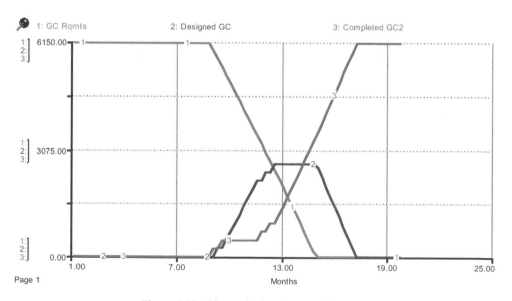

Figure 5.33. Glue code development dynamics.

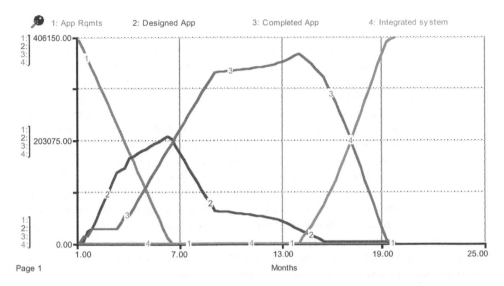

Figure 5.34. Application development and integration dynamics.

when 80% of application (custom-based) components are completed and integration should start when 30% of glue code is completed.

A general conclusion regarding the starting point is that glue code development has to start in the end of the application development, and the integration process has to start in the beginning of the glue code development.

Although software COTS products are attempting to simulate the "plug-and-play" capability of the hardware world, software COTS products seldom plug into anything easily. Most products require some amount of adaptation to work harmoniously with the other commercial or custom components in the system.

Integration of COTS software products requires adjustment and accommodations to the development process. Preparations must be made to start prototyping activities and integration activities immediately to take advantage of COTS products to accelerate development. Additional resources must be allocated late in the development cycle to provide maintenance and support to the software developers.

This simulation model can be enhanced for other aspects of the COCOTS model such as assessment, tailoring, and volatility. They include feedback to the COTS product selection process, feedback to the requirements definition for COTS products, and reevaluation of the COTS products.

5.6.2 Example: COTS-Lifespan Model

A COTS-Lifespan Model (COTS-LIMO) was proposed in [Abts 2000]. This model is conceptual and has not yet been elaborated into an executable model. The overall concept and basic reference behaviors have been defined, such that a system dynamics model could be developed. The description below is derived from [Abts 2000].

Anecdotal evidence collected during interviews to gather calibration data for the COCOTS model suggests that generally, though not universally, the more COTS software components you include in your overall software system, the shorter the economic life will be of that system. This is particularly true when doing present-worth analyses comparing alternative designs using various combinations of COTS components, or when comparing COTS-based designs to building the entire system from scratch.

This is due to the volatility of COTS components. By volatility is meant the frequency with which vendors release new versions of their products and the significance of the changes in those new versions (i.e., minor upgrades vs. major new releases). When you first deploy your system, you have selected a suite of components that will provide the functionality you require while at the same time work in concert with each other. Over time, however, those products will likely evolve in different directions in response to the marketplace, in some cases even disappearing from the market altogether. As a consequence, the ability of these diverging products to continue functioning adequately together if and when you install the newer versions will likely also become more problematic; the more COTS components you have, the more severe the consequences of these increasing incompatibilities will become.

Looking at the model behavior itself in Figure 5.35, the graph is broken into two regions bisected by the line *n*. As long as the number of COTS components in the system is less than *n*, the increase in experience gained by your system maintainers over time and, thus, the inherent improvements in their productivity will outpace the increased effort required to maintain the system as the COTS products it contains age and evolve

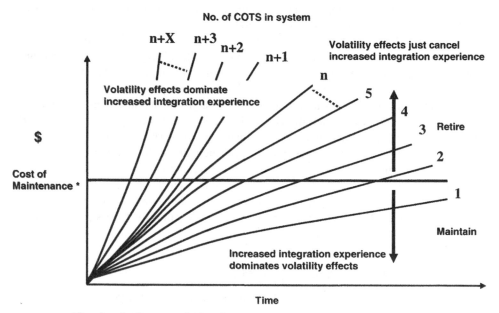

Figure 5.35. The COTS—LIMO model behavior.

in divergent directions. However, at some number of installed COTS components n, the breakeven point is surpassed and no matter how skilled and experienced your maintainers become, the increases in their efficiency at maintaining the system can no longer keep pace with the impact of the increasing incompatibilities arising in the evolving COTS components. At this point, you have reached the zone in which the useful life of your system has been shortened considerably and a decision to retire the system will soon have to be made.

The actual value of n, the specific shape of the individual contour lines, and the location of the M–R (maintain–retire) line will be highly context sensitive, differing for each software system under review. Abts has suggested that a meta-model could be developed using systems dynamics simulation. See the exercise at the end of this chapter that addresses the lifespan trade-offs described here.

5.7 SOFTWARE ARCHITECTING

The architecture of a system forms the blueprint for building the system and consists of the most important abstractions that address global concerns. Development of an architecture is an iterative process. Architecture is important to many modern, iterative life cycles such as the Rational Unified Process (RUP) and Model-Based Architecting and Software Engineering (MBASE). It is important to develop an architecture early on that will remain stable throughout the entire life cycle and also provide future capabilities. An example process model for architecting is described next.

5.7.1 Example: Architecture Development During Inception and Elaboration

The dynamics of the architecture development process were investigated by Nikunj Mehta and Cyrus Fakharzadeh at USC. They modeled architecture development in the MBASE inception and elaboration phases for their research. The model also studies the impact of rapid application development (RAD) factors such as collaboration and prototyping on the process of architecting. The following highlights are mostly taken from [Mehta, Fakharzadeh 1999].

The primary goals of the research were to:

- Investigate the dynamics of architecture development during early MBASE life-cycle phases
- Identify nature of process concurrence in early MBASE phases
- Understand impact of collaboration and prototyping on life-cycle parameters

Table 5.7 is a high-level summary of the model.

5.7.1.1 Background

The MBASE approach involves creation of four kinds of models—product, process, property, and success models—and their integration in an ongoing fashion. MBASE is

Table 5.7. Software architecting model overview

Purpose: Process Improvement, Planning
Scope: Portion of Lifecycle—Architecting

Inputs and Parameters	Levels	Major Relationships	Outputs

• Activity effort distributions
• Identified units
• Average duration
• Resource constraint
• Defect release
• Concurrence relationships
	• Architecture items Identified
	  Completed but not checked
	  To be iterated
	  To be coordinated
	  Prototyping required
		• Prototyping rate
		• Iteration rate
		• Basework rate
		• Approval rate
		• Initial completion rate
		• In-phase concurrence constraint
		• Interphase concurrence constraint
			• Staffing profiles
			• Architecture items
			• Schedule

also an architecture-centric approach and the architecture is constantly integrated with other models.

The process of architecting is still not a very well understood one and involves varying degrees of method, theft, and intuition. However, it is possible to model the concurrence relations among requirements and architecture activities.

5.7.1.1.1 EMPIRICAL REFERENCE DATA. Substantial empirical data was available for calibrating the process model. The model behavior is predicated on data collected from CS 577 graduate student team projects at USC. The data for the model was acquired from the CSCI 577a (Fall 1998) and CSCI 577b (Spring 1999) Weekly Effort Reports. The data is for effort for a standard set of activities, size (documentation), use cases, and requirements.

A summary of some of the data is shown in Table 5.8. It shows the individual activity person-hours and percentages to reach LCO, LCA, a Revised LCA (RLCA), LCA

Table 5.8. CSCI 577 effort distribution data

	LCO	%	LCA	%	RLCA	%	Total LCA	%	Overall	%	Adjusted
Management	230.8	40%	235	41%	112	19%	348	60%	578	38%	
Environment	110.1	60%	18	10%	55	30%	72	40%	182	12%	
Requirements	173.9	53%	103	32%	48	15%	152	47%	325	22%	50%
Architecture and Design	101	45%	64	28%	61	27%	125	55%	226	15%	34%
Implementation	36	36%	30	30%	33	34%	63	64%	99	7%	16%
Assessment	35	35%	41	40%	25	25%	66	65%	100	7%	
Total	686	45%	490.8	32%	334.7	22%	826	55%	1511.6	100%	100%

total, and overall. The adjusted column normalizes the percentages for the activities represented in the model. The entire dataset had more detailed activities. The original report has the full dataset, defines the activities in detail, and describes the effort adjustment algorithms.

5.7.1.2 Model Overview

The model simulates the two major activities of the front end of a software development project: requirements elicitation and architecture design. It also models the prototyping tasks in the development process as a supporting activity. Some features of the model include:

- Schedule as independent variable
- Iterative process structures
- Sequentiality and concurrency among phases (requirements and architecture/design) and activities (initial completion, coordination, quality assurance, iteration)
- Demand-based resource allocation
- External and internal precedence constraints

These features are addressed in the following sections.

The two activities are modeled separately in the model and a generic process structure is chosen to describe the internal dynamics of each activity with customizations performed to accommodate each activity's characteristics. The resource allocation in a concurrent model cannot be described by a static relationship with progress. Instead, the required resources are often dictated by resource availability. Once hired, these resources are dynamically allocated to various tasks based on the backlog of tasks of that kind. Three subsystems of this model are process structure, resources, and performance.

The flow of products between project activities is described in the project network diagram in Figure 5.36. Links between activities of the project are distinguished as car-

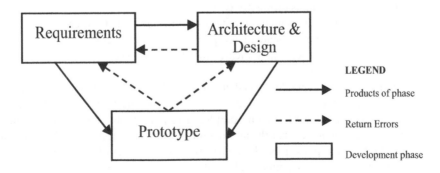

Figure 5.36. Activity network diagram.

rying products of an activity or returning errors from the following activity. The inter-activity interactions arise from the following:

- Requirements activity produces requirement descriptions that are available to the architecture activity.
- Architecture activity produces artifacts that are used in downstream activities but these downstream activities are not modeled.
- Architecture design reveals errors in the requirements definition that cause re-work in the previous phase.
- Prototyping activity is driven by both requirements and architecture activities and serves as a fast-track route for discovering the details that would otherwise require more effort and time.
- Once prototyping is performed, it uncovers information that is required to better describe and understand the products of each of the two principal activities. Prototyping is a supporting activity and does not by itself consume or produce any artifacts (assumed in this model, but prototypes are not always throw-aways).

The model is based on the assumptions that the projects are completed in a fixed time frame and that schedule is an independent variable. This assumption is necessary so that the model can be calibrated against a set of projects from the CSCI 577 courses.

Modeling a concurrent process requires a good understanding the relations of the various concurrent activities of the project. The model is based on the product development project model by Ford and Sterman [Ford, Sterman 1997], which describes the concurrency relationships that constrain the sequencing of tasks and interactions with resources. This model identifies a generic process structure that can be used to describe the iteration and completion of artifacts and the generation and correction of errors in each activity.

Process elements are organized in the form of a phase-activity matrix, so that both requirements elicitation and architecture design activities involve initial completion, coordination, QA, and iteration. All the rates and levels of the generic process structure are arrayed in two dimensions: activity and tasks.

The concurrence for requirements elicitation indicates that it experiences a fairly high rate of independence on its state of completion. The architecture concurrence is in the form of an S-shape curve. This indicates that there is a significant dependence of architecture on the requirements.

The only interactivity dependency is that between the requirements and architecture activity. It is modeled as shown in Figure 5.37, showing the fraction of architecture tasks available to complete the given completed requirements. The S-shaped curve starting at the origin indicates that the architecture design can start only after some requirements elicitation is performed. However, the steep incline of the curve indicates that once some information is available about the requirements, the rest of the architecture can be designed quickly.

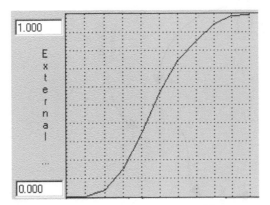

Figure 5.37. External concurrence constraint for architecture design activity (fraction of architecture tasks available to complete versus requirements completed).

The rate of iteration is determined by both the resource constraints on this rate as well as the minimum activity duration for iteration. A separate prototyping chain is created to handle the demand for prototyping and create the prototypes based on resource and process constraints.

The feedback loop diagram for the model is shown in the Figure 5.38. It shows the reinforcement feedback loop caused by initial basework when more items are completed as some items get completed. Another reinforcement loop is created due to prototyping; as more initial work is completed, the need for prototyping increases and, thus, the iteration rate increases as a result.

The main structures in the model are seen in Figure 5.39. Plots from some test runs are shown in Figure 5.40 and Figure 5.41. The first graph shows the levels of architecture items in different stages, whereas the second one shows the necessary personnel resources over time needed to support the architecting process.

5.7.1.3   Conclusions and Future Work

The model shows that initial completion rates for the requirements identification and architecture development activities significantly impact the number of approved items. Prototyping factors such as IKIWISI and collaboration also significantly affect the rates of completion and approval. The model also describes a declining curve for staffing analysts and a linear growth for architecting and design personnel. The model behavior is similar to RUP in terms of the effort distribution curves of the process.

This model is able to replicate the effort profiles for requirements and architecture/design activities based on a concurrent development model and a dynamic resource allocation scheme. Our model also provides a starting point to model many RAD opportunity factors for understanding the effects of RAD techniques on software life cycles. In essence, this model can be a handy test bed for designing

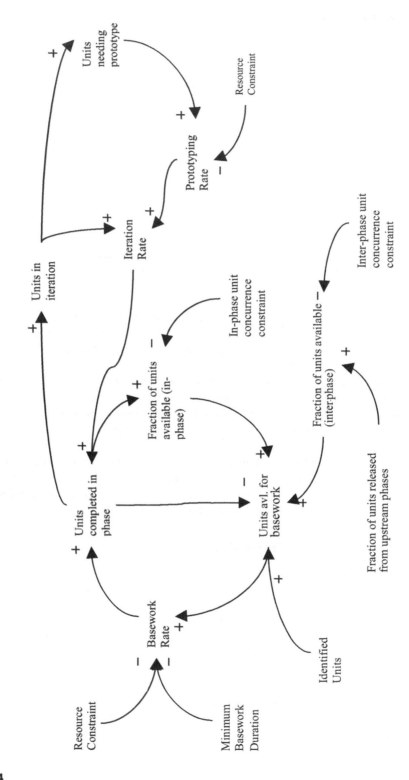

Figure 5.38. Main causal loop.

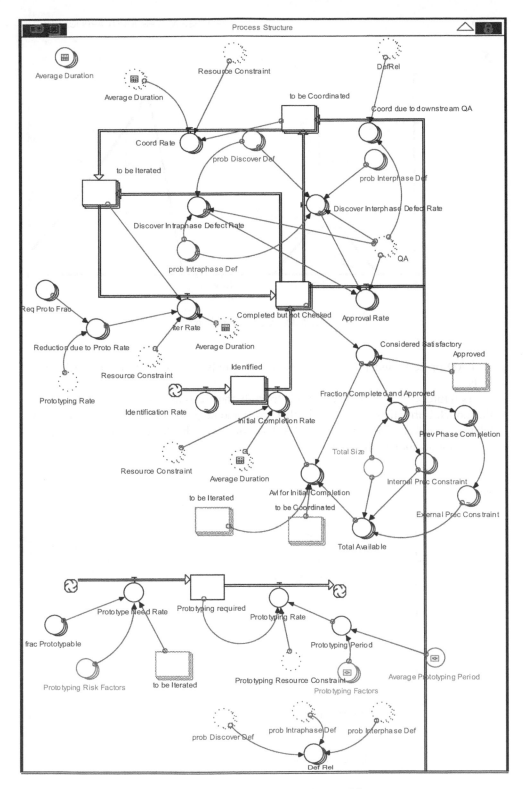

Figure 5.39. MBASE architecting model.

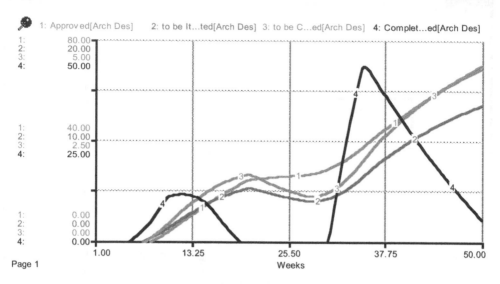

Figure 5.40. Architecture items.

an RAD process model. It can also be used to study staffing patterns for RAD projects.

As future work, it would be possible to study the creation and removal of defects in the model. Currently these are statically chosen and no probabilistic approach has been taken. The effect of peer reviews and walk-throughs on the defect rates can also serve as a major addition to the model.

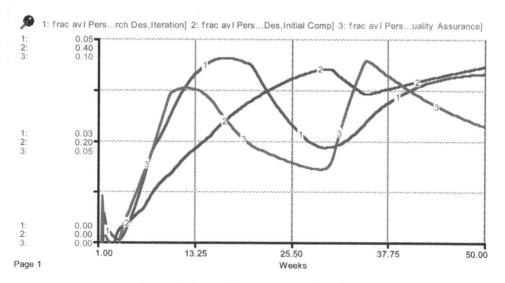

Figure 5.41. Architecture personnel fractions.

5.8 QUALITY AND DEFECTS

Software quality means different things to different people. The relative importance of different characteristics or attributes depends on who is assessing the software and what they need or expect from it. Utility can be considered in many ways. Users frequently are concerned about the number and type of failures that occur during usage. Hence, the number of defects is a measure of quality but there are many other possible measures.

A list of representative quality attributes was introduced earlier in the chapter in Section 5.1. Working definitions of these attributes are provided in [Madachy, Boehm 2005] using a value-based stakeholder perspective. Product attributes are not always independent and the relationship between technologies for achieving product measures is not easy to model. See [Boehm et al. 2004] for further details and discussion of the attributes.

The value-based product model described in detail in Chapter 6 addresses the attributes *reliability, affordability,* and *timeliness* in a commercial market context. The stakeholder business value being optimized is profit, and the goal is to maximize profit from investing in processes that contribute to reliability. The model is primarily covered in the organizational applications chapter because the primary result variables used to gauge the decision options are organizational financial measures.

However, there is a major relationship between product characteristics and their impact on business value. The quality of a product is a primary factor in sales. Achieving revenue from a reliable product is balanced against its affordability and timeliness of delivery. The model demonstrates a value-based framework for decision analysis by modeling dependability impact on costs and profit of achieving different reliability levels.

In order to assess quality, there should be provisions for representing defects since latent ones may impact a system with respect to quality attributes. A way to model different defect severities or types of defects using system dynamics is to have separate flow chains to represent the different categories.

The number of defects is generally considered a rough measure of overall quality, but is most closely tied to the attribute *correctness* (depending on the stakeholder perspective). Modeling the resources expended on defect detection and removal supports trade-off decisions to achieve product goals.

Defect analysis is a primary strategy for facilitating process improvement. Defect categorization helps identify where work must be done and to predict future defects, whereas causal analysis seeks to prevent problems from reoccurring. Defect prevention is a highly relevant area that modeling and simulation can specifically address. It is a high-maturity, key process area in process improvement frameworks including the SW CMM and CMMI.

A number of organizations are using process modeling as a preventive measure to improve their process performance. One example is Motorola, which has been modeling defect generation and prevention as part of their overall efforts to improve software processes [Eickelmann et al. 2002]. They have used combined approaches that use discrete aspects to tie a variety of attributes to defects, including different severity levels and corresponding defect-finding effectiveness values. They have also used ODC attributes in their process modeling. The advantage of assigning detailed attributes is a primary reason that companies addressing defect prevention resort to discrete event or combined modeling.

5.8.1   Example: Defect Dynamics

The integrated model developed by Abdel-Hamid [Abdel-Hamid, Madnick 1991] included defect flows and interventions, including quality assurance and testing. Table 5.9 is a high-level summary of the QA sector model.

The flow chains in Figure 5.42 were used to model the generation, detection, and correction of errors during development. The chains are simplified and only show the connections to adjacent model elements. There are two types of errors in the model, called passive and active. Active errors can multiply into more errors whereas passive ones do not. All design errors are considered active since they could result in coding errors, erroneous documentation, test plans, and so on. Coding errors may be either active or passive.

There is a positive feedback loop between the undetected active errors and the active error regeneration rate. Potentially detectable errors are fed by an error generation rate. The errors committed per task is defined as a function against the percent of job worked. The workforce mix and schedule pressure also affect the error generation rates. The model addresses both the growth of undetected errors as escaped errors and bad fixes that generate more errors, and the detection/correction of those errors. Figure 5.43 shows a graph of some of the important quantities for a representative simulation run.

Table 5.9. Quality assurance sector model overview

Purpose: Planning, Process Improvement
Scope: Development Project

Inputs and Parameters	Levels	Major Relationships	Outputs

• Daily manpower for QA (from manpower allocation sector)
• Daily manpower for rework (from manpower allocation sector)
• Multiplier for losses (from software productivity sector)
• Percent of job worked (from control sector)
• Average QA delay
	• Tasks worked
	• Errors
	   Potentially
	     detectable
	   Detected
	   Reworked
	   Escaped
		• Error generation rate
		• Nominal errors committed
		• Error multiplier due to schedule pressure
		• Error multiplier due to workforce mix
		• Nominal QA manpower needed per error
		• Nominal rework manpower needed per error
		• Multiplier due to error density
			• Detected errors

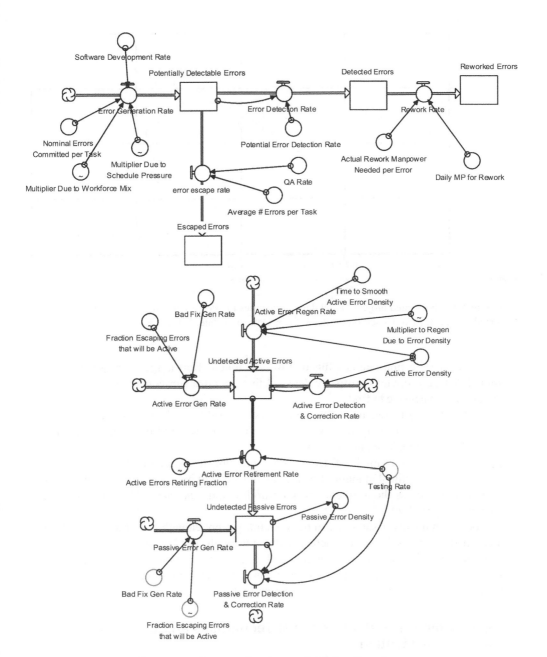

Figure 5.42. Integrated project model defect flow chains.

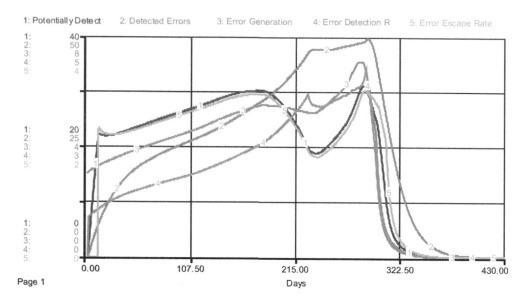

Figure 5.43. Integrated project model defect dynamics (1: Potentially Detectable Errors, 2: Detected Errors, 3: Error Generation Rate, 4: Error Detection Rate, 5: Error Escape Rate).

The error detection rate is a function of how much effort is spent on QA. It is assumed that easy, obvious errors are detected first, and that subsequent errors are more elusive and expensive to find.

System testing is assumed to find all errors escaped from the QA process and bad fixes resulting from faulty rework. Any remaining errors could be found in maintenance, but is not included in the model.

A representative example of determining "how much is enough" was provided by the model. The optimal amount of quality assurance activities was experimentally determined to address the attributes of *affordability* and *timeliness*. The trade-offs are shown in Figure 5.44.

Too much quality assurance can be wasteful, yet not enough will impact the effort and schedule adversely because defects will get through. The key is to run a simulation at applicable values across the spectrum and determine the optimum strategy or sweet spot of the process. Based on their assumptions of a project environment, about 15% of the total project effort was the optimal amount to dedicate to quality assurance.

5.8.2 Example: Defect Removal Techniques and Orthogonal Defect Classification

At USC, we are currently developing simulation models for NASA* to evaluate the effectiveness of different defect detection techniques against ODC defect categories.

*This work is sponsored by NASA Ames Cooperative Agreement No. NNA06CB29A for the project *Software Risk Advisory Tools*.

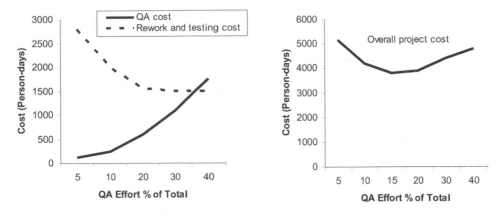

Figure 5.44.   Quality assurance trade-offs.

This section summarizes a continuous-risk model that extends the Constructive Quality Model (COQUALMO) [Chulani, Boehm 1999]. The model uses standard COCOMO factors for defect generation rates and defect removal techniques for automated analysis, peer reviews, and execution testing and tools. A summary of the simulation model is in Table 5.10.

COQUALMO is a static model, which is a form not amenable to continuous updating because the parameters are constant over time. Its outputs are final cumulative quantities, no time trends are available, and there is no provision to handle the overlapping capabilities of defect detection techniques. The defect detection methods (also called V&V techniques) are modeled in aggregate and it is not possible to deduce how many are captured by which technique (except in the degenerate case, where two of the three methods are zeroed out).

The primary extensions to COQUALMO include:

- Defect and generation rates are explicitly modeled over time with feedback relationships.
- The top-level defects for requirements, design and code, are decomposed into ODC categories.
- The model is calibrated with relevant NASA data.
- There are trade-offs of different detection efficiencies for the removal practices per type of defect.

The system dynamics version can provide continual updates of risk estimates based on project and code metrics. The simulation model is easily updated as more data becomes available and incorporated into the calibration. The current ODC defect distribution pattern is per JPL studies [Lutz, Mikulski 2003]. This model includes the effects of all defect detection efficiencies for the defect reduction techniques against each ODC defect type.

Table 5.10. Model summary table

Purpose: Process Improvement, Planning, Control, and Operational Management
Scope: Development Project

Inputs and Parameters	Levels	Major Relationships	Outputs
• SLOC	• Defects	• Defect generation rates (10 defect types)	• Defect generation curves (10 defect types)
• Effort coefficient	Requirements— Correctness	• Defect detection rates (10 defect types)	• Defect detection curves (10 defect types)
• Schedule coefficient	Requirements— Completeness	• Defect elaboration functions	• Final defects (10 defect types)
• Automated analysis setting	Requirements— Consistency	• Composite defect detection efficiencies	• Effort
• Peer review setting	Requirements— Ambiguity/ Testability		• Schedule
• Execution testing and tools setting	Design/Code—Timing		
• 180 defect detection efficiencies (10 defect types – 3 defect reduction techniques · 6 settings per technique)	Design/Code—Class/ Object/Function		
• Generation buildup parameter (3)	Design/Code—Method/ Logic/ Algorithm		
• Detection buildup parameter (3)	Design/Code—Data		
• Nominal design start time	Design/Code— Values/Initialization		
• Nominal code start time	Design/Code— Checking		
	• Defects found		
	Requirements— Correctness		
	Requirements— Completeness		
	Requirements— Consistency		
	Requirements— Ambiguity/Testability		
	Design/Code—Interface		
	Design/Code—Timing		
	Design/Code—Class/ Object/Function		
	Design/Code—Method/ Logic/Algorithm		
	Design/Code—Data		
	Design/Code—Values/ Initialization		
	Design/Code—Checking		

Figure 5.45. Defect removal settings on control panel (1 = very low, 2 = low, 3 = nominal, 4 = high, 5 = very high, 6 = extra high.

The defect removal factors are shown in the control panel portion in Figure 5.45. They can be used interactively during a run. A simplified portion of the system diagram (for completeness defects only) is in Figure 5.46. The defect dynamics are based on a Rayleigh curve defect model of generation and detection. The buildup parameters for each type of defect are calibrated for the estimated project schedule time, which may vary based on changing conditions during the project.

The defect detection efficiencies are modeled for each pairing of defect removal technique and ODC defect type. Examples of how the defect detection techniques have different efficiencies for different defect types are shown in Figure 5.47 and Figure 5.48. Peer reviews, for instance, are good at finding completeness defects in requirements but not efficient at finding timing errors for a real-time system. Those are best found with automated analysis or execution and testing tools. These differences for peer reviews are reflected in the graphs for defect detection efficiency for the different defect types.

The scenario is demonstrated in Figure 5.49 through Figure 5.51, showing the dynamic responses to changing defect removal settings on different defect types. Figure 5.49 shows the defect removal settings with all defect removal practices initially set to nominal. At about 6 months, automated analysis goes high and then is relaxed as peer reviews is kicked up simultaneously. The variable impact of the different defect types can be visualized in the curves.

The requirements consistency defects are in Figure 5.50, showing the perturbation from the defect removal changes. The code timing defects is evident in Figure 5.51. Near the end, the setting for execution testing and tools goes high, and the timing defect detection curve responds to find more defects at a faster rate.

5.9 REQUIREMENTS VOLATILITY*

Requirements volatility refers to growth or changes in requirements during a project's software development life cycle. It could be due to factors such as mission or user interface evolution, technology upgrades, or COTS volatility. The requirements volatility phenomenon is a common ailment for an extremely high percentage of software pro-

*Ashwin Bhatnagar initially created this section on requirements volatility as a graduate student at USC and wrote most of the description of the software project management simulator example.

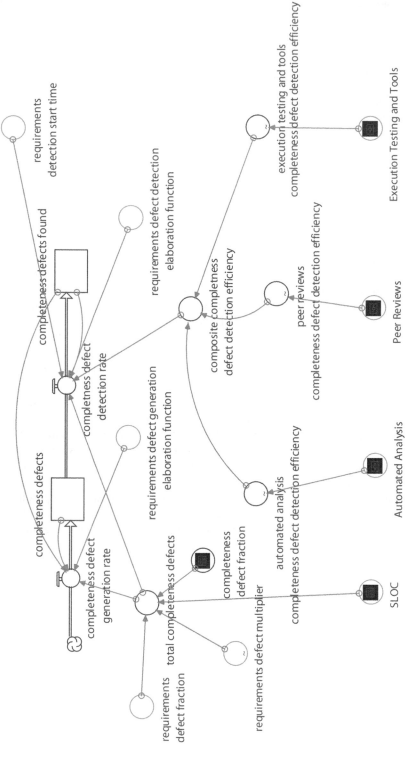

Figure 5.46. Model diagram portion (completeness defects only).

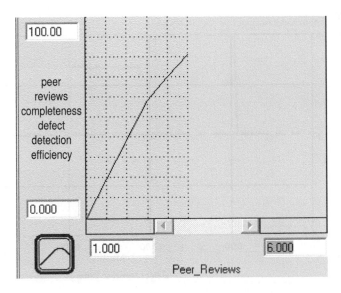

Figure 5.47. Peer review detection efficiency for requirements completeness defects.

jects. In addition, the effects of requirements volatility on critical project success factors such as cost, schedule, and quality are not well documented nor well understood.

The situation is made more complicated by the growth of the IKIWISI (I'll Know It When I See It) syndrome. Traditional waterfall life-cycle philosophy dictated that requirements had to be frozen before the design of the project was initiated, but this form

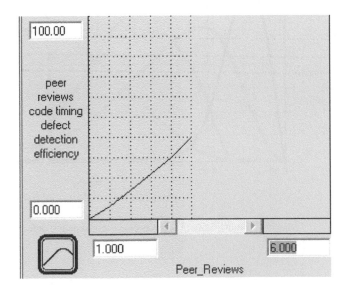

Figure 5.48. Peer review detection efficiency for code timing defects.

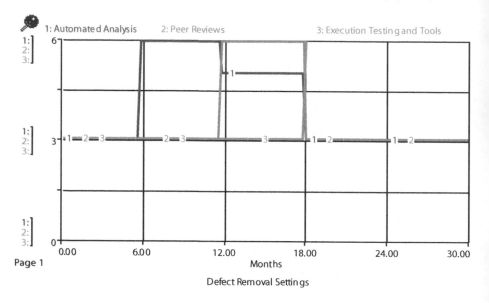

Figure 5.49. Defect removal settings.

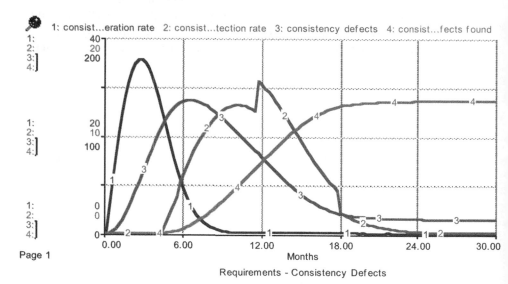

Figure 5.50. Requirements—consistency defects.

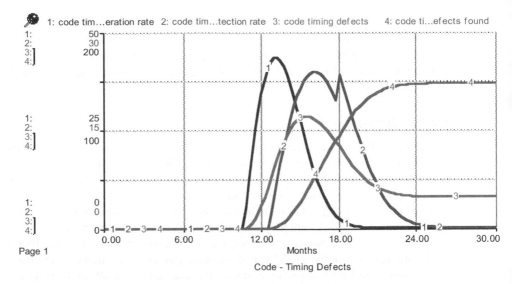

Figure 5.51. Code—timing defects.

of project development is unrealistic [Reifer 2000]. Requirement changes can be initiated in any phase of the software development life cycle and are unavoidable [Kotonya, Sommerville 1998]. Requirement changes can even be introduced after project completion.

As a result, the practice of requirements engineering, which deals with processes to generate and maintain the software requirements throughout the duration of the software life cycle, is receiving increased attention. Requirements volatility factors are now considered to be of paramount importance in order to assess critical project success factors such as cost, schedule, and quality.

For example, our COCOMO II research [Boehm et al. 2000] led us to introduce a factor for Requirements Evolution and Volatility (REVL) to adjust the effective size of the product caused by requirements evolution and volatility. REVL is the percentage of code discarded due to requirements evolution from any sources. With a larger effective size in COCOMO due to REVL, the effort includes the extra work due to requirements volatility and not just the work associated with the final kept software.

In [Pfahl, Lebsanft 2000] a simulation model demonstrated the impact of unstable software requirements on project duration and effort. It allowed one to determine how much should be invested in stabilizing requirements for optimal cost effectiveness. Another model for requirements volatility was developed in [Ferreira et al. 2002] and is described next.

5.9.1 Example: Software Project Management Simulator

An effort to model and illustrate the far reaching effects of requirements volatility on the software development lifecycle was carried out at Arizona State University by Susan Ferreira, James Collofello and colleagues in [Ferreira et al. 2003]. This initiative is of particular interest because previous requirements volatility models were specific to an organization or had limited inclusions of requirements volatility and requirements generation. Table 5.11 is a high-level summary of the model with different work phases abstracted out.

5.9.1.1 Background

The Software Project Management Simulator (SPMS) model is targeted at a software development project manager or a manager who wishes to better understand the effects of requirements engineering and requirements volatility on critical project factors such as cost, quality, and schedule. The model is relatively complex and assumes that the user has prior knowledge of simulation models. The model relies on a significant and proven foundation of software project management and simulation research.

Development of the model was started with an extensive review of related literature on the subject. Before the model was developed, however, requirements engineering process model and workflows, an information model, and a causal model were developed in order to better understand the involved relationships.

Table 5.11. Requirements volatility model overview (abstracted)

Purpose: Planning, Process Improvement
Scope: Development Project

Inputs and Parameters	Levels	Major Relationships	Outputs

• Change requests
• Change request acceptance rates
• Requirements volatility rates
• Staffing profiles
• Productivity rates
• Quality assurance effectiveness
• Rework policies
	Requirements sector only:
	• Requirements
	  Undiscovered
	  Additional
	  To be worked
	  Generated
	  Awaiting review
	  Reviewed
	  With errors
	  With errors reworked
	• Requirements product
	  with defects
	  With defects reworked
	• Requirements changes
	  To be reworked
	  Generated
	  Awaiting review
	  Reviewed
	  With errors
	  With errors reworked
		• Schedule pressure effects on error generation
		• Process delays
		• Productivity functions
		• Review backlog tolerances
			• Effort
			• Schedule
			• Defects

An information model, which covered part of the model's context, was developed in order to gain further knowledge about requirements and change requests prior to modeling. The identification of relevant factor relationships led to the development of the causal model shown in Figure 5.52. Factors such as the review of relevant literature and discussions with various software engineering experts contributed greatly to the development of the causal model.

Concurrently, a use case along with various user scenarios were created to make the model development more focused and to serve as a training tool for others. These scenarios also helped identify additional elements that needed to be added to the model and to check parameter coverage.

A number of walk-throughs and reviews were held with selected researchers. The model was modified to incorporate the key suggestions of the reviewers and the model was then considered ready to receive quantitative data.

In order to populate the model with relevant data, a survey was developed and conducted. The survey was used to obtain data for only a subset of the causal model factors as relevant data for some relationships were already available. The survey was sponsored by the Project Management Institute Information Systems Specific Interest Group. In addition, the survey also targeted the members of the SEI Software Process Improvement Network (SPIN) and individual professional contacts. Over 300 software project managers and other development personnel responded to the survey, and 87% of them were project managers or had some kind of a lead role.

The survey showed that 78% of the respondents experienced some level of requirements volatility on their project. The survey showed that the effects of requirements volatility extended to:

- Increase of job size
- Major rework
- Morale degradation
- Increase in schedule pressure
- Decrease in productivity
- Increase in requirements error generation

The histogram in Figure 5.53 indicates the percent change in project size with the corresponding number of projects (frequency). Note the positive skew of the distribution, indicating that, in almost all cases, requirements volatility serves only to increase the project size. On an average basis, survey results showed 32.4% requirements-volatility-related job size increase.

Figure 5.54 shows the distribution of the requirements volatility job size change of a typical project across 10 equal time intervals. The figure clearly demonstrates how requirements volatility is a factor that needs to be considered throughout the entire phase of the project development life cycle. Greater detail on the survey findings showing primary and secondary effects of requirements volatility are discussed in [Ferreira et al. 2002].

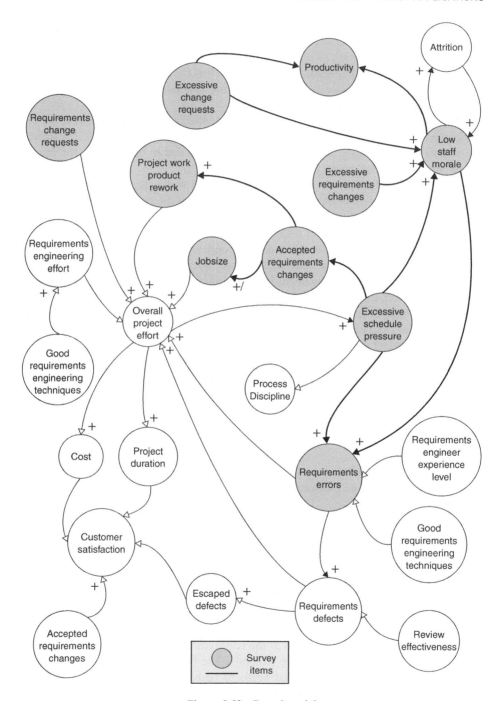

Figure 5.52. Causal model.

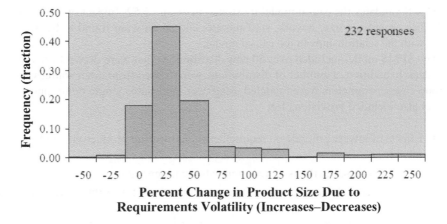

Figure 5.53. Distribution of requirements volatility percent change in product size.

5.9.1.2 Simulation Model

The SPMS was evolved from several previous models. Dan Houston reused and modified the Abdel-Hamid model [Abdel-Hamid, Madnick 1991], integrated it with John Tvedt's dissertation model [Tvedt 1996], and added risk-based extensions to create the SPARS model [Houston 2000]. The SPARS model was further enhanced with requirements engineering extensions and requirements volatility effects to create SPMS.

SPMS facilitates the addition of the requirements engineering phase through the test phase of the software development life cycle, and the requirements volatility effects through the development and test phase of the life cycle. The model also covers change requests, change request analysis, review activities, and their dispositions.

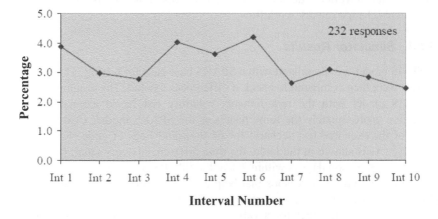

Figure 5.54. Requirements volatility job size change averages, per time interval.

SPMS validates the causal model illustrated in Figure 5.52. Impact of requirements volatility on project size, rework, staff morale, and so on were found to be in agreement with the relationships in the causal model.

The SPMS model included over 50 new distributions that were drawn from the survey data. In addition, a number of distributions were reused from other sources and, in certain cases, parameters were modeled using user modifiable single point inputs. The model also included provisions for:

- Effects of lowered morale on requirements engineering productivity and requirements
- Schedule pressure effects on requirements error generation
- Requirements defect detection effectiveness effects for software development milestones
- Relative work rates of requirements-volatility-related activities compared to their normal work rates
- Addition of requirements engineering staff type
- Addition of requirements engineering support activities

The model is segmented into 20 sectors. Figure 5.55 provides an overview of the requirements engineering work flow sector. The connections on the right of the sector are bidirectional, connecting to the development and test work flow sectors. In the requirements work flow sector, any product in which errors are detected is removed and reworked before flowing into the development and test sectors. In addition, requirements defects caught at later stages also come back to this sector to be reworked. The reworked product then flows back into the development and test sectors. Additions to job size due to volatility and underestimation flow into the normal work flow through the course of the project.

The lower half of the sector includes the requirements change rework flows and contains separate requirements-error-related activities. Rework due to requirements volatility is taken from the development and test work flows and is worked though the requirements change rework work flow.

5.9.1.3 Simulator Results

The SPMS model was populated with a SPARS base case for testing. The SPMS model results were then compared to check if differences existed. The assumption was that the SPMS model with the requirements volatility risk-based extensions removed should give approximately the same results as the SPARS model. Cost and schedule outputs of the executed test scenario for 64 thousand lines of code (KSLOC) are in Table 5.12. As is shown in the table, the time difference is very small (< 1 day). The cost in terms of person days is within 7% of the SPARS base case.

There are a number of reasons that help explain the difference in the values. The SPMS model uses function points as inputs whereas the SPARS model uses KSLOC based units. Hence, in order for a valid comparison to be made, the function points were converted to equivalent KSLOC values using a language conversion factor and a backfiring value, which may not always be a 100% accurate. Certain input factors in SPMS are stochastic, implying that a 100% results match between the values produced by SPMS and SPARS will not always be possible. In addition, the SPMS model has certain extensions which provide for recognition of requirements defects in later project phases. This is not modeled in the SPARS model.

A separate set of results shows the comparison between the base case runs and the runs with the requirements volatility risk-based extensions actualized. The results are displayed in Figure 5.56 and Figure 5.57.

Box plots are used as the results produced by the test runs are positively skewed. The box plots graphically display the center and the variation of results. As can be seen in both Figure 5.56 and Figure 5.57, the baseline results also show some degree of probability due to the stochastic nature of inputs. This implies that probabilistic results may appear, even with the requirements-volatility-based extensions turned off. The large variation in outcomes for both cost and schedule clearly demonstrate the potential for unpredictable results due to requirements volatility.

5.9.1.4 Summary

The SPMS model clearly shows the effects of requirements volatility on critical project factors such as cost and schedule. In addition, the simulator can also be used to evaluate potential courses of action to address the risk of requirements volatility. The work helps to better understand the intricate relationships that exist in a software development lifecycle. In addition, the data that was gathered through the survey has helped to fill in important quantitative gaps in project relationships.

5.10 SOFTWARE PROCESS IMPROVEMENT

Software process improvement (SPI) at an organizational level is one of the most important applications in this book. Virtually all companies are (or should be) concerned with continuous process improvement, or they risk languishing behind their competitors. Many companies allocate substantial resources for SPI initiatives and they expect returns. Modeling can frequently give them a better idea of where to put resources and provide insights into organizational policies and expected results. Several SPI frameworks were introduced in Chapter 1. The reader is encouraged to review that section and CMM introductory concepts as background for this section, as necessary.

An important study of process improvement dynamics in a high-maturity organization was commissioned by the SEI and conducted by Steve Burke [Burke 1996]. He developed an extensive model at the Computer Sciences Corporation (CSC) using the NASA Goddard Space Flight Center Software Engineering Lab (NASA SEL) environment to model software development and SPI processes. This report is recommended reading for those interested in using simulation to analyze SPI potential and is reviewed in the example section below.

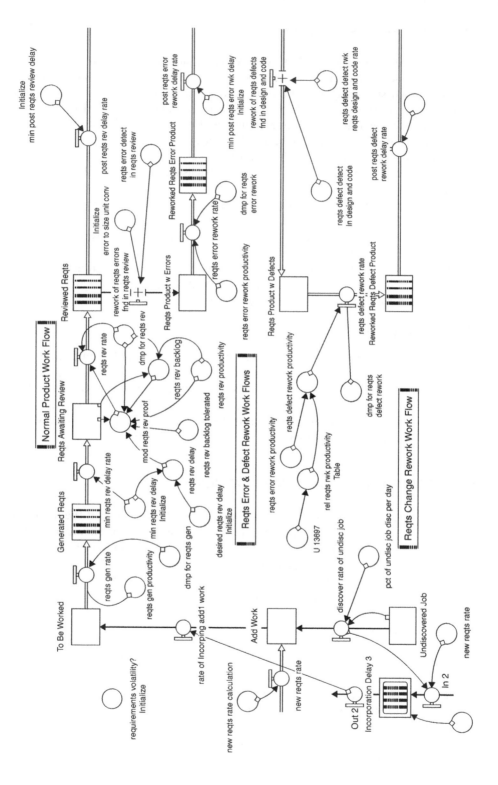

344

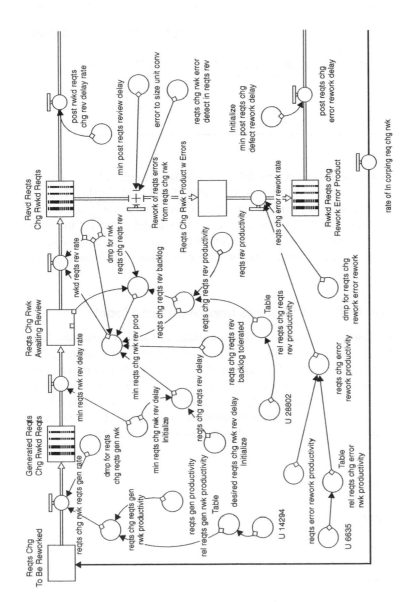

Figure 5.55. SPMS requirements work flow sector sample.

Table 5.12. Test runs comparison between the SPARS and the SPMS models

	Schedule (days)	Cost (person days)
SPARS	383	3606
SPMS	384	3870

Experience with a system dynamics model for studying strategic software process improvement in the automotive industry is described in [Pfahl et al. 2004a]. The collaborative effort with DaimlerChrysler AG aimed to explore the level of process leadership to be achieved by one of the divisions. By identifying and determining the influence factors and expected measures of process leadership, a generic modeling structure was developed that can serve as a framework for other companies examining improvement strategies.

5.10.1   Example: Software Process Improvement Model

The original goal in [Burke 1996] was to find the quantitative value of improving from CMM Level 3 to Level 5. However, NASA SEL uses a different process improvement mechanism than the CMM, called the "Experience Factory." The slightly refined goal was to determine the impact of various management-level policy decisions. The resulting model shows the value of high maturity in general, the value of the Experience Factory in particular, and how the Experience Factory can relate to the CMM in a very generalized sense. As discussed later and used in the Xerox adaption study, there is a

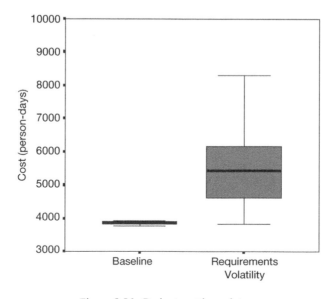

Figure 5.56. Project cost box plot.

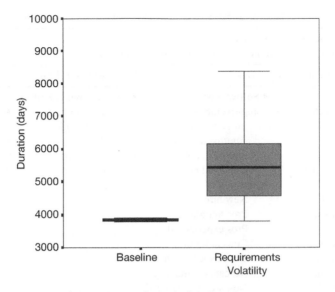

Figure 5.57. Project schedule box plot.

fair equivalence between Key Process Areas (KPAs) and "Major SPI suggestions" in the model. The latter are used as surrogates for KPAs.

The model was used by a number of major companies to evaluate process improvement options. This author was briefed on a major effort undertaken by Hughes Spacecraft and Communications (now Raytheon) to adapt the model internally and perform extensive sensitivity analyses. The Xerox adaptation of the model and their experience is covered later in this section. Table 5.13 is a high-level summary of the model.

5.10.1.1   High-Level Feedback

Figure 5.58 shows a high-level diagram of the model and the key feedback relationships. The basis of the simulation representing the software development and process improvement processes used by the NASA SEL is described in the following causal loop:

1. Major software process improvement (SPI) efforts are piloted and deployed based on project cycle time (i.e., piloted on one project, tailored and deployed on the subsequent project).
2. Major SPIs increase maturity (the probability of successfully achieving your goals).
3. Increased maturity attracts new hires and retains experienced staff that are "pro SPI" (they support and participate in SPI activities and are attracted to success and innovation).
4. Pro-SPI staff makes minor SPI suggestions.
5. Major and minor SPIs decrease cycle time.

Table 5.13. Software process improvement model overview

Purpose: Process Improvement, Planning
Scope: Multiple Concurrent Projects, Long-term Organization

Inputs and Parameters	Levels	Major Relationships	Outputs
• Size	• Software process	• SPI deployment rates	• KPAs by phase
• Initial workforce	improvements	• SPI adoption rate	• Effort
• Pro/con ratio	Initial major	• People attitude	• Schedule
• Cutout flag	Approved major	transfer	• Errors
• Initial major SPIs	Piloted major	• Hiring policies	• Staffing by type
• Suggestion per	Deployed major	• Error rates	• SPI major
pro per cycle	• Personnel	• Delays	maturity
• Minor ROI	New hires		• SPI minor
improvement	Pros in training		maturity
• Percent of	Pros experienced		
suggestions	Cons in training		
from outside	Cons experienced		
• Active hiring	No-cares in training		
• Quit rate	No-cares experienced		
	• SPI size		
	• SPI schedule		
	• SPI effort		
	• SPI errors		

6. Decreased cycle time enables more major and minor SPIs to be accomplished.

7. Go back to 1 and repeat the cycle.

This high-level feedback is further elaborated in the model and its subsystems are described next. The top-level mapping layer of the model in Figure 5.59 shows "process frame" building blocks. These are the important aspects of the system that can be drilled into. The arrows linking the process frames in the diagram show the relationships between the various pieces of the model.

Control Panel I in Figure 5.60 is the "dashboard" or "cockpit" from which to perform flight simulation test runs. This control panel is the major user interaction area for this particular study, which shows the following parameters available for change via knob inputs:

- Size of the project in KSLOC
- Initial organization pro/con ratio
- Cutout or Noncutout

It also shows a graph output to display cumulative major SPIs being piloted or deployed as the model runs in real time. Numeric display bars show outputs such as improved size and schedule numbers and others.

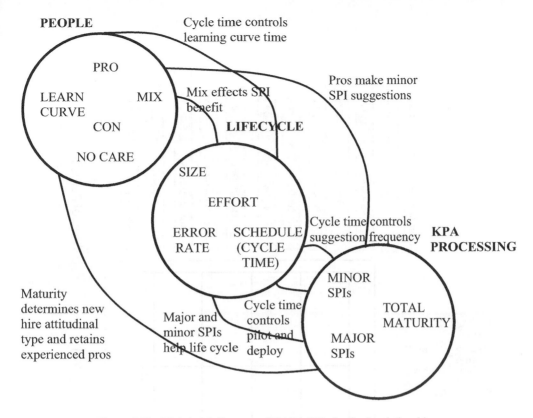

Figure 5.58. High-level diagram of NASA SEL feedback relationships.

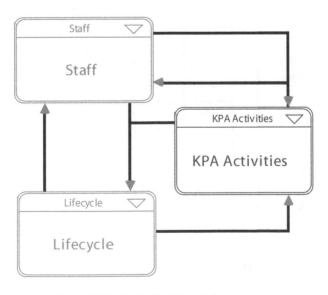

Figure 5.59. Model high-level diagram.

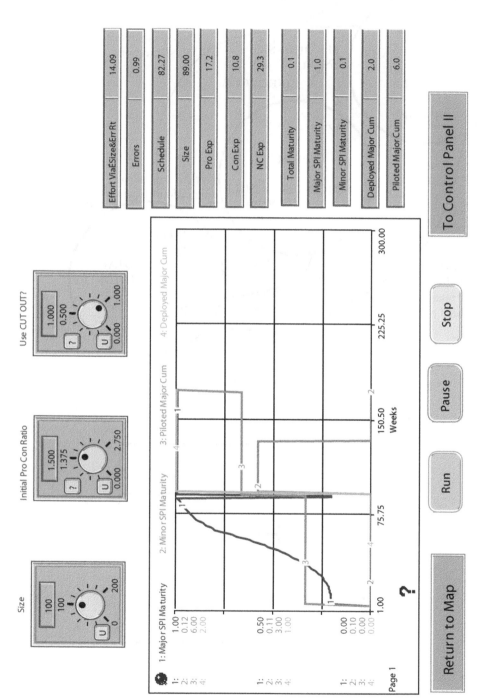

Figure 5.60. Control Panel I.

Control Panel II in Figure 5.61 groups various input parameters used by different sections of the model, and enables easy adjustment of the parameters for test runs. The model subsystems are described next.

5.10.1.2   Life-Cycle Subsystem

The life-cycle process model shows how software size, effort, quality, and schedule relate to each other in order to produce a product. They could be changed by process improvements or by each other as one process improvement rippled through the four at-

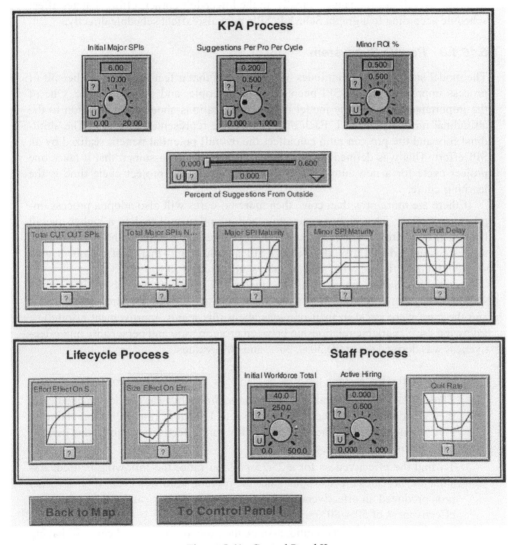

Figure 5.61. Control Panel II.

tributes. SPI benefits are modeled as percent reductions in size, effort, error rate, or schedule.

The life-cycle subsystem is shown in Figure 5.62. Starting at the upper left-hand corner and working clockwise, the personality (attitude) mix converter adjusts any of the schedule, size, ROI rates based on the pro-to-con ratio. Moving over to the top center, cumulative size SPIs affect the rate of change of size. In the upper-right corner, size changes affect error rate according to a defined graph. Also, an SPI may affect the error rate directly. In the lower-right corner, the impact that size or error rate might have on effort is modeled. In the lower-center part of the diagram, changes in effort due to size or error rate changes are combined with changes in effort due to effort SPIs to model overall effort changes. Finally, in the lower-left corner, effort changes affect schedule according to a graph. Schedule SPIs may also affect schedule directly.

5.10.1.3 People Subsystem

The model simulates three attitudes of project staff that affect the potential benefit of process improvement: pro-SPI people, con-SPI people, and no-care people. One of the important lessons of the model is that organizations should pay attention to the attitudinal mix of personnel. Each of the types are represented as levels. The attitudinal mix and the pro/con ratio can affect the overall potential benefit realized by an SPI effort. This was defined as the attitude impact. It also assumed that it takes one project cycle for a new hire to become experienced. The project cycle time is the learning curve.

If there are more pros than cons, then more no-cares will also adopt a process improvement effort. This higher penetration and adoption will realize a higher overall benefit. If there are a lot of cons, then a lot of people may not adopt the SPI effort. Interviewees agreed that attitude affected SPI adoption and that staff members with strong attitudes affected other staff members' adoption of SPI.

A subjective survey on an Ada/reuse major SPI effort showed about 30% of the staff said they were pro-Ada, 20% were con-Ada, and 50% did not care. Both the pros and the cons were vocal in their opinions about this major improvement effort. The following "soft" variable relationship between pro/con ratio and personality mix effectiveness was derived using the 30%, 20%, and 50% values:

1. At a 30/20 ratio, assume the 50% no-cares go along with the pros.
2. Thus, 80% of the total staff are virtual pros. Since this was the documented case, their personality mix effectiveness was set to 1. That is, if an SPI effort claims to give a benefit of 50%, then the personality mix effectiveness given this personality mix is 50% times 1, or 50%.
3. To find the effectiveness for a 25/25 pro/con ratio, the following is used: Assume the no-cares are also split, since the pro/con ratio was even. If 80% virtual pros produced an effectiveness of 1, then having 50% virtual pros produces an effectiveness of 50%/80% = 0.625.
4. If there is a 20/30 pro/con ratio, assume the no-cares are virtual cons. So having only 20% pros produces an effectiveness of 20/80 = 0.25.

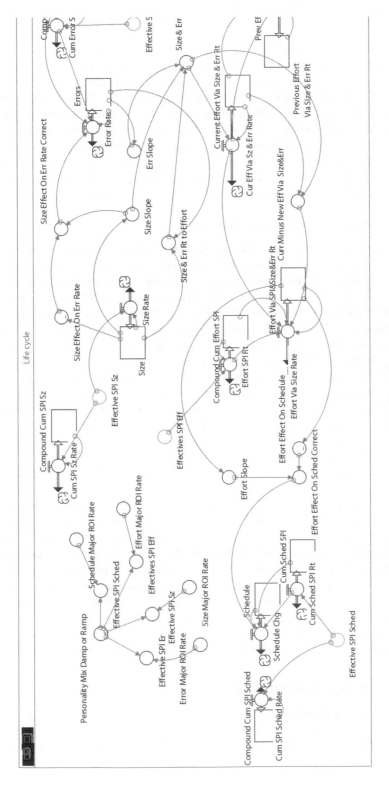

Figure 5.62. Life-cycle subsystem.

Referring to Figure 5.60 and starting at the right, experienced no-cares, cons and pros are separate flows that quit according to the quit rate. The quit rate itself changes with maturity. For each quit, a no-care, con, or pro new hire is determined by a Monte Carlo probability distribution that is also based on maturity (see the left part of the diagram). If an experienced con quits, a pro may replace him or her if the maturity is high. The time the no-cares, cons, or pros spend in training (the middle slotted boxes) is regulated by the current project schedule. As process improvements decrease cycle time, the learning curve time is also decreased. As process improvements increase maturity, the attitudinal mix based on the new pro and con totals also changes because new hires may have a different attitude than the experienced person who quit.

5.10.1.4 KPA Processing Subsystem

The KPA processing subsystem is the most complex subsystem. It models the timing of the flow of process improvements into the life cycle and people subsystems. There are two types of SPIs in Burke's model: major and minor. This maturity variable does not directly map to the five levels of the CMM, but uses adoption of SPIs and suggestions as surrogates for maturity levels. The total maturity is defined as being a composite of major SPI maturity and minor SPI maturity. Each of these was set on a scale of zero to one.

Figure 5.64 shows the KPA processing subsystem. The top half deals with major SPIs, and the bottom half models the minor SPI suggestion process. For the major SPI section starting from the left, major SPIs are piloted and deployed as regulated by schedule (see top center for the schedule box). In the center, the "Pilot Major Cum" and "Deployed Major Cum" receive the impulse of the completed piloted or deployed SPI at the end of a cycle and store the cumulative total. In the center, the "Total Major SPI" sends out the appropriate ROI percent based on when the pilots and deploys are complete. This ROI percent is sent out to one of either the "Size Major ROI," "Effort Major ROI," "Error Major ROI," or "Schedule Major ROI" flows located in the top-right corner.

For the bottom half that models the minor SPI suggestions, the bottom center shows the "Sug Frequency" being a product of "Total Maturity," number of pros, "Suggestions per Pro per cycle," and "Percent of Suggestions from Outside." The structure to the right of this causes the suggestions to be implemented in a "low-hanging fruit" fashion. That is, within a project cycle, a few suggestions are made at the beginning, many in the middle, then only a few at the end since all of the easy ones (the low-hanging fruit) were worked. The structure in the lower-left corner is needed to compute the average suggestion frequency for a floating period of one-half of a project cycle. As the suggestion frequency increases, the "Minor SPI Maturity" also increases because when an organization is mature, everyone is involved in making improvement suggestions.

5.10.2 Example: Xerox Adaptation

The Xerox Corporation adapted the Burke SPI model to support planning, tracking, and prediction of software process improvement activities for their Common Client & Server Development (CCSD) group. Jason Ho led the effort to model the scenario of

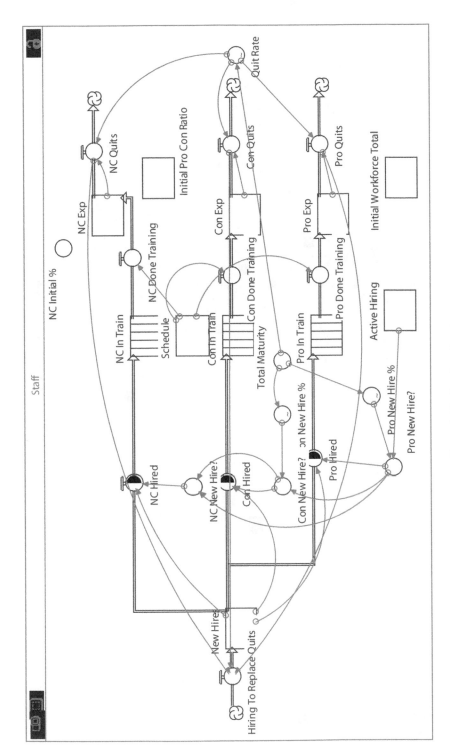

Figure 5.63. People subsystem.

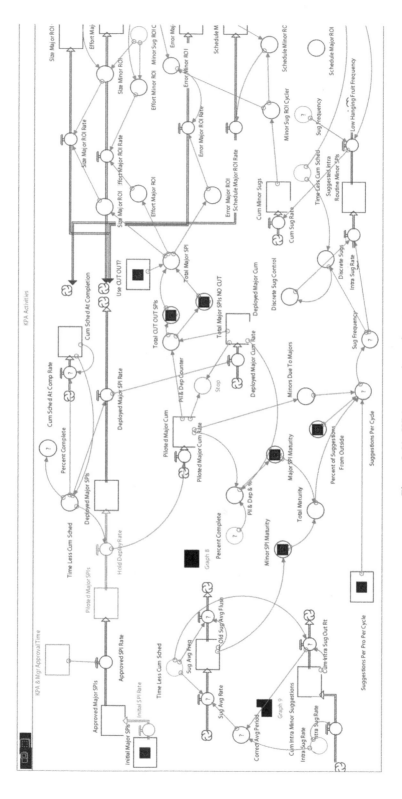

Figure 5.64. KPA processing subsystem.

the group working toward achieving CMM Level 3 after recently being assessed as a CMM Level 2 organization. Challenges to resolve in adopting Burke's model included modeling the Experience Factory versus the CMM and handling two types of process improvements. The original model had major and minor improvements versus the notion of KPAs in the CMM.

In order to reuse Burke's model for simulating Xerox software group's CMM SPI activities, the following assumptions and modifications were made:

- The basic model structure reflects a general software development organization's product life-cycle and process improvement behaviors, though it was specifically simulating NASA GSFS SEL with its own data.
- Xerox software organization data was used to calibrate the life cycle and the people processes replacing the calibration to SEL data.
- The definition of major SPIs in Burke's model can be equated to KPAs in CMM model.

Complete details can be found in [Ho 1999]. Following are highlights from that report. Changes were made to the subsystem models and the user interface, and new test cases were developed. Specific adaptations to the model sectors and their parameters are described next.

5.10.2.1 Model Changes

The life-cycle subsystem was left as is but a new calibration was desired. Initially, there was no data available from Xerox to recalibrate the percentage (reduced) effects for measuring the benefit of CMM KPAs to project life-cycle elements (size, effort, error rate, and schedule) in the model. NASA data on major SPI benefits was adopted for reference instead, until Xerox data became available.

The people subsystem was evaluated for relevance to Xerox. The people attitude phenomenon in the model was personally experienced within the Xerox software development group. Quick polls of the Xerox group under study showed that the nominal case of a 30/20 pro–con ratio and 50% no-cares seemed to hold true for the organization. This was used to set the attitude proportions for the Xerox environment.

The SEL reported that turnover started at about 10% per year, then decreased to 2–3% as maturity increased, then increased to about 6% toward the end of the 10-year period. For the previous five years, the turnover rate at the Xerox group under study had been flat at 5% year by year, regardless of process maturity. In the test run, "quit rate" was modified to reflect Xerox's situation.

The KPA processing model area was the major focus of the study for Xerox purposes. Given the assumption that the definition of major SPIs in Burke's model can be equated to KPAs in a CMM model, major SPI and CMM KPA can be used interchangeably in the model. There are seven major SPIs (seven Level 3 KPAs in the CMM) to be piloted and deployed by projects in order to reach the next level of maturity. Based on CMM assessment criteria, all KPAs must be implemented (piloted), plus some need to be repeated (deployed) to satisfy the institutionalization requirements. Thus, the pilot/deploy scenario simulated in Burke's model can be adopted to reflect the CMM assessment requirements.

Burke's model assumes that one can only pilot or deploy one major SPI per cycle (i.e., a project). Test runs verified that it will take too long to implement all seven CMM KPAs with the original model. Validated by Xerox CCSD's experience on achieving CMM Level 2, two KPAs can be implemented per project on average. To simulate the average of two KPAs rolled out per project, the rate of the following elements in the model (as shown in Figure 5.65) was changed from one to two for the Xerox CCSD nominal case:

- Initial SPI Rate
- KPA & Mgr Approval Time
- Piloted Major SPIs
- Hold Deploy Rate

Also, in order to capture the simulated lapsed time in implementing seven Level 3 KPAs, an element needs to be added to stop the model running after seven major SPI roll outs. In this particular Xerox CCSD case, the already implemented Level 3 activities is assessed as worth one full KPA. So the modification is to stop the model after six major SPIs have been piloted. Figure 5.66 shows the element added.

One of the major issues faced by Xerox was that there was no group of full time process people to help with process improvement activities, so the group had to use the same resources (people who did software development) to work on process related activities, such as to define an organizational process and plan for the roll out. In a general sense, this will prolong the process journey in reaching the next level of maturity on the CMM ladder. Moreover, in many cases, it is not the general approach taken by other major companies working on their CMM SPI. There is a similar condition simulated in Burke's model, called cutout versus noncutout cases.

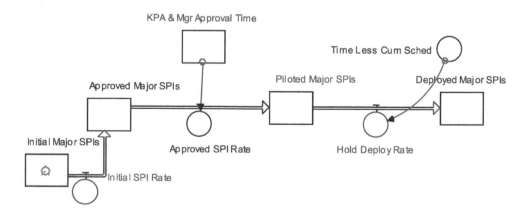

Figure 5.65. Changed KPA processing elements.

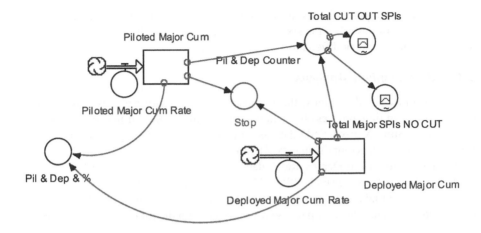

Figure 5.66. Added KPA processing elements.

In the cutout cases, projects accomplish SPI activities in isolation with no sharing of lessons. The noncutout case has a fully staffed group that would accomplish organization-level SPI activities across projects using the CMM Maturity Levels 4 and 5 key process area activities as a guide to pilot and deploy major SPIs across projects, extract lessons from projects, communicate them to other projects, and staff an organization-level metrics program. The SEL calls this staff the "Experience Factory" staff.

The Xerox case is a similar situation of the cutout case, which is the nominal case for the modified model. In addition, the comparison with the noncutout case would warrant the attention of management for the approach on SPI.

5.10.2.2   Test Runs

Test runs with the original and modified model are described here. Two test runs with the original Burke's model are described first, and then six runs that encapsulate Xerox data and calibrations.

5.10.2.2.1   ORIGINAL MODEL. The first test run was based on Burke's baseline case for NASA SEL. Values for the following variables were set: pro/con ratio at 1.5, project size at 100 KSLOC, and noncutout. The initial task force was changed to 40 people and the noncutout was changed to cutout, to reflect Xerox's condition. Results showed the group would not reach next level of maturity in the 10 years (500 weeks) time specified.

Based on the result from the first test run, the initial task force was changed to 100 people in the second run. This represents whether the management decided to grow the group because of extra process burden added. The run showed that the group will reach the next level of maturity in 430 weeks (about 8.3 years).

5.10.2.2.1.1   Modified Model. With the Xerox modified model, the initial task force is set at 40 (the group size of Xerox CCSD). Test runs were performed by changing the following input variables: project size, initial pro/con ratio, and cutout or non-cutout. Table 5.14 describes the six test runs and Table 5.15 shows a summary of the test results against the modified model for the cases.

5.10.2.3 Sensitivity Analysis

Given the model modifications, the purpose of a sensitivity analysis was to find a proper pattern of time progress for achieving a certain number of major SPIs (KPAs). Using the existing Xerox CCSD data as validation, it took four years to move from Level 1 to Level 2 (accomplishing six KPAs).

The parameter "Hold Deploy Rate" determines "Piloted Major Cum Rate," and is the factor that controls the stock "Piloted Major Cum"; see Figure 5.67.

The goal is to find the right major SPI deploy rate to reflect the Xerox CCSD's KPA implementation rate. The nominal case was defined with the following set parameters:

- The size of the project was set at 100 KSLOC
- The cutout versus noncutout flag was set to cutout

Table 5.14. Modified model test run descriptions

Test Run #	Description
1 (nominal Xerox case)	Representing the nominal case for Xerox CCSD, values for parameters were set at 100 KSLOC, 1.5 pro/con ratio, and cutout. Test results show 172 weeks (about three years) for accomplishing six major SPIs (KPAs), with the benefit of final size at 89 KSLOC. This represents the major output of this study—the Xerox CCSD group should make their commitment to the management of accomplishing CMM Level 3 in at least 3 years.
2	All the nominal case variable values stayed the same except that the cutout case was changed to noncutout. Test results show 121 weeks for accomplishing six major SPIs, with a significant benefit on the final size and schedule. This shows that using a different approach with support from a full-time process group would have saved the CMM journey a full year in getting to Level 3.
3	All the nominal case variable values stayed the same except size changed from 100 KSLOC to 200 KSLOC. Test results show 292 weeks for accomplishing six major SPIs. This shows that with a bigger project size, it will take longer to finish the project with the same amount of resources available. It will take longer to pilot out all the KPAs.
4	All the nominal case variable values stayed the same except Size changed from 100 KSLOC to 50 KSLOC. Test results showed 134 weeks for accomplishing six major SPIs. Compared to Test Run 3 with a smaller project size, it will be faster to finish the project and it will shorten the time to pilot all the KPAs. So it make senses to select some small projects for piloting the CMM KPAs, which was a good approach experienced by Xerox CCSD while working from Level 1 to Level 2.
5	Test Run 3 with the noncutout case.
6	Test Run 4 with the noncutout case.

Table 5.15. Xerox test run results.

Input Variables			Output Values				
Test Run #	Size	Pro/Con	Cut/noncut	CMM SCHD	EFF End	ERR End	SCHD End	Size End
1	100	1.5	Cut	172	14	1	82	89
2	100	1.5	Noncut	121	6.5	1	46	56
3	200	1.5	Cut	292	42	3.7	138	178
4	50	1.5	Cut	134	9	1.3	63	45
5	200	1.5	Noncut	180	12.8	1	78	112
6	50	1.5	Noncut	88	4	1	29	28

- The initial pro/con ratio was set to 1.5 (representing 30% pro SPI people, 20% con SPI, and 50% no-care

Several values for "Hold Deploy Rate" were used to see how the stock of "Piloted Major Cum" changes over time. Three values that are reasonable are 1, 2, and 3. The comparative run is shown in Figure 5.68.

The three curves all show the same pattern of step increase. The value to look for is six KPAs at about 208 weeks (4 years). Curve 1 shows six KPAs happen at between 375 to 500 weeks, which is too slow. Curve 3 shows six KPAs happen at between one to 125 weeks, which is too fast. Curve 2 shows it happens between 125 to 250 weeks, which is a reasonable range. So the pilot major SPI deploy rate of two is the value used in the model.

5.10.2.4 Conclusions and Ongoing Work

Results with the modified model satisfied the Xerox need to make the proper schedule commitment for CMM Level 2 to 3. The model helped quantify the duration of process

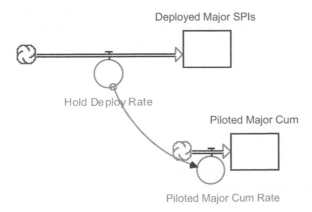

Figure 5.67. SPI accumulation substructure.

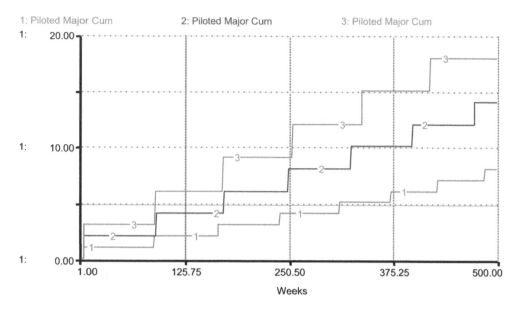

Figure 5.68. Comparative run of "Piloted Major Cum."

improvement and the value of improving software maturity, and brought to light lessons learned by other organizations that have improved. Many of the insights from the model were congruent with previous Xerox experience and data.

One of the most important lessons had to with the attitudinal mix of the software staff. The model showed that having some people with good, proactive attitudes toward process improvement helped instill the same behavior in others. If a critical mass of pro-SPI people are not in place first, then process improvement is much less likely to occur. This lesson is very important to consider when hiring people.

The model will be kept current and recalibrated with more Xerox data as it becomes available. Some specific parameters include recalibrating the KPA benefit percentage with Xerox data, and modifying "Effort Effect on Schedule" with Xerox data. Additionally, the model will be used for minor SPI suggestions and reaching levels beyond CMM Level 3.

5.11 MAJOR REFERENCES

[Abdel-Hamid, Madnick 1991] Abdel-Hamid T. and Madnick S., *Software Project Dynamics,* Englewood Cliffs, NJ: Prentice-Hall, 1991.

[Acuña, Juristo 2005] Acuña S. T. and Juristo N. (Eds.), *Software Process Modeling,* New York: Springer Science+Business Media Inc., 2005.

[Kruchten 1998] Kruchten P., *The Rational Unified Process,* Reading, MA: Addison-Wesley, 1998.

[Madachy 1996a] Madachy R., "System Dynamics Modeling of an Inspection-Based Process," in *Proceedings of the Eighteenth International Conference on Software Engineering*, Berlin, Germany, Los Alamitos, CA: IEEE Computer Society Press, 1996.

[Paulk et al. 1994] Paulk M., Weber C., Curtis B., and Chrissis M., *The Capability Maturity Model: Guidelines for Improving the Software Process*, Reading, MA: Addison-Wesley, 1994.

[SEI 2003] CMMI (Capability Maturity Model Integration) website, http://www.sei.cmu.edu/cmmi/.

5.12 PROVIDED MODELS

The models referenced in this chapter are provided for use by registered book owners and are listed in Appendix C. See the book website for model updates and additions.

5.13 CHAPTER 5 SUMMARY

Process and product applications cover broad areas and frequently coincide since software artifact quantities and their attributes are primary state variables for both. A majority of system dynamics applications have investigated process issues and not product aspects per se. Part of the reason for this is that other modeling techniques may address product analysis better, so combined approaches would be advantageous.

This chapter discussed some important process and product aspects including peer reviews, software reuse, software evolution, COTS-based systems, incremental and iterative processes, software architecting, quality, requirements volatility, and software process improvement.

Peer review models indicate that extra effort is required during design and coding for the reviews, but they are instrumental in producing higher quality software while also decreasing overall effort and time. Modeling the impact of formal inspections concluded this, and showed that testing effort and schedule were substantially reduced under nominal conditions. However, the cost-effectiveness of inspections varies according to factors like inspection efficiency, defect injection rates, defect amplification, testing, and fixing effort. Peer reviews in general are a good idea, but they should not be overdone as determined by local project conditions.

Software evolution is an iterative process largely driven by feedback as changes are initiated, driven, controlled, and evaluated by feedback interactions. Understanding and modeling global feedback can help address new and emerging trends such as globalization, COTS, or open-source development. A software evolution model for progressive and antiregressive work showed that the optimal level of antiregressive work varies from process to process and over the operational life of a long-lived software system.

Software reuse can provide high leverage in the process and help reduce cost and development time. A modeling study of fourth-generation languages revealed that a higher language level reduces the effort in design, code, and approval phases, but it does not reduce effort in the requirements phase.

Using COTS to develop products is a significant change in the way software systems are created, and CBSs continue to be more pervasive. COTS can help lower development costs and time. Using government/legacy off-the-shelf components is quite similar to COTS, but the use of open-source software presents some unique challenges.

With COTS there is no one-size-fits-all model. Assessment activities, tailoring, and glue code development are not necessarily sequential. A COTS glue code model indicated that glue code development has to start at the end of the application development, and the integration process has to start at the beginning of the glue code development.

Software architecting is a success-critical aspect of development that is iterative. An architecting model showed that initial completion rates for requirements and architecture development activities significantly impact the number of approved items. The model also describes a declining curve for staffing analysts and linear growth for architecting and design personnel.

Quality means different things to different people. Generally, stakeholders are concerned about failures that occur during usage or other operational difficulties. Thus, defect analysis is a primary strategy for facilitating process improvement. Defect categorization helps identify where work must be done and to predict future defects. Using separate flow chains to represent different categories of defects is a good way to model defect types or severities with system dynamics.

Project requirements may undergo much change throughout a life cycle. Requirements volatility can be attributed to factors such as user interface evolution, change of mission, technology updates, and COTS volatility. The SPMS model showed the effects of requirements volatility on critical project factors such as cost and schedule. The simulator can also be used to evaluate potential courses of action to address the risk of requirements volatility.

Software process improvement is a major thrust for organizations, involving a lot of investments. A comprehensive process improvement model included subsystems for the life cycle, people, and key process areas to model the timing of improvements to the subsystems. A primary insight of the model centered on people qualities: the attitudinal mix and the pro/con ratio seriously affect the overall potential benefit realized by SPI effort. People with good, proactive attitudes towards process improvement help instill the same behavior in others. Organizations including Xerox have used the model to quantify the duration of process improvement and the value of improving software maturity, using lessons learned by previous organizations that have improved.

5.14 EXERCISES

These application exercises are potentially advanced and extensive projects.

5.1. Choose a CMMI key process area and develop a model of the covered process activities. Enable your model to evaluate the effectiveness of different process strategies within that area. Higher level process areas based on

process feedback, such as causal analysis and resolution, organizational innovation and deployment, and organizational process performance, are good
candidates for automation of process evaluation.

5.2. Develop a defect propagation model based on the diagram below to represent the error flows in a process step. Each step receives errors from a previous phase, some of which are amplified, and new errors are generated before an imperfect detection filter allows errors to be passed on to the next
step. See [Pressman 2000] for some worked out examples using a waterfall
process. Adapt this kernel to the life-cycle process for your own environment. Alternatively, enhance it to be more granular for different types of error detection.

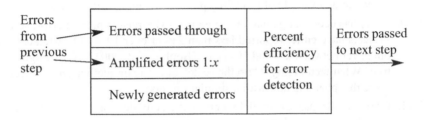

5.3. Compare and contrast some defect propagation models. Try to use empirical
data available from your own environment or the public domain to validate
the models.

5.4. a. Develop a defect introduction and removal model calibrated to empirical
data for your environment.

b. Develop and validate defect models to account for different severities,
types, priorities, or other classification of defects based on empirical data.

5.5. Integrate the provided Madachy and Tvedt inspection models to create a
model of both high-level and detailed-level effects.

5.6. Investigate other types of reviews or defect-finding activity by refining the
Madachy inspection model. You may also choose other proposed future directions for the model from this chapter or from [Madachy 1996b].

5.7. There are numerous defect-finding and removal methods (e.g., informal peer
reviews, formal inspections, pair programming, testing, automated checking,
etc.). Many of them overlap in terms of being able to find the same types of
defects; hence, there are some inefficiencies when combining techniques.
Develop a model that helps determine an optimal order, or sequence, of defect-finding activities.

5.8. Evaluate cost/quality trade-offs based on the COQUALMO extension of
COCOMO with a dynamic model. Like system dynamics, it uses a tank-
and-pipe analogy to defect introduction and removal. Defects come in
through various pipes (e.g., during requirements or design), and linger in the
system in "tanks" until they are eliminated through a defect-removal pipe

(e.g., peer reviews or testing). See [Chulani, Boehm 1999], which describes the extension that models defect introduction and elimination rates based on cost driver ratings.

5.9. An iterative version of a Rayleigh staffing curve model using arrays is provided in *Rayleigh iterative.itm* (see the list in Appendix C and Chapter 6 for more details). It enables one to create a project with multiple iterations using offset relationships to set the time phasing between iterations. Adapt and use the model for iterative planning or analysis. For example, the Rayleigh curve can be replaced with formulations for other types of processes and staffing models. The generalized Rayleigh curve generator in Chapter 3 could be integrated into the array structure. The iterative model can alternatively be reformulated into an incremental process model. Also see [Fakharzadeh, Mehta 1999] for an example of modeling process iterations with arrays.

5.10. There has been a large gap observed in COTS-related project effort statistics. Projects have either reported less than 2% or over 10% COTS-related effort, but never between 2% and 10% (see [Boehm et al. 2003]). Why might this be true? What factors might "tip the scale" one way or another on a project? Analyze this phenomenon with a simulation model.

5.11. Create a CBS process model whereby the activities for assessment, tailoring, and glue code development can be interchanged in different sequences. See [Port, Yang 2004] for a study of activity sequences. Experiment with different order sequences. You may also want to refer to [Kim, Baik 1999] for some ideas on modeling COTS-related activity sequences. Draw some conclusions from the model regarding the appropriate conditions for certain sequences. For simplification, you do not have to model all the different sequences that have been observed.

5.12. Investigate COTS lifespan issues suggested by the COTS Lifespan Model (COTS-LIMO) with a dynamic model. It should provide a framework for generating the cost of maintenance curves. A user would perform "what if" analyses by supplying specific values for the parameters in the model and generating sets of contour lines on a case-by-case basis. Controlled experimentation should produce families of breakeven curves for different COTS architectures, and the model should allow one to decide when to retire a CBS.

5.13. Develop some guidelines regarding optimal COTS refresh rates for a specific type of system. Model different dynamic scenarios for COTS product updates and consider overall costs, schedule, and risk.

5.14. Choose another important research issue for CBS that simulation can address and conduct a research project. Read ahead on the COTS section in Chapter 7.

5.15. Investigate the dynamic effects of software development tools across the life cycle. Develop a model so the user can choose different classes of tools and corresponding investment levels for them.

5.16. The PSP method has an important biofeedback-type process for estimation and defect prevention. Model the feedback inherent in the PSP.

5.17. Adapt the Burke process-improvement model for a specific organization. The Xerox adaptation example showed how it was interpreted for a CMM-based process improvement initiative. If your chosen organization is undertaking a Six Sigma initiative, is the model still valid? How might it be adapted for Six Sigma, or should it be superseded by a brand new model?

5.18. Once it is lost, quality is expensive to regain. Model the impact of restarting a process improvement program. Some factors might include a loss of trust or credibility in the organization. Make suggestions about keeping resources optimally allocated for continual process improvement.

6

PROJECT AND ORGANIZATION APPLICATIONS

6.1 INTRODUCTION

Applications for projects and organizations generally revolve around management issues such as estimating, planning, tracking, controlling, setting policies on how to do things, long-term strategies, and looking after people. Projects and organizations are where decisions are made, and largely direct how people and processes work to create products. Projects and organizations develop product visions and decide how processes should be set up to achieve the goals. Business cases are analyzed for developing software. Organizations derive product (line) strategies, plan individual projects that contribute to the larger strategies, and then execute the plans.

Projects and organizations provide the context to set goals and identify constraints for people to run processes and make products. These goals and constraints may apply at different levels such as individual projects or collective portfolios of projects. Strategic and tactical policies are analyzed and set with regard to people, processes, and products to achieve the goals within given constraints.

Decision structures are embodied in project and organization modeling applications. They frequently integrate the people/process/product structures to monitor status against plans, track expenditures and business value measures, and enable dynamic decisions to be made regarding people, processes, products, and so on.

Organizations are also responsible for people concerns: having people motivated and available, with the skills to perform their jobs, and ensuring their professional growth over time. Structuring teams in terms of desired skill sets and who should work

Software Process Dynamics. By Raymond J. Madachy
Copyright © 2008 the Institute of Electrical and Electronics Engineers, Inc.

together also comes under the purview of projects and organizations. Yet projects and organizations are comprised of people themselves, and it is those very people who collectively plan, track, decide, and so on. Thus, there is substantial overlap with people applications and, again, we conclude that focusing on people will improve organizational performance.

Allocation of people and other resources is a primary management function. Decisions must be made with respect to how many, who, when, and so on should be dedicated to particular tasks. Assessing which tasks are of higher priority or which defects should be fixed first are not easy decisions, but it will be seen that simple models can help make decisions as to where to place scarce resources.

Project and organization considerations are tightly congruent with each other, but organizations must consider initiatives or aspects outside the scope of individual projects or programs. They deal with aggregates of projects. Otherwise, projects and organizations are similar in topological structure and behavior. For example, an organization chart frequently shows major overlap of project and organization structures. They are alike but also affect each other greatly. Dynamic interactions between projects and their larger organizations occur in both directions.

The impacts of project and organizational factors in the COCOMO II model are shown in Figure 6.1. The factor for *Process Maturity* is listed because its rating stems from an organizational and/or project commitment even though it was also listed as a process factor in the last chapter.

An opportunity tree for projects and organizations is shown in Figure 6.2. Since an organization consists of projects and other entities, all project opportunities can also improve the organization at large and are shown on common branches. The management techniques on the top branch are traditionally applied on projects but are equally valid at a higher organizational level. For example, the methods can be applied to a portfolio that is a group of projects with something in common (department, product line, program, etc.).

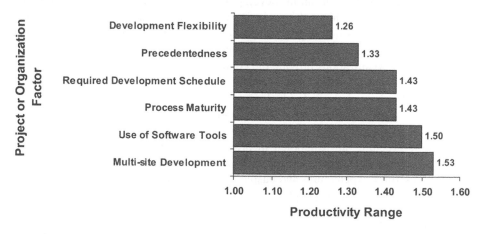

Figure 6.1. Project and organization impacts from COCOMO II—what causes these?

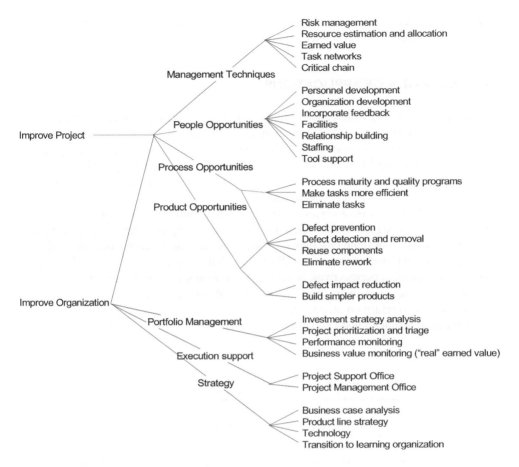

Figure 6.2. Project and organization opportunity tree.

The people, process, and product opportunities clearly impact projects and organizations. Because of the strong taxonomy overlap, the top-level branches of the respective opportunity trees in Chapters 4 and 5 are also shown here.

Simulation itself, as a relevant opportunity for organizations to improve, is perhaps best exemplified in the book, *Serious Play—How the World's Best Companies Simulate to Innovate* [Schrage 2000]. The book you are reading complements the organizational strategies described by Schrage by providing a simulation methodology and tools for companies that deal with complex systems and software.

6.1.1 Organizational Opportunities for Feedback

Understanding and leveraging system feedback is a primary theme of this book. Many forms of feedback may take place or be made available in order to improve projects and organizations. Table 6.1 is a list of possible feedback channels to be aware of and utilize for overall process optimization. Virtually all of them can be used to improve processes; if used improperly, they can lead to opposite results.

6.2 OVERVIEW OF APPLICATIONS

Abdel-Hamid's model of integrated project dynamics was the first major work applying system dynamics to software development phenomena [Abdel-Hamid, Madnick 1991]. It covers many important facets but primarily focused on project management. The first section provides detail of some of its structures for the integrated dynamics. A summary critique of the model is included due to its historical significance and substantial complexity touching on many areas.

Software business case analysis is a crucial responsibility of organizations that simulation is well-suited for. Value-based software engineering is an important thrust that integrates value considerations into software practices, and can be used to analyze business propositions. A model is illustrated that integrates business value with process and product perspectives. Several applied examples are shown for evaluating product strategies, and their effect on quality and business value measures such as market share and return on investment.

Allocating people to tasks and prioritizing their work involves additional detail be-

Table 6.1. Organizational feedback examples

Within a Project	Between Projects	Between Departments or Organizations	Between Stakeholder Communities
Earned value and progress measures	Postmortem and lessons learned reports	Postmortem and lessons learned reports	User/customer requests and complaints
Process performance metrics	Company newsletters and journals	Company newsletters and journals	Investor requests
Quality indicators and related metrics	Organizational metric reports	Organizational metric reports	Shareholder meetings
Status reports	Organizational Process Asset Library	Organizational Process Asset Library	Technical articles, journals,
Project meetings	(normally web-based)	Multidepartmental meetings	conferences,
Customer or peer reviews	Departmental meetings		workshops,
Problem reports	People talking and personal e-mail	People talking and personal e-mail	summit meetings
People talking and personal e-mail			
Project website or repository			
Project-wide bulletins and email			
Customer and other stakeholder communication			

yond overall staffing needs. Model structures are provided to simulate different allocation and prioritization policies, and the policies are compared in terms of their trade-offs.

Staffing and personnel allocation are primary responsibilities of project management. Several staffing models are reviewed that can be used for planning human resource needs over time. These include the traditional Rayleigh curve model of staffing, and process concurrence, which provides a more comprehensive way of analyzing staffing needs based on individual project characteristics.

The last section covers earned value, which is a popular and effective method to help track and control software projects. One can become a real-time process controller by using this technique to monitor dynamic trends. Earned value is explained in detail with examples because it is valuable to understand and use. It can also be misused, and some caveats are described. An original model of earned value is used that can be easily adapted. Some experiments are run with the model to evaluate project management policies. For example, it demonstrates that a policy of working hard problems first on a project is advantageous in the long run.

6.3 INTEGRATED PROJECT MODELING

6.3.1 Example: Integrated Project Dynamics Model

Abdel-Hamid's model was a complex integration of feedback structures between planning and control, software production, and human resource dynamics. Many of the structures and behaviors have already been reviewed in previous chapters on people and process applications, but this section provides more detail of its integrated aspects. This section overviews various sectors of the model, and present a few selected relationships and model diagram portions. The entire set of model diagrams and the equations can be found in the model provided. Important results from the model are discussed in several other sections of this book.

In [Abdel-Hamid 1989a] and [Abdel-Hamid 1989b], the dynamics of project staffing was investigated and validation of the system dynamics model against a historical project was performed. He synthesized the previous research into an overall framework in the book *Software Project Dynamics* [Abdel-Hamid, Madnick 1991], and this section describes his model contained in the book.

The model has four main components: human resource management, software production, controlling, and planning. The primary information flows between the model sectors that lead to dynamic behavior are shown in Figure 6.3. The structures of the different sectors are described in the following sections. The actual variable names used in the model show up in the narratives below. The provided model and much of its description in this section comes from [Johnson 1995].

The primary focus of the model is management of software production rather than software production itself. Relatively little structure is dedicated to software artifacts, though there is a detailed model of error propagation and detection. Much of the model is dedicated to planning and control, management perceptions, and personnel management. The simulation of management policies was derived from interviews, and

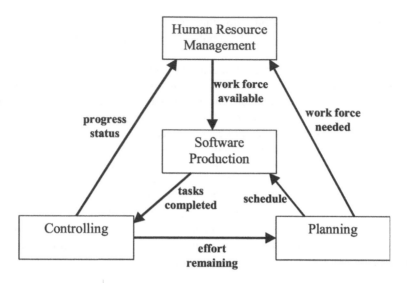

Figure 6.3. Top-level diagram of Abdel-Hamid model.

does not reflect decision-making structures in all organizations. See the last subsection on model critiques.

The software artifacts flowing through the model are defined as "tasks." A task is an atomic unit of work that flows through the project, where the units may differ among project phases. This is a simplifying abstraction for the sake of the model. Tasks are assumed to be interchangeable and uniform in size. Abdel-Hamid set a task equivalent to 60 lines of software, or roughly the size of a standard module. The simplified chain of flowing tasks is shown in Figure 6.4. A task changes from "developed" to "QAed" (gone through quality assurance) and finally to "tested." These are the only three levels associated with software artifacts. They represent the level of process visibility handled by the model; the product elaboration substates within development are not tracked.

Given the abstraction of flowing tasks, which is appropriate for a high-level management perspective, the model is not appropriate to use as a scheduling tool or for tracking milestones. Commensurately, the modeling of personnel with system dynamics does not lend itself to modeling individuals. All tasks and personnel are assumed to have "average" characteristics within any given level.

The Abdel-Hamid model has been mistakenly considered a deterministic "one size fits all" model that requires many inputs. Models should reflect the local organization. Obviously, one shoe does not fit all; each organization has unique aspects and associated problems with their processes. Thus, it is important to not mandate model structure for everyone; instead, allow flexibility and provide skills to adapt archetypes.

6.3.1.1 Human Resources Sector

The human resources sector contains structures for hiring, assimilation, training, and transferring of people off the project. See the Chapter 4 for details of the sector.

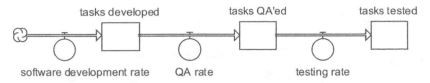

tasks developed   tasks QA'ed   tasks tested

software development rate   QA rate   testing rate

Figure 6.4. Software product chain.

6.3.1.2 *Planning Sector*

In the planning sector, initial project estimates are made and they are revised as necessary until the project ends. The sector contains elements for the desired number of people, a deadline date, and structures to revise and update estimates as the project progresses, depending on actual work accomplished. This sector works in conjunction with the human resources sector to determine the desired work force levels. Table 6.2 is a high-level summary of the model. The planning sector is shown in Figure 6.5.

The scheduled completion date is an important level used in this sector. It is adjusted by a "rate of adjusting flow," which depends on the perception of progress to date.

Table 6.2. Planning sector model overview

Purpose: Planning, Process Improvement
Scope: Development Project

Inputs and Parameters	Levels	Major Relationships	Outputs
• Scheduled completion date • Man-days remaining (from control sector) • Assimilation delay (from human resources sector) • Hiring delay (from human resources sector) • Total workforce level (from human resources sector) • Workforce level sought (from human resources sector) • Average manpower per staff (from human resources sector) • Schedule adjustment time • Maximum tolerable completion date	• Scheduled completion date	• Willingness to change workforce level	• Workforce level needed

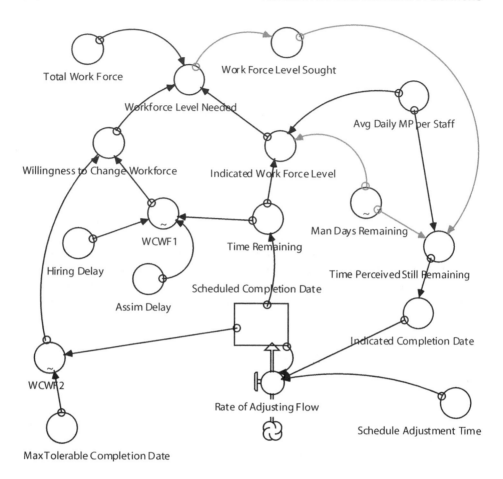

Figure 6.5. Planning sector.

This perception is captured in time perceived to be still remaining, which is added to the elapsed project time to determine the indicated completion date. The scheduled completion date is subtracted from the indicated completion date to determine a difference. The difference is divided by a delay for the schedule adjustment time to represent the change to the scheduled completion date.

The time perceived still remaining is determined with the man-days remaining (from the control sector). The man-days remaining is adjusted with the average daily manpower per staff (from the human resources sector). Workforce level sought (also from the human resources sector) is used to calculate time perceived still remaining by dividing man-days remaining by workforce level sought. Also, the indicated workforce level is determined by dividing time remaining by man-days remaining.

The workforce level needed is calculated from the indicated workforce level sought and a weighting factor for willingness to change workforce level. The weight represents the desire for a stable workforce, where a stable force does not have many new people on it. The willingness to change workforce level varies from 0 to 1. When it equals 1, the workforce level is set to the actual number perceived needed to complete the job. No weight is applied to the indicated workforce level in this case. But when the willingness is 0, the number of desired employees depends solely on stability concerns and the workforce level needed equals the total workforce. The workforce gap in the human resources sector equals zero, so no hiring or transferring is done.

The willingness to change workforce level (WCWF) has two components: WCWF1 captures the pressure for stability near the end of the project, whereas WCWF2 uses the difference between max tolerable completion date (a drop-dead time constraint) and the scheduled completion date. These are shown in Figure 6.6 and Figure 6.7. WCWF1 is affected by assimilation and hiring delays from human resources. Given these two delays, there is a reluctance to bring on new people as time remaining decreases even though there is a schedule crunch. WCWF2 rises gradually as the scheduled completion date approaches the maximum tolerable completion date. If WCWF2 exceeds WCWF1, then the weighting is dominated by schedule concerns to not go past the max tolerable completion date, and hiring takes place.

The sector thus determines the workforce level needed that is used by the human resources sector, and the two sectors interact with each other. When the total workforce increases and decreases due to hiring or transferring, the rate of change to the scheduled completion date slows down. Thus, two ways to deal with changes in the mandays remaining are to push back the scheduled completion date and to hire or transfer people.

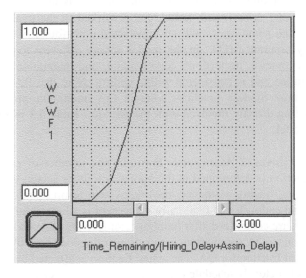

Figure 6.6. Pressure for workforce stability at end of project [willingness to change workforce versus time remaining/(hiring delay + assimilation delay)].

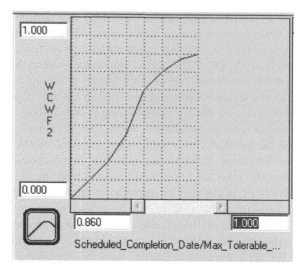

Figure 6.7. Pressure to change workforce during schedule crunch (willingness to change workforce versus scheduled completion date/maximum tolerable completion date).

6.3.1.3 Software Production Sector

The software production component has four sectors associated with it: manpower allocation, software development, quality assurance and rework, and system testing. The software development sector covers both design and coding, and they are aggregated together in a single level. Requirements analysis is not covered in the model. Developed software is reviewed, tested, and reworked in the quality assurance and rework sector, and some errors will go undetected until found in the system testing sector. Quality assurance (QA) in the model covers different techniques including walk-throughs, reviews, inspections, code reading, and integration testing. Unit testing is not included and is considered within coding. Note that this definition of QA differs from some modern practices wherein QA audits for process compliance, rather than getting directly involved with the product. Table 6.3 is a high-level summary of the model.

    6.3.1.3.1 MANPOWER ALLOCATION SECTOR. The number of people to work on software production is determined in the human resources sector, and allocations are made for training, quality assurance, rework, system testing, and software development (design and coding). The total daily manpower is adjusted for training overhead first; other tasks are considered after training resources are allocated.

    The allocation to QA comes from a converter influenced by a planned fraction for QA and an actual fraction for QA. The actual fraction is affected by schedule pressure from the control sector. If schedule pressure increases, then QA activities are relaxed. The default fraction of manpower for QA is 15% according to Abdel-Hamid's research, and the fraction is adjusted accordingly based on schedule pressure.

Table 6.3. Software production sector model overview

Purpose: Planning, Process Improvement
Scope: Development Project

Inputs and Parameters	Levels	Major Relationships	Outputs
• Nominal fraction of man-days for project • Nominal productivities • Exhaustion depletion delay • Maximum tolerable exhaustion • Nominal overwork duration threshold • Maximum boost in man-hours • Willingness to overwork • Rookies (from human resources sector) • Pros (from human resources sector) • Man-days remaining (from control sector) • Percent of job worked (from control sector)	• Actual fraction of man-days for project • Exhaustion	• Exhaustion flow • Potential productivity • Overwork duration threshold multiplier • Maximum shortage of man-days handled • Slack time growth • Communication overhead • Normal delay	• Software development productivity

Resources are allocated to error fixing as the errors are found through QA activities. The effort is based on a desired error correction rate and the perceived rework manpower needed per error. The difference between perceived and actual rework manpower needed stems from a delay in management between realizing a need for rework effort and acting on it. So a sudden increase in actual rework manpower needed does not affect allocation decisions until the increase has persisted for a while.

6.3.1.3.2 SOFTWARE DEVELOPMENT SECTOR. This sector is the simplest one in the model, and is shown in Figure 6.8. There is a main level for cumulative tasks developed that drives almost everything else in software production. The software development rate flowing into the level is based on the number of people working and their productivity. The productivity is determined in the software development productivity subsector.

The number of people working on software development is whatever is left over after training, QA, and rework allocations in the human resources sector. The people dedicated to software development gradually transition to system testing as the project progresses (determined by the parameter fraction of effort for system testing). The fraction is dependent on the project manager's perception, which comes from the perceived job size and tasks perceived to be remaining in the control sector.

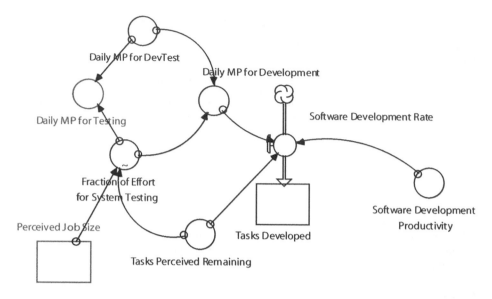

Figure 6.8. Software development sector.

6.3.1.3.2.1   Software Development Productivity Subsector. Figure 6.9 shows the software productivity subsector. The productivity model is based on the equation

actual productivity = potential productivity – losses due to faulty processes

Potential productivity represents the best possible use of resources. The nominal potential productivity is influenced by the experience level of the personnel, whereby an experienced person is set to 1 task/man-day productivity and new people to 0.5 task/man-day. So the overall potential productivity changes as does the mix of experienced and new people. There is also a learning curve effect that takes place throughout the project. It is an S-shaped multiplier curve set to 1 at the beginning and ends up at 1.25 at project end.

The difference between potential productivity and actual productivity is simulated with a multiplier for losses. The losses refer to communication overhead and motivational losses. The motivation impacts the slack time per day dedicated to personal matters, breaks, and so on. The slack time expands or contracts depending on project deadlines. With no deadline pressure, a nominal value of 60% is used for the fraction of a man-day on the project (40% of people's time is used on nonwork-related activities). The actual fraction can grow to 100% or more if pressure increases, but there is a threshold of time for which people will work in that mode.

The perceived shortage of man-days is an important factor in controlling the actual fraction of man-days for project work. If the difference between total man-days perceived to be still needed and man-days remaining is positive and below a threshold for the maximum shortage that can be handled, workers increase their effective hours by decreasing slack time or working overtime. The factors that affect the threshold are the

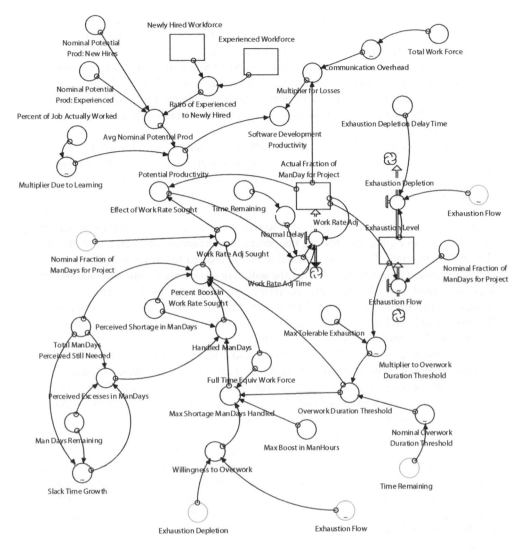

Figure 6.9. Software productivity subsector.

overwork duration threshold, full-time equivalent workforce (from the human re-sources sector) and the maximum boost in man-hours. The maximum shortage that can be handled varies.

Note that this productivity sector contains the exhaustion model highlighted in Chapter 4. Workers are less willing to work hard if deadline pressures persist for a long time. The overwork duration threshold increases or decreases as people become more or less exhausted. The exhaustion level also increases with overwork. See Chapter 4 for more details of the exhaustion model.

Other effects come into play if the project is perceived to be ahead of schedule. Slack time increases as people take care of personal matters, but only up to a threshold again. This time, management takes care of the threshold by adjusting the schedule.

Communication overhead is the other loss to productivity besides motivation. A graph function is used that relates the overhead to team size. The overhead is proportional to the square of team size. This is the initial formula used to model communication overhead in the Brooks's Law model in Chapter 1 (which only covers the region for 0–30 personnel).

In summary, the actual percentage of a day dedicated to project work is based on the current level of motivation after accounting for deadline pressures and exhaustion. The fraction is also adjusted for communication overhead, and the final result is the multiplier for losses.

6.3.1.3.3 QUALITY ASSURANCE AND REWORK SECTOR. The quality assurance and rework sector in Figure 6.10 models the generation, detection, and correction of errors during development. Potentially detectable errors are fed by an error generation rate. The error generation is the product of the software development rate and nominal errors committed per task. The errors committed per task is defined as a graph function against the percent of job worked. At the beginning of design, the nominal error rate is 25 errors/KDSI (KDSI stands for thousand delivered source instructions) and goes down to 12.5 errors/KDSI at the end of coding.

The workforce mix and schedule pressure also affect the error generation rates. It is assumed that new personnel generate twice as many errors as experienced people, as captured in the multiplier due to workforce mix. There is also a multiplier due to schedule pressure, defined as a graph function. As people work under more pressure, they become more tired and make more errors. The multiplier increases exponentially as schedule pressure increases.

Detection of errors is modeled with an error detection rate flowing out of potentially detectable errors and into a level for detected errors. The QA rate is modeled independent of effort and productivity. The QA function is assumed to be a prescheduled activity that processes all tasks in a fixed time. Thus, there is never a QA backlog, since all the work is done in the allocated timeframe. The QA rate is modeled as a simple delay of 10 days. The software tasks are considered QA'ed after that delay, independent of the QA effort. However, the effectiveness in terms of error detection rates is a function of how much effort is spent on QA.

A potential error detection rate is calculated as the QA effort (daily manpower for QA) divided by the QA manpower needed to detect an error. The nominal QA manpower needed per error is defined as a graph against the percent of job worked. Design errors are set to 1.6 times as costly to fix as a coding error, whereas the average is 2.4 hours to detect an error. The nominal value is also adjusted by the multiplier for losses defined in the software productivity sector. Finally, there is a multiplier due to error density used to adjust the QA manpower needed to detect an error. It is assumed that easy, obvious errors are detected first, and that subsequent errors are more expensive and difficult to find. The multiplier has no effect at large error densities, but it increases exponentially with smaller error densities. The error density (average number of er-

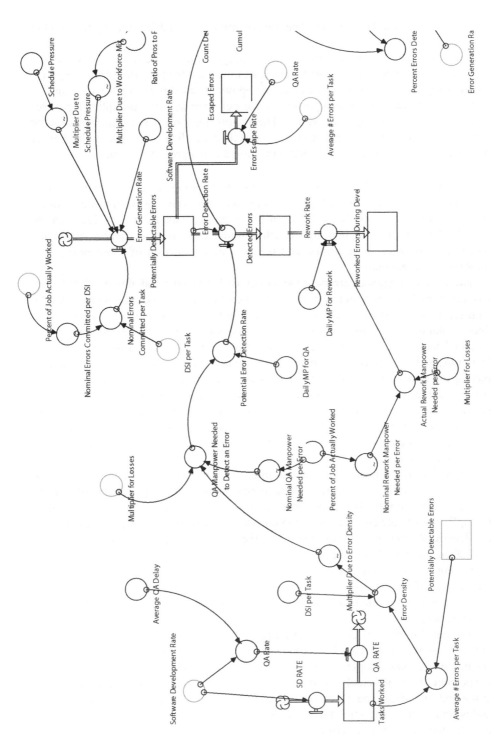

Figure 6.10. Quality assurance and rework sector.

rors per task) is calculated by dividing the potentially detectable errors by the number of tasks worked.

The errors found in QA are routed back to programmers to be fixed as rework. The rework rate is a function of effort (actual manpower needed per error) and manpower (daily manpower for rework). The actual manpower needed per error has two components: the nominal rework manpower needed per error and the multiplier for losses from the software productivity sector. The rework manpower is a function of error type, where a design error requires more effort than a coding error. The multiplier for losses accounts for lost effort on communication and nonproject activities.

6.3.1.3.4 SYSTEM TESTING SECTOR. The system testing sector is assumed to find all errors escaped from the QA process and bad fixes resulting from faulty rework. Any remaining errors could be found in maintenance, which is not included in the model. The sector models both the growth of undetected errors as escaped errors and bad fixes generating more errors, and the detection/correction of those errors. See Table 6.4 for a summary.

There are two types of errors in the model, called passive and active, whereby active errors multiply into more errors. Each type has a level associated with it. All design errors are considered active since they could result in coding errors, erroneous documentation, test plans, and so on. Coding errors may be either active or passive. The undetected active errors level has an inflow from escaped errors and bad fixes from QA, and regeneration of active errors. The outflow comes from finding and correcting the errors, or by making them passive. There is a positive feedback loop between the undetected active errors level and the active error regeneration rate. Undetected passive errors are fed by a flow from retired active errors and the generation of passive errors from QA escaped errors and bad fixes. The outflow is the rate of detection and correction of those errors. A simplified representation of the error flow model is shown in Figure 6.11.

The active error regeneration rate is a function of the software development rate and the active error density. A delay of three months is used for the generation of new errors from active errors. The active error regeneration rate uses a graph function called multiplier to activate error regeneration due to error density as a function of active error density. As the error density increases, the multiplier increases. However, a fraction of the errors will become passive and not multiply indefinitely. The active errors retirement fraction controls the active error retirement rate, and is a graph function of the percent of job actually worked. The fraction starts at 0 in the beginning and increases rapidly until the end of coding, whereby all active errors are retired and become passive.

Another flow into undetected active errors is escaped errors and bad fixes from the QA and rework sector. The flow is the escaped errors plus bad fixes, adjusted by the fraction of escaping errors that will be active. The fraction is another graph function of the percent of the job actually worked and varies from 1 in the beginning of design to 0 at the end of coding. The actual number of bad fixes is a function of the rework rate, and is set to 0.075. The same factors affect the passive error generation rate that flows into the undetected passive errors level.

Table 6.4. System testing sector model overview

Purpose: Planning, Process Improvement			
Scope: Development Project			

Inputs and Parameters	Levels	Major Relationships	Outputs

• Time to smooth active error density
• QA rate (from QA and rework)
• Daily manpower for testing (from manpower allocation sector)
• Multiplier for losses (from software productivity sector)
• Testing effort overhead
• Testing manpower per error
• Error escape rate (from QA and rework)
• Rework rate (from QA and rework)
• Percent bad fixes
• Percent of job actually worked (from control sector)
• Software development rate (from software productivity sector)
	• Errors
	   Undetected active
	   Undetected passive
	• Tasks
	   QA'ed
	   Tested
	• Testing man-days
	• Errors reworked in testing
		• Active error regeneration rate
		• Multiplier to regeneration due to error density
		• Fraction of escaping errors
		• Active error retiring rate
			• Tasks tested
			• Undetected active errors
			• Undetected passive errors
			• Testing man-days

The two stocks for active and passive errors are drained by a detection and correction rate for testing. It is defined as the daily manpower for testing divided by the testing manpower needed per task. The testing manpower needed per task uses the number of errors in a task and also considers the overhead of developing test plans (set to 2 man-days/KDSI, which can also be adjusted for motivation and communication losses). The error density of active and passive errors is multiplied by the testing manpower needed per error, which is set to 1.2 man-hours per error. Some levels are also present to accumulate the testing man-days, percent of tasks tested, total number of errors, and errors reworked in testing. These accumulations are used in the control sector.

6.3.1.4 Control Sector

The control sector measures project activities, compares estimates with actuals, and communicates the measurement evaluations to other segments of the model for readjusting project parameters. Progress is monitored by measuring the expended resources and is compared to plans. Many of the driving elements of other sectors are calculated

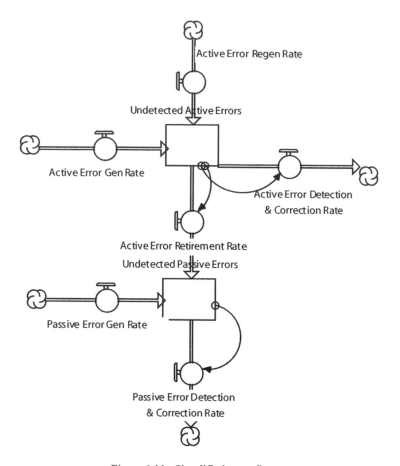

Figure 6.11. Simplified error flow.

in the control sector. See Table 6.5 for a summary. The detailed diagram for the control sector is in Figure 6.12 and Figure 6.13.

The initial value of the total job size in man-days is based on a Basic COCOMO [Boehm 1981] estimate, but it changes over the course of the project based on projected versus perceived progress, and undiscovered tasks being discovered.

One of the primary measures is total man-days perceived still needed, which represents the work for development, QA, rework, and system testing. There is an important distinction between man-days still needed and man-days remaining. Man-days still needed is based on the original plan, whereas man-days remaining is based on perception of actual progress. The two values are equal at the beginning of the project and diverge as the project continues. They essentially represent different modes of measuring progress.

Man-days perceived to be still needed for new tasks is determined by dividing tasks perceived to be remaining by the assumed development productivity. The latter

Table 6.5. Control sector model overview

Purpose: Planning, Process Improvement
Scope: Development Project

Inputs and Parameters	Levels	Major Relationships	Outputs

• Tasks developed (from software development sector)
• Cumulative man-days (from manpower allocation sector)
• Detected errors (from QA and rework)
• Perceived rework manpower needed per error (from manpower allocation sector)
• Time to smooth test productivity
• Delay in adjusting job size
• Delay in incorporating tasks
• Fraction of effort for testing (from software development sector)
• Reporting delay
• Tasks tested (from system testing sector)
	• Tasks
	  Undiscovered
	  Discovered
	• Perceived job size
	• Job size
	• Testing size
		• Assumed development productivity
		• Perceived testing productivity
		• Multiplier for development
		• Multiplier for resources
		• Fraction of additional tasks
		• Undiscovered tasks discovered per day
		• Percent development perceived complete
		• Percent tasks reported complete
		• Schedule pressure
			• Man-days remaining
			• Percent of job worked
			• Schedule pressure

is a converter that captures the perception change from "still needed" to "remaining" during the project. Assumed development productivity is a weighted average of projected development productivity and perceived development productivity. Projected development productivity is tasks perceived to be remaining divided by man-days perceived to be remaining for new tasks. This corresponds to productivity being a function of future projections early in the project. Whereas perceived development productivity is the cumulative tasks developed divided by the cumulative development man-days, representing productivity later in the project is a function of perceived accomplishments. The weight of projected productivity then varies from 1 to 0 over the project and is a product of the rate of expenditure of resources (multiplier for resources) and the rate of task development (multiplier for development).

The man-days perceived to be needed to rework detected errors is the product of detected errors (from the QA and rework sector) and the perceived rework manpower needed per error (from the manpower allocation sector). The man-days perceived

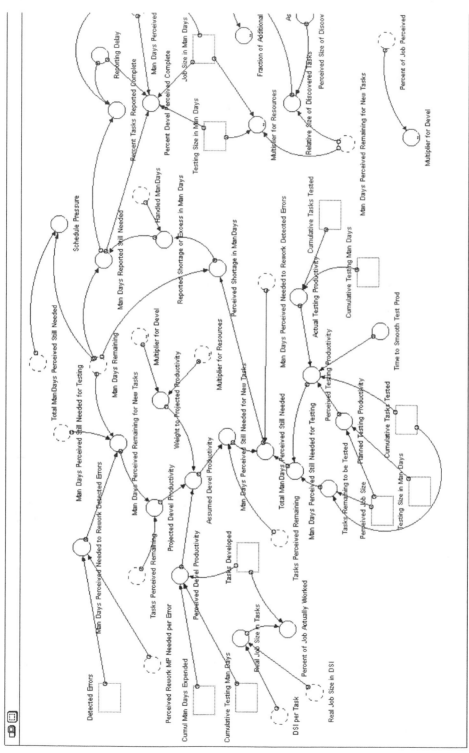

Figure 6.12. Control sector (left side).

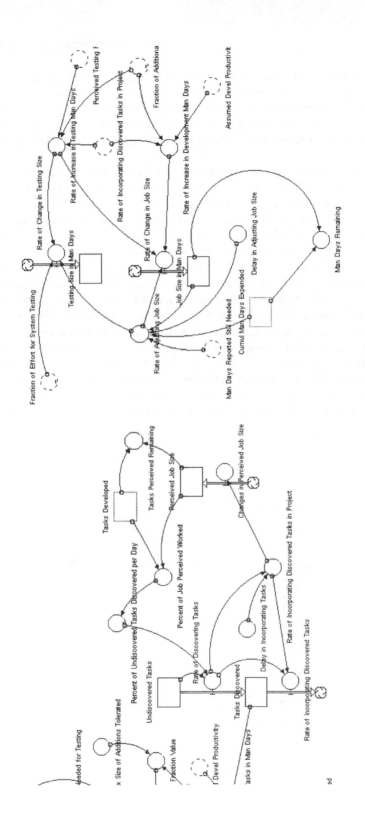

Figure 6.13. Control sector (right side).

389

to be still needed for testing converter is calculated as the tasks remaining to be test-ed divided by the perceived testing productivity. Tasks remaining to be tested is the difference between perceived job size in tasks and cumulative tasks tested (from the system testing sector). The perceived testing productivity equals the planned testing productivity at first, but actual testing productivity is used after testing actually be-gins.

The total man-days perceived to be still needed can be determined with the above. It is then compared with man-days remaining in the project to calculate the perceived shortage in man-days. The size of the project changes when the man-days reported still needed does not equal man-days remaining. The size change perception is trans-lated into a stock called job size in man-days. The adjustment is represented by the rate of adjusting job size calculated as (goal − current level)/adjustment time. The ad-justment time used is the delay in adjusting size, which is set to 3 days.

Job size can be adjusted for underestimation as well as falling behind in schedule. A parameter called task underestimation fraction is used to simulate the undersizing, as shown in Figure 6.14. Note that the project behavior modeled here is emblematic of some of the critiques in Section 6.3.1.5. The undiscovered job tasks are discovered at the rate of discovering tasks, which is a product of undiscovered job tasks and per-cent of undiscovered tasks discovered per day. A graph function is used that assumes that the rate of discovering previously unknown tasks increases as a project develops. This rate controls the flow of undiscovered tasks into the discovered tasks level, which is then drained by the delay in incorporating discovered tasks (set at 10 days delay).

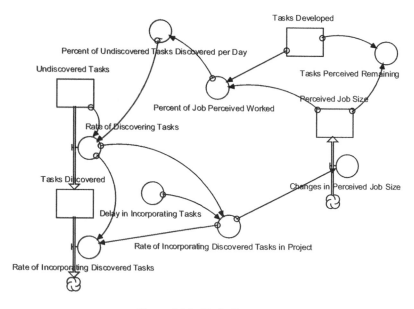

Figure 6.14. Task discovery.

The task underestimation effect is a major factor of the project dynamics in the Ab-del-Hamid model. The rise in perceived job size affects many interrelated functions. The summary graph of the model using default settings is shown in Figure 6.15. The task underestimation fraction is set to 0.67, which produces the rise in perceived job size and corresponding delayed rise in the scheduled completion date (both are shown highlighted in Figure 6.15).

The project's allocation of man-days changes when new tasks are discovered, but only when there is a significant amount. The perceived size of discovered tasks in man-days is divided by man-days perceived to be remaining for new tasks. If the relative size of discovered tasks is less than 1%, then nothing happens; if greater, then a portion of the additional tasks are translated into additional man-days using a graph function called fraction of additional tasks added to man-days. The new task effort is computed as the rate of increase in development man-days, and the testing effort is computed as the rate of increase in testing man-days.

There are also other converters calculated in this sector for use in other places. Man-days remaining is the difference between job size in man-days and cumulative man-days expended, and drives dynamics in the human resources and planning sectors. Schedule pressure is (total man-days perceived to be still needed–man-days remaining)/man-days remaining. This converter is used in the quality assurance and rework sector and manpower allocation sector. Other converters calculated here for other sectors are percent tasks reported completed, percent tasks perceived completed, real job size in tasks, and percent of job actually worked.

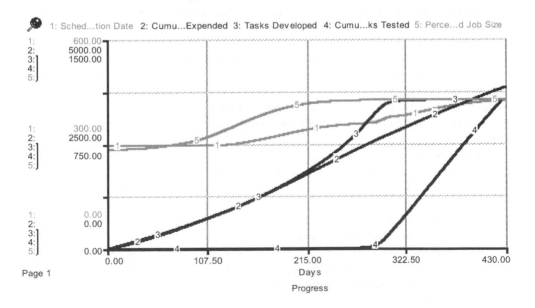

Figure 6.15. Task underestimation behavior (1: scheduled completion date, 2: cumulative man-days expended, 3: tasks developed, 4: cumulative tasks tested, 5: perceived job size).

6.3.1.5   Insights and Implications of Abdel-Hamid's Integrated Project Model

Abdel-Hamid's project model was a critical and highly enlightening work. However, all models are created to solve certain problems, come with specific assumptions, and cannot address everyone's needs. Abdel-Hamid's research issues and background were different from those of many readers, so this section summarizes the model's insights and implications to potentially be aware of. It is a very good model, but it models some poor behavior on software projects.

One advantage of the model is that it includes a good deal of important dynamic effects. It does well in illustrating some methods of poor software management (this can also be a downfall if certain policies are emulated, or the model becomes prescriptive instead of descriptive). It uses the very realistic notion that management perceptions, rather than true conditions, dictate actions. Delays in action are also important realistic considerations that the model covers well.

The inclusion of important personnel attributes like motivation, exhaustion, and schedule pressure effects are classic. These are vitally important considerations when managing a project. These structures of the model have been replicated and modified by many others.

The model is also strong in terms of planning and control structures. Many of these structures for project planning and control serve as good examples for other models. Abdel-Hamid showed in several of his publications how the planning and control policies embedded in the model make for interesting experiments with respect to usage of estimates [Abdel-Hamid 1993a] and making project judgments with fallible information [Abdel-Hamid et al. 1993]. However, the model contains too many elements for most managers to understand and use. For example, tracing the effects of Brooks's Law or schedule pressure through the entire model is difficult. The model also requires a good deal of parameters and functions to initialize for a particular environment. The experience has been that many of the inputs are very difficult to obtain without specialized collection efforts, and no known institution tracks the entire set of metrics by default. Some parts of the model also use idiosyncratic terminology. In particular, the error model is difficult for many to follow simply due to the semantics (e.g., active vs. passive errors).

Conversely, the software production model is not overly complex but very simplistic. Design and code are aggregated together. It does not provide the detailed visibility or management levers that would be of concern to many practitioners today.

The model may be wrongly used or overly relied on to perpetuate poor management practices, such as not being able to check status progress early on. Modern software management principles call for increased accounting and attention to earlier life-cycle activities. In the model, for example, the rate of discovering previously unknown tasks increases as a project develops, as opposed to a modern risk management approach with iterative processes that results in reduced volatility and less severe defect fixing as a project unfolds.

The control function uses a misleading indicator of progress to mimic previous projects based on interviews. Instead of measuring the tasks done, it defines progress as the effort expended against plan. This is a very dangerous policy (earned value can also be abused this way). The "plan" can change during the simulation, but checking the status of actual work accomplished is always preferred on a real project.

The planning and control structures do not describe all environments, especially those with more modern and enlightened management. In a sense, the control structures admit defeat in not being able to check the status of progress early on; a good deal of the structure is dedicated to this phenomenon, and actual accomplishments are used only very late in the project.

The definition of QA is nonstandard and the model represents a nonoptimized, dangerous policy for quality. The defect finding and fixing activities modeled as QA are in practice generally performed by the same people who develop software artifacts. They are implicitly considered part of standard development activities in most installations. The QA model assumes that all QA tasks are batch processed in an allocated fixed amount of time (10 days) as a separate activity tacked onto development. Regardless of error levels or the amount of software per QA batch, the same amount of work per week goes into finding and fixing defects before system testing. Quality can be undermined with this approach or effort can be wasted without considering the variable workloads.

Many of the dynamics arise from the parameter for task underestimation. This parameter is not known exactly prior to a project, but it could be accounted for much earlier by adjusting up the size for expected volatility in the beginning, or modeling size with a distribution. If the uncertainty is planned in from the outset, then the debilitating dynamics would not occur. Management reserves or buffers can be created with contingency plans to have more people ready to go when necessary. This would be prudent planning and management.

The model has been and will continue to be valuable for follow-on research by others. Different parts of the model can be incorporated into other models and/or used for directed experimentation. Thanks to the separation of sectors provided by Margaret Johnson for this book, component sectors of the model can be individually exercised and incorporated into other models; for example, the human resources sector can stand alone by itself as a distinct model.

It was not developed for future calibration. The values for productivity, error rates, and so on are hard-coded into many graph functions, making it difficult to calibrate the model for specific environments. The metrics also come from Abdel-Hamid's literature search and/or interviews, and often do not reflect currently expected values. These calibration issues should be addressed when adapting the model.

6.3.1.6 *Early Follow-ons to Abdel-Hamid's Work*

Abdel-Hamid's model was the basis for many of the subsequent early software process modeling efforts. Many of them were highlighted in a special issue of *American Programmer* [Yourdon 1993b] and another issue a year later [Yourdon 1994].

One of the first follow-on modeling efforts was performed at NASA Jet Propulsion Laboratories (JPL) by Chi Lin and others [Lin, Levary 1989, Lin et al. 1992]. She worked with Abdel-Hamid to extend his model for their projects to include requirements activities and multiple projects. In [Lin et al. 1992], some enhancements were made to the model and validated against project data. Several other organizations experimented with his model in the first few years.

One reason that few people were able to adapt the Abdel-Hamid model was its Dynamo implementation. His work at MIT was completed in the late 1980s when Stella with the Macintosh interface was just becoming popular. After that, few were willing to attempt the steep learning curve and legacy Fortran-like programming environment of Dynamo when much more user-friendly tools were available.

The divide between modern interfaces and the Abdel-Hamid model lasted for many years. It is certainly an arduous task to manually convert from a complex Dynamo model to another system dynamics tool, and several attempts were made to reverse engineer his model. Bellcore spent over a couple person-years to adapt the Abdel-Hamid model to Ithink for internal uses [Glickman 1994]. One adaptation used a more detailed implementation of COCOMO with effort adjustment factors.

Margaret Johnson produced a faithful reproduction of the Abdel-Hamid model in [Johnson 1995] and has provided it for the public domain through this book. Some of the examples in this book are derived from her work.

Johnson also worked with Ed Yourdon and Howard Rubin to further extend the Abdel-Hamid model. They investigated the effects of software process improvement through their adapted models [Rubin et al. 1994] and integrated system dynamics with the Estimacs cost estimation model.

Subsequent work was done by Abdel-Hamid in various experiments to test management policies afforded by the model. In [Abdel-Hamid 1993a], the problem of continuous estimation throughout a project was investigated. Experimental results showed that up to a point, reducing an initial estimate saves cost by decreasing wasteful practices. However, the effect of underestimation is counterproductive beyond a certain point because initial understaffing causes a later staff buildup.

Abdel-Hamid also developed a preliminary model of software reuse [Abdel-Hamid 1993b] with a macroinventory perspective instead of an individual project perspective. It captures the operations of a development organization as multiple software products are developed, placed into operation, and maintained over time. Preliminary results showed that a positive feedback loop exists between development productivity, delivery rate, and reusable component production. The positive growth eventually slows down from the balancing influence of a negative feedback loop, since new code production decreases as reuse rates increase. This leads to a decreasing reuse repository size since older components are retired and less new code is developed for reuse. The reuse inventory modeling effort is a prime example of modeling the process versus a project. The time horizon is such that there is no notion of a project start or end point.

The Abdel-Hamid model has lived on in various other forms over the years. It was a starting point for many of the other applications described in this book. For example, see the section in Chapter 5 on the SPMS model for requirements volatility and how its lineage can be traced back to the Abdel-Hamid model.

Abdel-Hamid's major publications in software-related journals are summarized in Appendix B: Annotated System Dynamics Bibliography. There are a few articles not listed from business journals and other venues, but they contain very little information beyond those already listed. The interested reader can look at *Software Project Dynamics* [Abdel-Hamid, Madnick 1991] or [Johnson 1995] for more details of the model.

6.4 SOFTWARE BUSINESS CASE ANALYSIS

It behooves every industrial software project or organizational process to have a business rationale for its existence, and it should be compatible with other plans, goals, or constraints. The business case helps sets the stage for an instantiated software process, and the relationship is a dynamic one.

Thus, the study of software business cases is important to understanding development and evolution processes. Executive decision making should be based on the best information available and linked to stakeholder value. Modeling is valuable if questions like the following need quantitative answers:

- How will customers, suppliers, partners, and competitors act in the future?
- How are changes in the market structure affecting business?
- What are the implications of trade-offs between financial and nonfinancial balanced scorecard measures?
- What effect will management actions have on internal processes and productivity?

[Reifer 2001] is a good reference on how to justify expenditures and prepare successful business cases. It provides useful examples of what to do and what not to do via the case study approach. Dynamic modeling is not explicitly addressed, but the general analysis methods are easily integrated with system dynamics. The examples in this section show how systems thinking and system dynamics can be brought to bear on business case analysis. This usage also falls under the general term of *business simulation,* by which one can quantify the time-based financial return from a software solution, explore alternative business scenarios, and support decision making to optimize business processes.

Business value attainment should be a key consideration when designing software processes. Ideally, they are structured to meet organizational business goals, but it is usually difficult to integrate the process and business perspectives quantitatively. The examples in this section are based on actual client experiences, but have been adapted for simplicity and recalibrated with nonproprietary data.

The first example shows how simulation can be used to assess product strategies from a value-based perspective in order to analyze business case trade-offs. The model relates the dynamics between product specifications, investment costs, schedule, software quality practices, market size, license retention, pricing, and revenue generation. It allows one to experiment with different product strategies, software processes, marketing practices, and pricing schemes while tracking financial measures over time. It can be used to determine the appropriate balance of process activities to meet goals.

Examples are developed for varying scope, reliability, delivery of multiple releases, and determining the quality sweet spot for different time horizons. Results show that optimal policies depend on various stakeholder value functions, opposing market factors, and business constraints. Future model improvements are also identified.

6.4.1 Example: Value-Based Product Modeling

Software-related decisions should not be extricated from business value concerns. Unfortunately, software engineering practice and research frequently lacks a value-oriented perspective. Value-Based Software Engineering (VBSE) integrates value considerations into current and emerging software engineering principles and practices [Boehm, Huang 2003, Biffl et al. 2005]. This model addresses the planning and control aspect of VBSE to manage the value delivered to stakeholders. Techniques to model cost, schedule, and quality are integrated with business case analysis to allow trade-off studies in a commercial software development context. Business value is accounted for in terms of return on investment (ROI) of different product and process strategies. Table 6.6 is a high-level summary of the model.

It is a challenge to trade off different software attributes, particularly between different perspectives such as business and software development. Software process modeling and simulation can be used to reason about software value decisions. It can help find the right balance of activities that contribute to stakeholder value with other constraints such as cost, schedule, or quality goals.

A value-oriented approach provides explicit guidance for making products useful to people by considering different people's utility functions or value propositions. The value propositions are used to determine relevant measures for given scenarios.

Two major aspects of stakeholder value are addressed here. One is the business value to the development organization stemming from software sales. Another is the value to the end-user stakeholder from varying feature sets and quality. Production functions relating different aspects of value to their costs were developed and are included in the integrated model.

Table 6.6. Value-based product model overview

Purpose: Strategic Management, Planning
Scope: Long-term Product Evolution

Inputs and Parameters	Levels	Major Relationships	Outputs
• Start staff • Function points • Manpower buildup parameter • Reliability setting	• Defects • Investments • Potential market share • Active licenses • Perceived quality • Cumulative investment • Cumulative revenue	• Market share production function vs. features • Sales production function vs. reliability • Quality perception • Defect rates • Staffing rate • Market dynamics	• Return on investment • Market share • Defects • Sales • Staffing

6.4.1.1   Model Overview

The model represents a business case for commercial software development in which the user inputs and model factors can vary over the project duration, as opposed to a static model. Input parameters can also be modified interactively by the user during the course of a run and the model responds to the midstream changes. It can be used dynamically before or during a project. Hence, it is suitable for "flight simulation" training or actual project usage to reflect actuals to date. The model can be used to assess the effects of combined strategies by varying inputs such as scope and required reliability independently or simultaneously.

The sectors of the model and their major interfaces are shown in Figure 6.16. The software process and product sector computes the staffing profile and quality over time based on the software size, reliability setting, and other inputs. The staffing rate becomes one of the investment flows in the finances sector, whereas the actual quality is a primary factor in market and sales. The resulting sales are used in the finance sector to compute various financial measures.

Figure 6.17 shows a diagram of the software process and product sector. It models the internal dynamics between job size, effort, schedule, required reliability, and quality. The staffing rate over time is calculated with a version of Dynamic COCOMO [Boehm et al. 2000] using a variant of a Rayleigh curve calibrated to the COCOMO II cost model at the top level. The project effort is based on the number of function points and the reliability setting. There are also some Rayleigh curve parameters that determine the shape of the staffing curve.

There is a simple defect model to calculate defect levels used in the market and sales sector to modulate sales. Defect generation is modeled as a coflow with the software development rate, and the defect removal rate accounts for their finding and fixing. See Chapter 3 for more background on these standard flow structures for effort and defects.

Figure 6.18 shows the market and sales sector accounting for market share dynamics and software license sales. The perceived quality is a reputation factor that can re-

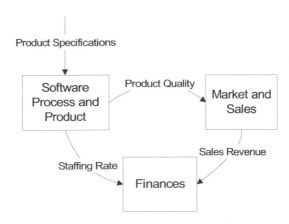

Figure 6.16. Model sectors and major interfaces.

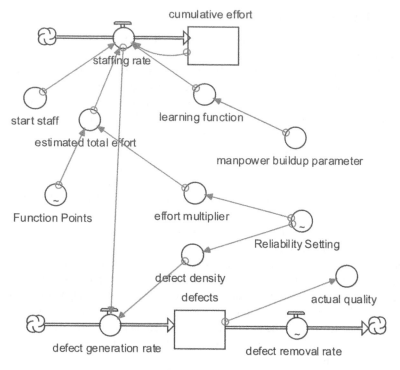

Figure 6.17. Software process and product sector.

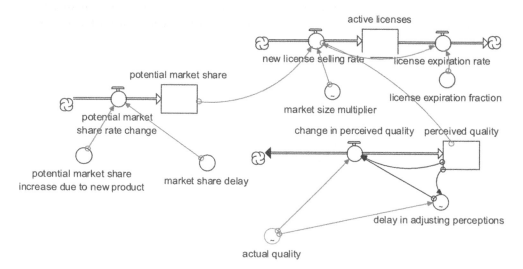

Figure 6.18. Market and sales sector.

duce the number of sales if products have many defects, as described in the next section. The market and sales model presented herein is a simplification of a more extensive model being used in industry that accounts for additional marketing initiatives and software license maintenance sales.

The finance sector is shown in Figure 6.19. It includes cash flows for investment and revenue. Investments include the labor costs for software development, maintenance, and associated activities. Revenue is derived from the number of license sales. Sales are a function of the overall market size and market share percentage for the software product. The market share is computed using a potential market share adjusted by perceived quality. The additional market share derivable from a new product is attained at an average delay time.

6.4.1.1.1 QUALITY MODELING AND VALUE FUNCTIONS. For simplification, software reliability as defined in the COCOMO II model [Boehm et al. 2000] is used as a proxy for all quality practices. It models the trade-off between reliability and development cost. There are four different settings of reliability from low to very high that correspond to four development options. The trade-off is increased cost and longer development time for increased quality. Table 6.7 lists the reliability rating definitions, the approximate mean times between failures, and relative costs from the COCOMO II model. This simplification can be replaced with a more comprehensive quality model to account for specific practices (see future work in Section 6.4.1.3 and the chapter ex-

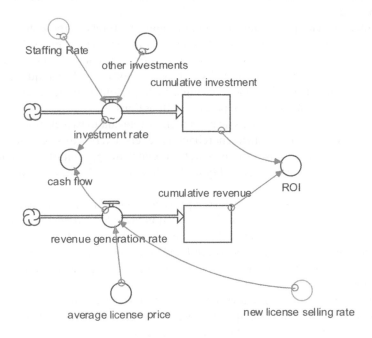

Figure 6.19. Finance sector.

Table 6.7. Reliability definitions.

Reliability Rating	Defect Impact	Approximate Mean Time Between Failure (Hours)	Relative Cost
Low	Small, recoverable losses	10	0.92
Nominal	Moderate, recoverable losses	300	1.00
High	Large, unrecoverable losses	10,000	1.10
Very High	Human life	300,000	1.26

ercises). The resulting quality will modulate the actual sales relative to the highest potential. A lower quality product will be done quicker; it will be available on the market sooner but sales will suffer from poor quality. The mapping between reliability and the relative impact to sales from iterated Delphi surveys is captured as a production function and used in the model.

Collectively, there are two value-based production functions in the model to describe value relationships (they are illustrated in the first applied example). A market share production function addresses the organizational business value of product features. The business value is quantified in terms of added potential market share attainable by the features. The relationship assumes that all features are implemented to the highest quality. Since the required reliability will impact how well the features actually work, the relationship between reliability costs and actual sales is needed to vary the sales due to quality.

The market share production function in Figure 6.20 relates the potential business value to the cost of development for different feature sets. The actual sales production function versus reliability costs is shown in Figure 6.21, and it is applied against the potential market capture. The four discrete points correspond to required reliability levels of low, nominal, high, and very high. Settings for the three cases described in the next section are shown in both production functions.

The value function for actual sale attainment is relevant to two classes of stakeholders. It describes the value of different reliability levels in terms of sales attainment, and is essentially a proxy for user value as well. It relates the percent of potential sales attained in the market against reliability costs. Illustrations of the production functions are shown in the next section.

The market and sales sector also has a provision to modulate sales based on the perceived quality reputation. A bad quality reputation takes hold almost immediately with a buggy product (bad news travels fast), and takes a long time to recover from in the market perception even after defects are fixed. This phenomenon is represented with asymmetrical information smoothing as shown in Figure 6.22 with a variable delay in adjusting perceptions.

The graph in Figure 6.22 shows a poor quality release at time = 3 years with a followup release to the previous quality level. Whereas the perceived quality quickly plummets after the bad release, it rises much more slowly even when the actual quality has improved. There are many historical examples of this phenomena.

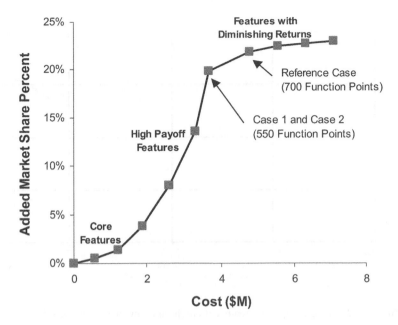

Figure 6.20. Market share production function and feature sets.

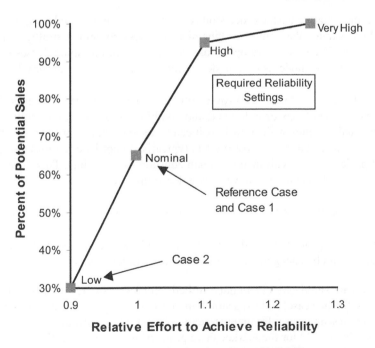

Figure 6.21. Sales production function and reliability.

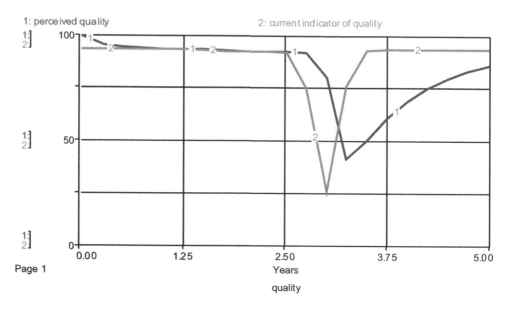

Figure 6.22. Perceived quality trends with high- and low-quality product deliveries.

6.4.1.2 *Applications*

Several representative business decision scenarios are demonstrated next. The first example demonstrates the ability to dynamically assess combined strategies for scope and reliability. The second example looks at strategies of multiple releases of varying quality. Finally, the model is used to determine a process sweet spot for reliability.

6.4.1.2.1 DYNAMICALLY CHANGING SCOPE AND RELIABILITY. The model can be used to assess the effects of individual and combined strategies for overall scope and reliability. This example will show how it can be used to change product specifications midstream as a replan. Static cost models typically do not lend themselves to replans after the project starts, as all factors remain constant through time. This dynamic capability can be used in at least two ways by a decision-maker:

1. Assessing the impact of changed product specifications during the course of a project
2. Before the project starts, determining if and how late during the project specifications can be changed based on new considerations that might come up

Three cases are simulated: (1) an unperturbed reference case, (2) a midstream descoping of the reference case, and (3) a simultaneous descoping and lowered required reliability. Such descoping is a frequent strategy to meet time constraints by shedding features. See Figure 6.20 for the market share production function and Figure 6.21 for the potential business value function for these three cases.

Figure 6.23 shows a sample control panel interface to the model. The primary inputs for product specifications are the size in function points (also called scope) and required reliability. The number of function points is the size needed to implement given features. The size and associated cost varies with the number of features to incorporate.

The reliability settings on the control panel slider are the relative effort multipliers needed to achieve reliability levels from low to very high. These are input by the user via the slider for "Reliability Setting." The attainable market share derived from the production function in Figure 6.20 is input by the user on the slider "Potential Market Share Increase."

Figure 6.23 also shows the simulation results for the initial reference case. The default case of 700 function points is delivered with nominal reliability at 2.1 years with a potential 20% market share increase. This project is unperturbed during its course and the 5 year ROI of the project is 1.3.

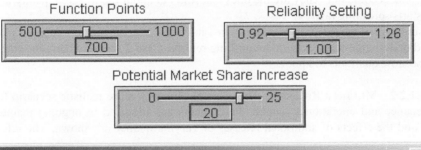

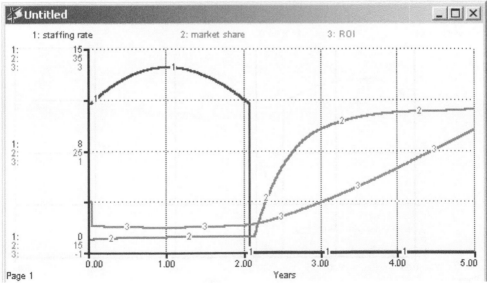

Figure 6.23. Sample control panel and reference case (unperturbed).

Case 1 in Figure 6.24 illustrates the initial case perturbed at 0.5 years to descope low-ROI features (see Figure 6.20 and Figure 6.21 for the points on the production function). The scope goes down to 550 function points and the staffing profile adjusts dynamically for it. The schedule is reduced by a few months. In this case, the potential market share increase is lowered by only two percentage points to 18%. With lower development costs and earlier delivery, the ROI increases substantially to 2.2.

A combined strategy is modeled in Figure 6.25 for Case 2. The scope is decreased the same as before in Case 1 (Figure 6.24), plus the reliability setting is lowered from nominal to low. Though overall development costs decrease due to lowered reliability, the market responds poorly. This case provides the worst return of the three options and market share is lost instead of gained.

In Case 2, there is an early hump in sales due to the initial attention paid to the brand-new product, but the market soon discovers the poor quality and then sales suffer dramatically. These early buyers and others assume that the new product will have the previous quality of the product line and are anxious to use the new, "improved" product. Some may have preordered and some are early adopters that always buy when new products come out. They are the ones that find out about the lowered quality and word starts spreading fast.

A summary of the three cases is shown in Table 6.8. Case 1 is the best business plan to shed undesirable features with diminishing returns. Case 2 severely hurts the enterprise because quality is too poor.

6.4.1.2.2 MULTIPLE RELEASES. This example shows a more realistic scenario for maintenance and operational support. Investments are allocated to ongoing maintenance and the effects of additional releases of varying quality are shown. The refer-

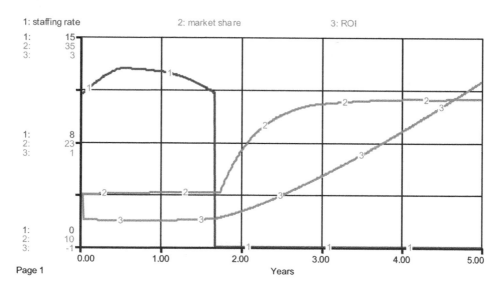

Figure 6.24. Case 1—descoping of low ROI features at time = 0.5 years.

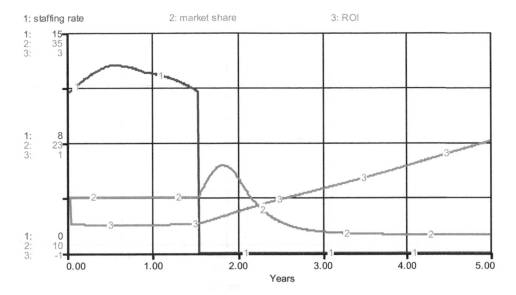

Figure 6.25. Case 2—descoping of low ROI features and reliability lowering at time = 0.5 years.

ence case contains two product rollouts at years 1 and 3, each with the potential to capture an additional 10% of the market share. These potentials are attained because both deliveries are of high quality, as seen in Figure 6.26 and Figure 6.27.

A contrasting case in Figure 6.28 and Figure 6.29 illustrates the impact if the second delivery has poor quality yet is fixed quickly (Figure 6.22 shows the quality trends for this case). This results in a change of revenue from $11.5 M to $9.6M and ROI from 1.3 to 0.9.

This example is another illustration of the sensitivity of the market to varying quality. Only one poor release in a series of releases may have serious long-term consequences.

6.4.1.2.3 FINDING THE SWEET SPOT. This example shows how the value-based product model can support software business decision making by using risk conse-

Table 6.8. Case summaries.

Case	Delivered Size (Function Points)	Delivered Reliability Setting	Cost ($M)	Delivery Time (Years)	Final Market Share	ROI
Reference Case: Unperturbed	700	1.0	4.78	2.1	28%	1.3
Case 1: Descope	550	1.0	3.70	1.7	28%	2.2
Case 2: Descope and Lower Reliability	550	.92	3.30	1.5	12%	1.0

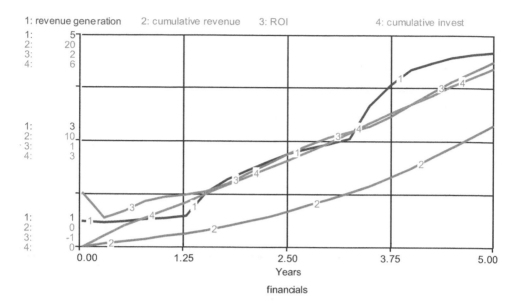

Figure 6.26. Reference case financials for two high-quality product deliveries (1: revenue generation rate, 2: cumulative revenue, 3: ROI, 4: cumulative investment).

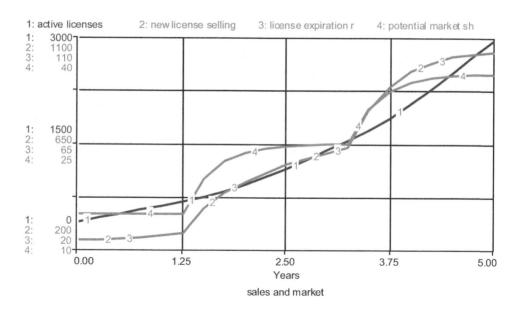

Figure 6.27. Reference case sales and market for two high-quality product deliveries (1: active licenses, 2: new license selling rate, 3: license expiration rate, 4: potential market share).

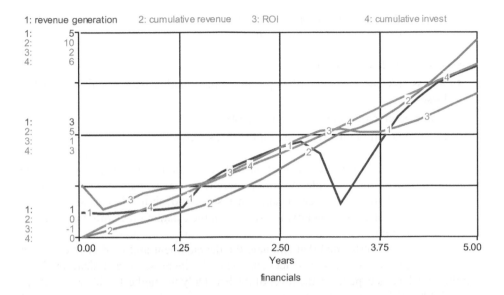

Figure 6.28. Financials for high- and low-quality product deliveries (1: revenue generation rate, 2: cumulative revenue, 3: ROI, 4: cumulative investment).

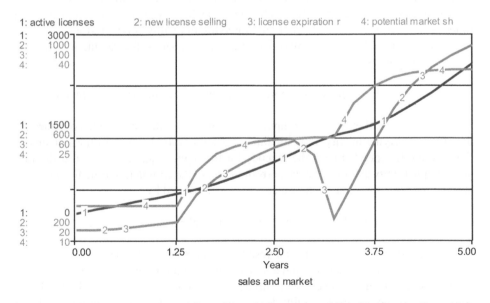

Figure 6.29. Sales and market for high- and low-quality product deliveries (1: active licenses, 2: new license selling rate, 3: license expiration rate, 4: potential market share).

quence to find the quality sweet spot with respect to ROI. The following analysis steps are performed to find the process sweet spot:

- Vary reliability across runs
- Assess risk consequences of opposing trends: market delays and bad quality losses
- Sum market losses and development costs
- Calculate resulting net revenue to find process optimum

The risk consequences are calculated for the different options. Only point estimates are used for the sake of this example. A more comprehensive risk analysis would consider probability distributions to obtain a range of results. Probability is considered to be constant for each case and is not explicitly used in the calculations. Only the costs (or losses) are determined.

A set of runs is performed that simulate the development and market release of a new 80 KSLOC product. The product can potentially increase market share by 30%, but the actual gains depend on the level of quality. Only the highest quality will attain the full 30%. Other parameterizations are an initial total market size = $64M annual revenue, the vendor has 15% initial market share, and the overall market doubles in 5 years.

A reference case is needed to determine the losses due to inferior quality. The expected revenues for a subquality delivery must be subtracted from the maximum potential revenues (i.e., revenue for a maximum quality product delivered at a given time). The latter is defined as delivering a maximum quality product at a given time that achieves the full potential market capture. The equation for calculating the loss due to bad quality is

$$\text{bad quality loss} = \text{maximum potential revenue with same timing} - \text{revenue}$$

The loss due to market delay is computed, keeping the quality constant. To neutralize the effect of varying quality, only the time of delay is varied. The loss for a given option is the difference between the revenue for the highest quality product at the first market opportunity and the revenue corresponding to the completion time for the given option (assuming the same highest quality). It is calculated by

$$\text{market delay cost} = \text{maximum potential revenue} - \text{revenue}$$

Figure 6.30 shows the experimental results for an 80 KSLOC product, fully compressed development schedules, and a 3-year revenue timeframe for different reliability options. The resultant sweet spot corresponds to reliability = high. The total cost consisting of delay losses, reliability losses, and development cost is minimum at that setting for a 3 year time horizon.

The sweet spot depends on the applicable time horizon, among other things. The horizon may vary for several reasons such as another planned major upgrade or new

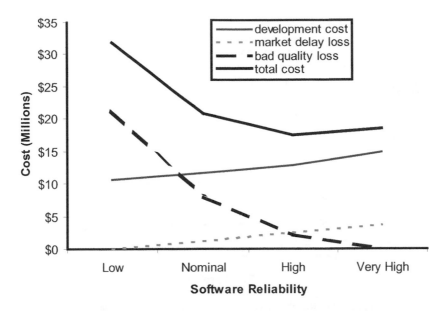

Figure 6.30. Calculating reliability sweet spot (3 year time frame).

release, other upcoming changes in the business model, or because investors mandate a specific time frame in which to make their return.

The experiment was rerun for typical time horizons of 2, 3, and 5 years using a profit view (the cost view is transformed into a profit maximization view by accounting for revenues). The results are shown in Figure 6.31. The figure illustrates that the sweet spot moves from reliability equals low to high to very high. It is evident that the optimal reliability depends on the time window. A short-lived product (a prototype is an extreme example) does not need to be developed to as stringent reliability standards as one that will live in the field longer.

6.4.1.3   Conclusions and Future Work

It is crucial to integrate value-based methods into the software engineering discipline. To achieve real earned value, business value attainment must be a key consideration when designing software products and processes. This work shows several ways that software business decision making can improve with value information gained from simulation models that integrate business and technical perspectives.

The model demonstrates a stakeholder value chain whereby the value of software to end users ultimately translates into value for the software development organization. It also illustrates that commercial process sweet spots with respect to reliability are a balance between market delay losses and quality losses. Quality does impact the bottom line.

The model can be elaborated to account for feedback loops to generate revised product specifications (closed-loop control). This feedback includes:

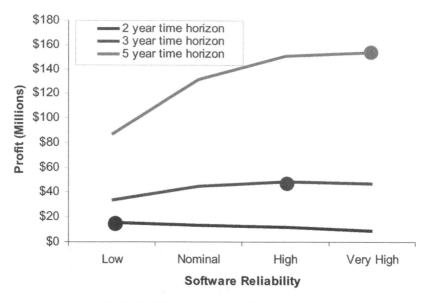

Figure 6.31. Reliability sweet spot as a function of time horizon.

- External feedback from user to incorporate new features
- Internal feedback on product initiatives from an organizational planning and control entity to the software process

A more comprehensive model would consider long term product evolution and periodic upgrades. Another related aspect to include is general maintenance by adding explicit activities for operational support.

The product defect model can be enhanced with a dynamic version of the Constructive Quality Model (COQUALMO) [Chulani, Boehm 1999] to enable more constructive insight into quality practices. This would replace the current construct based on the single factor for required software reliability.

Other considerations for the model are in the market and sales sector. The impact of different pricing schemes and varying market assumptions on initial sales and maintenance can all be explored. Some of these provisions are already accounted for in a proprietary version of the model.

The model application examples were run with idealized inputs for the sake of demonstration, but more sophisticated dynamic scenarios can be easily handled to model real situations. For example, discrete descopings were shown, but in many instances scope will exhibit continuous or fluctuating growth over time.

More empirical data on the relationships in the model will also help identify areas of improvement. Assessment of overall dynamics includes more collection and analysis of field data on business value and quality measures from actual software product rollouts.

6.5 PERSONNEL RESOURCE ALLOCATION

The proper allocation of people to different tasks is one of the most important jobs of software management. There are a variety of policies used for resource allocation, and this section overviews some ways to model them. Some of the referenced models are also provided for usage.

6.5.1 Example: Resource Allocation Policy and Contention Models

Several models of different resource allocation policies are described and analyzed below. The first one is a dynamic allocation policy whereby resources are allocated proportionally to larger tasks. Next are models for situations in which resource staffing can be described with parameterized shape profiles. Lastly is a simple project contention model that was used to examine and modify personnel allocation policies in industry.

6.5.1.1 *Squeaky Wheel Gets the Grease*

The infrastructure in Figure 6.32 is a modification of the resource allocation example in Chapter 3 that can be used to allocate resources among competing tasks. It is called

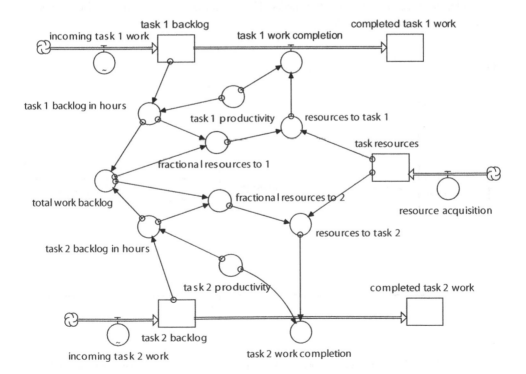

Figure 6.32. Fractional resource allocation structure.

the "squeaky wheel" algorithm because more fractional resources are allocated to those tasks with the highest backlog of work. Productivity serves as a weighting factor to account for differences in the work rates in calculating the backlog hours. The main equation that allocates the fraction of total resources to a given task is:

fractional resources to 1 = task 1 backlog in hours/total work backlog

This type of policy is used frequently when creating project teams. With a fixed staff size, proportionally more people are dedicated to the larger tasks. For example, if one software component is about twice as large as another, then that team will have roughly double the people. The component backlogs are monitored throughout a project, and people are reallocated as the work ratios change based on the respective estimates to complete.

Figure 6.33 shows the results of a simulation run in which both tasks start with equal backlogs and 50% allocations due to equal incoming work rates. At time = 6 more incoming work starts streaming into the backlog for task 2 (see the graph for incoming task 2 work). The fractional allocations change, and more resources are then allocated to work off the excess backlog in task 2. The graph for fractional resources to 2 increases at that point and slowly tapers down again after some of the task 2 work is completed. This example models the allocation between two tasks, but it can be easily extended to cover more competing tasks. The model is contained in the file *proportional resource allocation.itm.*

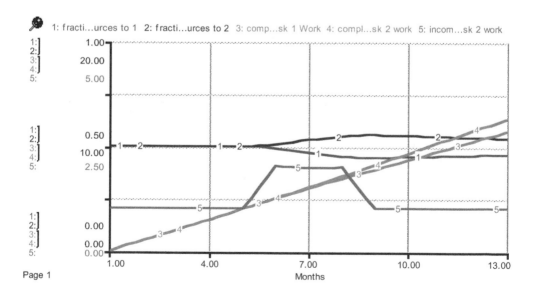

Figure 6.33. Fractional resource allocation simulation output (1: fractional resources to 1, 2: fractional resources to 2, 3: completed task 1 work, 4: completed task 2 work, 5: incoming task 2 work).

6.5.1.2 *Parameterized Allocation Profiles*

Some models use fixed resource levels or relative parameterized shapes that drive the simulation. One example is the portion of the Madachy inspection model in Chapter 5 that allocates staff for the primary development (a variable staffing portion is used for defect fixing based on the number of defects). Dynamic staffing profiles for design and coding activities are created based on the project size and complexity.

Figure 6.34 shows the dimensionless default staffing profile for design work that is proportionally sized for the project at hand based on the overall effort and schedule acceleration. It is a function of a schedule ratio of actual time to the initially estimated schedule time for development (consisting of design and coding activities that cover 85% of the overall lifecycle). The portion of staffing used for design, as defined by the graph in Figure 6.34, is taken from the overall manpower level to calculate the design manpower rate that actually drives the design activities. This structure is shown in Figure 6.35 without the other information links to the various model elements.

The inspection model also has provisions to add variable staff based on the defect levels. This is another type of allocation policy that adds the right amount of people to fix the defects that are detected. The following subsection discusses this and other defect-fixing allocation policies.

6.5.1.3 *Dynamic Resource Allocation with Initially Fixed Levels*

The previous discussion for using fixed resource levels is only applicable when the project scope does not change during the course of a simulation. In the Madachy inspection model, the overall project size stays constant (e.g., the design staffing will not change after the simulation starts) but the varying levels of defects impose different levels of fixing effort. The defect-fixing effort is modeled as a separate activity.

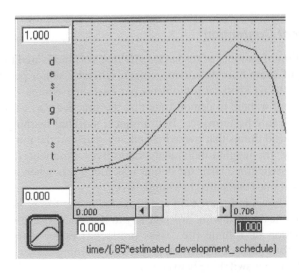

Figure 6.34. Adjustable design staffing curve.

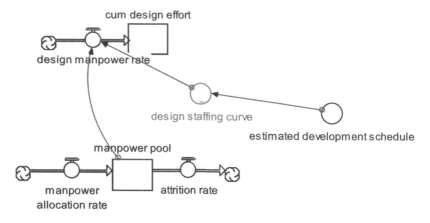

Figure 6.35. Structure to allocate fixed staffing level for design.

An example of staffing levels changing from initial simulation values is in the Abdel-Hamid project model. The initial values for personnel are calculated using the COCOMO model. However, the initial schedule and effort values are augmented by dynamic effects for task underestimation, other unexpected delays, and defect levels. The default run for the Abdel-Hamid model assumes a task underestimation factor of 0.67, so more staff is added as the additional work is needed. Thus, there are policy provisions for reassessing the project effort and allocating more people as necessary, given certain constraints for adding staff (see Section 6.3.1 for a detailed description of these constraints). It is important to note that the model has these factors for management and policy impact that are not included in traditional estimation models.

6.5.1.4 Project Contention

At Litton, creation of a model of resource switching was motivated by reactive behavior on the part of some executive management, whereby senior people were juggled between projects to fix short-term problems per customer whims. The software engineering department wanted to demonstrate that the practice was counterproductive in terms of cost/schedule performance. Both projects suffered learning curve and communication overhead drains that overwhelmed any gains on the initial "troubled" project. Additionally, the juggled individuals themselves experienced losses due to the multiple context switching. Their net output was much less when attempting to work on several tasks at once compared to a single task.

The model is shown in Figure 6.36 and provided in the file *project contention.itm.* Senior people are designated with "sr." One key to the model is expressing the learning curve as a function of volume (i.e., tasks produced) rather than time per se. See [Raccoon 1996] for a detailed discussion of software learning curves. When there are interruptions and context switching between projects, then an individual going back to a project requires longer than the interruption time to reach previous productivity levels.

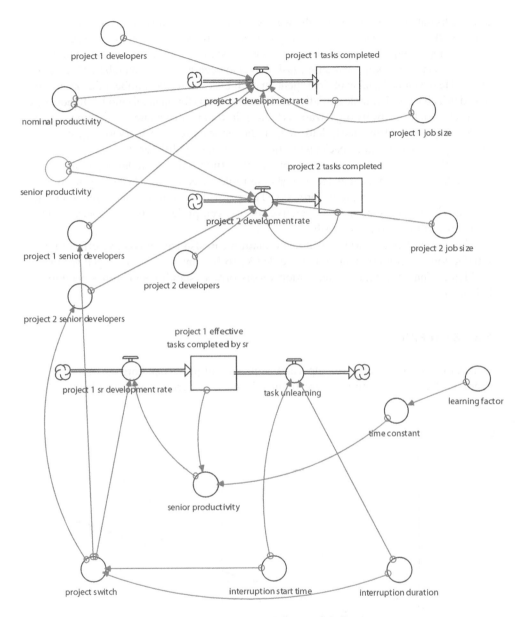

Figure 6.36. Project contention model diagram.

A Delphi poll and other queries were used to gauge the learning curve losses. It was estimated that 2–3 weeks are needed after a one-week break to get back into the productive mode of the original project. Added together, the respective losses and gains for the involved projects produced a net loss compared to not hot-switching personnel. Even more important, the anticipated schedule slips were directly correlated to customer (dis)satisfaction. These results were shown to the executives who could not disagree with the conclusions and changed their corresponding policies. Figure 6.37 shows sample output. The provided model can be studied for the detailed formulations.

The effects of working on multiple tasks has also been studied by Weinberg [Weinberg 1992]. He developed a table of time spent on each task versus the number of tasks, reproduced in Table 6.9. The table partially validates the results found in this model. It indicates a good lesson for software organizations to keep in mind—that context switching is costly. As people move from one task to another, they stop current work, try to remember the new project context, and go back and forth similarly among different tasks.

The effect of these multiple interruptions over time seriously reduces people's performance. To offset this, management should rank the competing tasks in priority and strive to have whole people on projects. The priorities might change over time, but people will generally be most productive for a given project if they can stay on that same project for as long as possible.

There is evidence, however, that team rotation can also have a positive effect on job satisfaction and commitment. Some people like to be continually challenged with new problems. Thus, the goals of innovation versus project stability sometimes need to be balanced.

6.6 STAFFING

Generating staffing plans is an important emphasis for project and organizational management. Cost estimation tools are frequently used to derive cost and schedule esti-

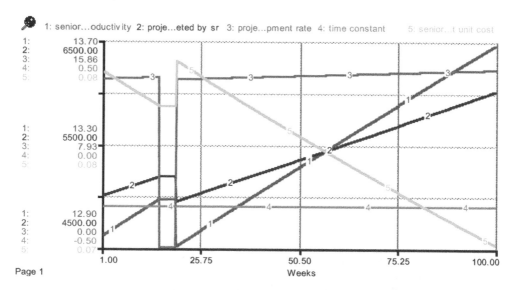

Figure 6.37. Project contention model results (1: senior productivity, 2: project 1 effective tasks completed by sr, 3: project 1 sr development rate, 4: time constant, 5: senior development unit cost).

Table 6.9. Productivity losses due to context switching from
[Weinberg 1992]

Number of Tasks	Time on Each Task
1	100%
2	40%
3	20%
4	10%
5	5%
More than 5	random

mates, and various models come into play to derive staffing profiles over time. A simple method to derive step function staffing profiles from a static cost estimate is to calculate average personnel levels per phase by dividing effort by schedule for each time
portion.

This section will cover different dynamic methods of estimating staffing needs.
They are contained in this chapter instead of in Chapter 5 on people applications because neither method models personnel levels explicitly as state variables. The
Rayleigh formulation uses a rate formula, which is interpreted as the staffing per time
period (only cumulative effort is a state variable), and process concurrence models
product characteristics (which can then be transformed into staffing needs).

Rayleigh curves have been traditionally used for many years to generate continuous
staffing profiles over time based on project characteristics. They are smoothed curves
that may reflect reasonable ramping up and ramping down, but frequently they pre-
scribe unrealistic staffing situations for organizations.

It is important to have the right number of people on a project at precisely the right
time, in order to not waste resources. In situations where a Rayleigh-like staffing curve
fits best, like an unprecedented system, a constant level-of-effort profile is inefficient.
It will waste people in the beginning and at the end, and will not have enough staff in
the project middle, as shown in Figure 6.38.

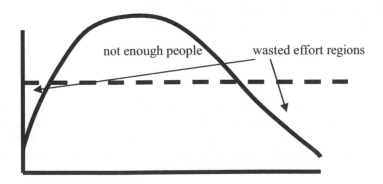

Figure 6.38. Ideal Rayleigh staffing versus level of effort.

Sometimes, a simple fixed staff size is reasonable for a project and/or it could also represent a real hiring constraint. A rectangular staffing pattern may be appropriate for situations including:

- Constrained staffing situations
- Well-known problems
- Mechanical translations
- Incremental development staffed-up portion

Modeling staffing needs is critical because otherwise many resources can be wasted and/or a project slowed down by not having resources at the right time. Modeling a fixed staff size is trivial, so the challenge is to model dynamic situations. Following are dynamic staffing models for Rayleigh curves and process concurrence approaches that can be adapted for many situations.

6.6.1 Example: Rayleigh Manpower Distribution Model

The Rayleigh curve (also called a Norden/Rayleigh curve) is a popular model of personnel loading that naturally lends itself to system dynamics modeling. It serves as a simple generator of time-based staffing curves that is easily parameterized to enable a variety of shapes. The Rayleigh curve is actually a special case of the Weibull distribution, and serves as a model for a number of phenomena in physics.

After analyzing hardware research and development projects, Norden put forth a manpower model based on Rayleigh curves. According to these staffing curves, only a small number of people are needed at the beginning of a project to carry out planning and specification. As the project progresses and more detailed work is required, the number of staff builds up to a peak. After implementation and testing, the number of staff required starts to fall until the product is delivered. Putnam subsequently applied the Rayleigh curve to software development [Putnam 1980], and it is used in the SLIM® and SEER® cost models among others.

One of the underlying assumptions is that the number of people working on a project is approximately proportional to the number of problems ready for solution at that time. Norden derived a Rayleigh curve that describes the rate of change of manpower effort per the following first-order differential equation:

$$\frac{dC(t)}{dt} = p(t)[K - C(t)]$$

where $C(t)$ is the cumulative effort at time t, K is the total effort, and $p(t)$ is a product learning function. The time derivative of $C(t)$ is the manpower rate of change, which represents the number of people involved in development at any time. Operationally, it is the staff size per time increment (traditionally, the monthly headcount or staffing profile).

The learning function is linear and can be represented by

$$p(t) = 2at$$

where *a* is a positive number. The *a* parameter is an important determinant of the peak personnel loading called the manpower buildup parameter. Note that the learning function actually represents increasing product elaboration ("learning" about the product), and is different from the people-skill learning curves discussed in Chapter 4. The distinction is discussed in the next section.

The second term $[K - C(t)]$ represents the current work gap; it is the difference between the final and current effort that closes over time as work is accomplished. The time convolution of the diminishing work gap and monotonic product learning function produces the familiar Rayleigh shape.

6.6.1.1 *System Dynamics Implementation*

The Rayleigh curve and much of Putnam's work is naturally suited to dynamic modeling. Quantities are expressed as first- and second-order differential equations, precisely the rate language of system dynamics. Table 6.10 is a high-level summary of the model.

Figure 6.39 shows a very simple model of the Rayleigh curve using an effort flow chain. The formula for effort rate (the manpower rate per time period) represents the project staffing profile. It uses a feedback loop from the cumulative effort, whereby the feedback represents knowledge of completed work.

The equations for the model are

$$\text{effort rate} = \text{learning function} \cdot \text{work gap}$$

$$\text{learning function} = \text{manpower buildup parameter} \cdot \text{time}$$

$$\text{work gap} = \text{estimated total effort} - \text{cumulative effort}$$

Figure 6.40 shows the components of the Rayleigh formula from the simulation model where estimated total effort is 15 person-months and the manpower buildup parameter is set to 0.5. The learning function increases monotonically while the work gap (the difference between estimated and cumulative effort used for effort rate) diminishes over time as problems are worked out. The corresponding effort rate rises and falls in a Rayleigh shape. The two multiplicative terms, the learning function and the work gap, produce the Rayleigh effort curve when multiplied together. They offset each other because the learning function rises and the work gap falls over time as a project progresses.

Table 6.10. Rayleigh curve model overview

Purpose: Planning, Training
Scope: Development Project

Inputs and Parameters	Levels	Major Relationships	Outputs
• Start staff • Function points • Manpower buildup parameter	• Effort	• Staffing rate	• Staffing • Effort • Schedule

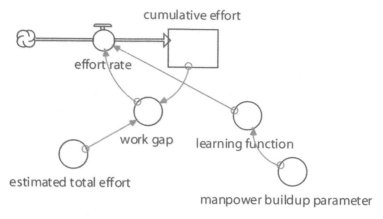

Figure 6.39. Rayleigh manpower model.

The Rayleigh model is an excellent example of a structure producing S-curve be-havior for cumulative effort. The learning function and work gap combine to cause the Rayleigh effort curve, which integrated over time as cumulative effort is sigmoidal. The cumulative effort starts with a small slope (the learning function is near zero), in-creases in slope, and then levels out as the work gap nears zero.

The learning function is linear and really represents the continued elaboration of product detail (e.g., specification to design to code) or increasing understanding about

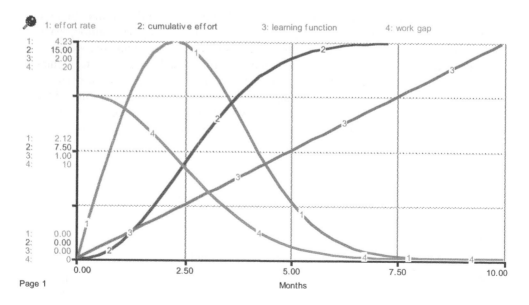

Figure 6.40. Rayleigh curve components.

the product makeup. A true learning curve has a different nonlinear shape (see Chapter 4). We prefer to call this an "elaboration function" to better represent the true phenomena being modeled. This is also consistent with the assumption that the staff size is proportional to the number of problems (or amount of detail) ready to be implemented. This is the difference between what has been specified (the elaboration function) and what is left to do (the work gap). Hence, we will use the term *elaboration function* in place of learning function from now on, except when the context calls for traditional Rayleigh curve terminology. See Section 6.6.3 for further relevance of this terminology.

Figure 6.41 shows the output staffing profile for different values of *a*. It is seen that the manpower buildup parameter *a* greatly affects the personnel loading curve. The larger the value of *a*, the earlier the peak time and the steeper the corresponding profile. For these reasons, *a* is also called the manpower buildup parameter (MBP). A large MPB denotes a responsive, nimble organization. The qualitative effects of the MBP are shown in Table 6.11.

It has been observed that the staffing buildup rate is largely invariant within a particular organization due to a variety of factors. Some organizations are much more responsive and nimble to changes than others. Design instability is the primary cause for a slow buildup. Top architects and senior designers must be available to produce a stable design. Hiring delays and the inability to release top people from other projects will constrain the buildup to a large extent. If there is concurrent hardware design in a system, instability and volatility of the hardware will limit the software design ready for programming solutions.

The Rayleigh curve is best suited to certain types of development projects like unprecedented systems. The Rayleigh curve can be calibrated to static cost models and

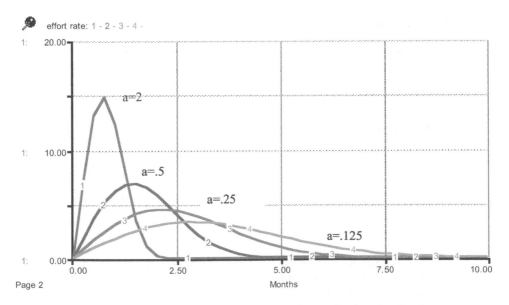

Figure 6.41. Rayleigh manpower model output for varying learning functions.

Table 6.11. Effects of manpower buildup parameter

Manpower Buildup Parameter	Effort Effect	Schedule Effect	Defect Effect
Low (slow staff buildup)	Lower $\downarrow$	Higher $\uparrow$	Lower $\downarrow$
Medium (moderate staff buildup)			
High (aggressive staff buildup)	Higher	Lower	Higher

used to derive dynamic staffing profiles. See Chapter 5 in [Boehm 1981] for examples or the model file *Rayleigh calibrated to COCOMO.itm* for an example.

6.6.1.2 Rayleigh Curve Versus Flat Staffing

In contrast to a Rayleigh curve buildup, a level-of-effort staffing may be possible for well-known and precedented problems that are ready for solution. An example would be a relatively simple porting between platforms of a software package with experienced developers. Since the problem has been solved by the people before, the task can be performed by an initial large staff. The project can be planned with a nearly linear trade-off between schedule and number of personnel (i.e., with a constant staff level, the porting will take about twice as long with one-half of the staff). Another example is an in-house organic project—many people can start the project compared to the slower Rayleigh buildup.

A high-peaked buildup curve and a constant level-of-effort staffing represent different types of software project staffing. Most software development falls in between the two behaviors. These two representative behaviors will be used as prototypical examples later when analyzing staffing curves.

6.6.1.3 Defect Modeling

The Rayleigh curve is also popular for modeling defect introductions and removals, as discussed in Chapter 5. Intuitively, the defect introduction curve should be very similar to the staffing curve, since the number of defects is expected to be proportional to the number of people working or the amount of work being produced.

6.6.1.4 Rayleigh Curve Enhancements

6.6.1.4.1 INCREMENTAL DEVELOPMENT. Some modeling approaches use a superposition of Rayleigh curves to represent parallel activities or phases. Figure 6.42 shows the output of an enhanced Rayleigh curve model for incremental development. Three increments are modeled with specified starting offsets, and the overall staffing shown is a superposition of the three increments. See the model file *rayleigh incremental.itm*.

6.6.1.4.2 DYNAMIC REQUIREMENTS CHANGES. Rather than assuming requirements specifications are fixed in the project beginning, it is more realistic to model changed requirements during the midst of a project. A simple model is provided that allows on-the-fly adjustments to the project size while the simulation is running.

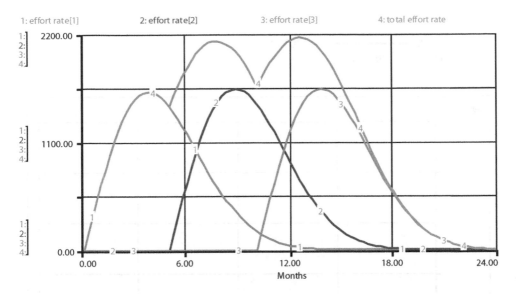

Figure 6.42. Rayleigh curves for incremental development.

The augmentation of the previous model in Figure 6.43 shows how the personnel rate is changed in response to additional requirements reflected in the project size. This mimics the effect of breakage or increased requirements. The slider is an interactive control that the user can adjust during a simulation run (purposely slowed to a human-controllable pace) to see the corresponding change in effort rate. Note that this represents an instantaneous decision regarding perceived additional effort. Only some projects can actually respond this quickly; thus, the modeler must be aware of these real-world constraints and account for them. Models can respond instantaneously, but actual processes may not. Metrics trends are more often analyzed at monthly intervals rather than every *dt* per the simulation, so there may delays in getting additional staff.

6.6.2 Example: Process Concurrence Modeling

Process concurrence is the degree to which work becomes available based on work already accomplished, and can be used to derive staffing profiles. It describes interdependency constraints between tasks, both within and between project phases. Concurrence relationships are crucial to understanding process dynamics. Internal process concurrence refers to available work constraints within a phase, whereas external process concurrence is used to describe available work constraints between development phases. A good treatment of process concurrence for general industry can be found in [Ford, Sterman 1997], and this book interprets and extends the concepts for software engineering.

The availability of work described by process concurrence is a very important constraint on progress. Otherwise, a model driven solely by resources and productivity

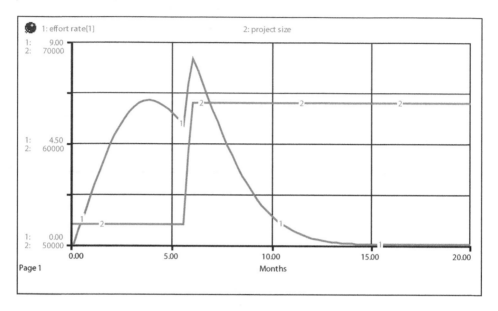

Figure 6.43. Interactive Rayleigh curve for requirements added midstream.

will allow a project to complete in almost zero time with infinite resources. Such is not the case with software processes in which tasks are highly interdependent, since some tasks must be sequential and cannot be done in parallel.

Process concurrence relationships describe how much work becomes available for completion based on previous work accomplished. These realistic bottlenecks on work availability should be considered during project planning and execution. There is a limit to the amount of concurrent development due to interdependencies in software processes. Concurrence relations can be sequential, parallel, partially concurrent, or other dependent relationships. Concurrence relationships can be elicited from process participants. A protocol for the elicitation is described in [Ford, Sterman 1998].

The definition of "task" in this context is an atomic unit of work that flows through a project, where the units may differ among project phases. This is the same treatment of tasks used in the Abdel-Hamid model and many others. Tasks are assumed to be interchangeable and uniform in size (e.g., the Abdel-Hamid task was equivalent to 60 lines of software). A task, therefore, refers to product specification during project definition, and lines of code during code implementation. The assumption becomes more valid as the size of the task decreases.

6.6.2.1 Trying to Accelerate Software Development

It is instructive to understand some of the phenomena that impede software processes. Putnam likens the acceleration of software development to pouring water into a channel-restricted funnel [Putnam 1980]. The funnel does not allow the flow to be sped up very much, no matter how much one pours into the funnel. This is like throwing a lot of software personnel at once into the development chute to accelerate things. They will not be able to work independently in parallel, since certain tasks can only be done in sequence. Figure 6.44 shows the limited parallelism of software tasks using a funnel analogy alongside the corresponding system dynamics structure.

There are always sequential constraints independent of phase. The elemental activities in any phase of software development include:

- Analysis and requirements specification; figuring out what you are supposed to do and specifying how the parts fit together
- Development of some artifact type (architecture, design, code, test plan, etc.) that implements the specifications
- Assessment of what was developed; this may include verification, validation, review, or debugging
- Possible rework or recycle of previous activities

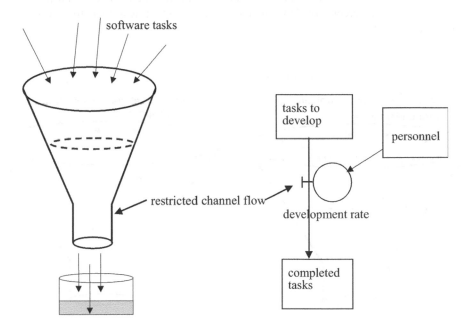

Figure 6.44. Funnel view of limited task parallelism and system dynamics corollary (partially adapted from [Putnam 80]).

These activities cannot be done totally in parallel with more applied people. Different people can perform the different activities with limited parallelism, but downstream activities will always have to follow some of the upstream ones.

The parallel constriction concept is further elaborated in Figure 6.45, which shows the constriction brought about by trying to parallelize sequential (or at least partially sequential) activities for a single thread of software. Tasks can only flow through in proper order.

In *The Mythical Man-Month* [Brooks 1975, 1995], Brooks explains these restrictions from a partitioning perspective in his Brooks's Law framework. Sequential constraints imply that tasks cannot be partitioned among different personnel resources. Thus, applying more people has no effect on schedule. Men and months are interchangeable only when tasks can be partitioned with no communication among them. Process concurrence is a natural vehicle for modeling these software process constraints.

6.6.2.2 *Internal Process Concurrence*

An internal process concurrence relationship shows how much work can be done based on the percent of work already done. The relationships represent the degree of sequentiality or concurrence of the tasks aggregated within a phase. They may include changes in the degree of concurrence as work progresses. Figure 6.46 and Figure 6.47 demonstrate linear and nonlinear internal process concurrence. The bottom right half under the diagonal of the internal process concurrence is an infeasible region, since the percent available to complete cannot be less than the amount already completed.

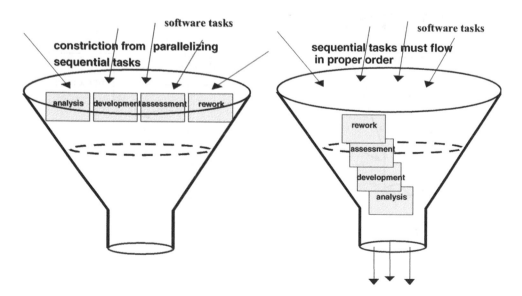

Figure 6.45. Trying to parallelize sequential tasks in the funnel.

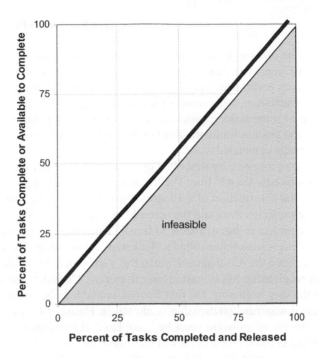

Figure 6.46. Linear internal process concurrence.

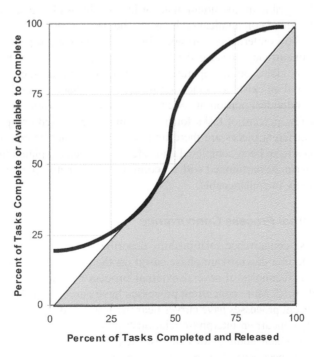

Figure 6.47. Nonlinear internal process concurrence.

The development of a single software task within a phase normally includes the sequences of construction, verification/validation, and, sometimes, rework. These cannot all be simultaneously performed in an individual task. There will always be an average duration of the subactivities, regardless of the resources applied to them. Additionally, the development of some tasks requires the completion of other intraphase tasks beforehand. Thus, the process limits the availability of work to be completed based on the amount of already completed work.

More concurrent processes are described by curves near the left axis, and less concurrent processes lie near the 45° line. The linear relationship in Figure 6.46 could describe the sequential construction of a 10 story building. When the first floor is complete, 10% of the project is done and the second floor is available to be completed, or 20% of the entire project is thus available to finish. This pattern continues until all the floors are done. This is sometimes called a "lockstep" relationship. The linear concurrence line starts above the 45° diagonal, since the y-axis includes work "available to complete." The relationship has to start greater than zero. Consider again a skyscraper being built. At the very beginning, the first floor is available to be completed.

A more typical nonlinear relationship is shown in Figure 6.47. For example, the overarching segments of software must be completed before other parts can begin. Only the important portions (such as 20% of the whole for an architecture skeleton, interface definitions, common data, etc.) can be worked on in the beginning. The other parts are not available for completion until afterward. This typifies complex software development tasks in which many tasks are dependent on each other. Men and months are not interchangeable in this situation according to Brooks because the tasks cannot be partitioned without communication between them.

Figure 6.48 shows internal concurrency for an extreme case of parallel work. There is very high concurrency because the tasks are independent of each other. Almost everything can be doled out as separate tasks in the beginning, such as a straightforward translation of an existing application from one language to another. Each person simply gets an individual portion of code to convert, and that work can be done in parallel. The last few percent of tasks for integrating all translated components have to wait until the different pieces are there first, so 100% cannot be completed until the translated pieces have been completed and released. Brooks explains that many tasks in this situation can be partitioned with no communication between them, and men and months are largely interchangeable.

6.6.2.3 External Process Concurrence

External process concurrence relationships describe constraints on amount of work that can be done in a downstream phase based on the percent of work released by an upstream phase. Examples of several external process concurrence relationships are shown in Table 6.12. More concurrent processes have curves near the upper-left axes, and less concurrent processes have curves near the lower and right axes.

The partially concurrent interphase relationship is representative of much software development in which complexities impose task dependencies and, thus, intertask communication is necessary. For example, a critical mass of core requirements must

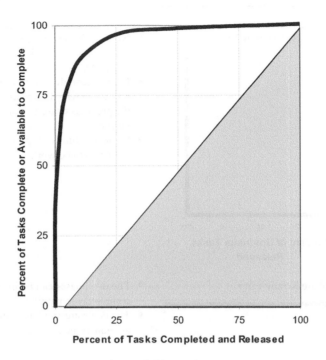

Figure 6.48. Nearly parallel internal process concurrence.

Table 6.12. External process concurrence relationships

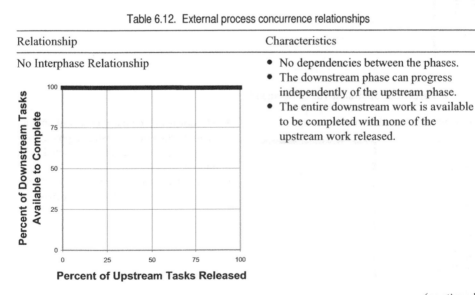

Relationship	Characteristics
No Interphase Relationship	• No dependencies between the phases. • The downstream phase can progress independently of the upstream phase. • The entire downstream work is available to be completed with none of the upstream work released.

(*continued*)

Table 6.12. *Continued*

Relationship	Characteristics
Sequential Interphase Relationship 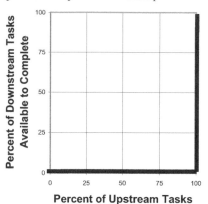	• None of the downstream phase can occur until the upstream phase is totally complete. • Like a theoretical waterfall development process in which no phase can start until the previous phase is completed and verified. • Same as a finish–stop relationship in a critical path network.
Parallel Interphase Relationship 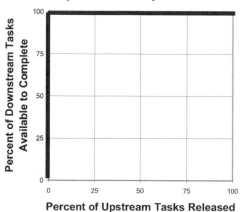	• The two phases can be implemented completely in parallel. • The downstream phase can be completed as soon as the upstream phase is started.
Delayed Start Interphase Relationship 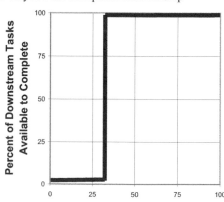	• The downstream phase must wait until a major portion of the upstream phase is completed, then it can be completed in its entirety. • Like a start–start relationship in a critical path network with a delay between the start times.

Table 6.12. *Continued*

Relationship	Characteristics
Lockstep Relationship 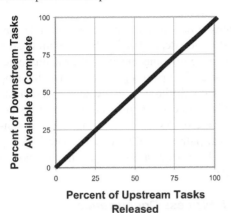	• The downstream phase can progress at the same speed as the upstream phase; thus, they are in lockstep with each other. • The downstream work availability is correlated linearly 1:1 to how much is released from upstream. For example, after 10% of system design is completed, then 10% of implementation tasks is available to finish. • This relationship is not available in PERT/CPM.
Delay with Partially Concurrent Interphase Relationship 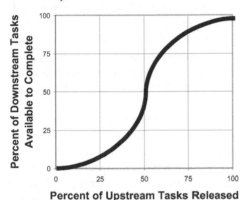	• The downstream phase has to wait until a certain percentage of upstream tasks have been released, and then can proceed at varying degrees of concurrence per the graph. • This relationship is representative of complex software development with task interdepencies. • This type of relationship is not available with PERT/CPM methods.
Leveraged Concurrence Relationship 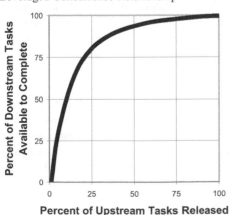	• This relationship exhibits a high degree of parallelism and leverage between phases. • Typical of Commercial Off-the-Shelf (COTS) products whereby one specifies the capabilities, and the system is quickly configured and instantiated. Also applicable for fourth-generation language (4GL) approaches.

be released before architecture and design can start. Then the downstream phase availability rate increases in the middle region (e.g., much design work can take place), and then slows down as the final upstream tasks are released.

External process concurrence relationships function like the precedence relationships in critical path and PERT methods to describe dependencies, but contain greater dynamic detail. For example, external concurrence relationships describe the phase dependencies for the entire durations. PERT and critical path methods only use the stop and start dates. They can also be nonlinear to show differences in the degree of concurrence, whereas PERT methods cannot. Lastly, process concurrence relationships are dynamic since the work completed could increase or decrease over time, but only static precedence relationships are used in critical path or PERT methods. The lockstep and delay of partially concurrent interphase relationships are situations that cannot be described with PERT or critical path methods.

6.6.2.4 *Phase Leverage Analysis with Process Concurrence*

The leverage in software development that we will examine refers to how much can be elaborated based on inputs from the previous phase. For example, a 4GL approach that generates code from requirement statements has much higher leverage than new code development. For about the same amount of effort expended on requirements, a great deal more demonstrative software will be produced with advanced 4GL tools compared to starting from scratch in each phase. Virtually all modern approaches to software development are some attempt to increase leverage, so that machines or humans can efficiently instantiate software artifacts compared to more labor-intensive approaches.

COTS is another good example of high phase leverage, because functionality is easily created after identifying the COTS package. If one specifies "use the existing XYZ package for library operations," then the functions of online searching, checkout, and so on are already defined and easily implemented after configuring the package locally.

Process concurrence is a very useful means of contrasting the leverage of different approaches, because the degree of concurrence is a function of the software methodology (among other things). When developing or interpreting external process concurrence curves for software development strategies, it is helpful to think of tasks in terms of demonstrable functionality. Thus, tasks released or available to complete can be considered analogous to function points in their phase-native form (e.g., design or code). With this in mind, it is easier to compare different strategies in terms of leverage in bringing functionality to bear.

6.6.2.4.1 RAD EXAMPLE OF EXTERNAL PROCESS CONCURRENCE. Increasing task parallelism is a primary opportunity to decrease cycle time in RAD. Process concurrence is ideally suited for evaluating RAD strategies in terms of work parallelism constraints between and within phases. System dynamics is very attractive for analyzing schedule time in this context compared to other methods because it can model task interdependencies on the critical path. Only those tasks on the critical path have influence on the overall schedule.

One way to achieve RAD is by having base software architectures tuned to application domains available for instantiation, standard database connectors, and reuse. This example demonstrates how the strategy of having predefined and configurable architectures for a problem domain can increase the chance for concurrent development between inception and elaboration.

6.6.2.4.1.1 Developing from Scratch. Suppose the software job is to develop a human resources (HR) self-service portal. It is to be a Web-based system for employees in a large organization to access and update all their personnel and benefits information. It will have to tie into existing legacy databases and commercial software packages for different portions of the human resources records. The final system will consist of the following:

- 30% user interface (UI) front end
- 30% architecture and core processing logic
- 40% database (DB) wrappers and vendor package interface logic (back-end processing)

Table 6.13 describes an example concurrence relationship between inception and elaboration for this system, where inception is defining the system capabilities and elaboration is designing it for eventual construction. The overall percent of tasks ready to elaborate is a weighted average. There is no base architecture from which to start from. Figure 6.49 shows a plot of the resulting external concurrence relationship from this worksheet.

6.6.2.4.1.2 Developing With a Base Architecture. Contrast the previous example with another situation in which there exists a base architecture that has already been tuned for the human resources application domain of processes and employee service workflows. It uses XML technology that ties to existing database formats and is ready for early elaboration by configuring the architecture. It already has standard connectors for different vendor database packages.

Figure 6.50 shows the corresponding process concurrence against the first example in which an architecture had yet to be developed. This relationship enables more parallelism between the inception and elaboration phases, and, thus, the possibility of reduced cycle time. When about 60% of inception tasks are released, this approach allows 50% more elaboration tasks to be completed compared to the development from scratch.

6.6.2.4.2 SYSTEMS ENGINEERING STAFFING CONSIDERATIONS TO MINIMIZE SCHEDULE. Staffing profiles are often dictated by the staff available, but careful consideration of the people dedicated to particular activities can have a major impact on overall schedule when there are no constraints. Consider the problem early in a project when developers might be "spinning their wheels" and wasting time while the requirements are being derived for them. Traditionally, the requirements come from someone with a systems engineering focus (though it is generally best when other disciplines also par-

Table 6.13. Concurrence worksheet for developing HR portal from scratch

| Inception (System Definition) | Elaboration (System Design) | | |
| | % of Inception Tasks Released | % of Components Ready to Elaborate | Overall % of Tasks Ready to Elaborate |
Requirements Released			
About 25% of the core functionality for the self-service interface supported by prototype. Only general database interface goals defined.	30%	20% UI 10% core 5% DB	11%
About half of the basic functionality for the self-service interface supported by prototype.	55%	40% UI 20% core 20% DB	26%
Interface specifications to commercial package defined for internal personnel information.	60%	40% UI 30% core 40% DB	37%
More functionality for benefits capabilities defined (80% of total front end).	75%	75% UI 60% core 40% DB	57%
Interface specification to commercial systems for life insurance and retirement information.	85%	75% UI 80% core 80% DB	79%
Rest of user interface defined (95% of total), except for final UI refinements after more prototype testing.	95%	95% UI 95% core 80% DB	89%
Time card interface to accounting package defined.	98%	95% UI 95% core 100% DB	97%
Last of UI refinements released.	100%	100% UI 100% core 100% DB	100%

ticipate). If those people are not producing requirements at a rate fast enough for other people to start elaborating on, then effort is wasted. The staffing plan should account for this early lack of elaboration, so that implementers are phased in at just the right times when tasks become available to complete.

Knowledge of process concurrence for a given project can be used to carefully optimize the project this way. The right requirements analysts (normally a small number) have to be in place producing specifications before substantially more programmers come in to implement the specifications. This optimizing choreography requires fine coordination to have the right people available at the right time.

To optimize schedule on a complex project with partial interphase concurrency, the optimal systems engineering staffing is front-loaded as opposed to constant level of ef-

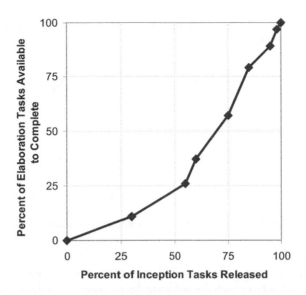

Figure 6.49. External process concurrence for HR system from scratch.

fort. As shown with process concurrence, the downstream development is constrained by the specifications available. Figure 6.51 shows two situations of awareness to achieve rapid application development (RAD) when there is partial interphase concurrency. The cases show what happens with (1) a constant staff size and (2) a peaked staffing profile for requirements generation. In the first case, there is a nonoptimal con-

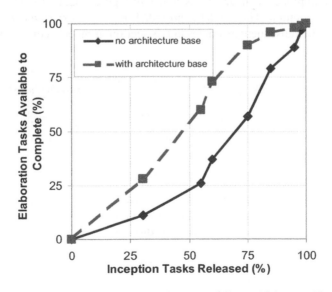

Figure 6.50. External process concurrence comparison with base architecture.

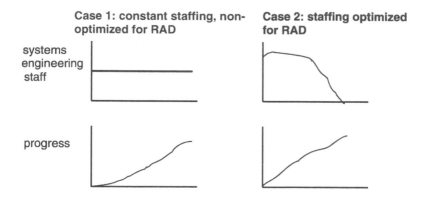

Figure 6.51.   Concurrence awareness for systems engineering staffing to achieve RAD.

stant staff level for systems engineering and overall progress is impeded. If a curvilinear shape is used instead to match the software development resources, then cycle-time gains are possible because programming can complete faster.

The figure denotes systems engineering staff, but the staff may be anyone specifying requirements with other titles (they may also be software engineers themselves). See the chapter exercise for testing the hypothesis in this section that to optimize schedule on a complex project with partial interphase concurrency, the optimal systems engineering staffing is front-loaded as opposed to constant level of effort.

6.6.2.4.3   EXTERNAL CONCURRENCE MODEL AND EXPERIMENTATION. A simple model of external process concurrence is shown in Figure 6.52, representing task specification and elaboration. This model is provided in the file *external.concurrence.itm* and is used for the subsequent examples in this section. It models concurrence dynam-

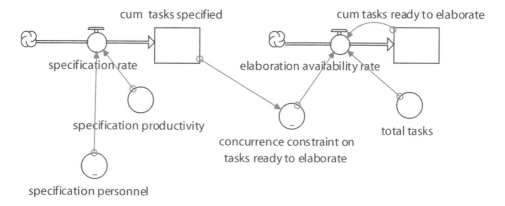

Figure 6.52.   External concurrence model.

ics in the elaboration phase of a typical project, and will be used to experimentally derive staffing profiles for different combinations of specification inputs and concurrence types. Table 6.14 is a high-level summary of the model.

The specification personnel parameter is a forcing function to the model, and is a graphical staffing profile that can take on various shapes. The specification input profile mimics how requirements are brought dynamically into a project. The concurrence constraint is also a graphical function drawn to represent different process concurrence relationships to be studied.

The time profile of tasks ready to elaborate will be considered proportional to an "ideal" staffing curve. This follows from an important assumption used in the Rayleigh curve that an optimal staffing is proportional to the number of problems ready for solution. It is very important to note that this model only considers the product view. The real-world process of finding and bringing people on board may not be able to keep up with the hypothetical optimal curve. Thus, the personnel perspective may trump the product one. Much experience in the field points out that a highly peaked Rayleigh curve is often too aggressive to staff to.

The model is used to experimentally derive optimal elaboration staffing profiles (from a product perspective) for different types of projects. We will explore various combinations of specification profiles and concurrence between specification and elaboration to see their effect. The staffing inputs include (1) flat staffing, (2) a peaked Rayleigh-like staffing, and (3) a COTS requirements pulse at the beginning followed by a smaller Rayleigh curve to mimic a combined COTS and new development. In addition, we will vary the concurrence types as such: (1) linear lockstep concurrence, (2) a slow design buildup between phases, (3) leveraged instantiation to model COTS, and (4) S-shaped concurrence that models a wide swath of development. COTS is a pulse-like input because the requirements are nearly instantly defined by its existing capabilities.

Table 6.15 shows outputs of the external concurrence model for a variety of situations. It is clear that optimal staffing profiles can be far different from a standard Rayleigh curve, though some of the combinations describe projects that can be modeled with a Rayleigh curve.

To further use these results for planning a real project, the ideal staffing curves have be modulated by relative effort. That is, implementing COTS or reused components generally require much less effort than new development. If a reused component takes

Table 6.14. External process concurrence model overview

Purpose: Planning, Process Improvement			
Scope: Portion of Lifecycle			
Inputs and Parameters	Levels	Major Relationships	Outputs
• Specification personnel • Specification productivity • Total tasks • Concurrence constraint relationship	• Cumulative tasks specified • Cumulative tasks ready to elaborate	• Elaboration availability rate	• Tasks ready to elaborate

438

Table 6.15. Elaboration availability simulation results

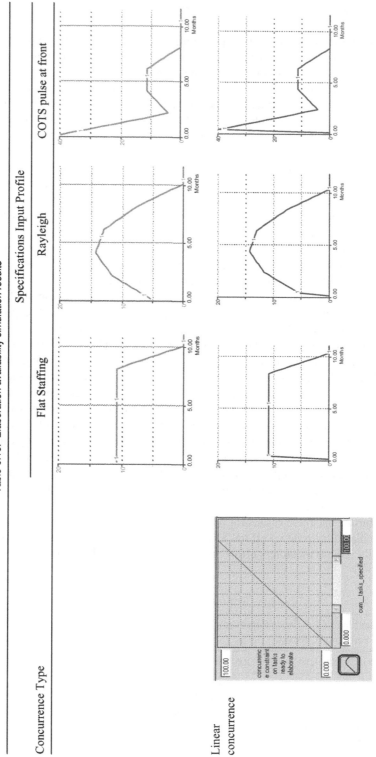

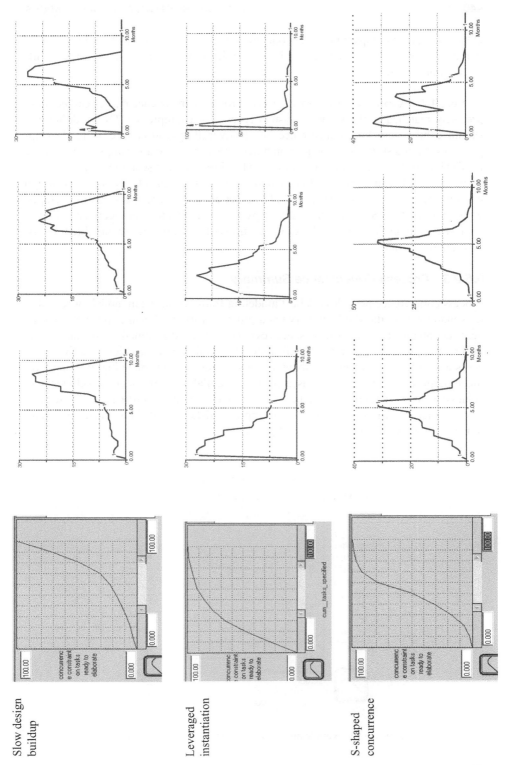

Slow design
buildup

Leveraged
instantiation

S-shaped
concurrence

439

20% of the effort compared to a new one, then the required staffing should be similarly reduced. So the staffing curves need further adjustments for the relative effort of different approaches.

6.6.2.4.4　ADDITIONAL CONSIDERATIONS. Process concurrence curves can be more precisely matched to the software system types. For example, COTS, by definition, should exhibit very high concurrence but an overall system can be a blend of approaches. Mixed strategies produce combined concurrence relationships. Concurrence for COTS first then new development would be similar to that seen in Figure 6.53. The curve starts out with a leveraged instantiation shape, then transitions to a slow design buildup. This type of concurrence would be better matched to the system developed with an initial COTS pulse followed by new software development, corresponding to the last column in Table 6.15. Many permutations of concurrence are possible for various actual situations.

6.6.2.5 Process Concurrence Summary

Process concurrence provides a robust modeling framework. It can model more realistic situations than the Rayleigh curve and produce varying dynamic profiles (see the next section on integrating the perspectives). It can be used as a method to characterize different approaches in terms of their ability to parallelize or accelerate activities. It gives a detailed view of project dynamics and is relevant for planning and improvement purposes. It can be used as a means to collaborate between stakeholders to achieve a shared planning vision as well as to derive optimal staffing profiles for different project situations. However, more empirical data is needed on concurrence relationships from the field for a variety of projects.

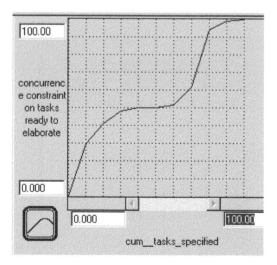

Figure 6.53. Sample process concurrence for mixed strategies.

6.6.3 Integrating Rayleigh Curves, Process Concurrence, and Brooks's Interpretations

There are connections between process concurrence and Rayleigh-curve modeling that are useful for understanding the dynamics and collectively provide a more robust framework for modeling processes. In fact, process concurrence can be used to show when and why the Rayleigh curve does not apply. Process concurrence provides a way to model the constraints on making work available in and between phases. The work available to perform is the same dynamic that drives the Rayleigh curve, since the staff level is proportional to the problems (or specifications) currently available to implement. S-curves result for expended effort over time (the accumulation of the staffing curve) or cumulative progress when a Rayleigh staffing shape applies.

However the Rayleigh curve was based on the initial study of hardware research and development projects that most resemble a traditional waterfall life cycle for unprecedented software systems. Now there are a great variety of situations that it does not match so well. Rayleigh staffing assumptions do not hold well for COTS, reuse, architecture-first design patterns, fourth-generation languages, or staff-constrained situations.

The underlying assumption that an "ideal" staffing curve is proportional to the number of problems ready for solution (from a product perspective only) still seems prudent. With modern methods, the dynamic profile of problems ready for solution can have far different shapes than was observed when the Rayleigh curve was first applied to software. Experimentation with the external concurrence model in Section 6.6.2.4.3 showed examples of this.

Iterative processes with frequent cycles or incremental development projects generally have flatter staffing profiles. Some would argue the flat profiles are the superposition of many sub-Rayleigh curves but, nevertheless, the initial assumptions were based on sequential, one-pass projects.

Other situations in which the Rayleigh curve does not apply too well are highly precedented systems for which early parallel work can take place and the project ends with a relatively flat profile, such as a heavy reuse or simple translation project, or any situation in which a gradual buildup is not necessary. Process concurrence can produce any number of dynamic profiles, and can thus be used to model more situations than the Rayleigh curve.

Schedule-driven projects which implement timeboxing are another example of projects that can have more uniform staffing distributions. These projects are sometimes called Schedule As the Independent Variable (SAIV) projects since cost and quality float relative to the fixed schedule. On such projects, there is no staff tapering at the end, because the schedule goal is attained by keeping everyone busy until the very end. Thus, the staffing level remains nearly constant.

We now have alternative methods of modeling the staffing curve. A standard Rayleigh formula can be used or process concurrence can replace the elaboration function in it. The first term in the Rayleigh equation that we call the elaboration function, $p(t)$, represents the cumulative specifications available to be implemented. The cumulative level of specifications available is the output of a process concurrence relationship that operates over time. Thus, we can substitute a process concurrence relationship in place of the elaboration function, and it will be a more general model for software processes since the Rayleigh curve does not adequately model all development classes. Process concurrence provides a more detailed view of the dynamics and is meaningful for planning and improvement purposes.

Recall the Rayleigh staffing profile results from the multiplication over time of the elaboration function and the remaining work left. The elaboration function increases and the remaining work gap decreases as work is performed. Figure 6.54 shows the idealized Rayleigh staffing components and the process concurrence analogy for the product elaboration function. Internal and external concurrence relationships that can replace the Rayleigh formula for this are in Figure 6.55.

Table 6.16 summarizes the process dynamics of tasks and personnel on prototypical projects per different modeling viewpoints that have been presented. The Rayleigh manpower buildup parameter a depends on the organizational environment and project type, so the relative differences in the table only address the effect of project type on staff buildup limits. A more precise assessment of the buildup parameter for a specific situation would take more into account.

6.7   EARNED VALUE

Earned value is a useful approach for tracking performance against plans and controlling a project. It provides important management indicators but does not have dynamics intrinsic to itself. This section, therefore, focuses on using an earned value simulation model for training and learning. Earned value helps you become a "real-time process controller" by tracking and reacting to the project trends. Monitoring cost and schedule performance against plans helps spot potential schedule slippages and cost overruns early in order to minimize their impact. Earned value refers to the monetary value of work accomplished, where the value of a given task is defined by a

Rayleigh staffing profile ≈ problems ready for solution

| Time | = | Time | · | Time |
| problems ready for solution | | product elaboration | | remaining work gap |

product elaboration ≈ tasks complete or available to complete (from process concurrence)

Figure 6.54. Rayleigh curve components and process concurrence analogy.

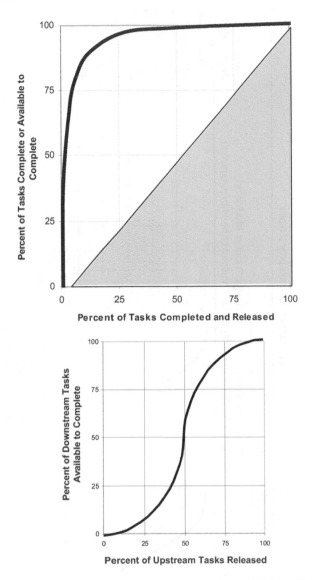

Figure 6.55. Process concurrence replacement for Rayleigh profile.

cost/schedule budget baseline. Earned value can also be implemented using straight labor hours rather than costs.

All work is planned, budgeted, and scheduled in time-phased increments constituting a cost and schedule measurement baseline. Value is earned after completion of budgeted milestones as work proceeds. Objective milestones consist of directly observable steps or events in the software process, and earned value is, therefore, a measure of progress against plan.

Table 6.16. Task and effort dynamics summary for major project types

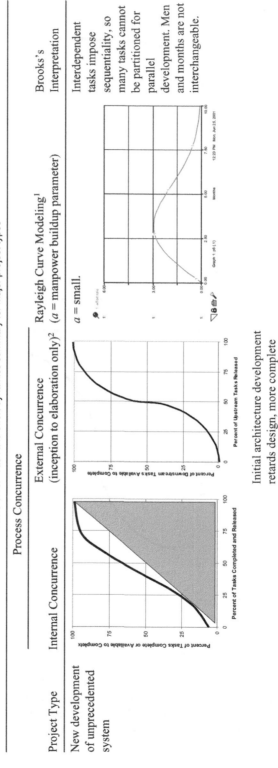

Project Type	Process Concurrency		Rayleigh Curve Modeling[1] (a = manpower buildup parameter)	Brooks's Interpretation
	Internal Concurrence	External Concurrence (inception to elaboration only)[2]		
New development of unprecedented system		Initial architecture development retards design, more complete definition enables parallel development, then last pieces cause slowdown.	a = small.	Interdependent tasks impose sequentiality, so many tasks cannot be partitioned for parallel development. Men and months are not interchangeable.

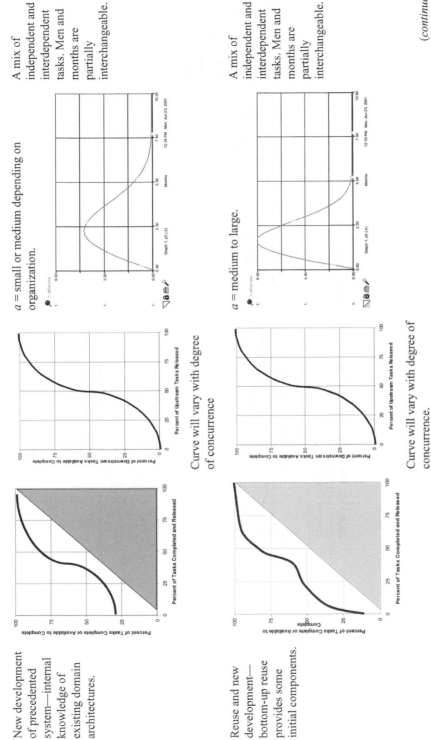

A mix of independent and interdependent tasks. Men and months are partially interchangeable.

a = small or medium depending on organization.

New development of precedented system—internal knowledge of existing domain architectures.

Curve will vary with degree of concurrence

A mix of independent and interdependent tasks. Men and months are partially interchangeable.

a = medium to large.

Reuse and new development— bottom-up reuse provides some initial components.

Curve will vary with degree of concurrence.

(continued)

Table 6.16. Task and effort dynamics summary for major project types (continued)

Project Type	Process Concurrence		Rayleigh Curve Modeling[1] (a = manpower buildup parameter)	Brooks's Interpretation
	Internal Concurrence	External Concurrence (inception to elaboration only)[2]		
COTS-based—most requirements predefined by COTS capabilities; some glue code development necessary.		Leveraged process instantiates software from defined COTS capabilities.	a = large—not a good fit for steady-state portions of rectangular staffing (but models extreme ramping up/down portions).	A mix of independent and interdependent tasks. Men and months are partially interchangeable.

Translation of existing application— pieces can proceed in parallel until final integration testing.

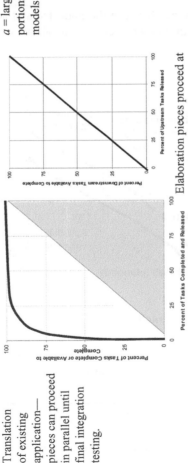

Elaboration pieces proceed at same rate as inception.

a = large—not a good fit for steady-state portions of rectangular staffing (but models extreme ramping up/down portions).

Tasks can mostly be partitioned with no communication between them. Men and months are largely interchangeable

[1]The generalized buildup patterns shown assume that all else is held constant between these examples except for the project type. Different organizations will exhibit different buildup patterns if they have to staff the same given projects. Some organizations will always be more nimble for quick staff buildup due to their internal characteristics.
[2]There is often self-similarity observed in the different phases. In many instances, the concurrence between elaboration and construction will be similar.

Cost expenditures and progress are tracked against previously defined work packages. Performance is measured by comparing three earned value quantities:

1. Budgeted cost of work performed (BCWP)
2. Actual cost of work performed (ACWP)
3. Budgeted cost of work scheduled (BCWS)

These quantities and other earned value parameters are displayed in Figure 6.56.

BCWP is the measure of earned value for work accomplished against the overall baseline plan. The accomplishment is stated in terms of the budget that was planned for it. BCWP is compared to ACWP to determine the cost performance (i.e., is the actual cost greater or less then the budgeted cost?). BCWS is the planned cost multiplied by the percentage of completion that should have been achieved according to the project baseline dates. Figure 6.56 shows these earned value quantities for an underperforming project with calculated variances and final projections based on extrapolating the actuals to date.

The cost variance is the difference between the budgeted and actual cost of work performed. Schedule variance quantifies whether tasks are ahead or behind of schedule

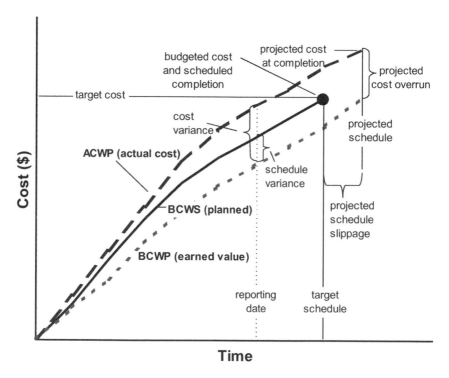

Figure 6.56. Earned value visualization.

at any point by taking the difference between the budgeted cost of work performed and the budgeted cost of work scheduled. These variance equations are:

$$\text{Cost variance} = \text{BCWP} - \text{ACWP}$$

$$\text{Schedule variance} = \text{BCWP} - \text{BCWS}$$

The variances are also visualized in Figure 6.56 with respect to BCWP, ACWP, and BCWS.

The cost performance index (CPI) represents cost efficiency against plan, or the ratio of budgeted cost for the work performed versus the actual cost of work performed for a specified time period. The schedule performance index (SPI) represents schedule efficiency against plan. Values greater than 1.0 represent performance better than planned, and less than 1.0 represent less efficient than planned. The performance indices are calculated as:

$$\text{CPI} = \text{BCWP}/\text{ACWP}$$

$$\text{SPI} = \text{BCWP}/\text{BCWS}$$

Earned value is highly recommended as an integral part of software project management. Trends should be evaluated often and remedial action taken quickly. Even if only 15% of progress has been completed and the budgets are being overrun, recovery is almost impossible. One should then focus on not getting worse, and adjust far-term projections based on current overruns.

An automated earned value system is particularly necessary to provide management visibility on large projects. In any case, a strong benefit to project understanding and organization is derived by thinking through project activities and assigning worth to them. More information on applying earned value concepts can be found in Reifer's software management tutorial [Reifer 2002].

However, there is an important caveat to standard earned value methodology. It may not be tracking the "real value" of a project. See Section 6.4 for more details of value-based software engineering and modeling examples for different stakeholder value functions.

6.7.1.1 General Project Procedures

Implementation of an earned value process can be scaled to fit projects of varied size and complexity. First establish a performance measurement baseline in monetary units such as dollars, or straight labor hours, to determine the budgeted cost of work scheduled for the life of the project. One should select the appropriate level of a work breakdown structure (WBS) for data gathering and appropriate means for determining earned value. This can range from a few top-level categories for which earned value is determined from percent completion estimates to projects for which earned value uses preplanned assignment of dollar values to completion of specific milestones or subtasks within tasks. For example, earned value can be determined by such methods as:

- Prorating value based on task percent completion
- Interim milestones with earned value linked to subtask completions, where a predetermined amount is accrued for each completed subtask
- Level of effort with no definable work product, whereby the budget is laid out as a function of time

BCWS is the planned performance measurement baseline. When the project schedule is expressed as budgeted dollars (or hours of work), BCWS can be determined at any point using work scheduled to have been accomplished under the baseline plan. For large projects, near-term work elements can be budgeted into work packages, whereas future tasks may have budget values allocated as future planning packages or as undistributed budget.

Project status should be evaluated relative to BCWS to assess earned value for completed tasks and those in progress. Determine earned value for work accomplished to date as BCWP. Summing earned value across the WBS determines BCWP. If the work is on schedule, the BCWS will be equal the BCWP (if the earned value accurately reflects performance). If the cost actuals are on target with the budget, the BCWP will be equal to the ACWP.

6.7.2   Example: Earned Value Model

The earned value model described here was developed and used in training venues, and is summarized in Table 6.17. It is a self-contained model that takes planned and actual values from the user. The best use of such as model would be to integrate it with a larger project model, such as Abdel-Hamid's, plugging in quantities for planned and actual progress (see the corresponding exercise at the end of the chapter).

The diagram for this model is shown in Figure 6.57, which implements the basic formulas for earned value using dynamic indicators. It has flow chains for product

Table 6.17. Earned value model overview

Purpose: Training, Control, and Operational Management
Scope: Development Project

Inputs and Parameters	Levels	Major Relationships	Outputs
• Planned productivity • Planned staffing profile • Actual productivity • Actual personnel • Budgeted cost per milestone • Labor rate	• Planned cumulative milestones • Actual cumulative milestones • Actual cost of work performed	• Performance indices	• Cost performance index • Schedule performance index • Budgeted cost of work performed • Actual cost of work performed • Budgeted cost of work scheduled

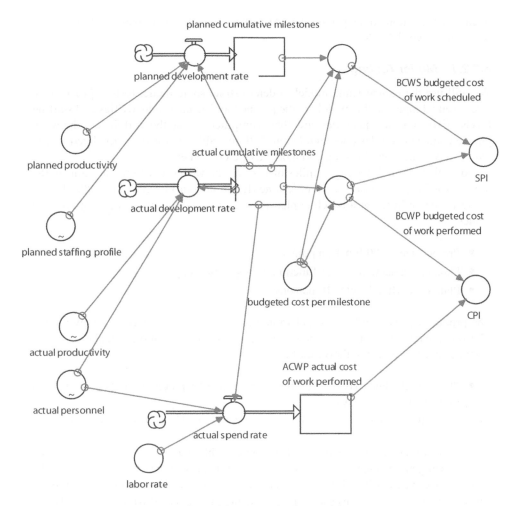

Figure 6.57. Earned value model.

tasks being developed—one for planned and one for actual. The user must input the planned number of people over time for the staffing profile, the planned productivity, and the budgeted cost per milestone.

Completed milestones are accumulated in the levels as a function of the development rates over time. The rates are determined with linear productivity formulas. The model also has a flow chain for actual money spent. For each time point in the simulation, the model compares actual progress to planned and computes the current earned value parameters, including SPI and CPI.

Task units are function points, since they apply across all project stages versus SLOC. Function points are also used as milestones in this case, and each function point is budgeted equally (an actual detailed plan could have unequally weighted milestones). The model is calibrated to a project plan for 100 function points to be developed at 0.1 function points/person-day. At $1000 for each person-day of labor, a function point is worth $10K.

6.7.2.1 Model Testing

We will use the earned value model to demonstrate some model testing procedures. The essential inputs to the model are the planned and actual productivities and staffing levels. Earned value quantities are then computed using the differences between planned and actual milestone completion. CPI and SPI are already normalized to 1.0, which makes the overall testing and model usage convenient.

To further simplify testing, a milestone is set equivalent to a function point in the model. The budgeted cost of each milestone (function point) is set to $10,000. Most of the tests shown here use a baseline plan for the project using the following nominal values:

- Project size = 100 function points
- Planned productivity = 0.1 function points/person-day
- Planned staffing level = 10 persons

The productivity is a middle-ground value that we used in the Brooks's Law model. The other parameters are also chosen to simplify the validation calculations. The planned schedule and cumulative cost are calculated as:

- Planned schedule (days) = 100 function points/(0.1 function points/person-days) · 10 persons = 100 days
- Planned cost (dollars) = 100 function points · $10,000/function point = $1 M

Four stages of testing are performed that progressively build confidence in the model by addressing more complex test cases. This is a typical sequence to take whereby the initial tests can be easily validated manually or with a spreadsheet, since rates remain constant. Once those test cases are passed, the model is assessed with increasingly dynamic conditions:

- Stage 1—use constants for all productivity and staffing levels
- Stage 2—use a mix of constants and time-varying inputs for actual productivity and staffing levels
- Stage 3—use time-varying inputs for actual productivity and staffing levels
- Stage 4—allow both planned and actual quantities to vary over time

Within each stage are subdivisions of test cases.

The testing is made convenient since all we have to change for the test cases are the productivity and staffing levels by drawing their time curves and/or typing in the numbers. See Figure 6.58 and Figure 6.59 for examples of specifying project actuals for a simulation run. These examples are intended to be realistic, whereby the productivity

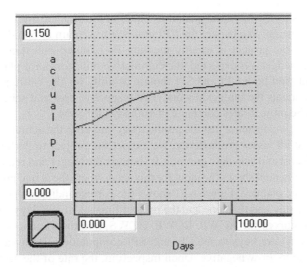

Figure 6.58. Example input for actual productivity (actual productivity vs. days).

shows a learning curve ramp and the staffing profile is tapered at the beginning and end.

The graphical productivity function can be replaced with another simulation model component, such as any of the other models in this book that calculate effective production rates. When using the earned value model in practice on a live project, the actual progress metrics should be substituted.

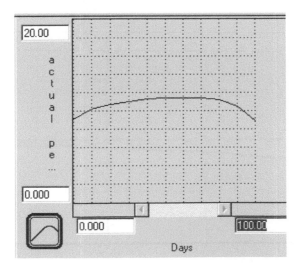

Figure 6.59. Example input for actual personnel (actual personnel vs. days).

The first test is to set the actual quantities equal to the planned ones, using constants for steady-state testing. We expect the CPI and SPI to remain at one during the entire simulation, since the project is exactly meeting its planned milestones on time and with the allotted budget. As expected, the cumulative milestones for planned and actual are equivalent, and both CPI and SPI remain at unity for the entire project because the actual work equals the budgeted work. The respective cost and schedule variances are both zero. The project does complete in 100 days for $1M.

In the next test, we decrease just the productivity and keep the actual personnel equal to the planned. With lesser productivity, we expect the project to perform worse than planned on both cost and schedule grounds. It should take longer and require more effort than planned. Figure 6.60 shows the input for this case, where the actual productivity never quite reaches the planned. Figure 6.61 shows the corresponding output. As expected, both CPI and SPI stay less than one and the project finishes in 108 days for $1.07 M.

The dynamic curves for ACWP, BCWP, BCWS, and the variances on the second chart in Figure 6.61 are keys to the CPI and SPI computation. Both variances start at zero and continue to grow negative. Upon inspection, the rate of the growing negative variances decreases as productivity starts to come close to the actual. The varying slopes of the variance curves can be studied to understand the progress dynamics and used to extrapolate where the project will end up.

To support further testing considering all ranges of values, a test matrix can be created that covers the different combinations of actual versus planned inequalities. The input conditions and expected outputs are shown in Table 6.18, where the inequalities are assumed to be for the entire project duration. This type of input/output matrix can help in model experimentation and validation.

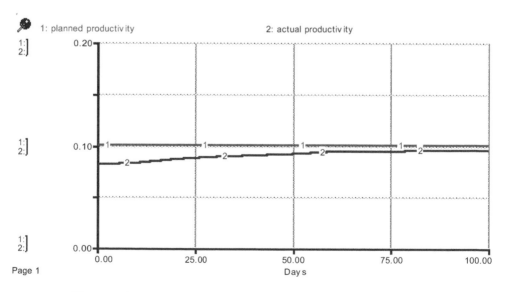

Figure 6.60. Test case inputs—actual productivity < planned productivity.

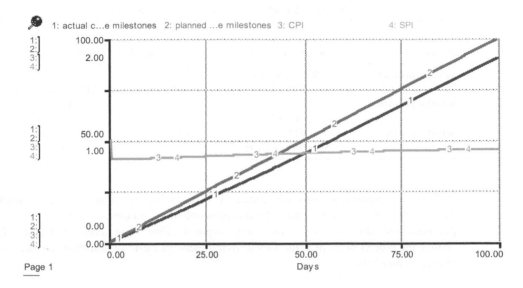

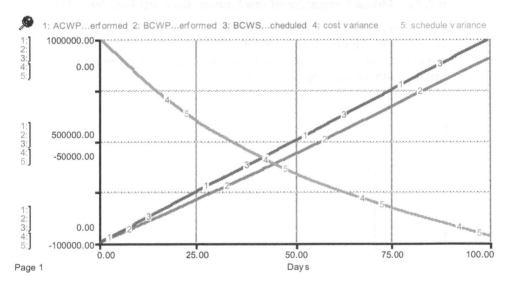

Figure 6.61. Test case results—actual productivity < planned productivity.

Figure 6.62 and Figure 6.63.show the progress and earned value outputs for the case of actual productivity being less than planned and actual personnel less than planned.

Based on the results of these first six tests, we have increased confidence that the model correctly calculates earned value dynamically. Subsequent testing with more variations to the planned quantities is left to the student (see the chapter exercises), and more applied examples follow later in this section.

Table 6.18. Earned value test matrix and expected results

Personnel	Productivity		
	actual > planned	actual = planned	actual < planned
actual > planned	CPI indeterminate	CPI > 1	CPI < 1
	SPI > 1	SPI > 1	SPI indeterminate
actual = planned	CPI > 1	CPI = 1	CPI < 1
	SPI > 1	SPI = 1	SPI < 1
actual < planned	CPI > 1	CPI < 1	CPI indeterminate
	SPI indeterminate	SPI < 1	SPI < 1

More interesting cases arise when the actual values fluctuate relative to the planned. The reader is encouraged to interact with the supplied model *earned value.itm* and experiment with different scenarios. Very minimal effort is required to graphically change the project plans or actuals by drawing them on a grid or, alternatively, keying in precise numbers.

6.7.2.2 Model Usage: Read the Slopes, Do Hard Problems First

To gain more insight into evaluating cost and schedule performance with CPI and SPI, we will play with the model to visualize the dynamic earned value trends. This is an example of using a model to further one's knowledge and management skills without making costly mistakes on an actual project.

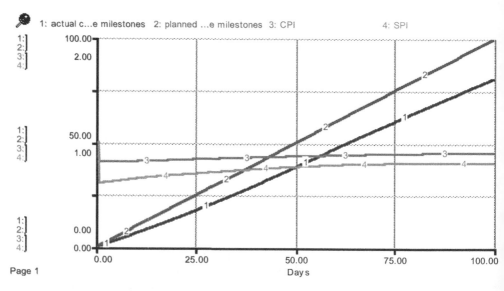

Figure 6.62. Actual productivity < planned productivity and actual personnel < planned personnel (1: actual cumulative milestones, 2: planned cumulative milestones, 3: CPI, 4: SPI).

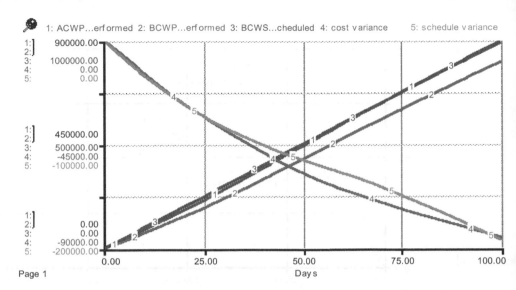

1: ACWP...erformed 2: BCWP...erformed 3: BCWS...cheduled 4: cost variance   5: schedule variance

Figure 6.63. Actual productivity < planned productivity and actual personnel < planned personnel (1: actual cost of work performed, 2: budgeted cost of work performed, 3: budgeted cost of work scheduled, 4: cost variance, 4: schedule variance).

We will demonstrate how to spot trends early in order to effect control. This is done by monitoring the *slope* of earned value trends as opposed to current static values only. A quick glance at early trends to assess task completion progress may be deceiving if the slopes (rates of change) are not considered.

For example, a project that starts out solving easy problems at a fast pace creates an illusion of early overall completion. But the slope of the progress line, also borne out in the dynamic CPI/SPI curves, clearly shows a worsening negative trend. The following case demonstrates this.

A partial simulation of two comparative projects stopped after about 25% completion is shown in Figure 6.64. The two projects are being simulated with the same planned progress. Assuming that the same trends continue, the question is, which project will finish first? Many people fail to consider the changing slopes of the initial progress trends, and erroneously choose which project will perform best.

The answer lies in the assessing the slopes of the actual progress lines, which are also reflected in the CPI and SPI curves. Figure 6.65 shows the final comparison between the progress trends, from which it is clear that project 2 finishes substantially sooner. The battery of trends for projects 1 and 2 are respectively shown in Figure 6.66 and Figure 6.67.

Figure 6.66 clearly shows that the rate of accomplishment continues to diminish for project 1; the slope of the actual progress line keeps decreasing. Likewise, the BCWP slope decreases. Accordingly, the CPI and SPI curves fall monotonically. But the slope of the actual progress line or BCWP for project #2 in Figure 6.67 keeps increasing, and

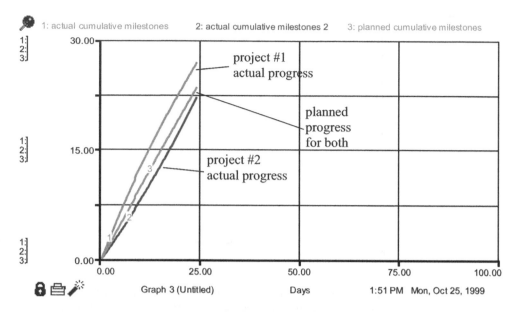

Figure 6.64. Early comparison of two projects.

the CPI and SPI measures continually improve to be greater than one. The lesson is to read, interpret, and extrapolate dynamic trends, rather than look only at static values for cost and schedule performance.

This example also demonstrates one of our primary recommendations: Do the hardest problems first (and mitigate the largest risks first). What drove this simula-

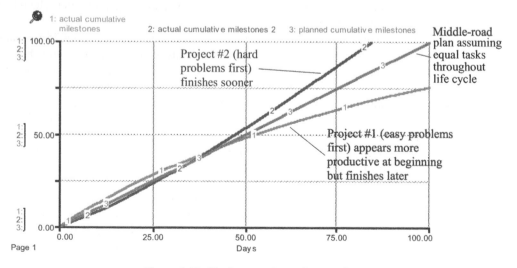

Figure 6.65. Final comparison of two projects.

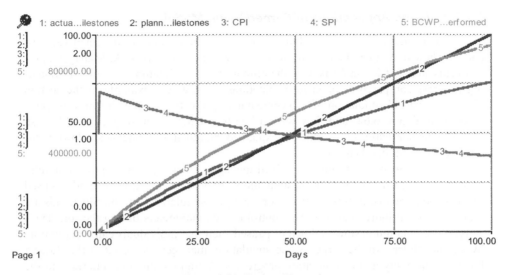

Figure 6.66. Project #1 trends.

tion example is varying the task difficulties. The planned progress assumed that all tasks were equal. Project #1 was modeled to do easy tasks first. This is what gave the illusion of early progress beating the plan. Project #2 was assumed to do hardest tasks first, and its rate of accomplishment continually increased. See the model *earned value project comparison.itm* to see how the varying task difficulty was implemented.

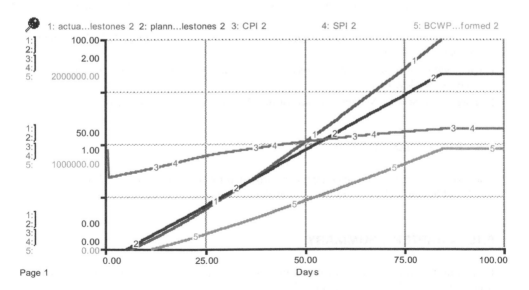

Figure 6.67. Project # 2 trends.

6.7.2.3   *Litton Applications of Earned Value Model*

The earned value model was used at Litton to (1) demonstrate what earned value is, and (2) show how it can be used to manage a project using feedback. Managers, project leads, and metrics analysts were the primary trainees. Examples involved evaluating progress compared to planned completions, such as the example in the section above. The partial simulation of two comparative projects was first shown to students (such as in Figure 6.64) and they were asked to predict which project would finish first. Further simulations were run and explained, and then the students sat down to interact with the model themselves.

The other part of the training involved managers interacting with project simulations as they are running in a "flight simulation" mode. The earned value model is used for hands-on practice in this manner. For example, simulated CPI and SPI trends are monitored by an individual who can control certain parameters during the run. Typically, the simulation is slowed down or paused such that individuals can react in time by varying sliders. In the earned value simulation, managers can control the staffing levels interactively as the simulation progresses. A flight simulation interface to the earned value model was developed, by which the user can adjust staff size during the project with a slider.

6.8   MAJOR REFERENCES

[Abdel-Hamid, Madnick 1991] Abdel-Hamid T. and Madnick S., *Software Project Dynamics*, Englewood Cliffs, NJ: Prentice-Hall, 1991.

[Biffl et al. 2005] Biffl S., Aurum A., Boehm B., Erdogmus H., and Grünbacher P. (Eds.), *Value-Based Software Engineering*, New York: Springer, 2005.

[Reifer 2001] Reifer D., *Making the Software Business Case*, Reading, MA: Addison-Wesley, 2001.

[Reifer 2002] Reifer D., *Software Management* (6th Edition), Los Alamitos, CA: IEEE Computer Society Press, 2002.

[Royce 1998] Royce W., *Software Project Management—A Unified Approach*, Reading, MA: Addison-Wesley, 1998.

[Schrage 2000] Schrage M., *Serious Play*, Boston, MA: Harvard Business School Press, 2000.

6.9   PROVIDED MODELS

The models referenced in this chapter are provided for usage to registered book owners and listed in Appendix C. See the book website for model updates and additions.

6.10   CHAPTER 6 SUMMARY

Project and organization applications include estimating, planning, tracking, controlling, setting policies on how to do things, long-term strategies, and looking after people. Projects and organizations provide the context for goals, constraints, and priorities of software development. Decision structures are embodied in project and organization applications to monitor status against plans, track expenditures and business value measures, and enable dynamic decisions regarding people, processes, products, and so on.

Organizations are typically collections of projects but also have broader initiatives (e.g., process improvements or shareholder return) and provide the supporting resources for them. Thus, the techniques for improving projects usually in turn benefit the organization. Organizations are responsible for people concerns and there is substantial overlap with people applications.

Abdel-Hamid's landmark model of integrated project dynamics has a primary focus on management of software production rather than software production itself. The model includes sectors for human resources, planning, controlling, software production, quality assurance and rework, and system testing. Many interesting results have been derived from experiments with the model, particularly in the area of software management policies. Retrospectively, the Abdel-Hamid model also illustrates some methods of poor software management. For example, the control function uses a dangerous policy of defining progress as effort expended against plan instead of measuring the tasks done.

Value-based software engineering considers different components of utility that software provides to stakeholders. It is different from earned value used to track a project and can be termed "real" earned value with respect to the stakeholders. Stakeholder objectives can be far and wide, and simulation can be used to evaluate and trade them off. For example simulation lends itself very well to assessing the business rationale of a software project and quantifying decision options.

A value-based product model incorporated two major aspects of stakeholder value: business value to the development organization stemming from software sales, and the value to the end-user stakeholder from varying feature sets and quality. The model helped identify features with diminishing returns and demonstrated that poor quality can severely hurt an enterprise, even after the problems are fixed. The model was also used to determine the optimal sweet spot of a process.

Personnel resource allocation is a most crucial aspect of management. Various models demonstrated different policies (e.g., needs-based or fixed allocation of resources), and can be used for actual decisions when parameterized for real projects. The adopted policies will depend on project context, constraints, and value priorities.

Some dynamic staffing models include the Rayleigh curve and process concurrence. One of the underlying assumptions of both is that the number of people working on a project is approximately proportional to the number of problems ready for solution at that time.

The Rayleigh curve when integrated is an excellent example of a structure producing an S-curve behavior for cumulative effort. The learning function component representing elaboration growth increases monotonically, whereas the work gap diminishes over time as problems are worked out. The corresponding effort rate rises and falls in a Rayleigh shape. It is been observed that the staffing buildup rate is largely invariant within a particular organization and reflects its characteristics. Despite the pervasiveness of Rayleigh-based estimation models, organizations cannot always respond as fast as some Rayleigh models dictate.

Process concurrence modeling can be used to see if and how much the software process can be accelerated. Both internal and external process concurrence relationships were explored. It was shown that process concurrence provides a robust modeling framework and can model more realistic situations than the Rayleigh curve.

Earned value is a valuable method for measuring performance with respect to plans and helping to control a project. It works best when thinking dynamically and can help develop such a mindset. The earned value model can be employed on projects, and was used in industry for earned value training showing how it can be used to manage a project using feedback. The model can be used to train managers to spot trends early in order to administer controlling corrective actions.

It was demonstrated that interpreting the slopes of earned value quantities provides much insight into trends not easily observed otherwise, and enables one to better extrapolate into the future. Static values do not allow this. One important lesson learned from experiments with the earned value model is that a policy of working hard problems first is advantageous in the long run.

6.11 EXERCISES

These application exercises are potentially advanced and extensive projects.

6.1. Consider the more modern practices in the Abdel-Hamid model. Define a project to modify some components of it but retain those parts that still apply for your environment. For example, you may choose to replace the software production sector or completely revamp the quality assurance sector for modern peer reviews or the team software process. You may get some ideas for improvement from the critique presented in this chapter. Define the problem(s) to address, include the usage context, conceptualize a high-level model, consider data sources to use, and begin model formulation. Elaborate further and implement the model depending on your goals and constraints.

6.2. Organizations often undergo simultaneous and/or sustained changes to processes, organizational structures, personnel, product lines, market shifts, and so on. However, organizations and their people ultimately have limits on the level of changes that can be absorbed at one time. How might one model the limiting factors? For example, it has been hypothesized that many organizations are averse to hiring more people when management overhead nears about 25% of the total workforce (since more managers are needed to supervise a larger workforce). Why might this limit be true? Give examples of other project or organizational situations for which change limits apply, investigate them through modeling, and draw conclusions.

6.3. Extend the value-based product model with a more comprehensive quality model. It should allow the user to experiment with details of different quality practices and assess the same process trade-offs already demonstrated.

6.4. Add a services sector to the value-based product model to replace revenues from product sales. In this context, an organization derives revenue from their developed software by using it to perform services to other parties. Model the services market and dynamics for your environment.

6.5. Consider how the views of different classes of project stakeholders may impact the degree of model aggregation. For example, does an oversight stakeholder need the same amount of detail on individual tasks as those working on implementation? Propose and justify appropriate levels of task aggregation to model production in the following scenarios:

- A three-person team developing an internal prototype in 5 weeks
- A RAD project with 15 people developing an e-commerce solution in 100 days with two team leads
- A software development team varying from 4 to 8 people working for about 18 months under one project manager
- A multicontractor distributed team of 500 people developing a large integrated system over the course of 4 years.

Identify the different stakeholders and their needs in representative situations. Consider anonymity issues within a team and external to a team. When is data on individual entities appropriate and useful and when should model entities be aggregated together? A goal–question–metric approach can be used to define appropriate metric indicators at different hierarchical levels of the project.

Software metrics "etiquette" should be followed. The table below from [Grady, Caswell 1992] provides some organizational guidelines for a metrics program.

Functional Management	1. Do not allow anyone in your organization to use metrics to measure individuals.
	2. Set clear goals and get your staff to help define metrics for success.
	3. Understand the data that your people take pride in reporting. Never use it against them; do not ever even hint that you might.
	4. Do not emphasize one metric to the exclusion of others.
	5. Support your people when their reports are backed by data useful to the organization.
Project Management	6. Do not try to measure individuals.
	7. Gain agreement with your team on the metrics that you will track, and define them in a project plan.
	8. Provide regular feedback to the team about the data they help collect.
	9. Know the strategic focus of your organization and emphasize metrics that support the strategy in your reports.

Project Team   10. Do your best to report accurate, timely data.
                11. Help your managers to focus project data on improving
                    your processes.
                12. Don't use metrics data to brag about how good you are or
                    you will encourage others to use other data to show the op-
                    posite.

6.6. Adapt the Brooks's Law model from Chapter 1 and implement the enhance-
     ments listed below.

- Add a stop to the simulation when all requirements are developed. This
  will prevent the model from running overtime.

- Add a simple feedback loop that controls the personnel allocation rate by
  comparing actual production to planned production. The existing model
  covers actual production; the planned production assumes a constant development rate with all 500 function points completed at 200 days.

- Add logic for a one-time-only correction when the difference between actual and planned is 65 function points. Run the model and show the results
  for adding 0, 5, 10, and 20 people.

- Make the model scalable for larger team sizes up to 60 people to overcome
  the current restriction on team size maximum. You might simulate team
  partitioning for this (see below).

Advanced Exercise

Add the effects of partitioning to the resulting model and try to validate it
against empirical data. You can use the data from [Conte et al. 1986] on
average productivity versus personnel level to help develop it (if you are
using an analytical top-level approach). It would be even better to model
the underlying mechanics of how teams are formed and use the data to test
your model as described below. [Briand et al. 1999] also provides data
analysis on the effect of team size on productivity. Normalize the empirical data on productivity into a relative relationship for evaluation against
the Brooks's Law model.

Test the revised Brooks's Law model by putting it into steady state and comparing it to empirical data on software productivity versus team size. Put it
into steady state such that personnel do not evolve into experienced people
(otherwise the results will be confounded). Make an array of runs to test
the model at different project sizes; show the results and discuss them.

Plot the results for individual productivity versus increasing team size. Productivity can be calculated as the overall software development rate divided by the team size for each simulation run for which team size was varied.
Compare the plot of individual productivity against the normalized relationship from empirical data. They should exhibit the same qualitative
shape.

Background

Brooks stated that adding people to a software project increases the effort in three ways: training new people, added intercommunication, and the work and disruption of partitioning. Repartitioning of teams is a particularly difficult effect to model, as witnessed by Brooks. In his 1995 updated version of *The Mythical Man-Month,* Brooks reviews the Abdel-Hamid Brooks's Law model and one by Stutzke [Stutzke 1994]. He concludes "neither model takes into account the fact that the work must be repartitioned, a process I have often found to be nontrivial." Our experience in assigning this as student homework attests to that fact.

During a real project, as the overall team grows in size, partitioning of teams does take place. More subteams will be needed on a 100-person project than a 10-person project. People naturally subdivide the work per their management instincts as the product design allows. Effects that come into play are two types of communication overhead: (1) the intrateam overhead that we have already modeled and (2) the interteam communication overhead. Either type can overwhelm a project if partitioning is done suboptimally. Any single team that is too large will be swamped with communication, whereas too many small teams will be burdened with trying to communicate between the teams. The team leads designated to coordinate with other teams will have no time for anything else if there are too many other teams to interface with. The balance that is to find is the right number of teams of reasonable size.

First, suppose a team grows from 20 people to 80 without reforming of teams. What does our current model show? The simple model is only scaled for teams up to 30 people, so it is restricted for larger team sizes. If we simply continue with the formula overhead $= 0.06 \cdot \text{team}^2$, then the equations quickly become greater than 100%. What is wrong with this? It does not account for repartitioning. It assumes that a single team will remain and continue to grow indefinitely in size without breaking into more teams.

Assume that the project acts like a self-organizing system. It will develop additional teams in a near-optimal manner to meet the demands of increased work scope. This is the self-partitioning effect we wish to model.

6.7. As a converse variation of the Brook's Law effect, model the impact of taking people off of a continuing project. There is extra coordination work required when people leave a project, associated with sorting out and covering the tasks of those leaving. Since there are fewer workers and the project is slowed down, management may increase pressure. This may then lead to others leaving. In this modeling context, the staff levels are reduced, leaving the same workload to be covered by fewer people.

6.8. The generic Rayleigh curve always starts out at zero, but in reality most projects start with a set number of staff. Planners adjust the Rayleigh curve in actual practice to start out with a more reasonable amount of people. Modeling this may involve clipping the curve or revising the equation parameters. Take the basic Rayleigh curve model and augment it with an initial offset to represent a starting point up on the curve. Parameterize the model so that users can input the desired initial staff size.

6.9. Some have theorized that aspects of software processes exhibit self-similar patterns at difference scales. Such phenomena have been described with chaos theory or fractals in other fields. Examine whether such techniques can be applied to superimposed staffing patterns like Rayleigh curves, process concurrence relationships, or any other aspect of software processes. For example, many small Rayleigh curves together can produce a larger Rayleigh curve, and ad infinitum.

6.10. Augment the Norden/Rayleigh model for the Putnam time constraint equations. Try to validate the time constraint formula against actual data and document your findings.

6.11. Develop a simple staffing model by replacing the $p(t)$ term in the Rayleigh formula with a manually drawn curve provided by the user that represents the accumulation of requirements available to be implemented.

6.12. Develop a model that replaces the $p(t)$ term in the Rayleigh formula with a process concurrence formula.

6.13. Evaluate the hypothesis that an organization striving to achieve RAD may choose to use a variable staffing profile as opposed to a constant profile for the upfront systems engineering effort. What conditions of the project environment make a difference as to which profile type is more suitable?

6.14. Adapt any of the provided process concurrence models or those of Ford and Sterman to be fully iterative. Model an iterative process like RUP or MBASE, including phases and activities. The model should be scalable for any number of iterations per phase. Calibrate it with available data.

6.15. Test the hypothesis that for best schedule performance, the optimal systems engineering staffing should be front loaded as opposed to constant level of effort on a complex project with partial interphase concurrency (see the process concurrence section). Assume a fixed project effort and standard percentage of systems engineering for the project (25% would be a reasonable figure). Compare the schedule performance for the level-of-effort systems engineering staffing with a front-loaded staffing profile. Vary the staffing profiles under comparison. Is there an optimal staffing profile for the concurrency relationship you used? Quantify the cost and schedule trade offs and draw conclusions.

6.16. Integrate the earned value model with an independent project model (such as Abdel-Hamid's or another), so that planned and actual quantities are computed internally instead of input directly by the user. Develop and run scenarios to assess various management actions using feedback from the earned value indicators.

6.17. Model the impact of requirements volatility in the context of earned value tracking. Suppose management wants to understand the consequences of taking on more requirements changes and they ask, "What will be the impact to our CPI and SPI with a given percentage of requirements volatility?" Start with the earned value model and analyze the impact of varying levels of requirements changes. You can report your results in two ways: (1) adjusting the earned value baseline assuming that the changes are out of scope and (2) taking on the changes without adjusting the baseline.

6.18. (This exercise is for the mathematically inclined.) Examine varying the choice of the *dt* interval in the Rayleigh curve generator and tie this to feedback delays. Can equivalent behavior be created between a Rayleigh curve and a substituted policy of hiring delays? Show your results and explain why or why not.

6.19. Model the "rubber-band" schedule heuristic identified and described in [Rechtin 1991]. He states that "The time to completion is proportional to the ratio of the time spent to the time planned to date. The greater the ratio, the longer the time to go." Use the schedule stretch-out experienced to date on a project to recalibrate and extrapolate the future remaining schedule. Alternatively, analyze this effect on a completed project using midpoint status references. Does it make sense to include this schedule effect in a cost estimation model? Describe what type(s) of projects and conditions it might hold true for.

6.20. Weinberg describes the dynamics of various management issues with causal-loop-type diagrams in [Weinberg 1992]. Choose one or more of them and elaborate them into simulation models. Experiment and derive policy conclusions from the results.

6.21. Compare and evaluate different product line strategies with a dynamic product line model. The provided COPLIMO static model spreadsheet or another referenced model can be used as a starting point. If a static model is adapted, then reproduce the static calculations first as a steady-state test before introducing test cases with dynamics.

6.22. Discuss and model the variability in metrics analysis intervals for different software processes. For example, effort reporting may only be available at monthly intervals but late testing activities may be statused on a daily basis. Run experiments to determine trade offs and to optimize the metrics feedback process for visibility and decision making.

7

CURRENT AND FUTURE DIRECTIONS

7.1 INTRODUCTION

There are many important problems and challenging opportunities for extensions of the work discussed in this book, as well as for the overall field of software process simulation. In general, the current and future directions presented here apply to all forms of simulation for software processes. System dynamics will be one of several techniques to further the theories and practice of software engineering as will discrete event methods, agent-based modeling, and others. The different techniques will also be used in combination with each other more frequently. System dynamics will be integrated with other process modeling aspects, similar to how software product architecture descriptions require multiple perspectives.

This chapter overviews some current (and presently apparent) future directions as of early 2006, but the list is certainly incomplete as new issues and technologies will arise. One thing we can be sure of is continued rapid change in the field. It is also inevitable that simulation will become more pervasive and integrated with everyday processes. This will be driven by advances in modeling and the practical need to be able to respond to changes.

Figure 7.1 shows a stack of software process simulation technologies, from the supporting infrastructures through simulation development environments and up to advanced new modes of simulation operations. Everything is built upon infrastructure software represented in the bottom tier, and the level of domain knowledge and sophistication of simulation increases up the stack. Like computer science in general, some

Software Process Dynamics. By Raymond J. Madachy

Process Mission Control Centers, Analysis, and Training Facilities
- Project and portfolio views
- Multiple model views and continuous model updating
- Use of real-time process data
- Virtual training integrated with actual process data
- Anticipation of change
- Distributed and networked across stakeholders

Integrated Models
- Combined application models of different aspects
- Hybrid models and combined approaches (e.g., continuous and discrete, static and dynamic, quantitative and qualitative)
- Model interface standards

Software Process Model Componentry
- Reusable structures and component interfaces

Simulation Environments and Tools
- Continuous, discrete, agent-based, qualitative, combined simulation
- Automated model building, input and output analysis
- Integration with analysis tools, spreadsheets, databases, enterprise software
- Incorporation of virtual reality, groupware, distributed computing, and so on

Computing Infrastructures
- Virtual reality, gaming, groupware technology, distributed computing, agent technology
- Operating systems, compilers, networks, databases

Figure 7.1. Software process simulation technology stack.

people create new operating systems and compilers upon which new applications are built, whereas others specialize in particular application areas. There are back-and-forth dynamics between the layers as new infrastructure creates new application opportunities, and application needs may fuel new infrastructure technology.

The technology layer for simulation environments and adjunct tools requires the basic computing infrastructures underneath. Applications are then created with the simulation environments, and may optionally be built using reusable model structures and components for the software process domain. The application models may be further combined with other applications or even other types of modeling techniques. The top layer represents advanced simulation operations in terms of how models are used, combined with other project management methods, or how they leverage more of the infrastructure technologies to increase simulation utility.

This chapter will describe future directions in all but the bottom infrastructure layer, which is outside the scope of process simulation, but it will assume continued advancements in the infrastructure areas. The middle tiers generally follow the book progression from simulation fundamentals to the higher-level applications based on the fundamentals. Part 1 of this book focuses on the modeling process, tools to a small extent, and the middle layer of software process model componentry. Part 2 looks at some applications for continuous systems modeling represented in the middle tier and a few integrated models belonging in the next tier up. The applications can be further integrated with other models of various types and brought into more advanced usage represented by the top two layers.

Simulation environments and tools will continue to advance in capabilities for automated model building, visualization, output analysis and optimization, model integration, and distributed usage across the Internet or other (sub) networks. Artificial intelligence and knowledge-based techniques will be used for some of the automation functions. Future environments that automate many aspects of model building will help minimize the effort for model development.

The trends of increasing computing power, distributed calculations across networks, and virtual reality provide new and unique advantages for users. These will lead to simulation software that employs parallel and distributed simulation techniques to execute computations and provide graphics-intensive simulations. Computer games and other software applications keep improving virtual reality to provide more interactive and lifelike simulation. The degree to which users can immerse themselves into a virtual environment will continue to grow.

Software process model componentry involves developing reusable modeling components across the industry (both macro- and microprocess views), refinement and enhancement of specific model structures, and incorporating object-oriented techniques with modeling structures. Application models will become easier to construct as componentry advances are made. Improved simulation environments will leverage the reusable components and provide more application-specific tools for software process aspects.

Future application models will be driven by new and emerging trends in software processes. These overlapping trends include increased globalization and distributed development, more open-source development and improved COTS, increased emphasis on the user and people concerns, new agile and hybrid processes, increased product demands for aspects such as security and quality, more complex systems of systems, and personnel shortfalls in skills and talent to meet the new demands. Increasingly rapid change permeates all of the above trends. Additionally, more of the applications will come from a value-based perspective and models will become more interdisciplinary, encompassing broader enterprise concerns.

Models will become more integrated not only in terms of different application areas, but also with respect to modeling techniques. For example, the need for combined continuous and discrete models is already apparent and the practice of hybrid modeling is gaining momentum. Other meta-modeling techniques such as analytic equations or heuristic approaches will be integrated with and/or compared to simulations. The practice of using different meta-models will support theory building in the field of software engineering.

It is also incumbent on modeling practitioners to improve their processes in conjunction with the advanced environments and new directions. For example, better modeling methods and empirical research to demonstrate model validation would help achieve wider acceptance of process simulation in the software industry.

Simulation and empirical software engineering methods will become more strongly connected. There is much synergy between them as each can help advance the other. As empirical research becomes more integrated with simulation, they will be used together for theory development and validation in the software field.

Simulation will become more commonly practiced and inherent in the software process. Models will not be so detached from everyday operations but instead will become a natural way of doing things. For example, project dashboards will include models and simulations and evolve into process "mission control" centers that are model-intensive. They will be used constantly for "what if" analyses and to respond to unanticipated changes. The models will be updated continuously in light of changing assumptions and more accurate data from the actual process, and they may also change as a result of machine learning from them.

With technology advances and improved data collection, many fields now depend on extensive use of simulation as a way of doing business, to test new theories and options. Other disciplines are also evolving their simulations into advanced modes of operation with the improved environments and computing infrastructures. The software process discipline will naturally progress as the other fields have. The rest of the chapter will describe some exciting current and future directions for applications and research, and how many of them are inextricably related to each other.

7.2 SIMULATION ENVIRONMENTS AND TOOLS

Advancing technology will lead to exciting new features in simulation environments and tools. There will be a host of new and improved ways to build models, simulate, interact with the simulations in stimulating ways, optimize them in a goal-driven manner, and automatically extract useful information from the simulation runs. There are more hybrid simulation approaches and toolsets being used. Tools are becoming better at integrating representation, guidance, simulation and execution capabilities.

Other disciplines have at least partially brought their simulations into advanced modes of operation, most notably war game simulations. They are currently the most complex simulations of man-made systems; they combine different simulation techniques in hybrid modeling approaches, they model entities in the thousands or even millions, and frequently use distributed computing and advanced supercomputing capabilities to crunch the numbers. They also use virtual reality and have a long history of using simulation for game playing and training.

The U.S. Defense Modeling and Simulation Office (DMSO) uses advanced modeling and simulation research that incorporates many of the concepts in this chapter [DMSO 2006]. They foster interoperability, reuse and affordability of modeling and simulation. They have developed a general-purpose simulation High Level Architecture (HLA) to support those goals. It is adopted as the standard architecture for all Department of Defense simulations and also for distributed simulation systems by the Object Management Group (OMG). Some of the ideas and standards from this domain can potentially be brought into the software process modeling domain. See [DMSO 2006] for extensive information and resources on simulation including the HLA.

The next subsections describe some new and future aspects of simulation environments and tools. They include recent and frequently limited examples of their application to software process modeling and simulation.

7.2.1 Usability

Even with modern computer tools, system dynamics can sometimes require a hefty intellectual investment, particularly if one has a nontechnical background. The Ithink, Vensim, and Powersim tools offer highly usable human interfaces, but the task of modeling becomes more difficult when domain knowledge comes into the picture. That is a reason why automated model building for specific domains would be a quantum leap of capability. Knowledge-based techniques can help, per Section 7.2.3, as can model componentry, per Section 7.3, and related methods such as system dynamics metamodeling for software processes [Barros et al. 2006a] (Section 7.3.2).

Some of the provided models in this book can be enhanced for usability by adding interactive control-panel capabilities. To support policy analysis and experimentation, user-friendly slide controls for varying model parameters, buttons, and dials can be employed with the system dynamics simulation software packages. Such an interface is more along the lines of a virtual dashboard for project control, per Section 7.7, Process Mission Control Centers.

Simulation tools, like many other software applications, will continue to evolve to become collaborative platforms for people to work in groups. New user-interface issues will arise as groupware technology becomes integrated into simulation environments.

Simulation tools will become easier for nontechnical people to use, much like spreadsheets have. However, there is a potential downside that the quality of these simulations may decrease as amateurs "do their own thing" without proper assistance [Nance 2000]. This argues for robust, automated, and application-specific simulation toolsets to reduce the risk of poor modeling as well as changing educational curriculums to introduce simulation to a wider variety of students.

7.2.2 Model Analysis

Techniques to analyze models, such as sensitivity analyses, were demonstrated in previous chapters. The study by [Houston et al. 2001a], for example, took the general approach of sensitivity analysis to compare and understand four different system dynamics software process models. However, new simulation environments will come with increased statistical support and experimental design facilities to ease the burden. There are advanced methods for evaluating models based on optimization and machine learning techniques described in this section and the next.

The verification and validation of models will always be challenging, and to some extent be a partial roadblock to widespread acceptance of simulation. Recent work addressing this problem in [Wakeland et al. 2005] illustrates the use of heuristic algorithms to improve the verification and validation of software process simulation models using system dynamics. In this approach, an optimization problem is formulated to guide a heuristic search algorithm that attempts to locate particular combinations of parameter values that yield surprising results. These results often help the modeler to identify flaws in the model logic that would otherwise remain undetected.

Advanced techniques for data mining or machine learning are other forms of model analysis. Machine learning is the ability of programs to improve performance over time by extracting rules and using them to solve new problems. Machine learning was not applied to software process simulation models until recent advancements in tools such as TAR2 [Menzies et al. 2002, Menzies et al. 2004a] made it possible. In these applications, treatments are learned from the models that improve the simulation outputs.

Treatment learners find the fewest factors that most influence a simulation model. The TAR2 tool is a data miner for performing automatic sensitivity analysis of large data files, looking for constraints or parameters that can most improve or degrade the performance of a system. Numerous Monte Carlo simulations are run, attribute values are ranked, treatments are built with a small number of attribute ranges with high rankings, and the new treatments are tested in fresh simulation runs.

Some examples of using machine learning on models for software cost estimation and risk assessment can be found in [Menzies, Richardson 2005]. TAR2 is applied to the static COCOMO cost estimation model [Boehm et al. 2000] and the Expert CO-COMO heuristic risk analyzer [Madachy 1997]. At USC, we are currently applying machine learning with the ODC defect model highlighted in Chapter 5 to assess risks for NASA flight projects.

Genetic programming is another machine learning technique that uses an evolutionary optimization algorithm [Koza 1992]. It imitates genetic algorithms, which use mutation and replication to produce algorithms that represent the "survival of the fittest." The integrated use of genetic programming and system dynamics modeling for software processes is described in [Ramesh, Abdel-Hamid 2003]. An application is shown of a decision support system enhanced with a genetic algorithm for optimizing quality assurance allocation.

7.2.3   Artificial Intelligence and Knowledge-Based Simulation

Simulation and artificial intelligence (AI) both try to model reality to solve problems, and can contribute to each other. Improvements in expert systems can potentially affect all aspects of simulation. Knowledge-based simulation (KBS) is the application of AI to simulation operations. Expert systems can be developed for a large list of tasks related to simulation. These include the use of AI knowledge representation techniques for the modeling of complex systems as well as the codification of simulation expertise to manage the simulation life cycle [Fox et al. 1989]. Intelligent simulation environments include automation of different simulation tasks, including model construction, verification, output analysis, experimental design, and documentation. See [Fox et al. 1989] for an overview of an artificial intelligence approach to system modeling and automating the simulation life cycle using knowledge-based techniques.

An interdisciplinary approach to modeling and simulation that incorporates the representational flexibility and ease of use that AI techniques offer is provided in [Weidman et al. 1989]. Another framework for integrating simulation and AI based on their similarities is described in [Doukidis, Angelides 1994].

Expert systems already exist for automating various simulation tasks such as checking input consistency, elaboration of high-level models for specific domains, statistical analysis and experimental design, analysis of output to determine model relationships, suggesting changes, and others.

A variety of enhancements and further research can be undertaken for the knowledge-based aspects of software process models. One drawback of system dynamics modeling tools is that they are relatively insular, and not easily amenable to integration with other tools such as expert system shells. A challenge is to overcome this current limitation and integrate them into unified applications.

It is unlikely that knowledge-based aids will completely automate simulation. There will always be a need for humans to interpret the output and apply contextual judgment. Since problems keep changing, there will always be new situations that automated solutions cannot handle.

7.2.4 Networked Simulations

The Internet has already revolutionized working modes in many regards, and network technology may provide substantial benefits for advanced uses of simulation. Simulation across the Internet includes models running in a distributed mode at multiple servers/clients, models accessing data across the Internet, models running at a server being accessed by users, and combinations of these modes [Jain 1999].

Many of the major system dynamics tool vendors already have some mechanism for running their simulations over the Internet [isee 2006, Powersim 2006, Ventana 2006], and some exclusively offer Web-based simulations [Forio 2006].

Improvements in distributed simulation coincide with project trends for distributed development in multiple locations. Not only can each location be simulated independently on a network, but each location can have its own respective simulations. For example, the hybrid model proposed in [Raffo, Setamanit 2005] is distributed in the sense that each development location has separate discrete-event submodels and separate system dynamics submodels. There is also a global continuous submodel for project-level dynamics in the proposed approach.

7.2.5 Training and Game Playing

Virtual simulation for training and game playing will become more common in the future, though it is already ubiquitous in aerospace and military applications. Most of the models presented in this book have been run in a detached mode without extensive user interaction. The mode of executing models by themselves (like batch jobs) is called constructive simulation. However, virtual simulation with people in the simulation loop can be quite powerful. The combination of system dynamics models with an immersive simulation technology is intriguing. Virtual reality and agent-based technologies have the potential to better integrate humans in the simulation loop.

Some experiences with simulation for personnel training were summarized in Chapter 4. Strong results from empirical experiments in [Pfahl et al. 2004b] demonstrate that a simulation-based role-playing scenario is a very useful approach for learning about issues in software project management. Favorable training results were also reported in [Collofello 2000] and [Madachy, Tarbet 2000].

An overview of issues in learning and decision support for software process management is described in [Pfahl et al. 2006b]. Examples in the automotive industry illustrate how simulation can become a useful management tool for the exploration and selection of alternatives during project planning, project performance, and process improvement. Also discussed are limitations, risks, and proposed future work.

The development of games for improving and enriching a student's learning experience is again on the rise. The beer game [Sterman 1989] in the field of system dynamics was developed to instill the key principles of production and distribution. Some recent game applications for software process applications are [Barros et al. 2006a], SimSE [Oh Navarro, van der Hoek 2005, Birkhoelzer et al. 2005], and SimVBSE [Jain, Boehm 2005].

A system-dynamics-based game for software project management was developed in [Barros et al. 2006a]. It describes a game intended for training purposes and the changes that were made to allow a system dynamics simulator to support game-like interaction. An experimental evaluation of the game's application to management students was performed, and they proposed models to describe the story underlying a game without programming.

SimSE is an educational software engineering simulation game that uses both predictive and prescriptive aspects [Oh Navarro, van der Hoek 2005]. It provides a simulated game with virtual office scenes for its players to take on the role of a project manager and experience the fundamentals of software engineering through cause–effect models. It supports the creation of dynamic, interactive, graphical models for software engineering process education. The authors have built an initial simulator of the waterfall lifecycle process to teach some process principles to students.

SimVBSE is a rule-based game for students to better understand value-based software engineering and its underlying theory [Jain, Boehm 2005]. It is also a medium to test hypotheses about value-based engineering theories. In SimVBSE, the player traverses through different rooms, gets briefed by virtual employees, and gets to choose various options, including changing project parameters, making strategic investments, and applying processes. The player gets to see relevant project metrics and his decisions involve the consideration of stakeholder value. Cause and effect rules are invoked and the student gets an assessment for his actions in each scenario.

Even though these simulation games are oriented toward educational applications, they can also be adapted for actual project environments (see Section 7.7, Mission Control Centers). Extensive use of simulation for training is also undertaken in military applications. See [DMSO 2006] for resources and information on use of simulation for training in a defense context.

7.3 MODEL STRUCTURES AND COMPONENT-BASED MODEL DEVELOPMENT

Chapter 3 introduced common structures that are reusable and adaptable for a variety of situations. The essential model elements are fixed, but all the generic flow processes, infrastructures and chains can be further investigated and refined. Chapters 4–6 presented models with some suggestions for modifications, and some of the changes are described in the chapter exercises. Many of the proposed future directions for the models involve revising model structures or creating new ones. Virtually all of the models could be enhanced to "drill down" further into various subprocesses. The reader is encouraged to look back at those chapters for more ideas on specific model componentry.

A framework for component-based model development would provide a higher level of abstraction for modelers, and could accelerate model creation. Development of models would be made easier, substantial effort could be saved, and modeling errors reduced. The reusable modeling structures presented in Chapter 3 are not yet provided in a "drag-and-drop" tool interface for easy incorporation into models. Making such structures more accessible for component-based modeling is a future challenge. Work in this area may lead to new language possibilities and simulation paradigms.

Methods for developing models with easily composable parts would be beneficial. Some model structures could become standard "plug and play" modules across the simulation community. A desired model could be developed with off-the-shelf elements or generation aids, similar to applications composition practices that rapidly compose programs from interoperable components, or applications generation whereby domain-specific programs are generated from high-level specifications. For example, a robust defect chain could be instantiated for a particular life-cycle process working at a high level of abstraction. The tedium of producing a defect model from the ground up and thoroughly testing it would be largely eliminated.

Component-based development takes advantage of patterns. All software programs are composed of patterns [Gamma et al. 1995]. So is process knowledge itself [Chang 2005], and simulation models are no exception. Entire models are thus constructed from basic patterns and the rules for putting them together can also be expressed as patterns. Software process patterns would be encapsulated as reusable building block components (see Section 7.3.2 on metamodels as an example).

The components would be assembled together with the help of predefined interfaces that describe their respective inputs and outputs, and modelers would simply "wire" them up accordingly. The predefined components serve as starting points and are not always cookie-cutter solutions, because new situations would frequently require their adaptation.

There are a variety of ways to ease the integration of model pieces. Making components easy to interface requires careful architecting. Interface specifications would have to be developed that enable disparate structures to be hooked together in a dynamic model. Some applied examples of submodel integration are shown in [Johnson 1995] using model variables common to multiple sectors of the Abdel-Hamid model as integration linchpins.

The GQM technique could be used to rigorously define data structures for models to adhere to. Simple examples of applying GQM to system-dynamics-based software process models were shown in Chapter 2, and [Pfahl et al. 2002] discusses a framework for using GQM to help integrate modeling with descriptive process and goal-oriented measurement. Also see the work on metamodels in Section 7.3.2 for composing and integrating software process models at a high level.

Submodels do not have to be directly connected if other data exchange methods are used. For example, XML is a possible way to integrate stand-alone submodels using it as an interchange standard to exchange data. XML would serve as a flexible glue between submodels while allowing substitution of other submodels that adhere to the XML schemas. XML is also discussed in Section 7.5.1 for unifying larger independent models. See [Diker, Allen 2005] for a proposed XML standard for system dynamics models.

Issues of reuse in software process modeling were described in [Neu, Rus 2003]. The authors looked at possible approaches in software engineering that may transfer over to simulation modeling. Some assets they identified that may be reusable include requirements, environment, scenarios, static process models or their components, influence diagrams, relations between process parameters, model design (patterns), executable model elements, and modeling knowledge. They also described ways to facilitate reuse in development environments.

7.3.1   Object-Oriented Methods

Object-oriented methods are a natural and convenient way to support component-based model development, and system dynamics lends itself to object orientation, as briefly discussed in Chapter 3. System dynamics structures and their behavior can be easily likened to classical "objects" with associated data items and methods. Elaborated models are comprised of instantiations of objects with levels, rates, and methods between them consisting of flow integration logic. (Note that in the section below on metamodels, "classes" are used in a more traditional object-oriented and fine-grained way to represent sets of elements such as "developers").

In object-oriented simulation, modular objects are used that encapsulate attributes and procedures. The objects are dynamic data types with fields and methods (procedures) that pass messages to invoke methods or update attributes. There are also inheritance of attributes/methods and polymorphism properties associated with them. These principles were shown in the Chapter 3 class hierarchy and demonstrated with example model components. Advantages of object-oriented simulation include easier reuse of process modules, modification of models, general ease of use, and reduction of modeling errors [Khoshnevis 1992].

7.3.2   Metamodels

Advanced work in the area of metamodels has been performed by Barros and colleagues [Barros et al. 2001b, Barros et al. 2002a, Barros et al. 2006b]. Metamodels are extensions to system dynamics that allow the development and specialization of domain models, providing a high-level representation for developers within domains. A domain expert develops a model, which conveys the relevant categories of elements that compose the domain and the relationships among those elements. A developer uses this model to describe a particular problem, by specifying how many elements of each category exist in the model of interest and the particular characteristics of each one. Finally, the model is translated to system dynamics constructors in order to be simulated and analyzed.

The authors have developed a metamodel that allows the development of software process models based on high-level constructors instead of mathematical equations. These constructors represent software process domain concepts such as developers, activities, resources, and artifacts. A domain model allows the translation of these concepts to traditional stock-and-flow diagrams, which can be simulated to evaluate the behavior of software process models. The approach helps inexperienced modelers build process models by reducing the semantic gap between system dynamics and the software process domain.

7.4   NEW AND EMERGING TRENDS FOR APPLICATIONS

Writing this book has amply demonstrated how dynamic the field is, as it was difficult to keep up with new and emerging trends in software technology, processes, and the business environment. This section identifies anticipated trends likely to impact the types of applications covered in Chapters 4–6. What is currently written as new and emerging trends may soon become the focus of robust, working models or be overtaken by other unprecedented trends.

Underlying all of this is the continued trend of more rapid change. The ability to adapt to change becomes ever more important for individuals and organizations alike. When added to the trend toward emergent requirements, the pace of change places a high priority on process agility and investments in continuous learning for both people and organizations. A major challenge in organizations is to determine which legacy processes and principles to keep, modify, or eliminate. The pace of change will inflict heavy penalties on overly bureaucratic and document-intensive software processes [Boehm 2005a].

The accelerated change is driven by technology trends such as Moore's Law about increasing computer capacity, the continuing need for product differentiation, and quick-to-market business strategies. Global connectivity also accelerates the ripple effects of technology, marketplace, and technology changes. Rapid change increases the priority of speed over cost to meet market windows. Simulation can be used to evaluate these trade-offs for new products (see the value-based product model in Chapter 6) as well as identify and prepare for major changes to legacy systems.

Ubiquitous change also prompts significant changes in software engineering education. Students should not only learn concepts, processes, and techniques, but also to learn how to learn [Boehm 2005]. Simulation and game technology are some powerful strategies for helping students learn how to learn, as described in section 7.2.5, Training and Game Playing. Fortunately, the educational applications can be modified for use on actual projects relatively easily.

Virtually all of the emerging phenomena described in this section cut across and inflict changes in people, process, product, project, and organization application areas. The concepts and boundaries of projects and organizations need to be rethought when considering trends such as open source and distributed development. People applications become ever more important in light of recent trends such as global, distributed development, more of a user focus, and multicultural concerns. There are process issues with regard to skills, distributed team structures, and culture matching.

Process and product application areas will be impacted by the proliferation of more complex systems of systems, hybrid processes, open source development, distributed global development, and more stringent product demands for higher security and quality. There are increasing needs for COTS, reuse, and legacy systems and software integration. Systems will need to interoperate with each other in ways they have not been designed for.

Project and organization applications will incorporate global collaboration processes. Even the definition of organization must now include distributed open source communities not tied to specific companies, and they have different goals/motivations for performing their work. Projects in open source development do not always have clearly defined beginning and end points.

The interaction of project and organizational dynamics is a complex area for future study. How do product lines, enterprise architectures, and standards interact with each other? The effect of mergers and acquisitions can be profound. Sometimes, organizations change overnight and such events put a big spike into projects and processes.

The new and emerging areas described will have major impacts and thus warrant focused study. They are new enough that substantive system dynamics modeling has not been applied yet, but almost certainly will be in a matter of time. It is expected that these areas will eventually be addressed more thoroughly by modeling and simulation, and some of them will become application areas with example models in the next edition(s) of this book. References are provided to current work in these areas and challenges for future modeling are identified. Additional details on the likely influences of many of these trends over the next couple of decades are in [Boehm 2005a], and trends for systems engineering processes are described in [Boehm 2005b].

7.4.1 Distributed Global Development

Economic trends are disrupting software business models as geographically distributed development processes are becoming ever more pervasive on modern software projects. Software is developed collaboratively in multiple locations around the world, and projects are being contracted out in whole or part for economic leverage. Projects are often split among distributed teams; the teams contribute different portions of work per phase to take advantage of their skill sets and rates. Thus, there is a need for new process models of global, distributed software development

Global development impacts many areas. New types of talent, people, and team-building skills are necessary. People have to collaborate in groups distributed across the globe, requiring new ways of working together with new supporting infrastructure. Processes and products are impacted tremendously. The acquisition of new systems needs to be rethought. These impacts from global development trends are briefly described below.

Strategies for global development cover different areas: product globalization, globally distributed processes, and people issues. These bring new challenges in all areas of products, processes, projects, and organizations. Even open source development is a variation of global development with unique characteristics. See Section 7.4.5, Open Source Software Development.

Global integration also shares characteristics of systems of systems; everything and everybody is increasingly connected to everything and everybody else. Projects are undertaken by multiple teams in different locations, requiring new group processes. Once-standalone systems become parts of large systems of systems they were not designed to interoperate with [Boehm 2005b].

Considerable personnel talent is necessary to succeed with new global opportunities. Distributed group collaboration, continuing education, career path development, and multinational teams provide opportunities for proactive organizations to grow and retain their talent base.

Global outsourcing and teambuilding also requires advanced acquisition management capabilities, including retraining software engineers to think like acquirers rather than like developers (see Section 7.5.2, Related Disciplines and Business Processes). User interfaces for developers, end users, and simulationists need to better reflect the transition from individual to group-oriented performance.

Global connectivity provided by the Internet provides major economies of scale and network-based economies that drive product and process strategies. Developing across multiple time zones may allow very rapid development via three-shift operations, though there are significant challenges in management visibility and control, communication semantics, and building shared values and trust. A groupware mission control concept is an attractive option for distributed process visibility and control (more details are in Section 7.7, Process Mission Control Centers).

Challenges for global collaborative processes include cross-cultural bridging; establishment of common shared vision and trust; contracting mechanisms and incentives; handovers and change synchronization in multitime zone development; and culture-sensitive, collaboration-oriented groupware. Culture matching and localization will be drivers for the new processes and supporting environments [Boehm 2005a].

There is an interesting tie-in between distributed global development and distributed simulation technology. The simulation model topology may resemble the form of the distributed process itself, whereby the nodes of the distributed simulation are coincident with the geographic nodes of the global development. One possibility is that each development site may be responsible for maintaining its own local simulation, and each local simulation may somehow be integrated into a master simulation of the distributed project at large.

An example of using distributed simulation for distributed development is proposed in [Raffo, Setamanit 2005]. This hybrid modeling approach would contain continuous and discrete event submodels. The continuous model portion with system dynamics would have a global submodel for overall project planning and controlling, and several continuous submodels for each development site to reflect differences in human resources and productivity. There would be discrete event submodels for each development site. Each site might have different steps, and artifacts could be passed between sites.

There are also new risks and entanglements with global development. On a multi-contractor global project in which different locations maintain their own local simulations, it is inevitable that disputes may arise due to differences in their simulation results and corresponding decision actions. The respective models will be the subjects of evidence for settling controversies.

7.4.2   User- and People-Oriented Focus

> Software is of the people, by the people, and for the people.
> —Barry Boehm and Rich Turner [Boehm, Turner 2004]

As the Lincolnesque quote above reminds us, software is by the people and for the people. They are both software users and producers. The universal proliferation of software and the Internet have made the overall population more computer savvy and, therefore, demanding better user interfaces and quality. For software processes, this begets an increasing emphasis on users and their value considerations.

The user emphasis also entails a global perspective for software used across the Internet and other distributed applications. Software must not only operate in different languages, but it needs to be increasingly culturally aware as well. This implies major interface and design challenges. The issues of culture matching and localization become important. For example, there is a much higher Chinese acceptance level of a workstation desktop organized around people, relations, and knowledge as compared to a Western desktop organized around tools, folders, and documents [Boehm 2005a].

For people issues in a software development environment, see [Acuña et al. 2005] for a process model handbook on how to best incorporate people's capabilities. A focus on people is also a main principle of agile processes, whereby processes are adjusted for individuals and their skillsets. See the next section for this aspect of people-orientation in the process (by the people) versus consideration of people as software consumers (for the people).

7.4.3   Agile and Hybrid Processes

Agile and lightweight processes requiring less rigor need to evaluated quantitatively. The question of scalability is of prime concern. Things are often done loosely without documentation for the sake of speed, and dense people interactions take place. Extreme Programming [Beck 2000] is a good example of a lightweight iterative process that seems to work in limited situations. Two developers share a single workstation and work side by side on the same software. One writes while the other observes, checks syntax, and reviews the work. They periodically switch roles. Even the originators admit that such processes do not scale above about 20 people. Why or why not is this the case? Maybe automated tools should do some of the checking. What dynamic effects occur above certain thresholds of people that impact a lightweight process?

People characteristics and their interaction dynamics are even more important in agile processes. The consideration of personality fit for different roles or processes is one area of study that spans behavioral sciences and software engineering. We have already seen a major model that accounted for different personality types in Chapter 5—the Burke SPI model that differentiated people by their attitudes toward process improvement. Organizations themselves often have distinct personalities that tend to draw certain types of people and reinforce certain behaviors. But exactly what types of people with what skill sets should companies try to find?

The heavy face-to-face interaction in agile processes is a process within itself that warrants examination. How much close working together can individuals perform? The amount is probably related to individual personality types, which implies that different people might be better suited for different processes.

The degree of change tolerated by people also covers a broad spectrum. Some prefer highly stable environments where they know the project and the organization will not be changing, whereas others enjoy the rapid dynamics typified by fast-paced Internet projects in which the business goals and development environment often change. Companies will always deal with finding the right balance between flexibility and discipline. Like crossing a chasm, they cannot lean too far on either side. And the balance shifts over times with market and other business trends.

Hybrid processes are emerging in several forms. On distributed, global projects they may be comprised of multiple local processes in conjunction with integrated processes with combined teams. Some projects may be combinations of open-source and closed-source development. On other large complex projects, they might be manifested as combined agile and disciplined processes. Hybrid processes may be composed of "hybrid" teams of different types of people skills, as a variant of Conway's Law.

For example, on large and complex systems-of-systems projects, strategies are being developed for balancing agility and discipline. Separate teams of people with different skills can be used to cope with rapid change while retaining project stability. Areas of faster product change are dealt with by separate teams of "agile" people equipped for assessing rapid change, whereas other more "disciplined" teams focus on stabilizing software baselines and plans amidst the changes. Development can be stabilized using short cycles and the right people on the right teams. Change can be foreseen, assessed, and built into the product architecture using as short increments as possible [Madachy et al. 2006].

Some people thrive on order and others thrive on chaos. These differences can be utilized for different aspects of a project to rebalance it when necessary. Agile-oriented people are rapid learners and good at assessing new technologies and COTS in light of unplanned changes. Plan-driven teams can develop the specifications in a more disciplined fashion. On larger projects, another team might consist of dedicated people who are continuously doing verification and validation (V&V). They would be good at critiquing but not necessarily very agile.

At USC, we are currently modeling hybrid processes for an extended spiral life cycle to address new challenges for software-intensive systems of systems (SISOS), such as coping with rapid change while simultaneously assuring high dependability [Madachy et al. 2006]. See the model highlighted in Chapter 4 for optimizing the number of agile people in a hybrid process.

Another recent effort at modeling agile processes is described in [Fernández-Ramil et al. 2005]. The authors use qualitative modeling to investigate agile processes after having success with qualitative modeling of open source community processes per [Smith et al. 2005].

7.4.4 Commercial Off-the-Shelf Software

COTS was briefly introduced and defined in Chapter 5, which highlighted a model for COTS glue code development and described a model concept for a COTS life-span model. However, those just addressed a very small part of the totality of COTS issues, which continue to change. This section will expand on the Chapter 5 introduction to address current and future trends of COTS.

The trend of building systems incorporating preexisting software is one of the most significant changes in software development. However, COTS products are examples of a disruptive technology with major potential advantages and major but poorly understood impacts on current practices. The use of COTS products generally introduces large, opaque, uncontrollable components with large multidimensional sources of advantages and disadvantages into a software application's solution space, causing fundamental changes in the nature of software requirements engineering, design, development, verification, evolution processes, methods, and economics.

To provide a focus on the types of applications for which COTS considerations significantly affect the dynamics of the development process, a COTS-based application (CBA) is defined as a system for which at least 30% of the end-user functionality (in terms of functional elements: inputs, outputs, queries, external interfaces, internal files) is provided by COTS products, and at least 10% of the development effort is devoted to COTS considerations. The numbers are approximate behavioral CBA boundaries observed in COTS-based system (CBS) projects [Boehm et al. 2003].

At USC, we have identified three primary sources of CBA project effort over years of iteratively defining, developing, gathering project data for, and calibrating the Constructive COTS (COCOTS) cost estimation model [Abts 2003]. These are defined as follows:

- *COTS assessment* is the activity whereby COTS products are evaluated and selected as viable components for a user application. This includes searching for suitable products, evaluating them with respect to the needs of the project and the capabilities of the developers, and choosing the best-fit candidate COTS products.
- *COTS tailoring* is the activity whereby COTS software products are configured for use in a specific context.
- *COTS glue code development and integration* is the activity whereby code is designed, developed, and used to ensure that COTS products satisfactorily interoperate in support of the user application. Glue code, also called "glueware" or "binding" code, is the code needed to get a COTS product integrated into a larger system (see the Chapter 5 example on glue code).

Other sources of effort not covered in COCOTS include:

- *COTS volatility* effort is that required to adapt to COTS product changes over time, including minor version updates and major new releases.
- *CBS evolution* refers to the ongoing modification, adaptation, and enhancement of a COTS-based system after its initial deployment. Sometimes, this effort can be quite substantial.

An important consideration is that there is no one-size-fits-all CBS process model. Assessment activities, tailoring activities, and glue code development are not necessarily sequential. Many different ordering and iteration patterns of these activities have been observed [Boehm et al. 2003, Port, Yang 2004]. Such differences in the activity sequences result from specific project characteristics and associated risks.

There has been also been a wide variation in the observed effort distribution of CBS assessment, tailoring, glue code development, and maintenance across projects [Boehm et al. 2003]. The assessment and tailoring efforts vary significantly by the class of COTS products (e.g., OS, DBMS, GUI, device driver, disk arrays, compilers, word processors).

CBS post-deployment costs may significantly exceed CBS development costs, and rise faster than linearly with the number of COTS products integrated. Although there is some anecdotal evidence for this, the greater than linear relationship is strongly suggested by the fact that n components will require on the order of n^2 interfaces to be considered, and the effort in developing and maintaining COTS-based systems generally lies in those interfaces. The implication is that short-term planning that often plagues new development is even more risky in CBS development projects. A summary of lessons learned from COTS system maintenance is presented in [Reifer et al. 2003].

New risks due to COTS products include:

- Having no visibility into COTS internals
- No control over COTS evolution
- Unpredictable interactions among independently developed COTS products

For such risks, traditional programming-oriented software engineering guidelines are occasionally useful, frequently irrelevant, and often dangerous. Examples of the latter are traditional approaches to software requirements, object-oriented design and development, and complementary black-box/white-box testing.

Traditional sequential requirements–design–code–test (waterfall) processes do not work for CBS [Benguria et al. 2002], simply because the design decision to use a COTS product constitutes acceptance of many, if not most, of the requirements that led to the product and to its design and implementation. Usually, a COTS product's capabilities will drive the "required" feature set for the new product rather than the other way around, though the choice of COTS products to be used should be driven by the new project's initial set of "objectives" rather than "requirements." Additionally, the volatility of COTS products [Basili, Boehm 2001] introduces some recursion and concurrency into CBS processes.

Glue code and overall CBS costs and risks can be reduced by investments in COTS assessment. The implication is that developing glue code or other CBS activities without sufficient COTS assessment may incur unexpected critical risks. Risk reducing assessment approaches include benchmarking, prototyping, trial use, and reference checking. COTS assessment is another source of effort for which "how much is enough?" can be answered via risk analysis. This involves balancing the risk exposure of doing too little COTS evaluation (picking the wrong combination of COTS products) with the risk of doing too much COTS evaluation (incurring too much delay).

The average COTS software product undergoes a new release every 8–9 months, and has active vendor support for only its latest several releases. Survey data supports the 8–9 months release cycle, whereas the evidence for the number of supported releases is anecdotal and varies widely. The implications are high adaptation costs not only during maintenance, but also during development and transition, especially if the CBS evolves in a different direction than the underlying COTS components.

There are a number of important research issues regarding the dynamic aspects of CBS development and evolution. These include adaptation to COTS releases, COTS refresh strategy analysis, balancing COTS risks, process concurrence, glue-code dynamics, tailoring, and more.

Software systems that contain multiple COTS packages often need to synchronize releases from several vendors with different update schedules. The challenge is timing the product "refresh" as new COTS releases are put out. The problem is exacerbated in complex systems of systems with distributed platforms. How frequently the components should be "refreshed" and the overall software rebuilt is a complex, dynamic decision.

Models describing the interrelated factors and feedback in complex CBS and evolution processes can help in decision making and process improvement. For example, the effects of interactions between COTS filtering, detailed package assessment, tailoring, glue-code development, integration with legacy systems and other applications, system testing, and evolution can be quantified and better understood. Users can assess different "what-if" scenarios and plan CBS projects with better information. Improved CBS processes can be defined from this.

Open-source development is a related topic that has much in common with developing systems with COTS. However, there are some unique differences. The open-source phenomenon is gaining a lot of ground but currently there are no modeling applications using system dynamics. This new and emerging area is discussed next.

7.4.5 Open Source Software Development

The phenomenon of open source software development has gained significant prominence in the last decade. There is still much to understand about the different people factors, group dynamics, quality attributes, overlapping project dependencies, different evolution dynamics, and other phenomena compared to more traditional closed source or COTS development. Open source is also a variant of global development, with many of the same considerations mentioned in Section 7.4.1, Distributed Global Development.

Open source development also has much in common with COTS-based systems, except for some unique characteristics. The source code is by definition available and transparent to all. Anyone can potentially have an influence on new features or participate in other aspects of development, so the processes used in the open source community present unique social interaction models.

Many point out the successes of the open source Linux operating system and other projects in terms of increased security, reliability and stability when compared to their closed source contemporaries. But some security experts are skeptical about the ability to assure the secure performance of a product developed by volunteers with open access to the source code. Proliferation of versions can also be a problem with volunteer developers. Open source may not be optimal for all classes of software. Feature prioritization by performers is generally viable for infrastructure software, but less so for corporate applications software [Boehm 2005a].

The usage and reach of the Internet as a universal communicational medium has helped fuel the recent tremendous growth in the open source movement. Traditionally, the communication overhead and complexity of a project increases by the square of the number of people. However, in open source development processes with thousands of programmers, the effects of onerous communication overhead are mitigated through the extensive use of a central versioning control system, a small core development group, a large set of beta testers, and frequent releases.

Quality dynamics are different in open source systems, partly because "Many eyes make all bugs shallow" (also called "Linus' Law) [Raymond 2004]. With so many open source testers, a high percentage of defects are found in every release. With frequent releases, updated and increasingly reliable software gets to the end user quicker. Open source development requires a critical mass of beta testers for this speedy feedback.

The success of open source development is highly dependent on the formation and evolution of their supporting communities, which may include end users, beta testers, developers, and others. Communities provide a sense of belonging and rapid feedback, and are why developers stay on projects [Jensen 2004]. Core developers listen closely to these communities and try to incorporate the suggested changes.

Group dynamics play a big role in open source development. Modeling the process factors of community peer review and collective decision making would enable better understanding of open source methodologies. These are also common concerns with (closed source) globally distributed development.

Few open source projects are started and built from scratch, and reuse is typically high. Usually, there is the presence of a critical starting mass of software elements, which themselves have to be open source in order to allow modifications. There are also aspects of product lines to consider. A large number of open source projects become dependent on one another, much due to the philosophy of code sharing. The interdependencies may be at different granular levels and have been studied in [Scacchi 2004a, Schach 2002, Smith et al. 2005].

People dynamics and their motivation are essential areas of study for open source development processes as the factors vary greatly when compared to traditional COTS processes [Scacchi 2004b]. Why do people come together and persist during the development of an open source product? Surveys have revealed that open source projects are viewed as a venue for learning, positions are based on interest, and a high percentage of participants contribute to multiple open source projects [Hann 2002, Hertel 2003]. Primary motivational factors are a sense of betterment of one's skills and self-satisfaction. A large majority of open source contributors develop a personal stake in their projects and many work tirelessly.

Web-based open source software development project communities provide interesting and unique opportunities for modeling and simulation of the process and people dynamics. Much of the process data is recorded and public, such as bug databases and code repository histories. This empirical data can be leveraged by researchers. For example [Jensen, Scacchi 2005] focuses on processes both within and across three distinct but related open source project communities: Mozilla, the Apache HTTP server, and NetBeans. They looked at the process relationships within and between these communities as components of a Web information infrastructure. This modeling helps to understand the open source development processes utilized by their respective communities and the collective infrastructure in creating them.

Open source systems may not neatly follow the well-known laws of software evolution in [Lehman 1980, Lehman 2002]. Recent modeling of open source software evolution is described in [Smith et al. 2005], where qualitative simulation is used to examine the general behavior of models of software evolution. This approach to the empirical study of software evolution system dynamics was used because neither the empirical data nor precise relationships were all available.

The qualitative modeling of open source growth trends and other empirical data in [Smith et al. 2005] looked at drivers of software evolution. The authors report on the application to data from 25 open source software systems. They compared model output with qualitatively abstracted growth trends, and looked at trends of functional size and complexity to those predicted by the models. The results suggest that the study of the relationship between size and complexity and its interaction via stakeholder feedback loops has a role in explaining the long-term evolutionary behavior of open source systems. This same qualitative approach is being extended for the evaluation of agile processes [Fernández-Ramil et al. 2005].

The same authors have applied an agent-based approach to studying open source processes. In [Smith et al. 2006], they model both users and developers in the evolution of open source software. They included factors for productivity limitations, software fitness for purpose, developer motivation, and the role of users. They compared the results against four measures of software evolution and found good fidelity with the model.

7.4.6 Personnel Talent Supply and Demand

There are global and national software skill concerns that warrant more rigorous examination. System dynamics has a long history of being applied at very high macro levels of people, such as an ongoing world model of population and resource dynamics [Forrester 1973]. One issue of prime importance for the software industry is the disparity between supply and demand for software engineers. The level of industrial demand versus the number of students being educated with requisite skills should be quantified for long-term policy making. All indications are that the growing demand for software will outstrip the supply in the foreseeable future.

With demands for software and information technology growing at a blinding pace, it is no surprise that there is a shortage of qualified personnel. A previous report [DoD 2000] suggested that there were more than 50,000 unfilled software jobs in the United States alone and that the number was growing at a rate of more than 45,000 jobs per year. Other sources indicate the current shortage as high as 400,000 jobs [DoD 2000]. This gap will continue to put pressure on the industrial base to maintain adequate staffing levels.

The shortages are industry-specific and caused by economic fluctuations. For example, aerospace and defense companies in the United States today typically have very highly experienced people. However, their workforce will be losing critical domain knowledge in the next two decades as these people retire. The tremendous growth of commercial software work has tipped the balance to attract the vast majority of entry level and early career software professionals away from aerospace and defense companies.

Witness also the impressive growth of software companies in India and China in recent years. They have produced some top-notch software development and consulting firms that can severely undercut United States labor rates. The impact to established consulting firms is being felt in terms of lost contracts.

In the discussion on agile and hybrid processes, the existence of radically different types of personalities was noted, as was the need to capitalize on their differences. Some people like fast-changing conditions, whereas others prefer stable environments. Some enjoy interacting with many people and some prefer to work alone in a corner. In today's world, with hybrid processes and so many different stakeholders to deal with, there is room for all types of people in software development and evolution.

7.5 MODEL INTEGRATION

7.5.1 Common Unified Models

The nature of process modeling is that different process concerns drive different factors to be included in particular models, but the concept of a unified model is attractive nonetheless. Different models can be integrated through combination and portion replacements. There are several candidate foundation models such as the Abdel-Hamid project model, but it is unlikely that a consensus set of models can be reconciled. Similarly, an attempt to combine the best of all software cost models is bound to fail just due to differing base assumptions. Business and market forces alone will keep models proprietary and insular, since in-house models use sensitive local data and sales of modeling products depend on having differentiating factors from competitive offerings.

Models for different life-cycle processes could be integrated in a unified system dynamics model for comparing multiple alternative lifecycle processes. It would be used to help select appropriate life-cycle process model(s) from the myriad of choices. An example of a life-cycle process model decision table can be found in [Boehm 1989], though it needs to be updated for modern practices.

An interchange standard for system dynamics models would go far to promote unification of different models. XML is a good candidate as a viable and natural solution for system dynamics model interchange. Details of a proposed approach for an XML-based standard are in [Diker, Allen 2005].

7.5.2   Related Disciplines and Business Processes

In most circumstances, the software process is one of several processes to be integrated in an enterprise. Businesses will be embedding simulation into larger enterprise-wide applications that encompass many disciplines. Some examples include systems engineering, business processes (e.g., sales, hardware development, supply chain, etc.), or acquisition processes undertaken by large governmental agencies. As described in the book *Serious Play* [Schrage 2000], organizations will increasingly continue to resort to heavy use of simulation to gain competitive advantage.

A prevalent trend is the increasing integration of software engineering and systems engineering disciplines. This is reflected in the CMM-I, superseding the Software CMM, the refocusing and expansion of many organizations to recognize and integrate both disciplines (even going so far as renaming their companies), and major conferences like the Systems and Software Technology Conference now incorporating both disciplines. There have not been any system dynamics models to date that exclusively focus on their integration dynamics. Process concurrence relationships between systems and software work phases could be applicable.

Integrated models will include more disciplines and business aspects, such as integrated systems and software engineering processes, business processes with software processes, and integrated views of acquisition processes and supplier development processes on large government projects with acquisition oversight. Simulation will also be integrated with more traditional project management tools. These include planning and scheduling tools, earned value reporting systems, and so on.

Simulation to support business case development was highlighted in some Chapter 6 applications. Software business value analysis is a crucial area that simulation will increasingly address. Business case simulation requires industry-specific knowledge to analyze particular software product markets and their associated business processes. Conversely, business considerations are a major external driver of software processes.

An integrated acquisition and software process model would involve modeling overall system feasibility as well as process development considerations (e.g., cost, schedule, quality). A virtual acquisition process was described in the SAMSA proposal [Boehm, Scacchi 1996], where system dynamics was incorporated for project modeling. A system dynamics model framework for a software supplier acquisition process for the automobile domain was described in [Haberlein 2004]. More recently, the acquisition process for a large-scale government system has been the focus of a multiyear research project at the Aerospace Corporation [Abelson et al. 2004, Greer et al. 2005].

[Greer et al. 2005] describes the results to date by the Aerospace Corporation for the use of simulation to better understand the software-intensive system acquisition process. A case-study approach is used to explore the dynamics of "disconnects" in baselines across multiple organizations in a large software-intensive space system development program. Disconnects are the latent differences in understanding among groups or individuals that can negatively affect the program cost, schedule, performance, and quality should they remain undetected or unresolved.

In [Greer et al. 2005] the authors have constructed a system dynamics model of communication effectiveness and delay across four organizations that sequentially and iteratively rely on each other for requirements and deliverables. Their analyses from multiple simulations suggest that the highest points of leverage in reducing disconnects are in increasing expertise levels, improving communication clarity, and accelerating the pace of assessing the impacts of changes in partner organizations' understandings and actions. These results oppose traditional assumptions that disconnects are due to external requirements changes and that speeding up organizational processes will reduce disconnects.

Chapters 3 and 6 provides some stock models of integrated systems engineering, hardware engineering, marketing, sales, and manufacturing processes. These may serve as starting points for integrated enterprise process models.

7.5.3 Meta-Model Integration

In this section, *model* is used in a meta sense; it refers to a general modeling technique or perspective and not specific instances like the application models.* Results in any scientific or engineering field are stronger when validated using different perspectives or models. A related best practice in software estimation we have been preaching for years is to estimate using several methods [Boehm 1981], compare the results, and hone in on a better result. If different approaches provide disparate results, then evaluate their respective assumptions to find discrepancies and iterate. Generally, the estimates converge and more confidence can be had in the results.

Likewise, system dynamics presents one way of viewing the world and it is best used to balance and complement with other modeling techniques. Meta-model integration may refer to the following types of models:

- Static and dynamic models
- Continuous, discrete, agent-based, and combined models
- System dynamics and analytic dynamic models (e.g., analytic Rayleigh staffing model)
- Quantitative and qualitative models
- Mathematical and heuristic models
- System dynamics in support of theory validation in general (see Section 7.6)

---

*The term meta-model refers to any type of model representation, as opposed to "metamodels" from [Barros et al. 2006b], which are system dynamics models specific to software processes.

Integration may take on several forms. It can include identifying model differences and similarities in assumptions or constructs, combining models that may or may not have common elements, taking selected parts of different models to create new ones, comparing and interpreting results between models, calibrating between models, or even simplifying models in light of each other.

One example of a modeling technique "filling the gaps" of knowledge for another is qualitative simulation in conjunction with system dynamics. If the system dynamics of a process are under investigation but empirical data and precise functional relationships are lacking, then a qualitative model can at least provide output results with general shapes and trajectories.

7.6   EMPIRICAL RESEARCH AND THEORY BUILDING

Simulation will increasingly be used to support empirical research in software engineering, and vice-versa, as simulation becomes more widely accepted and practiced. There are several ways in which simulation and empirical studies can be used together synergistically. Simulation models can support real experiments to strengthen other empirical methods and be used for evaluating theories [Munch et al. 2003, Rus et al. 2003]. Or empirical results can be used to develop better models. [Munch, Armbrust 2003] is an example of using empirical knowledge from replicated experiments for simulation.

Simulation can provide a virtual laboratory for low-cost experimentation compared to live experiments or field studies that require a lot of resources. Simulation is an efficient and powerful way to test theories this way. Empirical observations required for nonsimulation approaches may be very difficult and time-consuming to generate and assemble, and, thus, simulation can help accelerate progress in empirical research. When the empirical data is virtually impossible to obtain, such as trying to conduct a large industrial project more than one way to compare techniques, simulation may provide results when traditional methods cannot.

Simulation models can be calibrated with a relatively small amount of empirical data or expert-determined values. The scope of the models can potentially be broadened to include other factors that have been empirically determined or with expert judgment when empirical results are not available. Then experiments can be run without the need for actual projects or other expensive data collection. Sometimes, the models will also help identify new measurements that are necessary to fill gaps, so simulation may, conversely, help refocus empirical data collection.

In the traditional process of theory building, a problem is identified, a hypothesis is formulated, experiments are defined to test the hypothesis, resources are gathered for the experiments, and, finally, the experiments are executed and analyzed with respect to the hypotheses. Ideally, the experiments can also be independently replicated. Simulation provides an alternative way to prepare for and run the experiments, and the results of the simulations can be used for analysis.

Proposed theories can be incorporated and tested in a simulation framework, incrementally added to, or alternative theories can be substituted. By changing simulation parameters, each theory can be tested individually or combinations of noncompeting theories can be evaluated. If any fragments of relevant data do exist, they can be compared to the simulation results. As in other fields, a simulation framework can incrementally incorporate newly accepted theories to serve as a unified model and experimental testbed. The framework can potentially integrate both macro and micro process views as well.

Frequently, there are complications in the real world so experiments need to be iterated more than once. Sometimes, the results of live experiments indicate a need for revisions in the experimental design. As in all scientific studies, empirical research must also be repeatable by others to validate new theories. Simulation makes it much easier to rerun experiments for all these reasons. Independent researchers trying to replicate results can also resort to their own independent simulation models to validate the results of others. The practice of using alternative simulation models in parallel to test theories about complex phenomena is common in other disciplines.

The research in [Raffo et al. 1999a] identified the scarcity of empirical studies relating to the practical impact of process modeling and simulation. The authors addressed some relevant aspects of the multifaceted relationship between empirical studies and the building, deployment, and usage of software process models. They identified empirical issues encountered when trying to analyze the following:

- Process data used as direct input to simulation models and/or used to assist model building
- Model output data used to support management decisions about process alternatives
- Model structure in the context of evaluating the efficiency of a process
- The effectiveness of process models in supporting process change and improvement

Work needs to be done on techniques for empirical analysis of model inputs, analysis of simulation outputs, empirical evaluation of process models, and the empirical evaluation of process models in supporting process improvement. A recurrent theme is the complementary nature of modeling and measurement [Raffo et al. 1999a]. Simulation models provide a framework and focus for measurement programs.

7.6.1 Empirical Data Collection for Simulation Models

Simulation does not eliminate the need for empirical data collection, so there is still substantial future work to be done in this area. Progress in virtually all of the modeling application areas depends on real-world data for inspiration, analysis, and other usage in the models. Empirical data from real projects and experiments still needs to be continuously collected and analyzed. Accurate and consistent-quality data is desired and therein lays the challenge as in all software metrics activities.

Empirical data can be highly valuable for software process simulation studies, yet there are fundamental challenges in its acquisition and usage. Data is used in calibration and the driving of and validation of simulation models. When simulation is used for decision support, empirical data is used to describe the distributions for different decision options. Research results ideally can be validated by others with different sets of data from multiple sources.

Some potential problems to overcome when acquiring data for simulation models include:

- Large effort in generation, collection, and possible reformatting of data for simulation models
- Effort to locate and assess relevance of empirical data from external sources
- Existing data may not be commensurate with model constructs in terms of granularity, abstraction level, and so on
- There are so many different processes
- Field data does not represent hypothetical future processes
- The lack of data may constrain the scope of process models

The use of experimental data or observational field data for simulation depends on the goals and constraints. It is frequently desired to bolster models with data to reflect reality as closely as possible, but detailed data is not always warranted. Conversely if it is not available, its lack may become a constraint on the simulation study. As discussed in Chapter 2, a balance must be struck because such data rarely exists in perfect form, if at all. Some metrics frameworks to address these issues were described in Chapter 2 in Section 2.11, Software Metrics Considerations, including GQM, IMMoS, and the WinWin Spiral life cycle as a risk-driven approach to simulation studies.

Initiatives can also be undertaken in the larger software community to align diverse efforts for traditional experimentation and process simulation modeling. Such initiatives would define and implement research approaches that combine empirical measurement and process simulation. Researchers could work more closely with industry to obtain empirical data for their research. New techniques could be developed to transform data or deal with the lack of data. Improving access to and interpretation of existing empirical data and process models would also be a great advantage to the community.

Whereas organizations maintain local empirical data caches (to differing extents), there are no freely available public domain sources of comprehensive empirical data to validate research studies at large. Open source repositories of empirical data are one possible way to help alleviate the lack of data. For example, on a CeBASE research project sponsored by NASA we developed an online experience base for researchers on best practices related to high-dependability computing [Boehm et al. 2004]. Contextual interpretations were provided with the raw data. A long-range option is to extend this type of work and provide public sources of empirical software process data.

7.7 PROCESS MISSION CONTROL CENTERS, ANALYSIS, AND TRAINING FACILITIES

Simulation will become part of the process itself and a natural way of doing business. People will be using models much more frequently to help determine next steps and replans in response to changes. Project dashboards that provide "the big picture" are currently used as vehicles for management insight and project control, and they will evolve to include more models as views into projects. Risk mitigation and replanning will frequently involve a change of model(s) for all to see.

Measurement-driven dashboards provide a unifying mechanism for understanding, evaluating, and predicting the development, management, and economics of systems and processes [Selby 2005]. Dashboards enable interactive graphical displays of complex information and support flexible analytic capabilities for user customizability and extensibility. The displays help visualize data more intuitively, identify outliers, and support drill-down capabilities. Dashboards have been used on actual large-scale projects and empirical relationships have been revealed by the dashboards. In [Selby 2005], the dashboards revealed insights on leading indicators for requirements and design of some large-scale systems for feedback to the organization.

Several of the simulation applications in this book have demonstrated dashboard-like displays using top-level graphical interfaces with interactive gauges, sliders, input boxes, and output displays. The dashboard concept can be substantially extended by incorporating more models and interactive simulations, plugging into actual process data to drive the models, and allowing group interaction.

We will define a process "mission control center" as an extended dashboard concept employing multiple adaptive models with real-time data streams. It provides a model-pervasive, multidimensional view of processes. The model outputs are shown with past actual process data and extrapolated into the future. With multiple models that may indicate different outputs, decision makers can consider the context and applicability of the models in specific situations. Models can be deleted over time when they fall out of favor or are updated for improvements.

This usage of simulation brings it more into the fold for "control and operational management," which is one of the purposes of simulation identified in Chapter 1 but has very few examples. It goes much further than planning or tracking, by enabling users to make real-time control decisions using simulation results and actual project measurements.

The mission control center metaphor goes beyond traditional dashboards because it not only supports project tracking but, like space mission control centers, it supports preparations for major changes and unanticipated events through the models. "What ifs" can be conducted at any time, leveraging the actual process data, and models can be recalibrated or otherwise updated in real time as necessary. The data streams may be of different periodic rates, whether weekly and monthly metrics traditionally used for project tracking [Baumert et al. 1992, McGarry et al. 2002] or per minute telemetry such as provided by the Hackystat tool [Johnson et al. 2005].

During space missions, control centers are manned 24 hours each day, and such continuous monitoring would be relevant for large 24/7, globally distributed projects as multiple teams hand off work. Real-time trends of geographically distant teams would be instantly recognizable at all mission view centers.

As a model-intensive dashboard, the mission control center employs multiple simulations with possibly competing or contradictory models, allowing comparisons of alternative simulation approaches to help decide when one approach is more suitable.

Some may go out of use when they become irrelevant, events cause the assumptions of the model to be wrong, or they are judged too defective for repair. The models adapt over time as the "mission" unfolds. Behind the scenes are model learners to aid in the continuous model updating and deleting.

Suppose one aspect or portion of the mission control center is dedicated to defect trends. There will be arrays of continuous model outputs plotted against actuals and arrays of discrete mode results plotted against actuals. These kinds of simulations will be used to test changing assumptions. Some of the models will be recalibrated at some point and reflect their updated simulation results. Some models will be better predictors then others, possibly at different phases. Some of the models will be deleted or retired when they become irrelevant or invalid.

The control centers also have access to virtual reality simulations with humans in the loop to practice or test how people will react in a given situation. For example, a process performer can be inserted into a virtual environment like SimSE [Oh Navarro, van der Hoek 2005] that takes on the characteristics of the actual project. Or a manager can propose that a value-based decision be made in a SimVBSE environment [Jain, Boehm 2005]. The participant can use actual process measurements and simulations of his choice to help assess the value trade-offs and support his decision. The virtual environment can even include internal simulations for observation and manipulation.

All of the aforementioned elements of a process mission control center would share a common database of past and actual process data, and there would be conceptual links between the different model representations. For example, the individual discrete entities in a discrete event model would be the same ones aggregated in a continuous representation. The user view would depend on the modeling paradigm used and chosen level of aggregation.

7.8   CHAPTER 7 SUMMARY

Simulation usage will grow in diverse disciplines to extend knowledge, and software engineering should not be an exception. Improvements in simulation technology and underlying computing infrastructure will help fuel dramatic advances. Such advances are already happening in many fields and, likewise, software process simulation will continue to become more immersive and extensively used. But we also need to improve the practice of software process simulation to cope with perpetual rapid change.

Simulation will become the way to do business in the future. Simulation systems will often be used as part of larger decision support and enterprise systems, and major decisions will be assessed using simulations that encompass all aspects of business operations. Simulation software will become more open to allow integration with related applications. Simulation will be widely used, but people will be using more simulators specifically designed for their business processes instead of using generic simulation tools.

Many of the future thrusts described in this chapter are connected and will contribute to each other. For example, better modeling tools and methods will help simulation become more widely accepted and easy to use for software processes. As simulation becomes more accepted and usable, it will be applied more frequently in empirically based research. Seeing the fruits of simulation-based research will help spawn even better tools and methods, with increased usage by the practitioner community. The tools and methods include component-based modeling, automation of model building and output analysis, statistical support and experimental design, more interactive and lifelike simulations, enhanced project dashboards with simulation, game playing and training applications, and so on.

Simulation software of the future will provide enhancements for model creation, input data analysis, output data analysis, and decision making. Novel techniques such as machine learning or genetic algorithms will be used to better understand or update models. Improved graphics and virtual reality can make the environments more appealing and powerful. Environments will be customized for specific applications such as software processes, but also allow integration with other enterprise aspects and disciplines for modeling more comprehensive systems.

Model building will become more automated and domain-specific. Tool advancements such as component-based or automated model construction kits can make simulation resources more easily available to people. Tools will mature to optimize the creation of software process models specifically, and those models may be integrated with models developed with other tools optimized for their respective domains.

Object-oriented technologies have become pervasive in software development and will also be used more in simulation. Models will be created with object-oriented components and sometimes be driven by object-oriented databases, depending on the application. Techniques such as system dynamics meta-modeling will be used for construction and reuse of domain models.

In the future, simulation software will no longer be so cleanly divided among continuous, discrete event, or agent-based methods. Applications will incorporate hybrid modeling to capture different perspectives and allow multiple-view insights. The different methods can all share common data and be linked through intermodel relationships in many cases.

New application models will cover related trends such as globalization and distributed development, open source development, increased emphasis on the user and people concerns, new agile and hybrid processes, increased product demands with more complex systems, and personnel shortfalls to meet the new demands. These areas are additive to the types of applications already showcased in Chapters 4–6, and will be viewed from new perspectives such as value-based software engineering.

These application trends demonstrate increasing connectedness of people, processes, products, projects, and organizations. Similarly, there will be more connected models of all these aspects. Multidisciplinary teams will use integrated sets of simulators. Enterprises will continue to integrate simulations of all aspects of their operations. However, the traditional boundaries of projects and organizations will sometimes be redefined in light of new trends. Software process models will be components of more increasingly complex and integrated simulations encompassing more business aspects.

Many of the directions in this chapter have multiple new aspects to them, such as current efforts using both new modeling techniques and modeling new application areas of software processes. This belies the fact that rapid change is also occurring in software process modeling and simulation.

Simulation will strengthen and streamline many aspects of empirical research and theory building. When combined with empirical methods, simulation is a powerful way to test theories and extend knowledge in the field (partially aided by new simulation tools for experimental design). Some expensive and time-consuming empirical investigations can be reduced or totally eliminated through the use of simulation. This different mode of research is expected to provide new insights at a faster pace than in the past. This has already happened in other disciplines, and the only barriers in this field are more widespread acceptance and development of simulation skills/resources.

Extended dashboards and mission control centers will comprise many of the aforementioned concepts. They will be model-intensive interactive displays that are used in all aspects of process operations. Models will be phased out continuously, sometimes due to improved models (aided by model learners behind the scenes) or because the phase of a project or enterprise changes. As the real-life systems change, then corresponding simulation models need updating. For instance, when a software system goes into operation, its development models will be replaced or enhanced with models for its evolution.

This book proudly carries on the tradition of past pioneers such as Forrester, Abdel-Hamid, and others. It is hoped that this book will help guide others in their quest to have successful projects make useful software for people, through better understanding and informed decision making in complex scenarios.

We will have to change our ways of thinking because simulation will indeed be more pervasive in the future. As we practice simulation, it will induce even more changes about how we view and architect software processes. The models will change us, not just vice-versa. Modeling applications will be more sophisticated, with more impact on the bottom line and affecting the daily activities of many software professionals. It is time for serious play, so rev up your simulation engines.

7.9 EXERCISES

7.1. Choose one or more of the models provided in this book and improve their interfaces so that people can use them easier. Add control panel capabilities to make them more user friendly. Develop appropriate scenarios to run them interactively. If you have access to advanced rendering technology, you may investigate transforming them to be more graphical or potentially incorporate virtual reality.

7.2. Discuss issues related to groups of people accessing, modifying, and running common simulation models. Consider interface, configuration management, and other issues impacted by group usage.

7.3. Choose one or more of the models provided in this book and adapt them to run on the Internet or other network. Furthermore, adapt them for collaborative distributed usage across the network by multiple people.

7.4. Conduct research and write an essay on how system dynamics tools can be integrated with expert system shells. Note that several entries in the annotated bibliography address expert systems.

7.5. Apply machine learning techniques on a model chosen from this book or another source, or create another model and analyze it. Describe what was learned from the model and implications for model improvement.

7.6. Create a mockup of a process model construction utility for any chosen aspect(s) of software processes. You can focus on particular aspects such as effort or defect modeling, or be more comprehensive. You may also focus on particular applications such as product line modeling, global development, and so on. Develop use cases that describe the interaction with such a utility.

7.7. Investigate the integration of systems and software engineering processes. Create a model with policy levers to represent options on how the integration might work. Possible issues to analyze are having separate or conjoined processes, the timing of artifact handoffs (process concurrence might be handy), the effect of (non)participation of software engineering personnel on developing requirements, process serialization versus iterative parallel activities, and so on.

7.8. Assess and critique some of the stock models provided in Chapter 6 for integrated enterprise processes. If feasible, adapt them for software development scenarios for a chosen environment.

7.9. An older example of an application that embodies some of the ideas in this chapter was described in [Boehm, Scacchi 1996]. Tom DeMarco developed the hypothetical project simulation tool in Appendix 2 that provides the following abilities to multiple stakeholders (acquirer, user, developer, etc.):

- Simulating project outcomes under different what-if conditions
- Simulating different risk conditions to give managers a chance to work out reasonable responses
- Simulating later stages of project work from a base of actual performance to date (the model is updated with actual data as the project continues)
- Creating a common metaphor to allow program managers to interact fruitfully with their peers

   A simulation scenario and narrated experience of interacting with the tool is also described, whereby a user iteratively hones in on a suitable project scenario balanced by risk. He eventually locks in the required capability and specifies constraints until the risk is acceptable. Update this concept for other features of advanced simulation environments such as distributed usage, among others. Go further and develop a prototype or a working tool based on these concepts.

7.10. Choose any of the new and emerging application areas and develop a simulation research project around it.

7.11. Examine the future supply versus demand of software personnel for a chosen region (e.g., United States, India, the world). Identify important dynamic factors, indicators, and needs of the employment market. Analyze the experience levels and the number of well-trained people based on actual data. Project the future supply and represent the trend(s) in a system dynamics model. Extrapolate out 5 and 10 years into the future. What are the consequences? Are there any national or international policies to recommend?

7.12. Create a mockup of a process mission control center showing multiple models with updates and retirements. It can focus on a particular aspect and does not have to contain every item mentioned. Create storyboard(s) that describe the scenario of how the control center is used and what is being displayed. This may include project history to explain trends and model changes.

Appendix A

INTRODUCTION TO STATISTICS OF SIMULATION

This appendix covers basic probability concepts and statistical methods for simulation. Software processes are stochastic like other real-life processes. The mere presence of people alone guarantees a degree of uncertainty. Treating software processes as deterministic is a gross approximation. In order to build representative simulation models, the random effects present in a system must be simulated. This appendix will show methods to deal with random effects in the inputs to system dynamics models as well as analysis of stochastic simulation output. The modeling principles described up to this point have mostly treated simulation outputs as deterministic point estimates (except for a Monte Carlo example in Chapter 2).

However, a point estimate is only one of an infinite number of possibilities; hence, the probability of achievement is zero. One should evaluate the entire uncertainty range. The variance of outputs from multiple runs is used to quantitatively assess risk.

The stochastic nature of a system is thus an essential feature to consider. Bounds on the uncertainty and the implications of potential outcomes must be understood and evaluated. Analytical models have restrictive constraints on the number and kind of random variables that can be included, whereas simulation provides a flexible and useful mechanism for capturing uncertainty related to complex systems.

A simulation can be deterministic, stochastic, or mixed. In the deterministic case, input parameters are specified as single values. Stochastic modeling recognizes the inherent uncertainty in many parameters and relationships. Rather than using point esti-

Software Process Dynamics. By Raymond J. Madachy
Copyright © 2008 the Institute of Electrical and Electronics Engineers, Inc.

mates, stochastic variables are random numbers drawn from a specified probability distribution. Mixed modeling employs both deterministic and stochastic parameters.

It can be risky to draw conclusions based on the results of a single simulation run. One should not be blinded by deterministic point estimates. A point estimate may give a first-cut approximation or an initial handle on things, but stochastic analysis is much preferred. In a purely deterministic model, only one simulation run is needed for a given set of parameters, but with stochastic or mixed modeling the result variables differ from one run to another because the random numbers drawn differ from run to run. In this case, the result variables are best analyzed statistically across a batch of simulation runs (see the section on Monte Carlo analysis).

This appendix describes probability distributions and includes methods for analyzing input data, generating random variates, and analyzing the output of simulation models. More comprehensive treatments of these topics can be found in [Law, Kelton 1991] and [Khoshnevis 1992] (the latter is oriented toward discrete systems). It should be noted that many of the methods for discrete system analysis will not apply to continuous modeling. Autocorrelation from queuing processes and output data dependency are not problems in system dynamics. For example, analysis of queue waiting times via instrumentation of entities is not performed in traditional system dynamics since entity flow is aggregated together. Information on individual entities is generally not available with classic system dynamics simulation tools, though some tools allow limited attribute tracking.

[Sterman 2000] is another source for system dynamics model verification and validation techniques. Chapter 2 in this book already covered much of that same material, but [Sterman 2000] includes more procedures and tools with examples of statistical methods that can be applied to continuous models.

A.1   RISK ANALYSIS AND PROBABILITY

Risk means uncertainty that can be described with a probability distribution. Accordingly, risk analysis implies a study to determine the outcomes of decisions along with their probabilities. For example, answering the question "What is the likelihood of completing a software project within 10 calendar months?" is a risk analysis. A decision maker is often concerned with exploring options and evaluating the resultant probabilities that a project can be carried out with the time and money available. The risks of failure may differ between alternatives and should be estimated as part of the analysis.

In the context of software process management, risk analysis deals with identification of adverse impacts of process risks and determination of their respective probabilities. In decision making under uncertainty, risk mitigation aims to minimize the failure to achieve a desired result, particularly when that result is influenced by factors not entirely under the decision maker's control.

With stochastic analysis, the range of possible inputs and outputs is analyzed. Few parameters are known with certainty and few things in the software process are truly deterministic, so probability distributions are used to assess the effects of uncertainties. By looking at the range of possible results, risk analysis can help answer the question "how much is enough?" in terms of balancing process activities. Examples are shown in subsequent sections.

In probabilistic risk analysis, process model input parameters are specified as distributions. Corresponding output distributions reflect the stochastic ranges of the input parameters. Confidence level risk charts are based on the resulting output distribution. A point on the output distribution corresponding to a desired confidence level specifies the risk tolerance.

Confidence level refers to the probability of not exceeding a given value (e.g., a conservative 90% confidence level cost means a 10% chance of exceeding the cost based on the probabilistic inputs). A point estimate should always be reported with its associated confidence level. In lieu of any other information, the default assumption should be that an estimate refers to the 50% confidence level. This means that half the time the actual result will be less and half the time it will be greater.

One common method of probabilistic estimation involves inputting fixed probability distributions, and is described in the next section. The Monte Carlo simulation technique described later is another method used to analyze stochastic systems. Monte Carlo analysis is a "game of chance" technique used to solve many types of problems by applying random sampling methods. Risk analysis using Monte-Carlo simulation takes random samples from input probability distributions and computes corresponding output probability distributions. It estimates the likely range of outcomes by running a model a large number of times.

There are practical uses of the results of a probabilistic estimate. In terms of estimating costs, you may want to budget contingency funds to cover a comfortable part of the range. For fixed-price jobs, this can be especially important. For setting expectations, one should express size/cost/schedule estimates in terms of ranges rather than fixed numbers (point estimates). Stakeholders are better served by discussing the project in terms of its probability of completion (e.g., there is an 80% chance that effort will be less than 200 person-months).

A.2   PROBABILITY DISTRIBUTIONS

Probability is a quantitative measure of the chance or likelihood of an event occurring. The event may be the delivering of software by a certain date, keeping software costs within a given budget, software having a specified reliability, or having an earthquake on a given day.

A probability distribution is an arrangement of data that shows the frequency of measurements versus measurement values (also called a frequency distribution). See Figure A.1 for a general probability distribution function. The graph is also known as the probability density function $f(x)$ of the random variable x_i. The total area under a probability distribution function (PDF) is unity.

Distributions may be continuous (e.g., the height of people or the time of software development) or they can be discrete (e.g., the number of software defects). Intervals are sometimes used on the abscissa to show the number of measurements within discrete bins, and this bar chart depiction is called a histogram. For discrete functions,

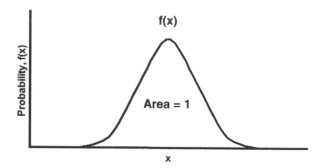

Figure A.1. Probability distribution function.

$F(X)$ is the summation of $f(x)$ and holds the same properties. See Figure A.2 for an example discrete PDF. Generally, we can use continuous probability distributions to also model discrete quantities in the process modeling context, so this section will focus on continuous distributions.

The integral or cumulative form of the PDF is called the cumulative distribution function (CDF). It is also sometimes called a probability distribution function, so we will use the term CDF to distinguish it. The CDF is defined as $F(X)$, the integral of $f(x)$:

$$F(X) = \int f(x)\, dx$$

The CDF has the following properties:

- $0 \leqq F(x) \leqq 1$ for all x
- $F(x)$ is nondecreasing

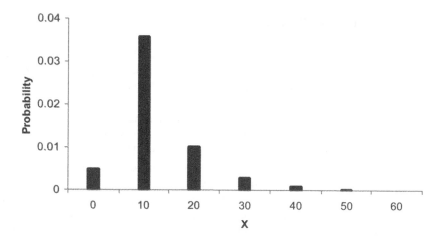

Figure A.2. Discrete probability function.

The CDF gives the probability that a random value x_i is less than or equal to x. This probability is expressed as

$$P(x_i < x)$$

The final value of a CDF is always one, since the entire area under the PDF is also one. Figure A.3 shows a general cumulative distribution corresponding to the PDF in Figure A.1. The PDF is the first derivative of the CDF, since the CDF is the integral of the probability distribution function $f(x)$. A common application of the cumulative distribution is to generate random variates for the Monte Carlo method, and is described in the next major section.

A.2.1 Interpreting Probability Distributions

Recall that the total area under a probability density function is unity. The area under a portion of the probability density function is the probability of a random measurement x_i lying between the two corresonding value x and $x + dx$. In a symmetric normal distribution, 50% of the values lie below the mean and 50% above.

For example, the shaded area in Figure A.4 corresponds to the probability of size being between 40 and 45. It equals the difference of cumulative probabilities evaluated at 45 and 40 shown on the cumulative distribution in Figure A.5, or $F(45) - F(40) = 0.309 - 0.159 = 0.150$. Thus, there is a 15% chance of the size lying between 40 and 45.

The cumulative form of a resulting output distribution can be used as a confidence level chart. Confidence level refers to the probability of not exceeding a given value. See Figure A.6 for a PDF and corresponding CDF that can be used to determine the confidence level as the cumulative probability for a given value.

A sample confidence level chart in the form of a transposed cumulative effort distribution is shown in Figure A.7. The figure represents the results of running many simulation runs, and can be used to assess project cost risk. For example, there is an 80% chance that the project will take 30,000 person-months or less.

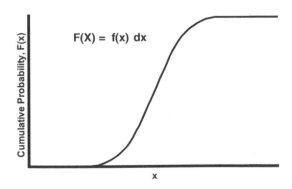

Figure A.3. Cumulative distribution function.

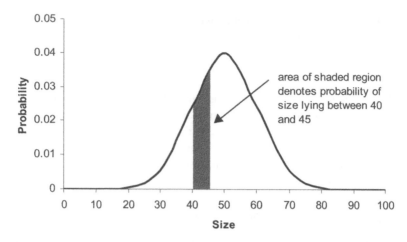

Figure A.4. Interpreting the probability region on a normal probability distribution.

A.2.2 Measures of Location, Variability, and Symmetry

Data and their probability distributions can be summarized in terms of their measures of location (usually a measure of central tendency), variability (referring to how the measures are bunched together or scattered apart), and symmetry. A measure of central tendency is not adequate to give a complete picture of a distribution. Following are the typical measures used:

Mean or average—the measure found by adding together all the measurements of a distribution and dividing by the total number of measurements

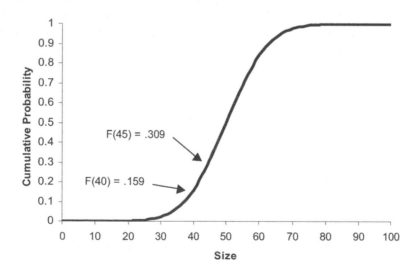

Figure A.5. Calculating probability from cumulative distribution.

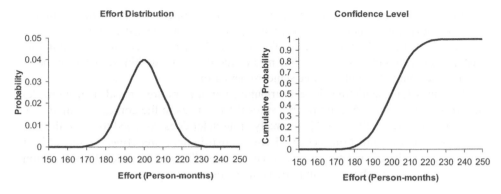

Figure A.6. Sample output distributions.

Median—the middle measurement in a distribution when the measures are arranged from largest to smallest

Mode—the measurement that occurs most often in a distribution

Range—the difference between the lowest and highest measurements

Deviation—the difference between an individual measurement and the mean of a distribution

Variance—the mean of the squared deviations in a distribution

Standard deviation—the square root of the variance; or the square root of the mean of the sum of the squared deviations in a distribution

Skewness—describes how a distribution is shaped in terms of symmetry

Standard deviation is more commonly used to describe the scatter than variance because it uses the same units as the measurements. Standard deviations give a good indication of how wide a distribution is. A small standard deviation indicates a much

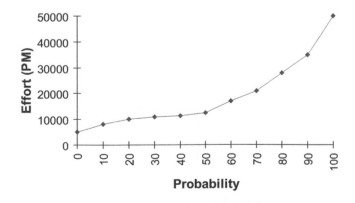

Figure A.7. Confidence level chart using transposed cumulative probability distribution.

narrower distribution than a large deviation. Thus, a statement of just the mean and standard deviation is enough to give a rough picture of a whole distribution.

In a normal distribution, for example, about 68% of measurements lie within one standard deviation on either side of the mean. About 95% lie within two standard deviations, and about 99% within three standard deviations.

Formulas for calculating these distribution parameters are provided in more detailed statistics books. A good reference for the formulas in the context of simulation modeling is [Law, Kelton 1991]. Normally, a modeler does not need to know the formulas since most simulation packages have the distributions predefined. A spreadsheet is another handy adjunct tool to create custom distributions outside of a simulation tool, and the data can be easily imported into a simulation.

A.2.3   Useful Probability Distributions

There are a very large number of probability distributions used in different fields. We will overview some of the simpler distributions that can be applied to software process modeling.

A.2.3.1   Uniform

A uniform distribution is one in which there are an equal number of measures in each interval. It represents an equal probability between its endpoints, as shown in Figure A.8. Any value in the range is equally likely. The uniform distribution $U(0,1)$ is essential for generating random values for all other distributions. It can be used as an initial model for a quantity that is felt to be randomly varying between a and b but about which little else is known.

A.2.3.2   Triangular

The triangular distribution is used when the minimum, maximum, and most likely values of a random variable are known but no other information. A triangular distribution

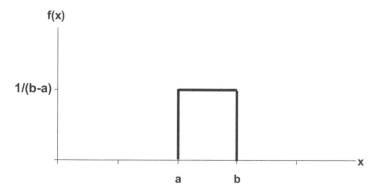

Figure A.8. Uniform distribution.

is often used as a rough model in the absence of data. It accounts for a tapered distribution with the values being centered around the c location parameter. The limiting cases where $c = b$ and $c = a$ are called right-triangular and left-triangular distributions respectively.

A.2.3.3   Normal

A normal distribution is symmetric around the mean and bell shaped (it is also called a bell curve). The most measures occur in the intervals closest to the center of the distribution and fewer in the intervals farther from the center. Figure A.10 shows sample normal probability distributions for the random variable size with different standard deviations (σ). All distributions in the figure have a mean of 50.

Figure A.11 shows the corresponding CDF for the normal distribution in Figure A.10.

A.2.3.4   PERT

The PERT probability distribution used in many cost estimation and scheduling tools is a form of a beta distribution. It is a rounded version of the triangular distribution that can be skewed or resemble a normal distribution. It is specified by three parameters: a minimum, a most likely, and a maximum value. Typically, the minimum and maximum represent 5% and 95% cumulative probabilities, respectively.

A.2.3.5   Lognormal

A skewed distribution is one in which the measurements cluster around a certain value, but that value is not in the center of the distribution. One example is the lognormal distribution, in which $\ln(x)$ is normally distributed. The distribution mean is the mean of $\ln(x)$, and the standard deviation is the standard deviation of $\ln(x)$. Figure A.13 shows three sample lognormal distributions in which the mean of $\ln(x)$ is 0 and standard deviations and 0.5, 1, and 1.5.

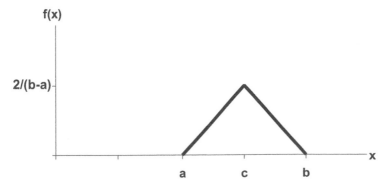

Figure A.9. Triangular distribution.

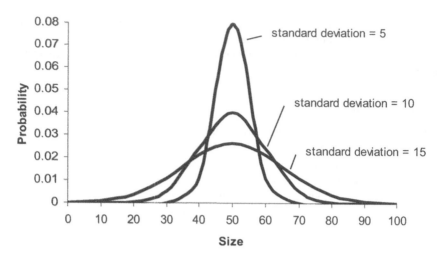

Figure A.10. Normal probability distributions (mean = 50).

The lognormal function can take on shapes similar to the gamma function or the Weibull distribution (the Rayleigh curve is actually a special case of the Weibull distribution). The density takes on shapes similar to gamma (a,b) and Weibull (a,b) for densities for $a > 1$, but can have a large spike close to $x = 0$.

One drawback of a lognormal function is that it frequently has an extremely long tail. Hence, we resort to a truncated lognormal function to bound the distribution to more realistic end values. The previous distribution is shown truncated in Figure A.14. This distribution is often a good one to model the overall size or complexity of a software project, as one tends to underestimate the maximum possible values. Studies have shown that a lognormal distribution describes the ratio of actual effort to estimates from completed projects.

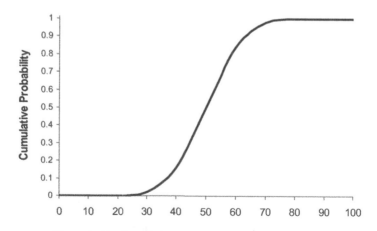

Figure A.11. Cumulative normal probability distribution.

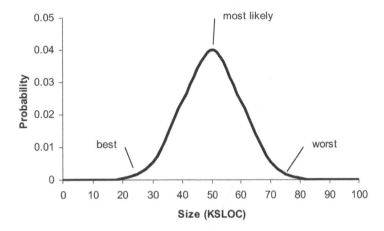

Figure A.12. PERT distribution.

A.2.3.6 Gamma

Another skewed distribution is the gamma function. It is shown in Figure A.15 with varying values of the beta parameter while holding alpha constant. It can be used to model the time to complete a task, or it can also be used in reliability studies to model the time to failure of a software component or system. The gamma function, the log-

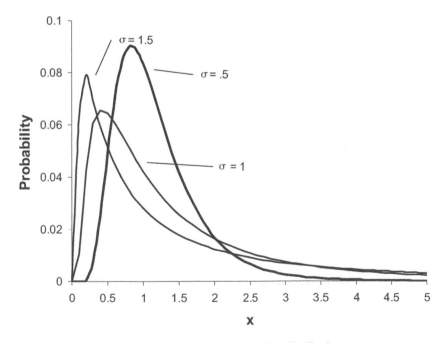

Figure A.13. Lognormal probability distribution.

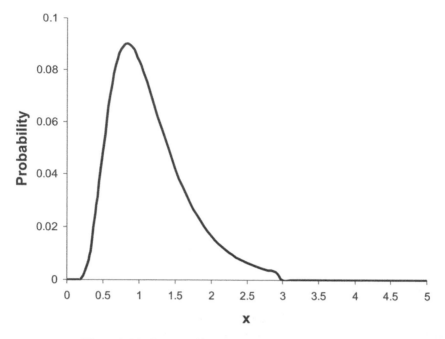

Figure A.14. Truncated lognormal probability distribution.

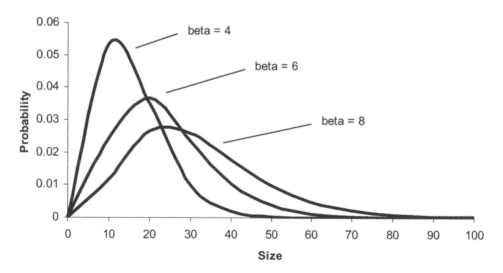

Figure A.15. Gamma probability distribution (alpha = 4).

normal distribution, and the Weibull distribution (Rayleigh curve) can take on very similar shapes.

A.2.3.7 Empirical Distributions

When actual observed data is available, an empirical distribution can be derived from it instead of resorting to a theoretical distribution. Sometimes, a theoretical distribution will not adequately fit the data, and often an empirical distribution will be more realistic since it is predicated on real data (assuming there is enough data). For example, some data might exhibit a bimodal distribution and the best way to represent it is building up your own empirical distribution.

A.2.3.8 Summary of Probability Distributions

A summary of the major characteristics of probability distributions is shown in Table A.1.

What are the best probability distributions to use for software processes? See Table A.2 for basic distributions that can be used in software process modeling. The uniform distribution is a simple one to start out with, and is relevant when there is an equal probability of a variable within a given range or no better information is known. Next in sophistication is the triangular distribution. It does not have to be symmetric, and some skewness can be modeled with it.

Table A.1. Probability distribution summary

	Probability Distribution		Cumulative Probability Distribution	
	Function	Graph	Function	Graph
Continuous	$P(x < x_i < x + dx) = f(x)$	frequency vs. measurement value	$P(x_i \leq x) = F(X)$	Cumulative percentage
	$f(x)$ is the first derivative of $F(X)$		$F(X) = \int f(x)dx$	
Discrete	$P(x < x_i, x + \Delta x) = f(x)$	frequency vs. measurement value	$P(x_i \leq x) = F(X)$	Cumulative percentage
	$f(x)$ is a term of $F(X)$		$F(X) = \Sigma f(x)$	

Table A.2. Basic distributions for modeling software processes

Distribution	Shape	Typical Applications
Uniform		• Used in the absence of distribution data • Used to represent equally likely outcomes (e.g., decision choices) • Software cost drivers
Triangle		• A rough model to use when the minimum, most likely, and maximum are known but no other distribution shape data • Software cost drivers, including size
Normal (or PERT)		• Personnel factors representing a normal spread of capability • Size, effort, complexity, and other project characteristics • PERT is available in many software project estimation or modeling tools; it can be used to approximate the normal and other distributions
Lognormal (or gamma)		• System size, effort, complexity • Accounts for typical underestimation of scope and system-wide effects
Truncated lognormal		• To prevent nonpositive values or other inconsistent values from a standard lognormal distribution (e.g., when the mean is close enough to zero that the spread goes negative)

A normal distribution can be used to model some quantities more realistically than a triangular distribution, but it is a symmetric distribution, and care should be taken when using it to ensure that the quantity being modeled is indeed symmetric. It can be used to model errors of various types, other process parameters like size and cost drivers, or quantities that are the sum of a large number of other quantities [according to the Central Limit Theorem (CLT)]. An application of the latter would be the roll-up summary of subhierarchical software components.

The PERT distribution is simple to implement and can approximate a symmetrical normal distribution or a skewed distribution like the triangle or lognormal. It is available in many packages and often gives good enough results given the inherent uncertainties. But if more precise information is known about a parameter distribution, then one should consider an alternative if the PERT is not a good fit and modeling precision is important.

Generally speaking, software engineers are an optimistic bunch when it comes to estimating and want to think that everything will go fine. Also, some aspects of the job are often ignored. Interfaces, glue code, and such are often not considered when estimating a system at the top level, and more often than not the size is under-estimated. To compensate for these tendencies, positively skewed distributions of size or effort with long tails are recommended to be realistic for many estimating situations.

The asymmetric log-normal distribution is relevant for modeling system size, complexity, or the time to perform some task, particularly since scope is usually underestimated and unconsidered details tend to increase the job size. It will account for the asymmetry in the expected outcomes. It is often useful for quantities that are the product of a large number of other quantities (by virtue of the CLT).

A.3   MONTE CARLO ANALYSIS

Monte Carlo analysis is a "game of chance" technique used to solve many types of problems by applying random sampling instead of analytic methods. Samples are taken from known input probability distributions to create output distributions. It estimates the likely range of outcomes from a complex random process by simulating the process a large number of times. It can be used to solve stochastic models in simulation, or to obtain approximate solutions for definite integrals, integrodifferential equations, and linear equations. It is an analysis method often referred to as Monte Carlo simulation, which does not necessarily imply continuous system simulation or even time-based simulation (it is often applied to static situations). The term *Monte Carlo analysis* is used to eliminate confusion.

The following steps are performed for *n* iterations in a Monte Carlo analysis, where an iteration refers to a single simulation run:

1. For each random variable, take a sample from its probability distribution function and calculate its value.
2. Run a simulation using the random input samples and compute the corresponding simulation outputs.
3. Repeat the above steps until *n* simulation runs have been performed.
4. Determine the output probability distributions of selected dependent variables using the *n* values from the runs.

A.3.1   Inverse Transform

Monte Carlo analysis uses random numbers to sample from known probability distributions to determine specific outcomes. The inverse transform technique for generating random variates is convenient for this. First, a random number r is chosen that is uniformly distributed between 0 and 1. It is set equal to the cumulative distribution, $F(x) = r$, and x is solved for. A particular value r_0 gives a value x_0, which is a particular sample value of X. It can be expressed as

$$x_0 = F^{-1}(r_0)$$

This construction is shown in Figure A.16 to generate values x of the random variable X that represents size. It graphically demonstrates how the inverse transform uses the cumulative probability function for generating random variates using random samples between 0 and 1 for input.

Referring to Figure A.16, first a random number between 0 and 1 is generated, then the cumulative distribution is used to find the corresponding random variate. In the example from a normal distribution, the first random number of 0.42 generates a value of size = 48. The second random draw of 0.86 produces a value of size = 61 per the figure.

There is a strong intuitive appeal to the inverse transform method. The technique works because more random number inputs will hit the steep parts of the CDF, thus concentrating the random variates under those regions where the CDF is steep, exactly the same regions where the PDF is high. Since the PDF is the derivative of the CDF $[f(x) = F'(x)]$, $f(x)$ can be viewed as the slope function of $F(x)$. Thus, the CDF rises most steeply for values of x where $f(x)$ is large and, conversely, it is flat where $f(x)$ is small.

The Monte Carlo method will fill out a distribution of random variates prescribed by the PDF, since most of them will be from the largest areas of the original distribution. The corresponding distribution of random variates will thus resemble the PDF after enough iterations. See the following example for an illustration of Monte Carlo analysis as applied to software effort estimation.

A.3.2   Example: Monte Carlo Analysis

This example will simulate the randomness of the size input to a dynamic effort model, and quantify the resulting output in probabilistic terms. Assume that the likely values for size can be represented with a normal probability distribution as shown in Figure A.17 with a mean of 50 KSLOC and a standard deviation of 10 KSLOC.

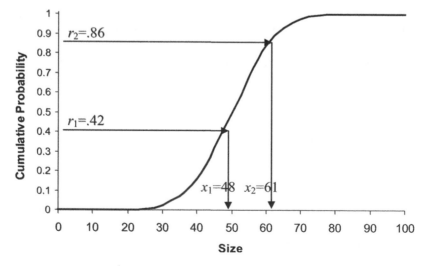

Figure A.16. Cumulative probability distribution and the inverse transform for two random draws.

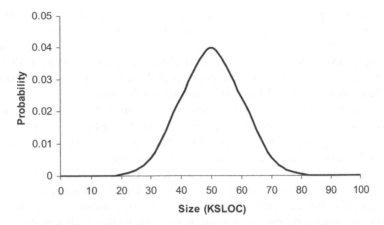

Figure A.17. Normal probability distribution representing size.

To implement Monte Carlo analysis, a small set of $n = 16$ random samples will be generated for size input to the Dynamic COCOMO model. In actual practice, 16 would be a very low number (except for very large and expensive simulation iterations). Generally, 50–100 iterations should be considered as a minimum for filling out distributions, and up to 1000 iterations will give good results in many situations.

First, 16 random numbers between 0 and 1 are generated. The inverse transform technique is then used to determine size by mapping the random numbers onto its cumulative distribution function. Table A.3 shows the set of 16 random numbers (r_i) and the generated size values $F^{-1}(r_i)$.

Table A.3. Monte Carlo analysis inputs

Iteration	Random Number (0–1)	Size (KSLOC)
1	0.321	45.4
2	0.550	51.3
3	0.091	36.6
4	0.807	58.7
5	0.427	48.1
6	0.667	54.3
7	0.451	48.8
8	0.003	22.7
9	0.727	56.0
10	0.360	46.4
11	0.954	66.8
12	0.371	46.7
13	0.224	42.4
14	0.704	55.4
15	0.787	57.9
16	0.202	41.7

Figure A.18 graphically illustrates the inverse transform technique using the same numbers to determine size 16 times via the cumulative distribution function. Note how the steepness in the middle of the CDF produces more size numbers in the central region compared to the more uniform spread of the initial random numbers. The reader is encouraged to eyeball the graph and notice that about 50% of the random spread in the middle maps into about 25% of the values per the distribution.

Dynamic COCOMO is then run 16 times with the respective size inputs. The simulation outputs for the personnel staffing curve in Figure A.34 demonstrate the model sensitivity to the size samples. Project effort is the area under a staffing curve. Table A.4 shows the cumulative project effort for the 16 iterations.

Figure A.20 shows the Monte Carlo results in terms of an effort distribution histogram and its continuous representation. It stacks up the 16 simulation outputs for the total project effort into respective effort bins. A smoother distribution would be seen filled out when more iterations are run and plotted beyond the small sample size of 16.

Figure A.21 shows the cumulative effort distribution used as a confidence level chart. With enough iterations, the cumulative chart could also be drawn on a standard continuous axis without the large bins. One can read that the 80% confidence level is at 290 person-months, which means there is a 20% chance of effort being greater than 290 person-months per the model.

A.3.2.1   Randomness for Multiple Parameters

This simple example only modeled the randomness of a single input parameter (size), and the same technique is used to simulate the random distributions of multiple input parameters at once. Random input samples are drawn for each parameter for each iteration.

Suppose in a given model that the dependent variable effort depends on size and

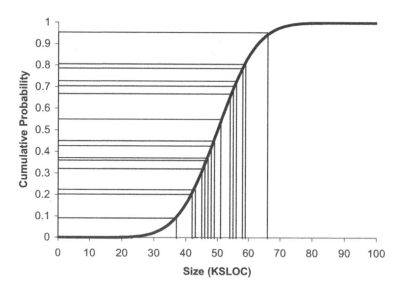

Figure A.18. Monte Carlo analysis using inverse transform technique.

personnel: 1 - 2 - 3 - 4 - 5 - 6 - 7 - 8 - 9 - 10 - 11 - 12 - 13 - 14 - 15 -

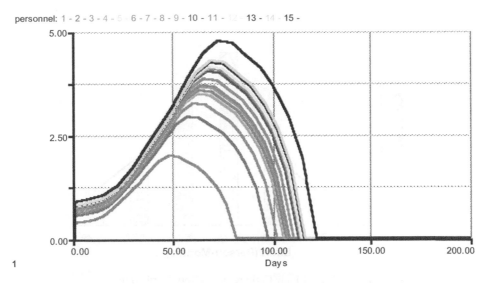

1

Figure A.19. Monte Carlo results: personnel staffing curves for 16 runs.

complexity:

$$\text{Effort} = f(\text{Size}, \text{Complexity})$$

Figure A.22 shows the Monte Carlo procedure for the two-parameter example.

Table A.4. Monte Carlo effort output

Iteration	Effort (Person-months)
1	217.7
2	252.2
3	168.6
4	296.5
5	234.0
6	270.4
7	237.5
8	94.9
9	280.7
10	223.9
11	346.7
12	225.6
13	200.9
14	276.6
15	292.2
16	196.6

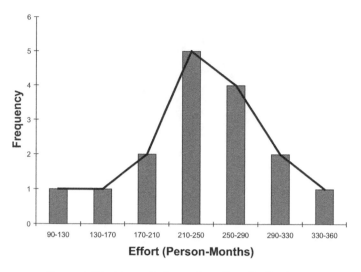

Figure A.20. Monte Carlo results: effort distribution.

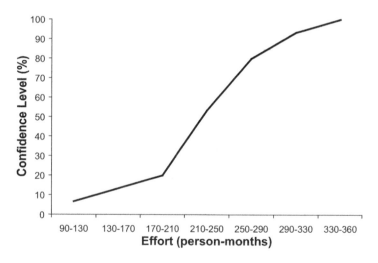

Figure A.21. Monte carlo results: confidence level chart (cumulative effort distribution).

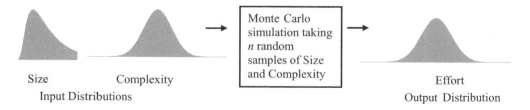

Figure A.22. Monte Carlo analysis for two parameters.

A.4   ANALYSIS OF SIMULATION INPUT

To build a representative simulation model, the random effects in a system must be recreated. This section describes some methods to analyze input data that go hand in hand with the probability concepts previously described. Top-level steps performed during input analysis are:

- Identifying system input variables
- Collecting data on the input variables
- Estimating the parameters of the data distribution
- Fitting known distributions to the data
- Hypothesis testing to validate the distribution
- Selecting a distribution and generating random numbers for the simulation.

One way of recreating random effects is to use a stream of data from real-world processes. There are a number of significant practical problems, though. Field data is usually limited and there is substantial effort and time associated with its collection and reformatting for simulation models. It could also be quite voluminous to use with a model. Field data, if available, is valid only for currently operating processes. However, the purpose of many simulation studies is to analyze hypothetical future systems. Lastly, it could be very difficult to perform sensitivity analyses on field data.

It is important to note that field data could be very useful for validity checking. A model subjected to input field data should ideally perform like the system being simulated, and its output statistics should match closely to the actual system.

Due to the practical limitations described above, a means for artificially generating random data to match certain specifications is desired. You should collect sufficient field data to serve as a reliable sample of the actual statistical population. Next, perform a statistical analysis of the collected sample to identify the probability distribution of the population from which the sample was taken, and then use a method to create random variates that represent the population.

It is desirable to use an available PDF that fits the field data in question. First, one must identify which theoretical PDF best fits the real world data. This can be done by various means such as statistical goodness-of-fit tests. Visual inspections of real data frequency histograms can be used as a first step to identify candidate PDFs before rigorous statistical testing.

A.4.1   Goodness-of-Fit Tests

A goodness-of-fit test is a statistical hypothesis test. It assesses whether data points are independent samples from a particular probability distribution. Two of the more popular goodness-of-fit methods include the older chi-square test and the Kolmogorov–Smirnov test.

In the chi-square test, a histogram of field data is built. The upper and lower bounds of each cell of the histogram are taken, and the probability of the random variable falling within each pair of upper and lower bounds is found. It essentially is a formal comparison of a histogram or line graph with the fitted density function. The following test statistic is calculated:

$$X_2 = \sum_{j=1}^{k} (N_j - np_j)^2/np_j$$

where N_j is the number of X_is in the jth interval, and pj is the expected proportion of of X_is that would fall in the jth interval. Since np_j is the expected number of n X_is that would fall in the jth interval if the hypothesis were true, we would expect X_2 to be small if the fit is good. Therefore, we reject the hypothesis if X_2 is too large.

The Kolmogorov–Smirnov test does not require a histogram of the field data like the chi-square test, and works well with a small number of data points. Its disadvantage is that it only applies to continuous distributions. The test is performed by developing an empirical cumulative probability distribution function based on the field data, and then comparing it with the cumulative probability function of the candidate theoretical distribution. The test is based on the largest absolute deviation between the empirical and theoretical CDF for every given value of x. The following five steps are performed:

1. Rank the field data in increasing order.
2. Compute the following using the theoretical CDF:

$$D^+ = \max_{1 \leq i \leq N} [i/N - F(x_i)]$$

$$D^- = \max_{1 \leq i \leq N} [F(x_i) - (i-1)/N]$$

3. Let $D = \max (D^+, D^-)$.
4. Find the critical value from a Kolmogorov–Smirnov table for a given significance level and sample size.
5. If D is less than or equal to the critical value, accept the candidate distribution as having a good fit to the field data. Reject it otherwise.

The chi-square test is more appropriate for large numbers of data points and discrete distributions. The Kolmogorov–Smirnov is better suited for smaller sample sizes and continuous distributions. Worked-out examples of these are shown in [Law, Kelton 1991], [Khnoshevis 1994], or other simulation analysis references. Other goodness-of-fit approaches have been developed. The reader is encouraged is study advanced statistical texts to learn more.

A.4.1.1 Example: Goodness-of-Fit Test

We will use the Kolmogorov–Smirnov test to assess whether a set of data on change request sizes is uniformly distributed between 1 and 2 with a significance level of $\alpha = 0.05$. Suppose we have five observations on the size of change requests in function points as follows: 1.38, 1.25, 1.06, 2.0, and 1.56. For the uniform distribution, the CDF is

$$F(x_i) = z/(b - a) \qquad a \leqq x \leqq b$$

When $b = 2$ and $a = 1$, $F(x_i) = z/2$. Table A.5 shows the calculations. $D = \max(0.02, 0.53) = 0.53$. The critical value from Kolmogorov–Smirnov tables for a sample size of 5 and significance level of 0.05 is 0.565. D is less than the critical value, so the hypothesis that the distribution of data is uniform between 1 and 2 is not rejected.

A.5 EXPERIMENTAL DESIGN

An "experiment" in our context is the execution of a computer simulation model. Experimental design is a way of deciding before runs are made which configurations to simulate so that the desired information can be obtained with a minimal amount of simulating. Carefully designed experiments will eliminate the "hit and miss" experience.

Parametric as well as structural changes to the model might be called for. Changing the length of each run, systematically changing the parameters, and multivariate comparisons are involved during experimentation. The experimentation ultimately should lead to an understanding of the simulated system and how to improve it.

In many cases, trial and error is necessary to try a large number of values to optimize system performance. (Note that some system dynamics simulation packages enable limited optimization.) Finding the optimal value for a system may require a heuristic search process using derivatives. There are other special search techniques that are beyond the scope of this book. Heuristic optimization is more valuable as the number of decision parameters increase. Otherwise, all possible combinations of variables must be tried, which can be prohibitively time-consuming.

A simulation model is a mechanism that turns inputs into output performance measures; in this sense, a simulation is just a function. In many cases a three-dimensional response surface can represent the output space of a simulation model. The next section shows an example output response surface. A whole area of response surface methodologies exists to seek the optimal configuration. Many of these techniques use a gradient approach.

Table A.5. Kolmogorov–Smirnov calculations

i	x_i	$F(x_i)$	i/n	$i/n - F(x_i)$	$F(x_i) - (i - 1)/n$
1	1.06	0.53	0.2	−0.33	0.53
2	1.25	0.625	0.4	−0.225	0.425
3	1.38	0.69	0.6	−0.09	0.29
4	1.56	0.78	0.8	0.02	0.18
5	2.0	1.0	1.0	0	0.2
				$D^+ = 0.02$	$D^- = 0.53$

The input parameters and structural assumptions are called factors, and the output performance measures are called responses. Which parameters and structures to keep fixed and which are factors to vary depends on the goals of the study rather than the form of a model. Factors are also classified as controllable or uncontrollable depending on whether they represent management options in the real-world system. Normally, we focus on the controllable factors.

The experimental design for a one-factor model is simple. Run the simulation at various values, or levels, of the factor. A confidence interval could be formed for the expected response at each of the factor levels. Suppose now there are k factors and we want an estimate of how each factor affects the response, as well as whether the factors interact with each other. The number of runs can balloon as all factors must be set at specific levels to test their interaction with a particular one. A 2^k factorial design is an economical strategy to measure interactions. It requires only two levels for each factor and then calls for simulation runs at each of the 2^k possible factor-level combinations. The reader should consult advanced statistical texts for more information on experimental design.

A.5.1   Example: Experimental Design and Model Response Surface

The simple Brooks's Law model is Chapter 1 is used to create a model response surface. The model output is defined as schedule gain relative to the original plan of 200 days. The two input parameters varied are the number of added staff and the progress gap threshold used before adding people. The experimental design will simply straddle the region described in the original example around a 15% gap threshold. The model is thus run at the gap thresholds of 5%, 10%, 15%, 20%, and 25%. The added staff varies from 0, 5, and 10 per the original example.

Figure A.23 shows the response surface generated from these experiments. Since schedule gain is plotted in the Z-dimension, a large value is a desired result. Thus,

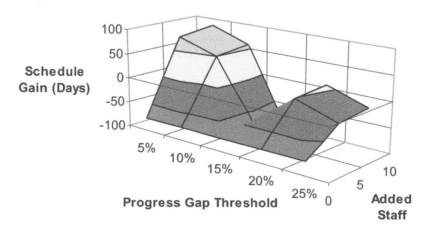

Figure A.23. Brooks's Law model response surface.

maxima can be interpreted as process optima or sweet spots. The behavior of the model can be analyzed from such a response surface.

A.6 ANALYSIS OF SIMULATION OUTPUT

Simulation models convert stochastic inputs and system components into statistical data output. Hence, simulation is another sampling method and the output is subject to statistical analysis. Some purposes of analyzing simulation output are

- To determine characteristics of certain variables for given inputs
- To compare variable characteristics under different conditions
- To improve a system or design a future one

As simulation is a sampling process, variable estimates are subject to sampling choice and sample size. Discrete event simulation has unique concerns that are not addressed here, such as data dependency. Independency of sample data allows use of classical statistical analysis; however, most discrete simulation models lack independence. Queuing processes, for example, usually lead to autocorrelation. Readers who are concerned with data dependency and discrete event modeling are encouraged to read general simulation texts to learn more.

Output analysis typically differs for terminating versus nonterminating systems. In the software process modeling arena, very few applications are for nonterminating systems, hence the distinction will not be addressed here.

A.6.1 Confidence Intervals, Sample Size, and Hypothesis Testing

We desire to know the true value of a simulation output parameter based on the results of many simulation runs. The accuracy of a statistical estimate is expressed over an interval. The confidence level is the probability that the interval contains the true value of the parameter. The confidence interval is updated after the result of each simulation run.

The interpretation of a confidence interval follows. If one constructs a very large number of $(1 - \alpha)$ confidence intervals each based on n observations, in the long run $(1 - \alpha)$ of the intervals contain the parameter value. The parameter α is also called the significance level, or the probability of rejecting a hypothesis when it is true.

For a given confidence level, a small confidence interval is preferable. For a given confidence interval, a higher confidence level is preferable. In practice, choose a confidence level. The sample size affects confidence level and interval, such that smaller confidence intervals require a larger sample size. The $(1 - \alpha)$ confidence interval relationship can be written as

$$P\{-Z_{\alpha/2} \leq Z \leq Z_{\alpha/2}\} = 1 - \alpha$$

where Z is distributed normally with a mean of zero and standard deviation of one. Z is expressed as

$$Z = (X - \mu)/\sigma_x$$

where X is the sample mean, μ is the population mean and σ is the standard deviation of the population of random variables. Substituting Z in the previous expression gives the confidence interval as follows:

$$P\{X - Z_{\alpha/2}\sigma/\sqrt{n} \leq \mu \leq X + Z_{\alpha/2}\sigma/\sqrt{n}\} = 1 - \alpha$$

Figure A.24 depicts the confidence interval using a normal distribution with a mean of one. The true mean falls in the confidence interval with a probability of $(1 - \alpha)$. Use normal distribution tables for Z if there are greater than 30 samples, and use the student t distribution when the sample size is less than 30.

The formulas for confidence intervals can be manipulated to determine the converse—the required sample size to attain a desired confidence interval width in conjunction with an estimated sample variance. Variance usually decreases with sample size. Other special variance reduction techniques are available, but these are important only for large models and have been deemphasized with modern computing power.

In hypothesis testing, you start with a null hypothesis and set the significance level α (the confidence interval is $1 - \alpha$). Example hypotheses can be that the parameter mean is in an interval or it is greater than a certain value or less than a certain value. You fail to reject the hypothesis if certain statistical relationships hold true. We already saw the formula for interval testing, and the ones for other comparisons are found in statistical texts.

Statistical techniques covered so far assume samples are independent and identically distributed. Independent replication is a technique that addresses the problem of autocorrelation that works as follows:

- Perform several short runs (replications) from time = 0.
- Use different random number seeds per run (or possibly different initial conditions) so replications are then independent of each other.
- Each replication mean is an independent observation.
- Compute the mean, variance, and confidence interval.

Batch means is a method that only applies to steady state analysis. It alleviates the problem of handling transitional periods during independent replications. You divide a single run into multiple intervals (batches). Batch mean values serve as independent samples. You can use the runs up and down test to detect dependencies, and determine optimal batch size to minimize data dependencies. The runs up and down test use sequential data points. A run is a succession of similar increasing or decreasing patterns in the sequence. The number of "runs" is counted, and equations computed for hypothesis testing.

More mathematical background on independent replications, batch means, and runs up and down can be found in [Khoshnevis 1991] or other discrete event simulation

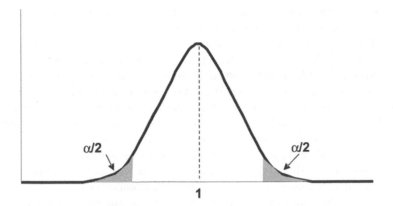

Figure A.24. Confidence interval.

texts. Also beware of nonnormality in the simulation data. This topic becomes quickly advanced and readers should consult more detailed statistics references.

A.6.1.1   Example: Confidence Interval Calculation

We will use the results of the Monte Carlo example simulation in Section A.3.2 to estimate the 90% confidence interval for the effort output. The array of outputs in Table A.4 is used to calculate a mean of 238 and a standard deviation of 58.8. For a sample size of 16, we resort to a standard t-distribution table and find a value of 1.75 corresponding to 15 degrees of freedom and t_{95}. Since we want a 90% interval, $\alpha/2 = 5\%$ and we keep 5% at each tail at the distribution by looking up the value for $1 - \alpha/2$. Thus the 90% confidence interval is

$$P\{238 - 1.75 \cdot 58.8/\sqrt{16}\} \leq \mu \leq \{238 - 1.75 \cdot 58.8/\sqrt{16}\} = 0.9 = \{212 \leq \mu \leq 264\}$$

Thus the 90% confidence interval for simulated effort is between 212 and 264 person-months, and we fail to reject the hypothesis that the means lies in that interval. The interval would be larger if we wanted 95% confidence.

A.7   MAJOR REFERENCES

[Law, Kelton 1991] Law M., and Kelton W., *Simulation Modeling and Analysis.* New York: McGraw-Hill, 1991.

[Khoshnevis 1992] Khoshnevis B, *Systems Simulation—Implementations in EZSIM.* New York: McGraw-Hill, 1992.

A.8   APPENDIX A SUMMARY

The random effects inherent in systems should be modeled to build representative simulations. It is prudent to look at the range of possible results from a model rather than be blinded by a deterministic point estimate. It is more meaningful to discuss projects in terms of ranges that represent uncertainty, or risk.

In risk analysis, one tries to gauge the adverse impacts and probabilities of risk items. Probability distributions are used to express the stochastic ranges of simulation inputs and outputs and account for the uncertainties. When a probability distribution is used to express the output of several simulation runs, its cumulative form can be used to assess the confidence level for a given value in the distribution. Stakeholders can gauge the associated confidence level of their plans to help risk manage the project and, in fact, every estimate should be reported with an associated confidence level. Otherwise, others should assume the 50% confidence level by default. The overall uncertainty of estimates should decrease over time, however, as a project progresses, because the product becomes more elaborated with less unknowns.

Several popular types of probability distributions can be used for the software process domain, including the uniform, triangle, normal, PERT, and lognormal and its truncated version. Standard parameters are used to describe their shapes. They are best applied in different situations per the guidelines described in the text.

The Monte Carlo method is one of the most convenient and popular ways to create random variates for simulation runs through the use of probability distributions and inverse transforms. Random numbers between 0 and 1 are used to index into a known cumulative probability distribution to generate the random variates. Those variates are then used as inputs to a simulation. Multiple input parameters can be used as random inputs to the Monte Carlo technique to better reflect the uncertainties. There are a variety of tools that can support Monte Carlo simulation.

Simulation input analysis looks at the pattern of real inputs and attempts to model them with appropriate distributions. Goodness-of-fit tests are used to test hypotheses about whether distributions are well fitted to data. The chi-square and Kolmogorov–Smirnov are two frequently used methods for this.

In experimental design, we decide before simulation on what configurations to run. These experiments should be carefully thought out in order to minimize the number of runs and get the maximum information from the simulations. Factors are chosen to be run at different values. A 2^k factorial design is an economical design strategy for larger models.

Simulation is a sampling method in itself and, correspondingly, its output is subjected to statistical analysis. We would like to determine the characteristics of specific outputs with known confidence. Statistical methods are used to determine the confidence intervals for output parameters. Hypothesis testing is used determine if a parameter is an interval or not, after setting the desired significance level and accounting for the sample size.

With proper experimental design, simulation is handy for process optimization to determine "how much is enough." Process models are run over reasonable ranges in order to find the optima. Typically, a balance needs to be found between counteracting effects. Process optimization also helps determine the break-even points where activities lost their cost effectiveness.

Process simulation techniques are crucial for good risk management, and they are highly complementary in nature. Process simulation can help in both the assessment and control of risks. Model factors provide a powerful mechanism to identify risks in union with simulation, so risks are not ignored. Models also support risk management by analyzing cost and schedule impacts, trade-offs, and sensitivities. Simulation can also help quantify the uncertainties in addition to the consequences of risk items. Sensitivity analysis is useful to determine the relative variance of outputs to changes in input parameters. Decision making is also supported by quantifying the risk-reduction leverage of different options.

But analysis is not a one-time event and changes occur. Risk assessment is a continuous process throughout a project life cycle and, commensurately, simulations should be frequently updated and rerun to provide the best information for risk management decisions.

Risk exposure is defined as the probability of a loss multiplied by the cost consequence of that loss. Risk exposure is a convenient framework for software decision analysis, and process modeling can contribute to analyses in several ways. Risk exposure analysis is a valuable framework to find the "sweet spots" of processes, such has how much testing or rigor is enough (Sections 4.6 and 6.4 show examples). By identifying the risks of doing too much and too little, summing risk exposure curves will find the sweet spots.

Process models easily support discrete trade-offs such as choosing between teams or toolsets. The relative costs, schedule, or other impacts can be quantified. Finally, they can help in the back and forth of project negotiations by quantifying the trade space for decisions to be made.

A.9 EXERCISES

A.1. Describe in your own words what a confidence level signifies.

A.2. a) Collect data on important software process measures in your organization and construct their probability distributions. Alternatively, use data from other sources and create representative probability distributions.

b) Now decide if any standard distributions are good fits to the data. Employ goodness-of-fit tests and report your results.

A.3. Here is a dataset of defect fixing times in person-hours: 3.5, 3.0, 17.1, 15.3, 10, 12.9, 4.5, 3.0, 19.4, 21.1, 17.4, 14.5, and 17.1. Construct its frequency histogram and cumulative distribution. Does it appear to be any of the standard distributions?

A.4. Review the basic distributions for modeling software processes. Critically analyze whether they are good representations or not. Suggest other distributions, as applicable.

A.5. Suppose someone tells you an estimate for a software project as a point estimate (single number) with no other information. What is your assumption with no other context given? What questions would you have and what suggestions for improved communication?

A.6. Generate 100 random variates with an exponential distribution and a mean of 15.

A.7. The PDF of function x is defined as

$$f(x) = x/16 \qquad \text{for } 0 \leqq x \leqq 4$$
$$f(x) = 1/4 \qquad \text{for } 4 \leqq x \leqq 6$$

Draw the PDF. Use the inverse transform method to develop the relationships to generate a random variate given a random number between 0 and 1. Describe in your own words how the Monte Carlo analysis technique works.

A.8. Using the inverse transform technique, develop the equations for creating triangularly distributed random variates.

A.9. Use one of the provided models in the book and modify it to run Monte Carlo simulations. Choose an appropriate variable in the model and create your own random variates for it. Make the runs and summarize your results.

A.10. Use a spreadsheet or other tool to create Monte Carlo inputs for (1) a normal, (2) a triangular, and (3) a truncated lognormal distribution.

A.11. Explain the difference in the procedure to determine the 90% confidence interval if 50 observations were available in Section A.6.1.1.

A.12. Construct the 85% and 95% confidence intervals for the Monte Carlo example results.

A.13. Name five specific examples whereby simulation can help in software risk management.

Advanced Exercises

A.14. Apply 2^k experimental design principles to the Chapter 1 Brooks's Law model.

A.15. Modify the Dynamic COCOMO model to accept two random inputs and run a Monte Carlo analysis.

ANNOTATED SYSTEM DYNAMICS BIBLIOGRAPHY

CONTENTS AND SOURCES

This section summarizes publications that involve system dynamics modeling of software processes. These same citations are listed in boldface in the references. Some grouped longitudinal bodies of work are listed with multiple citations. Only modeling with system dynamics is covered; therefore, important work with other techniques is not listed. Figure B-1 shows a Venn diagram of the current coverage. Some hybrid modeling with system dynamics and discrete event methods are included, less than 10% of the citations listed.

Publication titles in the bibliography with quotation marks are the original titles from the authors. Titles for groups of references describe the overall work and do not have quotations. Each entry in the bibliography also contains an abbreviation key for the type of reference per Figure B-2.

Books represented include the seminal *Software Project Dynamics* [Abdel-Hamid, Madnick 1991], recent edited compilations on software process modeling with chapters involving system dynamics [Acuña, Juristo 2005, Acuña, Sánchez-Segura 2006], other edited books with relevant chapters and even a novel on software project management [Demarco 1998].

The journals most frequently represented in the bibliography that publish about software process modeling with system dynamics are:

Software Process Dynamics. By Raymond J. Madachy
Copyright © 2008 the Institute of Electrical and Electronics Engineers, Inc.

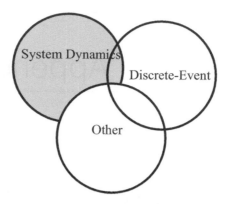

Figure B-1. Coverage of modeling techniques.

- *Software Process Improvement and Practice* (see special issues per Table B-1 at the end of this appendix)
- *Journal of Systems and Software* (see special issues per Table B-1 at the end of this appendix)
- *American Programmer* (see special issue per Table B-2 at the end of this appendix). This journal has since been renamed as *Cutter IT Journal.*

Other journals include:

- *Annals of Software Engineering*
- *Communications of the ACM*
- *IEEE Computer*
- *IEEE Software*
- *IEEE Transactions on Education*

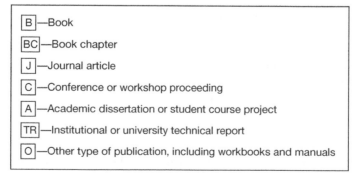

Figure B-2. Publication type legend.

- *IEEE Transactions on Software Engineering*
- *Information and Software Technology*
- *International Journal of Software Engineering and Knowledge Engineering*
- *Software Concepts and Tools*
- *Software Practice and Experience*

These journals in the above list are also the most likely sources for future work in the field.

Since 1998, the *International Workshop on Software Process Simulation and Modeling (ProSim)* has been the main venue for the field. It is now called the *International Conference on Software Process* after recently joining with the *International Software Process Workshop* (previously held since the 1980s) to become the leading event for systems and software process research. Each year, selected best papers are revised and published in a special journal. Table B-1 is an endnote to the bibliography that lists the year of the workshop and the corresponding journal issue with the revised papers. Only the journal versions are listed here for papers published in both places. If one is not available, then readers can consult the table to find the corresponding publication.

The *International System Dynamics Conference* is the leading venue for system dynamics and systems thinking that includes contributions from many disciplines besides software. There are other conferences and workshops represented that are related to software process improvement, cost modeling, software quality, and similar topics in software or systems engineering.

Numerous companies, government agencies, and universities have sponsored work listed in the tables. They are sometimes the sources for technical reports, dissertations, and other references. Companies have also published internal proprietary reports involving system dynamics not available to the public.

BIBLIOGRAPHY

[Abdel-Hamid 1984]　　　　　　　　　　　　　　　　　　　　　　　　　　　A
"The Dynamics of Software Project Staffing: An Integrative System Dynamics Perspective"
  This was Abdel-Hamid's Ph.D. dissertation of his integrated model for software projects. See [Abdel-Hamid, Madnick 1991] for full details of the model.

[Abdel-Hamid 1989a]　　　　　　　　　　　　　　　　　　　　　　　　　　　J
"The dynamics of software project staffing: A system dynamics based simulation approach"
  This describes the Abdel-Hamid model of software project staffing throughout the software development lifecycle. A case study is used to simulate staffing practices. The experiment provides insights into explicit and implicit policies for managing human resources. See [Abdel-Hamid, Madnick 1991] for the rest of the integrated model and more simulation experiments with it.

[Abdel-Hamid, Madnick 1989b] ☐J
"Lessons learned from modeling the dynamics of software development"
This article presents a version of the Abdel-Hamid integrated model of the dynamics of software development, and shows how it can provide insight and make predictions for the software process. It is a forerunner of the book [Abdel-Hamid, Madnick 1991].

[Abdel-Hamid 1990] ☐J
"Investigating the cost/schedule trade-off in software development"
In previous studies, schedule compression had been treated as a static decision that can be unambiguously measured. However, the study in this paper indicates that it is neither.

[Abdel-Hamid, Madnick 1991] ☐B
"Software Project Dynamics"
This is the landmark first book on using system dynamics for software development, where the Abdel-Hamid model is presented in detail. It describes an integrated dynamic model for software project management based upon extensive review of the literature supplemented by focused field interviews of project managers. The integrative model captures multiple functions of software development, including management functions of planning, controlling and staffing and software development functions like designing, coding, reviewing, and testing. It uses a case study to illustrate how the model was able to accurately replicate the actual development of a software project. It utilizes the model as an experimentation vehicle to study and predict the dynamic implications of managerial policies and procedures.

Some classic process effects are included in the model such as task underestimation, progress perception delays, schedule pressure, hiring policies, overwork, staff assimilation and attrition, and more. The book synthesizes previous work including [Abdel-Hamid 1989, Abdel-Hamid, Madnick 1989a], and some of his earlier publications. This model is featured in several chapters of this book and is used for experimentation by several others in the bibliography.

[Abdel-Hamid 1991] ☐J
"Organizational learning: The key to software management innovation"
This paper shows that organizational learning is the key to management learning. A case is made that accurate measurements are not necessarily better.

[Abdel-Hamid 1993a] ☐J
"Adapting, correcting, and perfecting software estimates: a maintenance metaphor"
This paper contends that continuous estimation models are needed that can constantly evaluate schedules. A hybrid estimation model is proposed. A demonstration of how to use this model is also given.

[Abdel-Hamid et al. 1993] ☐J
"Software project control: An experimental investigation of judgment with fallible information"
Heuristics are deployed to handle the problems of poor estimation and visibility that hamper software project planning and control. Also, the implications for software project management are presented. A laboratory experiment in which subjects managed a simulated software development project is conducted.

[Abdel-Hamid 1993b] ⊡J

"Thinking in circles"

Because most managers forget to think in circles, they get into trouble. Because managers continue to believe that there are such things as unilateral causation, independent and dependent variables, origins, and terminations, managerial problems persist.

[Abdel-Hamid 1993c] ⊡C

"Modeling the dynamics of software reuse: an integrating system dynamics perspective"

An integrating system dynamics approach is proposed for modeling software reuse. This approach integrates multiple functions of the software reuse process and uses feedback principles of system dynamics.

[Abdel-Hamid 1993d] ⊡J

"A multi-project perspective of single project dynamics"

The project-in-isolation assumption is relaxed to demonstrate that interactions and interdependencies among projects can have a significant influence on project behavior. A study is conducted on a multiproject system dynamics model that was developed on the basis of field studies in five organizations.

[Acuña, Juristo 2005] ⊡B

"Software Process Modeling"

This edited book focuses on new aspects of software process modeling. It deals with sociotechnological aspects, process modeling for new development types, and organization change management. See the chapters [Madachy, Boehm 2005] on software dependability applications including system dynamics, and [Lehman et al. 2005] on modeling with system dynamics for managing software evolution.

[Acuña, Sánchez-Segura 2006] ⊡B

"New Trends in Software Process Modelling"

This edited book addresses new trends in software process modeling related to open source software, system dynamics modeling, and peopleware: the importance of people in software development and by extension, in the software process. See the chapters [Pfahl et al. 2006b] on system dynamics for learning and decision support, and [Barros et al. 2006b] on system dynamics metamodels.

[Angkasaputra, Pfahl 2004], [Angkasaputra, Pfahl 2005] ⊡C

Agile and Pattern-based Software Process Simulation Modeling

One reason software process simulation is not yet widely accepted is the difficulty of delivering valid simulation models on time and within budget. As simulation models can be considered software, the authors believe that promising software development techniques such as agile methods and (design) patterns can be utilized to help solve the problem. They present a research plan that aims at enhancing IMMoS (see [Pfahl 2001]), a methodology for systematic simulation model development, by introducing agile techniques and design patterns. They provide an example of a design pattern for process simulation modeling. As research proceeds, it is expected that the new method, agile/P-IMMoS, will help shorten simulation model delivery time and cut down modeling costs without compromising model quality. In [Angkasaputra, Pfahl 2005] they identify the different possibilities to adopt the agile practices used in XP and present the enhanced IMMoS as a potential agile method for model development. It can shorten the model delivery, and be responsive to changes in the modeled process.

[Aranda et al. 1993]   [J]
"Quality microworlds: Modeling the impact of quality initiatives over the software product life cycle"

This work melds the concepts of Total Quality Management (TQM) with software development modeled as a stream of releases/versions. A long time horizon is used to model customer requirement evolution and released functionality separate from individual project perspectives. To no surprise, the model helps to demonstrate the leverage of long-term considerations. Both Ithink and Microworld Creator are used for implementation.

[Baik, Eickelmann 2001]   [C]
"Applying COCOMO II effort multipliers to simulation models"

This presentation describes work at Motorola integrating COCOMO II factors into dynamic simulation models. An example is shown for the system test process and future work is discussed.

[Barbieri et al. 1992]   [C]
"DynaMan: A tool to improve software process management through dynamic simulation"

These researchers created the Dynaman tool for implementing system dynamics as applied to software process management. This paper describes the first version of the tool.

[Barros et al. 2000a]   [C]
"Applying system dynamics to scenario based software project management"

Scenario-based software project management is an extension of the risk management paradigm that uses system dynamics abstract models to describe potential problems that can affect a software project. Dynamic models are also used to describe possible resolution strategies applicable to eliminate or reduce the potential problem impact. Scenarios are defined by integrating combinations of these models to another based on Abdel-Hamid and Madnick's model with relations among development staff, software products, quality, project control, and planning. The original model was adapted to allow a fine-grained description of project tasks, personnel abilities, and error propagation. The modified model also allows operational project monitoring. The proposed technique allows the development of a standard problem and resolution strategy model library, to be integrated to new and ongoing projects. These models are abstract, and simulation is only accomplished when they are integrated to the project model. Their variables and equations affect the project model behavior, replicating the impact promoted by the problems and resolution strategies that they describe. The system dynamics notation was expanded to allow the definition of the integration interface. Scenario analysis is a valuable tool to predict project results, such as cost, schedule, and effort, in face of several combinations of problems and resolution actions. System dynamics complements the technique, describing nonlinear relationships and feedback loops among model elements.

[Barros et al. 2000b]   C

"Using process modeling and dynamic simulation to support software process quality management"

The quality of a development process directly affects the quality of its produced artifacts. Based on this assumption, some research efforts have moved from improving just products to enhancing process quality. Different software process alternatives are possible for a software project. However, when several alternatives are made available, process improvement efforts are selected mostly based only on expert knowledge. This can be a risky selection method, due the complex nature of software development, which may induce counterintuitive reasoning and process behavior prediction. By considering the software development process as a complex dynamic system, this paper presents some applications of process modeling and dynamic simulation as tools for quality evaluation, prediction, and improvement of software processes. They explore a software project model and three simulation approaches, presenting an example of their application in project schedule prediction and quality assessment effort impact upon schedule.

[Barros et al. 2001a]   C

"Explaining the behavior of system dynamics models"

This paper presents a technique called Event Tracking that helps the analysis of system dynamics models and is applied to the Abdel-Hamid model. It maps simulation trends over time to predefined events. It uses state machines whose behavior can be traced to changes suffered by selected variables in a model. Changes to variable values trigger messages, which are presented to the model analyst to help the interpretation of the underlying model behavior. The technique maps results to natural language statements. It allows a trainer assistant to define the relevant events for a model, highlighting the model major features through event messages. The technique is implemented in the ILLIUM simulator and it allows a student to track model behavior, while executing a simulation and following the presented messages.

[Barros et al. 2001b], [Barros et al. 2002a], [Barros et al. 2006b]   C J BC

Metamodels for Software Process Modeling with System Dynamics

Metamodels are extensions to system dynamics that allow the development and specialization of domain models, providing a high-level representation for developers within domains. A domain expert develops a model, which conveys the relevant categories of elements that compose the domain and the relationships among those elements. A developer uses such model to describe a particular problem by specifying how many elements of each category exist in the model of interest and the particular characteristics of each one. Finally, the model is translated to system dynamics constructors in order to be simulated and analyzed. [Barros et al. 2001b] first shows these applied to software projects.

The authors have developed metamodels that allow the development of software process models based on high-level constructors instead of mathematical equations. These constructors represent software process domain concepts such as developers, activities, resources, and artifacts. A domain model allows the translation of these concepts to traditional stock-and-flow diagrams, which can be simulated to evaluate the behavior of software process models. The proposed approach helps inexperienced modelers to build process models by reducing the semantic gap between system dynamics and the software process domain. Thus, resulting models are more readable and easier to understand and maintain. [Barros et al. 2002a] provides an example of a process model built with the approach, presenting its translation and simulation processes. [Barros et al. 2006b] provides more detail of metamodels and improves upon [Barros et al. 2002a].

[Barros et al. 2002b]   C

"Evaluating the use of system dynamics models in software project management"
This paper presents an empirical study evaluating the application of system dynamics models in software project management. A project concerning the specification and implementation of part of an academic control system for a graduate department was proposed for several participants. The project was decomposed into an activity network and several developers were available to accomplish the activities. Each participant was asked to impersonate as the project manager and make decisions in order to finish the project in the least time possible. The results from the experimental study analysis show that, for the selected participants, managers using system dynamics models to support their decision perform better than managers who base their decisions only upon personal experience. This paper presents detailed results from the experiment and some directions to improve the application of system dynamics models in project management.

[Barros et al. 2003]   C

"System dynamics extension modules for software process modeling"
Scenario models are extension modules that allow the separation of facts from assumptions in system dynamics models, as opposed to metamodels, which are system dynamics extensions that allow the development and specialization of domain models (see [Barros et al. 2001b] etc.). Application of scenario models suggests that a model must contain only known facts about its knowledge area, whereas assumptions are separately modeled as scenarios. To analyze the impact of an assumption upon a model behavior, a scenario model must be built to represent the assumption and further integrated to the model. The integration process automatically adjusts model equations according to the scenario, presenting the impact of the assumption upon the original model behavior. The authors discuss the advantages of using scenarios models instead of the traditional control parameter approach to *"what-if"* analysis and present an application of such models to support managerial decision making and process improvement in software projects.

[Barros et al. 2004]   J

"Supporting risks in software project management"
This paper describes an approach to develop, retrieve, and reuse management knowledge and experience concerned with software development risks. Scenarios (see [Barros et al. 2003]) are used to model risk impact and resolution strategies efficacy within risk archetypes. A risk archetype is an information structure that holds knowledge about software development risks. A risk management process organizes the use of risk archetypes within an application development effort. The process resembles a reuse process framework, in which two subprocesses are respectively re-

sponsible for identifying and reusing risk information. Simulating the impact of the expected risks can support some of the decisions throughout the software development process. This paper shows how risk archetypes and scenario models can represent reusable project management knowledge. An observational analysis of applying such an approach in an industrial environment and a feasibility study are also described.

[Barros et al. 2006a]   [J]

"Model-driven game development: experience and model enhancements in software project management education"

This work presents experiences in developing system-dynamics-based games for software project management. It describes a project management game intended for training purposes and the changes that were made to allow a system dynamics simulator to support game-like interactions. It also describes an experimental evaluation of the game's application as a learning-by-doing environment for management students. On the basis of the experience acquired by building such an interface, they propose models to describe the story underlying a game and its graphical presentation. Such models allow the construction of games without programming, thus hastening the development of simulation-based games.

[Burke 1996]   [TR]

"Radical improvements require radical actions: Simulating a high-maturity software organization"

This study of process improvement dynamics in a high-maturity organization was commissioned by the SEI. Steve Burke of Computer Sciences Corporation (CSC) used the NASA SEL environment to model software development and software process improvement (SPI) processes. The model separates personnel into pro-SPI, con-SPI, and no-cares. One of the important lessons of the model is that organizations should pay attention to the attitudinal mix of personnel. This is recommended reading for those interested in using simulation to analyze SPI potential. An adaptation of the model is highlighted in Chapter 5 [Ho 1999].

[Chatters et al. 2000]   [J]

"Modelling a software evolution process: A long-term case study"

As part of the ongoing FEAST investigation into the effect of feedback on the long-term evolution of software systems, system dynamics models of the evolutionary processes of real-world software products are being developed. The model described here simulates the evolution over 13 years and many releases of one of the constituent parts of the VME mainframe operating system. The model reflects the assumption, supported by expert opinion, that, in addition to any exogenously generated demand for VME enhancements, enhancing VME itself results in demands for further enhancements. This circular process is embodied in the model structure. Model input parameters have been calibrated using metric data and collaborator experts' judgment. Comparisons of model outputs against actual values for implemented change requests and accumulated code size are shown. The feedback-based model provides a plausible explanation of trends in VME evolution, and that the successful calibration of a model abstracting lower-level dynamics such as release schedules suggests that these may have only limited influence on global process trends. These findings are broadly in line with the Laws of Software Evolution. The results of the work demonstrate that a simple model can successfully simulate the externally perceived behavior of the software process. See [Lehman 1996] and others for more information on FEAST and software evolution.

[Chichakly 1993] $\boxed{J}$

"The bifocal vantage point: Managing software projects from a systems thinking perspective"

The "bifocal" vantage point refers to systems thinking as keeping one eye on the big picture, and one eye on daily details. A low–medium complexity model implements some traditionally held views of software development.

[Christie 1998] $\boxed{C}$

"Simulation in support of process improvement"

This article shows how simulation including system dynamics supports software process improvement by enhancing process definition. It is shown how simulation can support activities at all five levels of CMM maturity, when the simulation capability matches the needs at each level. Simulation can start out being used qualitatively at the lower maturity levels and advance to quantitative prediction at the higher levels. At the lowest level, simulation can help improve awareness of process dynamic behavior and the sometimes insidious effect of feedback on process performance. As process maturity improves, simulation is increasingly tied to operational metrics, to validate one's understanding of process behavior and improve the simulations' predictive power. At level 5, for example, organizations now have detailed, validated models of their processes, and can quantitatively predict the impact of significant changes to these processes.

[Christie, Staley 2000] $\boxed{J}$

"Organizational and social simulation of a software requirements development process"

This work explores the organizational issues of requirements development and also the social issues, namely, how does the effectiveness of "people interactions" affect the resulting quality and timeliness of the output. It describes the modeling and simulation of requirements development since this early activity is crucial to the success of any software project. It models a Joint Application Development (JAD) process as implemented by the Computer Sciences Corporation. This process was used to identify detailed requirements for a large incremental release of a command and control system for the U.S. Air Force. Using the JAD process, system users and engineering specialists worked jointly in an electronic meeting environment and successfully reduced development time and failure risk. This model has both continuous and discrete modeling components.

[Collofello et al. 1995] $\boxed{A}$

"Modeling software testing processes"

To produce a high-quality software product, application of both defect prevention and defect detection techniques is required. One common defect detection strategy is to use unit, integration, and system testing. The authors propose utilizing system dynamics models for better understanding of testing processes.

[Collofello 2000] $\boxed{\text{J}}$
"University/industry collaboration in developing a simulation-based software project management course"
A significant factor in the success of a software project is the management skill of the project leader. The ability to effectively plan and track a software project utilizing appropriate techniques and tools requires training, mentoring, and experience. This paper describes a collaborative effort between Arizona State University and Motorola to develop a software project management training course. Although many such courses exist in academia and industry, this course incorporates a system dynamics simulator of the software development process. The use of this simulator to train future software project managers is analogous to the use of a flight simulator to train pilots. This paper describes the software project simulator and how it is utilized in the software project management training course. Feedback from the training course participants is also shared and discussed.

[Collofello et al. 1998] $\boxed{\text{C}}$
"A system dynamics process simulator for staffing policies decision support"
Staff attrition is a problem often faced by software development organizations. How can a manager plan for the risk of losses due to attrition? Can policies for this purpose be formulated to address his/her specific organization and project? The authors propose a software development process simulator tuned to the specific organization, for running "what-if" scenarios for assessing the effects of managerial staffing decisions on project's budget, schedule, and quality. They developed a system dynamics simulator of an incremental software development process and used it to analyze the effect of the following policies: to replace engineers who leave the project, to overstaff in the beginning of the project, or to do nothing, hoping that the project will still be completed in time and within budget. This paper presents the simulator, the experiments run, the results obtained, and analysis and conclusions.

[Collofello et al. 1996] $\boxed{\text{C}}$
"Modeling software testing processes"
The production of a high-quality software product requires application of both defect prevention and defect detection techniques. A common defect detection strategy is to subject the product to several phases of testing such as unit, integration, and system. These testing phases consume significant project resources and cycle time. As software companies continue to search for ways for reducing cycle time and development costs while increasing quality, software testing processes emerge as a prime target for investigation. This paper proposes the utilization of system dynamics models for better understanding testing processes. Motivation for modeling testing processes is presented along with an executable model of the unit test phase. Some sample model runs are described to illustrate the usefulness of the model.

[Cooper, Mullen 1993] $\boxed{\text{J}}$
"Swords and plowshares: The rework cycles of defense and commercial software development projects"
Rework dynamics are the focus of this modeling effort; it is well known that rework is an important consideration since it directly impacts profit margins. The

model does not represent only software aspects. An interesting presumption about the differences in perceived progress in commercial versus defense industries is made.

[DeMarco 1998]   B
"The Deadline"
This fictional novel on software project management vividly illustrates principles that affect team productivity. Coincidentally, a character by the name of Dr. Abdul Jamid helps management assess their project deadline with system dynamics modeling of the team and their productivity.

[Diehl 1993]   J
"The analytical lens: Strategy-support software to enhance executive dialog and debate"
In this article, MicroWorld S**4 is discussed. The three key elements of this tool that provide the needed flexibility to answer "what-if" and "why" questions are the following: flexible report generation, dynamic data analysis, and dynamic what-if analysis.

[Fakharzadeh, Mehta 1999]   C A
"Architecture Development Process Dynamics in MBASE"
The architecture of a system forms the blueprint for building the system and consists of the most important abstractions that address global concerns. It is important to develop an architecture early on that will remain stable throughout the entire life cycle and also future capabilities. The dynamics of the architecture development process were investigated on this research project at USC. They modeled architecture development in the MBASE inception and elaboration phases, and the impact of other factors such as collaboration and prototyping on the process of architecting. The primary goals were to: (1) investigate the dynamics of architecture development during early life-cycle phases, (2) identify the nature of process concurrence in early phases, and (3) understand the impact of collaboration and prototyping on life-cycle parameters. This model is highlighted in Chapter 5.

[Ferreira 2002], [Ferreira et al. 2003]   A C
Measuring the Effects of Requirements Volatility on Software Development Projects
This Ph.D. dissertation and follow-on work examines requirements volatility, a common software project risk that can have severe consequences resulting in cost and schedule overruns and cancelled projects. A system dynamics model was developed to help project managers comprehend the effects of requirements volatility. Requirements volatility and its effects were studied using various analyses and modeling techniques. Study results were used to design major simulator components that were integrated into a previously developed and validated simulator from [Houston 2000], leveraging pre-existing software-risk-related systems-dynamics research. The base simulator was also extended to provide an encompassing view of the requirements engineering process. The distributions used for stochastically simulating the requirements volatility risk effects and requirements engineering factors were derived from a survey that included over 300 software project managers. The simulator can be used as an effective tool to demonstrate the researched effects of requirements volatility on a software development project. [Ferreira et al. 2003] up-

dates the work in [Ferreira 2002] and provides empirical data on volatility. This model is highlighted in Chapter 5.

[Glickman 1994] |C|
"The Bellcore-CSELT collaborative project"
This presentation describes experience over a couple years at Bellcore to adapt the Abdel-Hamid model for internal uses.

[Greer et al. 2005] |C|
"Identifying and mitigating risk across organizational boundaries in software-intensive space system programs"
This paper describes work at the Aerospace Corporation on the use of simulation to better understand the software-intensive system acquisition process. A case-study approach is used to explore the dynamics of "disconnects" in baselines across multiple organizations in a large software-intensive space system development program. Disconnects are the latent differences in understanding among groups or individuals that can negatively affect the program cost, schedule, performance, and quality should they remain undetected or unresolved. The authors have constructed a system dynamics model of communication effectiveness and delay across four organizations that sequentially and iteratively rely on each other for requirements and deliverables. Their analyses from multiple simulations suggest that the highest points of leverage in reducing disconnects are in increasing expertise levels, improving communication clarity, and accelerating the pace of assessing the impacts of changes in partner organizations' understandings and actions. These results oppose traditional assumptions that disconnects are due to external requirements changes and that speeding up organizational processes will reduce disconnects.

[Haberlein 2004] |J|
"Common structures in system dynamics models of software acquisition projects"
Projects that contract third parties to develop software are even more unpredictable and underestimated by management than pure development projects and, thus, there is also a need to model and simulate these projects. This article deals with the design of system dynamics models of the unexplored domain, at least with respect to system dynamics, of software acquisition. A framework is described that captures causal structures common to all models of acquisition projects. Outputs of one concrete instance of the framework are presented.

[Hart 2004] |O|
"Bridging Systems Thinking and Software Quality Improvement: Initiating a Software Learning Organization"
This book draft portion shows that the systems thinking discipline is a critical part of any software organization's ability to adapt to change, how this discipline can give insights into more effective ways to enhance an organization's current software engineer and management activities, and how this skill is the foundation for developing skills in the other learning organization disciplines. It is the author's intent to also foster an awareness and appreciation in the software community for the value of replacing our existing obsession with software process maturity levels and certifications with a focus on learning as a basis of continuous performance improvement.

[Henderson, Howard 2000]   J
"Process strategies for large scale software development—simulation using systems dynamics"

CMPM, the Cellular Manufacturing Process Model, is an advanced component-based process strategy that uses concurrency and distribution to reduce cycle times. The aim of this research is to provide a simulation-based tool for designing and dynamically controlling CMPM processes. In CMPM, networks of semiautonomous cells cooperate to produce a complex large-scale system, and this paper examines some of the issues that affect the ability of cells to achieve their targets. The model views development as a manufacturing activity in which systems are built from components, which are a mixture of self-built components, reused components, and brought-in components. The model is hierarchical: any component may be a product of others. Predicting the cost, quality, and schedule outcome of CMPM depends upon the behavior within the cell (intracell) and the cooperative behavior between cells (intercell) in a dynamic environment.

[Ho 1999]   A
"Xerox SPI model study"

This graduate research on software process improvement was applied at Xerox. It adapts the NASA SEL process improvement model in [Burke 1996] for Xerox CMM-based process improvement. This work is highlighted in detail in Chapter 5.

[Houston 2000]   A
"A Software Project Simulation Model for Risk Management"

This Ph.D. dissertation developed a system dynamics model for risk management. The SPARS model is an adaptation of Abdel-Hamid's model [Abdel-Hamid, Madnick 1991] and Tvedt's model [Tvedt 1996]. The SPARS model is comprehensive in software project management scope and updated for more modern development practices. The consolidated model also incorporates the effects of a number of risk factors. Also see [Houston et al. 2001]

[Houston et al. 2001a]   J
"Stochastic simulation of risk factor potential effects for software development risk management"

One of the proposed purposes for software process simulation is the management of software development risks, usually discussed within the category of project planning/management. However, modeling and simulation primarily for the purpose of software development risk management has been quite limited. This paper describes an approach to modeling risk factors [Houston 2000] based on and simulating their effects as a means of supporting certain software development risk management activities. The effects of six common and significant software development risk factors were studied. A base model was then produced for stochastically simulating the effects of the selected factors. This simulator is a tool designed specifically for the risk management activities of assessment, mitigation, contingency planning, and intervention.

[Houston et al. 2001b]   J
"Behavioral characterization: finding and using the influential factors in software process simulation models"

Most software process simulation work has focused on the roles and uses of software process simulators, on the scope of models, and on simulation approaches. Little effort appears to have been given to statistical evaluation of model behavior through sensitivity analysis. Rather, most of software process simulation experimentation has examined selected factors for the sake of understanding their effects with regard to particular issues, such as the economics of quality assurance or the impact of inspections practice. In a broad sense, sensitivity analysis assesses the effect of each input on model outputs. Here, the authors discuss its use for behaviorally characterizing software process simulators. This paper discusses the benefits of using sensitivity analysis to characterize model behavior, the use of experimental design for this purpose, the procedure for using designed experiments to analyze deterministic simulation models, the application of this procedure to four published software process simulators, the results of analysis, and the merits of this approach.

[Houston 2006] ☐J☐
"An experience in facilitating process improvement with an integration problem reporting process simulation"
Software process improvement (SPI) has been a discernible theme in the software process simulation literature, which has recognized a wide variety of ways in which simulation can support SPI. This case study describes one of those ways—a very focused, retrospective modeling driven by integration delays in the development of an avionics system project. A simple simulation of the integration problem report flows offered a low-cost means of looking into the dynamics of the backlogged integration process and clearly seeing a basic development problem that was difficult to see from existing reports. The model became especially helpful when alternative scenarios were run in order to see the relative benefits that different types of actions would have provided to the integration process. These experiments clarified lessons learned from other sources and suggested a major improvement for the next release cycle. The actual results of improvements deployed in the next release cycle were a reduced problem report backlog (one-third that of the previous release) and 40% less test effort.

[Johnson 1995] ☐J☐
"Dynamic Systems Modeling: The Software Management Process"
This workbook by Margaret Johnson serves as a working companion to [Abdel-Hamid, Madnick 1991]. It includes a faithful reproduction of the Abdel-Hamid model in Ithink, which has been provided for the public domain through this book. It shows how to develop the Abdel-Hamid model from scratch, integrating model sectors and running sensitivity tests. Throughout, it also explains the software process phenomenology being modeled. It is a good end-to-end illustration of the modeling process and provides valuable modeling lessons.

[Kaghazian 1999] ☐C☐ ☐A☐
"Dynamic process of Internet companies: An abstract model"
This graduate research project investigated the dynamics of new Internet companies. One of the aspects of current shift in technology is the dynamic process of Internet companies. Financing, prototyping, teamwork, marketing, research and develop-

ment, and the whole process of current Internet companies have evolved in a new model. Companies with a great success in business have to develop their product in as short a time as possible and make if bug free as much as possible.

The paper provides an abstract model for the dynamic process of Internet companies, with emphasis on new features for Rapid Application Development. Four major factors are explained: outsourcing, hiring personnel, early error elimination, and instant bug fixing. The model is shown to be sensitive to a number of key factors such as personnel, the level of experience, outsourcing, integration, and the number of users who may access the site in a month.

[Kahen et al. 2001]   [J]
"System dynamics modelling of software evolution processes for policy investigation: Approach and example"

This paper describes one of the system dynamics models developed during the Feedback, Evolution and Software Technology (FEAST) investigation into software evolution processes (see [Lehman 1996] etc.). The intention of early models was to simulate real-world processes in order to increase understanding of such processes. The work resulted in a number of lessons learned, in particular with regard to the application of system dynamics to the simulation of key attributes of long-term software evolution. The work reported here combines elements of previous work and extends them by describing an approach to investigate the consequences on long-term evolution of decisions made by the managers of these processes. The approach is illustrated by discussion of the impact of complexity control activity. This model of the impact on product and global process attributes of decisions regarding the fraction of work applied to progressive and to antiregressive activities such as complexity control, for instance, exemplifies the results of the FEAST investigation.

[Kim, Baik 1999]   [A]
"Dynamic model for COTS glue code development and COTS integration"

This research project at USC sought to understand how the glue code development process and COTS integration process affect each other. The authors analyzed the effect on schedule and effort throughout a project lifecycle of glue code development and the ongoing integration of components into the developing system. This model is highlighted in Chapter 5.

[Kocaoglu et al. 1998]   [C]
"Moving toward a unified model for software development"

The scope and nature of software process models have been influenced by the tools available to construct the models. This work develops a unified model that unites the capabilities of both discrete and continuous simulation approaches. Although discrete modeling tools have captured the development process in rich detail, they do not capture the effect of continuously varying factors. Systems dynamics models capture the dynamic behavior of continuous project variables including their interaction and feedback, but do not capture process steps easily. A modeling tool is needed that models the creation of artifacts with attributes, modifies those attributes based on system variables, and allows the system variables to vary continuously.

[Lakey 2003] ☐C

"A hybrid software process simulation model for project management"
This paper introduces a hybrid software process simulation model that combines discrete event and system dynamics. The model supports software project estimation as well as project management. The model was originally constructed for a specific software organization and then been modified to make it more generic in nature. The model is fully functional but is intended primarily to offer a concrete theoretical framework for a hybrid approach to modeling specific software development projects. The theoretical basis for the model is documented in detail with a few examples of its behavior for varying parameters. The model description is followed by a general discussion of the following issues: utility of the modeling approach, adaptability of the theoretical framework to project-specific conditions, important modeling considerations, and other issues. The paper offers an approach that a model developer can use as the framework for developing a realistic project-specific model.

[Lehman 1996], [Lehman 1998], [Lehman, Ramil 1999], [Lehman, Ramil 2002], [Lehman, Ramil 2003], [Lehman et al. 2006] ☐J ☐C ☐J ☐J ☐J ☐BC

Software Evolution and Feedback: Background, Theory, and Practice
This body of work is based on 30 years of study of software evolution phenomenon by Manny Lehman and colleagues. It suggests that a constraint on software process improvement arises from the fact that the global software process that includes technical, business, marketing, user and other activities constitutes a multiloop, multilevel feedback system. To change the characteristics of such a system requires one to consider, design, or adapt and tune both forward and feedback paths to achieve the desired changes in externally visible behavior. [Lehman 1998] reviewed the difficulty of achieving major improvement in the global software evolution process and introduced the FEAST hypothesis that the global software process is a complex feedback system, and that major improvement will not be achieved until the process is treated as such. Results from the FEAST project support this hypothesis. The article presents results of exploring the feedback phenomena using system dynamics and black-box techniques applied to actual industrial data. See [Wernick-Lehman 1999] for a description of the system dynamics model and results, [Chatters et al. 2000] for another FEAST model, and [Kahen et al. 2001] for a later model for FEAST. [Wernick, Hall 2002] shows a model of the combined causal mechanisms for growth in the size of software products over many releases incorporating previous work.

   [Lehman, Ramil 2003] describes recent studies that have refined earlier conclusions, yielding practical guidelines for software evolution management and providing a basis for the formation of a theory of software evolution. Software that is regularly used for real-world problem solving or addressing a real-world application must be continually adapted and enhanced to maintain its fitness for an ever changing real world, its applications, and application domains. This adaptation and enhancement activities are termed progressive. As progressive activity is undertaken, the complexity (e.g., functional, structural) of the evolving system is likely to increase unless work, termed antiregressive, is also undertaken in order to control and

even reduce complexity. However, with progressive and antiregressive work naturally competing for the same pool of resources, management will benefit from
means to estimate the amount of work and resources to be applied to each of the two
types. The systems dynamics model in [Lehman et al. 2006] can serve as a basis of a
tool to support decision making regarding the optimal personnel allocation over the
system lifetime. The model is provided as an example of the use of process modeling in order to plan and manage long-term software evolution. See [Ramil et al.
2005] for more details of the antiregressive work model.

[Levary, Lin 1991]   J
*"Modeling the software development process using an expert simulation system hav-
ing fuzzy logic"*

A description of an intelligent computerized tool designed to aid managers of software development projects in planning, managing, and controlling the development
process of medium-to-large-scale software projects is given. The expert system having fuzzy logic handles the fuzzy input variables to the system dynamics simulation
model.

[Lin et al. 1992], [Lin et al. 1997]   TR J
"Software engineering process simulation model (SEPS)"

The Software-Engineering Process Simulation (SEPS) model developed at JPL is
described. It uses system dynamics to simulate the dynamic interactions among software life-cycle development activities and management decision-making processes.
This simulation model of the software project-development process is designed to
be a planning tool to examine trade-offs of cost, schedule, and functionality, testing
the implications of different managerial policies on a project's outcome.

[Lin, Levary 1989]   J
"Computer-aided software development process design"

A computer-aided software development process design is described in this paper in
the form of a computerized intelligent tool. This tool is designed to help managers in
planning, managing, and controlling the development process of medium-to-large-
scale software projects.

[Lin 1993]   J
"Walking on battlefields: Tools for strategic software management"

This article addresses the need for software management innovation and the importance of tools based on system dynamics to add a new dimension to software project
management. The dual life cycle is emphasized with a feedback structure of software engineering and management processes.

[Lo 1999]   A
"Reuse and high level languages"

This graduate research study investigated the dynamic effects of reuse and fourth-
generation languages in a rapid application development context for reducing schedule. Using different kinds of programming languages and levels of reuse affects the
schedule and effort, so understanding their effects on the software process will benefit management planning strategy. There are four phases represented in the model:
requirements, design, coding, and approval phases. See Chapter 5 where this model
is summarized.

[Madachy 1994b], [Madachy 1996a] A C
System Dynamics Modeling of an Inspection-Based Process
This Ph.D. research used a dynamic model of an inspection-based life cycle to support quantitative evaluation of the process. The model serves to examine the effects of inspection practices on cost, schedule, and quality throughout the life cycle. It uses system dynamics to model the interrelated flows of tasks, errors, and personnel throughout different development phases and is calibrated with industrial data. It extends previous software project dynamics research by examining an inspection-based process with an original model, and integrating it with the knowledge-based method for risk assessment and cost estimation. The model demonstrates the effects of performing inspections or not, the effectiveness of varied inspection policies, and the effects of other managerial policies. It was also modified for other types of peer reviews [Madachy, Tarbet 2000]. See the model in Chapter 5.

[Madachy 1995b] C
"System dynamics and COCOMO: Complementary modeling paradigms"
System dynamics and static models such as COCOMO rest on different assumptions, but the two perspectives can contribute to each other in a symbiotic and synergistic way. This paper compares and contrasts the underlying formulations, and demonstrates a dynamic model with relations to the static COCOMO. Static models were used to nominally calibrate the dynamic model, the dynamic model improved on static assumptions, and simulation results were used to generate a phase-sensitive cost driver for the static model.

[Madachy 1996b] C
"Tutorial: Process modeling with system dynamics"
This tutorial covered the modeling process with system dynamics with applications to software processes. Examples of software process infrastructures and working simulation models were demonstrated.

[Madachy 1996c] C
"Modeling software processes with system dynamics: Current developments"
This article describes the current developments in modeling software processes with system dynamics. It overviews different application areas in which system dynamics is being used and future research.

[Madachy, Tarbet 2000] J
"Case studies in software process modeling with system dynamics"
This describes the use of mostly small-scale models for investigating managerial process issues and supporting personnel training at Litton's Guidance and Control Systems (GCS) Division. At the project level, these include models for planning specific projects, studying Brooks' Law and hiring issues, an interactive earned value model, requirements volatility, and a detailed peer review model. The perspective of some of the models has been at a multiproject or departmental level, including domain learning, product-line reuse processes and resource contention among projects. Insights provided by the models supported decision making at different levels and helped galvanize process improvement efforts. The models helped managers understand the key factors in complex scenarios. The training applications added

spark to classes and improved overall learning for training of software managers and leads. Topics including earned value techniques, productivity estimation, requirements volatility effects, and extrapolation of project tracking indicators have been presented with simulation models. Some include "flight training" scenarios that the students interact with to practice project control, such as the use of earned value indicators for operational decision making.

[Madachy 1999] [A]

"CS599 Software Process Modeling Course Notes"
This course used early versions of portions of this book. The reference contains course slides, additional articles, links to models, and student work.

[Madachy, Boehm 2005] [BC]

"Software dependability applications in software process modeling"
Software process modeling can be used to reason about strategies for attaining software dependability. Dependability has many facets, and there is no single software dependability metric that fits all situations. A stakeholder value-based approach is useful for determining relevant dependability measures for different contexts. Analytical models and simulation techniques including continuous systems and discrete event modeling approaches can be applied to dependability, and the trade-offs of different approaches are discussed. Development process models mainly address software defect introduction and removal rates, whereas operational process models address the probability of various classes of failure. An overview of sample applications is presented, mostly using system dynamics. An elaborated example shows how modeling can be used to optimize a process for dependability.

[Madachy et al. 2006], [Madachy et al. 2007]

Assessing Hybrid Incremental Processes for SISOS Development
New processes are being assessed to address modern challenges for software-intensive systems of systems (SISOS), such as coping with rapid change while simultaneously assuring high dependability. A hybrid agile and plan-driven process based on the spiral life cycle has been outlined to address these conflicting challenges with the need to rapidly field incremental capabilities. A system dynamics model has been developed to assess the incremental hybrid process and support project decision making. It estimates cost and schedule for multiple increments of a hybrid process that uses three specialized teams. It considers changes due to external volatility and feedback from user-driven change requests, and dynamically reestimates and allocates resources in response to the volatility. Deferral policies and team sizes can be experimented with, and it includes trade-off functions between cost and the timing of changes within and across increments, length of deferral delays, and others. An illustration of using the model to determine optimal agile team size to handle changes is shown. Both the hybrid process and simulation model are being evolved on a very large scale incremental SISOS project and other potential pilots. [Madachy et al. 2007] builds on the work in [Madachy et al. 2006] by casting the results in a value-based framework accounting for mission value, and increasing the option space of the case study example. This model is highlighted in Chapter 4.

[Martin, Raffo 2000], [Martin, Raffo 2001], [Martin 2002]   J J A
Hybrid Modeling of the Software Development Process
   The Ph.D. dissertation in [Martin 2002] used a hybrid system dynamics and discrete
   event model and applied it to a project. Whereas models offer a means to represent
   the process, they also impose restrictions on those aspects of the system that can be
   addressed. [Martin, Raffo 2000] examined the possibility of a combined discrete
   and continuous simulation model that removes some of these limitations. They developed a method that combines the features of two well-known examples: the Abdel-Hamid system dynamics model and a discrete-event model of a standardized example of modifying a unit of code. The model was subsequently applied to a
   software development project [Martin, Raffo 2001].

[Pfahl 1995]   C
"Software quality measurement based on a quantitative project simulation model"
   The author outlines the system dynamics modeling and simulation approach called
   PROSYD, which stands for project simulation with system dynamics. The author
   discusses the relationship between software process modeling according to the
   PROSYD approach and metrics definition in addition to the relationship between
   project simulation, quality measurement, and process improvement.

[Pfahl, Lebsanft 1999], [Pfahl 2001], [Pfahl et al. 2002], [Pfahl et al. 2003], [Pfahl,
Ruhe 2005]   J J J C BC
Integrated Measurement, Modeling, and Simulation (IMMoS)
   Integrated measurement, modeling, and simulation (IMMoS) is an integrated approach for system dynamics modeling and software process measurement developed and validated by Pfahl and colleagues. The Ph.D. dissertation in [Pfahl 2001]
   describes the development, application, and initial validation of IMMoS. The goal
   of IMMoS is to support systematic development and usage of process simulation
   models. IMMoS combines system dynamics with static process modeling and goal-
   oriented measurement. The result is an integrated approach to simulation-based
   learning. It is based on lessons learned from industrial modeling and by combining
   system dynamics models with static models that contain qualitative or quantitative
   information. IMMoS combines system dynamics with descriptive process modeling
   and measurement-based quantitative modeling (which includes the goal–question–metrics method). Such a framework reduces the barriers to system dynamics
   modeling and places simulation under the umbrella of "goal-oriented" measurement
   and analysis. For example, it is seen how system dynamics may impose data collection requirements and how software metrics may be used to define reference modes
   for simulation models.
   The hybrid approach integrates the individual strengths of its inherent method-
   ological elements and concepts. First, it enhances existing guidance for SD modeling by adding a component that enforces goal orientation, and by providing a refined process model with detailed description of activities, entry/exit criteria,
   input/output products, and roles involved. Second, it describes how to combine system dynamics modeling with goal-oriented measurement and descriptive process
   modeling, thus improving efficiency and smoothly closing the gap to established
   methods in empirical software engineering. The effectiveness and efficiency of IM-

MoS is supported with empirical evidence from two industrial case studies and one controlled experiment. Also see [Angkasaputra, Pfahl 2004] about enhancing IM-MoS for agile modeling.

[Pfahl, Birk 2000] TR

"Using simulation to visualize and analyze product–process dependencies in software development projects"

The core element of the PROFES improvement methodology is the concept of product–process dependency (PPD) models. The purpose of PPD models is to help focus process improvement activities on those development technologies and processes that are most effective with regard to achieving specific customer-defined product quality goals. This paper describes how system dynamics simulation models can be used to check the plausibility of achieving positive effects on software product quality when implementing improvement actions derived from PPD models. This is done through extending an existing generic software project simulation model with structures that represent expected local cause–effect mechanisms of the PPD models.

[Pfahl, Lebsanft 2000a] J

"Using simulation to analyze the impact of software requirement volatility on project performance"

This paper presents a simulation model that was developed by Fraunhofer IESE for Siemens Corporate Technology. The purpose of this simulation model was to demonstrate the impact of unstable software requirements on project duration and effort, and to analyze how much money should be invested in stabilizing software requirements in order to achieve optimal cost-effectiveness. The paper reports in detail on the various steps of model building, discusses all major design decisions taken, describes the structure of the final simulation model, and presents the most interesting simulation results of a case study.

[Pfahl, Lebsanft 2000b] J

"Knowledge acquisition and process guidance for building system dynamics simulation models"

In this paper, experience with system modeling of software processes and projects within Siemens is reported. Special focus is put on problems encountered during knowledge acquisition for system dynamics model building, like inadequate guidance while conducting system dynamics modeling projects and insufficient methodical support for reusing available or generating missing knowledge. Both problems were addressed in a research project, jointly conducted by Fraunhofer IESE and Siemens Corporate Technology. One of the results of this project is a prescriptive process model for building system dynamics models. This process model, which is briefly outlined in the paper, provides guidance for a systematic development of system dynamics models in software organizations.

[Pfahl et al. 2001] J

"A CBT module with integrated simulation component for software project management education and training"

This describes a computer-based training (CBT) module for student education in software project management. The single-learner CBT module can be run using standard Web browsers, and the simulation component is implemented using system dynamics. The paper presents the design of the simulation model and the training scenario offered by the existing CBT module prototype. Possibilities for empirical validation of the effectiveness of the CBT module in university education are described, and future extensions of the CBT module toward collaborative learning environments are suggested (see [Pfahl et al. 2004a] for the follow-on work).

[Pfahl et al. 2004a] [C]

"PL-SIM: A generic simulation model for studying strategic SPI in the automotive industry"

This paper presents the approach, results, and conclusions of a simulation modeling activity conducted by Fraunhofer IESE with DaimlerChrysler AG to explore the level of process leadership (PL) that can be achieved by one of DaimlerChrysler's car divisions within the next five years. A crucial issue of the study was the identification and determination of influence factors and measures expected to have an impact on the level of PL. In order to help focus discussion and provide a quantitative basis for analyses, they jointly developed a system dynamics simulation model, PL-SIM. In a first assessment, the model was found to be useful for running experiments that qualitatively reflect the fundamental dynamics of the factors influencing PL. Though additional data needs to be collected in order to increase the model's accuracy and predictive power, its generic structure can easily be transferred into other companies and serve as a framework for exploring their specific SPI strategies.

[Pfahl et al. 2004b] [J]

"Evaluating the learning effectiveness of using simulations in software project management education: Results from a twice replicated experiment"

This paper presents the results of a twice replicated experiment that evaluates the learning effectiveness of using a process simulation model for educating computer science students in software project management (see [Pfahl et al. 2001] for a description of the model used in the experiments). While the experimental group applied a system dynamics simulation model, the control group used the COCOMO model as a predictive tool for project planning. The results of each empirical study indicate that students using the simulation model gain a better understanding about typical behavior patterns of software development projects. The combination of the results from the initial experiment and the two replications with meta-analysis techniques corroborates this finding. Additional analysis shows that the observed effect can mainly be attributed to the use of the simulation model in combination with a Web-based role-play scenario. This finding is strongly supported by information gathered from the debriefing questionnaires of subjects in the experimental group. They consistently rated the simulation-based role-play scenario as a very useful approach for learning about issues in software project management.

[Pfahl 2005] [BC]

"Software process simulation in support of risk assessment"

This chapter presents a five step simulation-based method to risk assessment, ProSim/RA, which combines software process simulation with stochastic simulation. Although the proposed method is not new, it is the first time that it was systematically described in detail based on an illustrative case example that served as a model for similar scenarios. By applying cost functions to the risk probabilities generated by ProSim/RA, the potential losses to the delivered product value can be calculated.

[Pfahl et al. 2006a]   C

"Simulation-based stability analysis for software release plans"

Release planning for incremental software development assigns features to releases such that most important technical, resource, risk, and budget constraints are met. The research in this paper is based on a three-staged procedure. In addition to an existing method for (i) strategic release planning that maps requirements to subsequent releases and (ii) a more fine-grained planning that defines resource allocations for each individual release, the authors propose a third step, (iii) stability analysis, which analyzes proposed release plans with regard to their sensitivity to unforeseen changes. Unforeseen changes can relate to alterations in expected personnel availability and productivity, feature-specific task size (measured in terms of effort), and degree of task dependency (measured in terms of workload that can only be processed if corresponding work in predecessor tasks has been completed). The focus of this paper is on stability analysis of proposed release plans. They present the simulation model REPSIM (Release Plan Simulator) and illustrate its usefulness for stability analysis with the help of a case example.

[Pfahl et al. 2006b]   BC

"Software process simulation with system dynamics—A tool for learning and decision support"

This chapter provides an overview of some issues in learning and decision support within the scope of software process management. More specifically, the existing work done in the field of software process simulation is presented, and the application of software process simulation models for the purpose of management learning and decision support is motivated and described. Examples of simulation modeling applications in the automotive industry are reported to illustrate how process simulation can become a useful management tool for the exploration and selection of alternatives during project planning, project performance, and process improvement. It concludes with a discussion of limitations and risks, and proposes future work that needs to be done in order to increase acceptance and dissemination of software process simulation in the software industry.

[Plekhanova 1999]   O

"A capability-based approach to software process modelling"

This unpublished paper presents a capability-based approach to stochastic software process modeling represented by a project schedule simulation, which is considered a combination of discrete event simulation and system dynamics modeling. The feedback path can be the reworking of a task or any sequence of project activities (i.e., step, phase, period, or stage). Since the number of loops is a random variable relevant to project resource capabilities, an integration of process simulation and system dynamics approach is used for stochastic modeling. A capability-based approach provides detailed process analyses, resource utilization, and how resources (people or team) fit a project not only at each discrete point in time, but also for each feedback path. Monitoring of performance feedback provides the determination of an optimal schedule. This ensures a simulation of a sequence of a random number of optimal schedules, which represents the evolution of the schedule, with feedback effect over time.

[Powell et al. 1999] ☐J

"Strategies for lifecycle concurrency and iteration: A system dynamics approach"

This paper documents the work in progress of a detailed model for investigating life-cycle concurrency and iteration to improve process performance. Based on the incremental life-cycle practices at Rolls Royce plc, the process is modeled that accounts for simultaneous, concurrent development between projects/phases, where time to market and business performance are key drivers. It also models the staged delivery approach and serves to evaluate combined strategies of concurrence and iteration to achieve improved cycle-time performance, increased product quality, and potentially lower overall development costs. Also see [Powell 2001].

[Powell 2001] ☐A

"Right on Time: Measuring, Modelling and Managing Time-Constrained Software Development"

This Ph.D. dissertation describes a technique to aid the management of time-constrained development with system dynamics modeling. The need to compress development timescales influences both the software process and the way it is managed. Conventional approaches to measurement, modeling, and management treat the development process as being linear, sequential, and static; but the processes used to achieve timescale compression in industry are iterative, concurrent, and dynamic. The Process Engineering Language (PEL) captures important elements of a process that are obscured by conventional approaches to data collection. These fine-grained measures are essential to observations of industrial process behavior within Rolls Royce and BAE Systems, and the isolation of three specific problems of time-constrained development: overloading, bow-waves, and the multiplier effect. In response, a new modeling technique, called Capacity-Based Scheduling (CBS), is proposed to control risk across a portfolio of time-constrained projects. Finally, industrial data from Rolls Royce is used to evaluate the validity and utility of the modelling approach and propose new strategies for the management of time-constrained software development.

[Raffo, Setamanit 2005] ☐C

"A simulation model for global software development projects"

Global software development is becoming a dominant paradigm in the software industry. Conducting development projects in multiple countries offers many potential benefits including significantly reduced cost and better response times. However, it also poses some difficulties and challenges in managing this kind of project. Software process simulation modeling can be used to support, enrich, and evaluate global development theories, to facilitate understanding, and to support corporate decisions. The discrete-event paradigm and system dynamic paradigm compliment each other and together enable the construction of models that capture both the dynamic nature of project variables and the complex sequences of discrete activities that take place. The authors argue that the ideal model for representing global projects would have to effectively support both system dynamics equations and discrete-event logic.

[Ramesh, Abdel-Hamid 2003]   BC

"Integrating genetic algorithms with system dynamics to optimize quality assurance effort allocation"

> This chapter describes the integrated use of genetic programming and system dynamics modeling. Genetic programming is a machine learning technique that uses an evolutionary optimization algorithm. It imitates genetic algorithms, which use mutation and replication to produce algorithms that represent the "survival of the fittest." An application is shown for optimizing quality assurance allocation.

[Ramil et al. 2005]   BC

"Simulation process modelling for managing software evolution"

> Software that is regularly used for real-world problem solving or addressing a real-world application must be continually adapted and enhanced to maintain its fitness in an ever changing real world, its applications, and application domains. This adaptation and enhancement activities are termed *progressive.* As progressive activity is undertaken, the complexity (e.g., functional, structural) of the evolving system is likely to increase unless work, termed *antiregressive,* is also undertaken in order to control and even reduce complexity. However, with progressive and antiregressive work naturally competing for the same pool of resources, management will benefit from means to estimate the amount of work and resources to be applied to each of the two types. After providing a necessary background, this chapter describes a systems dynamics model that can serve as a basis of a tool to support decision making regarding the optimal personnel allocation over the system lifetime. The model is provided as an example of the use of process modeling in order to plan and manage long-term software evolution (see [Lehman 1996] etc.). This model is highlighted in Chapter 5.

[Rodriguez et al. 2006]   J

"E-Learning in project management using simulation models: a case study based on the replication of an experiment"

> Current e-learning systems are increasing in importance in higher education, but e-learning applications do not achieve the level of interactivity that current learning theories advocate. This paper discusses the enhancement of e-learning systems based on replicated experiments with system dynamics models described in [Pfahl et al. 2004b].

[Roehling, Collofello 2000]   J

"System dynamics modeling applied to software outsourcing decision support"

> To illustrate some of the dynamics, potential benefits, and potential drawbacks of software outsourcing, this paper describes a simulation model software practitioners can leverage for useful insight and decision support. Practical benefits and a rationale for applying the model to the software outsourcing problem are provided. The model's applicability and usefulness is demonstrated with snapshots of simulation results, which are analyzed and discussed.

[Rothman 1996]   C

"Applying systems thinking to the issues of software product development"

> This paper discusses issues of software product development, such as meeting the schedule, implementing desired functionality, and removing a sufficient number of

defects. A systems thinking perspective is stressed in choosing the product's goal, planning the project, being aware of changing conditions, and changing the goals that will cause the schedule to slip.

[Rubin et al. 1994]   J
"With the SEI as my copilot: Using software process flight simulation to predict the impact of improvements in process maturity"
In this article, four distinct stages in the model construction life cycle of a process flight simulator are given. These are: establishing the scope of the simulation, constructing a model of the process being explored, turning the model into executable form by specifying the underlying mathematical measures and relationships, and turning the model prototype into a flight simulator by defining the key aspects of the "cockpit" or interface.

[Rubin et al. 1995]   J
"Software process flight simulation: Dynamic modeling tools and metrics"
Managers can get help in understanding the dynamics of new processes and technologies before they are introduced with process flight simulation tools. The authors show how these exploratory tools can be used for information systems (IS) project management, simple modeling of the software process, and modeling the dynamics of the IS organization in transition.

[Ruiz et al. 2001]   J
"A simplified model of software project dynamics"
In this work, several dynamic models were developed in order to simulate the behavior of software projects. From the comparison made between one of the best known empirical estimation models and dynamic estimation models, they analyzed the existing problems in dynamic models in order to make dynamic estimations at the early stages of software projects, when little information is available. The results are obtained from a reduced dynamic model developed to estimate and analyze the behavior of projects in the early phases, in which there is not much information regarding the project. The modeling approach followed to obtain this simplified model has been determined by the simplification of Abdel-Hamid and Madnick's model using the works of Eberlein about understanding and simplification of models.

[Ruiz et al. 2002], [Ruiz et al. 2004]   C J
An integrated framework for simulation-based software process improvement
These papers present a doubly integrated dynamic framework for CMM-based software process improvement that combines traditional static models with dynamic simulation. The aim is to support a qualitative and quantitative assessment for software process improvement and decision making to achieve a higher software development process capability according to the CMM. First, it is based on the systematic integration of dynamic modules to build dynamic models simulate each maturity level proposed in the reference model. As a consequence, a hierarchical set of dynamic models is developed following the same hierarchy of levels suggested in the CMM. Second, the dynamic models of the framework are integrated with different static techniques commonly used in planning, control, and process evaluation. The papers describe the reasons found to follow this approach, the integration process of models and techniques, and the implementation of the framework, and show an ex-

ample of how it can be used in a software process improvement concerning the cost of software quality.

[Rus et al. 1999]   J

"Software process simulation for reliability management"

This paper describes the use of a process simulator to support software project planning and management. The modeling approach here focuses on software reliability, but is just as applicable to other software quality factors, as well as to cost and schedule factors. The process simulator was developed as a part of a decision support system in [Rus 1998] for assisting project managers in planning or tailoring the software development process, in a quality driven manner. The original simulator was developed using the system dynamics approach. As the model evolved by applying it to a real software development project, a need arose to incorporate the concepts of discrete event modeling. The system dynamics model and discrete event models each have unique characteristics that make them more applicable in specific situations. The continuous model can be used for project planning and for predicting the effect of management and reliability engineering decisions. It can also be used as a training tool for project managers. The discrete event implementation is more detailed and therefore more applicable to project tracking and control. In this paper, the structure of the system dynamics model is presented. The use of the discrete event model to construct a software reliability prediction model for an Army project, Crusader, is described in detail.

[Rus, Collofello 1998]   C

"Software process simulation for reliability strategy assessment"

This paper describes the use of a process simulator for evaluating different quality-driven software reliability strategies. As part of a decision support system for project managers, different strategies can be compared via simulation for a project to choose from and tailor. The system also includes a rule-based fuzzy logic expert system component for suggesting alternative processes. Product and project factors that affect software reliability are modeled with other related project parameters. The effect of different software reliability practices impacting different factors is shown, as well as the impact on cost and schedule. This led to the dissertation in [Rus 1998].

[Rus 1998]   A

"Modeling the Impact on Cost and Schedule of Software Quality Engineering Practices"

This Ph.D. dissertation investigated how to design the process for developing software with given quality requirements, in order to achieve product requirements while maintaining the balance between software quality, project cost, and delivery time. The solution proposed is to develop a framework for customizing a project by selecting software reliability engineering practices for achieving specified software reliability requirements, and modeling the resulting process in order to assess, by simulation, the impact of these practices on project cost, schedule, and software quality throughout the development life cycle. The framework is implemented by a decision support system (DSS) for software reliability engineering strategy selection and assessment. This dissertation describes the framework and presents the methodology used for developing it, as well as framework implementation and the results of using the fuzzy expert system for strategy selection and the system dynamics process simulator for practices effect evaluation.

[Smith et al. 1993] ☐J

"Death of a software manager: How to avoid career suicide through dynamic process modeling"

Software managers commit career suicide each year because they do not alter their mental models that often stifle consideration of alternatives until they are exposed or fail dramatically. To improve software development both at an individual and corporate level, the authors feel that our mental models must expand to include new experiences and alternatives, and we need a way to collect and share experiences.

[Stallinger 2000] ☐J

"Software process simulation to support ISO/IEC 15504 based software process improvement"

A generalized system dynamics model of *"a set of improving software processes"* was developed to support SPI action planning at a tactical level. The basic intention is to determine the impact of a set of scheduled improvement actions on the strategic target variables of SPI (time to market, cost, quality, etc.). The approach integrates the two main "mental models" behind ISO/IEC 15504: the process model described textually as a network of processes and work products, and the model of maturing single processes describing the evolution of process capability through a series of process attributes. The development of the model is oriented toward organizations with lower capability and medium-sized development projects. The results of preceding software process assessments are used as a major source for model initialization. The feasibility of the approach is demonstrated by providing results from prototype applications to improvement projects, and insights and lessons learned on how to build such a model are described.

[Stallinger, Gruenbacher 2001] ☐J

"System dynamics modelling and simulation of collaborative requirements engineering"

Requirements engineering is a success-critical activity in the software development process. Within this context, this paper presents selected aspects of the system dynamics modeling and simulation of the EasyWinWin requirements negotiation methodology. EasyWinWin approaches requirements definition as a learning rather than a gathering activity and aims at fostering stakeholder cooperation and involvement. It is based on the WinWin requirements negotiation model and provides a set of collaborative techniques and tools to enable stakeholder interaction. The major goal behind the modeling and simulation effort is to assess the issues associated with the social and behavioral aspects of the EasyWinWin process and to explore how these issues affect the overall outcome of the process. This paper introduces the EasyWinWin process, presents the simulation model, and provides details and results of the requirements elicitation component of the model. It discusses model validation and calibration, and summarizes the conclusions and insights obtained.

[Sycamore 1995] ☐A

"Improving Software Project Management through System Dynamics Modeling"

This M.S. dissertation introduces a tool that gives accurate foresight into the dynamics of a system based upon intuitive managerial decisions for an incremental development process. The relationships among various components of a software system are described through equations that represent causal influences rather than statistical correlation.

[Taweponsomkiat 1996] A

"Report for re-engineering of concurrent incremental software development model"
A description of the process of reengineering a concurrent incremental software development model implemented in Ithink to the Extend simulation language is given. A rationale for the need for reengineering and a description of this process is also provided.

[Tvedt, Collofello 1995] C

"Evaluating the effectiveness of process improvements on software development cycle time via system dynamics modeling"
The objective is to provide decision makers with a model that will enable the prediction of the impact a set of process improvements will have on their cycle time. A description is given of the initial results of developing such a model and applying it to assess the impact of software inspections. This work pre-dated the dissertation in [Tvedt 1996].

[Tvedt 1995] A

"A system dynamics model of the software inspection process"
The author describes the modeling of software inspections used in predicting their impact on software development cycle time. Along with an overview of the software inspection process, a software inspection model is presented in this paper. Also see [Tvedt 1996].

[Tvedt 1996] A

"A Modular Model for Predicting the Impact of Process Improvements on Software Development Time"
This Ph.D. dissertation describes a model for concurrent incremental software development and applies it to assess the impact of software inspections. Reducing software development cycle time without sacrificing quality is crucial to the continued success of most software development organizations. Software companies are investing time and money in reengineering processes incorporating improvements aimed at reducing their cycle time. Unfortunately, the impact of process improvements on the cycle time of complex software processes is not well understood. The objective of this research was to provide a model that will enable researchers and software project managers to evaluate the impact a set of process improvements will have on their software development cycle time. The model enables researchers and software project managers to gain insight and perform controlled experiments to answer "what if" type questions, such as, "What kind of cycle time reduction can I expect to see if I implement inspections?" or "How much time should I spend on inspections?"

[Twaites et al. 2006] C

"Modeling inspections to evaluate prioritization as a method to mitigate the effects of accelerated schedules"
Inspections have long been accepted as one of the most efficient ways of detecting many types of product defects. Given sufficient time, trained reviewers are quite good at detecting defects. Unfortunately, there is often insufficient time in which to

perform a rigorous review. This paper uses a system dynamics model to assess the effect of prioritizing the items under inspection when presented with an accelerated schedule.

[Waeselynck, Pfahl 1994] ☐J

"System dynamics applied to the modelling of software projects"

A summary is presented of the major results of a study performed to review world-wide activities in the field of system dynamics modeling and simulation applied to software development projects. The five potential uses of this method for software development projects are the following: research, training, policy investigation, postmortem analysis, and monitoring ongoing projects.

[Wakeland et al. 2004] ☐J

"Using design of experiments, sensitivity analysis, and hybrid simulation to evaluate changes to a software development process: A case study"

Hybrid simulation models combine the high-level project issues of system dynamics models with the process detail of discrete event simulation models. Hybrid models not only capture the best of both of these simulation paradigms, but they also are able to address issues the other simulation paradigms are only able to address alone. This article describes a structured approach that applies design of experiments (DOE) and broad-range sensitivity analysis (BRSA) to a hybrid system dynamics and discrete event simulation model of a software development process. DOE is used to analyze the interaction effects. The sensitivity of the model to parameter changes over a broad range of plausible values is used to analyze the nonlinear aspects of the model. The end result is a deeper insight into the conditions under which the process change will succeed, and improved recommendations for process change design and implementation. In this particular study, significant interactions and nonlinearities were revealed, supporting the hypothesis that consideration of these complex effects is essential for insightful interpretation of model results and effective decision making.

[Wernick, Lehman 1999] ☐J

"Software process dynamic modeling for FEAST/1"

This article presents a high-level system dynamics model of software evolution developed for the FEAST project (see also [Lehman 1996] etc. on software evolution). The model investigates the role and effect of feedback in the global software process. It tests the FEAST hypothesis that the dynamics of real-world software evolution processes leads to a degree of process autonomy. It is shown that the model behavior closely reflects data from an actual defense project that involved successive releases with strict deadlines, and supports the contention that external feedback significantly influences progress. It demonstrates that a simple top-down model can reproduce real-world trends, and that some aspects of the process can be ignored when considering long-term software product evolution.

[Wernick, Hall 2002] ☐J

"Simulating global software evolution processes by combining simple models: An initial study"

A number of studies of the long-term evolution of commercial software products over many releases have established a consistent pattern for growth in the size of the systems examined. This shows a trend toward a progressive slowdown in growth over time. The work presented here is a step in developing a simulation of the combined effects of the causes of this trend. A number of simple system dynamics simulations, each capturing the causal structure and behavior of one of a number of causes are presented. These models are then combined into a single simulation model reflecting the effect of a combination of these causes. Possible causes considered here are the reduction over time in both the conceptual space, which can be searched for new uses of a system and the design spaces constraining developers' ability to modify their systems; the effects of the degradation of the structure of a software system as is it is evolved in unanticipated directions; and the reducing coverage of developers' knowledge of the structure of the system. The combined model incorporates all of these causal mechanisms and introduces a relative weighting for each. The long-term aim is to produce a simulation embodying those possible causes which are found to be supported by actual evidence.

[Williford, Chang 1999]   ⃞J

"Modeling the FedEx IT division: A system dynamics approach to strategic IT planning" This paper describes a model for long-term IT strategic planning at Federal Express. The macro-level model predicts staffing, training, and infrastructure needs over a five-year period. It was developed using actual metrics, expert judgement, and business predictions. Strategic factors that could be adjusted included process improvement programs, investment in tools and training, recruiting, and architecture strategies. The submodels include balancing of permanent employees with contract workers, and included staff retraining associated with the transition from mainframe to distributed systems. An infrastructure rollout model estimated server purchases to support computing workloads as they migrated, and incorporated Moore's Law to predict changing hardware costs. The model outputs were judged to be reasonable by participating management, and served to strengthen senior management's commitment to process improvement and, particularly, human resource strategies.

Table B-1. Special journals with ProSim and SPW/ProSim papers

International Workshop on Software Process Simulation and Modeling (ProSim) Year and Location	Journal Issue with Revised Papers
ProSim 1998 Portland, OR, USA	*Journal of Systems and Software,* Vol. 46, Issue 2-3, Elsevier, 1999
ProSim 1999 Portland, OR, USA	*Software Process Improvement and Practice,* Vol. 5, Issue 2-3, John Wiley & Sons, Ltd., 2000
ProSim 2000 London, England	*Journal of Systems and Software,* Vol. 59, Issue 3, Elsevier, 2001
ProSim 2001 Portland, OR, USA	*Software Process Improvement and Practice,* Vol. 7, Issue 3-4, John Wiley & Sons, Ltd., 2002
ProSim 2003 Portland, OR, USA	*Software Process Improvement and Practice,* Vol. 9, Issue 2, John Wiley & Sons, Ltd., 2004
ProSim 2004 Edinburgh, Scotland	*Software Process Improvement and Practice,* Vol. 10, Issue 3, John Wiley & Sons, Ltd., 2005
ProSim 2005 St. Louis, MO, USA	*Software Process Improvement and Practice,* Vol. 11, Issue 4, John Wiley & Sons, Ltd., 2006
SPW/ProSim 2006 Shanghai, China (first joint conference with International Software Process Workshop)	*Software Process Improvement and Practice,* Vol. 12, Issue 5, John Wiley & Sons, Ltd., 2007 (to be published)

Table B-2. Additional special journals on system dynamics for software processes

Journal Issue
American Programmer, Yourdon E (ed.), Cutter Information Group, New York, May 1993

Appendix C

PROVIDED MODELS

The models in Tables C-1 through C-6 are referenced in the chapters and provided to registered book owners. The list of models will be updated on the book's Internet site(s).

Table C-1. Chapter 1—Introduction Models

Model Filename	Description
brooks.itm	Example Brooks's Law model

Table C-2. Chapter 2—The Modeling Process with System Dynamics Models

Model Filename	Description
dynamic behaviors.itm	Example structures that produce typical dynamic behaviors
delay tests.itm	Demonstrates different time delay structures
test functions.itm	Demonstrates standard test input functions

Table C-3. Chapter 3—Model Structures and Behaviors for Software Processes Models

Model Filename	Description	External Source
rayleigh.itm	Rayleigh curve staffing rate	
resource allocation.itm	Resource allocation infrastructure where tasks with the greatest backlog receive proportionally greater resources ("squeaky wheel gets the grease")	Modified from isee systems

(*continued*)

Software Process Dynamics. By Raymond J. Madachy
Copyright © 2008 the Institute of Electrical and Electronics Engineers, Inc.

Table C-3. *Continued*

Model Filename	Description	External Source
production.itm	Simple software production structure with single stock for personnel	
reuse.itm	Demonstrates reuse economy	
example1.itm	Example project that combines software product development (see production.itm) with personnel chain	
example1 reuse.itm	Adds software reuse to product development and personnel pool in example1.itm	
example1 incremental.itm	Adds incremental development structure to example1.itm	
system development.itm	Detailed model of combined hardware/ software development includes competition and market factors	Modified from isee systems
product.itm	Product production infrastructure includes target inventory and experience effects	Modified from isee systems
perceived quality.itm	Models perceived quality with delay for adjusting perceptions	Modified from isee systems
single tier personnel chain.itm	Single-tier hiring and quitting infrastructure with target growth percentage and replacing for attritions	Modified from isee systems
interact.itm	Detailed organizational model showing interactions between human resources, finance, product quality, and clients	Modified from isee systems
two tier personnel chain.itm	Two-tier hiring and quitting infrastructure	Modified from isee systems
rookie.itm	Simple rookie and pro personnel chain	Modified from isee systems
wrkchain.itm	Work flow main chain infrastructure whereby tasks undergo inspections with applied resources	Modified from isee systems
hrprod.itm	Human resources productivity infrastructure with levels for motivation, knowledge, and experience	Modified from isee systems
hrchain.itm	Human resources main chain infrastructure with three levels of personnel experience, promotion delays, and quitting fractions	Modified from isee systems

Table C-4. Chapter 4—People Applications Models

Application Area	Model Filename	Description and External Source
Project Workforce Modeling	human resource management.itm	Human resource sector from Abdel-Hamid's integrated software project dynamics model. Provided by Margaret Johnson.
	rookie.itm	Simple rookie and pro personnel chain. Modified from isee systems.
	hrprod.itm	Human resources productivity infrastructure; includes levels for motivation, knowledge, and experience. Modified from isee systems.
Motivation	overtime.itm	Effect of overtime on productivity relationship
Exhaustion and Burnout	exhaustion.itm	Exhaustion submodel from Abdel-Hamid's integrated software project dynamics model
	burnout.itm	Alternate model of burnout dynamics. Modified from isee systems.
Learning	learning curves.itm	Demonstration and comparison of learning curve formulations
Personnel Hiring and Retention	hiring delay.itm	Simple hiring delay model
	single tier personnel chain.itm	Single-tier hiring and quitting infrastructure; includes target growth and attrition replacement. Modified from isee systems.
	two tier personnel chain.itm	Two-tier hiring and quitting infrastructure. Modified from isee systems.
	hrchain.itm	Human resources main chain, includes three levels of experience, promotion, and quitting. Modified from isee systems.
Team Communication	brooks.itm	Brooks Law example

Table C-5. Chapter 5—Process and Product Applications

Application Area	Model Filename	Description and External Source
Peer Reviews	inspections.itm	Dynamic project effects of incorporating formal inspections
	insp.itm	Version of Abdel-Hamid's integrated software project dynamics model (includes switch for inspections) (also see *base.itm* for incremental processes and inspections). Provided by John Tvedt.

(continued)

Table C-5. *Continued*

Application Area	Model Filename	Description and External Source
Peer Reviews (*cont.*)	wrkchain.itm	Simple work flow chain where tasks undergo inspections using a conveyer model. Modified from isee systems.
Software Reuse	reuse and language level.itm	Impact of reuse and language levels. Provided by Kam Wing Lo.
Global Process Feedback	global feedback.itm	Illustration of global feedback to software process (simplified version of Wernick-Lehman 98 model). Provided by Paul Wernick.
COTS-based Systems	COTS glue code integration.itm	Dynamics of glue code development in COTS-based systems. Provided by Jongmoon Baik.
Incremental and Iterative Processses	base.itm	Dissertation model for incremental development and inspections. Provided by John Tvedt.
	project increments.itm	Three-increment project model. Provided by Doug Sycamore.
	simple iterative process.itm	Highly simplified software development structure using arrays to model iterations
Software Architecting	MBASE architecting.itm	Software architecting using the MBASE framework; also includes iterations. Provided by Nikunj Mehta.
Quality	COQUALMO.xls	Spreadsheet version of the Constructive Quality Model (COQUALMO). Provided by the USC Center for Systems and Software Engineering.
Software Process Improvement	SEASauth.itm	Organizational process improvement. Provided by Steven Burke.
	Xerox SPI.itm	Xerox adaptation of Burke's process improvement model. Provided by Jason Ho.
Other—System Testing	STEAM.zip	System test and evaluation model (Extend model files and other assets). Provided by Greg Twaites.

Table C-6. Chapter 6—Project and Organization Applications Models

Application Area	Model Filename	Description and External Source
Integrated Project Modeling	integrated project.itm (and all sector submodels)	Abdel-Hamid's integrated software project dynamics model translated into Ithink. Provided by Margaret Johnson.
Earned Value	earned value.itm	Earned value project simulator and trainer
Staffing	rayleigh.itm	Rayleigh curve staffing model
	rayleigh interactive.itm	Interactive user control of requirements influx to gauge impact on Rayleigh curve staffing rate

Table C-6. *Continued*

Application Area	Model Filename	Description and External Source
Staffing (*cont.*)	rayleigh incremental.itm	Rayleigh curve model with array structure to model incremental development
	rayleigh COCOMO.itm	Rayleigh curve calibrated to COCOMO with parameterized staffing shapes
	external concurrence.itm	Generalized external process concurrence model
	1phase.itm	Single-phase dynamic development project model (with process concurrence and iteration). Provided by David Ford.
	DNFProjProcess.mdl	Multiple-phase dynamic development project model (with process concurrence and iteration). Provided by David Ford.
Personnel Resource Allocation	proportional resource allocation.itm	Resource allocation infrastructure where tasks with the greatest backlog receive proportionally greater resources ("squeaky wheel gets the grease"). Modified from isee systems.
	project contention.itm	Models the contention of senior developers between projects in terms of project transference losses
Product Line Strategy	COPLIMO.xls	Spreadsheet version of the Constructive Product Line Model (COPLIMO). Provided by the USC Center for Systems and Software Engineering.
	core product line reuse.itm	Top-level, nonexecutable model of product line core software reuse
Business Case Analysis	value based product.itm	Value-based product model with software process, quality, market/sales, and financial models
	system development.itm	Detailed model of combined hardware/software development with competition and market factors. Modified from isee systems.
	interact.itm	Detailed organizational model showing interactions between human resources, finance, product quality, and clients. Modified from isee systems.

REFERENCES

References shown in boldface involve system dynamics modeling for software processes and are summarized in the annotated bibliography in Appendix B.

[Abdel-Hamid 1984] Abdel-Hamid T, *The Dynamics of Software Project Staffing: An Integrative System Dynamics Perspective,* Ph.D. dissertation, Massachusetts Institute of Technology, 1984.

[Abdel-Hamid 1989a] Abdel-Hamid T, "The dynamics of software project staffing: A system dynamics based simulation approach," *IEEE Transactions on Software Engineering,* February 1989.

[Abdel-Hamid 1989b] Abdel-Hamid T, "Lessons learned from modeling the dynamics of software development," *Communications of the ACM,* December 1989.

[Abdel-Hamid 1990] Abdel-Hamid T, "Investigating the cost/schedule trade-off in software development," *IEEE Software,* January 1990.

[Abdel-Hamid 1991] Abdel-Hamid T, "Organizational learning: The key to software management innovation," *American Programmer,* June 1991.

[Abdel-Hamid, Madnick 1991] Abdel-Hamid T and Madnick S, *Software Project Dynamics,* Englewood Cliffs, NJ: Prentice-Hall, 1991.

[Abdel-Hamid 1993a] Abdel-Hamid T, "Adapting, correcting, and perfecting software estimates: a maintenance metaphor," *IEEE Computer,* March 1993.

[Abdel-Hamid 1993b] Abdel-Hamid T, "Thinking in circles," *American Programmer,* May 1993.

[Abdel-Hamid 1993c] Abdel-Hamid T, "Modeling the dynamics of software reuse: An integrating system dynamics perspective," Presented at the Sixth Annual Workshop on Software Reuse, Owego, NY, November 1993.

[Abdel-Hamid 1993d] Abdel-Hamid T, "A multi-project perspective of single project dynamics," *Journal of Systems and Software,* 22(3), 1993.

[Abdel-Hamid et al. 1993] Abdel-Hamid T, Sengupta K, and Ronan D, "Software project control: An experimental investigation of judgment/ with fallible information," *IEEE Transactions on Software Engineering,* June 1993.

[Abelson et al. 2004] Abelson L, Adams R, and Eslinger S, "Aquisition modeling: The key to managing acquisition complexity?" in *Proceedings of the Conference on the Aquisition of Software-Intensive Systems,* Software Engineering Institute, 2004.

[Abts 2003] Abts C, *Extending the COCOMO II Software Cost Model to Estimate COTS-Based System Costs,* Ph.D. Dissertation," University of Southern California, 2003.

[Abts, Boehm 1998] Abts C and Boehm B, "COTS software integration cost modeling study," USC-CSE Technical Report 98-520, 1998.

[Abts 2000] Abts C, "A perspective on the economic life span of COTS-based software systems: The COTS-LIMO model," USC Center for Software Engineering, USC-CSE-2000-503, 2000.

[Acuña 2002] Acuña S T, *Capabilities-Oriented Integral Software Process Model,* Ph.D. Thesis, Universidad Politécnica de Madrid, Madrid, 2002.

[Acuña, Juristo 2005] Acuña S T and Juristo N (Eds.), *Software Process Modeling,* New York: Springer Science+Business Media Inc., 2005.

[Acuña, Juzgado 2004] Acuña S T and Juzgado N J, "Assigning people to roles in software projects," *Software Practice and Experience,* 34(7), 675–696, 2004.

[Acuña et al. 2005] Acuna S, Juristo N, Moreno A, and Mon A, *A Software Process Model Handbook for Incorporating People's Capabilities,* New York: Springer, 2005.

[Acuña, Sánchez-Segura 2006] Acuña S T and Sánchez-Segura M I, *New Trends in Software Process Modelling,* Singapore: World Scientific Publishing, 2006.

[Acuña et al. 2006] Acuña S T, Juzgado N J, and Moreno A M, "Emphasizing human capabilities in software development," *IEEE Software* 23(2): 94–101, 2006.

[Agile 2003] Agile Manifesto Group, "Manifesto for Agile Software Development," *http://agilemanifesto.org,* 2003.

[Agresti 1986] Agresti W (Ed.), *New Paradigms for Software Development,* Washington, DC, Los Alamitos, CA: IEEE Computer Society, 1986.

[Angkasaputra, Pfahl 2004] Angkasaputra N and Pfahl D, "Making software process simulation modeling agile and pattern-based," in Pfahl D, Raffo D, Rus I, and Wernick P (Eds.), *Fifth International Workshop on Software Process Simulation and Modeling,* pp. 222–227, ProSim 2004, Edinburgh, Scotland—Proceedings. Stevenage: IEE Publishing, 2004.

[Angkasaputra, Pfahl 2005] Angkasaputra N and Pfahl D, "Towards an agile development method of software process simulation," in *Proceedings of 6th International Workshop on Software Process Simulation Modeling,* pp. 83–92, ProSim 2005, St. Louis, Missouri, 2005.

[Aranda et al. 1993] Aranda R, Fiddaman T, and Oliva R, "Quality microworlds: Modeling the impact of quality initiatives over the software product life cycle," *American Programmer,* May 1993.

[Baik, Eickelmann 2001] Baik J and Eickelmann N, "Applying COCOMO II effort multipliers to simulation models," in *Proceedings of the Sixteenth International Forum on COCOMO and Software Cost Modeling,* USC, Los Angeles, CA, 2001.

[Baik et al. 2001] Baik J, Eickelmann N, and Abts C, "Empirical software simulation for COTS glue code development and integration," in *COMPSAC 2001,* pp. 297–302, Chicago, 2001.

[Balzer et al. 1992] Balzer R, Cheatham T, and Green C, "Software technology in the 1990's: Using a new paradigm, *IEEE Computer,* pp. 39–45, November 1983.

[Barbieri et al. 1992] Barbieri A, Fuggetta A, Lavazza L, and Tagliavini M, "DynaMan: A tool to improve software process management through dynamic simulation," in *Proceedings, Fifth International Workshop on Computer-Aided Software Engineering,* Montreal, July 1992.

[Barros et al. 2000a] Barros M, Werner C, and Travassos G, "Applying system dynamics to scenario based software project management," in *Proceedings of the 2000 International System Dynamics Conference*, Bergen, Norway, 2000.

[Barros et al. 2000b] Barros M, Werner C, and Travassos G, "Using process modeling and dynamic simulation to support software process quality management," in *Proceedings of WQS'2000 Workshop Qualidade de Software*, vol. 1. pp. 295–305, Sociedade Brasileira de Computação, 2000.

[Barros et al. 2001a] Barros M, Werner C, and Travassos G, "Explaining the behavior of system dynamics models," in *Proceedings of the 2001 International System Dynamics Conference*, Atlanta, 2001.

[Barros et al. 2001b] Barros M, Werner C, and Travassos G, "From metamodels to models: Organizing and reusing domain knowledge in system dynamics model development," in *Proceedings of 2001 International System Dynamics Conference*, Atlanta, 2001.

[Barros et al. 2002a] Barros M, Werner C, and Travassos G, "A System dynamics metamodel for software process modeling," *International Journal of Software Process Improvement and Practice*, 7(3–4), 161–172, 2002. (Initial version in *Proceedings of ProSim Workshop 2001.*)

[Barros et al. 2002b] Barros M, Werner C, and Travassos G, "Evaluating the use of system dynamics models in software project management," in *Proceedings of 2002 International System Dynamics Conference*, Palermo Italy, Systems Dynamic Society, 2002.

[Barros et al. 2003] Barros M, Werner C, and Travassos G, "System dynamics extension modules for software process modeling," in *Proceedings of 2003 Software Process Simulation and Modeling Workshop*, Portland, OR, 2003.

[Barros et al. 2004] Barros M, Werner C, and Travassos G, "Supporting risks in software project management," *Journal of Systems and Software*, 70(1), 21–35, 2004.

[Barros et al. 2006a] Barros M, Dantas A, Veronese G, and Werner C, "Model-driven game development: Experience and model enhancements in software project management education," *Software Process Improvement and Practice*, 11(4), 2006.

[Barros et al. 2006b] Barros M, Werner C, and Travassos G, "A metamodel for software project model development with system dynamics," in Acuña S, Sánchez-Segura M I (Eds.), *New Trends in Software Process Modelling.* vol. 18, pp. 91–119, Singapore, World Scientific Publishing, 2006.

[Basili 1992] Basili V R, "Software modeling and measurement: The goal/question/metric paradigm," Technical Report, CS-TR-2956, Department of Computer Science, University of Maryland, College Park, MD 20742, September 1992.

[Basili, Turner 1975] Basili V and Turner A, "Iterative enhancement: A practical technique for software development," *IEEE Transactions on Software Engineering*, December 1975.

[Basili et al. 1994] Basili V, Caldiera G, and Rombach D H, "The goal question metric paradigm," in *Encyclopedia of Software Engineering*, vol. 2, pp. 528–532. Wiley, 1994.

[Basili, Boehm 2001] Basili V and Boehm B, "COTS-based systems top 10 list," *IEEE Computer*, May 2001.

[Baumert et al. 1992] Baumert J and McWhinney M, "Software measures and the capability maturity model," SEI Technical Report CMU/SEI-92-TR-25, September 1992.

[Beck 2000] Beck K, *Extreme Programming Explained*, Boston MA: Addison-Wesley, 2000.

[Benguria et al. 2002] Benguria G, Garcia A, Sellier D, and Tay S, "European COTS Working Group: Analysis of the common problems and current practices of the European COTS users," in *COTS Based Software Systems (Proceedings, ICCBSS 2002)*, Dean J and Gravel A (Eds.), pp. 44–53, New York: Springer-Verlag, 2002.

[Benington 1956] Benington H, "Production of large complex programs," reprinted in *Annals of the History of Computing,* 5(4), pp. 350–361, AFIPS Press, 1983.

[Bhatnagar 2004] Bhatnagar A, unpublished student report for CSCI 599, University of Southern California Computer Science Department, 2004.

[Biffl et al. 2005] Biffl S, Aurum A, Boehm B, Erdogmus H, and Grünbacher P (Eds.), *Value-Based Software Engineering,* Berlin: Springer, 2005.

[Birkhoelzer et al. 2005] Birkhoelzer T, Oh Navarro E, and Van der Hoek A, "Teaching by Modeling Instead of by Models," in *Proceedings of the 6th International Workshop on Process Modeling and Simulation (ProSim 2005),* IEE, 2005.

[Boehm 1976] Boehm B W, "Software engineering," *IEEE Transactions on Computers,* 25(12), 1226–1241, 1976.

[Boehm 1981] *Software Engineering Economics,* Englewood Cliffs, NJ: Prentice-Hall, 1981.

[Boehm 1987] Boehm B W. "Improving software productivity," *IEEE Computer,* September, 43–57, 1987.

[Boehm 1988] Boehm B W, "A spiral model of software development and enhancement," *IEEE Software,* May 1988.

[Boehm 1989] Boehm B W, *Software Risk Management,* Washington, DC: IEEE-CS Press, 1989.

[Boehm 1996] Boehm B, "Anchoring the software process," *IEEE Software,* July, 73–82, 1996.

[Boehm 2000] Boehm B, "Spiral development: Experience, principles, and refinements," Special Report CMU/SEI-00-SR-08, in Hansen W J (Ed.), *Spiral Development Workshop Final Report, http://www.sei.cmu.edu/cbs/spiral2000/february2000/BoehmSR.html,* June, 2000.

[Boehm 2005a] Boehm B, "The future of software processes," in *Proceedings of the International Software Process Workshop, SPW 2005,* Beijing, China, Springer-Verlag, 2005.

[Boehm 2005b] Boehm B, "The future of software and systems engineering processes," USC Technical Report, USC-CSE-2005-507, 2005.

[Boehm, Scacchi 1996] Boehm B and Scacchi W, "Simulation and modeling for software acquisition (SAMSA): Air Force opportunities," *http://www.usc.edu/dept/ATRIUM/Papers/SAMSA/samcover.html,* 1996.

[Boehm et al. 1998] Boehm B, Egyed A, Kwan J, and Madachy R, "Using the WinWin Spiral Model: A case study," *IEEE Computer,* July, 33–44, 1998.

[Boehm et al. 2000] Boehm B, Abts C, Brown W, Chulani S, Clark B, Horowitz E, Madachy R, Reifer D, and Steece B, *Software Cost Estimation with COCOMO II,* Englewood Cliffs, NJ: Prentice-Hall, 2000.

[Boehm et al. 2003] Boehm B, Port D, Yang Y, Bhuta J, and Abts C, "Composable process elements for developing COTS-based applications," in *IEEE/ACM International Symposium on Empirical Software Engineering 2003,* Italy, September 2003.

[Boehm, Belz 1988] Boehm B and Belz F, "Applying process programming to the spiral model," in *Proceedings, Fourth International Software Process Workshop,* ACM, May 1988.

[Boehm, Bose 1994] Boehm B and Bose P, "A collaborative spiral software process model based on Theory W," in *Proceedings, ICSP 3,* IEEE, Reston, VA, October 1994.

[Boehm, Huang 2003] Boehm B and Huang L, "Value-based software engineering: A case study," *IEEE Software,* 20(2), 2003.

[Boehm, Ross 1989] Boehm B, and Ross R, "Theory-W software project management: Principles and examples," *IEEE Transactions on Software Engineering,* pp. 902–916, July 1989.

[Boehm, Turner 2004] Boehm B and Turner R, *Balancing Agility and Discipline,* Reading, MA: Addison-Wesley, 2004.

[Boehm et al. 2004a] Boehm B, Huang L, Jain A, and Madachy R, "Reasoning about the ROI of software dependability: The iDAVE Model," *IEEE Software,* 21(3), 2004.

[Boehm et al. 2004b] Boehm B, Brown A W, Madachy R, and Yang Y, "A software product line life cycle cost estimation model," in *ISESE '04: The 2004 International Symposium on Empirical Software Engineering,* pp. 156–164, IEEE Computer Society, 2004.

[Box 1979] Box G E P, "Robustness in the strategy of scientific model building," in Launer R L, and Wilkinson G N, (Eds.), *Robustness in Statistics,* New York: Academic Press, 202, 1979.

[Briand et al. 1999] Briand L C, El Emam K, and Wieczorek I, "Explaining the cost of European space and military projects," in *Proceedings of the 16th International Conference on Software Engineering,* IEEE, Los Angeles, 1999.

[Brooks 1975] Brooks F, *The Mythical Man-Month,* Reading, MA: Addison-Wesley, 1975 (also reprinted and updated in 1995).

[Brownsword et al. 2000] Brownsword L, Oberndorf P, and Sledge C, "Developing new processes for COTS-based systems," *Software,* July/August, 48–55, 2000".

[Burke 1996] Burke S, Radical improvements require radical actions: Simulating a high-maturity software organization," CMU/SEI-96-TR-024, Software Engineering Institute, Pittsburgh, PA, 1996.

[Chang 2005] S. Chang (Ed.), *Handbook of Software Engineering and Knowledge Engineering,* vol. 3, Singapore: World Scientific Publishing, 2005.

[Charette 1989] Charette R N, *Software Engineering Risk Analysis and Management,* New York: McGraw-Hill, 1989.

[Chatters et al. 2000] Chatters B, Lehman M, Ramil J, and Wernick P, "Modelling a software evolution process: A long-term case study," *Software Process Improvement and Practice,* vol. 5, issue 2–3, John Wiley and Sons, 2000. (Initial version in *Proceedings of ProSim Workshop 1999.*)

[Chen et al. 2004] Chen Y, Gannod G C, Collofello J S, and Sarjoughian H S, "Using simulation to facilitate the study of software product line evolution" in *Seventh International Workshop on Principles of Software Evolution,* Kyoto, Japan, 2004.

[Chichakly 1993] Chichakly K, "The bifocal vantage point: Managing software projects from a systems thinking perspective," *American Programmer,* May 1993.

[Chillarege et al. 1992] Chillarege R, Bhandari I, Chaar J, Halliday M, Moebus D, Ray B, and Wong M, "Orthogonal defect classification—A concept for in-process measurements," *IEEE Transactions on Software Engineering,* 18(11), 943–956, 1992.

[Christie 1998] Christie A, "Software process simulation to achieve higher CMM levels," in *Proceedings of ProSim Workshop '98,* Portland, OR, June 1998.

[Christie 1999] Christie A M, "Simulation: An enabling technology in software engineering," *CrossTalk—The Journal of Defense Software Engineering,* April, 1999.

[Christie, Staley 2000] Christie A and Staley M, "Organizational and social simulation of a software requirements development process," *Software Process Improvement and Practice,* 5(2–3), 2000. (initial version in *Proceedings of ProSim Workshop 1999.*)

[Chulani, Boehm 1999] Chulani S, Boehm B, "Modeling software defect introduction and removal: COQUALMO (COnstructive QUALity MOdel)," USC-CSE Technical Report 99-510, 1999.

[Clements, Northrop 2001] Clements P and Northrop L M, *Software Product Lines: Practices and Patterns,* Reading, MA: Addison-Wesley, 2001.

[Cockburn 2001] Cockburn A, *Agile Software Development,* Reading, MA: Addison-Wesley, 2001.

[Cockburn, Highsmith 2001] Cockburn A and Highsmith J, "Agile software development: The people factor," *IEEE Computer,* November 2001.

[Collofello 2000] Collofello J, "University/industry collaboration in developing a simulation-based software project management course," *IEEE Transactions on Education,* 43(4), 2000.

[Collofello et al. 1995] Collofello J, Yang Z, Tvedt J, Merrill D, and Rus I, "Modeling software testing processes," Computer Science and Engineering Dept., Arizona State University, 1995.

[Collofello et al. 1998] Collofello J, Rus I, Houston D, and Smith-Daniels D, "A system dynamics process simulator for staffing policies decision support," in *Proceedings of 1998 Hawaii International Conference on System Sciences,* 1998.

[Collofello et al. 1996] Collofello J, Yang Z, Merrill D, Rus I, and Tvedt J D, "Modeling Software Testing Processes," in *Proceedings of the International Phoenix Conference on Computers and Communications (IPCCC'96),* 1996.

[Conte et al. 1986] Conte S, Dunsmore H, and Shen V, *Software Engineering Metrics and Models,* Menlo Park, CA, Benjamin/Cummings, 1986.

[Cooper, Mullen 1993] Cooper K and Mullen T, "Swords and plowshares: The rework cycles of defense and commercial software development projects," *American Programmer,* May 1993.

[Cost Xpert 2003] Cost Xpert Group, *Cost Xpert 3.3 User's Guide,* San Diego, CA, 2003.

[Curtis et al. 1992] Curtis B, Kellner M, and Over J, "Process modeling," *Communications of the ACM,* September 1992.

[Curtis et al. 2001] Curtis B, Hefley B, and Miller S, *The People Capability Maturity Model,* Reading, MA: Addison-Wesley, 2001.

[Davis 1995] Davis A, *201 Principles of Software Development,* New York: McGraw-Hill, 1995.

[Diehl 1993] Diehl E, "The analytical lens: Strategy-support software to enhance executive dialog and debate," *American Programmer,* May 1993.

[DeMarco 1982] DeMarco T, *Controlling Software Projects,* New York: Yourdon Press, 1982.

[DeMarco 1998] DeMarco T, *The Deadline,* New York: Dorset House Publishing, 1998.

[DeMarco 2001] DeMarco T, *Slack: Getting Past Burnout, Busywork, and the Myth of Total Efficiency,* New York: Random House, 2001.

[DeMarco, Lister 1999] DeMarco T and Lister T, *Peopleware, Productive Projects and Teams,* New York: Dorset House Publishing, 1999.

[Diker, Allen 2005] Diker V and Allen R, "It's about time: The why and how of using XML for developing an interchange standard for system dynamics models," in *Proceedings of the 2005 International System Dynamics Conference,* 2005.

[DMSO 2006] U.S. Defense and Modeling Office, http://www.dmso.mil, 2006 .

[DoD 2000] U.S. Department of Defense, *Report of the Defense Science Board Task Force on Defense Software,* Office of the Under Secretary of Defense for Acquisition and Technology, 2000.

[Donzelli, Iazeolla 2001] Donzelli P and Iazeolla G, "Hybrid simulation modelling of the software process," *Journal of Systems and Software,* 2001.

[Doukidis, Angelides 1994] Doukidis P, Angelides M, "A framework for integrating artificial intelligence and simulation," *Artificial Intelligence Review,* 8(1), 1994.

[Drappa, Ludewig 2000] Drappa A and Ludewig J, "Simulation in Software Engineering Training," in *Proceedings of the 22nd International Conference on Software Engineering,* 2000.

[Eick et al. 2001] Eick S, Graves T, Karr A, Marron J, and Mockus A, "Does code decay? Assessing the evidence from change management data," *IEEE Transactions on Software Engineering,* 27(1), 1–12, 2001.

[Eickelmann et al. 2002] Eickelmann N, Anant A, Baik J, and Hyun S, "Quantitative control of process changes through modeling simulation and benchmarking," in *Proceedings of the Seventeenth International Forum on COCOMO and Software Cost Modeling,* USC, Los Angeles, CA, 2002.

[Fagan 1976] Fagan M E, "Design and code inspections to reduce errors in program development," *IBM Systems Journal,* 15(3), 182–210, 1976.

[Fagan 1986] Fagan M E, "Advances in software inspections," *IEEE Transactions on Software Engineering,* SE-12(7), 744–751, 1986.

[Fakharzadeh, Mehta 1999] Fakharzadeh C and Mehta N, "Architecture development process dynamics in MBASE," University of Southern California, CS599 Final Report, http://sunset.usc.edu/classes/cs599_99/projects/MBASE.pdf, 1999 and *Proceedings of the 2000 International System Dynamics Conference,* Bergen, Norway, 2000.

[FEAST 2001] *Feedback, Evolution and Software Technology, http://www.doc.ic.ac.uk/~mml/feast/,* 2001.

[Feiler, Humphrey 1993] Feiler P and Humphrey W, "Software process development and enactment: concepts and definitions," in *Proceedings of the Second International Conference on the Software Process,* IEEE Computer Society, Washington DC, 1993.

[Fernández-Ramil et al. 2005] Fernández-Ramil J, Capiluppi A, and Smith N, "Understanding open source and agile evolution through qualitative reasoning," in *Proceedings of the 6th International Workshop on Process Modeling and Simulation (ProSim 2005),* IEE, 2005.

[Ferreira 2002] Ferreira S, *Measuring the Effects of Requirements Volatility on Software Development Projects,* Ph.D. Dissertation, Arizona State University, 2002.

[Ferreira et al. 2003] Ferreira S, Collofello J, Shunk D, Mackulak G, and Wolfe P, "Utilization of process modeling and simulation in understanding the effects of requirements volatility in software development," in *Proceedings of the 2003 Process Simulation Workshop (ProSim),* 2003.

[Ford, Sterman 1997] Ford D and Sterman J, "Dynamic modeling of product development processes," Technical report, Massachusetts Institute of Technology, MIT D-4672, 1997.

[Ford, Sterman 1998] Ford D and Sterman J, "Expert knowledge elicitation to improve formal and mental models," *System Dynamics Review,* 14(4), 1998.

[Ford, Sterman 2003] Ford D and Sterman J, "Iteration management for reduced cycle time in concurrent development projects," *Concurrent Engineering Research and Application (CERA) Journal,* March 2003.

[Forio 2006] Forio Business Simulations, *http://www.forio.com,* 2006.

[Forrester 1961] Forrester J W, *Industrial Dynamics,* Cambridge, MA: MIT Press, 1961.

[Forrester 1968] Forrester J W, *Principles of Systems,* Cambridge, MA: MIT Press, 1968.

[Forrester 1973] Forrester JW, *World Dynamics,* 2nd edition, Cambridge: Wright-Allen Press, Inc., 1973.

[Forrester, Senge 1980] Forrester J W and Senge P, *Tests for building confidence in system dynamics models,* in Legasto A et al. (Eds.), *TIMS Studies in the Management Sciences (System Dynamics),* The Netherlands: North-Holland, pp. 209–228, 1980.

[Fox et al. 1989] Fox M, Reddy Y, Husain N, and Roberts M, "Knowledge based simulation: An artificial intelligence approach to system modeling and automating the simulation life cycle," in Widman L E (Ed.), *Artificial Intelligence, Simulation and Modeling,* pp. 447–486, New York: Wiley, 1989.

[Freeman, Aspray 1999] Freeman P and Aspray W, *The Supply of Information Technology Workers in the U.S.,* Computing Research Association, Washington DC, 1999.

[Galorath 2005] Galorath Inc., *SEER-SEM User Manual,* 2005.

[Gamma et al. 1995] Gamma E, Helm R, Johnson R, and Vlissides J, *Design Patterns: Elements of Reusable Object-Oriented Software,* Reading, MA: Addison-Wesley, 1995.

[Ghosh 2000] Ghosh R, and Prakash V V, "The Orbiten Free Software Survey," *First Monday,* 5(7), July 2000.

[Glickman 1994] Glickman S, "The Bellcore-CSELT collaborative project," in *Proceedings of the Ninth International Forum on COCOMO and Software Cost Modeling,* USC, Los Angeles, CA, 1994.

[Goodman 1974] Goodman M R, *Study Notes in System Dynamics,* Cambridge, MA: Productivity Press, 1974.

[Grady, Caswell 1992] Grady R and Caswell D, *Practical Software Metrics for Project Management and Process Improvement,* Englewood Cliffs, NJ: Prentice-Hall, 1992.

[Greer et al. 2005] Greer D, Black L, and Adams R, "Identifying and mitigating risk across organizational boundaries in software-intensive space system programs," in *Proceedings of the 2005 Space Systems Engineering and Risk Management Symposium,* 2005.

[Haberlein 2004] Haberlein T, "Common structures in system dynamics models of software acquisition projects," *Software Process Improvement and Practice,* 9(2), 2004. (Initial version in *Proceedings of ProSim Workshop 2003.*)

[Hann 2002] Hann I-H, Roberts J, Slaughter S, and Fielding R, "Economic incentives for participating in open source software projects," in *Proceedings of Twenty-Third International Conference on Information Systems,* pp. 365–372, December 2002.

[Hars 2002] Hars A and Ou S, "Working for free? Motivations for participating in open source projects," *International Journal of Electronic Commerce,* 6(3), 2002.

[Hart 2004] Hart J, *Bridging Systems Thinking and Software Quality Improvement: Initiating a Software Learning Organization,* book draft, *http://www.stise.com/bridgingst2se/index.htm,* 2004.

[Henderson, Howard 2000] Henderson P and Howard Y, "Process strategies for large scale software development—Simulation using systems dynamics," *Software Process Improvement and Practice,* 5(2–3), 2000. (Initial version in *Proceedings of ProSim Workshop 1999.*)

[Hertel 2003] Hertel G, Neidner S, and Hermann S, "Motivation of software developers in open source projects: An Internet-based survey of contributors to the Linux kernel," *Research Policy,* 32(7), 1159–1177, 2003.

[Hines 2000] Hines J, *Molecules of Structure Version 1.4,* LeapTec and Ventana Systems, Inc., 2000.

[Ho 1999] Ho J, "Xerox SPI model study," University of Southern California, CS599 Final Report, http://sunset.usc.edu/classes/cs599_99/projects/SPI.pdf, 1999.

[Houston 2000] Houston D, *A Software Project Simulation Model for Risk Management,* Ph.D. Dissertation, Arizona State University, 2000.

[Houston 2006] Houston D, "An experience in facilitating process improvement with an integration problem reporting process simulation," *Software Process Improvement and Practice,* 11(4), 361–371, 2006. (Initial version in *Proceedings of ProSim Workshop 2005.*)

[Houston et al. 2001a] Houston D, Mackulak G, and Collofello J, "Stochastic simulation of risk factor potential effects for software development risk management," *Journal of Systems and Software,* 59(3), 247–257, 2001.

[Houston et al. 2001b] Houston D, Mackulak G, and Collofello J, "Behavioral characterization: Finding and using the influential factors in software process simulation models," *Journal of Systems and Software,* 59(3), 259–270, 2001. (Initial version in *Proceedings of ProSim Workshop 2000.*)

[Humphrey 1989] Humphrey W, *Managing the Software Process,* Reading, MA: Addison-Wesley, 1989.

[Humphrey 1997] Humphrey W, *Managing Technical People,* Reading, MA: Addison-Wesley, 1997.

[Humphrey, Konrad 2005] Humphrey W and Konrad M, "Motivation and Process Improvment," in Biffl S, Aurum A, Boehm B, Erdogmus H, and Grünbacher P (Eds.), *Value-based Software Engineering,* pp. 141–161, Berlin: Springer, 2005.

[IEEE 1991] IEEE, *IEEE Standard Glossary of Software Engineering Terminology,* IEEE-STD-610 ANSI/IEEE Std 610.12-1990, February 1991.

[IEEE 2002] IEEE, *IEEE Software,* special edition on software product lines, IEEE Computer Society, July/August 2002.

[IFPUG 2004] IFPUG, *Function Point Counting Practices Manual, Release 4.2,* International Function Point Users Group, 2004.

[Imagine 2006] Imagine That, *http://www.imaginethatinc.com,* 2006.

[isee 2006] isee systems, *http://www.iseesystems.com,* 2006.

[ISO 2005] ISO 9000 Web site, *http://www.iso.org/iso/en/iso9000-14000,* 2005.

[Jain 1999] Jain S, "Simulation in the next millennium," in *Proceedings of the 1999 Winter Simulation Conference,* 1999.

[Jain, Boehm 2005] Jain A and Boehm B, "SimVBSE: Developing a game for value-based software engineering," USC Technical Report, USC-CSE-2005-518, 2005.

[Jensen 2004] Jensen C and Scacchi W, "Collaboration, leadership, and conflict negotiation in the NetBeans.org community," in *Proceedings of 4th Workshop on Open Source Software Engineering,* Edinburgh, UK, May 2004.

[Jensen, Scacchi 2005] Jensen C and Scacchi W, "Process modeling across the Web information infrastructure," *Software Process Improvement and Practice,* 10(3), 255–272, 2005.

[Johnson 1995] Johnson M, *Dynamic Systems Modeling: The Software Management Process,* Bartz Associates, 1995.

[Johnson et al. 2005] Johnson P, Kou H, Paulding M, Zhang Q, Kagawa A, and Yamashita T, "Improving software development management through software project telemetry," *Software,* Vol. 22, No. 4, July 2005.

[Jones 1994] Jones C, *Assessment and Control of Software Risks,* Englewood Cliffs NJ: Yourdon Press, 1994.

[Jones 2000] Jones C, *Software Assessments, Benchmarks and Best Practices,* Reading, MA: Addison-Wesley, 2000.

[Kaghazian 1999] Kaghazian L, "Dynamic process of Internet companies: An abstract model," University of Southern California, CS599 Final Report, http://sunset.usc.edu/classes/cs599_99/projects/internet.pdf, 1999 and *Proceedings of the 2000 International System Dynamics Conference,* Bergen, Norway, 2000.

[Kahen et al. 2001] Kahen G, Lehman M M, Ramil J F, and Wernick P D, "System dynamics modelling of software evolution processes for policy investigation: Approach and example," *Journal of Systems and Software,* 59(3), 271–281, 2001. (Initial version in *Proceedings of ProSim Workshop 2000.*)

[Kellner 1991] Kellner M, "Software process modeling and support for management planning and control," in *Proceedings of the First International Conference on the Software Process,* pp. 8–28, IEEE Computer Society, Washington DC, 1991.

[Kellner et al. 1991] Kellner M, Feiler P, Finkelstein A, Katayama T, Osterweil L, Penedo M, and Rombach D, "IPSW-6 Software process example," in *Proceedings of the First International Conference on the Software Process,* IEEE Computer Society, Washington DC, 1991.

[Kellner, Raffo 1997] Kellner M and Raffo D, "Measurement issues in quantitative simulations of process models," in *Proceedings of the International Conference on Software Engineering (ICSE) Workshop on Models and Metrics,* Boston, IEEE Computer Society Press, May 1997.

[Kellner et al. 1999] Kellner M, Madachy R, and Raffo D, "Software process simulation modeling: Why? What? How?", *Journal of Systems and Software,* Spring 1999.

[Kelly, Sherif 1990] Kelly J and Sherif J, "An analysis of defect densities found during software inspections," in *Proceedings of the Fifteenth Annual Software Engineering Workshop,* Goddard Space Flight Center, 1990.

[Khoshnevis 1992] Khoshnevis B, *Systems Simulation—Implementations in EZSIM,* New York: McGraw-Hill, 1992.

[Kim, Baik 1999] Kim W K and Baik J, "Dynamic model for COTS glue code development and COTS integration," University of Southern California, CS599 Final Report, http://sunset.usc.edu/classes/cs599_99/projects/COTS.pdf, 1999.

[Kocaoglu et al. 1998] Kocaoglu D, Martin R, and Raffo D, "Moving toward a unified model for software development," in *Proceedings of ProSim Workshop '98,* 1998.

[Kotonya, Sommerville 1998] Kotonya G and Sommerville I, *Requirements Engineering: Processes and Techniques,* New York: Wiley, 1998.

[Koza 1992] Koza J R, *Genetic Programming: On the Programming of Computers by Means of Natural Selection,* Cambridge, MA: MIT Press, 1992.

[Kruchten 1998] Kruchten P, *The Rational Unified Process,* Reading, MA: Addison-Wesley, 1998.

[Lakey 2003] Lakey P, "A hybrid software process simulation model for project management," in *Proceedings of ProSim Workshop 2003,* Portland, OR, 2003.

[Lakhani 2002] Lakhani K R, Wolf B, Bates J, and DiBona C, "The Boston Consulting Group Hacker Survey," July 2002.

[Law, Kelton 1991] Law M and Kelton W, *Simulation Modeling and Analysis,* New York: McGraw-Hill, 1991.

[Lee 1996] Lee M J, *Foundations of the WinWin Requirements Negotiation System,* Ph.D. thesis,

Computer Science Department, University of Southern California, Los Angeles, CA 90089, August 1996.

[Lehman 1980] Lehman M M, "Programs, life cycles, and laws of software evolution," *Proceedings of IEEE,* 68, 1060–1078, 1980.

[Lehman 1996] Lehman M M, "Feedback in the software process," *Information and Software Technology,* Special issue on Software Maintenance, 38(11): 681–686, 1996.

[Lehman 1998] Lehman M, "The impact of feedback in the global software process," in *Proceedings of ProSim Workshop '98,* Portland, OR, June 1998.

[Lehman 2002] Lehman M M, "Software evolution," in Marciniak J (Ed.), *Encyclopedia of Software Engineering,* 2nd Edition, New York: Wiley, pp. 1507–1513, 2002.

[Lehman, Belady 1985] Lehman M M and Belady L A (Eds.), *Software Evolution—Processes of Software Change,* London: Academic Press, 1985.

[Lehman, Ramil 1999] Lehman M M and Ramil J F, "The impact of feedback in the global software process," *Journal of Systems and Software,* 46(2–3), 1999. (Initial version in *Proceedings of ProSim Workshop 1998.*)

[Lehman, Ramil 2002] Lehman M M and Ramil J F, "Software evolution and software evolution processes," *Annals of Software Engineering 2002,* Special issue on process-based software engineering, 14, 2002.

[Lehman, Ramil 2003] Lehman M M and Ramil J F, "Software evolution: Background, theory, practice," *Information Processing Letters archive,* Special issue contributions to computing science, 88(1–2), 2003.

[Lehman et al. 2006] Lehman M M, Kahen G, and Ramil J F, "Simulation process modelling for managing software evolution," in Acuña S T and Juristo N (Eds.), *Software Process Modelling,* International Series in Software Engineering, 10, Berlin: Springer, 2005.

[Levary, Lin 1991] Levary R R and Lin C Y, "Modeling the software development process using an expert simulation system having fuzzy logic," *Software—Practice and Experience,* February, 133–148, 1991.

[Lin 1993] Lin C, "Walking on battlefields: Tools for strategic software management," *American Programmer,* May 1993.

[Lin, Levary 1989] Lin C and Levary R, "Computer-aided software development process design," *IEEE Transactions on Software Engineering,* September 1989.

[Lin et al. 1992] Lin C, Abdel-Hamid T, and Sherif J, "Software-engineering process simulation model," TDA Progress Report 42-108, Jet Propulsion Laboratories, February 1992.

[Lin et al. 1997] Lin C Y, Abdel-Hamid T, and Sherif J S, "Software engineering process simulation model (SEPS)," *Journal of Systems and Software,* 38, 263–277, 1997.

[Lo 1999] Lo K, "Reuse and high level languages," University of Southern California, CS599 Final Report, http://sunset.usc.edu/classes/cs599_99/projects/reuse.pdf,.

[Londeix 1987] Londeix, B, *Cost Estimation for Software Development,* Cornwall, England: Addison-Wesley Publishing Co., 1987.

[Lutz, Mikulski 2003] Lutz R and Mikulski I, "Final report: Adapting ODC for empirical analysis of pre-launch anomalies," version 1.2, JPL Caltech report, December 2003.

[Madachy 1990a] Madachy R, "CASE and hypertext integration issues," presented at the Third Annual Teamworkers International User Group Conference, San Diego, CA, March, 1990.

[Madachy 1990b] Madachy R, "Directed research final report, class report," ISE 590, University of Southern California, May 1990.

[Madachy 1993] Madachy R, "Knowledge-based assistance for software cost estimation and project risk assessment," in *Proceedings of the Eighth International Forum on COCOMO and Software Cost Modeling,* SEI, Pittsburgh, PA, 1993.

[Madachy et al. 1993] Madachy R, Little L, and Fan S, "Analysis of a successful inspection program," in *Proceedings of the Eighteenth Annual Software Engineering Workshop, NASA/SEL,* Goddard Space Flight Center, Greenbelt, MD, 1993.

[Madachy 1994a] Madachy R, "Development of a cost estimation process," in *Proceedings of the Ninth International Forum on COCOMO and Software Cost Modeling,* USC, Los Angeles, CA, 1994.

[Madachy 1994b] Madachy R, *A Software Project Dynamics Model for Process Cost, Schedule and Risk Assessment,* Ph.D. Dissertation, Dept. of Industrial and Systems Engineering, University of Southern California, December 1994.

[Madachy 1995a] Madachy R, "Dynamic modeling of inspection-based process," in *Proceedings of the California Software Symposium,* UC Irvine, Irvine, CA, January 1995.

[Madachy 1995b] Madachy R, "System dynamics and COCOMO: Complementary modeling paradigms," in *Proceedings of the Tenth International Forum on COCOMO and Software Cost Modeling,* Software Engineering Institute, Pittsburgh, PA, October 1995.

[Madachy 1995c] Madachy R, "Process improvement analysis of a corporate inspection program," in *Proceedings of the Seventh Software Engineering Process Group Conference,* May 1995.

[Madachy 1995d] Madachy R, "Knowledge-based risk assessment and cost estimation," Automated Software Engineering, September 1995.

[Madachy 1995e] Madachy R, "Measuring inspections at Litton," in *Proceedings of the Sixth International Conference on Applications of Software Measurement,* Orlando, FL; *Software Quality Engineering,* October 1995; *Software Quality Assurance,* 3(3), 1996.

[Madachy 1996a] Madachy R, "System dynamics modeling of an inspection-based process," in *Proceedings of the Eighteenth International Conference on Software Engineering,* Berlin, Germany, IEEE Computer Society Press, March 1996.

[Madachy 1996b] Madachy R, "Tutorial: Process modeling with system dynamics," in *Proceedings of the Eighth Software Engineering Process Group Conference,* Atlantic City, NJ, May 1996.

[Madachy 1996c] Madachy R, "Modeling software processes with system dynamics: current developments," in *Proceedings of the 1996 International System Dynamics Conference,* Cambridge, MA, July 1996.

[Madachy 1997] Madachy R, "Heuristic risk assessment using cost factors," *IEEE Software,* May 1997.

[Madachy 1999] Madachy R, *CS599 Software Process Modeling Course Notes,* USC Center for Software Engineering, November 1999.

[Madachy 2001] Madachy R, "New processes for rapid software development," in *Proceedings of the Fifth World Conference on Systemics, Cybernetics and Informatics and the Seventh International Conference on Information Systems Analysis and Synthesis,* IEEE Computer Society, Orlando, FL, July 2001.

[Madachy 2002] Madachy R, "Tutorial: Use of cost models in risk management," in *Proceedings of the Seventeenth International Forum on COCOMO and Software Cost Modeling,* USC, Los Angeles, CA, October 2002.

[Madachy 2005] Madachy R, "Integrating business value and software process modeling," in

Proceedings of the 2005 Software Process Workshop, Beijing, China, Springer-Verlag, May 2005.

[Madachy, Boehm 2005] Madachy R and Boehm B, "Software dependability modeling," in *Software Process Modeling,* Acuña S T and Juristo N (Eds.), Springer Science+Business Media Inc., New York, 2005.

[Madachy, Tarbet 2000] Madachy R and Tarbet D, "Case Studies in software process modeling with system dynamics," *Software Process Improvement and Practice,* 5(2–3), 2000. (Initial version in *Proceedings of ProSim Workshop 1999.*)

[Madachy et al. 2006] Madachy R, Boehm B, and Lane J, "Spiral lifecycle increment modeling for new hybrid processes," in *Proceedings of the Software Process Workshop/Workshop on Software Process Simulation 2006* (SPW/ProSim 2006), Shanghai, China, Springer-Verlag, May 2006.

[Madachy et al. 2007] Madachy R, Boehm B, and Lane J, "Assessing hybrid incremental processes for SISOS development," *Software Process Improvement and Practice,* 12(5), pp. 461–473, 2007.

[Martin 2002] Martin R, *A Hybrid Model of the Software Development Process,* Ph.D. Dissertation, Dept. of Engineering Management, Portland State University, 2002.

[Martin, Raffo 2000] Martin R and Raffo D, "A model of the software development process using both continuous and discrete models," *International Journal of Software Process Improvement and Practice,* 5(2/3), June/July, 2000. (Initial version in *Proceedings of ProSim Workshop 1999.*)

[Martin, Raffo 2001] Martin R and Raffo D, "Application of a hybrid process simulation model to a software development project," *Journal of Systems and Software,* 59, 237–246, 2001. (Initial version in *Proceedings of ProSim Workshop 2000.*)

[McCracken, Jackson 1983] McCracken D and Jackson M, "Life-cycle concept considered harmful," *ACM Software Engineering Notes,* April, 29–32, 1982.

[McGarry et al. 2002] McGarry J, Card D, Jones C, Layman B, Clark E, Dean J, and Hall F, *Practical Software Measurement: Objective Information for Decision Makers,* Reading, MA: Addison-Wesley, 2002.

[Mehta, Fakharzadeh 2000] Mehta R and Fakharzadeh C, "Architecture development process dynamics in MBASE," in *Proceedings of the 18th International Conference of the System Dynamics Society,* Bergen Norway, 2000.

[Menzies et al. 2002] Menzies T, Raffo D, Setamanit S, Hu Y, and Tootoonian S, "Model-based Tests of Truisms," in *Proceedings of 2002 IEEE Automated Software Engineering (ASE),* 2002.

[Menzies et al. 2004a] Menzies T, Setamanit S, and Raffo D, "Data mining from process models," in *Proceedings of 2004 Process Modeling and Simulation Workshop (ProSim),* 2004.

[Menzies et al. 2004b] Menzies T, Smith J, and Raffo D, "When is pair programming better?" *http://menzies.us/pdf/04pairprog.pdf,* unpublished, 2004.

[Menzies, Richardson 2005] Menzies T and Richardson J, "XOMO: Understanding development options for autonomy," in *Proceedings of the 20th International Forum on COCOMO and Software Cost Modeling,* 2005.

[Mills 1987] Mills H, Dyer M, and Linger R, "Cleanroom engineering," *IEEE Software,* September 1987.

[Motorola 2006] Motorola, "Motorola University Six Sigma Articles," *http://www.motorola.com,* 2006.

[Munch, Armbrust 2003] Munch J and Armbrust O, "Using empirical knowledge from replicated experiments for software process simulation: Practical example," in *Proceedings of the 2003 International Symposium on Empirical Software Engineering (ISESE'03)*, p. 18, 2003.

[Munch et al. 2003] Munch J, Rombach D H, and Rus I, "Creating an advanced software engineering laboratory"," in *Proceedings of Software Process Simulation Modeling Workshop (ProSim 2003)*, Portland OR, May 2003.

[Nance 2000] Nance R, "Simulation education: Past reflections and future directions," in *Proceedings of the 2000 Winter Simulation Conference*, 2000.

[Neu, Rus 2003] Neu H and Rus I, "Reuse in software process simulation modeling," in *Proceedings of Software Process Simulation Modeling Workshop (ProSim 2003)* Portland OR, May 2003.

[Oh Navarro, van der Hoek 2005] Oh Navarro E and van der Hoek A, "Software process modeling for an educational software engineering simulation game," in *Software Process Improvement and Practice*, 10(3), 311–325, 2005.

[Osterweil 1987] Osterweil L, "Software processes are software too," in *Proceedings ICSE 9*, pp. 2–13, IEEE Catalog No. 87CH2432-3, March 1987.

[Osterweil 2005] Osterweil L, discussion at SPW/ProSim 2005, 2005.

[Osterweil 2006] Osterweil L, "Ubiquitous processe engineering: Applying software process technology to other domains," in *Proceedings of SPW/ProSim 2006*, 2006.

[Palmer et al. 1998] Palmer J, Speier C, Buckley M, and Moore J, "Recruiting and retaining IS personnel: factors influencing employee turnover," in *Proceedings of the 1998 ACM SIGCPR Conference on Computer Personnel Research*, ACM Press, 1998.

[Park et al. 1996] Park R, Goethert W, and Florac W, *Goal-Driven Software Measurement—A Guidebook*, CMU/SEI-96-HB-002, August 1996.

[Paulk et al. 1994] Paulk M, Weber C, Curtis B, and Chrissis M, *The Capability Maturity Model: Guidelines for Improving the Software Process*, Reading, MA: Addison-Wesley, 1994.

[Pfahl 1995] Pfahl D, "Software quality measurement based on a quantitative project simulation model," presented at European Software Cost Modelling Conference (ESCOM '95). Rolduc, The Netherlands, May 1995.

[Pfahl 2001] Pfahl D, *An Integrated Approach To Simulation-Based Learning In Support Of Strategic And Project Management In Software Organizations*, Ph.D. dissertation, University of Kaiserslautern, 2001.

[Pfahl 2005] Pfahl D, "ProSim/RA—Software process simulation in support of risk assessment," in Biffl S, Aurum A, Boehm B, Erdogmus H, Grünbacher P (Eds.), *Value-based Software Engineering*, pp. 263–286, Berlin: Springer, 2005.

[Pfahl, Birk 2000] Pfahl D and Birk A, "Using simulation to visualise and analyse product-process dependencies in software development projects," IESE-Report 013.00, University of Kaiserslautern, 2000.

[Pfahl, Lebsanft 1999] Pfahl D and Lebsanft K, "Integration of system dynamics modeling with descriptive process and goal oriented measurement," *Journal of Systems and Software*, 46(2–3), 1999. (Initial version in *Proceedings of ProSim Workshop 1998*.)

[Pfahl, Lebsanft 2000a] Pfahl D and Lebsanft K, "Using simulation to analyse the impact of software requirement volatility on project performance," *Information and Software Technology*, 42, 2000.

[Pfahl, Lebsanft 2000b] Pfahl D and Lebsanft K, "Knowledge acquisition and process guidance for building system dynamics simulation models. An experience report from software industry," *International Journal of Software Engineering and Knowledge Engineering* 10(4), 487–510, 2000.

[Pfahl et al. 2001] Pfahl D, Klemm M, and Ruhe G, "A CBT module with integrated simulation component for software project management education and training," *Journal of Systems and Software,* 3, 2001.

[Pfahl et al. 2002] Pfahl D, Ruhe G, Dorsch J, and Krivobokova T, "IMMoS. A methodology for integrated measurement, modelling, and simulation," *Software Process Improvement and Practice,* 7(3–4), 2002. (Initial version in *Proceedings of ProSim Workshop 2001.*)

[Pfahl et al. 2003] Pfahl D, Ruhe G, Dorsch J, and Krivobokova T, "Goal-oriented measurement plus systemd dynamics—A hybrid and evolutionary approach," in *Proceedings of the 2003 Software Process Simulation Modeling Workshop (ProSim),* Portland, OR, 2003.

[Pfahl et al. 2004a] Pfahl D, Stupperich M, and Krivobokova T, "PL-SIM: A generic simulation model for studying strategic SPI in the automotive industry," in *Proceedings of the 2004 International Workshop on Software Process Simulation and Modeling (ProSim),* Edinburgh, 2004.

[Pfahl et al. 2004b] Pfahl D, Laitenberger O, Ruhe G, Dorsch J, and Krivobokova T, "Evaluating the learning effectiveness of using simulations in software project management education: Results from a twice replicated experiment," *Information and Software Technology,* 46, 2004.

[Pfahl, Ruhe 2005] Pfahl D and Ruhe G, "System dynamics and goal-oriented measurement: A hybrid approach," in Chang S K (Ed.), *Handbook of Software Engineering and Knowledge Engineering, Vol 3: Recent Advances,* pp. 429–454, Singapore: World Scientific, 2005.

[Pfahl et al. 2006a] Pfahl D, Al-Emran A, and Ruhe G, "Simulation-Based Stability Analysis for Software Release Plans," in Qing W et al. (Eds.), *International Software Process Workshop and International Workshop on Software Process Simulation and Modeling, SPW/ProSim 2006—Proceedings,* pp. 262–273, Berlin–Heidelberg: Springer-Verlag (Lecture Notes in Computer Science 3966), 2006.

[Pfahl et al. 2006b] Pfahl D, Ruhe G, Lebsanft K, and Stupperich M, "Software process simulation with system dynamics—A tool for learning and decision support," in Acuña S T and Sánchez-Segura M I (Eds.), *New Trends in Software Process Modelling, Series on Software Engineering and Knowledge Engineering,* Vol. 18, pp. 57–90, Singapore: World Scientific, 2006.

[Piplani et al. 1994] Piplani L, Mercer J, and Roop R, *System Acquisition Managers Guide for the Use of Models and Simulations,* Ft. Belvoir, VA, Defense Systems Management College Press, 1994.

[Plekhanova 1999] Plekhanova V, "A capability-based approach to software process modelling," in *Proceedings of ProSim Workshop '99,* Portland, OR, June 1999.

[Powersim 2006] Powersim Software, *http://www.powersim.com,* 2006.

[Pressman 2000] Pressman R, *Software Engineering—A Practitioners Approach,* 5th edition, New York: McGraw-Hill, 2000.

[Port, Yang 2004] Port D and Yang Y, "Empirical analysis of COTS activity effort sequences," in *Proceedings of the 2004 International Conference on COTS-Based Software Systems,* Redondo Beach, CA, 2004.

[Porter 1982] Porter M, *Cases in Competitive Strategy,* New York: The Free Press, 1982.

[Powell et al. 1999] Powell A, Mander K, and Brown D, "Strategies for lifecycle concurrency and iteration: A system dynamics approach," *Journal of Systems and Software,* 46, 1999. (Initial version in *Proceedings of ProSim Workshop 1998.*)

[Powell 2001] Powell A, *Right on Time: Measuring, Modelling and Managing Time-Constrained Software Development,* Ph.D. Dissertation, University of York, 2001.

[Preece 2000] Preece J, *Online Communities: Designing Usability, Supporting Sociability,* Chichester, UK: Wiley, 2000.

[PRICE 2005] PRICE Systems, *TRUE S User Manual,* 2005.

[Prieto-Diaz, Arango 1991] Prieto-Diaz R and Arango G, *Domain Analysis and Software Systems Modeling,* Los Alamitos, CA: IEEE Computer Society Press, 1991.

[Putnam 1980] Putnam L, *Tutorial: Software Cost Estimating and Life-Cycle Control: Getting the Software Numbers,* New York: IEEE Computer Society Press, 1980.

[Raccoon 1996] Raccoon L, "A learning curve primer for software engineers," *Software Engineering Notes,* ACM Sigsoft, January 1996.

[Raffo 1995] Raffo D M, *Modeling Software Processes Quantitatively and Assessing the Impact of Potential Process Changes on Process Performance,* Ph.D. Dissertation, Graduate School of Industrial Administration, Carnegie Mellon University, Pittsburgh, PA, 1995.

[Raffo et al. 1999a] Raffo D, Kaltio T, Partridge D, Phalp K, and Ramil J, "Empirical studies applied to software process models," *Empirical Software Engineering,* 4(4), pp. 353–369, 1999.

[Raffo et al. 1999b] Raffo D, Vandeville J, and Martin R, "Software process simulation to achieve higher CMM levels," *Journal of Systems and Software,* 46(2/3) 15, April 1999.

[Raffo, Kellner 2000] Raffo D and Kellner K, "Empirical analysis in software process simulation modeling," *Journal of Systems and Software,* 47(9), 2000.

[Raffo, Vandeville 2004] Raffo D and Vandeville J, "Combining process feedback with discrete event simulation models to support software project management," in Madhavji N H, Lehman M M, Ramil J, and Perry D, (Eds.), *Software Evolution,* Hoboken, NJ: Wiley, 2004.

[Raffo, Setamanit 2005] Raffo D and Setamanit S, "A simulation model for global software development projects," in *Proceedings of the 6th International Workshop on Process Modeling and Simulation (ProSim 2005),* IEE, 2005.

[Ramesh, Abdel-Hamid 2003] Ramesh B and Abdel-Hamid T K, "Integrating genetic algorithms with system dynamics to optimize quality assurance effort allocation," in Khoshgoftaar T M (Ed.), *Software Engineering with Computational intelligence,* Norwell, MA: Kluwer Academic Publishers, 2003.

[Ramil et al. 2005] Ramil J F, Lehman M M, and Cohen G, "Simulation process modelling for managing software evolution," in Acuña S T and Juristo N (Eds.), *Software Process Modeling,* New York: Springer Science+Business Media Inc., 2005.

[Randers 1992] Randers J (Ed.), *Elements of the System Dynamics Method,* Cambridge, MA: Productivity Press, 1992.

[Raymond 2004] Raymond E, "The cathedral and the bazaar," *http://www.catb.org/~esr/writings/cathedral-bazaar/,* 2004.

[Rechtin 1991] Rechtin E, *Systems Architecting,* Englewood Cliffs, NJ: Prentice-Hall, 1991.

[Rechtin, Maier 1997] Rechtin E and Maier M, *The Art of Systems Architecting,* Boca Raton, FL: CRC Press, 1997.

[Reifer 1997] Reifer D, *Practical Software Reuse,* New York: Wiley, 1997.

[Reifer 2000] Reifer, D J, "Requirements management: The search for Nirvana," *IEEE Software,* 17(3), May/June, 45–47, 2000.

[Reifer 2001] Reifer D, *Making the Software Business Case,* Reading, MA: Addison-Wesley, 2001.

[Reifer 2002] Reifer D, *Software Management* (6th edition), Los Alamitos, CA, IEEE Computer Society Press, 2002.

[Reifer et al. 2003] Reifer D, Basili V, Boehm B, and Clark B, "Eight lessons learned during COTS system maintenance," *IEEE Software,* 20(5), 94–96, 2003.

[Repenning. 2001] Repenning N, "Understanding fire fighting in new product development," *Journal of Product Innovation Management,* 18, 285–200, 2001.

[Richardson, Pugh 1981] Richardson G P and Pugh A, *Introduction to System Dynamics Modeling with DYNAMO,* Cambridge, MA: MIT Press, 1981.

[Richardson 1986] Richardson G, "Problems with causal-loop diagrams," *System Dynamics Digest,* 1986.

[Richardson 1991] Richardson G P, "System dynamics: Simulation for policy analysis from a feedback perspective," in Fishwich and Luker (Eds.), *Qualitative Simulation Modeling and Analysis* Springer-Verlag, 1991.

[Richmond 1994] Richmond B, *System dynamics/systems thinking: Let's just get on with it,* Proceedings of the 1994 International System Dynamics Conference, Sterling, Scotland, July 1994 and http://www.hps-inc.com/st/paper.html.

[Richmond et al. 1990] Richmond B et al., *Ithink User's Guide and Technical Documentation,* Hanover, NH, isee systems Inc., 1990.

[Riordan 1977] Riordan J S, "An evolution dynamics model of software systems development," in *Software Phenomenology—Working Papers of the (First) SLCM Workshop, August 1977,* Airlie, Virginia, Pub ISRAD/AIRMICS, Comp. Sys. Comm. US Army, Fort Belvoir VA, 339–360, 1977.

[Rodriguez et al. 2006] Rodríguez D, Sicilia M A, Cuadrado J J, and Pfahl D, "E-Learning in project management using simulation models: A case study based on the replication of an experiment," *IEEE Transactions on Education,* 49, 451–463, 2006.

[Roehling, Collofello 2000] Roehling S and Collofello J, "System dynamics modeling applied to software outsourcing decision support," *Software Process Improvement and Practice,* 5(2–3), 2000. (Initial version in *Proceedings of ProSim Workshop 1999.*)

[Rothman 1996] Rothman J, "Applying systems thinking to the issues of software product development," in *Proceedings of the 1996 International System Dynamics Conference,* Cambridge, MA, July 1996.

[Royce 1970] Royce W, "Managing the development of large software systems," in *Proceedings IEEE Wescon,* 1970.

[Royce 1998] Royce W, *Software Project Management—A Unified Approach,* Reading, MA: Addison-Wesley, 1998.

[Rubin 1997] Rubin H, *The United States IT Workforce Shortage (Version 3.0),* META Research Report 1997.

[Rubin et al. 1994] Rubin H, Johnson M, and Yourdon E, "With the SEI as my copilot: Using software process flight simulation to predict the impact of improvements in process maturity," *American Programmer,* September 1994.

[Rubin et al. 1995] Rubin H, Johnson M, and Yourdon E, "Software process flight simulation: dynamic modeling tools and metrics," *Information Systems Management,* Summer 1995.

[Ruhe et al. 2003] Ruhe G, Eberlein A, and Pfahl D, "Tradeoff analysis for requirements selection," *International Journal of Software Engineering and Knowledge,* 13(4), pp. 345–366, 2003.

[Ruiz et al. 2001] Ruiz M, Ramos I, and Toro M, "A simplified model of software project dynamics," *Journal of Systems and Software,* 59(3), 2001. (Initial version in *Proceedings of ProSim Workshop 2000.*)

[Ruiz et al. 2002] Ruiz M, Ramos I, and Toro M, "Integrating dynamic models for CMM-based software process improvement," *Lecture Notes in Computer Science,* Vol. 2559/2002, *Product Focused Software Process Improvement: 14th International Conference, PROFES 2002,* Finland, Berlin / Heidelberg, Springer, 2002.

[Ruiz et al. 2004] Ruiz M, Ramos I, and Toro M, "An integrated framework for simulation-based software process improvement," *Software Process Improvement and Practice,* 9(2), 2004. (Initial version in *Proceedings of ProSim Workshop 2003.*)

[Rus et al. 1999] Rus I, Collofello J, and Lakey P, "Software process simulation for reliability management," *Journal of Systems and Software,* 46(2–3), 1999. (Initial version in *Proceedings of ProSim Workshop 1998.*)

[Rus 1998] Rus I, *Modeling the Impact on Cost and Schedule of Software Quality Engineering Practices,* Ph.D. dissertation, Computer Science and Engineering Dept., Arizona State University, March 1998.

[Rus, Collofello 1998] Rus I and Collofello J, "Software process simulation for reliability strategy assessment," in *Proceedings of ProSim Workshop '98,* Portland, OR, June 1998.

[Rus et al. 2003] Rus I, Halling M, and Biffl S, "Supporting decision-making in software engineering with process simulation and empirical studies," *International Journal of Software Engineering and Knowledge Engineering,* 13(5), 531–546, 2003.

[Schach 2002] Schach S R, Jin B, Wright D R, Heller G Z, and Offutt A J, "Maintainability of the Linux Kernel," *IEE Proceedings—Software,* 149(1), 18–23, February 2002.

[Scacchi, Mi 1993] Scacchi W and Mi P, "Modeling, enacting and integrating softare engineering processes," in *Proceedings of the 3rd Irvine Software Symposium,* Costa Mesa, CA, April, 1993.

[Scacchi 2004a] Scacchi W, "Understanding free/open source software evolution," in Madhavji N H, Lehman M M, Ramil J F, and Perry D (Eds.), *Software Evolution,* New York: Wiley, 2004.

[Scacchi 2004b] Scacchi W, "Socio-technical interaction networks in free/open source software development processes," in Acuña S T and Juristo N (Eds.), *Peopleware and the Software Process,* Singapore: World Scientific Press, 2004.

[Schmid, Verlage 2002] Schmid K and Verlage M, "The economic impact of product line adoption and evolution," *IEEE Software,* 19(4), 50–57, July 2002.

[Schrage 2000] Schrage M, *Serious Play,* Boston MA: Harvard Business School Press, 2000.

[SEI 2003] CMMI (Capability Maturity Model Integration) website, *http://www.sei.cmu.edu/cmmi/,* 2003.

[SEI 2005] ISO-15504 website, *http://www.sei.cmu.edu/ISO-15504/,* 2005.

[Selby 2005] Selby R, "Measurement-driven dashboards enable leading indicators for requirements and design of large-scale systems," in *Proceedings of the 11th IEEE International Symposium on Software Metrics (METRICS 2005),* 2005.

[Senge 1990] Senge P, *The Fifth Discipline,* New York: Doubleday, 1990.

[Senge et al. 1994] Senge P, Kleiner A, Roberts C, Ross R, and Smith B, *The Fifth Discipline Fieldbook,* New York: Doubleday, 1994.

[Sharma 2002] Sharma S, Sugumaran, and Rajagopalan B, "A framework for creating hybrid open-source software communities," *Information Systems Journal,* 12(1), 7–25, 2002.

[Smith 1999] Smith M and Kollock P (Eds.), *Communities in Cyberspace,* London: Routledge, 1999.

[Smith et al. 1993] Smith B, Nguyen N, and Vidale R, "Death of a software manager: How to avoid career suicide through dynamic process modeling," *American Programmer,* May 1993.

[Smith et al. 2005] Smith N, Capiluppi A, and Ramil J, "A study of open source software evolution data using qualitative simulation," *Software Process Improvement and Practice,* 10(3), 287–300, 2005.

[Smith et al. 2006] Smith N, Capiluppi A, and Ramil J, "Users and developers: An agent-based simulation of open source software evolution," in *Proceedings of the International Software Process Workshop and International Workshop on Software Process Simulation and Modeling (SPW/ProSim 2006),* Shanghai, China, Springer-Verlag, 2006.

[Sommerville et al. 1996] Sommerville I and Rodden T, Human, "Social and organizational influences on software processes," in Fugetta A and Wolf A (Eds.), *Software Process,* vol. 4 of *Trends in Software,* Wiley, 1996.

[Stallinger 2000] Stallinger F, "Software process simulation to support ISO/IEC 15504 based software process improvement," Software Process Improvement and Practice, 5(2–3), 2000. (Initial version in *Proceedings of ProSim Workshop 1999.*)

[Stallinger, Gruenbacher 2001] Stallinger F and Gruenbacher P, "System dynamics modelling and simulation of collaborative requirements engineering," *Journal of Systems and Software,* 59(3), 2001. (Initial version in *Proceedings of ProSim Workshop 2000.*)

[Sterman 1989] Sterman J, "Modeling managerial behavior: Misperceptions of feedback in a dynamic decision making experiment," *Management Science,* 35(3), 321–339, 1989.

[Sterman 2000] Sterman J, *Business Dynamics: Systems Thinking and Modeling for a Complex World,* New York: Irwin McGraw-Hill, 2000.

[Stutzke 1994] Stutzke R, "A Mathematical Expression of Brooks' Law," in *Proceedings of the Ninth International Forum on COCOMO and Cost Modeling,* Los Angeles, CA, 1994.

[Sycamore 1995] Sycamore D, *Improving Software Project Management Through System Dynamics Modeling,* M.S. Dissertation, Computer Science and Engineering Dept., Arizona State University, 1995.

[Taweponsomkiat 1996] Taweponsomkiat C, "Report for re-engineering of concurrent incremental software development model," Computer Science and Engineering Dept., Arizona State University, August 1996.

[Tvedt 1995] Tvedt J, "A system dynamics model of the software inspection process," Computer Science and Engineering Dept., Arizona State University, January 1995.

[Tvedt 1996] Tvedt J D, *An Extensible Model for Evaluating the Impact of Process Improvements on Software Development Cycle Time,* Ph.D. Dissertation, Arizona State University, 1996.

[Tvedt, Collofello 1995] Tvedt J and Collofello J, "Evaluating the effectiveness of process improvements on software development cycle time via system dynamics modeling," University of Arizona, 1995.

[Twaites et al. 2006] Twaites G, Collefello J, and Zenzen F, "Modeling inspections to evaluate prioritization as a method to mitigate the effects of accelerated schedules," in *Proceedings of the 12th ISSAT International Conference on Reliability and Quality in Design,* International Society of Science and Applied Technology, vol. 12, 2006.

[USC 2004] University of Southern California, *Software Engineering Economics,* CS510 Course Notes. USC Computer Science Department, 2004.

[Vennix, Vennix 1996] Vennix J A M and Vennix J A C, *Group Model Building: Facilitating Team Learning Using System Dynamics,* New York: Wiley, 1996.

[Ventana 2006] Ventana Systems, *http://www.vensim.com,* 2006.

[Verner, Tate 1988] Verner J and Tate G, "Estimating size and effort in fourth generation development," *IEEE Software,* pp. 15–22, July 1988.

[Waeselynck, Pfahl 1994] Waeselynck H and Pfahl D, "System dynamics applied to the modelling of software projects," *Software Concepts and Tools,* 15(4), 162–176, 1994.

[Wakeland et al. 2004] Wakeland W, Martin R, and Raffo D, "Using design of experiments, sensitivity analysis, and hybrid simulation to evaluate changes to a software development process: a case study," *Software Process Improvement and Practice,* 9(2), pp. 107–119, 2004. (Initial version in *Proceedings of ProSim Workshop 2003.*)

[Wakeland et al. 2005] Wakeland W, Shervais S, and Raffo D, "Heuristic optimization as a V&V tool for software process simulation models," *Software Process Improvement and Practice,* 10(3), 301–309, 2005.

[Weinberg 1992] Weinberg G, *Quality Software Management, Volume 1, Systems Thinking,* New York: Dorset House Publishing, 1992.

[Weinberg 1998] Weinberg G, *The Psychology of Computer Programming: Silver Anniversary Edition,* New York: Dorset House Publishing, 1998.

[Weiner 1961] Weiner N, *Cybernetics: or Control and Communication in the Animal and the Machine,* Cambridge, MA: The MIT Press, 1961.

[Weiss, Lai 1999] Weiss D and Lai C T R, *Software Product Line Engineering,* Reading, MA: Addison-Wesley, 1999.

[Wernick, Lehman 1999] Wernick P and Lehman M, "Software process dynamic modeling for FEAST/1," *Software Process Improvement and Practice,* 7(3–4), 2002. (Initial version in *Proceedings of ProSim Workshop 1998.*)

[Wernick, Hall 2002] Wernick P and Hall T, "Simulating global software evolution processes by combining simple models: An initial study," *Journal of Systems and Software,* 46(2–3), 1999. (Initial version in *Proceedings of ProSim Workshop 2001.*)

[Widman et al. 1989] Widman L, Loparo K, Nielson N, *Artificial Intelligence, Simulation, and Modeling,* New York: Wiley, 1989.

[Williams, Cockburn 2003] Williams L and Cockburn A, "Agile software development: It's about feedback and change," *IEEE Computer,* 36(6), 39–43, June 2003.

[Williford, Chang 1999] Williford J and Chang A, "Modeling the FedEx IT division: A system dynamics approach to strategic IT planning," *Journal of Systems and Software,* 46(2–3), 1999. (Initial version in *Proceedings of ProSim Workshop 1998.*)

[Wise 2006] Wise A, "Little-JHIL 1.5 language report," University of Massachusetts technical report, UM-CS-2006-51, 2006.

[Wise et al. 2000] Wise A, Cass A, Lerner B, McCall E, Osterweil L, and Sutton S, "Using Little-JIL to coordinate agents in software engineering," in *Proceedings of the Automated Software Engineering Conference (ASE 2000),* Grenoble, France, pp. 155–163, 2000.

[Wood, Silver 1995] Wood J and Silver D, *Joint Application Development,* 2nd edition, New York: Wiley, 1995.

[Wolstenholme 1990] Wolstenholme E, *System Enquiry: A System Dynamics Approach,* West Sussex, England: Wiley, 1990.

[Yamamura 1999] Yamamura G, "Process improvement satisfies employees," *IEEE Software,* September/October 1999.

[Ye 2004] Ye Y, Nakajoki K, Yamamoto Y, and Kishida K, "The co-evolution of systems and communities in free and open source software development," in Koch S (Ed.), *Free/Open Source Software Development,* pp. 59–82, Hershey, PA: Idea Group Publishing, 2004.

[Yourdon 1993a] Yourdon E, *Decline and Fall of the American Programmer,* Englewood Cliffs, NJ: Prentice-Hall, 1993.

[Yourdon 1993b] Yourdon E (Ed.), *American Programmer,* New York: Cutter Information Group, 1993.

[Yourdon 1994] Yourdon E (Ed.), *American Programmer,* New York: Cutter Information Group, September 1994.

[Yourdon 2004] Yourdon E, *Death March* (2nd edition), New York: Yourdon Press, 2004.

INDEX

Printed and bound by CPI Group (UK) Ltd, Croydon, CR0 4YY

27/10/2024

14580332-0005